A MODERN READER

A MODERN READER

Essays on present-day life and culture

SELECTED AND EDITED WITH THE COLLABORATION OF

WALTER LIPPMANN

AND

ALLAN NEVINS

D. C. HEATH AND COMPANY

BOSTON   NEW YORK   CHICAGO

ATLANTA   SAN FRANCISCO   DALLAS

LONDON

PRINTED IN THE UNITED STATES OF AMERICA

PREFACE

These essays upon present-day economics, politics, social life, and culture have been chosen for their pertinency, sparkle, and insight. Taken as a whole, we believe that they offer a fairly expert and comprehensive introduction to certain important sides of the modern world. We believe also that the ordinary reader — the high school student, the college student, the plain man or woman — will find them decidedly interesting, and that they present nothing esoteric or difficult. In making the selection, we have merely assumed that the reader has a certain grounding in the standard literature upon the subjects here treated, or will be inspired to acquire such a grounding through the use of this volume.

This is of course a rather large assumption, and it is perhaps proper to explain and modify it. To master any considerable part of the standard literature of the past is a tremendous task; the task of a lifetime. It can never be finished, and it is an unusual person who can truly say that he has made a fair beginning. Our belief is simply that use of this collection should either be preceded by or lead to such a beginning, and should not interfere with its enlargement. These essays on modern topics by modern writers who adopt a modern tone are intended to supplement, not exclude, older material. We think that no person should feel ready to grapple with present-day ideas in politics until he has some first-hand acquaintance with Aristotle's *Politics*, with John Locke's *Two Treatises on Government*, and with Mill's *On Liberty* (not to mention a few other titles). No one should feel ready to grapple with present-day writings upon economics who has not some thoughtful knowledge of Adam Smith, Ricardo, Karl Marx, and Bagehot. Scientific writings present more difficulty, for many former classics of science are not only dead but misleading; yet here too no one can understand the present without knowledge of Darwin, Huxley, and Spencer. In aesthetics and criticism all contemporaneous literature falls into insignificance beside the treasures of the past; not to know Coleridge, Hazlitt, Sainte-Beuve, and Matthew Arnold is not to know what is absolutely essential. It is obvious that not all this can be done at once; what is important is that the student achieve a fair conception of the domain of past ideas, become acquainted with its principal features, and resolve to continue his explorations. As he does this, he may well begin to acquaint himself with new ideas, new problems, and present-day authorities.

For the present-day world is confused, complex, challenging beyond all precedent. It changes with bewildering rapidity; it contains forces that are as baffling as they are powerful. It is no longer compartmentalized as it once seemed to be; economics and politics are more and more inextricably commingled, science alters the primary postulates of both, and letters and art mirror social changes and new scientific and philosophical concepts with marvelous celerity. It was once said that the world of McKinley differed more from that of Washington than Washington's differed from that of Caesar. So it might now be said that the world of today differs more from that of 1900 than the latter differed from Washington's. Certain verities are indeed eternal; but some ideas which we fondly thought verities have been as drastically questioned in recent years as the Newtonian physics itself — and who thought in 1900 that it would ever be questioned? A few ages in human history are distinctly revolutionary. It is probable that the period since 1914 will hereafter be classified under that heading as emphatically as the period 1789–1815. The learning of the *ancien régime*, if we may so term it, does not fit the new age. A distinct change in emphasis becomes necessary, and while many old classics do not lose an iota of their value, they must make shoulder-room for new writers and new points of view. If students are not given some acquaintance with the newer issues, the newer problems, and the most important of the newer arguments, they will feel very bewildered indeed when they walk out into the glare and clamor of the world.

The chief regret of the editors is that the present collection, large as it is, could not be much larger. We should have liked to present those very modern writers Thomas Jefferson and Jeremy Bentham, for example. We should above all have liked more room for writers of the second half of the nineteenth and the early twentieth century. It is regrettable that there is no essay here by William Graham Sumner; that we could not include a few burning pages from Henry George's *Progress and Poverty;* that there was no space for one of the "Short Studies on Great Subjects" in which J. A. Froude makes some momentous historical movement or issue glow with color; that we could not choose a few pages from Lecky's work on Rationalism, or Leslie Stephen's on Agnosticism; that Herbert Croly, to mention a later name, is unrepresented. Going further afield, and into more debatable ground, it would have been gratifying to include two or three of the Titans who raised their voices on moral, social, or political questions still much alive — Milton or Tolstoi. But the restrictions of general theme and unity have had to be considered as well as limitations of space. An effort has been made to hold the collection with some rigidity to issues of the present day, treated in terms of the present day, and with a catholic representation of all useful points of view.

We would emphasize this effort to represent with impartiality all honest and enlightening points of view. It is noteworthy that these essays fall to a great extent into the two general categories of conservative and liberal, or, if the word be preferred, radical. This is so whether politics, or morals, or literature is being discussed. It is noteworthy, too, how much evidence the collection gives of a rapid shift in the definition of these terms. What was the position of the radicals a generation ago is the position, in many instances, of the conservatives today. Mr. Herbert Hoover clearly took many of his political and economic ideas, as he took his word "regimentation," from Herbert Spencer. But the practical position taken by President Hoover in 1931–1933 would have profoundly alarmed Spencer. It is doubtless true today as in Gilbert and Sullivan's time

> That every boy and every gal,
>   That's born into the world alive,
> Is either a little Liberal,
>   Or else a little Conservative.

But as the social environment changes, the ideas bound up in these words change also. As between the extremes of opinion we have tried to avoid any show of bias. This was the easier because, in most instances, we do not lean to extremes in either direction, but sincerely prefer a median road.

The editorial notes are the work of Mr. Nevins.

WALTER LIPPMANN
ALLAN NEVINS

CONTENTS

I. THE CHANGING POLITICAL WORLD

II. THE CHANGING ECONOMIC WORLD

III. THE CHANGING SOCIAL WORLD

IV. WAR AND WORLD ORDER

CONTENTS

X. AMERICA, PAST AND PRESENT

I

THE CHANGING POLITICAL WORLD

THERE was a time before the World War when the political units of the globe were frequently thrust into the three simple categories of republics, constitutional or limited monarchies, and absolute monarchies. It was an unphilosophical and inexact classification, but it served, and it found implied acceptance even in such books as Woodrow Wilson's *The State*. Today the political situation throughout the world is more complex, confused, and unpredictable than would have been deemed possible a generation ago. Confidence in old forms of democracy no longer stands where it did when Sir Henry Maine's able exposure of their defects in *Popular Government* was received with resentment and derision. Students of government must take account of the great experiment in Communist control in Russia — communism combined with autonomous federalism on a far-reaching scale. They must take account of Hitler's totalitarian state in Germany; of the theoretical attempt at a corporative state under Mussolini in Italy. They cannot avoid the evidence that under Presidents Hoover and Roosevelt some wholly new concepts of the purposes and ends of government have been firmly implanted in the minds of the American people. In the section which follows, James Bryce deals with the old liberal ideals of democratic government; H. G. Wells with some of the new challenges to democratic forms; and John Dewey with the complexity of the problem presented to democracy. There follow careful analyses, all critical in temper, of Communism in Russia, Fascism in Italy, and Naziism in Germany. Finally, the evidence that democracy, despite the new forms that autocracy has taken in politically undeveloped lands, despite the economic tempest that came in the wake of the war, has fairly vindicated itself and proved its superior virtues, is summed up in the last article.

THE RESULTS DEMOCRATIC GOVERNMENT HAS GIVEN[1]

Lord Bryce

JAMES BRYCE was born in Belfast, Ireland, in 1838, the son of a Scottish schoolmaster. Educated at Glasgow and Oxford Universities, Bryce early showed signs of great brilliance. At twenty-six, when just beginning studies for the bar, he published his *Holy Roman Empire*, a work still authoritative and indispensable. After some practice in London, he was Regius Professor of Civil Law at Oxford from 1871 to 1893. He traveled widely; became a power in the Liberal Party; sat in the House of Commons; and held the Under-Secretaryship of Foreign Affairs in Gladstone's last Cabinet. In 1888 he published his classic work *The American Commonwealth*, which after fifty years is still of value. On his numerous visits to America he made a host of friends, and it was natural that he should be made Ambassador to the United States. This post he held from 1907 until 1913, performing services that were rewarded in 1913 by the title of Viscount. He died in 1922.

When he became Ambassador in 1907, James Bryce was already collecting material for a work upon modern democracy. Probably no man in the world was better equipped for such a study. His *American Commonwealth* had shown his mature knowledge of political ideals and practices in the United States; he had traveled and observed in all the British Dominions, in South America, and in Asia as well as Europe; he had practical experience of parliamentary administration. Indeed, he had taken pains since youth to give critical scrutiny to political institutions everywhere. He could say that he had collected impressions of government from the time he visited the tiny republic of Andorra in 1873 and chatted with its head, "a stalwart old peasant in a red flannel shirt threshing his own corn," until he watched the proceedings of China's brand-new parliament in 1913, with its frock coats and pigtails. And after the war he made special journeys to Switzerland, Canada, and the United States to bring his information up to date. His *Modern Democracies* deals with the governments of the United States, Canada, Australia, New Zealand, France, and Switzerland. His refusal to include Great Britain grew out of his fear that, having been involved in party issues there, he could not treat the subject with judicial detachment.

In *Modern Democracies* we have one of the great liberals of his generation testing, in balanced and penetrating fashion, a set of democracies by Liberal touchstones. Lord Bryce wrote with unflagging faith in the democratic ideal. He rejoiced in the creation of seven new democratic states in Europe after the World War. Yet he was aware that times were changing, as he indicated when he contrasted the old generation with the new. "That generation busied itself with institutions; this generation is bent rather upon the purposes which institutions may be made to serve."

---

[1] From *Modern Democracies*, by James Bryce. By permission of The Macmillan Company, publishers.

To test democracy by its results as visible in the six countries examined, it will be convenient to consider how far in each of them the chief ends for which government exists have been attained, taking these ends to include whatever the collective action of men associated for the common good can do for the moral and material welfare of a community and the individual citizens who compose it, helping them to obtain the maximum that life can afford of enjoyment and to suffer the minimum life may bring of sorrow.

These ends may be summed up as follows:

(1) Safety against attack on the community from without.

(2) Order within the community — prevention of violence and creation of the consequent sense of security.

(3) Justice, the punishment of offenses and the impartial adjustment of disputes on principles approved by the community.

(4) Efficient administration of common affairs, so as to obtain the largest possible results at the smallest possible cost.

(5) Assistance to the citizens in their several occupations, as, for example, by the promotion of trade or the regulation of industry, in so far as this can be done without checking individual initiative or unduly restricting individual freedom.

These may be called the primary and generally recognized functions of government in a civilized country. Other results, needing a fuller explanation, will be presently adverted to. I take first the five ends above named.

(1) Safety against external attack. In all the six democracies this end has been attained as fully as in most non-democratic governments, and in one respect better attained, because the necessary preparations for defense have not given reasonable ground to other nations to fear that armaments were being increased with a view to hostile aggression.

(2) In most of the six, internal order has been well maintained, best perhaps in Switzerland, least perhaps in parts of the United States, where, although the federal government has done its duty faithfully, some state governments have tolerated lynching and failed to check other breaches of the law. Rioting in connection with labor disputes has occurred everywhere, but except in some Australian cases the constituted authorities have shown themselves able to deal with it.

(3) Justice has been honestly and capably administered, quite as well as under other forms of government, in Switzerland, Canada, Australia, and New Zealand, and in France also, though perhaps with not so full a confidence of the people in the perfect honor of all the

courts. In the United States the federal courts are staffed (with few exceptions) by upright and capable men, and the same is true of certain states. In others, however, the judiciary is below the level of its functions, and in a few it is not trusted, while criminal procedure is cumbrous and regrettably ineffective.

(4) Civil administration has long been conducted with efficiency in France and Switzerland, and is now, since the partial abolition of the spoils system, beginning to be so conducted in the United States federal government and in many of the state governments. A similar improvement is visible in Canada. Australia and New Zealand have permanent services which are honest but as yet not more than fairly competent. Still possessed by the notion that one man is as good as another, the new democracies have not yet duly recognized the increased call for thorough knowledge and trained skill in handling the widened functions now imposed on governments, both in determining the principles of economic and social policy to be adopted and in carrying them out in a scientific spirit. That the management of national finances has, in every country except Switzerland, been lavish and frequently wasteful is the fault not of the civil services but of ministers and legislatures who have spent vast sums in that form of electioneering bribery which consists in making grants of money to particular classes (as in the United States to those who professed to be Civil War veterans), or to constituencies under the pretense of executing public works. . . .

(5) What further services, beyond those already mentioned, government may render to a community or to any class of its citizens by acquiring property to be used for the common benefit, or by embarking on industries or trading enterprises, or by aiding individuals to do so, is a question on which opinions differ so widely that no standard exists whereby to estimate the merits or defaults of governments. The only two countries that have gone far in this direction are New Zealand and Australia, with results which raise doubts whether democracy is a form of government fitted for such enterprises. Other matters, however, which are now generally deemed to fall within the sphere of legislation, such as public health and the conditions of labor and the regulation of the means of transportation, have received in all the six countries due attention, the newer democracies being in no wise behind their elder sisters.

Of the conduct of foreign policy, once deemed a department in which popular governments were inconstant and incompetent, nothing need be added to what has been said in a preceding chapter except

that the errors of the peoples have been no greater than those committed by monarchs, or by oligarchies, or in democracies themselves
by the small groups, or the individual ministers, to whose charge
foreign relations had been intrusted.

Outside and apart from these definite duties, legally assigned to
and discharged by government, there is a sphere in which its action
can be felt and in which both its form and its spirit tell upon the
individual citizen. When political institutions call upon him to bear
a part in their working, he is taken out of the narrow circle of his
domestic or occupational activities, admitted to a larger life which
opens wider horizons, associated in new ways with his fellows, forced
to think of matters which are both his and theirs. Self-government
in local and still more in national affairs becomes a stimulant and an
education. These influences may be called a by-product of popular
government, incidental but precious. Whoever has grown up in a
household where public affairs were followed with interest and constantly discussed by the elders and friends of the family knows how
much the boy gains by listening, asking questions, trying to understand the answers given; and the gain to the budding mind is greatest
when the differences of opinion he hears expressed are most frequent.
In Britain and America every general parliamentary or presidential
election marked for many a boy an epoch in the development of his
thought . . . . In the six democracies described this kind of education is always going on, and the process is continued in an even more
profitable form where the citizen, when he has reached the voting age,
is required to vote not only at elections but also, as in Switzerland and
some of the American states, on laws submitted to the people by
referendum and initiative.

Could this examination be extended to six other European countries,
Italy, Holland, Belgium, Denmark, Sweden, Norway, the results to
be described would not differ materially from those set forth as attained in the six countries examined. In none has justice or order or
the efficiency of civil administration suffered in the process of democratization which all have undergone within the last ninety years, and
in most these primary duties of government are better discharged.
We may accordingly treat the results our inquiry has given for the
six as substantially true for European democracies in general.

Here, however, a wider question arises. Someone may say:
"These attempts to estimate what government has done or failed
to do for the citizen do not convey a definite impression of what is
after all the thing of most worth: viz., the amount of satisfaction,

be it greater or less, with life and in life which democracy has brought to the modern world. What has it done for human happiness? Is it discredited, as some argue, by the fact that, after its long and steady advance, those civilized peoples which had hoped so much from popular government have seen in these latest years the most awful calamities which history records? Has it, if we think of the individual man, made him more or less disposed to say, taking the common test, 'If I could, I would live my life over again,' or does it leave him still in the frame of mind expressed twenty-three centuries ago by the Greek poet who wrote, 'The best thing for a man is never to have been born at all, and the next best to return swiftly to that darkness whence he came'?"

Shall we say, in the familiar lines of a later poet, that the question is idle, because governments have infinitesimally little to do with the matter?

> How small of all that human hearts endure,
> That part which laws or kings can cause or cure.

What is happiness? Nations as well as men have shown by their acts how differently they conceive it. Some, like Albanians and Afghans, cannot be happy without fighting, and the exploits of the heroes recorded in the Icelandic sagas as well as the feats of warlike prowess which fill the *Iliad* seem to show that the first European peoples to produce great literatures cherished the same ideals. Yet the ideals of peace also were never absent. Eris and Atē — Strife, and Sin the parent of Strife — loom large in the Homeric poems as figures to be hated, because they are sources of misery. That impassioned little poem, the hundred and forty-fourth Psalm, begins with the stern joy of battle in the verses:

Blessed be Jehovah my Strength who teacheth my hands to war and my fingers to fight.
My goodness and my fortress, my high tower and my deliverer, my shield and he in whom I trust.

And ends with a prayer for the blessedness of peaceful prosperity which the Almighty bestows:

That our sons may grow up like young plants and our daughters be as the polished corners of the temple:
That our garners may be full affording all manner of stores:
That our oxen may be strong to labour, that there may be no breaking in or going out, that there be no complaining in our streets.
Happy is the people that is in such a case; happy the people whose God is Jehovah.

So peace is for Dante the supreme good, which the government of an emperor commissioned from on high is to confer upon an Italy distracted by internal strife, leading men to the practice on earth of active virtue in this world, according to the precepts of philosophy, as the successor of Peter is to lead them to celestial felicity in the world to come. The Greek philosophers, however, and the Eastern mystics and the Christian theologians agree in regarding happiness as a thing which governments can neither make nor mar, since it is unaffected by the possession or the lack of earthly goods. From this exalted view there is a long downward scale, for the pleasures of sense must not be forgotten: many Europeans would deem happiness unattainable in a land where alcoholic stimulants were unprocurable; and among the various ideals of different modern countries there is that of the maximum of amusement with the minimum of toil, high wages and leisure for bullfights or horse races and athletic sports, in which many, and that not in Spain or Australia only, place their *summum bonum.*

Of democracy and happiness can more be said than this: that whatever governments can do to increase the joy of life is so slight in comparison with the other factors that tell on life for good and evil as to make the question not worth discussing on its positive side? With the negative side it is otherwise. The establishment of popular freedom has removed or at least diminished sources of fear or suffering which existed under more arbitrary forms of government. France has never returned to the oppressions and injustices, even the religious persecutions, which had lasted down to the days of Louis XV. In England, under the dawning light of popular power, the slave trade and the pillory and the cruel penal code and the oppressive restrictions on industry had begun to disappear even before the peaceful revolution of 1832; and slavery in every British dominion fell at once thereafter. In Germany, Switzerland, and Spain torture chambers had remained till the advent of the armies of republican France. Russia is the only country in which the overthrow of an old-established tyranny has not been followed by the extinction of administrative cruelty. Freedom of thought and speech, if not everywhere the gift of popular government, has found its best guarantee in democratic institutions.

It remains to see which, among the things expected from it by its sanguine apostles of a century ago, democracy has so far failed to bestow upon the peoples. To Mazzini and his disciples, as to Jefferson and many another fifty years before, democracy was a religion, or the natural companion of a religion, or a substitute for religion, from which effects on morals and life were hoped similar to those which the preachers of new creeds have so often seen with the eyes of faith.

What, then, has democracy failed to accomplish? It has brought no nearer friendly feeling and the sense of human brotherhood among the peoples of the world toward one another. Freedom has not been a reconciler.

Neither has it created good will and a sense of unity and civic fellowship within each of these peoples. Though in earlier days strife between classes had arisen, it is only in these later days that what is called class war has become recognized as a serious menace to the peace of states, and in some countries the dominant factor in political and economic conflicts. Liberty and Equality have not been followed by Fraternity. Not even far off do we see her coming shine.

It has not enlisted in the service of the state nearly so much of the best practical capacity as each country possesses and every country needs for dealing with the domestic and international questions of the present age.

It has not purified or dignified politics, nor escaped the pernicious influence which the money power can exert. In some states corruption has been rife, and the tone of public life no better than it was under the monarchies or oligarchies of the eighteenth century.

Lastly, democracy has not induced that satisfaction and contentment with itself as the best form of government which was expected, and has not exorcised the spirit that seeks to attain its aims by revolution. One of the strongest arguments used to recommend universal suffrage was that as it gave supreme power to the numerical majority, every section of the people would bow to that majority, realizing that their aims must be sought by constitutional methods, since a resort to violence would be treason against the people and their legal sovereignty. Nevertheless, in many a country revolutionary methods are now being either applied or threatened just as they were in the old days of tyrannical kings or oligarchies. If democracy is flouted, what remains? There was a Greek proverb, "If water chokes, what can one drink to stop choking?" If the light of democracy be turned to darkness, how great is that darkness!

Anyone can see that these things which have not been attained ought not to have been expected. No form of government, nothing less than a change in tendencies of human nature long known and recognized as permanent, could have accomplished what philosophies and religions and the spread of knowledge and progress in all the arts of life had failed to accomplish.   Christianity — a far more powerful force than any political ideas or political institutions, since it works on the inmost heart of man — has produced nearly all the moral progress that has been achieved since it first appeared, and can in individual men transmute lead into gold; yet Christianity has not done these things for peoples, because, checked or perverted by the worse propensities of human nature, it has never been applied in practice.   It has not abolished oppression and corruption in governments, nor extinguished international hatreds and wars; has not even prevented the return of hideous cruelties in war which were believed to have been long extinct.

Yet the right way to judge democracy is to try it by a concrete standard, setting it side by side with other governments.   If we look back from the world of today to the world of the sixteenth century, comfort can be found in seeing how many sources of misery have been reduced under the rule of the people and the recognition of the equal rights of all.   If it has not brought all the blessings that were expected, it has in some countries destroyed, in others materially diminished, many of the cruelties and terrors, injustices and oppressions, that had darkened the souls of men for many generations.

DEMOCRACY UNDER REVISION[1]

H. G. Wells

HERBERT GEORGE WELLS was born at Bromley, Kent, in 1866, and educated at the Royal College of Science in London. After some years spent in teaching science, he turned in 1893 to journalism and in 1895 published his first book, *Select Conversations with an Uncle*. Since then he has been one of the most prolific authors the world has ever seen; yet he has found time for much public activity. He became a member of the Fabian Society in 1903, later quarreling with it; he has traveled widely and reported many world events for the press with his own highly individual commentary; he has taken a practical interest in education; and in 1922 and 1923 he stood unsuccessfully as Labor candidate for Parliament.

Springing from an environment of lower middle class and shop life, Wells was intellectually awakened not only by the Royal College of Science but by wide reading, and by the ideas of the Fabian Socialists and such literary men as W. E. Henley. Learning to clothe scientific speculation in the garb of exciting fiction, he achieved a certain fame before he was thirty by his fantasy *The Time Machine* (1895). In the book-crowded years that followed, he produced works that chiefly fall into three categories: scientific romances like *The War of the Worlds* (1898), realistic novels like *Tono-Bungay* (1909), and sociological treatises (to which *The Outline of History*, 1920, belongs). Gifted with an independent and acute mind, with great earnestness, and with remarkable powers of imagination, he lacks profundity and the deeper type of originality. His vision of the future is thoroughly material: no New Jerusalem, but a scientific and sociological Utopia, of the earth earthy, to which mankind is to be lifted by the continuous development of invention, science, and education, and by the activities of governments remodeled along the wisest bureaucratic lines. He finds little spiritual inspiration in the older faiths of mankind; he pictures "the world set free" by forces which some other teachers of our time regard as dubious liberators — by machinery, by the state, by scientific fact.

But however limited and materialistic his vision may be, his keen and stimulating mind, his real insight into politics and economics, his intense interest in the pressing problems of the day and his ingenuity in propounding solutions for them, have made him one of the most powerful influences of the time. With the effectiveness almost of Voltaire, he has struck destructively at shams, fallacies, and evils. His attacks upon war, inefficiency, failure to use the latest technical resources of mankind, faulty educational systems, and religious and moral hypocrisy, have all been telling. His plans for reforming the present and building the future, though often hasty and sometimes lacking in tolerance for the views of others, have always been highly stimulative of thought. Taking due account of his novels, with their strong propagandist element, he may be called the ablest pamphleteer of his time in any language.

[1] From Sorbonne Lecture, 1927. L. and V. Woolf. Reprinted by permission of the author.

I propose to launch a generalization, a generalization about the probable forms of expression prevalent now and in the immediate future — expression in political, social, literary and artistic life. I am going to suggest that we are in the beginning of an age whose broad characteristics may be conveyed some day by calling it the Age of Democracy under Revision. That title I have chosen by way of defining its relation to the age which has been drawing to its close under our eyes: the Age of Democracy Ascendent.

Let us begin by exploring common ground. It would be easy to find quite a large number of intelligent and well-instructed people who would agree that the sixteenth century saw the germination, the seventeenth and the eighteenth the birth struggles, the nineteenth the rise and prevalence of something called Modern Democracy. Something not merely political, but social, and profoundly differentiating the literature and art of this time — quite as much as the political life — from those of any previous period. That ascendency of democracy has culminated; and like some wave that breaks upon a beach, its end follows close upon its culmination.

Now what do we mean by this word "democracy"? We are apt to say that such words as "democracy" and "socialism" may mean anything or nothing. But the truth is that, in spite of many variations and convolutions both these words retain very definite meanings indeed. One might compare them to little bags given to a multitude of children to collect anything they liked from a pebble beach. In such bags you might find at the end of the day a great variety of things; in no two bags would you find exactly the same things, and yet for all that in nearly all the bags would you find very much the same content.

I suppose we should, nearly all of us, be in agreement that what we meant by "democracy" — in the modern sense — was expressed morally by the statement:

All human beings are of equal value in the sight of God;

or legally: *All men are equal before the law;*

or practically: *One man's money is as good as another's.*

This implies a repudiation of caste, of inherent rank and function, of all privileges and all fixed subordinations. It is equalitarian or rebellious. And it is mildly paradoxical in the fact that, by insisting upon the importance of *all* individualities, it tends to restrain the exaltation of particular individuals; and by exalting all individuals to an equal level, it subordinates all individuals to the mass.

The democratic idea is no doubt very deeply rooted in the competitive and insurgent heart of man. It is implicit in Christianity and in Islam. But it was only in the sixteenth century, with the progressive decay of feudalism, that it began to be effective in the literary, political, and artistic expression of mankind. If you reflect, I think you will agree that its appearance was everywhere associated with the breakdown of outworn or outpaced systems, with processes of release and liberation, and generally also with processes of disintegration. Democracy to many minds will also involve the challenging and repudiation of authority. Some Catholic Democrats may question that, but I believe I shall have the general feeling with me in accepting that relaxation also as an aspect of democracy.

Now as democracy became ascendent in our world, its spirit produced new forms in political life, in literature, in art, in music. Let us consider these distinctive forms.

In politics it produced government by elected representative assemblies — elected by an ever-widening constituency of voters. We have Chambers of Representatives, Parliaments, spread throughout the world, and we have seen the franchise extend until manhood, and at last womanhood, suffrage seems everywhere in sight. It is strange to us nowadays to imagine a fully organized country without a constitution, a parliament, and periodic appeals to the mass of voters to indorse an elected government periodically replaceable. Yet six hundred years ago such a way of managing public affairs would have seemed fantastic. The Ancient World knew nothing of such devices. There were assemblies then, but not representative assemblies. The Greek democracies and republican Rome assembled all their citizens. Even countries like France and England before the sixteenth century, which had parliaments of a sort, did not conceive of them for a moment as governing bodies and kept the elected element in a minor position. I doubt if many of us fully realize the significance of the fact that the current political methods and assumptions of the world today, prevalent from China to Peru, would have been almost inconceivable even to highly intelligent human beings until twelve or fifteen generations ago.

So much for the political expression of democracy. In literature the democratic spirit found its natural vehicle in the novel. That too was new and distinctive. The tale, the story of adventures, mankind has had always — most usually of kings, princes, and heroic leaders — but it was only with the ascent of democracy that stories of characters, histories of common individual lives detached from politics, detached from any sense of social function, getting loose from any subordination or any responsibility, rose toward dominance in literature. At the very outset of the ascent of democracy came the great master Cervantes with his *Don Quixote*, scoffing at aristocracy, scoffing at privileged responsibility, mocking at the final futility of chivalrous mastery, putting his wisest words into the mouth of a clown and letting the flour mills of the common bread-eater overthrow his knight in armor. As Modern Democracy rose to its climax, the novel rose to its climax. The common characteristic of almost all the great novels of the nineteenth century, and up to our own time, is that they represent great crowds of individuals who follow trades, professions, and so forth, and who have either no public function or, if they have a public function, are not so differentiated by it that it is of any serious importance to the story and the values of the novel. The crowd of individuals and its interplay has become everything. Great ideas that bind people together into any form of collective life are disregarded. Great religious ideas, great political ideas and developments, are not there in any living, fermenting, debatable form — are even challenged and forbidden by the critics as having no place there. Consider Balzac, Dickens, Turgenev, Zola, and suchlike representative giants of this closing age. You think at once of a picture of humanity like a market place, like a fair, like the highroad to anywhere on a busy day. When political life appears, it appears just as any other sort of life. Here is a novel about elections and their humors, and here is one about peasants or fishermen. Just different scenery and costumes for the common story.

It strikes one at first as paradoxical that a period in which the exaltation of the individual has tended to make everyone a voter, a fractional sovereign of the whole world, should lead in the literary expression of the time to the disappearance, so to speak, of the whole world in a crowd of people. But the paradox involves no real inconsistency. What is everybody's business is nobody's business. The literature of the period of Democracy Ascendent displays what its political developments mask only very thinly — that Modern Democracy is not a permanent form of political and social life, but a phase of immense dissolution.

I think it would be comparatively easy to call the drama of the last three centuries to confirm the evidence of the novel. With the beginning of the period under consideration the miracle play which gave you Everyman and related him to God and Heaven and Hell gave place to Falstaff and his jolly companions, to the jealousy of Othello and the social aspirations of Monsieur Jourdain. If we turn to painting or to music we find all over this period the same effect of release — if you like — detachment, anyhow, from broad constructive conception and any sort of synthesis. There was very little detached painting in the old world. It was a part of something else. It decorated a building, it subserved a religious or political as well as a decorative purpose. If paintings were ever detachable, it was that they might be carried from a studio to an altar or a palace elsewhere. But with the sixteenth and seventeenth centuries painting became more and more liberated, said good-bye to the altarpiece and the palace and set out upon a life of its own. Now our painters are pure anarchists. They paint what pleases them for the sake of painting. They paint with a total disregard of any collective reality, and they are extremely offended when we build our houses with insufficient accommodation for their bright irrelevant observations upon the beauty of this and that.

So too music has broken loose. In the old world it was relevant and generally subordinate. I can imagine nothing more astonishing to a revenant from the ancient to our present world — not even a general election! — than a visit to a large concert hall during the performance, let us say, of Debussy's *L'Après-midi d'un Faune* or Ravel's *Septette* — this gathering of fortuitous people with no common function, to listen to music which, apart from its beauty, has no sort of collective meaning, no social object at all.

So far I have been attempting to make a case for the assertion that a consideration of the chief forms of human expression during the past age enables us to see in all of them democracy as a great process of loosening of bonds and general disintegration. But that loosening and disintegration were not universal. Now I would point out that in certain fields synthesis is so necessary, so inherent, that it has put up a very successful fight against the solvent tendencies of democracy.

In certain fields the ascent of democracy has not meant dissolution. No doubt the whole world of modern science became possible, and could only become possible, through the immense mental releases of ascendent democracy. But while in the realms of political, literary, and artistic expression democracy meant fragmentation and reduction to unorganized masses, in this newer world of science the onset of democracy was accompanied by synthesis of the most extensive sort. The development of science in the past three centuries has been dia-

metrically different from the political, literary, and artistic development of the same period. In the preceding ages, when everything
else was organized and relevant, science was a mere miscellany of
disconnected facts. With the release of the human mind from
authority, science began to be systematic and coherent. Release
from established traditions and precedences meant, in the world of
politics, literature, and art, limitless freedom. In science it meant
subjugation to experimental verification and the logical consistency
of fact with fact. So while the broad visible history of the Age of
Democracy so far has been one of release, escape, go as you please,
less conspicuous in laboratories and faculties and books and classes —
but in the end infinitely more significant — has been the growth of
one consistent vision of reality to which all things must be referred,
in which the moods of a man are made to march with chemical
changes, and the structure of the smallest atom is brought into relation
with the physics of the remotest star. To that release of synthetic
forces I shall presently return.

Next let me point out that this period of the ascent of democracy
has by no means been a period of easy, undisputed ascent. Nor has
it been merely a struggle against kings and aristocracies, privileges
and advantages, ancient traditions and old authority. The proposition that any man is as important as any other man has come hard
against certain mental and material realities. History, for the last
hundred years or so, has been largely the story of that collision.
This assertion of human equality has come against the severest
stresses at the boundaries where language meets language, and at
the geographical or social frontiers of dissimilar races. There the
common man, who has been willing to break down all the boundaries
between himself and his superiors, discovers deep instinctive dispositions to call a halt and draw the line. His mind is invaded by
an exaggerated sense of difference. He develops rivalries, suspicions,
antagonism. The Age of Democracy has also been the Age of
Nationalism. Never in the whole history of mankind have national
and racial antagonisms been so acute and conscious, so massive,
powerful, and dangerous as they have become during the ascent of
democracy. And yet that is entirely inconsistent with the larger and
completer aspirations of democracy, which have insisted always that
there shall be no distinctions of class or creed or race. One of the
most human and interesting things to watch at the present time is the
struggle of the labor parties in the European democracies against
their ingrained nationalist feelings and their belligerent patriotism.

And still more edifying are the fluctuations of the labor movement in such countries as Australia and South Africa with regard to yellow and brown immigration and the black vote.

But nationalism is not the greatest force that Modern Democracy has evoked against itself in its ascent. Far more fundamental is the synthetic drive in economic life, the enormous material pressure making for the replacement of individual and small competitive businesses by great and unifying enterprises, not merely in manufactures but in the production of such staples as coal, oil, iron and steel, cotton, food substances, and fundamental chemical products. The small man and the medium-sized business are pushed aside by highly organized and often quite scientifically organized concerns.

Here again the paradoxical aspect of democracy reappears. These great crystallizations of business — so large as to become at last monopolies — are plainly due to the releases of democracy, the freedom of science, invention, experiment, and enterprise, the lack of control and restriction the ascent of democracy has involved. But just as plainly do these crystallizations run counter to the more intimate feeling of democracy that every man is as good as every other man, that every man should be his own master and live his life in his own fashion after his own heart. Essential to the life and success of these big businesses is an intricate system of specialization and subordination of functions, and great freedoms of action for the executives. Most of those engaged in working them must be simply employed persons, and there must be great inequalities of authority and initiative between one man and another. In America a sort of reconciliation between this democratic reality of economic synthesis and democratic ideals of equality has been attempted by anti-trust legislation, and in England there is a small but delightfully logical movement for what is called the Distributive State, which is to cut up big businesses periodically and hand the bleeding fragments back to the common man. But the main expression of this conflict between synthesis and analysis in the democratic age has been the struggle for and against socialism. For there is scarcely any form of socialism that does not fall within the definition of an attempt to take the general economic life out of whatever hands control it at present and hand it over to the direction either of representatives elected by the workers, or of politicians elected by the voters of the entire community. Socialism is the attempt to democratize economic life as political life has already been democratized. And the final practical objection to socialism, partial or general — the objection that has usually carried the argument — has always been this: that politicians and elected people are not good enough for the job.

That brings me to the great conspicuous fact of our present time, to what I may call the arrest, the pause, in the advance of political democracy — to the fact that now and since the war there has been a growing distrust and discontent with the politicians and the political methods evolved by parliamentary democracy.

In two great Latin countries we have seen politicians and parliamentary institutions thrust aside with no signs of popular regret. In Russia a parliamentary republic appeared and vanished like a dream and gave place to a government by an organized association of a quite unprecedented pattern, the Communist Party, making only the slightest concessions to the representative idea. In China we see another extraordinary organization, the Kuomintang, consolidating the whole country with tremendous vigor in the face of the discredited parliamentarianism of Pekin. I will not discuss nor even raise other instances to enforce my argument that the magic has gone out of the method of government by general elections.

I have said enough, I think, to pose my essential question. Is the process of ascendent democracy played out? Or is it going on upon the old lines, in spite of these appearances? Or is it perhaps entering upon a new phase, a phase so different as practically to open a new age in the story of human experience? Are not its synthetic releases overtaking and mastering its tendency to fragmentation?

I have already betrayed, even in my title, the answer I am disposed to give to these questions, which is that democracy is entering upon a phase of revision in which parliaments and parliamentary bodies and political life as we know it today are destined to disappear. And that with the disappearance will come profound changes in all our methods of expression, indeed in all our lives.

For a number of generations the democratic process ruling the world has meant nothing but release, enfranchisement for freedom, the breaking down of controls and restraints and obstacles. There has been a world-wide detachment of individuals from codes and controls, subjugations and responsibilities, functions and duties. I suggest that this process of dissolution is at an end, and that mankind is faced — is challenged — by the need for reorganization and reorientation, political and social and intellectual, quite beyond the power of the negligent common voter and his politicians and the happy-go-lucky education and literature on which our minds are fed.

Let me state three great interrelated problems that have been facing mankind since the war, and let me remind you how futile so far have been the attempts of our modern democratic governments and communities to find solutions, to produce any hope of solutions, for these problems.

Foremost of these three in our consciousness is the problem of war. I need not dilate upon the cruelty, the horror, the sheer destructiveness into which the war process, equipped by modern science, necessarily develops. I will not talk of air bombardment, nor of poison gas and germs, nor of the practical abolition of the immunity of the non-combatant, nor of the complete economic and social disorganization that would probably ensue upon another group of wars. I take it that upon these matters you are of the same mind as myself. I take it that an enormous majority of humanity now wants no more war.

Yet consider how feeble have been the efforts of any government since 1918 to set up more than the flimsiest paper barriers against war. The sabers still rattle in Europe. The big guns are moved from position to position. In 1910 war hung over Europe, over the world, like a cliff we knew must fall. And it fell. Here and now, are we any safer? For what were these politicians elected? Little conferences, little junketings, little demonstrations of amiability — like tying back the cliff with colored cotton. Meanwhile the foundries go on making tanks, battleships, guns, all the world over.

And second of these three problems Modern Democracy has no power to handle is the monetary question. If anything is plain, if there is anything upon which everyone must be agreed, it is that for the proper working of contemporary civilization a stable money basis of world-wide validity is essential. Just so far as money is unstable, so far does speculation undermine and replace sound business enterprise and honest work for profit. For eight years now we have seen the exchanges of the world dance together. We have seen the effort for economic recuperation crippled and deflected by this drunkard dance of money. Each democratic government has pursued its own policy according to its lights and apparent interests. The bankers and financiers have performed their mysterious operations in obscurity. And nowhere, in any democracy, has the mass of voters shown the slightest understanding of, or ability to grasp, the processes which threw them out of employment, made their poor savings evaporate, and snatched the necessaries of life out of their reach.

But the military obsession with its war threat and the monetary tangle are, so to speak, merely complications of the more general riddle before mankind, which is that, chiefly through changes in methods of transport and the advance of science and invention, economic life has become world-wide and a certain economic unity is being imposed willy-nilly upon the globe. A vast change of scale is happening in economic life — a vast extension of range. So that the method of the small individual manufacturer and trader, the method even of the moderate-sized competing company, the method even of national groups, tend to be superseded, in the case of all our staple supplies, by combinations upon a universal scale. The master problem before us all, before our race, is how to achieve this world economic unity, how to produce a system of world controls with as little blind experiment as possible, without the sacrifice of countless millions, of whole generations, in the throes of this inevitable reconstruction. How to establish enough political unity in the world to insure peace; how to establish enough political unity to save industry and trade from becoming the mere preliminaries to a gamble with the exchange; how to establish enough political unity to control and direct the distribution of raw products, employment, and manufactured goods about the earth — that, in brief, is the present task before the human intelligence. And we have no governments, we have nothing in the world able to deal with this trinity of problems, this three-headed Sphinx which has waylaid and now confronts mankind.

Now the sense of the inadequacy of modern democratic governments for the task before them grows upon us all. What is going to be attempted, what is going to be done in the matter? We are all familiar nowadays with various projects of electoral reform. Some, such as the referendum, aim merely at restraining and paralyzing governments. Others, such as the proposal to have smaller representative bodies of members elected by large constituencies by the methods of proportional representation by the simple transferable vote, would no doubt give a more free and vigorous assembly, and go far to abolish political parties and the hack professional politician. But none of these electoral reform projects goes to the root of the trouble with Modern Democracy, which is the indifference, ignorance, and incapacity of the common man toward public affairs.

We have to recognize more plainly than is generally admitted today that the ordinary voter does not care a rap for his vote. He does not connect it with the idea of the world at large, nor use it to express any will or purpose whatever about the general conduct of things. I have already called attention to the fact that the novel, the characteristic literary form of Modern Democracy, and the modern drama ignore all comprehensive political and religious ideas. Thereby they display current reality with the utmost veracity. These forms, the novel and the play, have so far embodied no new concepts and directions about life as a whole; they have simply presented life at large released from preëxisting concepts and directions. Our modern democratic governments reveal as clearly that the onset of Modern Democracy did not mean a transfer of power from the few to the many, but a disappearance of power from the world. The vote is an instrument of defense, and not a constructive tool. Faced with gigantic constructive needs of ever-increasing urgency, political democracy fails. It cannot produce inventive and original governments; it cannot produce resolute governments; it cannot produce understanding, far-thinking governments. Its utmost act of will is the capricious or peevish dismissal of governments by a general election.

For a century or more it has worked well that the world should be undergoverned and underorganized. In that liberty science has won its way, established itself in a world-wide system of research and record, gained an invincible inertia. Music has achieved the most glorious developments, painting risen to unprecedented levels of technique, literature learned a new fearlessness, and industry and commerce have tried and expanded a thousand subtle and huge combinations no official control would ever have permitted. The mere breakdown of the cramping systems of the past, the escape from traditional privilege and authority, was enough to permit the great expansion of life that has gone on since the sixteenth century. But there is a limit to unguided and uncontrolled expansion, and at that limit we seem to have arrived with a war threat, a monetary instability, and a chronic conflict between the organic growth of economic processes and the desire of the worker for freedom and happiness, which none of the governments in the world seem to have the necessary initiative and vigor to meet.

We need now more definite direction and government in human affairs, on a scale and of a quality commensurate with the three mighty problems our race has to face. It is idle to talk of returning to the little royalties, aristocracies, and so forth, of the pre-democratic past. Are there any signs of a new, more decisive and more vigorously constructive form of government in our world? I submit there are, and on these signs I rest my anticipations of the Age of Democracy under Revision that is dawning upon us. Coming events cast their shadows before, and a keen eye can detect a number of shadows of what is coming. But the two shadows to which I would particularly draw your attention are the Communist Party and Fascism.

Let me be perfectly clear upon one point here. I am an unsparing hostile critic of Marxist communism. I have a strong dislike for many aspects of Fascism — including particularly its head. May I insist upon that? There is a mental disease about called "Seeing red," and I want to avoid any manifestations of that. I am not sympathetic with communist ideas. In my book, *The World of William Clissold*, you will find a most careful, elaborate, and destructive criticism of Marxism, and my treatment of Lenin has brought down upon me the violent vituperation of Mr. Trotsky. Quite as fervently have I plunged into conflict with Fascism. I am anti-communist and anti-Fascist. But what I am discussing now is not the mental content of these two movements, but their quality and spirit as organizations. . . .

They are both mainly composed of youngish people. They are so far democratic that they are open to anyone who will obey their disciplines and satisfy their requirements. Some of my hearers may know something of the intimate lives of young communists or young Fascists. The movement dominates the entire life. The individual gives himself — or herself — to the movement in a spirit essentially religious. It enters into the life and into the conscience as few religions do nowadays. Communism indeed claims that it is a complete substitute for religion. Everything else is to be subordinated to the ends of the movement. With the Fascist there is the supposed good of the Italian community; with the communist it is the supposed good of the whole world. These movements began as voluntary movements of young people, so concerned about public affairs as willingly to give themselves to the sacrifices and dangers — and adventure — involved. I submit it is a fact of profound significance that Fascism could attract enough vigorous young people to capture and hold and govern Italy, and that the Communist Party, with perhaps a hundred thousand members or so in Russia, could seize upon the ruins of that war-broken land and hold it against all comers.

One has to admit, in spite of many assertions to the contrary, that neither in Italy nor Russia do the masses of the population seem to resent the dictatorship of these associations. No vote famine has broken out in these disenfranchised countries. You do not find haggard peasants wandering about in search of a polling booth. So that our assertion that the average common man, the common voter, does not care a rap about the commonweal and his vote, has to be supplemented by the fact that there is an active-minded minority capable of so vivid an interest in the direction of public affairs as to make the most complete sacrifices to see things going in the way it considers right. This is most conspicuous in Russia and Italy, but in China students' associations, closely similar in character, are taking possession of the larger half of the country, and in Japan and many other countries kindred bodies of mentally energetic types are playing an increasingly important rôle in public life. In the nineteenth century such types were either not stimulated to activity, or their energies were spent upon parliamentary politics or diverted in other directions. Now all over the world a certain section of them is taking its activities out of parliamentary affairs and setting itself into vigorous competition with the parliamentary system.

You see I am building my expectation of a new phase in human affairs upon the belief that there is a profoundly serious minority in the mass of our generally indifferent species. I cannot understand the existence of any of the great religions, I cannot explain any fine and grave constructive process in history, unless there is such a serious minority amid our confusions. They are the salt of the earth, these people capable of devotion and of living lives for remote and mighty ends — and, unless the composition of our species has altered, they are as numerous as they have ever been. I see them less and less satisfied and used by existing loyalties and traditional faiths. I see them ready to crystallize about any constructive idea powerful enough to grip their minds. Is it not reasonable then to hold that these associations, these concentrations of mentally energetic types for political ends, these revelations of politico-religious fervor in the community — considerable as they are even now — are the mere beginnings of much greater things? The breakdown of the old loyalties and the old faiths in the past age has released this great fund of effort and synthetic possibility for new applications. And over against it we have the need for world peace — which can be achieved only by some sort of political unity — and for social adjustment, which seems only possible through the comprehensible handling of world economic affairs as one great system.

More than twenty years ago, in a book called *A Modern Utopia*, when there was not a fact on earth to support me, I sketched a World State ruled by a self-devoted organization of volunteers. Today, I can recall that conception of a future society and I can appeal to Russia, China, Italy, and much that is astir everywhere, to substantiate that possibility. I have spoken of the youth in these two specimen movements I have cited, but it is not merely the young who will be found willing to orient their dispersed lives to great aims and comprehensive ideas.   The pain of aimlessness and ineffectiveness can be aroused at any age with the realization of insecurity.   The search for a consuming objective ends only with life.   In short, we have the morally energetic types needed for such a movement in a released and nascent state.   We have the manifest need for such a movement.   We are gathering the creative ideas and accumulating the impulse for such a movement.   What is there to prevent a great politico-religious drive for social and world unity taking hold everywhere of the active and adventurous minority of mankind — that is to say, of all mankind that matters — even quite soon?

That is the essence of what I want to put before you. . . .   That is what I mean when I say that the phase of democracy as release has come to its end, and that we are already in the beginning of the phase of Democratic Synthesis, a great religious-spirited phase.   If you choose to link it to Christianity or Islam or Buddhism or any existing democratic religion; or with communism, that religious substitute; or call it in itself the Religion of Progress, nothing that I am saying here will stand in your way.   And if this diagnosis is correct, then necessarily the changing spirit of democracy, the change from fragmentation and irrelevance to synthesis and reference to directive general ideas on a universal scale, will become apparent in all forms of human expression.

Here I can but ask: Is that so?   In political life, is there any tendency among intelligent people to be dissatisfied with the passive rôle of voters and to attempt, in all sorts of ways, to exert a direct influence on common affairs?   In intellectual life, is there an increasing tendency to discuss world-wide problems — political, economic, social?   Is there a marked increase of such literature?   A livelier interest in such questions?   If this thesis is right, the novel and the drama should be changing.   They should both be bringing in great issues, a quasi-religious attitude to world affairs as a living part of the human story.   The novel should no longer be merely a picture of a spectacle relying for its interest upon adventures and the extraordinary traits of individual characters, in no way responsible for the whole.   It should be turning decisively toward responsibility, to what I might call creative propaganda.   It should be permeated by the question: What do these lives make for?   And the drama . . . should be no longer the well-made play grouping itself around a situation.   Is such a play as Shaw's *Saint Joan*, or Toller's *Masses and Men*, any intimation of Synthetic Democracy upon the stage?   Again, is there in painting and music any tendency to return from . . . pure painting and pure music to breadth and profundity of reference?

GOVERNMENT IN THE MACHINE AGE[1]

John Dewey

JOHN DEWEY was born in Burlington, Vermont, in 1859, and educated at the University of Vermont and Johns Hopkins. After teaching at the Universities of Michigan and Minnesota, he was asked by William Rainey Harper in 1894 to head the philosophy department of the recently founded University of Chicago. His first important writings were upon philosophy and psychology, but he soon turned to education, testing his ideas in the Laboratory School in Chicago in 1896–1903. During 1902–1904 he was also director of the Chicago University School of Education. In 1904 he went to Columbia University as professor of philosophy. Retirement from teaching in 1930 meant no cessation in his vigorous production of books and articles.

It is impossible to explain John Dewey's philosophy in simple terms and brief space without injustice to it. He began his career under the influence of Charles Peirce, chief founder of the distinctively American philosophy of pragmatism, and of T. H. Green and Bernard Bosanquet. It was one of Peirce's principles that, as William James put it, "the effective meaning of any philosophic proposition can always be brought down to some particular consequence in our future practical experience." Dr. Dewey has greatly developed some of Peirce's doctrines and combined them with ideas of his own; but all his work is governed by a belief that ideas should be instrumental in character, that the success of reflective thought is measured by the degree in which thinking disposes of some actual difficulty. In carrying out this doctrine he applies logic and philosophy to any number of practical questions. He did so with notable effect in education; he has done so with questions of morals; with the relations between public and state; with the relation of industrial arts to fine arts; with problems of religion and politics. In dealing with all the basic difficulties of modern life he would find answers by employing a general logic of experience for inquiry and interpretation. Hence it is that his writings, while compelling attention from philosophers, have won the interest of plain men and women absorbed in current issues. He has been the most influential philosopher the United States has yet known because he has done most to come down into the market-place.

Dr. Dewey's books, produced at fairly rapid intervals during nearly fifty years, indicate the breadth of his interest. They range from Leibnitz to Russia, from ethics to Darwin, from German philosophy to American politics. Among the more important titles are *School and Society* (1899); *How We Think* (1909); *Democracy and Education* (1916); *Reconstruction in Philosophy* (1920); *Experience and Nature* (1925); and *Individualism Old and New* (1930). He is without grace of style and often hard to read; he deals chiefly with difficult and technical questions; but he constantly inspires thought. As Morris R. Cohen writes, his ideas have won acceptance partly because they correspond to the prevailing American temper of the time. "Dewey appeals powerfully to the prevailing distrust of otherworldli-

[1] From *The Public and Its Problems*, by John Dewey. Reprinted by permission of Henry Holt and Company, publishers.

ness, a distrust which permeates even our theology with its emphasis on the social mission of the church. The doctrine that all ideas are and ought to be instruments for reforming the world and making it a better place to live in appeals at once to popular utilitarianism, to the worship of immediate practical results of which Theodore Roosevelt was such a conspicuous representative. . . . A philosophy which views nature as material to be transformed by our intelligence appeals to the prevailing light-hearted optimism which sees success as the constant reward of intelligent effort and finds no inherent obstacles to the establishment of a heaven on earth."

Optimism about democracy is today under a cloud. We are familiar with denunciation and criticism which, however, often reveal their emotional source in their peevish and undiscriminating tone. Many of them suffer from the same error into which earlier laudations fell. They assume that democracy is the product of an idea, of a single and consistent intent. Carlyle was no admirer of democracy, but in a lucid moment he said: "Invent the printing press and democracy is inevitable." Add to this: Invent the railway, the telegraph, mass manufacture, and concentration of population in urban centers, and some form of democratic government is, humanly speaking, inevitable. Political democracy as it exists today calls for adverse criticism in abundance. But the criticism is only an exhibition of querulousness and spleen or of a superiority complex, unless it takes cognizance of the conditions out of which popular government has issued. All intelligent political criticism is comparative. It deals not with all-or-none situations, but with practical alternatives; an absolutistic indiscriminate attitude, whether in praise or blame, testifies to the heat of feeling rather than the light of thought.

American democratic polity was developed out of genuine community life; that is, association in local and small centers where industry was mainly agricultural and where production was carried on mainly with hand tools. It took form when English political habits and legal institutions worked under pioneer conditions. The forms of association were stable, even though their units were mobile and migratory. Pioneer conditions put a high premium upon personal work, skill, ingenuity, initiative, and adaptability, and upon neighborly sociability. The township or some not much larger area was the political unit, the town meeting the political medium; and roads, schools, the peace of the community, were the political objectives. The state was a sum of such units, and the national state a federation — unless perchance a confederation — of states. The imagination of the founders did not travel far beyond what could be accomplished and understood in a congeries of self-governing communities. The machinery provided for the selection of the chief executive of the federal union is illustrative evidence. The electoral college assumed that citizens would choose men locally known for their high standing; and that these men when chosen would gather together for consultation to name someone known to them for his probity and public spirit and knowledge. The rapidity with which the scheme fell into disuse is evidence of the transitoriness of the state of affairs that was predicated. But at the outset there was no dream of the time when the very names of the presidential electors would be unknown to the mass of the voters, when they would plump for a "ticket" arranged in a more or less private caucus, and when the electoral college would be an impersonal registering machine, such that it would be treachery to employ the personal judgment which was originally contemplated as the essence of the affair.

The local conditions under which our institutions took shape is well indicated by our system, apparently so systemless, of public education. Anyone who has tried to explain it to a European will understand what is meant. One is asked, say, what method of administration is followed, what is the course of study, and what are the authorized methods of teaching. The American member to the dialogue replies that in this state, or more likely county, or town, or even some section of a town called a district, matters stand thus and thus; somewhere else, so and so. The participant from this side is perhaps thought by the foreigner to be engaged in concealing his ignorance; and it would certainly take a veritable cyclopedic knowledge to state the matter in its entirety. The impossibility of making any moderately generalized reply renders it almost indispensable to resort to an historical account in order to be intelligible. A little colony, the members of which are probably mostly known to one another in advance, settle in what is almost, or quite, a wilderness. From belief in its benefits and by tradition, chiefly religious, they wish their children to know at least how to read, write, and figure. Families can only rarely provide a tutor; the neighbors over a certain area, in New England an area smaller even than the township, combine in a "school district." They get a schoolhouse built, perhaps by their own labor, and hire a teacher by means of a committee, and the teacher is paid from the taxes. Custom determines the limited course of study, and tradition the methods of the teacher, modified by whatever personal insight and skill he may bring to bear. The wilderness is gradually subdued; a network of highways, then of railways, unites the previously scattered communities. Large cities grow up; studies grow more numerous and methods more carefully scrutinized. The larger unit, the state, but not the federal state, provides schools for training teachers, and their qualifications are more carefully looked into and tested. But subject to certain quite general conditions imposed by the state legislature, but not the national state, local maintenance and control remain the rule. The community pattern is more complicated, but is not destroyed. The instance seems richly instructive as to the state of affairs under which our borrowed English political institutions were reshaped and forwarded.

We have inherited, in short, local town-meeting practices and ideas. But we live and act and have our being in a continental national state. We are held together by non-political bonds, and the political forms are stretched and legal institutions patched in an *ad hoc* and improvised manner to do the work they have to do. Political structures fix the channels in which non-political, industrialized currents flow. Railways, travel and transportation, commerce, the mails, telegraph and telephone, newspapers, create enough similarity of ideas and sentiments to keep the thing going as a whole, for they create interaction and interdependence. The unprecedented thing is that states, as distinguished from military empires, can exist over such a wide area. The notion of maintaining a unified state, even nominally self-governing, over a country as extended as the United States and consisting of a large and racially diversified population would once have seemed the wildest of fancies. It was assumed that such a state could be found only in territories hardly larger than a city-state and with a homogeneous population. It seemed almost self-evident to Plato — as to Rousseau later — that a genuine state could hardly be larger than the number of persons capable of personal acquaintance with one another. Our modern state-unity is due to the consequences of technology employed so as to facilitate the rapid and easy circulation of opinions and information, and so as to generate constant and intricate interaction far beyond the limits of face-to-face communities. Political and legal forms have only piecemeal and haltingly, with great lag, accommodated themselves to the industrial transformation. The elimination of distance, at the base of which are physical agencies, has called into being the new form of political association.

The wonder of the performance is the greater because of the odds against which it has been achieved. The stream of immigrants which has poured in is so large and heterogeneous that, under conditions which formerly obtained, it would have disrupted any semblance of unity as surely as the migratory invasion of alien hordes once upset the social equilibrium of the European continent. No deliberately adopted measures could have accomplished what has actually happened. Mechanical forces have operated, and it is no cause for surprise if the effect is more mechanical than vital. The reception of new elements of population in large number from heterogeneous peoples, often hostile to one another at home, and the welding them into even an outward show of unity is an extraordinary feat. In many respects, the consolidation has occurred so rapidly and ruthlessly that much of value has been lost which different peoples might have contributed. The creation of political unity has also promoted social and intellectual uniformity, a standardization favorable to mediocrity. Opinion has been regimented as well as outward behavior. The temper and flavor of the pioneer have evaporated with extraordinary rapidity; their precipitate, as is often noted, is apparent only in the Wild West romance and the movie. What Bagehot called the cake of custom formed with increasing acceleration, and the cake is too often flat and soggy. Mass production is not confined to the factory.

The resulting political integration has confounded the expectations of earlier critics of popular government as much as it must surprise its early backers if they are gazing from on high upon the present scene. The critics predicted disintegration, instability. They foresaw the new society falling apart, dissolving into mutually repellent animated grains of sand. They, too, took seriously the theory of individualism as the basis of democratic government. A stratification of society into immemorial classes within which each person performed his stated duties according to his fixed position seemed to them the only warrant of stability. They had no faith that human beings released from the pressure of this system could hold together in any unity. Hence they prophesied a flux of governmental régimes, as individuals formed factions, seized power, and then lost it as some newly improvised faction proved stronger. Had the facts conformed to the theory of individualism, they would doubtless have been right. But, like the authors of the theory, they ignored the technological forces making for consolidation.

In spite of attained integration, or rather perhaps because of its nature, the public seems to be lost; it is certainly bewildered. The government, officials and their activities, are plainly with us. Legislatures make laws with luxurious abandon; subordinate officials engage in a losing struggle to enforce some of them; judges on the bench deal as best they can with the steadily mounting pile of disputes that

come before them. But where is the public which these officials are
supposed to represent? How much more is it than geographical
names and official titles? The United States, the state of Ohio or
New York, the county of this and the city of that? Is the public
much more than what a cynical diplomat once called Italy: a geographical expression? Just as philosophers once imputed a substance
to qualities and traits in order that the latter might have something
in which to inhere and thereby gain a conceptual solidity and consistency which they lacked on their face, so perhaps our political
"common sense" philosophy imputes a public only to support and
substantiate the behavior of officials. How can the latter be public
officers, we despairingly ask, unless there is a public? If a public
exists, it is surely as uncertain about its own whereabouts as philosophers since Hume have been about the residence and make-up of the
self. The number of voters who take advantage of their majestic
right is steadily decreasing in proportion to those who might use it.
The ratio of actual to eligible voters is now about one-half. In spite
of somewhat frantic appeal and organized effort, the endeavor to
bring voters to a sense of their privileges and duties has so far been
noted for failure. A few preach the impotence of all politics; the
many nonchalantly practice abstinence and indulge in indirect action.
Skepticism regarding the efficacy of voting is openly expressed, not
only in the theories of intellectuals, but in the words of lowbrow
masses: "What difference does it make whether I vote or not?
Things go on just the same anyway. My vote never changed anything." Those somewhat more reflective add: "It is nothing but a
fight between the ins and the outs. The only difference made by an
election is as to who get the jobs, draw the salaries, and shake down
the plum trees."

Those still more inclined to generalization assert that the whole
apparatus of political activities is a kind of protective coloration to
conceal the fact that big business rules the governmental roost in any
case. Business is the order of the day, and the attempt to stop or
deflect its course is as futile as Mrs. Partington essaying to sweep back
the tides with a broom. Most of those who hold these opinions would
profess to be shocked if the doctrine of economic determinism were
argumentatively expounded to them, but they act upon a virtual
belief in it. Nor is acceptance of the doctrine limited to radical
socialists. It is implicit in the attitude of men of big business and
financial interests, who revile the former as destructive "Bolshevists."
For it is their firm belief that "prosperity" — a word which has taken

on religious color — is the great need of the country, that they are its authors and guardians, and hence by right the determiners of policy. Their denunciation of the "materialism" of socialists is based simply upon the fact that the latter want a different distribution of material force and well-being than that which satisfies those now in control.

The unfitness of whatever public exists, with respect to the government which is nominally its organ, is made manifest in the extralegal agencies which have grown up. Intermediary groups are closest to the political conduct of affairs. It is interesting to compare the English literature of the eighteenth century regarding factions with the status actually occupied by parties. Factionalism was decried by all thinkers as the chief enemy to political stability. Their voice of condemnation is reëchoed in the writing of early nineteenth century American writers on politics. Extensive and consolidated factions under the name of parties are now not only a matter of course, but popular imagination can conceive of no other way by which officials may be selected and governmental affairs carried on. The centralizing movement has reached a point where even a third party can lead only a spasmodic and precarious existence. Instead of individuals who in the privacy of their consciousness make choices which are carried into effect by personal volition, there are citizens who have the blessed opportunity to vote for a ticket of men mostly unknown to them, and which is made up for them by an under-cover machine in a caucus whose operations constitute a kind of political predestination. There are those who speak as if ability to choose between two tickets were a high exercise of individual freedom. But it is hardly the kind of liberty contemplated by the authors of the individualistic doctrine. "Nature abhors a vacuum." When the public is as uncertain and obscure as it is today, and hence as remote from government, bosses with their political machines fill the void between government and the public. Who pulls the strings which move the bosses and generates power to run the machines is a matter of surmise rather than of record, save for an occasional overt scandal.

Quite aside, however, from the allegation that big business plays the tune and pulls the strings to which bosses dance, it is true that parties are not creators of policies to any large extent at the present time. For parties yield in piecemeal accommodation to social currents, irrespective of professed principles. As these lines are written a weekly periodical remarks: "Since the end of the Civil War practically all the more important measures which have been embodied in federal legislation have been reached without a national election which turned

upon the issue and which divided the two major parties." Reform of
civil service, regulation of railways, popular election of senators,
national income tax, suffrage for women, and prohibition are supported to substantiate the statement. Hence its other remark
appears justified: "American party politics seem at times to be a
device for preventing issues which may excite popular feeling and
involve bitter controversies from being put up to the American
people."

A negatively corroborating fact is seen in the fate of the child labor
amendment. The need of giving to Congress power to regulate child
labor, denied it by decisions of the Supreme Court, had been asserted
in the platforms of all political parties; the idea was endorsed by the
last three of the Presidents belonging to the party in power. Yet so
far, the proposed amendment to the Constitution has not begun to
secure the needed support. Political parties may rule, but they do
not govern. The public is so confused and eclipsed that it cannot
even use the organs through which it is supposed to mediate political
action and polity.

The same lesson is taught by the breakdown of the theory of the
responsibility of elected representatives to the electorate, to say
nothing of their alleged liability to be called before the bar of the
private judgment of individuals. Is it at least suggestive that the
terms of the theory are best met in legislation of the "pork barrel"
type? There a representative may be called to account for failure to
meet local desire, or be rewarded for pertinacity and success in fulfilling its wishes. But only rarely is the theory borne out in important
matters, although occasionally it works. But the instances are so
infrequent that any skilled political observer could enumerate them
by name. The reason for the lack of personal liability to the electorate is evident. The latter is composed of rather amorphous groups.
Their political ideas and beliefs are mostly in abeyance between
elections. Even in times of political excitement, artificially accelerated, their opinions are moved collectively by the current of the
group rather than by independent personal judgment. As a rule,
what decides the fate of a person who comes up for election is neither
his political excellence nor his political defects. The current runs
for or against the party in power, and the individual candidate sinks
or swims as runs the current. At times there is a general consensus of
sentiment, a definite trend in favor of "progressive legislation" or a
desire for a "return to normalcy." But even then only exceptional
candidates get by on any basis of personal responsibility to the

electorate. The "tidal wave" swamps some; the "landslide" carries others into office. At other times, habit, party funds, the skill of managers of the machine, the portrait of a candidate with his firm jaw, his lovely wife and children, and a multitude of other irrelevancies, determine the issue.

These scattered comments are not made in the belief that they convey any novel truth. Such things are familiar; they are the commonplaces of the political scene. They could be extended indefinitely by any careful observer of the scene. The significant thing is that familiarity has bred indifference if not contempt. Indifference is the evidence of current apathy, and apathy is testimony to the fact that the public is so bewildered that it cannot find itself. The remarks are not made with a view to drawing a conclusion. They are offered with a view to outlining a problem: What is the public? If there is a public, what are the obstacles in the way of its recognizing and articulating itself? Is the public a myth? Or does it come into being only in periods of marked social transition when crucial alternative issues stand out, such as that between throwing one's lot in with the conservation of established institutions or with forwarding new tendencies? In a reaction against dynastic rule which has come to be felt as despotically oppressive? In a transfer of social power from agrarian classes to industrial?

Is not the problem at the present time that of securing experts to manage administrative matters, other than the framing of policies? It may be urged that the present confusion and apathy are due to the fact that the real energy of society is now directed in all non-political matters by trained specialists who manage things, while politics are carried on with a machinery and ideas formed in the past to deal with quite another sort of situation. There is no particular public concerned in finding expert school instructors, competent doctors, or business managers. Nothing called a public intervenes to instruct physicians in the practice of the healing art or merchants in the art of salesmanship. The conduct of these callings and others characteristic of our time are decided by science and pseudo-science. The important governmental affairs at present, it may be argued, are also technically complicated matters to be conducted properly by experts. And if at present people are not educated to the recognition of the importance of finding experts and of intrusting administration to them, it may plausibly be asserted that the prime obstruction lies in the superstitious belief that there is a public concerned to determine the formation and execution of general social policies. Perhaps the apathy of the electorate is due to the irrelevant artificiality of the issues with which it is attempted to work up factitious excitement. Perhaps this artificiality is in turn mainly due to the survival of political beliefs and machinery from a period when science and technology were so immature as not to permit of a definite technique for handling definite social situations and meeting specific social needs. The attempt to decide by law that the legends of a primitive Hebrew people regarding the genesis of man are more authoritative than the results of scientific inquiry might be cited as a typical example of the sort of thing which is bound to happen when the accepted doctrine is that a public organized for political purposes, rather than experts guided by specialized inquiry, is the final umpire and arbiter of issues.

The questions of most concern at present may be said to be matters like sanitation, public health, healthful and adequate housing, transportation, planning of cities, regulation and distribution of immigrants, selection and management of personnel, right methods of instruction and preparation of competent teachers, scientific adjustment of taxation, efficient management of funds, and so on. These are technical matters, as much so as the construction of an efficient engine for purposes of traction or locomotion. Like it they are to be settled by inquiry into facts; and as the inquiry can be carried on only by those especially equipped, so the results of inquiry can be utilized only by trained technicians. What has counting heads, decision by majority, and the whole apparatus of traditional government to do with such things? Given such considerations, and the public and its organization for political ends is not only a ghost, but a ghost which walks and talks, and obscures, confuses, and misleads governmental action in a disastrous way.

Personally I am far from thinking that such considerations, pertinent as they are to administrative activities, cover the entire political field. They ignore forces which have to be composed and resolved before technical and specialized action can come into play. But they aid in giving definiteness and point to a fundamental question: What, after all, is the public under present conditions? What are the reasons for its eclipse? What hinders it from finding and identifying itself? By what means shall its inchoate and amorphous estate be organized into effective political action relevant to present social needs and opportunities? What has happened to the public in the century and a half since the theory of political democracy was urged with such assurance and hope?

Previous discussion has brought to light some conditions out of which the public is generated. It has also set forth some of the causes through which a "new age of human relationships" has been brought into being. These two arguments form the premises which, when they are related to each other, will provide our answer to the questions just raised. Indirect, extensive, enduring, and serious consequences of conjoint and interacting behavior call a public into existence having a common interest in controlling these consequences. But the machine age has so enormously expanded, multiplied, intensified, and complicated the scope of the indirect consequences, has formed such immense and consolidated unions in action, on an impersonal rather than a community basis, that the resultant public cannot identify and distinguish itself. And this discovery is obviously an antecedent condition of any effective organization on its part. Such is our thesis regarding the eclipse which the public idea and interest have undergone. There are too many publics and too much of public concern for our existing resources to cope with. The problem of a democratically organized public is primarily and essentially an intellectual problem, in a degree to which the political affairs of prior ages offer no parallel.

Our concern at this time is to state how it is that the machine age in developing the Great Society has invaded and partially disintegrated the small communities of former times without generating a Great Community. The facts are familiar enough; our especial affair is to point out their connections with the difficulties under which the organization of a democratic public is laboring. For the very familiarity with the phenomena conceals their significance and blinds us to their relation to immediate political problems.

The scope of the Great War furnishes an urgent as well as convenient starting point for the discussion. The extent of that war is unparalleled, because the conditions involved in it are so new. The dynastic conflicts of the seventeenth century are called by the same name: we have only one word, "war." The sameness of the word too easily conceals from us the difference in significance. We think of all wars as much the same thing, only the last one was horrible beyond others. Colonies were drawn in: self-governing ones entered voluntarily; possessions were levied upon for troops; alliances were formed with remote countries in spite of diversities of race and culture, as in the cases of Great Britain and Japan, Germany and Turkey. Literally every continent upon the globe was involved. Indirect effects were as broad as direct. Not merely soldiers, but finance, industry, and opinion were mobilized and consolidated. Neutrality was a pre-

carious affair.   There was a critical epoch in the history of the world
when the Roman Empire assembled in itself the lands and peoples of
the Mediterranean basin.   The World War stands out as an indubitable proof that what then happened for a region has now happened
for the world, only there is now no comprehensive political organization to include the various divided yet interdependent countries.
Anyone who even partially visualizes the scene has a convincing reminder of the meaning of the Great Society: that it exists, and that
it is not integrated.

Extensive, enduring, intricate, and serious indirect consequences of
the conjoint activity of a comparatively few persons traverse the
globe.   The similes of the stone cast into the pool, ninepins in a row,
the spark which kindles a vast conflagration, are pale in comparison
with the reality.   The spread of the war seemed like the movement of
an uncontrolled natural catastrophe.   The consolidation of peoples in
inclosed, nominally independent, national states has its counterpart
in the fact that their acts affect groups and individuals in other states
all over the world.   The connections and ties which transferred
energies set in motion in one spot to all parts of the earth were not
tangible and visible;   they do not stand out as do politically bounded
states.   But the war is there to show that they are as real, and to
prove that they are not organized and regulated.   It suggests that
existing political and legal forms and arrangements are incompetent
to deal with the situation.   For the latter is the joint product of the
existing constitution of the political state and the working of non-
political forces not adjusted to political forms.   We cannot expect the
causes of a disease to combine effectually to cure the disease they
create.   The need is that the non-political forces organize themselves
to transform existing political structures: that the divided and
troubled publics integrate.

THE POSITION AND PROSPECTS OF COMMUNISM[1]

Harold J. Laski

HAROLD J. LASKI was born in Manchester, England, in 1893, and educated at Oxford. He has lectured at Harvard and McGill Universities and been a visiting professor at Yale University; he has also served on various governmental bodies in Great Britain. Since 1926 he has been professor of political science in the University of London.

Mr. Laski is best known as the author of books upon the theory of sovereignty. His pluralistic view of sovereignty has attracted much attention. He attacks the doctrine that the power of the state should be absolute over the individuals and groups composing it, and that the state has moral title to a preëminent position. On the contrary, he asserts that the acts of the state are in reality merely the acts of those persons who happen to hold power, and that they therefore possess no special moral sanction. Moreover, the acts of the state must be tested by their usefulness and effectiveness; hence, such acts must compete with those of other associations, whose motives and aims may be quite as earnest and elevated, for the support or allegiance of individuals. In brief, Laski holds that the old doctrine of absolute sovereignty is a legal fiction and a barren concept; he applies a thoroughly pragmatic criticism to it. Among other writers who have written in stimulating fashion on the pluralistic theory of the state are G. D. H. Cole, S. G. Hobson, and Graham Wallas. Mr. Laski's ideas are set forth in a series of books — *The Problem of Sovereignty* (1917); *The Foundations of Government* (1921); *A Grammar of Politics* (1925); *Liberty in the Modern State* (1930); *The Dangers of Obedience* (1930); and *Democracies in Crisis* (1933).

I

"A specter is haunting Europe — the specter of communism." Eighty-five years have passed since the *Communist Manifesto* opened with those fateful words. It is little less since Tocqueville predicted that the democracy, weary of the inadequate results of their political emancipation, would one day turn to the destruction of the rights of property as the condition precedent to their economic emancipation. "In matters of social construction," he wrote, "the field of possibilities is much more extensive than men living in their various societies are willing to imagine."[2]

After the breakdown of the revolutions of 1848 there was little disposition among the statesmen of Europe and America to take the growth of socialism with any profound seriousness until the

[1] From *Foreign Affairs*, October, 1932. Reprinted by permission.
[2] *Recollections*, p. 101.

epoch of the war. A moment of horror at the events in Paris in 1871, a sense that the abortive revolution in Russia of 1905 might be the prelude to a vaster drama, exhausted the sense of doubt about the foundations of the social system. Neither the experience of France nor of Germany seemed to point to the likelihood of socialist governments; and as late as 1908, President Lowell, reflecting upon the English position at the close of his famous treatise,[1] concluded that "unless the Labor Party should grow in a way that seems unlikely" there was no prospect of a class division in English politics in the near future. Lord Grey, indeed, on the very eve of the war, was troubled by a sense that its prolongation might result in a repetition of 1848; but the universal welcome which greeted the March Revolution in Russia did not suggest that men had any doubts about the foundations of a capitalist society. At no time in American history prior to the war had the socialist movement made any profound impact upon American life.

The Bolshevik Revolution wrought an immediate and fundamental change in the perspective of public opinion. The very fact that Marxian principles could assume the guise of action made it evident that the foundations of capitalism had nothing like the security that had been assumed. As Lenin consolidated his position against both the attacks of the Allies and the impact of civil war, the Russian Revolution began to reveal itself as the profoundest change in the mental climate of the world since the Reformation. The proletariat in a state of one hundred and thirty millions had not merely challenged the rights of property, it had overthrown them. Before five years had passed it was obvious that the Russian Revolution was not, as its enemies hoped, a temporary portent. It had affected the psychological fabric of all civilization. Ideas like the class war, the dictatorship of the proletariat, the expropriation of the capitalist, had passed at a single bound from books to action. What seemed in 1914 an underground and unimportant conspiracy had become, ten years later, a state. And it was obvious that the fact of such a state's existence, the knowledge that it could survive and grow, had turned men's thoughts into new directions. For the first time in history, a proletarian state was an actual, and not merely an ideological, inspiration; and for the first time in history, also, capitalist society met a direct and thoroughgoing challenge.

The impact of Russia upon the Old World and the New cannot be expressed in simple terms. Certainly there were few thoughtful

[1] *Government of England*, Vol. II, p. 534.

minds whom it did not compel to a revaluation or, at least, a reassess-
ment of the basic principles of politics. The pre-war state-system
emerged from the great conflict far more shattered than was apparent
in the mood of vindictive triumph embodied in the Peace of Versailles.
It had to grapple with a *damnosa hereditas*. The necessities of war
had given an enhanced status to the working classes of the belligerent
countries; and it was necessary to satisfy their new claims. National
feeling had been profoundly inflamed by the conflict; and since nationalism took the form of an intense revival of neo-mercantilist
doctrine, a community of states emerged whose political practices
were increasingly at variance with the objective needs of the world
economic market. The problems created by debts and reparations,
the control of imports and migration in the interest of the several
states, the new levels of taxation rendered necessary by the demands
of social legislation, the refusal of the Far East any longer to accept
the domination of Western Europe and America, all implied the
futility of believing that the old *laissez faire* was compatible with the
attainment of social good. It had become clear to every careful
observer that it was necessary either deliberately to plan the post-
war civilization or to perish.

For a brief period, the sudden prosperity of America (though
much more confined than was generally realized) concealed from
many the realities of the situation. It was argued that the condition of Russia was a special one; that elsewhere the problem was
rather one of dealing with the excrescences of the capitalist system
than with capitalism itself. As late as 1928 President Hoover felt
able to announce to an awe-struck world that America had (under
God) solved the problem of poverty. Two years later, it was clear
that his announcement was premature. The world (including
America) was caught in the grips of a depression more intense and
more widespread than any other recorded in history. The unemployed
could be counted in millions in capitalist countries. The mood of
pessimism was universal; men spoke gravely of a possible collapse of
civilization. At a time when science had made possible a greater
productivity than in any previous age, the problem of distribution
seemed insoluble. All the nations demanded the removal of barriers
against world trade; despite pious recommendations, like those at
Geneva in 1927, they did not seem able to remove them. All the
world agreed upon the necessity of disarmament; the conference at
Geneva to attain it would have been farcical if it had not been tragic.
The dislocation of currency methods deprived commerce of that

automatic measure of value upon which the lifeblood of trade depended. Thirteen years after the end of the war, the perspective of capitalist civilization revealed an insecurity, both economic and political, which made justifiable the gravest doubts of its future. .

Russian development was in striking contrast. The Five Year Plan gave it an integrated and orderly purpose such as no capitalist country could rival. Productivity increased at a remarkable rate; unemployment was non-existent. If the standard of living was low compared with that of Great Britain or the United States, its tendency was to increase and not to decline. The whole population was united in a great corporate effort at material well-being in which there was the promise of equal participation. Where Europe and America were sunk in pessimism, the whole temper of Russia was optimistic. The authority of its government was unchallenged; its power to win amazing response to its demands was unquestionable. Granted all its errors, no honest observer could doubt its capacity both to plan greatly and, in large measure, to realize its plans. No doubt its government was, in a rigorous sense, a dictatorship. No doubt also it imposed upon its subjects a discipline, both spiritual and material, such as a capitalist civilization would hardly dare to attempt. No doubt, again, its subjects paid a heavy price for the ultimate achievement to which they looked forward. Yet, whatever its defects and errors, the mood of the Russian experiment was one of exhilaration. While the rest of the world confronted its future in a temper of skepticism and dismay, Russia moved forward in a belief, religious in the intensity of its emotion, that it had a right to ample confidence in its future.

II

No one can understand the character of the communist challenge to capitalism who does not grasp the significance of this contrast. A hundred years ago the votaries of capitalism had a religious faith in its prospects. They were, naturally enough, dazzled by the miracles it performed, confident that the aggregation of its individual successes was coincident with the social good, happy in a security about the results of their investment which seemed to entitle them to refashion the whole world in their own image. The successful business man became the representative type of civilization. He subdued all the complex of social institutions to his purposes. Finance, oil, coal, steel, became empires of which the sovereignty was as unchallenged as that of Macedon or of Rome. Men so different as Disraeli and

Marx might utter warnings about the stability of the edifice. Broadly speaking, they were unheeded in the triumphs to which the business man could point.

But those triumphs could not conceal the fact that the idol had feet of clay. The price to be paid for their accomplishment was a heavy one. The distribution of the rewards was incapable of justification in terms of moral principle. The state was driven increasingly to intervene to mitigate the inequalities to which capitalism gave rise. Vast and costly schemes of social legislation, militant trade unionism, a nationalism of pathological proportions, imperialist exploitation with its consequential awakening of nationalism among the peoples exploited,[1] were all inherently involved in the technique of a capitalist civilization. Nationalism meant imperialism; imperialism meant war; in the struggle for markets there was involved an inescapable threat to the security of the whole structure. That became finally evident in the Great War and its aftermath. A world of competing economic nationalisms could not avoid inevitable conflict.

Nor is this all. The condition for the survival of an acquisitive society is twofold. There must be no halt in its power to continue its successes; and it must be able so to apportion their results that the proletariat do not doubt their duty to be loyal to its institutions. This condition has not been realized. Economic nationalism has given birth to a body of vested interests which impede in a fatal way the expansion of world trade. On the one hand, the power of productivity makes the ideal of self-sufficiency incapable of realization; on the other, the capture of foreign markets means commercial warfare which issues into actual warfare. The individual ownership of the means of production is incompatible with the kind of planning necessitated by the interrelations of a world reduced to the unity of interdependence.

The failure to maintain the allegiance of the proletariat, though different in degree in different countries, is nevertheless universal. Its danger was foreseen by Tocqueville nearly a century ago. "The manufacturer," he wrote, "asks nothing of the workman but his labor; the workman expects nothing from him but his wages. The one contracts no obligation to protect, nor the other to defend; and they are not permanently connected either by habit or by duty. . . . The manufacturing aristocracy of our age first impoverishes and debases the men who serve it, and then abandons them to be supported by the charity of the public. . . . Between the workman and the master

[1] See my *Nationalism and the Future of Civilization* (1932).

there are frequent relations but no real partnership."[1] Everything
that has happened since Tocqueville wrote has combined to give
emphasis to his insight. The decay of religion has intensified the
appreciation of material well-being. The growth of education has
made working-class resentment at the contrast between riches and
poverty both keener and more profound. Universal suffrage has
made necessary a far wider and more costly response to the demands
of the proletariat; and the perfection of party organization has made
the struggle for political power one in which the offer of bread and
circuses is an essential part.

Men, in short, accept a capitalist society no longer because they
believe in it, but because of the material benefits it professes to
confer. Once it ceases to confer them, it cannot exercise its old
magic over men's minds. It has become, writes Mr. Keynes, "absolutely irreligious, without internal union, without much public spirit,
often, though not always, a mere congeries of possessors and pur-
suers."[2] Once its success is a matter of dubiety, those who do not
profit by its results inevitably turn to alternative ways of life. They
realize that the essence of a capitalist society is its division into a small
number of rich men and a great mass of poor men. They see not only
the existence of a wealthy class which lives without the performance of
any socially useful function; they realize also that it is inherent in such
a society that there should be no proportion between effort and reward.
They see this when the decline of capitalist prosperity makes the
payment of the price demanded for their allegiance to the system
one it is increasingly difficult to pay without destroying the position of advantage which the rich enjoy in society. The social service
state can only be maintained at a level which satisfies the worker
in a period of increasing returns. Once its benefits have to be diminished, the moral poverty of capitalism becomes apparent to all
save those who live by its preservation. There arises an insistent
demand for economic and social equality — such a distribution of the
social product as can rationally be referred to intelligible principle.
Resistance develops to the normal technique by which capitalism
adjusts itself to a falling market. The growth of socialism in Great
Britain, the dissatisfaction with the historic parties in the United
States, the rise of Hitlerism in Germany, the profound and growing
interest, all over the world, in the Russian experiment, are all of them,
in their various ways, the expression of that resistance. Men have

---

[1] *Democracy in America*, Part II, Book II, Chapter XVIII.
[2] *Essays in Persuasion*, p. 306.

begun to ask, upon a universal scale, whether there is not the possibility of consciously building a classless society in which the ideal of equality is deliberately given meaning.

It is not, I think, excessive to argue that the experience of this generation leads most socially conscious observers to doubt the desirability of relying upon the money motive in individuals automatically to produce a well-ordered community. It is at least a matter of universal recognition that the collective intelligence of society must control all major economic operations. But the translation of that recognition into policy encounters difficulties of which the importance cannot be emphasized. For it asks men to part with power on an unexampled scale. It changes a system of established expectations profoundly rooted in the habits of mankind. It disturbs vested interests which are well organized, both for offense and defense, and accustomed by long tradition to have their way. No governing class in the history of the world has consciously and deliberately sacrificed its authority. It has gone down fighting, as in France and Russia; it has coöperated with the *novi homines* of the industrial revolution, as in England or Germany. But the call to socialism, which the anarchy of capitalist society has produced, is at bottom a demand for economic egalitarianism in which the possessors are invited to sacrifice their power, their vested interests, their established expectations, for the attainment of a common good they will no longer be able to manipulate to their own interest.

The socialist parties of Western civilization have conceived a simple formula upon which to place reliance. They will win a majority of the electorate to their side; and they will proceed, by legislative enactment, gradually to introduce the socialist commonwealth. Possessing themselves of the constitution of the state, they assume that they can operate the machinery to their own purposes. They argue that if the pace is not too violently forced, the instinct for law and order will enable them to consummate their revolution with good will because their policy will proceed by reasonable stages. That has been the policy of the two Labor governments which arrived in office, a little accidentally perhaps, in Great Britain; and in their different ways it has been the policy of such socialist governments as have held office elsewhere. Of them all it is not unfair to say that they nowhere made any essential difference to the foundations of capitalist society. Of them, also, it is true to say that if they showed signs of seriously compromising those foundations, they were driven to surrender power to their rivals. And in that event it was the bankruptcy, rather than the success, of gradualist change which became apparent.

In this context, what is important is the underlying assumption of socialist gradualism: it builds upon the persistence of constitutional democracy. But not only — as Italy, Jugoslavia, and the rest make plain — is that persistence a dubious matter in practice; the persistence of constitutional democracy depends upon the further assumption that men are agreed upon the fundamental principles of policy. In a broad way, this was true as between Liberals and Conservatives in the nineteenth century; experience has demonstrated how little ground there is for believing that it is true when the choice is between a capitalist and a socialist way of life. No one who meditates upon the prospect of large-scale socialist experiment can conclude that it is likely to go into operation without grave challenge. No one, either, can argue that such a challenge will permit the principles of constitutional democracy to survive unimpaired.

III

It is at this point that the communist hypothesis becomes of such overwhelming importance. It points to the inherent contradictions of capitalist society. It denies that there is in it any longer the power to resolve those contradictions within its assumptions. It insists that no socialist government can attempt seriously to put its principles into practice without encountering determined resistance which will issue in civil war. To maintain socialist principles, in short, socialists will be driven to become communists or to betray their socialism. If they become communists, they will find themselves involved in the grim logic of Leninism — the dictatorship of the proletariat, the drastic suppression of counter-revolution, the confiscation of the essential instruments of production, the building of the state, in a word, upon the principles of martial law until the security of the new order is firmly established. The transformation of capitalism into socialism means revolution, and that implies an experience akin to that through which Russia has passed.

I do not see how it is reasonable to deny the possibility — to put it no higher — that the communists are right. The threat of war is implicit in our society, and war means revolution all over the world. Even if that revolution assumed a Fascist form, communism would be its inevitable antithesis; and, in that event, sooner or later communism would move to the assault. To avoid the threat of war, the degree of self-reformation which capitalist states must undertake would leave them unrecognizable as capitalist. The observer of England, of America, of France is entitled to doubt whether there is in the possessing classes of any of them that will to self-reformation which would make it effective. The change of heart required would involve a transvaluation of all values, the supersession by agreement of money as the dominant motive to action. It is only the acceptance of new values with an intensity almost religious in character which could effect that supersession; and that possession of a body of alternative values held with religious intensity is, to put it quite bluntly, practically a monopoly of the communists at the present time.

That, indeed, is the secret of its strength. Its devotees believe in it with a faith so absolute that there is no sacrifice they are not prepared to make in its name. Communism has succeeded in Russia for the same reasons that brought triumph to the Jesuits, the Puritans, the Jacobins in an earlier period. Willing the end, the communists have not shrunk from the application of any means likely to attain that end. They have consistently opposed an unshakable will to the resistance they have encountered. They have disdained both compromise and hesitation. In the service of no other social system in the world today can it be said that these qualities are enlisted. No one defends the acquisitive society save in the most mitigated terms. No capitalist society could attempt experiment on the Russian scale without risking the willingness of the working classes to observe the demands of law and order. Not even the most intense propaganda in capitalist countries has prevented the working classes from feeling a proud interest in every success the Russian experiment can show. "Perhaps," wrote Mr. Keynes, "Russian communism does represent the first confused stirrings of a great religion."[1] That is a widespread and growing feeling among all who are disturbed by the contradictions of capitalism; and it is an emotion far more profoundly diffused among the workers than is realized by the rulers of alternative systems.

The unity, in fact, of capitalist society has been broken. No country is prepared to pay the price which its simple rehabilitation demands; and to attempt the enforcement of that price would involve disorders of which no one could predict the outcome. That is the significance of the point made earlier in this essay that the Russian Revolution shapes the perspective of men's thoughts. Lower the standards of life, whether by decreases in wages or by economies in social legislation, diminish the worker's security, sharpen the contrast between poverty and wealth, and it at once comes into the worker's

[1] *Essays in Persuasion*, p. 309.

mind that in Russia, if the standard is low, it is rising, and that the hope of still greater rises is profound, that all social legislation is in the proletarian interest, that the contrasts between poverty and wealth are largely without meaning. A state has been built upon the exaltation of the common man; it is inevitable that the common men of other states should have its existence and its possibilities increasingly in their minds.

Capitalist society, in other words, is running a race with communist society for the allegiance of the masses. The terms upon which the former can be successful are fairly clear. It has to solve the contradiction between its power to produce and its inability to distribute income in a rational and morally adequate way. It has to remove the barriers which economic nationalism places in the way of an unimpeded world market. It has to remove the fear of insecurity by which the worker's life is haunted. It has to end the folly of international competition in wage rates and hours of labor; it has to find ways of saving Western standards from the slave labor of the East. It has, not least, to cut away the jungle growth of vested interests which at present so seriously impair its efficiency. Even a capitalist society will not long endure the spectacle of the cotton and coal industries of Great Britain or the power trust in the United States. Above all, perhaps, it has to find some way of removing from the clash of competing imperialisms those structures of armed power which, clothed in the garb of national sovereignty, make certain the perpetual threat of insecurity and, born of it, the advent of war.

Let me emphasize again that to meet successfully the challenge of communism a capitalist society has to show itself immensely more successful than the former. This does not, of course, mean that communism, in its Russian expression, does not confront its own grave problems. Broadly, they are of two kinds. It is necessary, by economic success, to maintain the exhilaration, the enthusiastic will to sacrifice, of the first great period of striving; and it is necessary, in the second, to relate Russia more adequately to the conditions of the external world. For, in the context of the first condition, it must not be forgotten that Russia was to some extent fortunate in her situation. Not only was she dealing with a people accustomed to the psychology of an autocratic discipline; she was also able to take advantage of a profound patriotism engendered by external attack. The Soviet State cannot go on perpetually demanding the postponement of consumption for the sake of a future which does not arrive.

They must come to a point where the maintenance of enthusiasm for the new régime is the outcome of having conferred tangible benefit. Nor will it be possible over any considerable period to maintain the dominating grip of the Communist Party over the whole political life of Russia. That grip has been acquiesced in because of the social circumstances confronting the new régime; no acquiescence in a dictatorship is ever permanent in character. There must, that is to say, not only be economic success in the new Russia; there must come also a time when restriction is relaxed and room is found for the admission of freedom. The permanence of communist society depends upon its ability to meet these issues creatively. For any new social order that seeks to become universal must be able to correlate its economic advance with spiritual growth.

No doubt, of course, spiritual growth, and especially that temper of tolerance which is the groundwork of all intellectual achievement, is, in its turn, dependent upon economic advance. Periods of revolutionary poverty rarely synchronize with periods of great scientific or literary production; for the atmosphere of dictatorship, the preoccupation with material well-being, are stifling to that atmosphere of experiment upon which intellectual advance depends. It is not accidental that neither the Puritan nor the French Revolution has left behind it a great cultural impact upon the mind of the world; the spiritual fruits of each were gathered after men could in leisure and in safety seek to prove their implications. It is therefore reasonable to argue that the success of Russian communism depends upon the maintenance, at least for a considerable period, of world peace. For if Russia becomes involved in any serious military conflict the transformation of its energies will dangerously impair the prospect of its economic policy. More than this, the intensification of the dictatorship involved in war might easily, if the struggle were at all prolonged, result in the kind of internal conflicts within the Communist Party which, in the French Revolution, made ultimately possible the emergence of Napoleon.

It would be folly to deny the possibility of Russia becoming involved in war within the next decade.[1] The clash of interests with Japan in the Far East is a grave one. The fear of the effect of Russian exports of butter, timber, oil, coal, and wheat on a depressed market already gives birth to those economic reprisals out of which war has so often come. The instability of Europe is fed by Russian propaganda;

<hr />

[1] On this see Mr. R. D. Charques's admirable résumé, *The Soviets and the Next War* (1932).

and the very fact that communism expects a world revolution to come by way of war gives to that propaganda the psychological perspective which so easily makes expectancy fact. The failure of disarmament, the dissatisfaction of minorities, the intensity of social revolutionary movements in the East, all of these point to that kind of collapse in the system of international regulation which is the prelude to conflict. And it is useless to deny that there are, all over the world, important interests which would welcome an attack on Russia before its success is beyond question as the surest way of ending that implicit challenge to capitalist society which it represents. Certainly militant communism and militant capitalism cannot exist side by side, especially in a period of serious economic stress. It is important that Moscow is the Mecca of the discontented and disinherited of the whole world; it is not less important that Moscow is ideologically driven to the encouragement of their hopes. No one who surveys at all objectively the relations of Russia with the external world can possibly be optimistic about their outcome.

I do not think that a war against Russia would destroy communism there though I believe it would enormously increase the price of its accomplishment; but I do believe it would be fatal to the maintenance of capitalist society at least in Europe and the Far East. Probably its cost would be a period of anarchy comparable to the Dark Ages, with every sort and kind of dictatorship emerging to supply for brief periods an uneasy semblance of order. Ultimately, I think, Russia would be the first state to emerge from that chaos with something like the hope of recovery; and its authority, under those circumstances, would be far more compelling than it is today, its challenge more direct and explicit. In the long run, in a word, the price of challenging communism to military conflict would be not its defeat but its victory.

IV

The future of communism is a function of the capacity of capitalist society to repair its foundations. The success — despite the appalling cost — of the Russian experiment has made it the one effective center of creativeness in a world which, otherwise, does not seem to know how to turn its feet away from the abyss. Capitalist society since the war has adopted every expedient of self-destruction. The Peace of Versailles, the tangled mess of war debts and reparations, the struggle for power concealed beneath the myth of national sovereignty, the failure to respect the League, all of these were implicit in its ultimate disrespect for moral principle. The social habits of its votaries, its literature with its insistent note of cynical skepticism, its philosophy which sought refuge in mysticism and impulse to shut out the still small voice of reason, a press which (not least notably in its dealing with Russia) could make miraculous propaganda but could not tell the truth, its religions in decay, its political and economic institutions hopelessly remote from the realities they confronted, its leaders like straws caught in the eddies of an ever-quickening stream — it is not in such a society as this that one looks for the spring of a new hope. On the credit side, no doubt, there was a science more renascent than at any time since the seventeenth century; but it was also more dangerous because the formula seemed lost by which it could be bent to social purposes.

Such a society cannot meet the challenge of communism, because its faith in itself is not sufficient to give it a victorious destiny. It may postpone defeat; it cannot finally elude it. For in the conflict of ideologies victory always goes in the end to men who are willing to sacrifice material power for spiritual conquest. Communism interests the new generation because, alone among the welter of competing gospels, it has known how to win sacrifice from its devotees in the name of a great ideal. It offers the prospect — the clue to the success of all the great religions — of losing one's life in order to find it. There is poverty, there is intellectual error, there is grave moral wrong; but there is also unlimited hope. These have been characteristic of all great religious movements. They do not seem to disturb their power eventually to triumph.

The chance for a capitalist society in contest with communism lies in its ability to remake its own creed. Its danger is the ease with which it attacks the symptoms of communism instead of its causes. It is afraid of the propaganda of the Third International instead of the conditions which make that propaganda fall on fertile soil. It is afraid of the bold imagination which underlies the Five Year Plan; but instead of planning more boldly and more imaginatively itself, it spends its time dourly foretelling its inevitable failure. It attacks with passion the outrageous injustices of which communism has been guilty, its stifling of initiative, the reckless cruelty of the Ogpu, the relentless attack on the Kulaks. But it does not stay to remember that its own Sacco-Vanzetti case, the Polish treatment of minorities, the dreary wastage of its own unemployment, bear the same lesson to the masses, and that for them the costs of Russia are expended for the advantage of the many, while the costs of the capitalist society are paid for the profit of a few. There is an uncomfortable sense in the world that what is happening in Russia may be the prelude to a renaissance of the human spirit. There is no such prophetic confidence in capitalist society. Its very leaders look less like great adventurers than men who scan a gray horizon without confidence of a dawn.

The principles which govern capitalist society are, in fact, completely obsolete before the new conditions it confronts; and it seems to lack the energy to bend itself to their revision. It needs a new scheme of motivation, a different sense of values. It needs the power and the will to move from the era of economic chaos to a system which deliberately controls economic forces in the interests of justice and stability. To do so there are required far more pervasive international controls, on the external side, and far greater equality in matters of social constitution, on the internal. To find equilibrium by the blind adjustment of competing interests is simply to court disaster. Yet, generally speaking, the men who govern the old world can think in no other terms.

It is true there are men about us who voice a different philosophy. Rathenau, Keynes, Salter — these have endeavored, as best they could, to insist that the way to survival lies along the road to profound reconstruction. They have seen that a temper is required which gives new significance to the claims of the common man, which recognizes the dangers inherent in a system which identifies self-good and social. They admit the need for sacrifice as the price of reconstruction. They see all the cost involved in a clash of ideologies which seek to test their respective strengths in terms of powder. But theirs, if I may say so, is an aristocratic approach, a cool and skeptical impatience of dogma, a passion for the rational solution of questions in their nature essentially rational, of which the appeal is by its nature a limited one. They underestimate the inertia of the existing order, the irrationality with which men will cling to vested interests and established expectations even when their title to response is no longer valid. Given something like a geological time, such rationalism might prevail against the passions which stand in its path. The tragedy of our present position is that the voice of the Mean is unlikely to win attention until humanity has been sacrificed to the call of the Extreme.

THE FASCIST DECADE[1]

Count Carlo Sforza

COUNT CARLO SFORZA, born at Lucca, Italy, in 1872, was trained for the diplomatic service. Beginning his career as secretary of the embassy in London, he became Minister to China in 1911 and to Serbia in 1916, and Under-Secretary for Foreign Affairs in 1919. When Giolitti formed his Cabinet in 1920, Sforza was made Foreign Minister, and in that capacity negotiated the Treaty of Rapallo. He was also responsible for Italy's denunciation of her agreement to cede twelve of the Dodecanese Islands in the eastern Mediterranean to Greece. On the accession of Mussolini to power late in 1922, Sforza resigned, and became one of the principal leaders of the Anti-Fascist Party in the Italian Senate. He is the author of a number of books, the chief being one on *European Dictatorships*.

This year completes a decade of Signor Mussolini's rule in Italy; but it would not be fully accurate to say that it completes a decade of Fascist dictatorship. The Fascist dictatorship in its present characteristic form began only on January 3, 1925, when Signor Mussolini declared in Parliament that he took upon himself responsibility for the murders and other forms of violence which had torn Italy since the advent of Fascism in the autumn of 1922. . . .

After ten years of rule, eight of them absolutely dictatorial, a régime might fairly be judged on its results. But although much has been written on the nature of Fascist doctrine, it may first of all be useful to sum up the characteristics of the Italian dictatorship, not as they were stated by early admirers and enemies of the régime, but as they stand out in comparison with such dictatorial régimes as have prevailed in Europe since the fall of the most conspicuous of them all, the Empire of the first Bonaparte.

I

In the first place, friends or foes are bound to admit that there is an immense difference between Fascism in power and Fascism as a revolutionary movement immediately after the war. That early Fascism was not lacking in a certain sincere and naïve passion for democratic renovation; the movement recruited its adherents from among the ex-service men home from the trenches, men who did not want to belong either to the Catholic organizations or to the Socialist Party, which in their eyes had been guilty — especially the second one

[1] From *Foreign Affairs*, October, 1932. Reprinted by permission.

— of having been averse to the war. But this Fascist movement was entirely lacking in political experience or tradition; in the main it was given substance by syndicalistic doctrines such as those preached before the war by a French writer who had gained more vogue in Italy than in his own country, Georges Sorel. It was mainly his theory of "violence" which most appealed to those crude youths who had just stepped out of the unsurpassed violence of four years of war.

Had this movement found a really strong personality to guide it, as happened in the case of the Russian Bolsheviks with Lenin, Fascism might perhaps have represented a genuinely original historical phenomenon. Such was not the case, however. The political ripeness and originality of its leader may be judged by the program he wrote for his party in 1919, a demagogic program in which momentous aims such as the abolition of the Senate, of compulsory service, and of stock exchanges were thrown in at random on a par with the suppression of titles of nobility and of orders of knighthood.

When chance and the infinite stupidity of the Facta Cabinet brought this movement and its leader to power at the end of 1922, and events turned to tragedy, there rapidly occurred the transformation of what had been revolutionary Fascism into the most complete police state ever seen in modern times. It was its way of meeting the growing opposition of the masses.

Almost all the present laws of the Fascist régime are reproductions of measures invented by the government of Napoleon III between 1852 and 1867 to destroy the French democratic opposition. Napoleon III kept up Parliament as a decoy but reduced it to impotence, and so did Fascism. Napoleon III made the prefects of the provinces omnipotent, and so did Fascism. Local government was destroyed under the Second Empire; and the same happened in Italy with much more serious consequences, since in municipal life the Italians are among the best in Europe — a legacy of the old Italian love for the *libero Comune*. In the two periods similar laws were enforced to get rid of judges who refused to obey governmental orders and to muzzle university professors, editors, and publishers. Most historic and political parallels smack of literary artifice, but one cannot help feeling that seldom in history has an analogy been so complete as that between the French Second Empire and Italian Fascism.

The analogy may be detected even in the foreign policy of the two régimes — in the psychological motives prompting them (which is what really counts), if not in external appearances. And nothing is more natural, for régimes which have suppressed the freedom which the people formerly enjoyed seek to divert their minds with successes abroad, and when success does not come turn to boastings about imperialistic conquest in the future. The foolish Napoleonic expedition to Mexico finds, morally speaking, its equivalent in the Fascist expedition to Corfu (1923), Fascism's first attempt to show the Italian people its diplomatic capacities.

Compelled under British pressure to evacuate Corfu, Fascism had the wisdom to realize that the foreign policy of a great country could not be managed on the *Strafexpedition* lines which had been the main method adopted by the Fascists to seize power at home. And we had in 1924 an agreement with Jugoslavia, based on the principles of political and moral collaboration with Italy's new eastern neighbor which I had inaugurated in 1920 with the Treaty of Rapallo and the anti-Hapsburg convention, and which constituted an application of Mazzini's great conception in the 'fifties: the independence of the Balkan nationalities oppressed by Austria is the necessary corollary of the independence of Italy.

Unfortunately, a few years later Fascist diplomacy gave the impression of reverting to the old paths; and the intimate relations which grew up between Fascist Rome and the aristocratic oligarchy governing Hungary led the governments of Prague and Belgrade to believe that the Fascist régime was seeking success at their expense. Here again, to mention it for the last time, stands out a similarity with the Second Empire. Napoleon III needed to give the French "glory," and his diplomacy, in search of territorial conquests, fluctuated feverishly between one contradictory method and another: secret negotiations with Prussia to win the annexation of Belgium, and shortly afterward a declaration of war on this same Prussia.

Fascism has often shown the same hesitations. The signature of the Kellogg Pact in 1928 is a case in point. Fascism did not dare not to sign. But the personal organ of Signor Mussolini, the *Popolo d'Italia* (he was its editor until the very day he became Prime Minister), commented as follows on the value of the Pact on the morrow of its signing:

France, England, and the United States may well speak with horror of the war which would alter the present *status quo;* but we, who breathe with great difficulty, we can but see in every League, in every collective move of those who have and will give nothing, an Insurance Committee working against the interest of the rising peoples. The result is that August 27 cannot be a feast day for us.

In a speech in Parliament on December 8, 1928, Signor Mussolini himself, in an ironical mood, declared:

We have signed the Kellogg Pact which I declare sublime, so much so that one might even call it transcendental. Were there other pacts ahead we should hasten to sign them. But above, below, and alongside of these pacts is a reality which we may not ignore if we do not want to be guilty of high treason toward the nation. This reality is as follows. The whole world is arming. Every day the newspapers publish information concerning the building of submarines and other engines of war. We must not delude ourselves regarding the political state of Europe. When the storm is brewing everyone speaks of calm and peace, as if prompted by a deep urge of the mind. We do not want to upset the balance of Europe, but we must keep ourselves in readiness. . . .

Toward the League of Nations, Fascist tactics may be divided into three distinct periods: the first, all contempt and irony; the second, when Signor Grandi (appointed as Foreign Minister in September, 1929) began admitting, under the influence of the permanent officials of the Foreign Office, that it was no use ignoring the League, the while his chief went on with his customary warlike speeches; the third, lasting until Signor Grandi's dismissal on July 20, 1932, during which time unanimity was reached in the Fascist language and everybody was advocating disarmament and Geneva collaboration.

The first period corresponds too closely with the original slogans of Fascism to be worth while considering.

The second period began in 1930 when for the first time a Fascist Foreign Minister, Signor Grandi, went to Geneva as Italian delegate to the Council of the League. The *Popolo d'Italia* explained on January 12, 1930, that this change of tactics was made advisable by the need for "wary and vigilant" Fascist delegates to watch over the numerous "all-invading" advisory and deliberative bodies of the League. It added: "Too often the skepticism shown and boasted of by Italians concerning the work, authority, and efficacy of the League of Nations has played into the hands of our adversaries, and contributed toward the success of certain shows of wordy pacifism and . . . imperialistic internationalism which a less indifferent attitude on our part would have lessened or even smothered in the cradle. Italy's share in the debates of the League of Nations cannot be either passive or merely decorative."

On May 9, 1930, Signor Grandi declared in a speech to the Chamber of Deputies that "the idiotic calumny" representing Italy "full of warlike truculence" had exploded forever. "Mussolini's Italy," he added, "asks only to be able to progress freely in a pacified and quiet Europe: the words 'equal rights and equal duties' express the only foundation upon which one may build a lasting understanding."

The newspapers with the text of Signor Grandi's speech were still being read when his chief began a tour of the Tuscan cities. On May 11 he said to the Fascist crowds at Leghorn:

Before your sea — that sea which is ours — after having visited your yards where keen workers are building the future war units, I want to say to you — and not only to you, but to the whole Italian people and to the peoples beyond our frontiers — that we do not desire hasty adventures, but that, should anyone strike at our independence or our future, he does not know to what a temperature I would bring the whole Italian people. He does not know how tremendously I would work up the passion of the whole Italian people if the Revolution of the Black Shirts were hindered in its development. Then the people, old and young, peasant and workers, armed and unarmed, would form one human mass — and more than a mass, a projectile, ready to be hurled against anyone, anywhere.

And six days later, in Florence:

Nothing is more insulting to the pride of the Italian people than to doubt the fulfillment of our naval program. I here again affirm that this new program will be carried out, ton for ton, and that its twenty-nine units will put to sea. . . .

During the last part of Signor Grandi's tenure of office the discrepancy between the speeches for foreign and home consumption seemed, as I said above, to have been eliminated. The feeling both in Italy and in the rest of Europe was that the new tactics were dictated by the economic and financial situation, which (as we shall see in a moment) has been especially cruel in Italy. If world opinion was somewhat skeptical of this sudden turn, the partisans of Fascism should acknowledge that they therein simply paid the price for the style of their régime. When the policy of a great country depends upon one man, and on a man at that who has often changed, there is no assurance that a certain policy, newly adopted, will be lasting. The fact that the dictator's change may even be made in all good faith is of little importance: he also, in his turn, pays for the fact that he is no longer enlightened as to the demands of public opinion; a dictator ends by mistaking for the opinion of the country what is but organized praise prepared by his own press service.

One therefore understands the doubts expressed abroad as to the genuineness of Fascism's conversion to the pacific life. . . .

Personally I am convinced — trying to see things without party bias — that the changes which occurred in the phraseology of Fascist foreign policy were something more than a modification of diplomatic tactics.   The point is that, hidden by the notes of a press which obeys as an orchestra obeys its conductor, a deep change — hardly visible to strangers — is asserting itself in Italian public opinion.   Sensational speeches with no subsequent results have not only ceased to work; they have become a nuisance for the prestige of Fascism itself. And its leader has probably begun to realize that it does not pay to go on relying too much on the wild Fascists whom Theodore Roosevelt would have put in his "lunatic fringe."

The future alone will tell whether Fascism can renounce for good the risky nationalistic ideologies which are in such violent opposition to the democratic principle of international justice. . . .

II

The minorities problem in the form in which it has developed in Italy under the Fascist régime is linked with the whole general conception which Fascism apparently has of life among nations.   That is why a short study of the question may be useful.

The problem was novel in Italy.   Before the war Italy was one of the most homogeneous nations in the world.   It was through the Treaty of St. Germain (September 10, 1919), which brought the frontiers of Italy to the natural confines of the Alps, and through the Treaty of Rapallo (November 12, 1920), the first of all post-war treaties to be based essentially on mutual understanding more than on force, that Italy received 215,345 Germans and 468,378 Jugoslavs. On December 1, 1919, opening the first Parliament elected after the war, the King solemnly said: "The territories newly annexed to Italy confront us with new problems.   Our liberal tradition will show us the way to find their solution, in respecting autonomous institutions and local usage as much as possible.   No trouble and no sacrifice should be avoided to the end that — after inevitable forcible measures — the return of these lands to their natural unit may not in their eyes represent a retrograde step or a decrease in prosperity. We know that in our subjects in the mountains and on the seacoast we shall find precious collaborators in the progress of the nation."

During the discussion in Parliament of the Treaty of Rapallo I made the following even clearer statement, which was strongly approved by the Chambers and by leaders of all parties: "We shall guarantee most ample liberty of language and culture.   This will be for us at once a point of honor and an act of political wisdom. Let us be certain, therefore, that in this respect also our new citizens will soon feel satisfied in belonging to a Great Power which, strong in her incomparable culture, respects their local life with jealous care."

Facts were true to words; and the administration of the new Italian provinces, as long as the Liberal governments were in power in Italy, could be pointed to as an example of real respect for the rights and traditions of annexed populations, and also — I am proud to add as an Italian — as a model of political wisdom. If Liberal methods had continued, the national minorities would almost unconsciously have identified themselves in a few decades with the great body of Italians.

The exactions of Fascist rule have worked dead against the very aim which they pursued. Today the rift is deep. The Fascist government has: (1) destroyed the provincial and municipal auton- omy of the new provinces; (2) shut down schools teaching in any language other than Italian, and by every means eliminated the use of foreign languages in education, government, justice, and the church; (3) changed even the family names; (4) suppressed rights of associa- tion; (5) suppressed all freedom of the local press; (6) forbidden any and every form of political life; (7) set up a rule of terror and violence, legal and illegal (though, truth to tell, not more violent than in the rest of Italy).

The suppression of provincial and municipal autonomy was par- ticularly resented by the populations which had belonged to the Austro-Hungarian Empire, for they had possessed complete machinery for collaborating in political, administrative, and social matters with the central government. The provincial Diets which existed in the Hapsburg realm exist no longer. Fascist authority changed the elec- ted mayors for extraordinary commissioners or *podestà* appointed by the Fascist Party, who may be removed without explanation of any sort by the prefect or on orders from Rome. The prefect also has the right to join several *comuni* together or divide them up as he pleases.

On the other hand the Fascist régime seems to have been unable to realize that by adopting and intensifying the measures which the Hapsburg monarchy used to suppress its Italian and Slav subjects, it has only mangled the victory over Austria-Hungary which cost the lives of 500,000 Italians dead on the blood-stained rocks of the Carso and on the Alpine chain. Italy's victory might have been one of the cleanest of the war; for it might have given not only independence to all Italians but also contentment to the peoples transferred from

Austro-Hungarian to Italian rule. It was Mazzini's great dream.
Fascism has destroyed it.

III

In yet another field has Fascism gone entirely against the Italian
Liberal traditions established by Cavour in the 'fifties — in the relations of church and state.   In this field Fascism has made an achievement which one may criticize or approve, but which is important:
the official reconciliation with the Vatican and the setting up of a
Vatican State.   These were the results of the Lateran Treaties signed
on February 11, 1929.

I have written "official reconciliation."   A *de facto* conciliation
existed already under the Liberal governments; one may even add
that to most European statesmen it appeared the embodiment of
practical wisdom.   As I have explained at length elsewhere,[1] the
Popes used to declare in an encyclical, every two or three years,
that the state of things created for them in Rome by the Italian
government was "intolerable"; the Italian government took care
not to make any answer.   On the following day — as on the previous
day — confidential agents from the Vatican would come to see Italian
officials (or sometimes the Italian Minister himself, as more than once
happened to me) and quietly and successfully arrange questions such,
for instance, as those concerning Italian missionaries and bishops
abroad.   The settlement of this question is now quoted as if it were
something new, and is painted as one of the advantages the Italian
Kingdom will reap from the Lateran agreements.

Benedict XV, the predecessor of the present Pope Pius XI, did
not in the least favor the schemes brought forward by Germans
during the war for the reconstitution of a small papal state.   His
essential aim was the maintenance of the old Italian Law of Guaran-
tees which had satisfactorily worked since 1871, but backed by a new
Christian Democratic Party, strong enough to withstand any possible
(if improbable) anticlerical excesses from the Left parties.   But Pius
XI (contrary to Benedict, who was probably the most intelligent of
modern Popes) was and is hostile to ideas of liberty; moreover, he is
a scholar grown up in libraries, afraid of life, and believing that a
treaty provides safer ground than the eternally shifting sands of
democracy.   The Fascist régime was ready to pay any price to win
the moral prestige which reconciliation would bring.   So the treaties
were signed.

[1] *Makers of Modern Europe.*   Bobbs Merrill, 1930.   Chapter XXXII, "Pius XI,
or The Roman Church and Fascism."

Who is the winner? To my mind, neither the church nor the state; for both are faced with the danger of some future reaction, which might bring forth a harvest of violence in the religious field such as the tolerant history of Italy has not yet seen. If either has gained, it is the Fascist government. At any rate, the transaction has given it the certainty that the Vatican, at least for as long as the present Pope is alive, is bound — out of common interest — to support it.

IV

About the economic situation of Italy during the Fascist régime much has been written. But the control over debates in Parliament and the muzzle on the press have eliminated the best sources for an investigation. The Fascist government may be right in complaining that certain criticisms of its economic policy are unfair; if so, these could easily be disposed of if impartial writers could draw on the sources of information which usually are available in a free country.

The economic situation of any one country may be studied at present only in the light of the world crisis. It may be difficult, therefore, for foreigners to realize that the present Italian economic crisis has not very much to do with the general world crisis. The general world crisis is a crisis of overcapitalization, while the crisis in Italy is one of lack of capital. There are direct proofs of this assertion. The Italian crisis began several years before the American and general crises — precisely, between 1924 and 1926. Evidence is found in statistics like the following:

1. *Bankruptcies.* In 1922, the last year of the pre-Fascist régime, there were 3,607 bankruptcies; in 1926, after four years of the Fascist régime, this figure had more than doubled, i.e. it had reached 7,631; in 1927 it had become 10,366, and in 1929 it had reached 11,106. In other words, the greatest increase in bankruptcies took place before the American crisis and only under the influence of the Fascist administration.

2. *Unemployment.* In 1926 there were 181,493 unemployed in Italy; in 1927 there were 414,283; in 1928, 439,211; in 1929, 489,347.[1] Which proves that the most serious jump in unemployment took place before the American crisis.

3. *Reduction of Foreign Trade.* In 1925 Italy's imports were valued at 26 billion lire; the figure was 22 billion in 1928. The value of Italian exports during the same period fell from 18 billion lire in 1925 to 14 billion in 1928.

[1] These are the official figures. In reality the unemployment situation is infinitely more serious.

Still another proof that the Italian crisis is different from the international one and that it is in part due to special causes may be seen in the fact that the general crisis has been accompanied by a slump in prices, while prices in Italy have had a tendency to rise — a tendency fought against in vain by Fascist police regulations. Nor could it have been otherwise, in view of the increasing lack of capital revealed by the feverish quest of the Fascists for loans.

What, then, have been the real causes of the Italian crisis? The general cause is found in the squandering of capital on the sort of unproductive expenditures in which dictatorships always indulge — unnecessary public works, the upkeep of the 300,000 men of the Fascist militia, and so on. One specific cause was the revaluation and stabilization of the lira, which Signor Mussolini fixed in 1928 at an exceptionally high rate, despite contrary advice from American experts. While France stabilized her franc at 25 to the dollar, Italy, a far less wealthy country, stabilized the lira at 19 to the dollar. Only in one event might stabilization at such a rate, determined solely by considerations of prestige, have caused less serious harm: if the government had reduced taxation and expenses in proportion to the new value of its monetary unit. But nothing of the kind was done in Italy. Taxation and public expenses constantly increased.

The Fascist government committed another specific error which had bad consequences of no trifling importance in the present Italian crisis. It practically forbade emigration. Before the war the annual exodus of some 600,000 Italians contributed largely to Italian prosperity. After the war, as a consequence of various foreign restrictions, these figures went down to 300,000; but even only 300,000 were still an effective source of riches for Italy. Then, as part of his scheme of international pressure, Signor Mussolini invented his slogan, "Expand or explode," and forbade all emigration. In this way he dried up a source of important revenue and aggravated the Italian economic situation. . . .

After ten years of Fascism the results of its financial policy may be summed up as follows: a tremendous decrease of Italian agricultural and industrial exports; unemployment, much greater than official statistics show; an increase in tax burdens to an extent which people who belong to naturally rich countries can hardly realize.

It would be impossible in the bounds of a single article to study otherwise than rapidly, and therefore inadequately, the whole series of problems — administrative, colonial, educational — which have, at least in the moral field, a bearing on the subject which we are considering. Instead, I shall single out one of these, the draining of marshlands and swamps, because readers will find in it two traits common to all the problems of Italian life under Fascist rule: the cleverness of the advertising policy of the Fascist régime; and the way in which this policy — contrary, I am willing to believe, to the intentions of its authors — always ends in the abuse of the secular efforts, as splendid as they are silent, of the Italian nation. . . .

It is a favorite legend of the Fascists that only Fascism could have saved Italy from Bolshevism; while the truth, of course, is that all revolutionary danger had disappeared by the time Fascism came into power.[1] A minor legend of later years, but a tough one, concerns the marvelous work done by Fascism in reclaiming lands. This is one of the sad cases where the interests of a faction go counter to the good name of a country. The truth is as follows. The Italian people, very densely settled on a very poor soil, has always been one of the most tirelessly laborious people on the face of the earth. The creation of agricultural Italy is the work of the Italian people. Thus the rich plains of Lombardy were, until the fifth century, nothing but a string of desolate swamps. Professor Valenti, one of the greatest European authorities on agrarian questions, wrote in 1919: "The richest Italian lands, in Lombardy, around Bologna, and in the Venetian provinces, have all of them been slowly reclaimed through long generations of workers, helped by capital." The progress of this agrarian revolution since the unification of Italy in 1860 is shown in the following figures: *Lands tilled and sown:* 1869, 12 million hectares; 1914, 13 million hectares. *Meadows and pasture lands:* 1864, 7 million hectares; 1914, 10 million hectares. *Wheat output:* 1864, 36 million hectoliters; 1914, 50 million hectoliters. *Cattle:* 1864, 18 million head; 1914, 27 million head.

A general survey of all lands to be reclaimed in Italy was made in 1882. It recorded a total of 1,839,411 hectares. At the end of 1922, 840,000 hectares, or nearly half of the total, had already been reclaimed, and work had been started on an important part of the remaining 999,000 hectares. It therefore is impossible that between 1922 and 1930 the Fascist government has done anything more in this field than the previous Liberal government did. True, in December, 1928, a law was passed stating that all unreclaimed land should be reclaimed within fourteen years; but this law only became effective

[1] Signor Mussolini himself wrote in his *Popolo d'Italia* on July 2, 1921, eighteen months before his appointment as Prime Minister: "To say that a Bolshevist danger still exists in Italy means taking base fears for reality. Bolshevism is overthrown."

in 1929.   It is evident, then, that the Fascist boast of having reaped wheat on lands which were reclaimed by the energy and foresight of Mussolini has no foundation in fact.

In this, as in other forms of political activity, Fascism has probably copied the Soviet government.   In Russia, the state, source and sole regulator of all life — just as Fascism wants to be in Italy — has decided on a momentous industrial and agrarian transformation, to be carried out in a comparatively short lapse of time.   But in Rome they forgot there is an important difference between Russia and Italy.   In Russia it was a question of changing the cultivation of lands which are among the richest and most fertile in the world; for those lands, little is needed but machines to plow, and men able to do the simplest sort of agricultural work.   In a word, the main element — the land — exists already in Russia, and work on it gives immediate results.   In Italy the situation is just the reverse.   Therefore an artificial reclamation policy is a drain on capital, which in consequence is lacking for more immediate and productive agricultural enterprise.

Readers will understand that I have lingered on this apparently technical problem because it is an example — one of many — of the way in which a régime responds to the need for cultivating prestige even (if it must) in opposition to the real progress of a nation.

From a moral point of view, which is, after all, what matters most, there is the risk that a policy of show and prestige, accentuated by the unanimity of a press bound never to admit a criticism and always to declare everything marvelous, will end by having an unfavorable influence on the critical sense of a nation. . . .   Mental prostration before dogmas and formulas and men (exalted today on order, forgotten tomorrow on order, as now happens constantly in Soviet Russia and in Italy), must be, in the long run, morally degrading. Whoever has traveled in the East has seen races poisoned incurably by long generations of subjection to despots.

Thucydides said of old: "The strength of a city is not ships or walls, but men."   Sharing that belief I conclude that even though a dictatorship may accomplish so much good as to have "the trains run on time," the net effects none the less will be lethal to the nation. I sometimes wonder to what extent Americans still remember Samuel Gompers.   Of all the thousands of idealistic utterances during the Paris Peace Conference few seemed to me as rich in deep, wholehearted sincerity as the following sentence of the American labor leader: "Men do not know how safe a thing freedom is."

GERMANY: BATTLEFIELD OF THE MIDDLE CLASSES [1]

Sigmund Neumann

Lecturer in sociology at Wesleyan University

The chief aim of Germany's post-war foreign policy has been to get rid of the burden of Versailles. Whether by destroying the treaty by means of her own power; or through an alliance with Russia to combat the "Western capitalistic system" and the treaty that was its symbol; or by a rapprochement with England and Italy which might make them new allies; or by means of a direct understanding with France — whatever the form, Germany's aim has always been the destruction of the intolerable treaty. In this aim all her politicians agreed. Their differences seemed to be a matter of political temperament. But it was more than that. There were different types of politicians fighting for the upper hand. They belonged to different social worlds, or at least they thought so.

The struggle over the course to be taken by the German Republic in foreign affairs was fought out in three phases, which marked off at the same time three main periods of internal development. The first epoch ended with the liquidation of the Ruhr struggle and the stabilization of the German mark; the second ended with the Hague settlement and the collapse of the great coalition between the German People's Party and the Social Democratic Party; the third reached its culmination in the seizure of power by the National Socialists in 1933.

The first five years after the Armistice were marked, so far as internal politics went, by the effort to establish and consolidate the Republic. There can be no question that the masses generally longed for peace after the convulsions and losses of war; but from the very first day of the breakdown of 1918 there existed also the idea of a *levée en masse*. The warrior had not yet returned home. A part of the fighting spirit was preserved in the revolutionary spirit.

Every decision in German foreign affairs during this epoch was unstable. The internal struggle regarding the acceptance of the Treaty of Versailles remained undecided until the last minute. The reception of the London ultimatum (1921) and the development of the struggle in the Ruhr demonstrated the unsteadiness of German

[1] From *Foreign Affairs*, January, 1935. Reprinted by permission.

policy at this time.   This instability was in no small degree caused
by the policy of the victorious Powers, which made it difficult even
for those groups which aimed to bring about a reconciliation to persist
in their ideas.   In this sense there was no clear distinction between
Right or Left wings.   The political fronts coincided only superficially
with the party groups.   A struggle went on daily in the soul of every
German. . . .

The first epoch was brought to a close by the conflict in the Ruhr.
This had started as a demonstration of the whole German people's
united spirit of resistance; its collapse seemed to end the hope of a
military solution of Germany's problems.   For France it connoted the
end of an epoch as well, because the occupation had not been a success.   The French elections and the victory of the Left Cartel proved
this.   Thus the Ruhr adventure cleared the atmosphere by demonstrating the limits of direct action.

After this, politics took a fresh turn.   The new era was clearly
characterized by the personalities of Briand and Stresemann, and it
proved to be the only post-war epoch during which there were real
French-German conversations.   These were possible because the
meetings between Stresemann and Briand and Herriot were meetings
of representatives of the European burgher class, speaking the same
language and holding the same values.   Upon this fact depended the
whole policy of Franco-German understanding and the so-called spirit
of Locarno.

Stresemann had grown up with the ideals of 1848.   As a student he
had opposed the changes in those ideals that overtook the majority
of German students; as a minister he tried to make those ideals appeal
to a new student generation.   He was almost the only republican
minister who awakened some response in academic circles.   Meantime the ideals of 1848 had changed considerably.   The German
national liberalism of the Bismarckian era had brought about a characteristic union of "property and culture."   That made it the representative of the upper middle classes.   Idealism and practical policy
became insolubly combined; and with them, in a very strange mixture, liberty and power.   This led to the stabilization of constitutional law at home and a powerful policy in foreign affairs, i.e. economic expansion and the building up of sea power.   As a matter of
fact, the middle classes resigned their influence upon internal affairs.
What remained was only an apparent retention of the constitution.
This was the compromise which the middle classes accepted after their
political defeats of 1848 and the so-called conflict of the constitution

between 1862 and 1866. The middle classes were deprived of all
sense of political responsibility; but it was only after the war that the
serious consequences of this became evident. With these developments came a decisive change in the middle classes themselves, characterized by the replacement of a politically-minded "burgher" by an
economically-minded "bourgeois."

The German Republic offered the chance for a retransformation,
for the rebirth of a political middle class. Stresemann seemed to be
the clear expression of this tendency — the reawakening of the traditions of 1848 and the enlargement of those traditions by the adoption
of the world-wide view of national policy which opened up early in
the new century. Stresemann showed this peculiar mixture of idealism and realism. This dreamer with the eyes of Coepenick Street
(the miserable district of Berlin where he was born) was a connoisseur
of literature and at the same time head of an industrial association.
It was by no mere chance that he became the founder and leader of
the German People's Party. Even in pre-war times Stresemann,
by founding and leading the industrial association of Middle Germany,
fought for small industry against the domination of the heavy industry of the Ruhr. He really represented the German people;
even in outward appearance he was of a type usual in Germany. . . .

Stresemann was not a revolutionary; he was at bottom uncom-
plicated, simple, affirmative. He was not shaken by crises in belief.
He was not an insurgent by nature. He was a liberal in the fullest
sense of the word, particularly in his idea of mankind. His nature
was happy, impulsive, with strong tensions but reconciled contrasts.
Almost automatically he achieved an inner harmony, and transferred
it from his personal philosophy to the world. Thus with that naturally liberal optimism which regards the whole process of the world's
history as nothing but a gradual evolution toward the good, he saw
great perspectives opening up where others scarcely perceived the
first feeble tendencies. It was said quite rightly that his approach to
Lord D'Abernon, the British Ambassador, rested upon simply a lack
of mistrust.

Here lies the basis of Stresemann's whole foreign policy. His first
success rested upon his going halfway to meet his adversary. He did
not claim the maximum in order to get half. But the Locarno Pact
was not the result of just a tactical manoeuvre. Stresemann's policy
of understanding raised the dispute over Versailles to another level,
and brought at least a temporary economic solution in its turning
away from the Dawes Plan to the Hague Conferences. The under-

standing with Briand, however, was more than that. It was based upon a common human ideal, the same social standard of values. It happened that two European statesmen met. But it is not chance that the meeting was the most fruitful of the long series of German-French discussions since the war. It is a tragic fact, as Professor Toynbee has rightly pointed out, that the Stresemann-Brüning régime in Germany and the Herriot-Daladier régime in France were not only not contemporaneous, but actually did not overlap — except in this Locarno period, which was only a beginning.

This policy of understanding — the second period of Germany's post-war foreign policy — was frustrated just when it had apparently triumphed with the evacuation of the Rhineland. This can be explained only superficially by Stresemann's death.

At bottom the third epoch which then began, and in which the rise of National Socialism was already foreshadowed, demonstrated how fragile was the basis of Stresemann's policy. In the economic field this became generally evident in the banking crisis of June, 1931. The prosperity of 1924–1929 was only a boom on credit produced by foreign loans for German finance. Thus the consolidation of the Republic in this epoch proved to be only apparent. This was true in a much deeper and non-economic sense. At the beginning came the inflation — in many respects the price paid for stabilization. Business, freed from debts and obligations, found a new starting point. But it was not until five years later that the social effect of the inflation, and the political consequences, became evident. It meant the beginning of the end for the middle classes. And this occurred just at the advent of an epoch which promised under Stresemann's leadership to give the middle classes predominance. From now on it was not only a middle class broken by the pre-war development in Germany and handicapped by its own lack of political consciousness; now it had been shaken to its very foundations. The year 1929 demonstrated just how far the "property and culture" of the former liberal middle classes had disappeared. From now on they were without their original power of resistance and capacity for influencing their environment. After this convulsion the king-pin of middle class values — the idea of security — was shattered.

The process began with the shrinking of all economic security in the period of inflation, which withdrew the guarantee which middle class people enjoyed by virtue of their training, occupation, and standard of life. The authority of money was diminished. Money had been the measure of social prestige in the nineteenth century, identifying, according to Guizot's well-known formula, wealth and the moral good in middle class civilization. The hierarchy of property still existed *de facto* but no longer *de jure.* The possession of property was more and more generally condemned in the popular judgment and even among well-to-do people. In any case, with the loss of property the burgher ideals of property and saving lost ground. From this side, too, the ideal of the individual was attacked. It is no mere accident that (as Pierre Vienot rightly pointed out in his *Incertitudes Allemandes*) in Germany at that time one did not ask: "How are your affairs?" or: "Do you earn much?" but: "How is the economic situation?" This tells only a little about the current practice but much about the public's opinion of the validity of the economic system. Here is the social-psychological root of socialism, even though of a vague and ambiguous variety. . . .

In 1929 the economic world crisis began. In Germany it revealed the breakdown of a surface boom. Simultaneously Germany experienced — as did other countries in lesser degree — the rebirth of the war as reflected in literature. After a period of ten years there was a peculiar revival of interest in war experiences. It was at once the resurrection of the warrior and a demonstration of antagonism toward him. The soldier had never been absent in Germany during Stresemann's period. His unrest had not been overcome and subdued. He had only stepped into the background. He lived on in many military political leagues. And now he got into touch with the new social groups that were pushing toward an anti-bourgeois reaction. The social revolution massed them together and gave them a revolutionary impulse.

It has been sufficiently demonstrated in political literature that this crisis extended far beyond the economic realm. It invaded all spheres of life and affected — maybe as an outpost's skirmish — the whole of European thinking. No wonder it touched general European foreign policy, which was substantially the burgher policy of security. In Germany, the Stresemann effort at reconciliation seemed to be submerged. The various inconclusive moves of German foreign policy (such as the proposal of an Austro-German tariff union in 1931) pointed to a revolutionary change.

It is, however, true that the Stresemann influence extended further into this third period, which reached its culmination in Hitler's seizure of power, than the collapse of the Stresemann policies seemed to indicate. The years 1924–1929 in Germany, although in retrospect they seemed to be merely a surface boom, diffused an extraordinary

amount of burgher philosophy even among the proletariat classes.
The economic crisis and the following enormous unemployment
eventually destroyed this development. Nevertheless these years
of stabilization to a certain extent brought about a social readjustment
by providing a rest period in which burgher values could revive.
This had a definite influence on the generation then growing up.
Simultaneously the pre-war generation staged a "comeback." The
war had meanwhile killed the best representatives of the wartime
generation, and had destroyed the bourgeois way of life for many of
those who returned home. They seemed almost forgotten. Grandfathers and grandsons now joined hands over their heads, leaving
them behind as unfit for the daily struggle.

This break disturbed the inner continuity between one generation
and the next. Forces accumulated, ready to burst through in a
crisis. When the crisis came the forgotten generation and the
youngest generation joined hands. It was this reinforcement of the
warriors of 1918 by the post-war generation — more bourgeois-
minded, yearning for order and security — and their joint success in
winning over some bourgeois pre-war politicians, which laid the foundations of the victorious National Socialism of 1933. Thereby it differed from the first insurrection of 1923, which had been destined to
fail because it was an incipient revolution of the warriors alone.
National Socialism meanwhile turned to legal methods, not only out
of tactical considerations, but because it found itself face to face with
a society which had undergone *Verbuergerlichung* (the process of
becoming bourgeois-minded) in the period of stabilization. And in
spite of all its penetration by revolutionary doctrine, National Socialism itself became to a considerable extent bourgeois-minded. . . .

The widespread consternation abroad which followed the National
Socialist seizure of power in Germany was quite similar to the general
suspicion in which Russia and Italy were held for many years after
the Bolshevist and Fascist revolutions. Different principles of foreign
policy seemed to confront one another. Real coöperation with foreign
Powers was impossible because the approach to international problems
was fundamentally different on each side. The world of the burgher,
which evidently also included large masses of the skilled workers, was
confronted by a new revolutionary world which doubted all its values.
An entirely new idea of foreign policy seemed to prevail.

In the burgher's world a fixed system of security, a comprehensive organization, and the legal regulation of contracts guaranteed
property and stability. French post-war foreign policy was based

upon such principles and determined to a large extent the whole European post-war diplomacy. The idea of the League was also to some degree based upon these principles, although overshadowed by the fact that the French system of security practically meant a guarantee for the Treaty of Versailles.

In a modern realistic view, Geneva may be defined as the chess-board on which the great game of world diplomacy is being played. For many of the League's champions, however, it means much more than that. For them, behind this institution stands the middle class idea. The world parliament took over into the sphere of international relations the internal methods and institutions of parliamentarism, the basis of which was reliance upon discussion and negotiation instead of force and violence to settle group conflicts. Discussions and publicity and their result — generally recognized laws — were the fundamentals of the parliamentarian state. It grew up during the period of enlightenment. There existed only one ideal state, just as there was only one way of arriving at truth — that is, by reason, which was the yardstick for every deed and attitude. This epoch of rationalism coincided with the awakening of the modern European middle class and gave clear philosophical expression to its ideals and aims in all spheres of life. Just as in economics, according to the classical theory, competition between supply and demand finally created the "just price," automatically restoring the general harmony of the community by the peaceful struggle of private interests, so in politics the open fight in parliament — the political market place — brought together the competitors in politics, the political parties. The "just price" in their case is composed of recognized, reasonable, and calculable laws.

From this point of view the League of Nations is a recent transfer of the general ideals of the middle class into international relations. But it was organized just at the time when their fundamental belief in a universally valid truth was being shattered by the World War and the post-war difficulties. It was organized when the foundations of the European middle class had been shaken to the bottom.

It was the attempt of the champions of the League of Nations to restore confidence in the ideals of security and order. Post-war statesmen like Briand, Chamberlain, Stresemann, and Herriot fought for the ideal of the burgher's foreign policy. In their hands, however, it lost its characteristic stiffness and narrowness because of the cosmopolitan ideals which they had drawn from their common European culture. Their type was the result of a long process of development;

in them the burgher politician had taken on the outlook and manners
of the aristocrat who had been the representative politician in pre-
burgher times and who had not completely disappeared. To this
aristocrat, whose habits of thought the bourgeois inherited, foreign
policy meant a sphere of close relationships and personal encounters.
He did not regard the representatives of other peoples as essentially
strange personalities. He considered the foreigner as a relative, as to
a certain degree a part of the entity to which he himself belonged. . . .

The real enemy of both middle class security and the cosmopolitan system is a revolutionary foreign policy represented in European history by the Jacobin. For him international policy does not
mean fixed boundaries or a discussion between the members of an
international community. For him foreign countries offer the battlefield, to be overcome by his ideas and conquered by his warriors.
In his psychology, military and revolutionary ideas are often closely
connected. "Ideas have no boundaries." The burgher fears the
Jacobin just because of his missionary power, because of his immeasurable dynamics, because of the unrest he brings into a secure
and clearly circumscribed world. Every revolution which claims
to be more than a mere change of governments and which pre-
tends to create a new social order must also influence neighboring
countries and awaken in them a spirit of deep unrest. This is the
more true if the revolution embodies political ideas which touch
upon foreign affairs. For then, finding natural confederates abroad
— perhaps a movement of social internationalism or a movement to
further some pan-nationalist idea — the revolution sets to work to
bore from within by propaganda and by inciting to civil war. Nowadays this is a very efficacious method of expansion, and at the same
time a substitute for military invasion. The readiness of a revolutionary country to abandon it is a visible sign that it is turning back
to a burgher policy and that it is paying the price claimed for its
readmission to the family of nations.

At first every revolution means a break with the common order
of the family of nations, and a danger to it. Usually it starts with
the suspension of international payments. The extraordinary importance of economics in modern international affairs makes the
attitude of a revolutionary country toward the debt question the
touchstone of political orientation. Often it is the banking and
business community which decides the foreign policy of the government. The world's reception of the Third Reich is an illuminating
example. The degree of Germany's readiness to pay or not to pay

was one of the main factors deciding her prestige. The moratorium of June, 1934, made a deeper impression abroad than the withdrawal from the League in October, 1933.

Nevertheless the causes of tension are more deeply rooted than what has just been said would indicate. The economic is only a part — though a very important part — of a nation's general attitude. Economic unrest is heightened so long as the inner forces of the revolutionary state remain uncertain, and hence so long as the tendencies of its foreign policy are not clear. Even a leader's true wish for peace may be weakened by the inner dynamics, the revolutionary driving power, of his movement. Sometimes his revolutionary speeches which so alarm the world are only meant for home consumption. In those cases they are evidence of inner tension and represent an attempt to divert attention from domestic to foreign problems. Modern European history gives us many examples of such a relationship between internal difficulties and adventures in the foreign field.

The acute need of a dictatorship based upon "plebiscites" and popular acclaim to show successes in foreign affairs is illustrated by the policy and destiny of Napoleon III. Bismarck, his greater and more successful opponent, seems to have been right when he said: "With foreign political successes you can win over your internal opponents. Give the people glory in foreign politics and they will be ready to renounce domestic rights."

This connection between foreign affairs and internal politics is especially revealed in the so-called totalitarian state. Its claim to totality in inner politics is generally based on a real or presumed danger from abroad. In wartime all opposition and discussion must cease; personal liberty no longer exists. The best argument for this sort of suppression is the country's peril. War is a dictatorship's beginning, its demand, its test. Therefore it centers its propaganda on building up the fighting spirit. The younger generation especially may not take the propaganda platonically, but literally. It may prefer the dangers and the power of a soldier's life to the security of the burgher's.

It is, finally, the missionary idea of every revolution, its internationalism, which stirs its neighbors. As long as there is no proof that the revolution will stop at its own boundaries, it is suspected of endangering the peace of an ordered world. Fascist Italy has gone through a period of world suspicion. Soviet Russia's foreign affairs have been even more marked by the tension arising out of such suspicion. Its recent approach to the states of Western Europe is based upon its definite adoption of an outspoken burgher policy in international relations. Litvinov's system of pacts is in one line with French policy. The Soviet Union is no longer outside the League of Nations. This change was preceded by a long inner struggle, part of the historical fight between Trotsky and Stalin. It may be that internal considerations dictated the cessation of the foreign revolutionary activity of the Third International and its diversion into efforts to make a success of repeated five-year plans. But it was more than the renunciation of aggressive policy which calmed the European Powers; it was the Soviet Union's adoption of a European policy of security through mutual pacts. Security against foreign interference had indeed become a prerequisite for the development of Soviet Russia's own internal plans. Thus she seems to have become a strong ally in the fight for the European *status quo* and against every revolutionary peril which might endanger her own internal development. It may be only tactics; if so, these tactics are very efficacious in the present European situation.

In its fear of a new revolutionary power, Europe makes its peace with the old revolutionary who offers at least a truce. Here is the explanation of the radical change in European politics since the rise of the Third Reich. In the end, Germany, too, may tend toward the same burgher policy as the other countries. But the mere possibility that Germany is leaving the common line of European policy threatens European security. By her geographical position Germany is the "heart of Europe." The effort of the European Powers, led by France, is to forestall the revolutionary peril by binding it by obligations and treaties and security pacts. But the real desire for security is not satisfied so long as there is no trust in the fidelity of those who pledge their faith. Trust presumes a common world in which all are partners. Doubt is sufficient to make every treaty ineffectual.

We cannot yet decide where Germany really stands in the struggle to determine Europe's future. Yet the deep causes of the violent tension pervading Europe become clearer when we consider the struggle over social principle which underlies the day by day development of German foreign policy. Germany has become the battlefield of the European burgher. The fight is not yet ended. Foreign affairs — seemingly on the periphery of these social developments — not merely reflect the course of this struggle but become in the end the historical test of the burgher order.

THE STRENGTH OF DEMOCRACY[1]

Walter Lippmann

WALTER LIPPMANN, formerly associate editor of the *New Republic* and editor of the New York *World*, is now on the staff of the New York *Herald Tribune*, writing articles ("Today and Tomorrow") which are syndicated nationally. Among his books are *A Preface to Politics; Drift and Mastery; The Stakes of Diplomacy; Liberty and the News; Public Opinion; The Phantom Public; A Preface to Morals; Interpretations* (two series); *The Method of Freedom;* and *The New Imperative.*

The triumph of Hitler has reduced still further the domain of popular government in the world, and it is but natural that men should wonder whether it can hope to survive anywhere. Yet this impression that autocracy is sweeping the world is something of an optical illusion. The fact is that this far at least the old democracies have withstood the impact of war and revolution and deep financial disorder. Wide as is the extension of autocracy today, except in one important country, it is no more widely extended than it was before the war. The exception is Italy, and Italy happens to be the one Great Power which had most recently achieved its national unity and had had the shortest experience in the conduct of representative government. For the rest it may be said that the Fascist and Communist victories of the last fifteen years have been won only where democracy had not yet been established.

Thus in Russia the dictatorship of Lenin and Stalin was founded on the collapse of tsarism. Japan, of course, has never had more than a faint imitation of popular government. The dictatorships of Central Europe and of the Balkan peoples had never known even one generation of political liberty and political responsibility. Hitler has overthrown a republic which was half strangled from the hour of its birth. But the old democracies of Scandinavia, of Switzerland, and of France, of Britain and of the Dominions, and of the United States, are still in being: the peoples which knew democracy in the nineteenth century, the peoples who have lived under the heritage of liberalism, have not fallen into disorder and have not surrendered to dictators.

A wise man once remarked that revolutions do not overthrow

[1] "Today and Tomorrow," March 30, 1933.

governments; governments collapse and revolutions ensue. The history of the last fifteen years offers impressive proof of this generalization. Kerensky did not overthrow the Tsar. Kerensky attempted to organize a government on the ruins of the tsarist régime. He failed and Lenin organized a government.

The German republicans did not overthrow the Hohenzollerns. The Kaiser had fled and his government was demoralized. The Weimar system failed to provide a government. In a half-dozen inconclusive elections the German people proved to themselves that they had not yet learned to make representative government effective. Only then did Hitler come into power.

The crises of the last few years have revealed the essential differences between the democracies which have a capacity to endure and the democracies which have not had it. The ineffective democracies disintegrate in a storm. Solid democracies are capable of uniting their forces, of concentrating power in an emergency, and then of relaxing when the crisis has been surmounted. The first great democracy to demonstrate this capacity was France in 1926. Confronted with what appeared to be an uncontrollable inflation, political power was concentrated in the hands of Poincaré, and order was restored. The second democracy to prove its strength was the British. In 1931, confronted with what might easily have become a catastrophe, the British people concentrated authority and mastered the danger. The third democracy to vindicate itself is our own during the last few weeks.

It is entirely misleading to look upon the concentration of national authority which took place in France in 1926, in Great Britain in 1931, and in the United States in 1933, as part of the tide of autocracy which has been sweeping over Asia and over Europe. What has happened in these three nations is the exact opposite of what has happened where there has been a collapse in dictatorship. The French, the British, and ourselves have been able to fortify democracy because popular government was inherently strong. Fascism has been overthrowing democracy where it is inherently weak.

Thus we are entitled to believe that democracy, once it is solidly founded in the traditions of a people, may be the toughest and most enduring of all forms of government. The generation through which we have lived seems to have given substantial proof that while popular government is difficult to establish, and must be learned by living with it, once established it will stand through very foul weather indeed.

II

THE CHANGING ECONOMIC WORLD

EVEN had the World War never occurred, the economic structure of the globe and of the United States would doubtless have changed with unparalleled rapidity in the two decades between 1915 and 1935. For a century there had been a steadily accelerating pace in such change. But the war threw the world into confusion. It was responsible for a tremendous stimulation in some economic fields, a powerful retardation in others; its terrific costs threw an unprecedented burden upon mankind; the changes in boundaries, the disruption of old lines of trade, the growth of economic nationalism to keep pace with the new political nationalism, all produced deplorable and incalculable effects. In much of the world (Great Britain was a conspicuous exception), the years immediately after the war witnessed an unexpected and illusory revival. This season of "prosperity" was most exuberant and extravagant in the United States, where it came to an abrupt and calamitous end with the crash of 1929. The result has been, throughout the world but most of all in the United States, a drastic revision of certain economic ideas popular in the flush days of the boom, and a searching reëxamination of old concepts of the proper relation between government and industry. It is with this revision and reëxamination that this section is concerned. The excerpt from the report of the Committee on Recent Economic Changes gives an expert résumé of developments immediately preceding the great crash. The selection from Mr. John Maynard Keynes offers the view of one authority upon the changes now certain in the relation of government to economic life; that from Sir Arthur Salter upon the changes required in world organization. Mr. Norman Thomas presents a Socialist opinion, and Dr. Benjamin Anderson the view of one fearful of too much state control. Mr. Marquis W. Childs presents a sketch of a nation where governmental intervention has gone far but has achieved outwardly successful results.

RECENT ECONOMIC CHANGES IN AMERICAN LIFE[1]

President Hoover's Committee on Recent Economic Changes

THE COMMITTEE ON RECENT ECONOMIC CHANGES grew out of President Harding's Conference on Unemployment in 1921. After a long period devoted to organization and accumulation of materials it began its work in January, 1928, under the chairmanship of Herbert Hoover, and completed it in 1929 under the acting chairmanship of A. W. Shaw. Its two-volume report offers the best analysis in print of the economic development in America between the World War and the Great Depression; but it must be said that the depression has compelled a wholly new attitude toward many of the problems treated. The report includes chapters by experts on Industry, Transportation, Labor, Agriculture, and like subjects, with a final summary, from which the selection here printed is taken, by Wesley Clair Mitchell of Columbia University. Dr. Mitchell, who was born at Rushville, Illinois, in 1874, and educated at the University of Chicago, is best known for his important work on business cycles, a subject upon which he has published several books and many articles.

THE STANDARD OF LIVING

Current impressions of the prevailing standards of living in the United States rest in the main on well-known index numbers of real earnings. All such measures point to a substantial rise in American standards in the past six years[2] and probably to a considerable widening of the margin between American and European standards of material well-being as contrasted with the state of affairs before the war.

Such measures are defective because they do not account for all of the elements of family income, on the one hand, and also because they fail to make proper allowance for fundamental changes in the amount, quality, and character of the things people buy and use. It is neither possible to discover and measure all sources of family income nor to account completely for far-reaching changes in consumption. Certain types of income can, however, be estimated and the outstanding changes in consumption described. For instance, the income repre-

[1] From *Recent Economic Changes in the United States*, Report of the Committee on Recent Economic Changes of the President's Conference on Unemployment, Herbert Hoover, Chairman; including the reports of a special staff of the National Bureau of Economic Research, New York, McGraw-Hill Book Company, Inc., 1929.

[2] 1922–1928.

sented by the free public services of education, charity, recreation, and health and sanitation increased from $859,336,000 in 1915 to $2,860,935,000 in 1926.

Surveys of the use of food, manufactured goods, automobiles, and housing reveal radical modifications in the habits of American consumption. New studies of family budgets will be necessary to correct erroneous impressions and to throw light on the sources and magnitude of prevailing family income.

Physiologically, per capita food requirements have declined, and are still tending to decline, especially in respect to quantities required for maintaining body heat and furnishing energy for work. With higher incomes per capita, higher standards of wholesomeness due to trade action and public inspection, a wider variety of foods available in all seasons and in all parts of the country, fuller knowledge of nutrition, and more widespread information on dietetics, there is reason to believe that the actual diets of today more nearly meet the physiological needs than has ever before been true for the population as a whole.

Food standards have risen notably in respect to auxiliary satisfactions derived from food. The diet of today contains an unprecedented proportion of elements appealing to the appetite, the senses of sight, taste, and smell, and other aesthetic desires. It is strikingly diversified in the individual meal, from meal to meal, from day to day, from season to season. It is eaten with a substantial degree of assurance that the elements are wholesome. It permits of ready adjustment to individual idiosyncracies of need or taste, and to changes in the family income.

Present-day food standards have also risen greatly in respect to economies in household expenditures of time and effort. To an increasing extent, food is purchased for the needs of the day. Less and less household labor is required in preparation, preservation, and storage.

The present diet is expensive in the sense that it entails a larger expenditure of purchasing power than is true in most other countries, or than was true in the United States in earlier years. Increasing congestion of population alone tends toward higher costs of distribution, which have been only partially offset by economies in production and marketing. Many of the grains already mentioned have entailed additional costs which are, for the most part, reflected in the prices of particular foods or food outlays as a whole. This is especially the case in respect to economies in household efforts, for small packages, prepared foods, prompt delivery, etc., entail heavier costs than bulk purchases of foods in an unprepared state, carried home by the consumer.

Considering, however, the character of the food consumed and the size of consumers' incomes, food costs cannot be accounted heavy. By and large, a smaller proportion of the family income is required, under present conditions, to secure a safer, better balanced, more varied, more appetizing diet than formerly.

There is still room for substantial improvement in food standards and substantial economies in food costs. While dietary improvements have been almost universal, large classes of the population can well make further advances in each of the three lines indicated. Avoidable malnutrition has not been eliminated. Much misinformation is widely circulated. Ideal standards of wholesomeness and honesty are by no means attained. Wastes of foodstuffs and of labor in connection with food are excessive from producer to consumer. Apart from the matter of suitable diets from the standpoint of nutrition, the food problems pressing for solution in America today are less those of the consumer, and more largely those of the farmer, the manufacturer, the wholesaler, and the retailer.

In the heterogeneous category of manufactured goods, the striking rise in output, and hence in consumption, has come in the manufacture of many mechanical articles of household equipment and of such new devices as the radio. The dramatic revolution, of course, is represented by the growth in the use of the automobile and by a current production of more than four million cars a year.

Staple consumers' goods have not shown a great increase, as indicated by the slow growth of flour milling, slaughtering, cotton and woolen goods, and clothing. The industries manufacturing cigars, chewing and smoking tobacco, and snuff have shown practically no growth, while the output of cigarettes has greatly expanded. In the textile and clothing group, including leather and its products, there has been no marked growth except for millinery, lace goods, and men's furnishings. Among textile materials there has been a great advance in the production of silks and rayon, knit goods, and carpets and rugs.

The volume of residential construction has increased more rapidly than population, and the quality of housing appears to show marked improvement, although very little material is available to show how large a part of our wage-earning population is still inadequately housed.

More than 40 per cent of the total farm population now living on low-value farms have not improved their standards of living in the period under review, and appear to have sustained such standards as they have by the use of a vast mortgage indebtedness. The 57.8 per cent of population living on high-value farms presumably have raised their standard since 1922.

INDUSTRY

When industries are measured according to the average number of wage-earners per establishment, wide differences appear. There is no noticeable trend toward production on a larger scale. The tendency is rather for the extremes to move toward the middle, and points of concentration are appearing: about 20 workers per establishment and 100 workers per establishment.

However, using horsepower per establishment as the basis for measurement, the increase in the scale of production is evident. There has been a general and marked increase in horsepower, and the development has by no means reached its culmination.

The implications of these two tendencies are significant in many respects. Plants can take on additional wage-earners without the assistance of financial institutions, but large increases in machinery necessitate corresponding initial outlays. In addition to its interest for the investment banker, this increase in the capital structure has significance for the business cycle analyst. As long as the chief expense is labor cost, the manufacturer, by means of discharging employees, can reduce costs as his receipts are reduced. But with a large investment in machinery, his interest charges will continue whether he operates or not. From the point of view of the worker, it means that more and more of the actual labor is done by the machine, and we are coming more and more to merit the designation of the "machine age."

It is evident that there are many combinations among industrial units. According to income tax returns, one-half of the largest enterprises in the country are engaged in manufacturing. However, the numbers in this field are not increasing so rapidly as in trade, banking, and other types of economic endeavor.

The records of mergers in recent years indicate that it has been a general movement, rather than one confined to any particular industries. It has been greatest among public utilities, reaching its height there in 1926. In manufacturing industry, the tendency to merge appears to follow the business cycle, but the general trend has been upward since 1922.

The present mergers are unlike those of the great combination period at the end of the nineteenth century.   In the earlier instances, the incentives were usually either the formation of a monopoly or profits of some promoter.   The present mergers often appear to be quickly followed by new financing, thus implying that the desire for additional capital is an important motive.   A further incentive, in certain industries, has come from modern marketing methods, in which the concern which is large enough to undertake national advertising has a definite advantage over its smaller rivals.

It has long been claimed that large-scale operation offered many potential economies.   It is evident that the most efficient size at which an industrial plant may operate has increased greatly during recent years.   However, as regards combinations among such plants, the facts are entirely inadequate.   The few available do indicate that, as often as not, these potential economies are more than offset by real losses in efficiency.

Over against this fact is the probability that the large concerns are taking an increasing part of the nation's business.   This also reflected in the record of the stock market, in which three of the four industries studied recorded the greatest advances made by the securities of the larger companies.   Again, we conclude that this larger share in the nation's business is not owing to ability to produce at a lower cost, but to greater success in the field of marketing.   An interesting side light on this development is the present status of the Sherman and Clayton Acts, which tend to encourage combinations, since the merged companies can adopt a uniform marketing policy which would be illegal if undertaken as independents.

In the case of random or casual fluctuations, small enterprises record wider variations than large concerns.   This appears to be true both of unemployment and of earnings.

In the case of cyclical fluctuations, the data indicate that large corporations are subject to wider fluctuations in production and employment than the smaller concerns, but that their earnings are more stable.   This seems to be the result of a more or less conscious policy to shut down the plant and accept the losses resulting from idleness rather than to offer their products at greatly reduced prices, thus accepting the loss on inventory, but maintaining operation.   The general tendency is therefore toward production cycles rather than price cycles.

The movement of industry among the areas of the country has tended definitely toward a more equal distribution of manufacturing.

The rapid industrial growth of the South and the decline of New England and the Middle Atlantic States illustrate this tendency.

Quite as important is the shift from city to country. The records indicate a definite decline in manufacturing activity in the larger cities, and an actual gain in the rural areas, particularly in the East North Central and South Atlantic divisions. There is a marked increase in size in these rural enterprises, which have heretofore always been much below the general average.

The third step in this tendency toward the more equal geographical distribution of industry is the breaking down of local concentration in the historical centers of specific industries.

LAND TRANSPORTATION

From 1920 (when railway property investment was slightly in excess of twenty billion dollars) to 1927, inclusive, the railways have made gross expenditures of nearly six billion dollars for additions to and betterments of facilities and equipment, an average annual expenditure of three-quarters of a billion. Of the total sum, approximately one-half has been devoted to roadway and structures, principally in additional running tracks, sidings, and yards; improved terminals and structures; additional automatic and other signaling; heavier rail; more and better ties; and more and better ballast. The other one-half has been devoted to betterments of equipment. The number of equipment units shows little change — a slight increase in freight cars but actual decreases in locomotives and passenger cars — but the average and the aggregate capacity of the units have increased, and particularly in locomotives, there have been notable improvements in design and economic effectiveness. In the first few years of the post-war period, the expenditures for equipment were greater than those for roadway and structures, but during the latter part of the period the proportions have been reversed. Because of the more effective use of equipment, the additional traffic has been handled with the same or even less units, and orders for new locomotives and cars have been mainly for replacement of units retired. . . .

Railway freight traffic since 1920 has had a general (but slight) upward tendency. The ton-miles of 1923 and 1926 were of record-breaking volume. The former peak loads were in 1918 and 1920. Taking 1918, a war year, as 100, the successive peaks were 101 in 1920, 102 in 1923 and 1925, 109 in 1926, and 106 in 1927. The number of loaded cars shows relatively greater increases than ton-miles, but the loaded-car unit does not take into account the tendency toward a smaller carload. Railway passenger traffic, in contrast to the slight increase in freight, is steadily and seriously diminishing in volume. Since 1920, each year, with the exception of 1923, has had a smaller total passenger-miles than the preceding year. The passenger-miles in 1927 were 28 per cent less than in 1920. The loss is almost entirely in local passengers, and is owing mainly to motor vehicle competition. Long-distance passengers and commuters have been increasing slightly.

The effect of motor truck competition on railways, while it has diminished the volume of less-than-carload freight and has taken away some tonnage in carload lots in a few other commodities, is not serious. Relatively, the freight lost to trucks is a small part of the total, and it is the least remunerative of railway freight. The small-shipment, short-haul freight traffic is burdensome in its demands upon equipment and facilities, and the railways are better off when the equipment and facility capacity released by the loss of freight to trucks is employed for the long-distance bulk freight which is more attractive from the point of view of net revenue. In railway passenger service, however, the loss in local passengers to automobiles and motor coaches is substantial and serious, and is narrowing the already small spread between railway passenger revenues and passenger expenses. To meet the new form of competition, the railways are improving the schedules and equipment of the through trains . . . and are entering the motor coach service. The greatest loss to the railways, however, is not in the passengers taken by motor coaches, but in the greater use of the private automobile as a substitute for railway transportation. . . .

The most notable achievement in railroad administration since the war has been the marked increase in the efficiency with which equipment has been utilized and trains operated. The car-miles per car-day have been increased from 25.1 in 1920 to 30.3 in 1927, and the ton-miles per car-day from 498 to 518. The 11 per cent more ton-miles of 1926 (the high record), compared with 1920, were produced with but 2 per cent more freight cars, notwithstanding a smaller average carload (over which the railways have little control) and a larger percentage of empty car-miles resulting from centralized distribution in shifting surplus cars from one region to another as needed for prospective loading. Unserviceable freight cars and locomotives have been reduced materially in number. In train service, there has been a steady and consistent gain in the train load from year to year since 1920, with a similar consistent gain in train speed through a reduction in road delays. In 1920, the gross load per train (cars and contents) was 1,443 tons; in 1927 it was 1,780 tons, a gain of 24 per cent. In 1920, the average train speed between terminals was 10.3 miles per hour; in 1927, it was 12.3 miles per hour, an increase of 19 per cent. . . .

From the railway point of view, the only important unfavorable element in the present situation is the low net return on value. The 1920 law was intended by Congress to give the railways a reasonable assurance of a fair return, but the rate-making policy of the Interstate Commerce Commission has not been consistent with that intention. The Commission, effective in 1922, defined a fair return as $5\frac{3}{4}$ per cent on value, but in no year since the law was enacted in 1920 have the railways earned that return. The work of valuation of railroad property is not complete, and in its present stage is surrounded by many uncertainties which are yet to be cleared up by the Supreme Court, but it seems not at all unlikely that the final value, when determined, will be little different from the investment cost carried on the railway books. On that value, plus working capital in cash and materials held for use, the net return in operating income was 2.9 per cent in 1921, with a gradually increasing rate up to 4.8 per cent in 1925 and 5.2 per cent in 1926, the year of greatest freight traffic volume and greatest gross revenues. In 1927, with slightly less traffic, the return was but 4.5 per cent, and for the first ten months of 1928 it was at the rate of 4.7 per cent. The average for the seven years ending with 1927 was 4.3 per cent, a rate inadequate as a reward for taking the risks of investment, and plainly below the reward that Congress intended as an incentive to adequate transportation service to the public when the Transportation Act was passed. The additional investments of the past eight years have been made with faith in the assurance of a fair return. Although the fair return has not been earned upon the total investment, it is likely that it would have been less without the additional investments, as they not only made it possible to produce the greater volume of transportation since 1923 but also to produce it at a lower cost. There is a limit, however, to the extent to which new dollars can be devoted to saving old dollars already invested, and the present policy of betterments cannot long be continued on an average return of 4.3 per cent on the whole.

Little progress has been made in carrying out the provisions of the Transportation Act pertaining to the consolidation of all railways into a limited number of systems of fairly equal financial strength.

The purpose of that part of the Act was to simplify the problems of rate-making, and to insure reasonably uniform returns under uniform rates to all of the railways in any region. The Interstate Commerce Commission was directed to prepare a final plan to which all proposals should conform, but the Commission has reached the conclusion that the task is too difficult, and no final plan has been published. In the meantime, no consolidations can take place because, according to law, none can be approved unless it is in harmony with the Commission's final plan not yet prepared. All that can be done is to approve unifications by lease or stock control, but short of actual consolidation. A few such proposals have been approved and others are before the Commission, but the law instead of bringing about the intended large-scale consolidations has, because of the inability of the Commission to prepare a final plan, acted as a brake upon the long-time natural process under which the existing systems have grown. An amendment to the law, proposing a period in which consolidations, when believed by the Commission to be in the public interest, may be effected voluntarily without regard to a comprehensive plan, was favorably considered by Congress early in 1928, but was crowded off the calendar in the closing days of the session.

From the public point of view, the outstanding railway development since the war has been the marked improvement in transportation service. The adequacy, speed, and dependability in freight movement have never been better. The improvement is seen in freedom from car shortages, embargoes, and other restrictions, and in close adherence to scheduled transit times. The number of scheduled fast freight trains has been increased and the speed bettered so as to give earlier deliveries at destination. Incidental services have been extended, and throughout the whole service there is greater effort to apply modern merchandising principles in the development and sale of transportation. The regularity of movement and dependability in rail service have given impetus to the general practice among manufacturers and merchants of carrying smaller inventories of raw materials and merchandise. Better rail service cannot be credited wholly with this economic development, but it called attention to the possibilities and led to the general movement. Certain it is that the smaller stocks would not afford adequate protection were rail service less prompt and reliable. The general reductions in inventories have released sums of capital which in the aggregate are enormous, and in buying habits have brought about profound changes which are far-reaching in their economic effects.

MARKETING

It often is stated that marketing costs, in contrast to production costs, have been tending to rise, in ratio to sales, over a period of years. That statement probably is true, but it cannot be proved statistically with the data now available. Furthermore, significant counter-tendencies have been at work, which have partially offset some of the increases. Some manufacturers, in order to increase their volume of sales, either with a view to securing production economies or to having the pleasure of doing a bigger business, have increased their expenditures for selling and sales promotion more rapidly than their sales have grown. Other manufacturers have followed a similar course with the hope of stabilizing their operations and their earnings. Still other manufacturers and wholesalers have been forced to increase their selling expenses because of their customers' growing practice of buying from hand to mouth. The changes in retail trading areas and the competition of chain stores have had the effect of increasing the expense ratios of numerous wholesalers. In department stores, too, there has been a tendency for the expense ratios to increase. On the other hand, many manufacturers have had no increase in their marketing expense ratios; chain stores have reduced the costs of retail and wholesale marketing in numerous lines; and some of the coöperative associations of farmers have succeeded in cutting marketing costs. Undoubtedly, the application of more scientific methods will result eventually in large economies in marketing. A detailed discussion of that problem, however, would take us far beyond the scope of this survey. The significant point for the task at hand is that during the period from 1922 to 1928 substantial reductions in marketing costs did not occur in most industries. The conditions which have existed during this period have led manufacturers and merchants in most instances to seek to stimulate and to satisfy demand rather than to reduce their marketing expenses.

During the period since 1922, the rise in standards of living, changes in methods of living, new inventions, and the exercise of merchandising ingenuity by manufacturers and merchants, have combined to cause large-scale changes in the character of the demand in the United States. Among these changes, the introduction of new types of merchandise, the broader emphasis on fashion, and the increased rapidity of style changes have been especially noteworthy. The result of these changes has been to yield prosperity for some industries and to necessitate retrenchment and reorganization for others. A premium thus has been placed on constructive merchandising ability, and more attention has come to be given, therefore, to specialized merchandising management. By no means all the problems growing out of these changes in demand have yet been solved.

The automobile has been one of the most pervasive influences affecting marketing as well as production during recent years. In addition to its direct influence on demand, its use as a transportation agency, supplemented by the construction of good roads, has facilitated changes in demand in many communities and has led to the widening of retail trading areas. These changes also have enhanced the prosperity of some groups of manufacturers and merchants and have created conditions which have necessitated, or will necessitate in the near future, readjustment in operating methods for many other manufacturers and merchants. . . .

In the field of distribution, the most notable change during the last eight years has been the expansion of chain stores. They have attained dominant positions in the gasoline and variety goods businesses and rapidly have been approaching dominance in the grocery, drug, and shoe trades.. The changes in buying habits in rural communities and small towns, with their impending effect on mail order sales, presumably impelled two of the largest mail order companies to launch chains of stores. The concentration of retail buying power in chain store companies and other large retail organizations not only has been cutting down the wholesalers' fields of activity and lessening the scope of opportunities for small-scale business enterprises, but it is also bringing to the fore a new problem of public policy in dealing with discriminations in terms of sale. . . .

Installment selling has been one of the most discussed marketing topics during the last four years. From the analysis of the subject in this survey, however, it appears doubtful if installment sales have increased more rapidly than total retail sales since 1923. Agricultural implement manufacturers increased their sales on installments in order to meet agricultural credit needs. Aside from agricultural implements, the chief industries in which sales on installments increased were those where the total demand was increasing and where the particular products were especially suited to that type of sales promotion. The sales of electric refrigerators and radio sets, for example, could be facilitated by means of installment terms, just as the same terms previously had been used for the sale of sewing machines and pianos. There is no real evidence to indicate that installment selling has been undermining the integrity of the credit structure or becoming more of a financial hazard than it was, for example, in 1920. The companies and institutions financing installment sales have learned the necessity of exercising discretion in the selection of credit risks and of avoiding excessively liberal terms.

Advertising has been a positive factor in stimulating the increase of sales in numerous industries since 1921. From 1921 to 1927, the total annual expenditures for advertising in the United States probably increased about 50 per cent. The increases were especially notable in 1923 and 1926. The industries in which particularly noteworthy increases in advertising expenditures took place were: radio sets, electric refrigerators, automotive equipment, foods, home equipment, soaps and cleansers, silverware, clocks and watches, pens and pencils, and toilet articles. Several of these industries were those whose sales expanded with especial rapidity. . . .

The chief characteristics of the advertising developments since 1921 are typical of nearly the whole field of marketing activities. The major changes represent the culmination of influences at work prior to 1920. The war period and the crisis of 1920, by upsetting traditions and adding a new spur of necessity, may have accelerated some of the changes, but the foundations had been laid before. Most of these changes, furthermore, are not yet completed. In fact, in view of the conditions now existing and in light of the opportunities almost untouched by scientific research, it seems probable that there are impending changes in marketing methods even greater than those that have occurred since 1921.

THE END OF *LAISSEZ FAIRE*[1]

John Maynard Keynes

JOHN MAYNARD KEYNES, born at Cambridge, England, in 1883, and educated there, entered the British civil service in 1906. The year 1915 found him, after service in the India Office, connected with the Treasury, where he did valuable work in connection with British loans to the Allied nations. At the Paris Peace Conference, of which he was a caustic observer, he was chief representative of the British Treasury, and he was deputy for the Chancellor of the Exchequer on the Supreme Economic Council in 1919. Since the war he has been fellow and bursar of King's College, Cambridge, chairman of a British weekly, *The Nation*, now extinct, and chairman of the National Mutual Life Assurance Society.

Keynes was an economist of merely national reputation when at the close of 1919 he published his now famous *Economic Consequences of the Peace*. This volume, a condemnatory analysis of the economic provisions of the treaty just signed at Versailles, instantly caught the world's attention. This was in part because of its vivid and arresting description of the leaders of the Peace Conference and the methods of their work, one of the most scathing bits of criticism that these years produced; in part because of the evident expertness and soundness of its economic views. The volume has remained memorable because of the singular completeness with which time has vindicated its bold prophecies. Its principal contentions were that the financial claims which the Allies were making against Germany (and which he estimated at 32 to 44 billion dollars) were impossible of payment; that to attempt seriously to collect them would result in ruinous losses to everyone; but that if they were reduced to legitimate demands, they would be within Germany's capacity to pay — which he placed at 10 billions of dollars. Mr. Keynes's subsequent books include *A Revision of the Treaty* (1922) and *Essays in Persuasion* (1931).

I

Economists, like other scientists, have chosen the hypothesis from which they set out, and which they offer to beginners, because it is the simplest, and not because it is the nearest to facts. Partly for this reason, but partly, I admit, because they have been biased by the traditions of the subject, they have begun by assuming a state of affairs where the ideal distribution of productive resources can be brought about through individuals acting independently by the method of trial and error in such a way that those individuals who move in the right direction will destroy by competition those who move in the wrong direction. This implies that there must be no mercy or protection for those who embark their capital or their labor in the wrong direction. It is a method of bringing the most successful

[1] From *The End of Laissez Faire*, London (Hogarth Press), 1926.

profit-makers to the top by a ruthless struggle for survival, which selects the most efficient by the bankruptcy of the less efficient. It does not count the cost of the struggle, but looks only to the benefits of the final result which are assumed to be permanent. The object of life being to crop the leaves off the branches up to the greatest possible height, the likeliest way of achieving this end is to leave the giraffes with the longest necks to starve out those whose necks are shorter.

Corresponding to this method of attaining the ideal distribution of the instruments of production between different purposes, there is a similar assumption as to how to attain the ideal distribution of what is available for consumption. In the first place, each individual will discover what among the possible objects of consumption *he* wants most by the method of trial and error "at the margin," and in this way not only will each consumer come to distribute his consumption most advantageously, but each object of consumption will find its way into the mouth of the consumer whose relish for it is greatest compared with that of the others, because that consumer will outbid the rest. Thus, if only we leave the giraffes to themselves, (1) the maximum quantity of leaves will be cropped because the giraffes with the longest necks will, by dint of starving out the others, get nearest to the trees; (2) each giraffe will make for the leaves which he finds most succulent among those in reach; and (3) the giraffes whose relish for a given leaf is greatest will crane most to reach it. In this way more and juicier leaves will be swallowed, and each individual leaf will reach the throat which thinks it deserves most effort.

This assumption, however, of conditions where unhindered natural selection leads to progress, is only one of the two provisional assumptions which, taken as literal truth, have become the twin buttresses of *laissez faire*. The other one is the efficacy and, indeed, the necessity of the opportunity for unlimited private money-making as an *incentive* to maximum effort. Profit accrues, under *laissez faire*, to the individual who, whether by skill or good fortune, is found with his productive resources in the right place at the right time. A system which allows the skillful or fortunate individual to reap the whole fruits of this conjuncture evidently offers an immense incentive to the practice of the art of being in the right place at the right time. Thus one of the most powerful of human motives — namely, the love of money — is harnessed to the task of distributing economic resources in the way best calculated to increase wealth.

The parallelism between economic *laissez faire* and Darwinism is now seen, as Herbert Spencer was foremost to recognize, to be very close indeed. Just as Darwin invoked sexual love, acting through sexual selection, as an adjutant to natural selection by competition, to direct evolution along lines which should be desirable as well as effective, so the individualist invokes the love of money, acting through the pursuit of profit, as an adjutant to natural selection, to bring about the production on the greatest possible scale of what is most strongly desired as measured by exchange value.

The beauty and the simplicity of such a theory are so great that it is easy to forget that it follows not from the actual facts, but from an incomplete hypothesis introduced for the sake of simplicity. Apart from other objections to be mentioned later, the conclusion that individuals acting independently for their own advantage will produce the greatest aggregate of wealth depends on a variety of unreal assumptions to the effect that the processes of production and consumption are in no way organic, that there exists a sufficient foreknowledge of conditions and requirements, and that there are adequate opportunities of obtaining this foreknowledge. For economists generally reserve for a later stage of their argument the complications which arise (1) when the efficient units of production are large relatively to the units of consumption; (2) when overhead costs or joint costs are present; (3) when internal economies tend to the aggregation of production; (4) when the time required for adjustments is long; (5) when ignorance prevails over knowledge; and (6) when monopolies and combinations interfere with equality in bargaining — they reserve, that is to say, for a later stage their analysis of the actual facts. Moreover, many of those who recognize that the simplified hypothesis does not accurately correspond to fact conclude nevertheless that it does represent what is "natural" and therefore ideal. They regard the simplified hypothesis as health, and the further complications as disease.

Yet, besides this question of fact, there are other considerations, familiar enough, which rightly bring into the calculation the cost and character of the competitive struggle itself, and the tendency for wealth to be distributed where it is not appreciated most. If we have the welfare of the giraffes at heart, we must not overlook the sufferings of the shorter necks who are starved out, or the sweet leaves which fall to the ground and are trampled underfoot in the struggle, or the overfeeding of the long-necked ones, or the evil look of anxiety or struggling greediness which overcasts the mild faces of the herd.

But the principles of *laissez faire* have had other allies besides economic textbooks. It must be admitted that they have been confirmed in the minds of sound thinkers and the reasonable public by the poor quality of the opponent proposals — protectionism on one hand, and Marxian socialism on the other. Yet these doctrines are both characterized, not only or chiefly by their infringing the general presumption in favor of *laissez faire*, but by mere logical fallacy. Both are examples of poor thinking, of inability to analyze a process and follow it out to its conclusion. The arguments against them, though reinforced by the principle of *laissez faire*, do not strictly require it. Of the two, protectionism is at least plausible, and the forces making for its popularity are nothing to wonder at. But Marxian socialism must always remain a portent to the historians of opinion — how a doctrine so illogical and so dull can have exercised so powerful and enduring an influence over the minds of men, and, through them, the events of history. At any rate, the obvious scientific deficiencies of these two schools greatly contributed to the prestige and authority of nineteenth century *laissez faire*.

Nor has the most notable divergence into centralized social action on a great scale — the conduct of the late war — encouraged or dispelled old-fashioned prejudices. There is much to be said, it is true, on both sides. War experience in the organization of socialized production has left some near observers optimistically anxious to repeat it in peace conditions. War socialism unquestionably achieved a production of wealth on a scale far greater than we ever knew in peace, for though the goods and services delivered were destined for immediate and fruitless extinction, none the less they were wealth. Nevertheless the dissipation of effort was also prodigious, and the atmosphere of waste and not counting the cost was disgusting to any thrifty or provident spirit.

Finally, individualism and *laissez faire* could not, in spite of their deep roots in the political and moral philosophies of the late eighteenth and early nineteenth centuries, have secured their lasting hold over the conduct of public affairs if it had not been for their conformity with the needs and wishes of the business world of the day. They gave full scope to our erstwhile heroes, the great business men. "At least one-half of the best ability in the Western world," Marshall used to say, "is engaged in business." A great part of "the higher imagination" of the age was thus employed. It was on the activities of these men that our hopes of progress were centered. "Men of this class," Marshall wrote, "live in constantly shifting visions, fashioned in their own brains, of various routes to their desired end; of the difficulties which Nature will oppose to them on each route, and of the contrivances by which they hope to get the better of her opposition. This imagination gains little credit with the people, because it is not allowed to run riot; its strength is disciplined by stronger will; and its highest glory is to have attained great ends by means so simple that no one will know, and none but experts will even guess, how a dozen other expedients, each suggesting as much brilliancy to the hasty observer, were set aside in favor of it. The imagination of such a man is employed, like that of the master chess-player, in forecasting the obstacles which may be opposed to the successful issue of his far-reaching projects, and constantly rejecting brilliant suggestions because he has pictured to himself the counter-strokes to them. His strong nervous force is at the opposite extreme of human nature from that nervous irresponsibility which conceives hasty Utopian schemes, and which is rather to be compared to the bold facility of a weak player, who will speedily solve the most difficult chess problem by taking on himself to move the black men as well as the white."[1]

This is a fine picture of the great Captain of Industry, the Master Individualist, who serves us in serving himself, just as any other artist does. Yet this one, in his turn, is becoming a tarnished idol. We grow more doubtful whether it is he who will lead us into Paradise by the hand.

These many elements have contributed to the current intellectual bias, the mental make-up, the orthodoxy of the day. The compelling force of many of the original reasons has disappeared, but, as usual, the vitality of the conclusions outlasts them. To suggest social action for the public good to the City of London is like discussing the *Origin of Species* with a bishop sixty years ago. The first reaction is not intellectual, but moral. An orthodoxy is in question, and the more persuasive the arguments the graver the offense. . . .

II

Let us clear from the ground the metaphysical or general principles upon which, from time to time, *laissez faire* has been founded. It is *not* true that individuals possess a prescriptive "natural liberty" in their economic activities. There is *no* "compact" conferring perpetual rights on those who Have or on those who Acquire. The world

---

[1] "The Social Possibilities of Economic Chivalry," *Economic Journal* (1907), Vol. XVII, p. 9.

is *not* so governed from above that private and social interest always coincide.   It is *not* so managed here below that in practice they coincide.   It is *not* a correct deduction from the principles of economics that enlightened self-interest always operates in the public interest. Nor is it true that self-interest generally *is* enlightened; more often individuals acting separately to promote their own ends are too ignorant or too weak to attain even these.   Experience does *not* show that individuals, when they make up a social unit, are always less clear-sighted than when they act separately.

We cannot therefore settle on abstract grounds, but must handle on its merits in detail, what Burke termed "one of the finest problems in legislation: namely, to determine what the state ought to take upon itself to direct by the public wisdom, and what it ought to leave, with as little interference as possible, to individual exertion." [1]   We have to discriminate between what Bentham, in his forgotten but useful nomenclature, used to term *Agenda* and *Non-Agenda*, and to do this without Bentham's prior presumption that interference is, at the same time, "generally needless" and "generally pernicious." [2]   Perhaps the chief task of economists at this hour is to distinguish afresh the Agenda of government from the Non-Agenda; and the companion task of politics is to devise forms of government within a democracy which shall be capable of accomplishing the Agenda.   I will illustrate what I have in mind by two examples.

(1) I believe that in many cases the ideal size for the unit of control and organization lies somewhere between the individual and the modern state.   I suggest, therefore, that progress lies in the growth and the recognition of semi-autonomous bodies within the state— bodies, whose criterion of action within their own field is solely the public good as they understand it, and from whose deliberations motives of private advantage are excluded, though some place it may still be necessary to leave, until the ambit of men's altruism grows wider, to the separate advantage of particular groups, classes, or faculties — bodies which in the ordinary course of affairs are mainly autonomous within their prescribed limitations, but are subject in the last resort to the sovereignty of the democracy expressed through Parliament.

I propose a return, it may be said, toward mediaeval conceptions of separate autonomies.   But, in England at any rate, corporations are

---

[1] Quoted by McCulloch in his *Principles of Political Economy*.

[2] Bentham's *Manual of Political Economy*, published posthumously, in Bowring's edition (1843).

a mode of government which has never ceased to be important and is
sympathetic to our institutions. It is easy to give examples, from
what already exists, of separate autonomies which have attained or
are approaching the mode I designate — the Universities, the Bank
of England, the Port of London Authority, even perhaps the railway
companies. In Germany there are doubtless analogous instances.

But more interesting than these is the trend of joint-stock institutions, when they have reached a certain age and size, to approximate
to the status of public corporations rather than that of individualistic
private enterprise. One of the most interesting and unnoticed developments of recent decades has been the tendency of big enterprise
to socialize itself. A point arrives in the growth of a big institution —
particularly a big railway or big public utility enterprise, but also a
big bank or a big insurance company — at which the owners of the
capital, i.e. the shareholders, are almost entirely dissociated from the
management, with the result that the direct personal interest of the
latter in making of great profit becomes quite secondary. When this
stage is reached, the general stability and reputation of the institution
are more considered by the management than the maximum of profit
for the shareholders. The shareholders must be satisfied by con-
ventionally adequate dividends; but once this is secured, the direct
interest of the management often consists in avoiding criticism from
the public and from the customers of the concern. This is particularly the case if their great size or semi-monopolistic position
renders them conspicuous in the public eye and vulnerable to public
attack. The extreme instance, perhaps, of this tendency in the case
of an institution, theoretically the unrestricted property of private
persons, is the Bank of England. It is almost true to say that
there is no class of persons in the Kingdom of whom the Governor
of the Bank of England thinks less when he decides on his policy
than of his shareholders. Their rights, in excess of their conventional dividend, have already sunk to the neighborhood of zero. But
the same thing is partly true of many other big institutions. They
are, as time goes on, socializing themselves.

Not that this is unmixed gain. The same causes promote conservatism and a waning of enterprise. In fact, we already have in
these cases many of the faults as well as the advantages of state
socialism. Nevertheless we see here, I think, a natural line of evolution. The battle of socialism against unlimited private profit is being
won in detail hour by hour. In these particular fields — it remains
acute elsewhere — this is no longer the pressing problem. There is,

for instance, no so-called important political question so really unimportant, so irrelevant to the reorganization of the economic life of Great Britain, as the nationalization of the railways.

It is true that many big undertakings, particularly public utility enterprise and other business requiring a large fixed capital, still need to be semi-socialized. But we must keep our minds flexible regarding the forms of this semi-socialism. We must take full advantage of the natural tendencies of the day, and we must probably prefer semi-autonomous corporations to organs of the central government for which ministers of state are directly responsible.

I criticize doctrinaire state socialism, not because it seeks to engage men's altruistic impulses in the service of society, or because it departs from *laissez faire*, or because it takes away from man's natural liberty to make a million, or because it has courage for bold experiments. All these things I applaud. I criticize it because it misses the significance of what is actually happening; because it is, in fact, little better than a dusty survival of a plan to meet the problems of fifty years ago, based on a misunderstanding of what someone said a hundred years ago. Nineteenth century state socialism sprang from Bentham, free competition, etc., and is in some respects a clearer, in some respects a more muddled version of just the same philosophy as underlies nineteenth century individualism. Both equally laid all their stress on freedom, the one negatively to avoid limitations on existing freedom, the other positively to destroy natural or acquired monopolies. They are different reactions to the same intellectual atmosphere.

(2) I come next to a criterion of Agenda which is particularly relevant to what it is urgent and desirable to do in the near future. We must aim at separating those services which are *technically social* from those which are *technically individual*. The most important Agenda of the state relate not to those activities which private individuals are already fulfilling, but to those functions which fall outside the sphere of the individual, to those decisions which are made by *no one* if the state does not make them. The important thing for government is not to do things which individuals are doing already, and to do them a little better or a little worse; but to do those things which at present are not done at all.

It is not within the scope of my purpose on this occasion to develop practical policies. I limit myself, therefore, to naming some instances of what I mean from among those problems about which I happen to have thought most.

Many of the greatest economic evils of our time are the fruits of risk, uncertainty, and ignorance. It is because particular individuals, fortunate in situation or in abilities, are able to take advantage of uncertainty and ignorance, and also because for the same reason big business is often a lottery, that great inequalities of wealth come about; and these same factors are also the cause of the unemployment of labor, or the disappointment of reasonable business expectations, and of the impairment of efficiency and production. Yet the cure lies outside the operations of individuals; it may even be to the interest of individuals to aggravate the disease. I believe that the cure for these things is partly to be sought in the deliberate control of the currency and of credit by a central institution, and partly in the collection and dissemination on a great scale of data relating to the business situation, including the full publicity, by law if necessary, of all business facts which it is useful to know. These measures would involve society in exercising directive intelligence through some appropriate organ of action over many of the inner intricacies of private business, yet it would leave private initiative and enterprise unhindered. Even if these measures prove insufficient, nevertheless they will furnish us with better knowledge than we have now for taking the next step.

My second example relates to savings and investment. I believe that some coördinated act of intelligent judgment is required as to the scale on which it is desirable that the community as a whole should save, the scale on which these savings should go abroad in the form of foreign investments, and whether the present organization of the investment market distributes savings along the most nationally productive channels. I do not think that these matters should be left entirely to the chances of private judgment and private profits, as they are at present.

My third example concerns population. The time has already come when each country needs a considered national policy about what size of population, whether larger or smaller than at present or the same, is most expedient. And having settled this policy, we must take steps to carry it into operation. The time may arrive a little later when the community as a whole must pay attention to the innate quality as well as to the mere numbers of its future members.

III

These reflections have been directed toward possible improvements in the technique of modern capitalism by the agency of collective action. There is nothing in them which is seriously incompatible with what seems to me to be the essential characteristic of capitalism: namely, the dependence upon an intense appeal to the money-making and money-loving instincts of individuals as the main motive force of the economic machine. Nor must I, so near to my end, stray toward other fields. Nevertheless I may do well to remind you, in conclusion, that the fiercest contests and the most deeply felt divisions of opinion are likely to be waged in the coming years not round technical questions, where the arguments on either side are mainly economic, but round those which, for want of better words, may be called psychological or, perhaps, moral.

In Europe, or at least in some parts of Europe — but not, I think, in the United States of America — there is a latent reaction, somewhat widespread, against basing society to the extent that we do upon fostering, encouraging, and protecting the money motives of individuals. A preference for arranging our affairs in such a way as to appeal to the money motive as little as possible, rather than as much as possible, need not be entirely *a priori*, but may be based on the comparison of experiences. Different persons, according to their choice of profession, find the money motive playing a large or a small part in their daily lives, and historians can tell us about other phases of social organization in which this motive has played a much smaller part than it does now. Most religions and most philosophies deprecate, to say the least of it, a way of life mainly influenced by considerations of personal money profit. On the other hand, most men today reject ascetic notions and do not doubt the real advantages of wealth. Moreover, it seems obvious to them that one cannot do without the money motive, and that, apart from certain admitted abuses, it does its job well. In the result the average man averts his attention from the problem, and has no clear idea what he really thinks and feels about the whole confounded matter.

Confusion of thought and feeling leads to confusion of speech. Many people, who are really objecting to capitalism as a way of life, argue as though they were objecting to it on the ground of its inefficiency in attaining its own objects. Contrariwise, devotees of capitalism are often unduly conservative, and reject reforms in its technique, which might really strengthen and preserve it, for fear that they may prove to be first steps away from capitalism itself. Nevertheless a time may be coming when we shall get clearer than at present as to when we are talking about capitalism as an efficient or inefficient technique, and when we are talking about it as desirable or objectionable in itself. For my part, I think that capitalism, wisely managed, can probably be made more efficient for attaining economic ends than any alternative system yet in sight, but that in itself it is in many ways extremely objectionable. Our problem is to work out a social organization which shall be as efficient as possible without offending our notions of a satisfactory way of life.

The next step forward must come, not from political agitation or premature experiments, but from thought. We need by an effort of the mind to elucidate our own feelings. At present our sympathy and our judgment are liable to be on different sides, which is a painful and paralyzing state of mind. In the field of action reformers will not be successful until they can steadily pursue a clear and definite object with their intellects and their feelings in tune. There is no party in the world at present which appears to me to be pursuing right aims by right methods. Material poverty provides the incentive to change precisely in situations where there is very little margin for experiments. Material prosperity removes the incentive just when it might be safe to take a chance. Europe lacks the means, America the will, to make a move. We need a new set of convictions which spring naturally from a candid examination of our own inner feelings in relation to the outside facts.

THE NEED FOR A NEW ECONOMIC SYSTEM[1]

Sir Arthur Salter

SIR ARTHUR SALTER has had rare opportunities to observe at first hand the principal economic currents of the world during and since the Great War, and the policies of the major Powers in relation thereto. Born at Oxford in 1881, and educated in Oxford University, he entered the British civil service in 1904. During the World War he was Assistant Director of Transports for the Admiralty and played an important part in the carrying of millions of Britons, Canadians, Australians, New Zealanders, South Africans, and finally Americans to the seat of war. In 1918 he was Director of Ship-Requisitioning for Great Britain, and secretary of the Allied Maritime Transport Council. For two years after the war, 1920–1922, he was general secretary of the Reparations Commission. He then became director of the Economic and Finance Section of the League of Nations, and held that post until 1930. It required him to become familiar with economic tendencies everywhere, and his books show both expert knowledge and breadth of view. The most important of these books are *The World's Economic Crisis* (1932), a volume of lectures in which other British economists are represented; *Recovery: The Second Effort* (1932); and *Toward a Planned Economy* (1933). He takes the view that the astonishing recovery of the world after the war was really fictitious; that radical errors were made with disastrous consequences; but that by wise action (for which he offers suggestions) mankind can correct them and inaugurate a new and sounder recovery. For doctrines of economic nationalism he has little mercy. Sir Arthur Salter is now a professor in Oxford University.

I propose in this first lecture to discuss why planning is now necessary to supplement the working of the competitive price system; to argue that the controls and restrictions of which the world is now full are not examples of planning because they have been improvised by opportunists, and that their replacement by planned control is now essential, and that this task cannot be carried out by government alone but needs the coördinated action of unofficial institutions. . . .

I think it is of the most vital importance that economists should now squarely face the question whether the actual economic life of the world in the future is likely to be within a framework substantially like that of the nineteenth century or profoundly different; and if they conclude that the latter is inevitable, that they should work intensively on the question of the modification which that will entail to economic doctrine and especially to its application. I can understand the reluctance of both the economic historian and the theoretical

[1] From *The Framework of an Ordered Society*, by Sir Arthur Salter. By permission of The Macmillan Company, publishers.

economist to contemplate any really fundamental change in the situation. The former has vividly in his mind the triumphs of the nineteenth century system, which encouraged and harvested the application of scientific invention to industrial technique, so that within a framework merely of law, gold currencies, and elementary social safeguards, individual enterprise was free to exploit the riches of the new discoveries, while supply adjusted itself to demand, and each one of an infinitely intricate series of economic processes and activities to every other, without either the painful effort or restrictive discouragements of deliberate planning and control.   None at least can withhold an honorable tribute at its passing to a system which sheltered hundreds of millions in a comfort known before by only as many thousands, and which decade by decade absorbed an increasing population and supported it at higher standards of living.   The reluctance of the theoretical economist is no less intelligible.   To pass from a system in which economic phenomena are determined by the motives of innumerable economic men, whose individual caprices do not exist or cancel out, to one in which they are profoundly affected by the deliberate and fallible reason of a few hundreds, is to pass from a comparatively exact to a mainly empirical science.   The theoretical and mathematical science based upon the assumptions that make exact conclusions possible may still remain and cultivate itself with ever-increasing subtlety; but if it fails to adjust itself to facts, it must lose even the semblance of any important relation to the practical life of man. Under a functioning *laissez faire* system the economist had the best of two good worlds; the satisfaction which intricate and exact intellectual reasoning gives, and the equally pleasing but usually incompatible satisfaction of exercising power.   It is a privilege hard to abdicate.

Nevertheless, I believe it is clear that an objective consideration of the actual forces and tendencies now in the world shows conclusively that this situation must be faced.   It is indeed possible, as it is certainly to be ardently hoped, that some of the impediments to the free working of automatic adjustments can be removed or reduced, that here and there a field of free action can be cleared.   If, however, we consider the factors which, as compared with the last century, are novel in degree and indeed in kind, and which tend to restrict and disturb the normal free adjustments, we shall, I think, realize that the automatic system can never again be relied upon to function as easily and frictionlessly as it did in the past.

Let us take, for instance, the character of the industrial organization of a considerable part of the largest industries in the most advanced countries. The steel industry in America, for example, is so nearly a monopoly that it can within considerable limits establish the price at which it will sell its products. Such effective competition as exists, in the case of industries organized upon this scale, is a competition with producers of substitute articles (oil instead of coal, etc.) rather than with producers of the same article, and often the most effective force tending to keep prices down is not the competitive price of the article but what the market will stand. The consideration which determines the price that is fixed is based upon whether reduction will tap a large additional demand or increase will kill it. The same applies to commercial organizations, where there are rings or semi-monopolies, or understandings. The consumer loses his "rent" and those with whom the decision rests are able to choose at a time of falling wholesale prices whether they will reduce their own prices correspondingly or lose the chance which reduced prices would give of maintaining or extending their custom. Whenever these conditions apply it is clear that the automatic adjustment of the old system works much less effectively than in the past.

A similar impediment to adaptation is of course created by all the organizations and the forces which tend to make wages rigid. This impediment is of special importance at a time when monetary or other causes are creating considerable changes in the general level of prices, but it is of importance at all times. The same is true also of the extending social legislation which has been so rapid a phenomenon of this century, especially in this country.

Not less important than the above factors is economic nationalism, expressing itself in tariff and other commercial policy. This has been steadily growing ever since the war and has now reached a height for which we can find no precedent in recent history. It is true that some of the causes of this movement may be temporary and that some retracing of our steps may be possible. It is difficult, however, to anticipate in any easily foreseeable future that we shall have a system favoring the free movement of trade as much as that of the nineteenth century did, even after the protection initiated by Germany in its later decades. We may reasonably hope for an improvement of the present position in some respects. In particular we may hope that tariffs will become more stable after the present financial crisis is past. But no prophecy surely could be safer than that, in the world as a whole, tariffs will for many years remain as a principal factor in determining the economic structure of most countries and the volume and character of the trade between them.

When again we turn from the sphere of economics to that of monetary policy and finance, we must surely contemplate not less but more control than was exercised in the years immediately preceding the crisis. The crisis itself indeed has demonstrated the impossibility of a system which combined almost complete freedom in the movement of capital, and in all capital operations, with such severe restrictions upon the movement and distribution of trade.

Wherever we turn, therefore, we have a prospect of extensive control and restriction upon the free development of enterprise and of trade. I have mentioned only some of the more striking examples of permanent and, for the most part, increasing importance. Now all of these, whether they are wise or foolish, whether they are improvised or planned, have one characteristic in common. They interfere with the free working of the automatic system of competitive price adjustment; they make it more rigid and less quickly and readily adaptable.

With this loss of elasticity in the system we are confronted with the other principal phenomenon of our age, the unprecedentedly rapid extension of mechanization and the improvement in industrial technique, which makes rapid adaptability in the economic system more essential if the most disastrous reactions and dislocations are to be avoided. Every new invention, displacing men, changing the distribution of purchasing power and consequently the direction of demand, will cause waste and unemployment unless the economic system is so elastic and responsive as to make the new demand quickly effective, to adjust supply to it, to transfer and absorb the displaced workers. There is indeed much exaggeration and folly associated with the "technocracy" which has recently been so much discussed in America. Many of those who have been dazzled by the staggering results of new technical inventions in particular industries, where a 90 per cent economy or more has been effected in man power, have assumed that this represents a process likely to extend in a similar degree over most human activities. This is, of course, a wild exaggeration. Some have fallen into the even more absurd error of thinking that man's increase of power over nature, instead of being as it is a promise of immensely greater prosperity, must inevitably entail permanent and increasing unemployment and impoverishment. Others again have, with equal folly, advocated the adoption, as the basis of currency systems, of a "unit of energy," failing to realize that the physical power used in production bears a changing and diminishing relation to economic values and human activities as a whole, and that it is therefore completely unsuitable either to determine the total amount of currency required at a given period, or to secure adjustment between different human activities, or to afford a measure of relative reward.

It is also true that new technical inventions, in spite of the displacement of labor which they involve, do not constitute the main origin of our present troubles; nor can they be regarded as solely responsible for the continuance of the unemployment which they cause by displacement. It would be more exact to say that when the adaptability and absorptive capacity of the economic system have, for other reasons, been reduced, the rapidity of technical invention is an aggravating factor. "Technological unemployment" is a substantial part of the present unemployment in the world and, in one sense, it can be approximately measured. Three separate estimates, for example, by competent economists have recently put the figure at one million out of the five million out of work in Germany. It would, however, be a mistake to conclude from this that if there were no general depression there would be in Germany a million unemployed through technological displacement. A large proportion of those who have become unemployed through this cause would in other circumstances be absorbed into other work and only remain unemployed now because the depression, itself due mainly to other causes, has temporarily reduced the absorptive capacity of the economic system.

Nevertheless, when we have stripped "technocracy" of all its fallacies and its exaggerations, this at least remains true. The combination of an increase in the rapidity of technical inventions and processes with the increased impediments to automatic adjustment which have been mentioned above must result, in any foreseeable future, in a substantial mass of "technological unemployment" unless we can restore the absorptive capacity of the economic system; and since many of the new impediments to automatic adjustment are likely to be permanent, we can only do this if we supplement it by some form of deliberate planning.

There are indeed, as I have suggested, many special features and causes of the present depression — some of which are unprecedented and will, we may hope, be neither permanent nor recurrent: a mass of indebtedness left after the war; a passionate nationalism expressing itself in economic policy; a monetary disturbance which has resulted from these and in turn has aggravated their consequences. But when all these have been dealt with, or have worked out their own solution, much will remain to differentiate both the system and the problems of our period from those of the last century.   I am convinced that the task of the future is not merely that of removing unwise restrictions, though much of this is required, but that of replacing foolish and improvised control by wisely planned control.

I do not think that many will dispute that the great mass of the present restrictions, controls, and recent interferences with the working of the automatic system has been improvised, and foolishly improvised.   Demonstration is therefore unnecessary, and a few illustrations will suffice to remind us of what we all know.

Let us consider, for example, in broad outline the character of state action within the sphere of commercial policy.   I do not now propose to discuss the general merits of protection and free trade.   I assume that, whether we like it or not, some measure of state protection in most countries will be a fundamental feature in the world's economic system for many years to come.   My present point is that the present tariffs are scarcely ever the expression of what in any reasonable sense can be called either national or any kind of policy.   It is rarely possible to discover in the mind of any government a general conception of economic policy for their country of which their detailed tariffs are the logical development.   Ideas of improving the balance of trade, or of securing self-sufficiency, or of making the foreigner pay, float about, but they operate, not to determine the character and proportions of the actual tariff system, but merely as arguments and forces to secure the acceptance of tariffs.   The tariffs themselves are selected, and their height determined, in most cases as the net result of organized competitive pressures.   For some years at Geneva, during the tariff negotiations there, I tried to discover what were the real springs of action, what were really the dominant anxieties and preoccupations in the minds of Ministers of Commerce and their chief officials when they were defending existing tariffs or proposing changes.   In nearly every case, when it was possible to penetrate behind the words to the thoughts of the persons concerned, it was not a conception, whether wise or unwise, of general economic national policy, but a calculation of prospective political forces, that was determining action.   Tariffs as we have them now in the world have not been planned but improvised, and improvised under organized pressure.

It is the same when we turn from tariffs to other forms of commercial policy.   Let us take a few examples from our own country of the selective encouragement by state action of particular kinds of production.   The most notable schemes that have been actually put into operation have concerned, in chronological order, rubber, sugar, and wheat.

It seems incredible, in retrospect, that any government could have employed official action to enforce a restriction scheme of which the ultimate effect was bound to be merely to profit the Dutch competitor. Had it been possible to secure the inclusion of the Dutch rubber planters, the scheme, whether or not defensible or desirable on other grounds, would at least have been a practicable one. But it should have been obvious, and would have been obvious to any body of competent and disinterested persons who had been given a week to examine the situation, that in their absence nothing but permanent harm could result. What happened was exactly what could have been anticipated. Great profits were made by speculators, and even greater profits by the Dutch planter, who enjoyed the full benefit of the higher prices which the restriction caused, while being himself free not only to continue his full protection but to expand it; and in these circumstances the price ultimately fell again, as it was bound to, but with the difference that the British share of the world market was left on a permanently lower level. When this had happened, and the harm done was irreparable, the scheme was brought to an end. My point is that the explanation of this ill-conceived venture is that a harassed, preoccupied, overworked, and inexpert government succumbed to the pressure of a concentrated and organized interest, as it is always apt to unless it has at its disposal, and utilizes, a machinery and procedure which will provide a safeguard against such follies. Had a committee selected from among such persons as are now associated with the present Economic Advisory Council been called to examine the proposal and report, there can be no doubt that their conclusions would have been strongly adverse. It does not follow, of course, that their advice would have been accepted; the government might, under the pressure of the interests concerned, have still sinned against the light.

I will now take two examples affecting agriculture in this country — the subsidies given to sugar and wheat. Again, I do not now propose to argue whether, by government action, and at some public expense to either the taxpayer or the consumer, it is wise to expand agricultural production in this country beyond the point which it would reach under a system of free competition with the outside world. If, however, we assume that this is our policy, surely one thing is clear: that the kind of agricultural production we should especially encourage is that for which the country has the best natural advantages.

Now it is obvious that as regards meat, fruit, poultry, and dairy produce this country has a natural advantage in that all these articles deteriorate in time or lose something of their quality by preservation, so that it is a good thing for the producer to be near his market.   In contrast with these, sugar and wheat lose nothing by lapse of time, and cost very little to transport or store.   Moreover, owing to the way in which our land is parceled up, and the tenure under which it is held, we are obviously at a great disadvantage in comparison with other countries from which we might import.   Sugar is just as good if it is transported over the world, and is indeed better if it comes from Java or the West Indies where a tropical sun has transmitted sweetness through the cane.   Wheat too is obviously produced more advantageously in lands where large spaces facilitate mechanized processes. There is another consideration, too.   There is a natural long-term tendency of the world demand for fresh meat, fruit, and dairy produce to increase, not only proportionately to the increase of population, but also with a rising standard of living, since they are relatively luxury foods.   On the other hand, it had long been obvious that sugar and wheat were likely for years to come to be produced in excess of an almost stationary demand.   A policy definitely designed to make us self-sufficient in wheat, in view of the risks of war, would of course be logically defensible, though very expensive and perhaps impracticable. But no such policy was at the basis of our action.   If that consideration is excluded it is obvious that a policy of agricultural protection, which had been planned and thought out with care, would have put wheat and sugar at the bottom, not at the top, of its list.   It is a good illustration of our present unplanned control that it was these two commodities which were selected for first and special encouragement.   The wheat subsidy, at the expense of the consumer, is relatively recent. The sugar subsidy has been in operation long enough for us to see its results.   It has proved so extravagant that the public (as taxpayer and consumer) was paying more than two pounds for every pound's worth of sugar even before the recent abnormal fall of world prices.

If we turn from commercial policy to monetary policy, the case is perhaps not quite so clear.   Here there has obviously been deliberate planning and direction.   The planning has, however, been incomplete and to a large extent ineffective.   To some extent this is due to the impact of forces of exceptional strength, resulting from war disturbance, both internal and external.   Exclude these, however, and we cannot fail to admit in retrospect that, if our own monetary policy was based upon a very definite view of London as a financial center, and England as a creditor, it was not planned in relation to a balanced view of all the varied interests of the country. It is clear that if there had been an equal consideration of the whole economic situation of the country, with due regard to the new rigidities of the price and wage structure, the pound would not have been so light-heartedly stabilized at 4.86, with the facile assumption, so commonly made by Treasuries trained under a more elastic system, that the economic adjustments of prices would follow automatically.

The instances discussed above of official intervention in schemes affecting production are not isolated or exceptional. On the contrary they are typical of the greater part of the world's commercial policy, which has been built up by successive concessions to interested pressure. It is the most serious, and the most unjust, obstacle to the schemes not only of socialists but of all those who desire any system in which the public interest is adequately protected by public control, that the present commercial policies of the world constitute a kind of bastard socialism, conceived not in the public interest but pressed upon harassed governments by strong sectional organizations. Nor is this accidental or fortuitous. It results inevitably from the unsuitability of the present procedure and traditions of representative government for the economic tasks of the present period.

It has, I think, become abundantly clear that, for such responsibilities, the machine of government as we know it in countries with free democratic institutions is incompetent. The system, its methods and its traditions, grew up when the bulk of the work of government was political and its tasks in relation to economic development either secondary or only occasional. There is a complete and fundamental difference between these two categories of tasks and the kind of government which is suitable for each. Political problems, whether they are internal, turning for example on the extension of the full rights and opportunities of citizenship to hitherto unfranchised or unprivileged classes, or external, turning upon disputes with other countries, may be both difficult and dangerous. But they are relatively simple in their content, discontinuous, disconnected, and terminating. A new extension of the franchise is given or denied; a dispute is settled and ended. Each may be a precedent or an occasion for a new problem; but there is not normally any such essential unity or interrelation between them as there is, or should be, between separate and successive measures of economic policy.

For economic problems, however, unless successive acts of government are to lead to continually increasing confusion, deliberate planning, consecutive thinking, and careful elaboration of the main policy without the disturbing influence of sectional pressure are essential.

Parliamentary government, as it now operates, makes this impossible. Parliament consists of a heterogeneous mass of persons distinguished from their fellows by the qualities that please electors or party committees, or who have more means and leisure than other men; in their contact with the executive's task of continuous government and elaboration of economic policy they are at once inexpert and sectionally-minded, at once ineffective and exacting. In such an environment a minister cannot plan; he can only improvise. The daily impact of successive visitors, combined with the inconsecutive, troublesome, urgent difficulties of daily administration, pouring in from every sphere of governmental activity and from every quarter of the world, makes consecutive thinking impossible. A modern minister is *ex officio* an improviser and an opportunist; and he is *ex officio* a weary man — perhaps a weary Titan, but certainly weary. And this is true not only of ministers, but of the relatively small number of officials who are consulted on major policy. Now, unhappily, the first instinct of every tired man is to reject new or external assistance as likely only to give him new work and worry. On a short view this is always true, and it is always the short view that the tired and overworked man tends to take. The best chance a government or a minister has of giving effect to a well-considered and deliberately thought-out policy is that they will have occupied a preceding period of opposition and relative leisure in thinking it out. But this is unlikely and unsatisfactory, for a policy worked out in opposition is likely to be determined too much by reaction from the opposing principles or proposals of rival parties; it suffers from the absence of expert opinion and the sense of responsibility which office gives; and, as events change quickly, it may be out of date. Moreover, the permanent advisers enjoy no such respite or opportunities. They are subject, without intermission, to the successive minor difficulties of daily administration; they see policy from the point of view of these near and narrow problems, and of a single, departmental point of view — and are likely therefore to fail to see the wood for the trees. Departmentalism, a conservative clinging to traditions and precedents unsuited to changed conditions, and an opportunist attitude to such new problems as cannot be ignored, are almost inevitable characteristics of an official system; and unless they are corrected by a wider vision and a more broadly conceived policy brought from outside by ministers and those consulted by them, the results must be disastrous.

It is in large measure the change in the character of modern tasks of government which explains the discredit, the deterioration, and in many cases the replacement, of free representative institutions. In Russia we have a centralized system which enforces planning at the expense of political, personal, and economic liberty alike. In Italy we have a Fascism which, at the expense of political freedom, has retained a measure of controlled economic freedom. In Germany and other countries we see a similar development. Even here, the establishment of the Tariff Advisory Committee, and the reasons by which it was explained, are a tentative step toward the removal from Parliament of powers previously exercised by it. It is becoming clear that either representative government must be replaced — at what a terrible price and by what methods I will not stop to inquire — or it must reform itself and its methods. I believe myself that the latter course is practicable. I do not believe that the only alternatives before us are a communism which destroys both political and economic freedom, or a Fascism which, at the expense of political liberty, leaves a limited freedom for capitalists; or the inefficiency which follows the assumption of new and more complex tasks by a representative government as it now functions. I believe that we can both plan and preserve freedom on three conditions: that parliaments will delegate some of their functions to the executive, without abdicating their ultimate responsibility; that the executive will fit those who direct the actual economic activities of the country; and that these in turn will assume the task of collectively controlling and planning their own activities, in association with government and through an appropriate organization.

THE ESSENTIAL CONDITION OF ECONOMIC PLANNING[1]

Norman Thomas

NORMAN M. THOMAS began his career as a minister, sprang to public notice as an author and publicist, and finally became famous as the principal leader of American Socialism. He was born in Marion, Ohio, in 1884, and educated at Princeton University and the Union Theological Seminary. In 1911 he was ordained as a Presbyterian minister, and soon attracted attention by his eloquence in the pulpit of the Brick Presbyterian Church in New York. But he found the temptation to seek a wider audience irresistible. In 1918 he founded *The World Tomorrow* and edited it for three years, and in 1921–1922 he was associate editor of *The Nation*. He then became director of the League for Industrial Democracy, an organization for the dissemination of advanced ideas in labor relations and governmental affairs. In 1924 the Socialist Party in New York nominated him for governor; in 1925 and again in 1929 he ran as a Socialist for mayor; and in 1928 and 1932 he was the Socialist nominee for President. Meanwhile he had published a series of thoughtful and influential books. One, the product of the World War, was *The Conscientious Objector in America* (1923); another, on disarmament, peace, and internationalism, was *The Challenge of War* (1925); one dealt with the labor question, *What Is Industrial Democracy?* (1927); and in a fourth he expounded the ideas of his party, *Socialism of Our Times* (1929).

A sorely chastened world is turning to the magic of economic planning as medicine for its wounds. I speak of *magic* advisedly, for in a great deal of what has been said and written there is more of simple faith in a word or a vague idea than of real plan. Nevertheless, the noble army of volunteer planners who do have something more or less specific to offer grows apace. To veterans like Stuart Chase have been added such diverse new recruits as Matthew Woll, acting president of the National Civic Federation and vice-president of the American Federation of Labor, Dean Donham of the Harvard School of Business Administration, President Nicholas Murray Butler, and last and greatest of all, Mr. Gerard Swope of the General Electric. Mr. Donham makes his appeal to business men in whose desire or capacity for planning he has little confidence — less, by his own admission, than in the ability of Russia to produce skilled workers. Mr. Woll generously includes labor (but specifically excludes the government) in his proposal for a conference to set up a plan. Pre-

[1] From *As I See It*, by Norman Thomas. By permission of The Macmillan Company, publishers.

sumably that plan would give respectful attention to Mr. Woll's pet hobbies of even higher tariffs and a world boycott on Russia, in which case it should be labeled: "A Plan to Make World War Certain." It must be added that Mr. Woll's inclusion of labor — that is, the A. F. of L. — in his proposals for conference, is less significant than it ought to be because of the weakness of the A. F. of L. or any other labor organization in all the key industries except transportation.

So popular is the word "plan" or "planning" that even President Hoover calls his faith that somehow the sturdy economic individualism of America will muddle through to new prosperity the "American Plan"!

At the opposite pole from such inaccurate looseness in the use of an important word are such detailed plans as Mr. Stuart Chase and Professor Charles A. Beard have placed before us. Mr. Chase draws inspiration from wartime experience and puts much faith in the value of regional boards. Professor Beard has gone even farther into the heart of the problem and proposes an immediate beginning at setting up syndicates of affiliated corporations in different industries (including agriculture) and their correlation under a National Economic Council, with which a Board of Strategy and Planning will be associated. His plan comes nearer giving us a possible framework for a transitional period of reorganizing a chaotic capitalist system into a virtual socialism than anything proposed by a non-socialist. Under his scheme the private stockholders would be taxed and stripped of power to the point of elimination.

Yet even Mr. Beard does not bring into the forefront of thinking the essential question of purpose. He leans over backward to prove the native, non-Russian origin of planning in general, and the consistency of his own very advanced proposals with American customs and traditions. Most of the other plans avowedly are directed to salvaging capitalism, profits and all. And some of them are not plans at all, but incantations.

The most important of all proposed plans, for the simple reason that it comes from one of our authentic captains of industry, is Mr. Gerard Swope's plan for a kind of capitalist syndicalism, a stabilization of industry by trade associations subject to federal regulation. Elsewhere in this book[1] I have suggested that this plan looks to an American Fascism. It cuts the ground from under the older competitive capitalism as completely as socialism. But it is vitally concerned still to preserve private property for power and private

[1] See the essay "The Next Decade," in Mr. Thomas's *As I See It*.

profit. It ignores, therefore, all questions of landlordism, market speculation, and the relation of the profit system, no matter how well stabilized, to cyclical depression. It is not an adequate plan, it is not a popular plan even with business, and to the degree that it might work for a time it would give us a certain stability at the price not only of true prosperity and reasonable economic equality but of liberty. It is a sadly belated effort of the new capitalism to save itself.

Nevertheless, this eagerness of a world that starves because it has produced so much, to find some plan by which to use the machinery it has had the wit to make, is of itself an immensely important sign of the times. It was the essence and the strength of the older economics that it taught faith in automatic processes and laws. Let each man intelligently seek his own good and the ever blessed laws of supply and demand would take care of the rest. Competition assured not only the survival of the strongest but guaranteed that the strongest would be the fittest and the most worthy to survive. Competition — not economic plan — was the guarantor of the general good.

Naturally enough such faith fitted into, and found confirmation from, the prevailing religious beliefs.

Years ago in an old library I came across a little book on theism dating from the early nineteenth century, which soberly advanced as one of the soundest arguments for the existence of God the fact that when every man sought his own good the good of all was advanced.

Who but an omnipotent God could arrange matters as nicely as that? Now behold the change. In the very citadels of capitalism, in complete disregard of the assumed efficacy of automatic economic processes, men talk plan.

Nor is it only in the ranks of the capitalists that this great change has occurred. Suppose pre-war anarchists, syndicalists, or even most socialists had been told that by 1931 the great achievement of a communist revolution would have been a five-year plan, not evolved spontaneously by emancipated peasants and workers, but imposed on them from on top by an iron discipline which resorted to the piecework and speed-up system, made labor unions the creatures of the dictatorship, and reduced nominal workers' control in factories to a shadow — would it not have been a vast and unwelcome surprise to men who had been proclaiming that all that was really necessary was to break the yoke of capitalism and destroy the profit system and set the workers free? Logically in socialism the notion of planning, especially during a transition period, was always implicit. But it certainly assumed no such commanding place in radical thinking as it has assumed today in Russia, and as it must assume if ever power-driven machinery is to be our salvation and not our destruction.

Perhaps the greatest triumph of the Russian dictatorship to date is this: it has taught the lesson that has been implicit in the specialization and interdependence of the machine age — plan or perish. And this lesson has been tragically emphasized for the Western world by a degree of economic insecurity, hunger, and actual starvation which we are solemnly told is due to overproduction under our hit-or-miss system.

Now of the necessity of planning no one is more fully persuaded than I. But most talk of planning in our capitalist world leaves me a bit cold and skeptical. Some of this talk of planning is consciously or subconsciously presented as a vague but glorious hope of an earthly heaven to dull the discontent of workers in the present hell of unemployment. It rarely takes account of the immediate emergency. It almost always ducks the questions: For whom are we planning, investors, speculators, or workers? Are their interests identical, and if so, how far? To men in earnest, the first step in curing our sick society is not plan but purpose. The truly revolutionary decision concerns not the kind of planning commission we shall set up to harness the "billion wild horses" of a machine age, but whether we seriously intend that they shall work for the use of workers rather than the profit of private owners. The Russian Revolution preceded the Five Year Plan. And while I profoundly hope that we may learn from Russian experience without repeating it in all its details, we cannot possibly beg the question of socialism versus capitalism by appointing a planning commission. That is several degrees worse than the utopian hope of a "scientific" tariff to be devised by a commission irrespective of determining the previous questions, why a tariff, what sort of tariff, and for whose benefit. A commission on planning may have to compromise on tactics and next steps; it cannot get far and compromise on principles. Principle or philosophy underlies plan.

Stuart Chase, writing on a Ten Year Plan for America in *Harper's Magazine*, has vividly reminded us of the success with which we went in for planning in war days. He may be right that physically the task of peace planning is easier because it concerns only raising the standard of living, while war planning added to that feeding the maw of the insatiable monster, War itself. But he omits or minimizes two considerations:

1. Economically, war planning did little or nothing to interfere with time-honored methods of financing — Liberty Loans, etc. —

or with profits; witness the 25 per cent average profits of steel companies. These profits did not break down planning while the war was on because War ever cried for more. The crisis inherent in the diversion of profit was postponed to post-war deflations. The economic set-up for successful peace planning must be very different and cannot allow for an orgy of high profits, even with rising wages, if we want to escape recurring crises.

2. Psychologically, the compulsions of war were understood and had traditionally a force that the compulsions of unemployment under a capitalist régime decidedly lack. Even so, notwithstanding the war compulsions and the tradition of discipline for war, the indecent haste with which the planning Mr. Chase praises was scrapped, when the Armistice was signed, shows how alien was planning to the spirit of capitalism. It will take a terror not yet inspired by too docile workers to force on capitalism such a degree of planning as will begin to approximate the wartime experiment.

But may not the growing concentration of power to which Mr. Gardiner C. Means calls attention alter some of the factors? May we not expect some general planning from "the less than two thousand" directors of the two hundred largest non-financial corporations which in 1927, according to Mr. Means, controlled "over 45 per cent of the assets of all non-financial corporations, received over 40 per cent of corporate income, controlled over 35 per cent of all business wealth, and between 15 and 25 per cent of national wealth"? The *New Republic*, which editorially is somewhat optimistic on this point, is candid enough to admit some of the difficulties. And to its list others can be added. Great as is the control of these corporations, it does not extend to such vital matters as farming, bituminous coal mining, building, and textiles. There is little evidence that these two hundred great corporations have tackled or desire to tackle the general economic problem. Mr. Swope's plan has not met with the universal applause of his fellow industrialists. The most the best of them have done is to make some beginning of stabilization within their own industries. Stabilization of employment has its merits, but the plain truth is that its general adoption at the present level of economic activity and at the present rate of technological advance threatens us with the creation of a standing army of the permanently unemployed. All these great corporations shared in the general speculative debauch; they are dominated by the prevalent acquisitive and competitive temperament. They exist to make profits, and production for profit inevitably means a greater or less degree of both technological and cyclical unemployment. Why, for instance, are new machines installed or new technical processes used save to reduce costs? Which means, almost every time, to cut payrolls by firing workers! Finally, there is no sign at all that the little group in legal control of our two hundred greatest corporations will invite that labor participation in general economic planning which is essential to any reasonable scheme for an economic general staff.

Nevertheless, the persistent discussion of planning, and the fact that big business is strategically and probably psychologically in a better position than a multitude of little businesses to play with this idea, means that we may find ourselves with some sort of planning commission (or commissions) on our hands which may at least spy out the land, make public its findings, and indulge in some useful suggestions. It could conceivably, as Mr. Chase insists, make forecasts that would advise the investor and so guide investment and credits — a guidance without which planning would be nothing but a joke. It might in like fashion aid the correlation of industries. That would be a beginning, and a beginning on which a society resolved to go socialist might well build. It would at least be a denial of the genius of capitalism with its "automatic laws." It is not likely, however, that any scheme of planning under capitalism would make a forthright attack on the heart of our problem, which is the redistribution of the national income. Without this the evils of underconsumption will persist.

The basic truth remains: Before society can plan for general use rather than for private profit it must own or at least control the vital economic enterprises for which it plans. All of which is a way of saying that socialism is the essential condition of planning even as planning is the essential tool of successful socialism. There remains the question whether socialism can impose the requisite degree of planning without the power of an iron dictatorship behind it. This in turn divides into two questions, one political or perhaps psychological, and the other economic. The first is: Can planning coexist with political democracy? The second: Can planning on a scale sufficient to banish unemployment and reduce waste permit any effective degree of consumers' choice, or must we all be rationed, fed, clothed, housed, and entertained much as any army is fed, clothed, housed, and entertained, with the inevitable corollary that we shall be assigned jobs much as soldiers are assigned jobs?

Neither question can be answered with absolute certainty. Planning under a democracy will succeed in proportion as the democracy is committed to the philosophy of socialism and to the necessity for intelligence in operating it. If these two ideas become dominant, democracy may provide a more orderly and less dangerous way to determine the human desires and prejudices of which even a dictatorship has to take account. Planning in Russia, notably in agriculture, has traced and retraced its steps as a result of Communist Party conflicts and compromises and Stalin's judgment of the strength of peasant resistance. At no time, not even now, could any economic commission, even with all the power of the dictatorship behind it, move the masses absolutely as they desired. Nevertheless, it will take a democracy capable of understanding and sharing a general interest rather than a democracy immersed in local, sectional, and other divisive interests — as our American democracy usually is — to make possible competent and adequate planning. The political democracy that gives sway to logrolling minorities to make tariff laws and pass pension legislation is not a democracy from which one may hope too much. But then the present democracy is thoroughly capitalist in its philosophy and loyalty.

The other question concerns the possibility of achieving a sufficient degree of economic planning to abolish unemployment without conscripting the workers as producers and rationing them as consumers. I have put this question in an extreme form. Neither the degree of economic planning which served war needs nor the economic planning which serves Russia today has entailed conscription and rationing of workers like soldiers. Indeed, the present tendency in Russia seems to be to increase the inducement of differential rewards of labor as opposed to military conscription and to decrease the amount of rationing of goods that has been necessary. If economic planning means even in a transitional period a degree of bureaucratic control which denies consumers' choice and conscripts workers with the aid of the secret police to the degree now practiced in Russia, it will seem well-nigh intolerable to the average American and it will probably result sooner or later in a dangerous stagnation in the industrial arts. Though I do not think the Russian government gets its astonishing results primarily by terror, I agree, in the main, with Professor Beard's vigorous statement: "One thing, however, is certain: the Russian government rules by tyranny and terror, with secret police, espionage, and arbitrary executions. The system may be adapted to a people who endured Tsarist despotism for centuries, but to suppose that it could be transported intact to the United States, even if deemed successful in its own bailiwick, is to ignore the stubborn facts of American life and experience — the long practice of self-government in towns, villages, and states, the traditions of personal liberty, the established public school system, and a thousand other elements that stand out like mountains in the American scene."

There is, moreover, a risk that too rigid a degree of planning will break down of its own weight and paralyze initiative by red tape. A machine age, already highly collectivized, must increasingly depend upon the initiative of the engineer rather than of the entrepreneur. But even the initiative of the engineer can be crushed by routine and the rigor of a system which tries the vain task of providing in advance for every conceivable contingency. At present the Russian dictatorship is bringing vigor and imagination to planning. It is easier to apply these qualities to catching up in an industrially backward country than to keeping up. Rather it is easier in some respects to industrialize a country than to manage the production and distribution of the things a nation needs after it is industrialized. Moreover, it is easier for a dictatorship to be vigorous and imaginative and honest in a revolutionary period than when it has settled down. These are not arguments against the success of the Russian experiment; they are reasons why it, and even more certainly any plan in the United States, must leave room for meeting emergencies and for developing initiative. Its very perfection on paper may paralyze it.

The best bureaucracy tends to be static and suspicious of those new things and new methods which invention gives us. But I cannot agree with those critics who think economic planning will either completely paralyze the consumers' right to turn from, let us say, coal to oil for domestic heating or will break on a vain attempt at such control. Logically, planning can reckon with change and leave a margin for experimentation. At any rate, there is more reason to expect this adaptability and to work for it than to endure the wastes of a planless economic order for which technological progress is poor compensation.

The hope of a sufficient economic planning to meet the problems of an interdependent society and still permit a high degree of choice of work and consumers' goods under a political democracy lies in three things: (1) the possibility of learning the average tendency of consumers' choices and even educating it so that a reasonable forecast can be made of the number of factories necessary for shoes, radios, automobiles, etc.; (2) the fact that the productivity of machinery allows for a very considerable amount of waste from an abstract standpoint without breaking down the system; and (3) that, short of conscription, workers can be guided by information and induced by differential rewards to take the necessary jobs. In a country as far advanced industrially as the United States, a country which does not have to pay to industrialize itself out of its food and clothing, a country already disciplined in factory labor, the degree of rationing and conscription practiced in Russia ought not to be necessary. It would at any rate be impossible without a large-scale war.

In short, while production for use rather than profit requires planning and alone makes possible adequate planning for a machine age, such planning will probably be more aided than hurt by keeping money and the mechanism of profit to permit men a very considerable choice both of what goods they will take and at what jobs they will work. That is to say, workers will be paid in money, and goods will be sold, as they are now, by consumers' coöperatives, on a basis of profit, which profit can be refunded either in increased return to the workers, or dividends to purchasers, or reductions of price the next year, or by some combination of these methods. At the same time, successful planning will enormously enhance the social income of parks, playgrounds, libraries, museums, and a hundred and one things that men may enjoy in the increased leisure which the efficient harnessing of the billion wild horses of machinery will give them. But this will require far more than trying to plaster planning on our capitalistic chaos. Important, difficult, and deserving of discussion as are questions of the nature of a desirable plan, the way it should be set up and the manner in which its commissions, regional and national, should be constituted, the primary question for America and the world is not: How shall we plan? but: For whom and for what shall we plan? What sort of society do we really want?

A PLANNED ECONOMY AND A PLANNED PRICE LEVEL[1]

Benjamin M. Anderson, Jr.

BENJAMIN M. ANDERSON was born at Columbia, Missouri, in 1886, and educated at the Universities of Missouri and Illinois, and at Columbia University, where he took his doctorate in 1911. He was instructor in economics at Columbia for two years, and assistant professor in that subject at Harvard from 1913 to 1918. After a brief service as economic adviser to the National Bank of Commerce in New York, he became economist for the Chase National Bank in 1920, a post he still holds. Though he has published several volumes, notably *The Value of Money* (1917) and *The Effects of the War on Money, Credit, and Banking in France and the United States* (1919), he is best known as editor of the monthly publication of his bank, the *Chase Economic Bulletin*, and as a lecturer. Particularly during the Great Depression, 1929–1935, his analyses of current business and economic problems attracted much attention.

ECONOMIC REVOLUTION OR ECONOMIC REVIVAL?

We must be clear as to our objectives. To my mind, the great and vital problem confronting the United States and the world today is that of getting many millions of men back to work, getting business going again, getting goods moving throughout the country and throughout the world, increasing enormously the volume of production in the world, so that the volume of consumption may also be greatly increased. But among the proposals which purport to have this economic revival for an objective there are not a few which really look toward different ends. There are, as usual, social revolutionaries who like to fish in troubled waters, who would seek radically to recast the whole economic system, to shatter the sorry scheme of things and "then remold it nearer to the heart's desire."

Whatever else measures of this sort might accomplish, they would not, in the near future, restore production and consumption in the world, or set men to work. And there are many much more moderate proposals which, while they might or might not be meritorious in themselves, if adopted in a tranquil time when the general economic machinery is functioning well, would, none the less, interfere with

[1] An address delivered before the Pilgrims of the United States, at a dinner given in honor of Sir Josiah Stamp, at the Plaza Hotel, New York City, on Thursday evening, June 8, 1933. Reprinted by permission of the author from *Chase Economic Bulletin*, June 9, 1933. Only a portion is given here, and the essay if possible should be read in full.

economic revival if adopted today. There are schemes for the redistribution of wealth, which schemes may or may not have merit, considered as long-pull measures, but they certainly are not revival measures. There are other proposals, growing out of the righteous anger of honest men who have discovered iniquity, which are punitive in their nature, and which can easily go so far as to impair the efficiency of existing economic machinery which is necessary to facilitate revival. We must be clear as to our objectives. If, as an incident to revival measures, or if, as contributing to revival measures, we can end old abuses and can improve the general economic system, so much the better. But we must not permit the present unhappy state of the world and the present flux of bewildered political opinion to be capitalized by those who advocate new and untested economic theories in the making of hazardous experiments. This sick economic world of ours is a patient in a hospital, not a subject for experimentation in a laboratory. And if, as I believe is the case, we can cure this patient by tried and tested measures, surely we have no right to discard those tried and tested measures and to turn the patient over to a new school of physicians who have some theories that have never been known to work.

In medicine, when radical new measures are proposed, it is at least the common practice to try them out on animals first, and then, after long and careful experimentation, to try them out tentatively on human beings. We must certainly ask the new schools of economic practitioners to try things out on a small scale first, tentatively and cautiously, before they ask us to transform the whole economic system radically.

OLD ECONOMICS AND NEW ECONOMICS

We have heard a great deal about the failure of the so-called old economics, and the need for new doctrines. I think it can safely be said that there has been no failure of the old economics in this post-war period, because so little of what the old economics advocates has been done. The old economics taught, and teaches, that tariffs should not be unduly high, and that goods should move with reasonable freedom across national borders. The post-war period has seen a steadily mounting body of tariffs and other trade barriers, choking the flow of goods across national borders.

The old economics taught that excessive credit and artificially cheap money would generate great speculation and the piling up of unsound debts which could not be paid and which, in their qualitative deterioration and collapse, would create crisis and panic. But we spent the post-war years, especially from 1922 into 1928, in an altogether unprecedented expansion of credit at artificially low interest rates, with rediscount rates held below the market instead of above the market as the old rules prescribed, and we generated a credit bubble and a speculative bubble, the collapse of which has brought us untold disaster.

John Stuart Mill knew the dangers both of excessive tariffs and of excessive credit. No new economics was needed to avert them.

The old economics taught that international debts must be paid primarily with goods and services. It taught that the debtor country, in the period when it was borrowing, would have an import surplus, but that when it began to repay, it must have an export surplus, sending out more goods than it consumed, and it taught that a creditor country, when the time came to receive payments, must receive an import surplus, a so-called "adverse balance of trade." But the old economics also knew what the new economics seems unwilling to admit: namely, that it was good for a creditor country to receive an excess of imports, that the term "adverse balance of trade" under these circumstances was a meaningless and misleading phrase. The old economics taught that when goods come into a country in payment of debts they do not reduce the ability of the country to buy the products of its own labor, but, rather, increase its total income and its total consumption. The foreign goods coming in in payment of debts are sold in the creditor country and the proceeds in money are not taken out, but, rather, are turned over as income to people within the creditor country, increasing their incomes by the same amount in money as the goods which come in in payment of the debts, and leaving them with undiminished buying power for their domestic products. But the new economics seems to be returning to seventeenth and eighteenth century policies with respect to these matters, seems to be afraid of good, afraid of production, afraid of income, and afraid of an abundance of goods for consumption.

The old economics knew very well that it was absurd to try to expect any definite equivalents in imports and exports as between two particular countries. It understood triangular and quadrangular trade. It knew that if a country's general balance of trade with the whole world was in proper adjustment to its creditor or debtor position things were going right, and that nothing need be done about it. The new economics seems to be veering strongly toward the notion that the volume of exports and imports with every particular country must be regulated, and that trade must be discouraged with every country which does not buy more from us than it sells to us. It is not pleasant to see this recrudescence of sixteenth and seventeenth century fallacies!

The old economics taught that there is no such thing as a general overproduction. It taught that the power to consume grows out of the power to produce, that consumption grows out of production. A man producing one commodity, as automobiles, contributes to the *supply* of automobiles, to be sure, but equally contributes to the *demand* for wheat, for silk, for cotton, and for other commodities which he wants. And the man producing cotton or cotton goods contributes to supply of these things, but also to demand for silk, for sugar, for automobiles, and for other things which he wants. The old economics recognized that things could be produced in wrong proportions, some things too much, others too little, and that then great abnormalities and distortions would come. The old economics recognized that when you had overproduction of certain things and underproduction of other things, the terms of exchange between them could be so deranged that the buying power of the producers of the excessive commodities would sink very low, and then even the underproduced commodities would seem to be overproduced, because they could not be sold. But it sought the remedies in better balance and better proportion, and not in a general contraction of all production. The old economics saw purchasing power growing out of production, and it held that a good equilibrium among the various elements of production meant large aggregate purchasing power, which could take care of large aggregate production. The new economics separates production and buying power. It looks on goods on the one hand and buying power on the other hand as separate and independent things, and it proposes artificial increases of buying power through currency and credit manipulations.

A PLANNED ECONOMY

One of the most dangerous of the proposals of the new economics is that of a so-called "planned economy." Economic life as we have known it has been, in large measure, an unconscious thing in the sense that no mind or no group of minds has seen the whole picture, and certainly no one mind or group of minds has directed the whole picture. Intelligence runs through it, but it is the intelligence of individuals or organizations seeking their own particular wages or their own particular profits, seeing their own sources of supply, seeing their own markets, but not seeing with any great clearness the movements of the system as a whole.

Automatic versus Conscious Control. In general it is not the function of government under the present system to produce goods or to perform economic services. The actual direction of industry, the decision whether more wheat shall be planted and less corn, or more shoes shall be produced and less hats, is not made by the state or by collective society, but is left to the choice of independent producers. These independent producers make their decisions with reference to the state of the markets. The up and down movements of prices and wages determine whether more or less of a given thing shall be produced. If prices are rising in a given industry and falling in another, the tendency is for labor and capital to flow from the industry where prices are falling to the industry where prices are rising. The tendency is, moreover, for consumers to consume less of those goods the prices of which are rising, and to consume more of those goods the prices of which are falling. Oversupply of any given commodity, accompanied by falling prices, thus tends to correct itself, since production declines and consumption increases, whereas the shortage of supply of another commodity, accompanied by rising prices, likewise tends to correct itself through an increase of production and a curtailment of consumption. Under this system of free private enterprise with free movement of labor and capital from industry to industry, the tendency is for an automatic balance to be maintained and for goods and services to be supplied in right proportions. A social order is created, a social coöperation is worked out, largely unconscious and largely automatic, under the play of the impersonal forces of market prices and wages.

This system obviously predicates a sound money which men can trust. The success of this system, moreover, depends upon its flexibility and the quickness with which readjustments can be made, and this, in turn, depends largely upon the extent to which it is competitive and free from unified conscious control. If a government of a collective system undertakes to regulate the business of a country as a whole and to guide and control production, there is required a central brain of such vast power that no human being who has yet lived, or can be expected to live, can supply it. When millions of people are working, each at his own special problem, studying his own special market, making his readjustment piecemeal, under the guidance of market prices, the problem is manageable. If a central brain must do the thinking for all of them, chaos is inevitable.   Great mistakes are made and these mistakes are carried much farther than would be possible under the competitive system, controlled by free prices.

Here then is the central contrast between our present system and a planned economy — in the problem of coördinating the economic activities of men and making a social order.   Our present system relies upon the unconscious, automatic functioning of the markets. A "controlled economy" must do it, if at all, by conscious public planning, a central brain guiding, controlling, and regimenting the masses of men, controlling production, controlling consumption, controlling the distribution of wealth, and, in a large measure, regulating the lives and activities of men.

The Limits of Economic Theory and Statistics.   If we wish revival without an early relapse into chaos, I do not think we shall go far with the advocates of the planned economy.   They cannot make a comprehensive plan.   The ablest and best trained brains, given unlimited power, could not do it.   The ablest students of economic theory can, for a little while, at times when their energies run high, see in theoretic outline, in schematic outline, an abstract picture of the economic order.   The concatenation of prices and costs, the interrelations among the industries, the international interrelations, the relations of capital market, money market, securities market and industry — there is a body of economic theory dealing with these matters sufficiently definite and sufficiently clear to enable us to reach some very important practical conclusions regarding public policy.   But to put flesh and blood upon this abstract skeleton, so as to make it a thing adequate for conscious control of industrial life, is an impossibility.   We have an immense mass of statistical detail regarding many phases of economic life, but not nearly enough for purposes of this sort, and not, moreover, in manageable form.   Further, it cannot be assembled with sufficient speed to enable one central planning body or one central brain to use it in making day by day decisions.   Neither economic theory nor statistics begins to supply the necessary foundation for dealing with such a problem.   The best industrial and financial intelligence sees only a part of the picture with definite realism.   The coördination of the multitudinous elements must be through the markets, and not through a central brain or central authority.

Economics Must Yield to Politics in Practical Administration. But, further, no one supposes that if we are to have a planned economic order the matter would be turned over to the men who have trained themselves to see the whole economic picture. They would not be regarded as competent to handle the administrative problem — and they would not be. The thing would be turned over to practical administrators, chosen primarily with respect to their ability to get along with men, and with respect to their acceptability to controlling political groups, and instead of *economic planning* we should get *political compromise*. The plans that would be made would be only partially harmonious from the standpoint of economic consistency. They would be, in large part, a mere resultant of political pressures, contradictory in their economic implications.

The administrative problem would be an impossible problem, particularly difficult in the United States because of our conflicts of state and federal jurisdictions and our constitutional limitations. With the control of industry, it would involve an immense bureaucracy — a bureaucracy so great that it might, indeed, go far in solving the problem of unemployment!

We used to have an immense respect for the power of the federal government to give us clean and efficient administration. In the old days, when the federal government had very limited functions, our Internal Revenue Service was extraordinarily clean and efficient (if one forgets the scandals of the 'seventies), there was immense respect for federal law and its administration, and we made frequent contrasts between the efficiency of federal administration and the inefficiency of state and local administration. But, when we gave the federal government problems similar to those of the states and municipalities, as in the case of prohibition, we saw the same evils creep in, the same abuses, the same corruption of federal law enforcement officers as we had had when the states and municipalities alone dealt with the liquor problem. The regulation of industry and the enforcement of regulation is increasingly impossible to the extent that it is thoroughgoing. Let federal agents go about inspecting the affairs of business men, and you will have a multiplication of the evils and abuses, including bribery and blackmail, that we see in our municipalities enforcing building codes, tenement house regulations, and so on.

Wartime Experience Inapplicable. It is urged that we have an experience on which to build in this connection. During the war, we did have a good deal of regulation and control of industry, and it is thought that this experience can be applied today. I believe that that wartime experience would be largely useless as applied to our present problem. The objectives in the wartime were simple and clear.

We were overstraining our productive capacity, and the problem was to produce essential goods. So and so many tons of steel were needed for such and such definite purposes. So and so much wheat was needed to go across the water. There was a definite military problem, and the big purpose of the war control was to hold down the production of non-essential commodities to provide resources for essential commodities. There was the definite further problem of holding prices down and limiting profits, along with the maximization of the production of specifically needed goods. There was unlimited demand and limited supply, and the problem was to restrict demand and to direct supply.[1]

The present problem is radically different. It is the problem of getting men to work producing goods that can be sold. No central brain can know which these goods are. The markets know. The individuals in charge of industries, each studying his own specific market, can know, but not even they can know how much demand can be increased as they and their fellows each increase production, each take on new employees and generate new buying power for all other products.

Who Will Coördinate the Trade Associations? I am particularly apprehensive regarding the proposal to allow trade associations on a great scale to get together, with the Sherman Law waived, to raise prices and limit output, euphemistically called "adjusting supply to demand." If one industry alone does this, it may, if it does not overdo it, increase its profits, although even one doing it could easily mean less men at work. But if all of them do it, they will simply strangle one another.

Here there would not be one central plan, but merely a central validation of a multitude of conflicting special plans.

The great and growing increase in demand which should come as men are steadily added to the payrolls, and as more and more raw materials are used, increasing the buying power of producers of raw materials, would simply not materialize. There is no surer anti-revival measure than a widespread application of this plan.

The Plan Would Prevent the Restoration of Balance between Manufactures and Raw Materials and Foods. One of the great troubles in the present situation has been that manufacturing has curtailed output, "adjusting supply to demand," as the phrase goes, on a colossal scale, while agriculture and raw material production have gone on

[1] See the paper by the present author, "Value and Price Theory in Relation to Price-Fixing and War Finance," in the *American Economic Review*, March, 1918.

largely unchecked. There is an immense unbalance between extractive industries, on the one hand, and manufacturing on the other, manifest in the exceedingly low prices of raw materials and agricultural products as compared with the prices of manufactured goods.

We want this unbalance corrected, and the great correction will come through the expansion of manufacturing activity at home and abroad. The lowering of the tariffs, permitting manufactured goods to come in from abroad, but, much more important, enabling foreign countries to buy on a great scale the raw materials and foods in this country which they need, will restore this balance. It will lead to an almost explosive rise in the prices of foods and raw materials in the United States, and to an almost explosive expansion of manufacturing industry here and abroad. Our own factories, sharing an expanding market with reasonable foreign competition, will produce and sell vastly more goods than they can do with exclusive control of the depressed agricultural market and the depressed raw materials market.

Special Cases — Wasting Natural Resources. I am not wholly hostile to some measure of coöperation under government auspices, looking toward the restriction of output in certain raw material lines, particularly where wasting natural resources are involved. We probably need it in the extraction of crude petroleum from the ground. Here supply is little influenced by price, but rather is governed by the discovery of new fields, and by the necessity which every producer faces of pumping oil if his neighbor is pumping, in order to protect his own oil from being drained away. Natural gas may present a similar case. Lumber possibly does. And the long-sick bituminous coal fields may well justify careful study and conscious public planning. But I know no case of manufacturing, refining, or processing industries where I should be willing to see trade associations get together, with the Sherman Law waived, to raise prices and restrict output. I should regard that as a measure tending to increase, rather than to diminish, the unbalance between raw material production and manufacturing, and I should regard it as an anti-revival measure.

Political Conflicts and Compromises. I have indicated that economic planning cannot be done on strict economic lines. It inevitably involves political compromises and the conflict of political purposes which will make the plan an economic disharmony. There will be conflicts among different trades, steel wanting higher prices, the railroads wanting lower steel rail prices. There will be conflicts between labor and capital. There will be political manœuvres and pressures. Congressmen and senators, under bombardment from their constituents, will be spending an ever-increasing amount of energy in putting political pressure upon the coördinator to favor this or that or the other special interest — and the Congressmen and Senators are sufficiently overburdened with private affairs at the present time not to welcome much more of this kind of thing. Let us hope that the administration will use these vast new powers with the greatest caution, in the most tentative manner, try them out on a very small scale, and extend the application very gradually. A sudden sweeping application could create a fearful chaos.

SWEDEN: WHERE CAPITALISM IS CONTROLLED[1]

Marquis W. Childs

MARQUIS W. CHILDS is a journalist who, after service on New York and other newspapers, is now (1935) a member of the staff of the St. Louis *Post-Dispatch*. He has contributed articles to various magazines, including a series on Samuel Insull published in 1932 in the *New Republic*.

I

If one were compelled to select in the present moment of flux and chaos a certain area of the earth's surface in order to show the highest good that Western civilization had up to the present achieved, one might go farther and do worse than to choose Scandinavia. One would include, of course, besides the Scandinavian peninsula proper, Denmark, which is allied to it by every tie of race and culture. And by "good" one would mean the greatest good for the greatest number of people: a civilization in which all the arts and sciences of the West are employed to enable man to live in comfort and peace surrounded by a considerable degree of beauty and order and cleanliness.

The Scandinavian countries have developed during the past hundred years more or less apart from the violent national and political passions of continental Europe. Aside from a healthy national rivalry, they have lived in peace and harmony. Within the past three or four decades they have evolved what may in many respects be considered a new form of economic life. They have achieved a planned internal economy. Wherever the direct interest of the consumer has been involved — the necessities of shelter, food, light, heat, clothing — the profit motive has been drastically curbed or abolished. It is a process of socialization that has gone forward unevenly, quietly, steadily. But the objective has not been a utopian state built in conformity with the blueprints of some arbitrary theory. The objective has been a practical one: to lower the cost of good living; a pragmatic test has been applied to all reforms. The objective is expressed in the slogan of the Social Democratic Party in Sweden: "Comfort in the home for all classes." It is as modest as that.

And it has worked. The standard of living in Denmark and Sweden has been the highest in Europe. (The standard in Norway has been

[1] From *Harper's Magazine*, November, 1933. Reprinted by permission.

130

lower because of large untillable land areas, the bleakness and sparseness of much of the country.) While it is difficult to make an exact comparison, it is probable that the standard of living of the mass of the people in Sweden and Denmark has been — and remains today — higher than the standard for the mass in the United States. These are, too, the most modern countries in Europe, with more motor cars and telephones per capita and more electric lines per unit area of population.

The fact that the Scandinavian countries have had a planned domestic economy has not made them proof against the effects of the depression. But it has now become obvious that the structure of international finance and trade was so complex that it could not be disrupted without harming every nation in the world — every individual in the world, one might almost add. Even in Russia, where the entire economy, trade within the country and with other nations, is unified under control of the state, the chief obstacles in the way of building an industrial civilization have been those encountered in international trade. Since the Scandinavian countries have shipped from 20 to 25 per cent of their goods into the international market, it is obvious that they have felt during the past three years the dire effects of world-wide unemployment.

But because they have had, in effect, a planned domestic economy, at every point vital to the consumer, the ravages of the depression have been less serious than elsewhere. The standard of living has not been battered down as it has in America. It is easy, of course, to dismiss the example of these northern countries; to say that they are small, that their population is homogeneous and highly educable; and that they have never been under the necessity of maintaining the difficult and dangerous rank of a major Power. But when one has made all these, and other, qualifications, the significance of what has happened in Scandinavia remains and has, I believe, a bearing upon certain problems that confront the world today and in particular those that confront the United States.

The Scandinavian countries in their present development stand midway between the uncontrolled capitalism of America before the crash and the arbitrary Marxian communism of Russia before the Stalin modifications of a year ago. They have arrived at this middle course by modifying and altering the economic forms of capitalism; by adopting practices from other economic systems; and by evolving new forms of their own. They have achieved that control of capitalism which is sought in the United States by the laws passed at the insistence of President Roosevelt during the last session of Congress. In Scandinavia this control has been attained during a period of thirty years or more; by the coöperation of aggressive groups of consumers; by the active and intelligent participation of the state in important industrial fields such as power; by virtue of an impregnable labor movement; by a long process of social education. Remarkably enough, this process of education has touched even the point of view of the capitalist and to such a degree that he has, in certain instances, it is said, lent his support to the movement to strengthen the domestic economy along coöperative lines.

The division, particularly in Sweden, is sharp and striking. To one group of capitalists — really to one family — has fallen virtually the whole business of manufacture for export and shipping. This group of capitalists has carried on in the international market by the same methods as other international traders — that is, by fighting fire with fire. They have of late years levied a comparatively slight tribute from the domestic consumer. Their source of profit has been almost entirely in the international market. It was so with Ivar Kreuger, whose operations were in many respects typical of the international financier, having little relation to domestic finance. The Kreuger crash, it may be noted here, worked more hardship in America than it did in Sweden. The virtual surrender of the domestic market by the Wallenbergs, the dominant capitalists in Sweden for nearly three generations, was not brought about without a conflict. The coöperative societies and the state have competed with private enterprise in one field after another, and on even terms with no favors asked; and they have won by virtue of their efficiency and acumen, and, it goes without saying, by virtue of the fact that they have not been under the constant necessity of surrendering to ownership a sizeable surplus.

II

In showing how this planned domestic economy has been achieved Sweden serves as the best example, because it is more highly industrialized than either Norway or Denmark. And the Swede is closer to the American than is the Norwegian or the Dane, if only for the reason that he believes in a high standard of living and spends his money freely for those things that in most European countries are regarded as luxuries for the rich — that is, for a little summer cottage, for a motor boat (instead of a motor car). These the Swedish worker regards almost as necessities of life.

The state had an investment in business undertakings in 1929 — the last year for which complete figures are available — of $613,452,000. On this investment in that year there was a net return of 6.08 per cent. And it must be recalled that this is in a country of six million population, distributed over a large area, much of which is mountainous or forest-covered. The activities of the state are many and varied. The state owns and operates at a profit nearly one-fourth of the forest area. The state controls and derives a considerable profit from the operation of about one-third of the mines. The state owns and operates at a profit railway, telegraph, and telephone systems. The state generates 34 per cent of the electricity used, and this represents about 80 per cent of the amount used by householders. The state controls and derives a considerable profit from the sale of tobacco and liquor and the broadcasting of radio programs. And it is now proposed to make the importation and wholesaling of coffee and the manufacture and export of arms and munitions also state monopolies.

In other fields coöperation has served to curb the profit motive to the great advantage of the consumer. Coöperative societies own and operate an estimated 10 per cent of all industry, for the most part manufacture for domestic consumption. The coöperatives control between one-third and one-half of the wholesale and retail trade of the nation in food, shoes, clothing, and certain other commodities. Coöperative societies, together with municipal organizations, have built and sold, on a coöperative basis, about one-fourth of the housing in the two principal cities, Stockholm and Gothenburg. They sell insurance, market agricultural produce, make motion pictures (chiefly for propaganda purposes), and engage in many other activities.

What proportion of the total trade of the country is carried on by the state and by the coöperative societies, it is difficult to say. But it has been sufficiently large to serve as an effective brake upon capitalist exploitation in the domestic market. Prices of the principal commodities, rentals, and utility service charges have been forced downward, often with dramatic suddenness, by the aggressive competition of the state and the coöperatives.

How this has been done can be shown perhaps best in the field of electric power. And in this connection I am tempted to recall a conversation in Sweden in 1930. Motoring through the pleasant Swedish countryside with the editor of one of the large Chicago newspapers, we talked of this business of putting the state in competition with private power companies. The editor had only a blustering impatience for such an arrangement. "We don't need anything like that in Chicago," he said. "We have Samuel Insull and he gives us our power and light cheap enough." Events that came to light a year later disclosed that Mr. Insull was not solely interested in providing Chicago with electric power at a fair rate.

In Sweden there has never been any attempt to regulate power distribution and cost through monopoly franchise and the functioning of an elaborate legal structure. There is in effect almost complete *laissez faire* in the power field. Under Swedish law two or more electrical companies may compete for business in the same district. It is only necessary to secure a concession from the state, which is merely an authorization to string wires and erect poles. But instead of chaos there is today an orderly distribution of power at a fair price.

When the state entered the power field nearly twenty-five years ago, it owned several important waterfall sites; private concerns and certain of the larger towns were already established and were beginning to develop water power for their own requirements. Methods were wasteful, rates were high. And yet competition was such that there was little or no profit in the industry. Gradually the state built up its own power block. There was at the head of the Royal Board of Waterfalls a man of great ability, W. Borgquist. He developed the state's power system by the addition of one station after another so that it soon occupied a strong, strategic position with lines stretching down the whole length of the country. It was operated in the most efficient fashion to produce power at the lowest possible cost to the consumer.

One of the first effects of this competition by the state was to eliminate weak and inefficient private companies. At the same time those that survived were compelled to reduce their rates and, therefore, to increase their efficiency. If the state had an advantage in that it was not under compulsion to yield a large annual tribute to ownership and to management, it was also under a decided disadvantage in that it was compelled to develop so-called cultural power lines in backward agricultural areas where a company organized solely for profit might never have entered. And the Board of Waterfalls has observed always the strictest accounting practices; that is, all fixed charges have been deducted, as with a private company, in estimating the net profit of the operations.

For 1932 the state operated its power system at a profit of $288,604 — this after all interest and tax charges had been deducted — on 1,700,000,000 kilowatt hours of power. While this sum is a small profit, it must be remembered that the state has had a heavy social responsibility; first, it has fixed its rates as low as possible; and second, it has developed backward regions. Sixty per cent of the land under tillage in Sweden has been provided with electricity, a higher percentage than exists in any other country.

There has come about, since the end of the era of wild competition, a working understanding between the state and the private electrical systems. On occasion they coöperate to their mutual advantage. For example, the parliament has recently ordered that the state railway line between Storvik and Ange be electrified. To supply the electricity that will be necessary for this project the Board of Waterfalls will construct a new power line, a branch of the major system. But it will be some time before this will be completed, and the board has made an agreement with a private company to supply the railway during this interval. Such agreements are not uncommon. It is almost as though there were one centralized power system operating for the good of the whole country.

Much of the power in Sweden, which ranks second only to Switzerland in power production, is distributed on a coöperative basis. This is particularly true of the agricultural areas. Rural districts form their own coöperative societies, construct the necessary local supply systems for 3,000 volts, the transformer stations necessary to step the energy down to low tension, and the requisite local supply lines. The operation and upkeep of the local lines and the delivery of energy in the territory of the society are also the business of the individual coöperatives. The capital to build and run the coöperative distributing system is contributed by members of the society in proportion to the amount of land owned, the number of rooms in a dwelling, or, if it is a shop, the number of lighting and motor installations. The larger societies are able to take advantage of an industrial rate offered by the state, so that they pay about 1.58 cents a kilowatt hour for power. The smaller societies take the district rate and pay 1.82 cents. To this must be added, in fixing the price to the ultimate consumer, the cost of distribution within the coöperative system.

Most of the cities and towns have their own distributing systems. There are special rate schedules whereby current taken in excess of a fixed number of kilowatt hours a room or square feet of floor space is supplied at a very much reduced price. This has resulted in the widespread electrification of Swedish households, as in certain towns, Kiruna in the far north, for example, electricity is supplied for as low a rate as 3 cents a kilowatt hour. In many communities in the industrial north 60 per cent of the households use electricity for cooking.

By intelligent coöperation these northern people have conquered the long, dark winters. There is in abundance, and at a price which puts it within the reach of all, artificial light and heat.

Power is only one, although perhaps it is the most important, of the fields in which the state has been successful in direct operation. There are other lines in which the state has delegated primary authority to a nominally private, limited dividend company. This has been done, for example, with the sale of liquor and the manufacture and sale of tobacco. Here it was felt that direct operation by the state might result in the manifold evils of bureaucracy.

There were two reasons why the state some sixteen years ago took over the sale, both wholesale and retail, of wines and spirits. First, it was felt, as the result of the efforts of the great reformer, Dr. Ivan Bratt, that it was important from the social point of view to remove the element of private profit from the liquor trade. Second, it was important to develop a new source of revenue for the state. These two reasons dovetailed nicely. The state, while retaining actual control, delegated the wholesale liquor trade to the Wine and Spirits Central, a private company paying a dividend limited to 5 per cent on a small share capital which is in the possession of a board of directors, all of whom must be approved by the government. The retail trade was delegated to a series of System Companies, organized on the same basis.

The intelligence of the social phases of the Swedish liquor plan, the use of pass books to restrict individual consumption of spirits, and so forth, has often been stressed. But sufficient emphasis has not been placed upon the economic side of the system. This is possibly more important than the social phase. In the opinion of the Swedes themselves, the removal of the profit motive was the essential factor in the success of the Bratt system.

The total amount spent by Swedish consumers on wine and spirits in 1931 was approximately $48,240,000. Of this amount the state received, through taxes and through the excess profits of the Wine and Spirits Central and the System Companies, $28,408,000, or 58.7 per cent of the whole. The cost of the liquors, the total cost of administration, and the cost of local taxation amounted to but 34.6 per cent of the total gross revenue. And liquor prices in Sweden are not high when it is taken into account that all except the local *brannvin* must be imported. That is, prices are not proportionately higher than in England or France. (This gives, incidentally, some idea of the enormous profits in the liquor trade.)

When broadcasting first appeared as a commercial possibility, the state retained the monopoly right to broadcast. At the end of an experimental period a similar private limited dividend company was formed to which the government granted the right to do all broadcasting. The source of revenue is, as in England, a moderate tax upon radio sets. As with the liquor monopoly, the excess profits, beyond the cost of administration and the amount paid to the holders of the small share capital, go to the government. This form of administration of a state monopoly has been so successful that it has been proposed for the manufacture of munitions and for the importation, processing, and wholesaling of coffee. If the latter is made a monopoly of the state, administered by a limited dividend company, as the Social Democrats propose, it would be purely for fiscal reasons. The manufacture of munitions, however, like the sale of liquor, is charged with significant social implications. It has been argued that, as with liquor, if there is no incentive to sell, there will be no forcing of sales by high-pressure methods. But this argument is somewhat redundant, since the Bofors plant in Sweden, employing two thousand men, is, like all other European munitions plants, at work on orders that are three years in advance; and most of these orders, under the Geneva Traffic in Arms Act, are for nations other than Sweden.

III

Thus far only the activities of the state have been considered. Through coöperation by consumers radical changes in the domestic economy of the country have come about. Coöperation is almost unknown in the United States. There are agricultural marketing coöperatives, and successful ones; but coöperation by consumers in the manufacture and sale of goods is all but unknown. Nor is it realized what a significant part this has played in Europe. The widespread development of consumer coöperatives in Russia was one of the few elements from the old régime which the Bolsheviks could employ in the construction of a socialist state. In England and Scotland more than 50 per cent of all consumers are members of coöperatives. Mussolini in reorganizing the economic life of Italy after seizing political power made use of the highly developed coöperatives then in existence for his own purposes. And Hitler in Germany is now emulating that example.

While scarcely more than a third of the consumers in Sweden are organized, it is possible that coöperation has had an even wider influence than in England. And the reason for this is the practical direction of Swedish coöperation. In England the coöperatives have been more or less institutional in character; their business has been largely exempt from taxation; the coöperative movement has had a strong political cast. In Sweden the opposite has been true: the first and foremost objective has been to reduce prices to the consumer, regardless of the social and political implications of the means employed to that end. That ultimate socialization of trade and manufacture is a possible goal of the coöperatives is a fact with which the directors of the movement have been only incidentally concerned.

In Sweden the coöperatives compete on equal terms, in regard to taxation and all other considerations, with private enterprise. The central organization is the Coöperative Union, which is the wholesaler and manufacturer for the 786 societies with their membership of 512,968 families (in 1932). In rural areas these societies own and operate usually only one store. The Consumers' Coöperative Society of Stockholm has 340 stores. These stores are specialized to sell food, clothing, meat, bread, and pastry. They are efficient and attractive, such shops as one sees in the smarter streets of an American city. The consumer buys at prices that are customarily a little lower than those of the private stores. Besides this outright saving, he is paid at the end of each year a dividend of 2 per cent on all his purchases. Consumers who are not members of the coöperative society may buy at the shop, but only members are entitled to the dividend.

It is of great interest to note the way in which coöperation has worked to drive prices downward for the whole mass of the buying public. It was not until the Coöperative Union and its affiliated societies were relatively strong that an attack was made upon the trusts. It was considered essential first to have a considerable consumer loyalty. The coöperators' first attack was directed against the margarine trust. Because so much butter is exported to the continent from Scandinavia, margarine is an important article of diet. The directors of the Coöperative Union knew that the price charged by the margarine trust was higher than was justified by the cost of manufacture. At the outset the coöperative directors tried to persuade the trust to reduce its prices. Next a threat was tried: the Union would begin the manufacture of margarine if prices were not lowered.

It was not that the coöperative directors particularly desired to go into the manufacture of margarine; they merely wanted lower prices and better quality. The trust ignored their demands, for the Union had not yet demonstrated its efficiency in the field of manufacture.

At last, in 1921, the Union carried out its repeated threats and constructed a margarine factory. This has been expanded several times until it is today the largest and most modern of its kind in the country. And the margarine trust soon lost its power, a fact reflected by successive price reductions from which the whole public benefited.

In the flour-milling industry the coöperators broke the power of another trust in a similar way. Today the Union owns the largest mills. In Sweden overshoes are a necessity of life during the winter, and the Coöperative Union next came to grips with a trust that had for long kept the price of this necessity at an unreasonable level. In this instance the first step taken by the Union was to issue a general proclamation, urging the public to subscribe to an industrial fund. This action alone was sufficient to cause the trust to cut its price on overshoes more than 50 cents a pair. The directors of the Union felt, however, that even this reduction did not bring the price to a figure based on a fair proportion between the cost of production and the selling price and so the Union went ahead with still another factory.

Even more striking is the success of the Union in breaking the grip of the international electric lamp cartel. In 1928 an investigation was begun into the cost of electric bulbs. Despite the fact that the trust dominated the whole European market, the investigators discovered the widest price discrepancies from country to country. The price for a 25 watt lamp was 37 cents in Sweden, 30 cents in Holland and Germany, 27 in Denmark, as low as 18 in Hungary, and 52 cents in England.

Careful estimates showed that the capital outlay for an up-to-date electric lamp factory was not prohibitive, amounting to less than the monthly net surplus of the various coöperative enterprises in Sweden. Nevertheless, as electric lamps play a comparatively minor part in the economy of the average household, it was debated for some time whether the Union should tie up its capital in such an enterprise. It was estimated that a saving of 12 cents on each lamp could be effected, a total annual saving to the country of about $1,500,000, and this, it was finally decided, was worth while. The decision was confirmed by a stroke of good luck which occurred at this time. Owing to the merger of two of the trust's lamp plants there became available the services of a technician capable of directing the construction and operation of a modern lamp factory. (There are very few such technicians and most of them are tied to the trust by long-term contracts.) Also, at this time the patents controlled by the trust expired.

In the face of dire warnings from the trust, the Union built the plant. From the outset it had been intended that the factory should be a common North European enterprise. As construction went forward, on capital supplied by the Coöperative Union, discussions were carried on with the central coöperative societies of Denmark, Norway, and Finland. On May 28, 1931, there was formed the North European Luma Coöperative Society which took over the then completed factory. Thus was formed the first truly international coöperative, with the consumer societies of all four countries each owning a proportionate share and each having a voice in the direction of the business through representatives on the board of directors.

The effect on the price of electric bulbs in Scandinavia was striking. Even while the Luma factory was in course of construction, the trust lowered the Swedish price from 37 cents to 27 cents. Soon after the coöperative lamp came on to the market the trust met the Luma price of 22 cents. With this the Luma price was cut to 20 cents, at which figure it is still possible to manufacture with a comfortable margin of surplus. On July 26, 1932, Luma turned out its five-millionth lamp. Each of the purchasers of the five million lamps received a dividend on his purchase from the surplus accumulated. The success of Luma has led English coöperatives to consider a similar manufacturing venture, and the price of bulbs in England has already dropped 10 cents.

It has been suggested that the central English coöperative society might build a plant in England which would be still another branch of the international coöperative enterprise. Swedish coöperators are strongly opposed to the practice of the English coöperators in selling their surplus manufactures abroad at a profit. This, it is said in Sweden, is not true coöperation and may give rise to the same frictions in international trade that occur at present with large corporations competing against one another in the international market. While they are modest in their hopes for the immediate future, the coöperative leaders in Sweden believe that this system is capable of almost infinite extension in the international field. And they are proud to have given to the world first a practical example of true international coöperation.

IV

Throughout the depression the Coöperative Union has continued to grow. During the past three years the books show gains in every department, the only decline being in the number of societies, the result of a policy of merging small societies to form stronger units. The number of stores owned by the local societies was 2,411 in 1926, 3,510 in 1931, and 3,716 in 1932. And the annual turnover rose correspondingly from $71,046,800 in 1926 to $94,006,360 in 1932. Because the directors of the Coöperative Union had faced the full implications of a possible world depression as early as 1930, the economy of the local societies has been directed during the past three years along the most strict lines. In 1932 the financial position of the Union and of the societies was stronger than ever before. Trade debts have been reduced on the joint balance sheet from 38 per cent to less than 6 per cent.

Coöperation has been markedly successful in the field of housing since the war. Here another group succeeded in bringing about a sharp decline in rentals through precisely the same methods. H.S.B., the coöperative housing society, has built during the past ten years a whole series of model apartment houses in Stockholm and in the second city, Gothenburg. These apartments were cheaper and far more desirable than the majority of flats in the older buildings. The power of what was equivalent to a housing trust was broken by H.S.B. three years after its organization.

All the achievements which have been recited here have been modest. They have been modest in aim and in attainment. They have been gained through patient, painstaking effort over a period of three decades. They have enlisted, it is almost needless to say, the services of men who have had not only a social point of view but who have possessed business acumen and organizing skill. Albin Johansson, the head of the Coöperative Union, is conceded by all factions to be the keenest merchant in the country. (To his ability the conservatives ascribe the success of the coöperative movement, but it has long since passed beyond the stage of dependence upon a single individual.)

Modest as they are, these successful economic experiments by the state and by the consumers themselves have been sufficient to control the capitalist in his operations within the country; in the domestic market it has been made impossible to exploit the consumer to the ultimate limit of his capacity to pay. As a cushion to absorb the worst shocks of the depression Sweden has had also during the past two years a currency managed, and successfully managed, in relation to commodity prices rather than to an arbitrary metallic standard. It is this managed currency which Professor Irving Fisher and other economists have for some time been urging upon the world at large.

The depression interrupted what might well have continued to be an orderly, evolutionary approach to socialism. That was the goal of the Social Democrats, who have held office six times within the past twenty years. Before the depression the party had considered the socialization of certain of the major export industries, notably paper, as a next step. The immediate problems arising from the crisis have made it impossible to contemplate this goal, even remotely, at the present time. The Social Democrats have just made into law a drastic unemployment program, designed, like the proposal of J. M. Keynes, to restore purchasing power virtually to the level of 1930. These and other emergency matters have occupied the government. But the Social Democrats have not forgotten their ultimate goal. It is possible that, if world capitalism now gains a breathing space, there may be completed in Sweden the gradual and orderly transition from one type of economic life to another. The very fact that such a transition may be possible is enormously heartening.

THE BASIS OF ECONOMIC PLANNING[1]

Lionel Robbins

LIONEL CHARLES ROBBINS has been professor of economics in the University of London since 1929. Born in England in 1898, he was educated at the University of London, fought in the World War, and then taught at Oxford and in the London School of Economics. He has published works on wages and on the nature of economic science, and has collaborated with Sir William Beveridge on a volume called *Tariffs: The Case Reëxamined*.

But on what basis is planning to take place?[2] The rationale of a planned society must surely be that it serves some purpose outside the plan. It must be planned for something. There are few who would regard the mere imposition of a pattern as an end in itself. What purpose is the plan to serve? Whose preferences are to govern the organization of production?

If the question is put in this way the answer seems obvious. A democratic community, at any rate, will attempt to organize production to meet the preferences of consumers. It will not value branches of production as such. It will value them for the various individual satisfactions which they make possible. It will not decide that the production of boots must be a certain absolute volume before it has ascertained the relative strength of the demand for boots and the demand for the products whose production has to be sacrificed if capital and labor are put to this job rather than to others. It will seek to distribute the factors of production between different lines of industry in such a way that it will be impossible to withdraw them from any one line and put them to any other without the products sacrificed being of greater value than the products gained. And if wants change, or if the means of satisfying them alter, it will seek to rearrange production so as once more to attain this end.

But how is this to be done? What mechanism is available for ascertaining the complex and changing tastes of the millions of different individuals constituting the community? And what means are present for deciding the relative efficiency of the different factors of

[1] From *The Great Depression*, by Lionel Robbins. Reprinted by permission of The Macmillan Company, publishers.

[2] The argument which follows owes much to the work of Professor Ludwig von Mises. See especially his *Gemeinwirtschaft*. A translation of this important book is shortly to appear in English.

production for satisfying these ends? How will the organizers of the planned economy choose between the production of boots and the production of potatoes? And having chosen, how will they decide the most expeditious methods of production?

Let us examine first the ascertainment of the preferences of consumers. It should be quite clear that this is not a matter which can be satisfactorily settled by the methods of political election. The problem of the planning of production concerns a vast multiplicity of alternatives. It is not a matter of "Vote for Jones and more umbrellas" or "Vote for Smith and more waterproof suiting." Thousands of commodities are involved, and the possibilities of alternative grouping run into many millions. It is clear that to attempt to solve the problem this way would result in complete chaos — a chaos which would result, not in consumers getting what they wanted, but in their being given simply what the planning authority on quite arbitrary principles decided that they ought to want — which would be by no means the same thing.

At first sight there seems ready to hand a much more efficient mechanism. If the various individuals constituting the community were given sums of money and were left free to bid for the various commodities available, there would result a series of prices which would be the objective register of their various preferences. The market in this respect may be compared to a continuous election with proportional representation. Every shilling spent is a vote for a particular commodity. The system of prices as a whole is the register of such an election.

It might be supposed then that a democratic community, determined to plan production, would attempt to resort to the market as a means for ascertaining the relative urgency of the demand for the various commodities available. A plan which was based upon the preferences of consumers would seek so to distribute its productive resources that the demand for all commodities was satisfied to the same level of urgency. If in making clothes a given quantity of labor produced less value in price terms than it would produce in the making of, let us say, fireworks, it would be withdrawn from the one and devoted to the other. And so with all the multitudinous instruments of production.

But it is one thing to sketch the requirements of the plan. It is another thing to conceive of its execution. It is in carrying out these requirements of productive organization that the project of planning to meet consumers' demands seems likely to encounter obstacles of a quite fundamental character — obstacles of whose existence the majority of the advocates of planning do not seem to have the slightest suspicion.

The requirement of a rational plan, as we have just seen, is that the factors of production (the land, capital, and labor) should be so distributed between the various alternatives of production that no commodity which is produced has less value than the commodities which might have been produced had the factors of production been free for other purposes. But how is this to be carried out? How is the planning authority to decide what distribution of resources satisfies this requirement? We have seen that it can do something to ascertain the preferences of consumers by permitting the pricing of the different commodities they consume. But clearly this is not enough. It must know also the relative efficiencies of the factors of production in producing all the possible alternatives.

On paper we can conceive this problem to be solved by a series of mathematical calculations. We can imagine tables to be drawn up expressing the consumers' demands for all the different commodities at all conceivable prices. And we can conceive technical information giving us the productivity, in terms of each of the different commodities, which could be produced by each of the various possible combinations of the factors of production. On such a basis a system of simultaneous equations could be constructed whose solution would show the equilibrium distribution of factors and the equilibrium production of commodities.

But in practice this solution is quite unworkable. It would necessitate the drawing up of millions of equations on the basis of millions of statistical tables based on many more millions of individual computations. By the time the equations were solved, the information on which they were based would have become obsolete and they would need to be calculated anew. The suggestion that a practical solution of the problem of planning is possible on the basis of the Paretian equations simply indicates that those who put it forward have not begun to grasp what these equations mean. There is no hope in this direction of discovering the relative sacrifices of alternative kinds of investment. There is no hope here of a means of adjusting production to meet the preferences of consumers.

Under competitive conditions this problem is solved by a comparison of costs and prices. In a free capitalistic society, the business man, deciding in what line to extend his enterprise, will take two things into consideration: on the one hand, the prices at which various commodities may be expected to sell; on the other, the costs which their production by various technical methods may be expected to incur. His expectations of price are based upon his knowledge of markets; his expectations of cost on technical information coupled with knowledge of the prices for the various factors of production. But the prices of the various factors of production, which are the resultant of the competitive bidding of the different entrepreneurs, tend to reflect the value of their contribution to the production of different products. If, therefore, costs are below prices in any line, that is an indication that additions to production in that line are more valuable in terms of consumers' preferences than the things which are being produced elsewhere — that transfer would result in a distribution of factors more in accordance with the preferences of consumers. If, under competitive conditions, the cost of producing potatoes is above the price which potatoes will fetch, that is an indication that some of the resources devoted to producing potatoes would produce things of more value elsewhere. Computations of costs and prices under competitive conditions are, as it were, a short cut to the solution of the millions of equations whose multiplicity we found such an obstacle to planning. The free market does the rest.

But, unfortunately, it is not easy to see how such computations could be made by a planning authority. For the possibility of computations of relative profitability of this sort involves the existence, not merely of a market for final products, but also of markets for all the multitudinous elements entering into costs: raw materials, machines, semi-manufactures, different kinds of land, labor, expert guidance, and, last but not least, free capital — with the entrepreneurs constituting the sellers and buyers, each acting according to his anticipation of the prices in the various markets in which they operate. But, by definition, the central planning authority has abolished all that. It disposes of all resources. There is no division between buyers and sellers. A plan is the centralized disposal of the factors of production precludes the existence of free markets. The planning authority can order production to be organized how it wishes. But it does not seem to be in a position to keep accurate accounts. How, then, can it plan in the spirit we have postulated?

It is sometimes thought that this difficulty can be surmounted by the creation of fictitious markets. The planned society is to be broken up again into semi-independent productive units, and the management of these units must, as it were, *play* at competition. They will bid against each other for factors of production, sell their products competitively, in short behave *as if* they were competitive capitalists. In this way the planned society will be realized.

There is a certain aesthetic attraction in the contemplation of a project which, setting out to eliminate the institutions of a "planless" society — the "chaos of competitive enterprise" — arrives finally at an attempt to reproduce them. Unfortunately there does not seem reason to suppose that the reproduction would be successful. The propounders of such schemes conceive of the problem in altogether too static and *simpliste* a manner. They conceive of competitive prices as springing from the demands of clearly demarcated administrative units whose continuity can be postulated without destroying the hypothesis that competitive prices are realized. But this is not the case. The conditions of demand and supply are continually changing. Tastes change. Technique changes. The availability of resources and the supply of labor and capital is in process of continual alteration. Competitive prices in the factor markets are the resultant of all this multiplicity of forces influencing the disposal of individual capital. For competition to be free the entrepreneur must be at liberty to withdraw his capital altogether from one line of production, sell his plant and his stocks, and go into other lines. He must be at liberty to break up the administrative unit. It is difficult to see how liberty of this sort, which is necessary if the market is to be the register of the varying pulls of all the changes in the data, is compatible with the requirements of a society whose *raison d'être* is ownership and control at the center. No doubt capitalism as we know it, encumbered on all sides by interventionism and state-created monopoly, and distorted by the vagaries of mismanaged money, is very far short of the accuracy of competitive adjustment. But with all its deficiencies in this respect, it seems a much more flexible mechanism than the collectivist alternatives. The path toward a completely planned economy is not a path toward, it is a path away from, the organization of production which would fulfill most completely the preferences of consumers.

In fact, of course, there is very little reason to suppose that the authorities of a planned society would resort to pseudo-competition. It is much more probable that they would fall back upon frankly authoritarian planning. They would attempt to manage production as a whole as the general staff manages an army at war. They would probably retain the price mechanism as an agency for distributing consumers' goods, supplementing it when anything went very wrong by the device of rationing, as in Russia at present. But for the rest they would dictate production from the center, choosing what kinds and qualities seemed to them most desirable. Such decisions, as we have seen, could not be based on an accounting system with any very precise meaning. The planning authorities would have no way of discovering with any accuracy whether the ends they chose were being secured with an economical use of means. In particular lines of production they could no doubt erect an apparatus which, from the technical point of view, would be very imposing. The Pharaohs did not need a price system for the erection of the pyramids. But at what sacrifice of other goods its products would be secured, at what economic, as distinct from technical efficiency,[1] it functioned, could not be ascertained. The system would require the complete regimentation of individuals considered as producers. As consumers they could choose between the commodities available. But on the choice of commodities to be produced they would have relatively little influence. They would have to take what it was decided to produce. And what it was decided to produce would be the resultant, not of the conflicting pulls of prices and costs, but of the conflicting advice of different technical experts and politicians with no objective measure to which to submit the multitudinous alternatives possible.

Is it certain that such a system would be more efficient than capitalism? Is it certain that the friends of liberty and progress who are also friends of planning have sufficiently considered the compatibility of these aims?

[1] For a more extensive discussion of the difference between the economic and the technical see my *Essay on the Nature and Significance of Economic Science*, Chapter II; also my article on "Production" in the *Encyclopaedia of the Social Sciences*, Vol. 12. It is perhaps no exaggeration to say that failure to distinguish between the technical and the economic lies at the root of nearly all the major confusions of contemporary economic discussion.

THE PERMANENT NEW DEAL[1]

Walter Lippmann[2]

I

It would be useful to know whether the many experiments of the past six years are merely a response to a passing emergency or whether they signify lasting changes in the relation between government and the economic order. A satisfactory answer to this question would not stop with a general conclusion that this is a rapidly changing world. The answer ought to carry conviction only if it identifies an important new function of government, defines it, and demonstrates the reason why there is a presumption of permanency. Burke has said that "one of the finest problems in legislation" is "to determine what the state ought to take upon itself to direct by the public wisdom, and what it ought to leave, with as little interference as possible, to individual exertion." Our inquiry is to find out, if we can, whether it has already been determined by historical circumstance that the state must henceforth direct certain affairs which hitherto have been left to private exertion.

It may be that we no longer have that perfect freedom of choice which Burke's remark implies, that a fundamental decision has already been made, and that our freedom to choose what ought to be the province of government is limited by that decision. Thus, for example, the question of American independence was a real one before 1776; it was no longer an open question after the surrender of Cornwallis. The issue of a federal government as against a loose confederation was decided when Washington was inaugurated. The right of secession ceased to be real after Appomattox. President Wilson's plan of January, 1918, to create a federal state out of the old Austro-Hungarian Empire passed into limbo when the subject nationalities revolted and declared their independence. After each of these decisive events the real issues were transformed. Must it be said that in an analogous sense we have recently passed decisively into a new relation between the government and the national economy?

[1] Reprinted from the June, 1935, issue of *The Yale Review*, copyright Yale University Press, by permission of the Editors.

[2] For biographical note, see page 73.

Obviously, a contemporary opinion of this sort will be highly vulnerable. Not all the seedlings will become trees; to attempt to say which ones will flourish, which ones will wither away, is to enter a realm where certainty is impossible. Yet the living generation can hardly defer the attempt to understand its own actions because posterity will understand them better. Posterity will know — whereas we can only predict. It will see the consequences. We can only anticipate them. It will not be biased by our interests and our ignorance and our moods. We can only attempt to discount them. The disadvantages of foresight as compared with hindsight are insuperable. Yet somehow or other we have to find a method of analysis that will discount our bias and provide a reasonably objective criterion with which to distinguish the transitory from the permanent.

It has occurred to me that by a rather extraordinary accident there has been something like a controlled scientific demonstration. Perhaps we can take advantage of it in this inquiry. The Great Depression has run nearly six years. During the first half of this period Mr. Hoover and the Republicans were in power; during the second half, Mr. Roosevelt and the Democrats. They profess to be deeply opposed. Would it not be reasonable to assume that where we find a new principle and a new function of government common to both Mr. Hoover and Mr. Roosevelt, there is a strong presumption that we are in the presence of a change due to historical forces that transcend individuals and parties and their articulate programs? It is not proof. But proof is not to be had. It is merely a presumption. Is it not a strong presumption? Is there any other criterion available which is less likely to be the rationalization of our individual preferences? Is there any which more effectively discounts partisan bias? Or any which conforms more closely to ordinary experience? When men who think differently behave alike, is it not probable that they are both responding to forces strong enough to deserve our attention?

Before we can begin to use this method of analysis we have to deal with the impression that the two Administrations are so radically different that they have nothing important in common. The partisans of both have tried to fix this opinion in the public mind. They would like us to believe that a new era began on March 4, 1933. They would have us believe that Mr. Hoover was the faithful defender of the established traditions and that Mr. Roosevelt is the revolutionary pioneer of a New Deal. Though it will outrage the supporters of both men, I must argue that this is not history but partisan mythology: that though the two Presidents have somewhat different sympathies and allegiances, though they profess somewhat different purposes, though they have somewhat different constituencies to please, though they have resorted to somewhat different devices, yet in their fundamental conceptions of the functions of government they are much nearer to one another than either is, let us say, to Calvin Coolidge or to Grover Cleveland.

I shall have to contend that if there has been anything in the nature of a sharp break with the past, the break occurred not in March, 1933, when Mr. Roosevelt was inaugurated, but in the autumn of 1929 when, with the collapse of the post-war prosperity, President Hoover assumed the responsibility for recovery. No doubt, it was inevitable that he should have done this since he had been elected on the promise of four more years of prosperity. But that does not alter the fact that the policy initiated by President Hoover in the autumn of 1929 was something utterly unprecedented in American history. The national government undertook to make the whole economic order operate prosperously. In the language of Burke, the state attempted to direct by the public wisdom a recovery in the business cycle which had hitherto been left with as little interference as possible to individual exertion. President Hoover, let us remember, did not merely seek to create an atmosphere of confidence in which private initiative could act; he intervened at every point in the national economy where he felt that something needed to be done.

For that reason, it may be said, I believe, that his historic position as a radical innovator has been greatly underestimated and that Mr. Roosevelt's pioneering has been greatly exaggerated. It was Mr. Hoover who abandoned the principles of *laissez faire* in relation to the business cycle, established the conviction that prosperity and depression can be publicly controlled by political action, and drove out of the public consciousness the old idea that depressions must be overcome by private adjustment.

Whether that was good or bad, necessary or unnecessary, does not concern us here. The point is that a radically new conception of the functions of government was established in the autumn of 1929. The subsequent course of events becomes utterly unintelligible if we accept naïvely what the partisans of Mr. Hoover and of Mr. Roosevelt say today. Only those who have forgotten the inclusive and persistent experimentation before March, 1933, can, I think, fail to see that most of President Roosevelt's recovery program is an evolution from President Hoover's program; and that there is a continuity of principle; and that both programs are derived from the unprecedented doctrine that the government is charged with responsibility for the successful operation of the economic order and the maintenance of a satisfactory standard of life for all classes in the nation. After October, 1929, that doctrine was the major premise of the Hoover Administration. It is the major premise of the Roosevelt Administration. Never, except in time of war, has it been the major premise in the policies of any other President. Did Harding in 1921 or Cleveland in 1893 or Grant in 1873 suppose that it was the President's duty to tell farmers and business men and bankers, debtors and creditors, employers and employees, governors and mayors, what to do in order to restore prosperity, or that he had a right to draw upon all the powers of government and all the resources of the nation?

Yet that is precisely what President Hoover, beginning in the autumn of 1929, took to be his duty and his right. Not until his time had any American President assumed this specific responsibility with all the expansion of the functions of government which it necessarily implies. Yet when the change occurred, there was almost no comment. Almost no one raised his voice to challenge Mr. Hoover on the ground of the individualistic tradition or of the accepted limitations of the federal power. So we have a strong presumption that the great change was generated by historic circumstances that are stronger than the ordinary opinions of men.

II

On August 11, 1932, in accepting his renomination, President Hoover declared that when "the forces of destruction" invaded the American economy and brought about "bank and business failures, demoralization of security and real property values, commodity prices, and employment . . . two courses were open. We might have done nothing. That would have been utter ruin. Instead, we met the situation with proposals to private business and the Congress of the most gigantic program of economic defense and counter-attack ever evolved in the history of the Republic."

Mr. Hoover made it perfectly plain that he had departed from the individualistic doctrine that depression must be liquidated by individual adjustment. "The function of the federal government in these times," he said, "is to *use its reserve powers* and its strength *for the protection of citizens and local governments* by support to our institutions *against forces beyond their control.*" He was insistent that this defensive and compensatory action by the government should not destroy but should on the contrary revive private and local enterprise and responsibility. But he had no doubts, theoretical or practical; indeed he proudly declared that "we have not feared boldly to adopt unprecedented measures to meet the unprecedented violence of the storm."

He then went on to describe his unprecedented measures. He had called the leaders of business and of labor and of agriculture "to meet with me and induced them, by their own initiative, to organize against panic":

(1) "To uphold wages until the cost of living was adjusted."

(2) "To spread existing employment through shortened hours."

(3) "To advance construction work, public and private, against future need."

He then described how he had mobilized the relief agencies and "when it became advisable to strengthen the states who could no longer carry the full burden of relief to distress, I held that the federal government should do so through loans to the states." He said that "in aid to unemployment we are expending some six hundred millions in federal construction and such public works as can be justified as bringing early and definite returns"; that in addition he had made "provision of one billion five hundred millions of loans to self-supporting works so that we may increase employment in productive labor."

He went on to tell how he had used government credit (1) to strengthen the capital of Federal Land Banks, (2) to lend money to farmers' coöperatives to protect farm prices and to home-owners in danger of foreclosure, (3) to set up the Reconstruction Finance Corporation "with a capital of two billions to uphold the credit structure of the nation."

He stated that "we expanded the functions and powers of the Federal Reserve Banks that they might counteract the stupendous shrinkage of credit due to fear, to hoarding, and to foreign withdrawals."

He pointed out how, parallel with his expansion of the extraordinary expenditures of the government, he was seeking to retrench on the normal expenditures and to increase taxes to balance them.

Finally, he announced that "I am today organizing the private and financial resources of the country to coöperate effectively with the vast governmental instrumentalities which we have set in motion."

When Mr. Hoover declared that "these programs" were "unparalleled in the history of depressions in our country and in any time," he had perhaps overlooked a few other countries, but his claim was quite correct when confined to the United States. His program was unparalleled. But what interests us about it is that it lays down the fundamentally new principle that it is "the function of the federal government in these times to use its reserve powers and its strength" to regulate the business cycle, and that in applying this general principle Mr. Hoover formulated a program which contains all the more specific principles of Mr. Roosevelt's recovery program.

Let us fix in mind the working principles of Mr. Hoover's recovery program:

(1) To counteract deflation by a deliberate policy of inflating the base of credit.

(2) To draw upon the government credit in order to supplement the deficiency of private credit.

(3) To reduce the normal expenses of government but to incur extraordinary expenditures covered not by taxation but by deficit financing.

(4) To expand public works in order to create employment.

(5) To have the federal government assume the ultimate responsibility for relief of destitution where local or private resources are inadequate.

(6) To reduce the hours of labor while maintaining wage rates.

(7) To peg farm prices and encourage farmers to organize to curtail production.

(8) To organize industry with a view to adopting common policies in respect to wages, hours, prices, and capital investment.

Apart from the Roosevelt measures of reform, which we shall have to examine later, all the main features of the Roosevelt program were anticipated by Mr. Hoover.

III

The only important difference between the monetary policies of the two Administrations is that Mr. Hoover attempted to regulate the internal value of the dollar whereas Mr. Roosevelt is attempting to regulate its external value as well. Mr. Hoover was just as eager as Mr. Roosevelt has been to bring about a rise in the wholesale prices of staple commodities, particularly the politically sensitive farm products and raw materials whose prices are fixed by international competition. He was just as eager to stop the general deflation and to bring about a reflation. Nor did he hesitate to use monetary measures, sometimes called "currency tinkering."

The measures he used consisted in expanding the base of credit by open-market operations in the Federal Reserve system and in lowering the discount rates. This was the policy of the President, of the

Treasury, and of his appointees on the Federal Reserve Board. It was carried out in spite of some opposition from some of the Federal Reserve Banks, and though the government's right to regulate the volume of credit was not formally avowed, as it is in Governor Eccles's banking bill, the power was, in fact, exercised.

Mr. Roosevelt has continued this policy. He has supplemented it by measures designed to regulate the international value of the dollar in terms of gold, silver, and the foreign exchanges. But the major premise, which was that the regulation of the purchasing power of money is a function of government and is not automatic, was accepted and acted upon by the Hoover Administration. However great may be the differences of opinion as to how the purchasing power of money should be regulated, however much men may disagree as to who shall exercise the power to regulate, it would therefore seem reasonable to assume that the effort to manage the purchasing power of money will continue to be a function of government.

Legally it has, of course, always been a function of government, and ever since the war we have had a managed monetary system. Neither Mr. Hoover nor Mr. Roosevelt invented a managed currency. Yet they have changed the conception of what the object of management should be. It had previously been assumed, though not with entire consistency, that the dominant purpose of management should be to keep the currency stable in terms of gold. Mr. Hoover did that though he wished at the same time to regulate the currency in terms of its purchasing power. When the value of gold changed violently between 1929 and 1933, he was caught on the horns of a dilemma. If he regulated the currency to maintain a stable gold content he had a currency which was catastrophically unstable in its purchasing power. Mr. Roosevelt resolved the difficulty in 1933 by abandoning stability in terms of gold in order to achieve control in terms of purchasing power. But in 1934 he returned to stability in terms of gold, and ever since the American price level has once more been under the disturbing influence of the instability of gold itself. The effort to manage the value of gold by manipulating the value of silver followed. It is too early to judge the experiment when this is written. Whether it fails or succeeds, whether the outcome is a new international gold standard, or bimetallism, or a second abandonment of the gold standard, is outside this discussion. The idea that it is a function of public authority to regulate the purchasing power of money is not likely to be abandoned, whatever may be the fate of the particular measures now used to regulate it.

The use of the national credit to support and to supplement local and private credit is not, strictly speaking, a radically new innovation. It was practiced during the World War and in the first post-war depression. President Hoover adopted the policy on a grand scale when he created the Reconstruction Finance Corporation and various farm credit agencies. Mr. Roosevelt has continued the policy and has extended it. A substantial part of the deficits incurred in both Administrations is due not to the expenses of government but to this banking operation. Neither President has believed that the money borrowed by the government for this banking operation should be balanced by taxes. Both have acted on the principle that this banking operation should be supported by deficit financing. It is reasonable to suppose that this principle will become orthodox and that in future emergencies government borrowing will be resorted to when private credit is deficient.

The questionable element of the Roosevelt budgetary program is in that part of the deficit which is being deliberately incurred in irre-coverable expenditures — for relief and for public works that are not "self-liquidating." Mr. Hoover had deficits of this sort. But he had a bad conscience about them, whereas Mr. Roosevelt has seemed to look upon them as preferable in principle to the deflationary effect of greatly increased taxes or of drastic retrenchment. But while Mr. Hoover was not in favor of deficits to finance public works, he was, of course, an early and conspicuous promoter of the idea that government enterprises should be expanded when private enterprises contract. He formulated the principle during the depression of 1921, acted upon it in 1930, and pointed to it with pride in 1932. Mr. Hoover believed in the principle of "pump-priming." In actual fact, he financed his pump-priming with deficits just as Mr. Roosevelt has done. In theory, he would presumably have preferred to finance them by taxes in order to keep the budget in balance, and presumably he would today prefer to give up the pump-priming in order to balance the budget.

In their relations to agriculture and to industry there is no sharp break between the two Administrations. Both have recognized that the agricultural staples have unsheltered prices whereas most manufac-tured goods have sheltered prices, and that this produces a disparity which it is a function of government to correct. The superior position of industry lies in the fact that it can benefit by the tariff, that much of it is under a centralized control in which prices can be maintained by regulating the supply through curtailment of production. The agricultural staples, on the other hand, cannot without special devices take advantage of tariffs, and the farmers are the most highly individualistic and competitive of all producers. President Hoover made many attempts to remedy this disparity. He increased the tariff on farm products. He used government money in an effort to control the supply offered in the markets. He advised the farmers to curtail production, and he contemplated the government rental or purchase of marginal lands in order permanently to reduce production. The Roosevelt agricultural policy has followed those same principles. It has used government money to regulate the supply offered for sale. It has supplemented Mr. Hoover's advice to curtail production by levying a tax to pay farmers who follow the advice, and it is withdrawing marginal lands permanently. Both Presidents recognized that a satisfactory domestic solution of the farm problem is very unlikely; both have wanted to see a revival of foreign markets; neither was able or willing to expand agricultural exports by reducing the tariff on industrial goods.

As regards their relations to industry, if we strip the N.R.A. of its ballyhoo, of the more or less unenforceable and unenforced labor provisions, we find the trade associations (which Mr. Hoover did so much to promote as Secretary of Commerce) freed of the menace of the anti-trust laws (which Mr. Hoover as President did so little to enforce). The N.R.A. extended the principle of organization to industries and trades that had not been organized previously. It tightened up the organization all along the line. It made price-fixing and production control and marketing quotas more general, more effective, more respectable. But in embryo, in all its essential features, the substance of N.R.A. existed before the Blue Eagle was hatched. The National Industry Recovery Act was little more than the substitution of legal for companionate marriages in the realm of private monopoly.

Even the wage policy of N.R.A. was a continuation of a policy inaugurated by Mr. Hoover in the autumn of 1929 and maintained by him throughout his term. It consisted in the preservation of the rate of wages regardless of the income received by the wage-earner. Mr. Hoover threw the whole weight of his influence against reduction in the rate of wages, as Mr. Roosevelt did in 1933 and until very recent times. He believed what the labor leaders believed, what the N.R.A. economists believed, what Mr. Roosevelt in his first year believed, that the purchasing power of labor could be maintained by a high hourly rate. That the high hourly rate in the face of falling prices was a sure way to increase and perpetuate unemployment was

denied in both Administrations, though I suspect that neither Mr.
Hoover nor Mr. Roosevelt would deny it today.

In rough fashion, this covers the ground usually marked out as the
recovery program.   I do not see how one can fail to conclude that in
all essential matters of policy — monetary management, the budget,
the agricultural disparity, and industrial "stabilization" — there has
been no break in principle, and that the Roosevelt measures are a
continuous evolution of the Hoover measures.

IV

What about the reforms?   In one sense the most radical of all the
reforms are these very recovery measures themselves: the acceptance
by the government of responsibility for recovery, and the corollaries
of that — the resort to monetary management, the use of government
credit, the expansion of government enterprise, and the organization
of agriculture and of industry under government auspices for the control of production and of supply in the markets.   These mark great
changes in a political system which until 1929 was committed to the
general doctrine of *laissez faire*.

The measures which are specifically called the "reforms" are distinguished from the others by the fact that, except as a response to
the challenge of popular discontent, they were not dictated by the
emergency and might have been imposed later and in more leisurely
fashion.   But it is clear, I think, that though the reforms might have
been delayed, and though they might have been different in detail,
their essential principles are derived directly and inevitably from the
fundamental assumption of the whole period since 1929, that we have
a national economy and not a mere aggregation of individual enterprises.

The reforms extend into new fields: the regulation of private
enterprises, on the one hand, and the expansion of government enterprises, on the other.   Some of the new regulation is merely the
logical development of well-established principles.   The clearest example in this category is the legislation as to busses and trucks and
other common carriers in order to bring about parity of competitive
conditions with the railroads.   Another example in the same category
is the proposal to bring gas and electricity under more complete
regulation.   These reforms involve no new principles, and the fundamental questions they raise are not novel and are not radical.

In the present Administration we come soon, however, to regulations
which are novel and radical.   In the Securities Act and in the Stock

Exchange Act and in certain parts of the Banking Act of 1933, the orbit of public authority is enlarged.   In substance, these reforms lay down the principle that corporations financed by public subscription are publicly accountable.   They require a disclosure, particularly of the whole process of capital investment, which is intended to take from private management much of its former privacy.   The under-lying theory of the legislation is that when the ownership of corpora-tions is widely diffused, when corporations are financed out of the savings of large masses of people, it is an anomaly that those who control and manage them but do not own them should have the kind of privacy in their corporate conduct which men have in their genu-inely personal affairs and in the handling of truly personal property. The legislation in these three Acts is not socialism.   It does not substitute government ownership or government management for private ownership and management.   It lays down the rule that private management shall operate in the public view in order to make it accountable to the great mass of its owners, its creditors, its cus-tomers, and its employees.

The officers of corporations are in effect required to submit to the same standards which they would have to meet if they were public officials.   The doctrine that public office is a public trust is supple-mented by the doctrine that corporate office is a public trust.   From this doctrine there follow inevitably the prohibitions in the new laws against being on both sides of a transaction.   Just as a public official may not have a private interest in a contract with the government, so under the new laws bankers may not sell to their depositors securi-ties which they have issued; utility holding companies may not sell services at their own price to operating companies they control; it is made hard for the officers and directors of corporations to use their special knowledge for their private advantage, and they are required to disclose their private interests in the corporations they manage.

That this development of public policy is the logical consequence of the corporate form of industry seems plain.   It might have come more slowly had the public not suffered such losses after 1929, and if there has not been so many flagrant examples of the abuse of positions of trust.   But once so important a part of the property of the nation became organized in large corporations, it was only a question of when and of how they would be recognized as being public institutions in all their essential relations.

The transition to this new conception of policy might possibly have been delayed a few years had the accidents of politics brought a conservative rather than a progressive Administration into power in 1933. The impulses of reform generated in the upheaval of the 'nineties were held back for a few years by the reaction against Bryanism and the distraction of the Spanish War. They became effective about 1902 and were not exhausted until the World War introduced a new diversion of the national energy. The reforms of Theodore Roosevelt and of Woodrow Wilson brought under some regulation large areas of private enterprise: the railroads, the central banking function, the public domain and natural resources, foods and drugs. These present reforms extend to private finance, generally, and to the capital market, the underlying assumptions which were applied to railroads and central banking in the preceding era of reforms.

In addition to this extension of the regulatory functions of government, there has been an extension of government enterprise. A part of it is simply a development of the conservation movement. Reforestation, measures against soil erosion, the protection of water courses are not new in principle: it has long been recognized that there were certain kinds of capital investment which, because they could not be profitable to private enterprise, had to be undertaken collectively. Mr. Roosevelt has, however, made a departure in at least two important directions. The first is represented by the Tennessee Valley Authority; here collective enterprise has been deliberately undertaken for the purpose of making a competitive demonstration against the electric utility companies. The second is the social insurance program: here the federal government enters a field heretofore left to individual or local action.

It would be an exaggeration to say that either of these Roosevelt reforms represents a clean break with the past. No other President, it is true, ever sought to regulate electric utilities by forcing them to face the competition of government-owned utilities. But other Presidents have sought to regulate railroad rates by building canals, and President Hoover himself promoted the St. Lawrence Seaway as a competitor with the railroads. As for social insurance, while it represents a new function of the federal government, it is not a new function in state government, and Republican leaders, including Mr. Hoover, have endorsed it in principle.

We must conclude, I think, that however startling they may have seemed, however inadvisable or inexpedient it may have been to impose them at this time, the Roosevelt reforms are far less novel or radical in their implications than is the recovery program which

Mr. Hoover and Mr. Roosevelt have both followed. To regulate large corporations and high finance, to extend government enterprise into fields unoccupied by private enterprise, to use government enterprise as a threat to compel private monopoly to reduce its rates, to insure the weaker members of the community by collective action — none of these things is new in principle. They are all the continuation of a movement in American politics which goes back at least fifty years, and there is little if anything in the New Deal reforms which was not implicit in the New Nationalism of Theodore Roosevelt or the New Freedom of Woodrow Wilson.

The recovery program, on the other hand, is new and is radical. For here we have an assumption of responsibility for the operation of the whole national economy and the conviction that all the reserve power of government and all the resources it can command may and must be used to defend the standard of life of the people "against forces beyond their control."

This represents a far more radical change in the conception of government in America than is to be found in any of the reforms. For if it is now the responsibility of the government to protect the people against the consequences of depression, then inevitably the government must regulate the prosperity which precedes depression and produces it. If government is responsible for the downward phase of the business cycle, it has a responsibility in the whole business cycle. If it is fitting and necessary to manage the currency, the national credit, budgetary expenditures, and the like to counteract deflation, then it is fitting and necessary that they may be managed to counteract inflation.

It would seem that the decision which Mr. Hoover took in the autumn of 1929 is irreversible: he committed the government to the new function of using all its powers to regulate the business cycle. With this precedent established it is almost inconceivable that any of his successors should in another depression refuse to act. The knowledge that the government will have to act to offset depression compels it to act to prevent depression. Because Mr. Hoover and Mr. Roosevelt have regulated a slump, their successors will also have to regulate a boom. The business cycle has been placed within the orbit of government, and for *laissez faire* and individual adjustment and liquidation there has been substituted conscious management by the political state.

It is perhaps possible to go further and indicate why it is that this very great new duty has been imposed upon the state. The recovery

program since 1929 has rested on the basic assumption that the
"fixed costs" in a modern economy are rigid: that debts, contracts,
wage rates, taxes cannot be reduced quickly or easily or sufficiently
to liquidate the depression.   Part of the recovery program under both
Mr. Hoover and Mr. Roosevelt has in fact been a defense of rigid wage
rates and debts.   The classic remedy, the only remedy known to
laissez faire, is therefore impracticable.   But if "fixed costs" are
rigid, then flexibility must develop somewhere else in the economy
if there is not to be complete paralysis followed by a social collapse.
The flexibility to compensate for the rigidity of "fixed costs" has been
found in the currency, in the national budget, and in public expenditure.

Unless one is to suppose that the proportion of fixed debt in the
modern economy will be drastically reduced, that long-term contracts
and rentals will become easily amended, that salaries, wages, and
pensions will become easily adjustable, we may take it as certain that
we shall not return to *laissez faire* in the business cycle.   If we do not
return to it, then the management of money and the use of the
national credit to expand and to contract government expenditures
must be regarded as permanently new functions of the American
government.

No one will imagine that I am saying that the particular devices
employed by Mr. Hoover or Mr. Roosevelt were well conceived or
effectively administered.   To judge them, they would have to be
examined on their merits.   But I am saying that when we examine
them, we are compelled to judge them on the presumption that, because our economy has become too rigid to readjust itself by individual
action, it will henceforth be a normal function of government to
attempt to regulate the business cycle.   We have come on to a new
plateau from which it is not likely that we shall easily descend.   On
this plateau the issues of the near future will be fought out, and there
it will be determined whether a system of private enterprise, which
has lost much of its power to adjust itself, can be preserved in working
equilibrium by the compensatory action of the state.

III

THE CHANGING SOCIAL WORLD

A HUNDRED writers have pointed out that, thanks to the achievements of science and invention, mankind now possesses the means to furnish ample security, leisure, and comfort to the people of the Western nations. For countless centuries men labored to solve the problem of producing enough food, fuel, and clothing to save them from want; now that problem is more than solved, and the new task is to find means of distributing the wares that technology could easily make superabundant. The contrast between the existing state of society, harassed by war, poverty, and a hundred other ills, and the peaceful and abundant state that ought now to be obtainable, sharpens the pens which castigate our social order and which present plans for altering it. Social criticism has never been more abundant, social Utopias have never been presented more alluringly. There are those who look back to the "happy" Middle Ages, like Belloc and Chesterton, and those who look forward many centuries, like Wells. There are men who live in the practical everyday Western world, like Charles A. Beard, and are intent simply on the next practical steps here; while we have prophets of the ideal, like Bertrand Russell, and philosophers like G. Lowes Dickinson, who contrast the serenity of Oriental civilization with the sick hurry of Western civilization. Some men, believers in equality, would trust for movement forward to the masses, while others, believing in inequality, trust for progress to an aristocracy of leaders. The debate between the two is presented in this section by Harold J. Laski and Aldous Huxley. Finally, there are the individualists, represented here by the Canadian administrator Dr. Oscar D. Skelton, and the socialists, represented by the British writer G. D. H. Cole. But for limitations of space it would be possible to present other important points of view; for society is changing fast, will change faster, and the pattern of its transformation will be the subject of fierce contention.

WHITHER MANKIND?[1]

Charles A. Beard

CHARLES A. BEARD, born at Knightstown, Indiana, in 1874, studied at De Pauw, Cornell, Oxford, and Columbia Universities, taking his doctorate at the last-named in 1904. From 1907 to 1917 he taught politics in Columbia University, resigning because his views on issues growing out of the World War clashed with those of President Butler. He was then director for five years of the Training School for Public Service in New York. He went to Japan in 1922 to direct the Institute for Municipal Research in Tokyo, and next year was adviser to Viscount Goto, Japanese Minister for Home Affairs, after the great earthquake. Thereafter he devoted himself to writing and to activity in the affairs of civic and learned organizations, varied by attention to a large dairy farm at New Milford, Connecticut.

Dr. Beard's original interest lay in European and especially English history, and he collaborated with James Harvey Robinson in widely used textbooks upon the development of modern Europe. But as he taught American politics at Columbia, he soon turned to the political history of the United States and the forces governing it. He developed the thesis that political thought and action are swayed primarily by the economic interest of parties, and not by sentiment or by abstract theory. He first illustrated his ideas upon this subject by three notable works upon the formative elements of the American nation and American parties: *The Supreme Court and the Constitution* (1912); *The Economic Interpretation of the Constitution* (1913); and *The Economic Origins of Jeffersonian Democracy* (1915). His special doctrine of the economic interpretation of American history, while somewhat overstated, was in general well buttressed by research, and has been highly influential upon subsequent historical writing. Of the three books the second was the most important. It has since been generally accepted that the American Constitution was the work of those whose property would be enhanced in value by its creation, and served the interests of security-holders and mercantile groups; how direct or conscious was the operation of selfish motives is another matter. Dr. Beard's most important work since has been *The Rise of American Civilization* (1927), written in collaboration with his wife, Mary Ritter Beard. This two-volume history of the American people, which in spirit owes something to John Richard Green, gives emphasis to ideas and interpretation rather than fact, and is marked throughout by originality of view; but it also shows not a little independent research. It is easily the best survey of American history available in such compass. Among Dr. Beard's other books should also be mentioned his *Economic Basis of Politics* (1922), and his two volumes on America's economic and political position in the world, *The Idea of National Interest* (1933) and *The Open Door at Home* (1935).

[1] From *Whither Mankind?* by Charles A. Beard. Reprinted by permission of Longmans, Green and Company, publishers.

165

I

What is called Western or modern civilization by way of contrast with the civilization of the Orient or mediaeval times is at bottom a civilization that rests upon machinery and science as distinguished from one founded on agriculture or handicraft commerce. It is in reality a technological civilization. It is only about two hundred years old, and, far from shrinking in its influence, is steadily extending its area into agriculture as well as handicrafts. If the records of patent offices, the statistics of production, and the reports of laboratories furnish evidence worthy of credence, technological civilization, instead of showing signs of contraction, threatens to overcome and transform the whole globe.

Considered with respect to its intrinsic nature, technological civilization presents certain precise characteristics. It rests fundamentally on power-driven machinery which transcends the physical limits of its human directors, multiplying indefinitely the capacity for the production of goods. Science in all its branches — physics, chemistry, biology, and psychology — is the servant and upholder of this system. The day of crude invention being almost over, continuous research in the natural sciences is absolutely necessary to the extension of the machine and its market, thus forcing continuously the creation of new goods, new processes, and new modes of life. As the money for learning comes in increasing proportions from taxes on industry and gifts by captains of capitalism, a steady growth in scientific endowments is to be expected, and the scientific curiosity thus aroused and stimulated will hardly fail to expand — and to invade all fields of thought with a technique of ever-refining subtlety. Affording the demand for the output of industry are the vast populations of the globe; hence mass production and marketing are inevitable concomitants of the machine routine.

For the present, machine civilization is associated with capitalism, under which large-scale production has risen to its present stage, but machine civilization is by no means synonymous with capitalism — that ever-changing scheme of exploitation. While the acquisitive instinct of the capitalist who builds factories and starts mass production is particularly emphasized by economists and is, no doubt, a factor of immense moment, it must not be forgotten that the acquisitive passion of the earth's multitudes for the goods, the comforts, and the securities of the classes is an equal, if not a more important, force, and in any case is likely to survive capitalism as we know it. Few choose nakedness when they can be clothed, the frosts of winter when they can be warm, or the misery of bacterial diseases when sanitation is offered to them. In fact, the ascetics and flagellants of the world belong nowhere in the main stream of civilization — and are of dubious utility and service in any civilization.

Though machine civilization has here been treated as if it were an order, it in fact differs from all others in that it is highly dynamic, containing within itself the seeds of constant reconstruction. Everywhere agricultural civilizations of the pre-machine age have changed only slowly with the fluctuations of markets, the fortunes of governments, and the vicissitudes of knowledge, keeping their basic institutions intact from century to century. Pre-machine urban civilizations have likewise retained their essential characteristics through long lapses of time. But machine civilization based on technology, science, invention, and expanding markets must of necessity change — and rapidly. The order of steam is hardly established before electricity invades it; electricity hardly gains a fair start before the internal combustion engine overtakes it. There has never been anywhere in the world any order comparable with it, and all analogies drawn from the Middle Ages, classical antiquity, and the Orient are utterly inapplicable to its potentialities, offering no revelations as to its future.

II

Granted that these essential characteristics of so-called Western civilization — namely, its mechanical and scientific foundations — are realistic, is it a mere "flash in the pan," an historical accident destined to give way to some other order based upon entirely different modes of life, lifting mankind "above the rudeness of the savage"? Now, if the term "decline" in this connection means anything concrete, it signifies the gradual or rapid abandonment of the material modes of production prevailing in any particular age and the habits and arts associated with them. Conceivably the Prussianism of the Hohenzollerns, described so well in Spengler's *Prussianism and Socialism*, may decline — is declining. It is highly probable that the petty tenure system of the French peasantry, the now sadly diluted aristocracy inherited from the eighteenth century, the church of little mysteries and miracles may decline, but these things are not the peculiar characteristics of the West. They are the remnants of the agricultural complex which the machine is everywhere steadily subduing. The real question is this: Can and will machine society "decline"?

It is generally agreed among historians that the decay of agriculture, owing to the lack of scientific management and fertilization, was one of the chief causes for the breakdown of the Roman state. Is it to be supposed that the drive of the masses of mankind for machine-made goods will fail, that large-scale production will be abandoned, that the huge literature of natural science will disappear in the same fashion as most of the literature of ancient Egypt, that the ranks of scientific men will cease in time to be recruited, that the scientific power to meet new situations will fail? An affirmative answer requires a great deal of hardihood. The scientific order is not recruited from a class, such as the patricians of ancient Rome; nor is scientific knowledge the monopoly of a caste likely to dissolve. Unless all visible signs deceive us, there is no reason for supposing that either machinery or science will disappear or even dwindle to insignificance. And they are the basis of the modern civilization.

If Western civilization does not break down from such internal causes, is there good reason for supposing that any of the races now inhabiting Asia or Africa could overcome the machine order of the West by any process, peaceful or warlike, without themselves adopting the technical apparatus of that order? No doubt, some of them are already borrowing various features of machine society, but slowly and with indifferent success. The most efficient of them, the Japanese, still rely largely upon the West for a substantial part of their mechanical outfit — for inventiveness and creative mechanical skill. Unless there is a material decline in Western technology — and no evidence of such a slump is now in sight — then it may be safely contended that none of the agricultural civilizations of Asia or Africa will ever catch up with the scientific development of the West. As things stand at present, none of them gives any promise of being able to overrun the West as the conquerors of Rome overran the provinces of that empire. Certainly there is not likely to be, in any future that we can foresee, such an equality of armaments as existed between the best of the Roman legions and the forces of their conquerors. Hence the downfall of the West through conquest may fairly be ruled out of the possibilities of the coming centuries. If, in due time, the East smashes the West on the battlefield, it will be because the East has completely taken over the technology of the West, gone it one better, and thus become Western in civilization. In that case machine civilization will not disappear but will make a geographical shift.

Defining civilization narrowly in terms of letters and art, are the probabilities of a "decline" more numerous? Here we approach a more debatable, more intangible, topic. With reference to letters, taking into account the evidence of the last fifty years, there is no sign of a decay — at all events, a decay like that which occurred between the first and the sixth century in Roman history. Indeed, there are many cautious critics who tell us that the writers of the past hundred years, with the machine system at a high pitch, may be compared in number, competence, and power without fear with the writers of any century since the appearance of the Roman grand style. Granted that we have no Horace, Shakespeare, or Goethe, we may reasonably answer that literature of their manner has little meaning for a civilization founded on a different basis. Considered in relation to their environment rather than some fictitious absolute, the best of modern writers, it may well be argued, rank with the best of the Middle Ages and antiquity. If poetry sinks in the scale and tragedy becomes comical, it may be because the mythology upon which they feed is simply foreign to the spirit of the machine age — not because there has been a dissolution of inherited mental powers. The imagination of an Einstein, a Bohr, or a Millikan may well transcend that of a Milton or a Virgil. Who is to decide?

The case of the arts is on a similar footing. For the sake of the argument, it may be conceded that the machine age has produced nothing comparable with the best of the painting, sculpture, and architecture of antiquity and the Middle Ages. What does that signify? Anything more than a decline in the arts appropriate to an agricultural and market-city era? The machine age is young. As yet it can hardly be said to have created an art of its own, although there are signs of great competence, if not genius, about us — signs of a new art appropriate to speed, mechanics, motion, railway stations, factories, office buildings, and public institutions. Using the lowest common denominator in the reckoning, there is no evidence of a decay in artistic power such as appears in the contrast between the Pantheon of Agrippa and the rude churches of Saxon England. To say that the modern age has produced no ecclesiastical architecture comparable with that of the Middle Ages is to utter a judgment as relevant to our situation as a statement that the mediaeval times can show no aqueducts or baths equal to the noblest structures of pagan Rome. It may be that the machine age will finally prove to be poor in artistic genius — a debatable point — but it can hardly be said that it has produced its typical art, from which a decline may be expected.

Passing to a more tangible subject, is it possible that machine civilization may be destroyed by internal revolutions or civil wars such as have often wrecked great states in the past? That such disturbances will probably arise in the future from time to time cannot be denied, and the recent Bolshevik Revolution in Russia is often cited as a warning to contemporary statesmen. If the revolutions of antiquity be taken as illustrations, it must be pointed out that the analogies are to be used with extreme care in all applications to the machine age. When the worst has been said about the condition of the industrial proletariat, it must be conceded that as regards material welfare, knowledge, social consideration, and political power, it is far removed from the proletariat of Rome or the slaves of a more remote antiquity. The kind of servile revolt that was so often ruinous in Greece and Rome is hardly possible in a machine civilization, even if economic distress were to pass anything yet experienced since the eighteenth century. The most radical of the modern proletariat want more of the good things of civilization — not a destruction of technology. If the example of Russia be pressed as relevant, the reply is that Russia possessed not a machine, but an agricultural civilization of the crudest sort; peasant soldiers supplied the storm troops of the November Revolution, and the Bolsheviki are straining every nerve to maintain their position by promising the peasants and urban dwellers that the benefits of a machine order will surely come. There will be upheavals in machine civilizations, no doubt, and occasional dictatorships like that in the United States between 1861 and 1865, but the triumph of a party dedicated to a deliberate return to pre-machine agriculture with its low standards of life, its diseases, and its illiteracy is beyond the imagination.

Finally, we must face the assertion that wars among the various nations of machine civilization may destroy the whole order. Probably terrible wars will arise and prove costly in blood and treasure, but it is a strain upon the speculative faculties to conceive of any conflict that could destroy the population and mechanical equipment of the Western world so extensively that human vitality and science could not restore economic prosperity and even improve upon the previous order. According to J. S. Mill, the whole mechanical outfit of a capitalistic country can be reproduced in about ten years. Hence the prospect of repeated and costly wars in the future need not lead us to the pessimistic view that suicide is to be the fate of machine civilization. We may admit the reality of the perils ahead without adopting the counsel of despair. If Europe and America were absolutely devastated, Japan with her present equipment in libraries, laboratories, and technology could begin the work of occupying the vacant areas, using the machine process in the operation.

For the reasons thus adduced it may be inferred: that modern civilization founded on science and the machine will not decline after the fashion of older agricultural civilizations; that analogies drawn from ages previous to technology are inapplicable; that according to signs on every hand technology promises to extend its area and intensify its characteristics; that it will afford the substance with which all who expect to lead and teach in the future must reckon.

III

Such appears to be the promise of the long future, if not the grand destiny of what we call modern civilization — the flexible framework in which the human spirit must operate during the coming centuries. Yet this view by no means precludes the idea that the machine system, as tested by its present results, presents shocking evils and indeed terrible menaces to the noblest faculties of the human race. By the use of material standards for measuring achievement, it is in danger of developing a kind of ignorant complacency that would make Phidias, Sophocles, Horace, St. Augustine, Dante, Michelangelo, Shakespeare, Lord Bacon, Newton, Goethe, Ruskin, and Emerson appear to be mere trifling parasites as compared with Lord Beaverbrook, Hugo Stinnes, John Pierpont Morgan, and Henry Ford. To deny the peril that lies in any such numerical morality would be a work of supererogation. More perilous still is the concentration on the production of goods that will sell quickly at the best price the traffic will bear and fall to pieces quickly — mass production of cheap goods — rather than concentration on the manufacture and exchange of commodities with the finest intrinsic values capable of indefinite endurance. What the creed of "give as little as you can for as much as you can get" will do to the common honesty of mankind, if followed blindly for centuries, can readily be imagined. Finally, it must be admitted that the dedication of the engines of state, supported by a passionate and uninformed chauvinism, to the promotion and sale of machine-made goods is creating zones of international rivalry likely to flame up in wars more vast and destructive than any yet witnessed.

To consider for the moment merely the domestic aspects of the question, the machine civilization is particularly open to attack from three sides.

On aesthetic grounds, it has been assailed for nearly a hundred years, England, the classical home of the industrial revolution, being naturally enough the mother of the severest critics — Ruskin, Carlyle, Kingsley, and Matthew Arnold. The chief article in their indictment, perhaps, is the contention that men who work with machinery are not creative, joyous, or free, but are slaves to the monotonous routine of the inexorable wheel. In a sense it is true that, in the pre-machine age, each craftsman had a certain leeway in shaping his materials with his tools and that many a common artisan produced articles of great beauty.

Yet the point can be easily overworked. Doubtless the vast majority of mediaeval artisans merely followed designs made by master workmen. This is certainly true of artisans in the Orient today. With respect to the mass of mankind, it is safe to assume that the level of monotony on which labor is conducted under the machine régime is by and large not lower but higher than in the handicraft, servile, or slave systems of the past. Let anyone who has doubts on this matter compare the life of laborers on the latifundia of Rome or in the cities of modern China with that of the workers in by far the major portion of machine industries. Those who are prepared to sacrifice the standard of living for the millions to provide conditions presumably favorable to the creative arts must assume a responsibility of the first magnitude.

Indeed, it is not certain, so primitive as yet are the beginnings of machine civilization, that there can be no substitute for the handicrafts as aesthetic stimulants, assuming that mechanical industry is not favorable to the creative life. The machine régime does not do away with the necessity for designing or reduce the opportunities for the practice of that craft: it transfers the operation from the shop to the laboratory; and it remains to be seen whether great aesthetic powers will not flourish after the first storm of capitalism has passed. In any case, it must be admitted that the "cheap and nasty" character of machine-made goods, so marked everywhere, may really be due to the profit-making lust and the desire of the multitude to have imitations of the gewgaws loved by the patricians, not to the inherent nature of machine industry. Possibly what is lost in the merits of individual objects of beauty may be more than offset by city and community planning, realizing new types of aesthetic ideals on a vast, democratic basis. Certainly the worst of the aesthetic offenses created by the machine — the hideous factory town — can be avoided by intelligent coöperative action, as the garden-city movement faintly foreshadows. In a hundred years the coal-consuming engine may be as obsolete as the Dodo, and the Birminghams, Pittsburghs, and

Essens of the modern world live only in the records of the historians. However this may be, the aesthetes of the future will have to work within the limitations and opportunities created by science and the machine, directed, it may be hoped, by a more intelligent economy and nobler concepts of human values.

Frequently affiliated with aesthetic criticism of the machine and science is the religious attack. With endless reiteration, the charge is made that industrial civilization is materialistic. In reply, the scornful might say, "Well, what of it?" But the issue deserves consideration on its merits, in spite of its illusive nature. As generally used, the term "materialistic" has some of the qualities of moonshine; it is difficult to grasp. It is the fashion of certain Catholic writers to call Protestantism materialistic, on account of its emphasis on thrift and business enterprise — a fashion which some radicals have adopted: Max Weber in Germany and R. H. Tawney in England, for example. With something akin to the same discrimination, Oswald Spengler calls all England materialistic, governed by pecuniary standards — as contrasted with old Prussia where "duty," "honor," and "simple piety" reigned supreme. More recently, André Siegfried, following a hundred English critics, with Matthew Arnold in the lead, has found materialism to be one of the chief characteristics of the United States, as contrasted with the richer and older civilizations of Europe, particularly France. And Gandhi consigns every one of them — England, Prussia, France, and America — to the same bottomless pit of industrial materialism. When all this verbiage is sifted, it usually means that the charge arises from emotions that have little or no relation to religion or philosophy — from the quarrels of races, sects, and nations.

If religion is taken in a crude, anthropomorphic sense, filling the universe with gods, spirits, and miraculous feats, then beyond question the machine and science are the foes of religion. If it is materialistic to disclose the influence of technology and environment in general upon humanity, then perhaps the machine and science are materialistic. But it is one of the ironies of history that science has shown the shallowness of the old battle between materialist and spiritist and through the mouths of physicists has confessed that it does not know what matter and force are. Matter is motion; motion is matter; both elude us, we are told. Doubtless science does make short shrift of a thousand little mysteries once deemed as essential to Christianity as were the thousand minor gods to the religion of old Japan, but for these little mysteries it has substituted a higher and sublimer mystery.

To descend to the concrete, is the prevention of disease by sanitation more materialistic than curing it by touching saints' bones? Is feeding the multitude by mass production more materialistic than feeding it by a miracle? Is the elimination of famines by a better distribution of goods more materialistic than prevention by the placation of the rain gods? At any rate, it is not likely that science and machinery will be abandoned because the theologian (who seldom refuses to partake of their benefits) wrings his hands and cries out against materialism. After all, how can he consistently maintain that Omnipotent God ruled the world wisely and well until the dawn of the modern age and abandoned it to the Evil One because Henry VIII or Martin Luther quarreled with the Pope and James Watt invented the steam engine?

Arising, perhaps, from the same emotional source as aesthetic and religious criticism is the attack on the machine civilization as lacking in humanitarianism. Without commenting on man's inhumanity to man as an essential characteristic of the race, we may fairly ask on what grounds can anyone argue that the masses were more humanely treated in the agricultural civilization of antiquity or the Middle Ages than in the machine order of modern times. Tested by the mildness of its laws (brutal as many of them are), by its institutions of care and benevolence, by its death rate (that telltale measurement of human welfare), by its standards of life, and by every conceivable measure of human values, machine civilization, even in its present primitive stage, need fear no comparison with any other order on the score of general well-being.

Under the machine and science, the love of beauty, the sense of mystery, and the motive of compassion — sources of aesthetics, religion, and humanism — are not destroyed. They remain essential parts of our nature. But the conditions under which they must operate, the channels they must take, the potentialities of their action are all changed. These ancient forces will become powerful in the modern age just in the proportion that men and women accept the inevitability of science and the machine, understand the nature of the civilization in which they must work, and turn their faces resolutely to the future.

WHAT MAKES A SOCIAL SYSTEM GOOD OR BAD?[1]

Bertrand and Dora Russell

BERTRAND RUSSELL was born at Trelleck, England, in 1872, a grandson of the statesman Lord John Russell. He was educated at Cambridge; and after a brief experience in the British foreign service, devoted himself to thinking, studying, and writing, with occasional periods of political activity. When the World War began he opposed conscription, was fined £100 as author of a pamphlet describing an early Christian conscientious objector, and lost part of his library when it was seized to pay the fine. Later, in 1918, he was sentenced to six months in jail for an article attacking the war, and wrote one of his best books, *Introduction to Mathematical Philosophy*, in prison. After the war he lectured at Peking University, almost dying of pneumonia during his stay in the Orient. Upon his return to England, he made a simple livelihood by journalism and public speaking. He has also lectured repeatedly in the United States. In 1927 he founded with his wife a school for young children. He has since become Earl Russell.

Earl Russell has told us that he began life both with a passionate interest in mathematics and science, and a passionate desire to be of some public use. Finding that he had a pronounced talent for mathematics but no ability whatever in science, he dropped the latter; but he quickly found a substitute interest. He had always possessed an intense skepticism. At the age of fifteen, he states, "I wrote in my diary that no fact seemed indubitable except consciousness." He therefore turned to philosophy in order to discover whether any certain knowledge exists. He devoted himself to mathematics, logic, and philosophy; and collaborating with Alfred N. Whitehead, he completed in 1911–1913 his great work *Principia Mathematica*. He was as skeptical of knowledge as ever; nothing in mathematics, logic, or the external world seemed to him certain. But he and Dr. Whitehead had discovered a new branch of mathematics, had invented a new method of philosophy, and had offered a detailed demonstration of their thesis that mathematics and formal logic are strictly identical. Already his interests had begun to expand, for he had written on German socialism and campaigned for woman's suffrage.

The World War experiences described above naturally awoke him to vigorous activity as a publicist. Unable to accept the myths about the conflict which all governments disseminated, profoundly alarmed by the discovery that civilization had the power to generate forces which might accomplish its own destruction, he dropped abstract pursuits and attempted to do his part in educating men to build a pacific society. His volume of 1915, *Why Men Fight*, was an analysis of what he conceived the true principles of social reconstruction. Since the war, while traveling, lecturing, and studying the civilizations of Soviet Russia, China, the United States, and Europe, he has hammered out in detail his view of the future of mankind — lucidly expressed in *Proposed Roads to Freedom*, *Education and the Good Life*, and *The Prospects of Industrial Civilization*. He believes in combining in-

[1] From *Prospects of Industrial Civilization*, by Bertrand and Dora Russell. Used by permission of D. Appleton — Century Company, Inc.

dustrialism with leisure, individual liberty, and the cultivation of art. He believes that this new civilization may easily be created if mankind will but establish three bases for it: first, a more equal distribution of goods; second, the abolition of war; third, the acceptance of a stationary or but slowly rising level of population. The essay here presented indicates the richness but hardly the scope of Earl Russell's thought, to appreciate which the three books just named should all be read.

I

Any man who desires, as I do, a fundamental change in the structure of society is forced sooner or later to ask himself the question: What is it that makes one social system seem to him good and another bad? This is undoubtedly very largely a matter of individual caprice. In history, for example, some prefer one epoch, some another. Some admire the polished and civilized ages, while others profess to admire the rude virtues of more barbarous times. One does not wish to think that one's political opinions result from mere fanciful preferences of this sort, yet I believe that an enormous proportion of political opinion comes, in the last analysis, from some untested, unexamined, almost unconscious love for a certain type of society actual or imagined. I think it is possible to arrive at something less subjective than such tastes and fancies, and I think the advocate of fundamental change, more obviously than anyone else, needs to find ways of judging a social system which do not embody merely his individual tastes.

Men's proximate political opinions are defended by arguments — arguments as to the effect of this course or that: such a course will lead to war; such another to economic slavery; such another to starvation. But in choosing the danger we most wish to avoid or the advantage we most wish to secure, we are almost all of us dominated by some more or less vague picture of the sort of society we should like to see existing. One man is not afraid of war because he has a picture of Homeric heroes whose fighting he finds it agreeable to contemplate. Another is not afraid of economic slavery because he thinks that he himself and his friends will be the slave-drivers rather than the slaves. Another is not afraid of starvation because he has a secret hoard and therefore believes that privation brings out the latent heroism in men. And so they differ as to the course which is best to be pursued, and the grounds of their differences remain obscure to themselves and others. Being obscure, they are suitable subjects for endless quarrels. The only way to make people's political judgments more conscious, more explicit, and therefore more scientific is to bring to the light of day the conception of an ideal society which underlies each man's opinion, and to discover, if we can, some method of comparing such ideals in respect of the universality, or otherwise, of their appeal.

I propose first of all to examine some ways of judging a social system which are common but which I believe to be erroneous, and then to suggest the ways in which I think such judgments should be formed.

Among most people at most times, the commonest way of judging is simply by inherited prejudices. Any society which is not in a state of rapid transition has customs and beliefs which have been handed down from previous generations, which are unquestioned, and which it appears utterly monstrous to go against. Such are the customs connected with religion, the family, property, and so on. The peculiar merit of the Greeks was due largely to the fact that, being a commercial and seafaring people, they came across the customs and beliefs of innumerable and widely differing nations and were thus led to a skeptical examination of the basis of all such customs, including their own. If my memory serves me, there is somewhere in Herodotus a story of a conversation between some Greeks and a barbarian tribe, in which the Greeks expressed horror of the barbarians for the practice of eating their dead; but the barbarians expressed quite equal horror of the practice of burying the dead, which to them was just as shocking as the other to the Greeks. Such experiences of intercourse with other nations diminish the hold which merely inherited beliefs have upon the man who lives in a fixed environment. In our age, this effect is produced not only by travel and commerce, but also by the changes in social custom inevitably produced by the growth of industrialism. Wherever industry is well developed and not very new, one finds that religion and the family, which are the twin props of every merely traditional social structure, lose their hold over men's minds. Consequently the force of tradition is less in the present age than it has ever been before. Nevertheless, it is even now as great probably as all other forces combined. Take, for example, the belief in the sacredness of private property — a belief bound up originally with the patriarchal family, the right which a man was supposed to have to the produce of his own labor, and the right which he was able to extort to what he had conquered by the sword. In spite of the antiquity and diminishing strength of these ancient grounds of belief in private property, and in spite of the fact that no new grounds are suggested, the enormous majority of mankind have a deep and unquestioning belief in its sacredness, due largely to the taboo effect of the words "Thou shalt not steal." It is clear that private property *private property system prevents fair distribution & products of society's labor.*

is an inheritance from the pre-industrial era when an individual man or family could make an individual product. In an industrial system a man never makes the whole of anything, but makes the thousandth part of a million things. Under these circumstances, it is totally absurd to say that a man has a right to the produce of his own labor. Consider a porter on a railway whose business it is to shunt goods trains: what proportion of the goods carried can be said to represent the produce of his labor? The question is wholly insoluble. Therefore it is impossible to secure social justice by saying that each man shall have what he himself produces. Early socialists in the days before Marx were apt to suggest this as a cure for the injustices of capitalism, but their suggestions were both utopian and retrograde, since they were incompatible with large-scale industry. It is therefore evident that the injustice of capitalism cannot be cured so long as the sacredness of private property is recognized. The Bolsheviks have seen this and have therefore confiscated all private capital for the use of the state. It is because they have challenged men's belief in the sacredness of private property that the outcry against them has been so great. Even among professing socialists there are many who feel a thrill of horror at the thought of turning rich men out of their mansions in order to make room for overcrowded proletarians. Such instinctive feelings are difficult to overcome by mere reason. The few men who do so, like the leading Bolsheviks, have to face the hostility of the world. But by the actual creation of a social order which does not respect merely traditional prejudices, more is done to destroy such prejudices in ordinary minds than can be done by a century of theoretical propaganda. I believe it will appear, when time enables men to see things in due proportion, that the chief service of the Bolsheviks lies in their practical challenge to the belief in private property, a belief existing by no means only among the rich, and forming at the present time an obstacle to fundamental progress — so great an obstacle that only its destruction will make a better world possible.

Another thing which affects people's instinctive judgment of a social system, whether actual or imagined, is whether it would provide a career for the sort of person they think they are. One cannot imagine that Napoleon, even in youth, could have been very enthusiastic about dreams of universal peace, or that captains of industry would be attracted by Samuel Butler's *Erewhon*, where all machines were illegal. Similarly, the artist will not enjoy the thought of a society where no man is allowed to paint unless his pictures are pleasing to the town council. And on this ground many artists are opponents of socialism. Men of science struggled against the system which existed in the seventeenth century and compelled them to teach nothing contradictory to revealed religion; and in like manner intellectuals in Russia object to having to teach their subjects from a Marxian point of view. People who find a pleasure in ordering others about (and this includes most of the energetic people in the world) will not like anarchism, where every man can do as he pleases. They will be in rebellion against existing authority unless they are part of it, but will wish to replace it by their own authority, not to abolish it, because in a world where every man could do as he pleases executive people would find no career. On the other hand, easy-going people will hate strenuous systems. They will oppose the setting up of drill and severe educational methods. During the war, they called such things "Prussianism." If they were better informed about Russia, they would now call them "Bolshevism." I confess to a temperamental sympathy with this point of view, and my sympathy was confirmed by what I saw of China, the most easy-going country left in the world. But this is not an easy-going age, nor one in which such temperamental preferences can be allowed to weigh. It is an age in which we have to think less of the present than of the future, less of the lives of our own generation than of the lives they are preparing for the generations to come.

Another thing which influences people, more or less unconsciously, in their judgment as to a suggested social system, is the question whether the activities involved in the creating of it would be agreeable to them. I fear that revolutionaries are not always exempt from this motive. There are certainly some in whom hatred of the possessing classes is stronger than love for the dispossessed; there are some to whom mere benevolent feeling appears to be repulsive humbug, and who derive the zeal of their revolutionary ardor mainly from the delight which they feel in the thought of punishing the bourgeoisie. Such men will, of course, always be found among the advocates of violent tactics, since without violence there is no satisfaction for their impulses. Patriotism and militarism have, in many men, a similar origin. The thought of fighting, or, more probably, the thought of setting others to fight, is delightful to them, and patriotism recommends itself to them as a creed likely to produce fighting. I do not mean that men are conscious of these impulsive sources of their beliefs, but I do mean that such impulses operate in the kind of way studied by psychoanalysis, and I believe that it is of great importance to drag the operation of these impulses into the light of day, to be aware of their operation in ourselves, and to do what we can to make others similarly aware; for an underground, unconscious force operates against reason, eludes discussion, and makes objectivity impossible while it remains undetected.

Among writers on sociology and political theorists generally, a very common way of judging the social structure is by whether it constitutes a pleasant pattern to contemplate. Many social theorists forget that a community is composed of individuals, and that whatever of good or bad it may contain must be embodied in those individuals. They think of the state as something having a good of its own, quite distinct from the good of the citizens; and what they call the good of the state is usually, unconsciously to themselves, what gives them a certain aesthetic or moral satisfaction. We know that when God created the world he saw that it was good, obviously not from the point of view of the unfortunates who have to live in it, but from a higher point of view, presumably that of aesthetic contemplation. In like manner, social theorists create worlds in their imagination which they also see to be good in spite of the fact that they would be intolerable to live in. Such worlds are neat and tidy; everybody does at each moment something which is in accordance with the central plan; they obey the will of the administrator as the universe obeys the will of God. The theorist, of course, is always in imagination himself the administrator. This kind of social theory was made popular among professors by Hegel; it was used by him to laud the Prussian state, and has been used by his academic followers to support the conservatisms of their several countries. Since the war, the Hegelian theory has been at a discount, having been supposed in some mysterious way to have inspired the invasion of Belgium; but in other forms a similar outlook remains common. Much of the belief in industrialism, particularly as applied to backward countries, is of this sort; it is intolerable to the industrially-minded to think of lazy populations sitting under banana trees, eating the fruit as it drops, and being happy in unproductive idleness. Some forms of socialism are not free from this defect: they aim rather at creating the kind of state which is pleasing to theoretical contemplation than the kind which will suit the temperaments of its citizens. A very great deal of imperialism is also of this sort; it is pleasant to see much of one's national color on the map, and it is unpleasant to see one's dominions jagged and scattered owing to the intrusion of foreign territories. The habit of judging the state as it is to contemplate, not as it is to live in, arises from giving more importance to the faint and transient sentiments of an observer (when that observer happens to be oneself) than to the vivid and continual experiences of those who have to live under the government of the state. It is certainly a very potent source of bad social theory. Whoever wishes to be a social theorist should daily remind himself of the very simple but important maxim that a state is something in which people have to live, and not merely something to be read about in books, or contemplated as we contemplate the view from a mountain-top.

II

So far we have been concerned with ways of judging a society which we believe to be mistaken. It is time to turn to those to which we can assent.

There are two elements in a good society: namely, first, the present well-being of those who compose it; and secondly, its capacity for developing into something better. These two do not, by any means, always go together. Sometimes a society in which there is little present well-being may contain within itself the seeds of something better than any previous system. Sometimes, on, the other hand, a society in which there is much diffused well-being may be unprogressive, for a time static, and ultimately decadent. It is, therefore, necessary to take account of both elements as independent ingredients of the sort of society we should wish to see existing. If the science of social dynamics were more developed and the art of prophecy less insecure, progressiveness would be a much more important quality in a society than present well-being. But politics is so far from scientific, and the social future so very uncertain, that present well-being, which is indubitable, must be allowed as much weight as an uncertain future good, although this future good, if realized, will outweigh anything merely present because of its longer extension in time. "A bird in the hand is worth two in the bush"; and this is particularly true when we are not sure there are any birds in the bush at all. Let us therefore begin with what makes the present well-being of a community.

In judging of the present well-being of a community, there are two opposite fallacies to be avoided. We may call these, respectively, the fallacy of the aristocrat and the fallacy of the outside observer. We considered a moment ago the fallacy of the outside observer. The fallacy of the aristocrat consists in judging a society by the kind of life it affords to a privileged minority. The ancient empires of Egypt and Babylonia afforded a thoroughly agreeable existence for

kings and priests and nobles, but the rest of the community were
mostly slaves or serfs, and must have had an existence composed of
unremitting toil and hardship.   Modern capitalism affords a delightful existence for the captains of industry: for them there are adventure and free initiative, luxury and the admiration of contemporaries.
But for the great mass of the workers, there is merely a certain place
in the great machine.   To that place they are confined by the need of
a livelihood, and no effective choice is open to them except the collective stopping of the whole machine by strikes or revolutions, which
involve imminent risk of starvation.   Defenders of the capitalist
régime are apt to vaunt the liberty which it grants to men of enterprise, but this is an example of the aristocratic fallacy.   In new countries, such as the United States used to be, and such as South America
still is, there may be some truth in it, and therefore in such countries
one sees capitalism at its best; but in older countries, whose resources
are developed and whose population is nearly as great as present
methods of industry can support, the supposed freedom of enterprise
exists only for a few.   The early history of railways in the United
States is full of bold piratical adventures; the railroad kings of that
period remind one of Elizabethan buccaneers.   But a railway in
modern England is a very sober affair: its capital is held largely by
innumerable maiden ladies and orphans whose funds are administered
by trustees; its directors are sleepy peers; its policy is traditional;
and it does nothing to encourage new men with bold schemes.   This
is not due, as superficial observers suppose, to a difference between the
British and American temperaments, but to a difference in their
geography and industrial antiquity.   But even taking the capitalist
case at its best, even considering America as it was forty years ago,
it was only the men of unusual enterprise and push and unscru-
pulousness who came to the top.   Such men are, by definition, the
minority, and a society which suits only them cannot be considered
satisfactory except by one who commits the aristocratic fallacy.   I
am afraid there are many socialists who commit the same fallacy;
they imagine industry developed under state control, and they visual-
ize themselves in that future millennium as part of the state control,
not as part of the ordinary workaday labor.   In a system of centralized bureaucratic state socialism, those who direct the machine will
have all the advantages at present enjoyed by the captains of industry,
with the exception of enormous wealth, which to a vigorous, executive,
and combative person is one of the smallest advantages of business
success, being valued mainly as a tangible proof of ability and power

and as a means of acquiring the respect of the herd. But it is not only the great captains of industry who will enjoy an exceptionally agreeable life under state socialism; it is also the whole army of officials. It is obvious that the man who sits in a government office, and spends his time interfering with the other people, has a pleasanter life than the man who works in a mine or stokes a liner. Yet there are many forms of socialism which would do nothing to remedy this inequality. The industrial machine as it has been developed by capitalism is full of injustices other than the inequality of wealth. Unless these other injustices are also remedied, a socialistic society may be scarcely pleasanter to the average manual worker than the existing system. This is concealed from labor politicians and from men with bureaucratic minds because they envisage themselves in the new order as leaders or officials, not as ordinary workers. Their judgment of the society they aim at creating is, in fact, vitiated by the aristocratic fallacy. It may be that the evils of the present world must be cured one by one, that inequality of wealth must be tackled first, leaving inequality of power for a later stage, and inequality in the pleasantness of labor for perhaps a still later stage. It may be that a bureaucratic centralized state socialism is the necessary first step. It is not this that I am denying. What I am denying is that such a society is good in itself, and I do not think that anyone who imagines with equal vividness the lives of all the members of the community can remain contented with an ideal which confines initiative, power, and the use of intelligence to a few.

A society which is to bring diffused well-being not only to one class or to one type of character, but as far as possible to every member of the community, must not be too systematic nor too orderly. It must not be the kind of society which a man of administrative temperament plans in his head and enforces by bayonets and the criminal law. Different individuals have different needs, and it is important to suit all needs that can be suited without damage to others. It is, of course, necessary to restrain predatory impulses. The insufficient amount of such restraint is one of the greatest evils of the world as it is. But it is at least equally disastrous to restrain creative impulses. This is the danger of what one may call tight systems. A military machine or an industrial machine treats men as all alike, with the exception of the privileged few who direct it; it has no room for other exceptions, no desire for the kind of work that would not be ordered from above, no toleration for the kind of person to whom it is difficult to become a mere cog in the machinery.

Perhaps the most important of all the qualities that a social system can possess is that it must be such as people can *believe* in. Europe during the last five centuries has advanced with quite extraordinary rapidity in all that makes what we call civilization, but step by step with this advance has gone a progressive disintegration of belief. I do not mean merely belief in religious dogma, though this also has played its part. I mean belief in all the assumptions on which the social order is based; all the sources of authority have become suspect, and all inherited institutions have ceased to command assent. The war and the Russian Revolution gave the *coup de grâce* to such beliefs as remained. At the beginning of the war, democracy was still a fighting creed, something for which men were willing to die. At the end, poor President Wilson was left its one remaining votary, proclaiming his gospel in pathetic isolation to a world which shrugged its shoulders and went about its business as if he had not spoken. It may be that some element of injustice is essential to the existence of a social order, at any rate for many ages to come. But in ages of faith men believe in the social order even when it makes them suffer, even when they are victims of what to a later age appears unmerited misfortune. Nowadays this is not the case. The only men nowadays who believe in injustice are those who profit by it, and even they in their hearts feel that their belief is not genuine but merely an embodiment of self-interest. I except from this indictment the big capitalists of America, who are more naïve, more untouched by modern thought, than any other set of men with the exception possibly of a few Central African Negroes. American business men still believe in the capitalist system, but business men elsewhere merely hope it will last their lifetime, provided they can obtain sufficient machine guns and ships to shoot down or starve those who advocate systems which, in their hearts, they know to be better. Such half-hearted belief does not bring happiness. The capitalists tried to persuade themselves that their war against Russia was a holy crusade, but in this attempt they were very unsuccessful throughout Europe. And everybody except the capitalists is unable to create in himself even a semblance of belief in the old order, the order which made the war and blockaded Russia, the order which devastated Ireland, starves Germany and Austria, imprisons or kills socialists, and, amid the tottering ruins of our old civilization, pursues the old absurd diplomatic game of haggling for territories and arming against nominally friendly nations. This old order is no longer capable of bringing happiness. It is not only its nominal victims who suffer; it is not only the defeated nations or the proletarians who find that life has lost its meaning. Even the well-to-do classes of Western Europe have no longer the sense of anything to live for. Having no purpose in life, they have plunged into a frantic pursuit of pleasure. But with every added pleasure comes added unhappiness; while the senses are gratified, the soul remains hungry — there is no inward sense of well-being, but only futility and despair.

There is only one cure for this despair, and that is a faith that a man can believe. No man can be happy unless he feels his life in some way important; so long as his life remains a futile round of pleasures or pains leading to no end, realizing no purpose that he can believe to be of value, so long it is impossible to escape despair. In most men at the present time this despair is dumb and unconscious, and, because it is unconscious, it cannot be avoided. It is like a specter always looking over a man's shoulder and whispering acid words into his ear, but never seen, never looked at face to face. Once acknowledged, once faced, this despair can be coped with, but it can be coped with only by a new belief, by something which supersedes the search for pleasure. Although it may sound old-fashioned to say so, I do not believe that a tolerable existence is possible for an individual or a society without some sense of duty.

There is only one kind of duty that the modern man can acknowledge without superstition, and that is a duty to the community. There was a time when such ideals as God, country, family, could move men. That time is past. All such ideals were used by elderly rulers throughout the war to drive the young to slaughter each other in futile carnage. Most of the young at the time believed that the war was about something important, but, now that it is nominally over, they see their mistake. Nothing good has come out of it except revolt against the system which caused it; the vices of the vanquished have been acquired by the victors, and the only new hope has come from Russia, the most defeated of all the nations in the Great War. Socialism is, I believe, the only faith which can restore happiness to the world, which can cure it of the sickness left by the war, which can give men the sense that their lives are capable of something better than pleasure and can end the despair that drives men to frivolous cruelty. The faith of the Russian communists in the new thing they are endeavoring to create is rather crude, rather ruthless, possibly rather premature, but it makes their lives happy as hardly any Western life is happy; it enables them to endure privations and dangers, and preserves throughout a kind of joy and freshness in the soul such as one does not find in the weary West. If there were no other argument for socialism, the fact that it is a creative faith which the modern man can believe would be alone enough to make it the hope of the world.

And this brings me to the second of the two characteristics which a good society must have. It must be progressive; it must lead on to something still better. Now fundamental progress seldom comes from those who fit comfortably and easily into the existing system. It is not, for example, from trust magnates that we expect the inauguration of the new era. In like manner, if we imagine socialism established, it will not be from those who administer it or from those who have least difficulty in adapting themselves to it that new growth will come. New growth will come from the creative people, the men of science, the artists, the thinkers, many of whom very probably will be critics of the new order. Under the influence of commercialism, many men have come to think that the important progress is progress in the technical methods of production, better machinery, better means of communication, and so on. This has been true, since in the past labor was not sufficiently productive to provide a good life for all. But it is true no longer, and with our existing technical knowledge, if we had a scientific socialist organization, every man could have enough without long hours of work. When once men have enough of material commodities, there is no great importance in providing them with a superfluity. It is only commercialism, the competitive struggle for markets, as reinforced by the luxury of the very rich, that has made mere quantity of goods seem so important. We have reached the point where we could organize our material resources in a way that would leave sufficiency and leisure for all. Therefore the important progress now is not in industrial production but in ideas. One might hope that under socialism the energy liberated from the production of luxuries and armaments would be employed in the pursuit of knowledge and in the beautifying of life, bringing back for the many that artistic excellence which existed in the pre-industrial era for the few. But if this is to happen, there must be freedom for the creative people, the men of science and the artists. They must not be controlled at every point by state officials, or obliged to do work at every moment which is pleasing to existing prejudices. Without freedom, the man who is ahead of his age is rendered impotent. All innovations are, to begin with, displeasing to the majority; yet without innovations no society can progress. Freedom for exceptional people, provided their work is creative and not predatory, is the most important condition of progress in any society. There is always a tendency for the administrator to think of himself as God Almighty and to imagine himself capable of judging the good or bad in every new idea. This tendency is dangerous, and would be particularly dangerous in the earlier phases of socialism, where the administrator may be expected to have more power than he has ever had before. The danger can only be met by acknowledging the importance of creative work and the fact that the best creative work often does not commend itself to contemporaries. It is not in the least necessary that the artists and men of science should be rewarded for their work, since the best of them are indifferent to rewards and do their work merely because they love it. But it is necessary that they should be free to do it and free to make it known — that, for example, a man of science should be able to print his work without having first to find favor in the eyes of officials. All this will come about of itself if socialism comes as a liberation for the many, not as a punishment for the few; if it is love for the good we are creating that inspires us, and not merely hatred for the evil we are destroying. It would be demanding the impossible to suggest that hatred should be wholly absent as a generator of energy in the time of transition, but it is important that it should not be the fundamental motive. If hatred is the fundamental motive, the régime created will be oppressive and restrictive, not only where it must be, but also in many directions where oppression and restriction must be avoided if progress is not to cease. It is a world full of hope and joy that we must seek to create, not a world mainly designed to restrain men's evil impulses. Evil impulses must be restrained, especially during the time of transition while they are still strong, but this is an incidental part of our task, not its main purpose or inspiration. The main purpose and inspiration of any reconstruction which is to make a better world must be the liberation of creative impulses, so that men may see that out of them a happier life can be built than out of the present frantic struggle to seize and hold what others desire. Socialism, once established, may so regulate the material side of existence as to enable men to take it for granted and to leave their minds free to employ their leisure in those things which make the true glory of man.

ORIENT AND OCCIDENT[1]

G. Lowes Dickinson

GOLDSWORTHY LOWES DICKINSON, son of the English artist Lowes Dickinson, was born in 1862, educated at Cambridge, and spent a long lifetime as fellow at King's College. He died August 3, 1932.

Dickinson became famous early in the century for philosophical works which were scholarly and often profound, but at the same time lucid in thought and charming in style. The important development of his ideas had begun with *The Greek View of Life*, published in 1896; he first rose to international notice in *Letters from a Chinese Official: Being an Eastern View of Western Civilization* (1901). William Jennings Bryan paid this the compliment of believing it the work of an authentic Oriental. Then in 1905-1908 came *Religion: A Criticism and a Forecast, A Modern Symposium*, and *Justice and Liberty*. Mr. Dickinson called himself a socialist. But his socialism is of a very different type from that of — say — H. G. Wells or G. D. H. Cole. Moved like them by a profound dislike of the existing social order, he looks rather to the past than to the future; to things of the spirit rather than to continued material progress. In *Justice and Liberty* he voices his indignation against modern society as "a silly, sordid muddle, grown up out of centuries of violence and perpetuated in centuries of stupidity and greed." But looking at the past, he states (in *The Greek View of Life*) that "with the Greek civilization, beauty perished from the world"; that Grecian civilization was the "fairest and happiest halting place in the secular march of men." And he makes the bland Chinese official say for him: "Your triumphs in the mechanical arts are the obverse of your failure in all that calls for spiritual insight. . . ." The views of such a man upon the Orient were certain to be sympathetic and penetrating; sent thither by the trustees of the Albert Kahn Travelling Fellowships, he made a striking brief report upon the spiritual and cultural estates of India, China, and Japan. His other works include *The International Anarchy, 1904-1914* and *Causes of International War* (1920).

As a result of a survey of the present condition of the principal countries of the Far East, I find myself face to face with one of the fundamental issues of modern civilization. The East, it is clear to me, has developed types of life having beauties and advantages which we have lost in the modern West. The great mass of the people live, as they always have lived, on the soil. They have a hard life, a life exposed to great physical disasters, a life at the mercy of nature. But also, it is a life *in* nature; and though the people may not be consciously alive to the beauties and sublimities of the natural world, I cannot doubt that they are aware of them and derive from them, if not happiness, at least a certain dignity and breadth of outlook. We ought not,

[1] From *An Essay on the Civilizations of India, China, and Japan*, by G. Lowes Dickinson. Reprinted by permission from Doubleday, Doran & Company, Inc.

on this point, to generalize from our own agricultural laborers, and infer a necessary degradation as the consequence of life on the soil. It is the peasants we have destroyed, those who lived on the land when England was "merry England," in whom we ought to seek an analogy for the life of Oriental peasants; and these, I suspect, have a solidity, a sense of the fundamental realities, and the possibility of a really religious outlook on the world which it will be hard to parallel among city dwellers.

Again, throughout all the East there has been a development of culture in some respects more important and higher than that of the modern West. Under culture I include religion, literature, and art. And I regard these, not as being, in themselves, the purpose of human life, but rather as signs that that purpose is being fulfilled; that men, having satisfied, without too much exertion and exhaustion, their material needs, are living a life of rich and fine feeling, are contemplating nature and their own lives and purposes in rituals, pictures, poems, and songs. This kind of culture the East, I think, has always had in a finer sense than the modern West.

On the other hand, for causes which it would be interesting to try to trace, the East has fallen far behind the West in what I may call the machinery of life, and in all that kind of intellectual effort and achievement on which the command of that machinery depends. The West has invented, if not science, the applied sciences; and in so doing has made the externals of life, for the well-to-do at any rate, and perhaps also, when all is said, for the poor, immensely more comfortable than they have ever been before. It has made it possible for a much greater number of people to live on a given area; but at the same time it has almost destroyed the beauty of life and the faculty of disinterested contemplation. It is not really creditable, in the West, to be anything but a man of business, in the widest sense of the term; to live in any way which cannot be shown directly or indirectly to increase the comforts and facilities of life or diminish its detriments. This, of course, is especially true of the new countries, where there are no traditions and no ancient culture; but it is becoming increasingly true in Europe too. Now I do not myself think that this attitude is merely contemptible, and convicts the West of sheer materialism. I believe that, under all this, hardly conscious of itself, is a great impulse which may fairly be called spiritual. The West is doing more than it knows it is doing; it is endeavoring to lift the general level of material life in order that there may be more leisure, more education, more capacity and opportunity for that impassioned reflection on life which is the essence of what I mean by culture. The pre-occupation of the West with material things does not really imply materialism; and it necessitates an intensity of life, a development of brain and will-power hitherto unknown in the history of the soul.

Still, the pace at which we are living, the competition of every kind, the intensity, the fatigue, the nerve strain, involve a dislocation of the moral equilibrium of life. The East lives, and has always lived, at a lower tension; but it has kept a better balance between the active and the contemplative faculties. It is in that balance that I see civilization. The West will have to recover it, and I used to think that it might learn to recover it from the East; that it might take from the East, and the East from it, what each required, and that a synthesis might result which would be more comprehensively human. My journey to the East has somewhat shaken my belief in this possibility. Civilization is a whole. Its art, its religion, its way of life, all hang together with its economic and technical development. I doubt whether a nation can pick and choose; whether, for instance, the East can say, "We will take from the West its battleships, its factories, its medical science; we will not take its social confusion, its hurry and fatigue, its ugliness, its overemphasis on activity." So, also, I doubt whether the West can say, "We will take from India its contemplative and religious spirit; but we will maintain our own pre-eminence in the material arts, our popular and democratic institutions, our science, theoretic and applied." The West may receive a stimulus from the East, it can hardly take an example; and the East, taking from the West its industrial organization, will have to take everything else.

I should look, therefore, for a redress of the balance in the West, not directly to the importation of ideals from the East, but to a re-action prompted by its own sense of its excesses on the side of activity. And on the other hand, I expect the East to follow us, whether it like it or no, into all these excesses, and to go right through, not round, all that we have been through on its way to a higher phase of civilization. In short, I believe that the renewal of art, of contempla-tion, of religion, will arise in the West of its impulse; and that the East will lose what remains of its achievement in these directions and become as "materialistic" (to use the word) as the West, before it can recover a new and genuine spiritual life.

A SACRED MOUNTAIN[1]

G. Lowes Dickinson[2]

It was midnight when the train set us down at Tai-an-fu.[3] The moon was full. We passed across fields, through deserted alleys where sleepers lay naked on the ground, under a great gate in a great wall, by halls and pavilions, by shimmering, tree-shadowed spaces, up and down steps, and into a court where cypresses grew. We set up our beds in a veranda, and woke to see leaves against the morning sky. We explored the vast temple and its monuments — iron vessels of the Tang age,[4] a great tablet of the Sungs,[5] trees said to date from before the Christian era, stones inscribed with drawings of these by the Emperor Chien Lung, hall after hall, court after court, ruinous, overgrown, and the great crumbling walls and gates and towers. Then in the afternoon we began the ascent of Tai Shan, the most sacred mountain in China, the most frequented, perhaps, in the world. There, according to tradition, legendary emperors worshiped God. Confucius climbed it six centuries before Christ, and sighed, we are told, to find his native state so small. The great Chin-shih-Huang was there in the third century B.C. Chien Lung in the eighteenth century covered it with inscriptions. And millions of humble pilgrims for thirty centuries at least have toiled up the steep and narrow way. Steep it is, for it makes no detours, but follows straight up the bed of a stream, and the greater part of the five thousand feet is ascended by stone steps. A great ladder of eighteen flights climbs the last ravine, and to see it from below, sinuously mounting the precipitous face to the great arch that leads on to the summit, is enough to daunt the most ardent walker. We at least were glad to be chaired some part of the way. A wonderful way! On the lower slopes it passes from portal to portal, from temple to temple. Meadows shaded with aspen and willow border the stream as it falls from green pool to green pool. Higher up are scattered pines. Else the rocks are bare —

[1] From *Appearances; Being Notes of Travel*, by G. Lowes Dickinson. G. Allen, publisher.

[2] For biographical note, see page 188.

[3] Tai-an-fu: a city in the Chinese province of Shantung, near Tai Shan, the sacred mountain.

[4] Tang age: the golden age of Chinese literature, under the rule of the Tang dynasty (A.D. 618–907).

[5] The Sungs: a later dynasty (A.D. 960–1126), noted for its philosophers.

bare, but very beautiful, with that significance of form which I have found everywhere in the mountains in China.

To such beauty the Chinese are peculiarly sensitive. All the way up, the rocks are carved with inscriptions recording the charm and the sanctity of the place. Some of them were written by emperors; many, especially, by Chien Lung, the great patron of art in the eighteenth century. They are models, one is told, of calligraphy as well as of literary composition. Indeed, according to Chinese standards, they could not be the one without the other. The very names of favorite spots are poems in themselves. One is "the pavilion of the phoenixes"; another "the fountain of the white cranes." A rock is called "the tower of the quickening spirit"; the gate on the summit is "the portal of the clouds." More prosaic, but not less charming, is an inscription on a rock in the plain, "the place of the three smiles," because there some mandarins, meeting to drink and converse, told three peculiarly funny stories. Is not that delightful? It seems so to me. And so peculiarly Chinese!

It was dark before we reached the summit. We put up in the temple that crowns it, dedicated to Yü Huang, the "Jade Emperor" of the Taoists;[1] and his image and those of his attendant deities watched our slumbers. But we did not sleep till we had seen the moon rise, a great orange disk, straight from the plain, and swiftly mount till she made the river, five thousand feet below, a silver streak in the dim gray levels.

Next morning, at sunrise, we saw that, north and east, range after range of lower hills stretched to the horizon, while south lay the plain, with half a hundred streams gleaming down to the river from the valleys. Full in view was the hill where, more than a thousand years ago, the great Tang poet Li-tai-po retired with five companions to drink and make verses. They are still known to tradition as the "six idlers of the bamboo grove"; and the morning sun, I half thought, still shines upon their symposium. We spent the day on the mountain; and as the hours passed by, more and more it showed itself to be a sacred place. Sacred to what god? No question is harder to answer of any sacred place, for there are as many ideas of the god as there are worshipers. There are temples here to various gods: to the mountain himself; to the Lady of the mountain, Pi-hsia-yüen, who is at once the Venus of Lucretius — "godness of procreation, gold as the clouds, blue as the sky," one inscription calls her — and the kindly mother who gives children to women and heals the little

[1] Taoists: one of the chief religious sects of China.

ones of their ailments; to the Great Bear; to the Green Emperor, who clothes the trees with leaves; to the Cloud-compeller; to many others. And in all this, is there no room for God? It is a poor imagination that would think so. When men worship the mountain, do they worship a rock, or the spirit of the place, or the spirit that has no place? It is the latter, we may be sure, that some men adored, standing at sunrise on this spot. And the Jade Emperor — is he a mere idol? In the temple where we slept were three inscriptions set up by the Emperor Chien Lung. They run as follows:

Without labor, O Lord, Thou bringest forth the greatest things.
Thou leadest Thy company of spirits to guard the whole world.
In the company of Thy spirits Thou art wise as a mighty Lord to achieve
    great works.

These might be sentences from the Psalms; they are as religious as anything Hebraic. And if it be retorted that the mass of the worshipers on Tai Shan are superstitious, so are, and always have been, the mass of worshipers anywhere. Those who rise to religion in any country are few. India, I suspect, is the great exception. But I do not know that they are fewer in China than elsewhere. For that form of religion, indeed, which consists in the worship of natural beauty and what lies behind it — for the religion of a Wordsworth — they seem to be preëminently gifted. The cult of this mountain, and of the many others like it in China, the choice of sites for temples and monasteries, the inscriptions, the little pavilions set up where the view is loveliest — all go to prove this. In England we have lovelier hills, perhaps, than any in China. But where is our sacred mountain? Where, in all the country, that charming mythology which once in Greece and Italy, as now in China, was the outward expression of the love of nature?

    Great God, I'd rather be
    A pagan suckled in a creed outworn;
    So might I, standing on this pleasant lea,
    Have glimpses that would make me less forlorn.

That passionate cry of a poet born into a naked world would never have been wrung from him had he been born in China.

    And that leads me to one closing reflection. When lovers of China — "pro-Chinese," as they are contemptuously called in the East — assert that China is more civilized than the modern West, even the candid Westerner, who is imperfectly acquainted with the facts, is apt to suspect insincere paradox. Perhaps these few notes on Tai Shan may help to make the matter clearer. A people that can so consecrate a place of natural beauty is a people of fine feeling for the essential values of life. That they should also be dirty, disorganized, corrupt, incompetent, even if it were true — and it is far from being true in any unqualified sense — would be irrelevant to this issue. On a foundation of inadequate material prosperity they reared, centuries ago, the superstructure of a great culture. The West, in rebuilding its foundations, has gone far to destroy the superstructure. Western civilization, wherever it penetrates, brings with it water-taps, sewers, and police; but it brings also an ugliness, an insincerity, a vulgarity never before known to history, unless it be under the Roman Empire. It is terrible to see in China the first wave of this Western flood flinging along the coasts and rivers and railway lines its scrofulous foam of advertisements, of corrugated iron roofs, of vulgar, meaningless architectural forms. In China, as in all old civilizations I have seen, all the building of man harmonizes with and adorns nature. In the West everything now built is a blot. Many men, I know, sincerely think that this destruction of beauty is a small matter, and that only decadent aesthetes would pay any attention to it in a world so much in need of sewers and hospitals. I believe this view to be profoundly mistaken. The ugliness of the West is a symptom of disease of the soul. It implies that the end has been lost sight of in the means. In China the opposite is the case. The end is clear, though the means be inadequate. Consider what the Chinese have done to Tai Shan, and what the West will shortly do, once the stream of Western tourists begins to flow strongly. Where the Chinese have constructed a winding stairway of stone, beautiful from all points of view, Europeans or Americans will run up a funicular railway, a staring scar that will never heal. Where the Chinese have written poems in exquisite calligraphy, they will cover the rocks with advertisements. Where the Chinese have built a series of temples, each so designed and placed as to be a new beauty in the landscape, they will run up restaurants and hotels like so many scabs on the face of nature. I say with confidence that they will, because they have done it wherever there is any chance of a paying investment. Well, the Chinese need, I agree, our science, our organization, our medicine. But is it affectation to think they may have to pay too high a price for it, and to suggest that in acquiring our material advantages they may lose what we have gone near to lose, that fine and sensitive culture which is one of the forms of spiritual life? The West talks of civilizing China. Would that China could civilize the West!

A PLEA FOR EQUALITY[1]

Harold J. Laski[2]

I

At no period since the French Revolution has there been a skepticism of democracy so profound as at the present time. Its unquestioned supremacy as an ideal is gone, and there are few now so poor as to do it reverence. Some speak with contempt of the bourgeois notions it embodies; others insist upon its futile inefficiency; to others, again, democracy has broken upon the impregnable rock of scientific analysis. It is based, we are told, upon the exploded myth of equality. It is the unnatural offspring of Romanticism, the fruit of a dubious marriage between Envy and Rousseau. Its principles, it is insisted, do not survive examination. Liberty is meaningless save in terms of law; and law demands authority and subordination as conditions of its life. Equality, could it be realized, would merely level the claims of the best to the plane of mediocrity; and it would compel the able and the energetic to fit a Procrustes' bed of identity for which Nature did not create them. Fraternity, moreover, is simple folly in a world where ruthless struggle is the law of life; we cannot love our fellow men until we have won security, and in the uneasy pyramid of society there is no security save as we trample upon our neighbors. All over the world the institutional system, which to the nineteenth century was the pattern laid up in Heaven for emulation, has been challenged; and there is no way to gain a reputation so easily as by insisting that the age of enthusiasm for democratic institutions is now drawing to its close.

Yet a shrewd observer would be a little skeptical of this temper. The democratic movement is not an historic accident. It arose from intelligible causes, and it is still referable to intelligible principle. It arose as a protest against the possession of privilege by men whose supremacy was not found to be intimately connected with the well-being of society. Men discovered at long last that exclusion from privilege is exclusion from benefit. They learned that if, over any considerable period, they are governed by a section of themselves, it

[1] From *The Dangers of Obedience*, by Harold J. Laski. Reprinted by permission of Harper & Brothers, publishers.
[2] For biographical note, see page 37.

is in the interest of that section that they will be governed. Grim experience taught them that power is poisonous to its possessors; that no dynasty and no class can exclusively control the engines of power without ultimately confusing their private interest with the public well-being. They learned that interest elevates prejudice to the level of principle, and that reason is then used, not to satisfy objective need, but to justify postponement of desirable change. They found, in a word, that if popular well-being is to be the purpose of government, popular control is the essential condition of its fulfillment.

Almost a century and a half has passed since 1789, and we can begin to assess the results of that gigantic upheaval. Broadly, it may be said to have brought the middle class business man to power; and its chief consequence has been the abolition of that political privilege which was the chief obstacle to his ascent. In the Western world, at least, men can now enjoy the major political freedoms. There is universal suffrage; there is a relatively wide liberty of speech and association; there is opportunity for the humble to elevate themselves to a part in the governance of the state. The old view of government as the natural field of an hereditary aristocracy has been definitely relegated to the museum of historic antiquities; and it is certainly difficult not to feel that the scale of life today is for the average man ampler than at any previous time. Given political-mindedness, he can hope to play his little part upon the national stage. Given the sense of organization, and any will widely representative of popular desire can expect to find its place, after due effort, in the statute book. The political state is a democratic state in the important sense that it is no longer built upon a system of deliberate exclusions.

But if the political state is democratic, it cannot be said that we are members of a democratic society. The outstanding fact in the political sphere is equality. Bismarck's insistence that the best form of government is a benevolent and rational absolutism no longer commands general assent because historic experience has shown that no absolutism is ever capable of continuing either benevolent or rational. Any form of government other than the democratic suffers from the fatal defect of preventing the natural expansion of the human spirit. It thwarts the progress of civilization because it belittles men. It elevates the few at the expense of the many in terms which reason cannot justify. When the monarchy governed France, when the aristocracy governed England, those who obtained the fruits of the adventure were rarely those who toiled for its enlargement. The democratic principle had at least this major advantage: that it offered a plane where the claims of men to a share in the common good could be admitted as equal. Personality as such was dignified by its recognition as citizenship. To open to ordinary men new avenues of creative effort was not merely to raise their moral stature; it enlarged also the quality of the political state by enabling it to base its experiments on a far wider induction than at any previous time. Political democracy, as Tocqueville regretfully admitted, more securely civilized the masses than has ever been the case under alternative systems.

II

But political democracy implies only political equality; and though it is not necessary to minimize the significance of political equality, neither is it necessary to magnify it. In most states of the modern world it has not been followed by equality either in the social or in the economic spheres. And since politics, after all, is relatively a small part of life, the ambit of territory within which the continuous expansion of personality is permitted, in which, that is to say, the spirit of the individual has genuine elbowroom, remains notably small. The distribution of wealth is notoriously unequal; the distribution of educational opportunities hardly less so. The degree to which occupations in the modern world are, America apart, stereotyped from father to son is astonishing to the observer. The democratic political state has, so far, been curiously unable to alter the inequalities of the social fabric. The result everywhere is grave dissatisfaction, a sense that political institutions are less capable of themselves effecting basic social change than merely of recording in legislation changes that have been effected by revolutionary means. The nineteenth century preached the doctrine that the ballot box was the highroad to the realization of social good. The twentieth century seems not unlikely to urge that violence is the true midwife of radical betterment. That difference in outlook — with all the dangers it implies — is born of nothing so much as our failure to apply the idea of equality outside the merely political sphere. For without equality there cannot be liberty, and without liberty there cannot be the humanization of mankind.

Without equality, I say, there cannot be liberty. All history goes to show that interdependence. For if liberty means the continuous power of expansion in the human spirit, it is rarely present save in a society of equals. Where there are rich and poor, educated and un-educated, we find always masters and servants. To be rich is to be

powerful; to be educated is to have authority.   To live in subordination by reason of poverty or ignorance is to be like a tree in the shade
which perishes because it cannot reach the light.   Poverty and
ignorance benumb the faculties and depress the energies of men.   It
is, of course, true that there are those who by the very strength of the
conditions which suppress them are goaded to conquest of their environment.   But with ordinary men this is not the case.   On the contrary, the sense of inferiority which an unequal society inflicts upon
them deprives them of that hope which is the spur of effort.   They
remain contented with a condition in which they cannot make the
best of themselves.   The distance which separates them from the
wealthy and the cultured is so vast that they are never stimulated to
make the effort to overpass it.   They remain uncivilized because
power and consideration are objects too refined for their understanding.   They are satisfied with the crude in arts and letters, the brutal
in sensual pleasures, the material and the vulgar in objects of desire.
And because of their inferiority, they are judged incapable of advancement.   Aristocracies, whether of wealth or birth, have never understood the secret of this degradation.   In part, they have accepted it
as proof of their own superiority; and in part they have welcomed it
as a safeguard of their security.   They take the deference they are
accorded as the proof of their inherent worth; and they do not
examine into the causes of its reception.

Aristocracies, historically, have always suffered from an incapacity
for ideas.   They cannot share the wants or the instincts of the rest
of the society of which they are a part.   And they always fail, accordingly, to realize that the desire of equality is one of the most permanent
passions of mankind.   At the very birth of political science, Aristotle
had already seen that a failure to satisfy it is one of the major causes
of revolutions; it is not less so today.   For where there are wide
differences in the habits of men, there are wide differences in their
thoughts.   To think differently is to lose hold of a basis of social
unity.   A house divided against itself, the Bible says, cannot stand;
a nation divided into rich and poor is a house divided against itself.
It is only where men have an equal interest in the result of the common
effort that there is a bond of genuine fellowship between them.   A
realization of unequal interest means, inevitably, the growth of a sense
of injustice.   That sense fastens itself upon the perception of an
unequal return to effort; and an abyss is precipitated between classes
of which, in the end, revolution is always the outcome.

It appears, therefore, that the less obvious the differences between men in the gain of living, the greater the bond of fellowship between them. And in a society like our own the differences between men are intensified by the fact that they are rarely referable to rational principle. We have wealthy men and women who have never contributed a day's effort to the sum of productivity; and we have poor men and women who have never known relaxation from unremitting toil. Wealth, with us, is so often the result of accident, of corruption, of a power to satisfy demand not inherently social in character, that there is little relation between its possession and a criterion of social benefit. The economic inequalities of society, that is to say, do not so explain themselves that men can regard them as just. Those who support them as necessary are always on the defensive; and they are always occupied in searching for possible concessions to the poor whereby they can be the better preserved. Philanthropy and social legislation are the taxes the rich must pay to keep the poor in order; and instead of a stimulus to cease from poverty they act as an incentive to remain in a routine where the service performed prevents by its character the emergence of a civilized quality in the performer. Our inegalitarian system corrodes the conscience of the rich by extracting ransom from them; and it destroys the creativeness of the poor by emphasizing their inferiority in the very conference of benefit. The rich hate the process of giving, and the poor hate them because they are compelled to receive.

The system, moreover, weakens from decade to decade. It weakens because in the first place it is no longer supported by the authority of religion, and, in the second, because the growth of education is increasingly destructive of the habit of deference. Where poverty was accompanied by deep religious feeling it rarely awoke envy, either because the poor man felt in duty bound to accept the will of God, or because he had an intimate assurance of a due reward in the after life. But he has no longer the sense of being selected for salvation; and despite the development of an increasingly Corybantic Christianity, he insists more and more that his Heaven must be realized in the present life. It is necessary, moreover, continually to raise the standard of education, in part because an intelligent worker is a condition of our scale of productive effort, and in part because an educated democracy is a primary condition of social peace. Yet the first result of education among the masses is the perception that whatever inequalities may be justified by social needs, the present inequalities are incapable of justification. The more we educate, in short, the more we reveal to the multitude the inadequacy of the moral principle upon which our civilization is based. Since we have given political power to that multitude, either it will use the institutions of democracy to rectify the inadequacy or it will search for some other institutional principle whereby the rectification can be made.

III

"Our inequality," said Matthew Arnold, "materializes our upper class, vulgarizes our middle class, brutalizes our lower." It does this, moreover, in proportion to the degree of inequality that exists among us. Anyone who considers the habits of our plutocracy will see how the crass stupidity of their standards is reflected in every nook and cranny of society. The fact that they govern because they are rich means that wealth is the mark of consideration. What is held out to other classes for admiration is not elevation of mind, dignity of character, or beauty of life, but position, show, luxury, or any other mark by which riches may be displayed. There is absent, that is to say, from an admiration for this plutocracy any quality that is likely to ennoble the mind. Those who feed it merely develop in themselves the zest for ostentation, crude as it is, that they admire. By maintaining inequality, in fact, we maintain the conditions which inhibit the process of civilizing men. For where those who are held up to us for emulation are those whose only qualities are either a genius for acquisition or a capacity to preserve what someone else had acquired, there cannot be growth of spiritual stature. The religion of inequality, indeed, has not even the advantage of mysticism; it is too solid, crude, brutal for that. And, like all religions void of graciousness, it fashions its acolytes in its own image.

There is, moreover, another aspect from which our religion of inequality must be regarded. One of the first considerations in any society is the need for the equal protection of the laws. What is certain in our society is that an unequal distribution of wealth means unequal protection in the courts. The rich man can almost always secure bail; not so the poor. A fine means nothing to the rich; but it may well destroy the poor man's home, or, in default, send him to prison. The rich man has at his disposal all the resources of legal technic; the poor man, for the most part, must either take what lawyer he can get, or rely on the power of the judge to penetrate through his own stumbling inarticulateness. Nor does the difference end here. What we call embezzlement in a junior clerk becomes high finance in a millionaire. What is disorderly conduct in the East End of London becomes high spirits west of Temple Bar. What is theft in Poplar is kleptomania in Kensington. We have no conscience about the fate of Sacco and Vanzetti; but Mr. Thaw's millions enable him to escape their fate. There is, in fact, equality before the law only when there is equal wealth in the parties; and the measure of justice they will obtain is very largely a function of their balance at the bank.

Or consider, from the same angle, the consequence of inequality in the sphere of education. Even where we have conquered illiteracy, education, for the overwhelming majority, ends at fourteen years of age; which means, for most, that the necessary tools of intellectual analysis are incapable of being used. Knowledge and the power to make experience articulate become the monopoly of the few. An inability in the uneducated to state their wants leads, at its lower levels, to a wantlessness which utterly degrades the human spirit. Most men and women go through life completely ignorant of the intellectual heritage of civilization. Yet, personal relations apart, no one who has been vouchsafed companionship in the investigation of that heritage but knows it as the source of the main joy life can offer. To deprive men of access to it does not destroy the impulse of curiosity; it merely deflects into it channels from which no social good can emerge. Education is the great civilizer; and it is, above all, absence of education which provokes the brute in man. The price we pay for that absence anyone can see in Manchester or the under-world of Chicago. Above all, an inequality in this sphere is paid for by the inability of the ignorant to realize the fragility of civilization. They have a sense of angry despair or sodden disillusion; they do not know how to formulate the source either of their anger or their hopelessness. We leave them to destroy because we have not taught them how to fulfill.

There is, moreover, a psychological result of inequality upon which too much stress can hardly be laid. Inequality divides our society into men who give and men who receive orders. The second class, being deprived of initiative, is robbed of the possibility of freedom. Its members spend their lives as prisoners of an inescapable routine they have had no part in making. When their life is compared with that of their governors, whose power of self-controlled initiative is continuous and unbroken, it is obvious enough that distinctiveness of personality has there little chance of survival. And the orders received are irresponsible since, in general, they are born, not of function, but of the possession of wealth. The farm laborer, the domestic servant, the factory worker realize in a high degree that definition of

an animate tool which Aristotle insisted was the quintessence of slavery.   In the psychological sphere their experience means a continuous
inhibition of natural impulse, a want of room to experiment with
themselves, which is disastrous to the expansion of personality.
Economic equality, for them, would mean the end of government by
a narrow oligarchy of wealth whose sole purpose in life is personal
pleasure or personal gain.   We can understand the need for obedience
to a doctor, a tax collector, a policeman.   There, as we can realize,
the rules they enforce are born of principles of which they, not less
than we, are servants; and their relation to the result is a disinterested
one.   But the orders of the narrow group who own economic power
are rarely disinterested and never born of principle unless they choose
so to make them.   The result is the loss of freedom in those whom
they command because they dictate the rules of authority to ends in
which their servants cannot share.

It is partly a result of this dictation that it should be incompatible
also with freedom in the sphere of the mind.   To preserve inequality
in social life, the pattern of mental experience must be controlled for
the majority.   The press, broadly speaking, is a servile instrument of
wealthy men. . . .   Our governors may well adapt to themselves the
aphorism of Fletcher of Saltoun and say that they care not who has
the making of the nation's laws so long as they have the making of its
news.   It is difficult for any observer, however much he strive for
impartiality, to see the facts through the clouds of bias, suggestion,
and suppression with which he is confronted; and it is the deliberate
purpose of those clouds to screen from view the actual workings of a
system of which inequality is the basic principle to be defended.

In a less degree, yet still very notably, the same is true of the educational system.   It is dangerous in school and university alike to obtain
a reputation for political or economic radicalism.   The authorities
who control appointments are the nominees of the conquerors; and,
from dismissal to loss of the chance of promotion, they have at their
disposal weapons which effectively prevent any ultimate freedom of
thought in their servants.   Anyone who scrutinizes the long list of
investigations by the American Association of University Professors,
or who analyzes the history of those teachers who have affiliated
themselves to trade unions, will realize amply enough that liberty of
thought in the teaching world is, at the point where the thought
touches the existing disposition of social forces, broadly impossible
for most.   There have not, perhaps, been in England some of the
more egregious outrages which have characterized American experi-

ence; but that is because there the selection has been more carefully made and dismissal, *a priori*, has been less necessary. For in the theological realm the English record is not an honorable one; and even today, in Oxford and Cambridge, theological teaching is a jealously guarded monopoly of the Church of England. In the result, both in school and university, the picture of the system presented is bound in the overwhelming majority of the cases to be that intellectually necessary for the preservation of the existing order. Exactly as in Soviet Russia where truth means "communist" truth, with a *ne varietur* written over the halls of instruction, so, if more subtly, the actual institutions of an unequal society are presented as though they were the inescapable inevitabilities of the social order. Our educational system is used, not to train the mind as an instrument of critical inquiry, but to bend it to the services of certain presuppositions profitable to the oligarchy which lives by their results.

IV

The price we pay for this inequality is a heavy one. The masses are dehumanized. The middle class is, in general, so wrapped up in its pursuit and worship of property that it has hardly the time, and rarely the inclination, for continuous experience of spiritual values. The wealthy pass their lives in feverish search for aimless pleasures which satiate at the moment of their attainment. Social prestige and conventional respectability are not ideals likely to produce a great civilization when they are regarded as ends in themselves. Yet they are the inevitable outcome of a society which regards inequality as its first and most natural law. For what it must do to maintain them as ideals is to frown upon those who do not follow the beaten track. Our personalities must be cast into molds which satisfy the norms of this pitiful principle. Even our charities are thought of, not in terms of their objects, but of those who support them. An English social worker who desires to raise funds for his organization knows perfectly well that he can double his subscriptions if he can persuade the Prince of Wales to permit the use of his name. A theatrical performance for charity in New York in one of the great houses, with members of the Junior League as its pathetic exponents, would raise far more money than one given by the Theatre Guild. Incredible organizations like the Primrose League in England and the Daughters of the American Revolution in America live by their ministration to the instinct for snobbery in an unequal society. What are so curiously termed the great hostesses entertain Mr. Shaw and Mr. Wells, Professor Einstein, and Mr. Ramsay MacDonald, not out of interest in, or sympathy for, their ideas, but for the advertising value of their presence at a social function.

The unequal society demands a standardized and uniform outlook as the condition of its preservation. It is fatal to individuality, because individuality implies the novel and the unexpected; and these are dangerous to conventional habits. It has to impose upon its members beliefs, ideas, habits, rules which prevent that affirmation of self from which the increase of civilization flows. To offer us the type of life our acquisitive society practices is to offer us a religion which leaves unsatisfied the claims alike of knowledge, of beauty, and of manners. The claims of knowledge: for we cannot afford the truth about social or economic organization. We cannot give more than the smatterings of education to the multitude if it is to remain properly subservient to its masters. On most of the vital aspects of sex we maintain a deliberate conspiracy of silence; and the very implications of the phrase "a good marriage" are tragi-comic evidence of the way in which the ideal of sexual comradeship is perverted. The claims, also, of beauty: for these always make room — as our slums, our factories, and our egregious villadom proclaim — to the demands of property. Successful art is either art which meets a vulgar demand or that which receives temporary canonization because it pleases the powerful; and when England wants a trustee of the National Gallery, it selects, not Roger Fry, but Lord Curzon, not Laurence Binyon, but Sir Philip Sassoon. The claims, finally, of manners: at the base, it is clear enough that manners will not emerge where overcrowding makes impossible the observance of the elementary decencies of life. The middle and the apex of the pyramid have been amply described for us by Mr. Galsworthy and Proust. Manners do not mean, as our system makes them mean, the uneasy and apprehensive search to maintain one's social position which gives to New York and London, to Paris and Rome, their pathetically elaborate code of trivialities, their ludicrous formalism, their contemptible craving for the publicity of the social column. The Duc de Guermantes, who calls for his ticket at the theatre and is able to show a greater courtesy to the attendant than a nobleman of lesser rank because he has a more assured social prestige, is a real symbol of our society.

We live in terror of doing the wrong thing instead of in hope of finding the right. We lack a healthy individualism which might give us the courage to experiment with ourselves. Instead of developing a self-respect born of a satisfied and harmonious personality, we sacrifice ourselves on the Procrustes' bed of traditional conventions, each one of which thwarts impulses that are basic to our character. We are trying to have our cake and eat it — a matter of impossibility in affairs of social logic. We have given the people power in the realm of politics, and we are trying to pretend to ourselves that the equalization of authority therein implied may rightly cease at its boundaries. The pretense is folly. The whole principle of democracy is nothing less than the affirmation by the people of its own essence; and this is incompatible with irrational privilege in any sphere. The law of democracy is the attachment of prestige, not to the accident of birth or wealth, but to the performance of social function. A democracy can understand why the President of the United States is important; but sensibly enough, it resents the attachment of importance and power to a leisured aristocracy with no duties save the pursuit of pleasure. It will give its respect to great artists, poets, scientists, philosophers, but it sees no reason to revere Commodore Vanderbilt or that Duke of Norfolk upon whose marriage the London *Times* of half a century ago bestowed the incredible epithalamium of a leading article.

The democratic demand for social and economic equality is, in fact, built upon the simple insistence that without it first things cannot come first. And that simple insistence is impossible in any community where, because the rights of property are unequally distributed, all other rights are modeled in their image. That is not, it is perhaps worth while to remark, the affirmation of dangerous radicalism. Conservative philosophers like Aristotle, publicists of genius like Harrington in England and Madison in America, critics of society like Matthew Arnold, all alike have insisted that as the rights of property are, so the complexion of society will be. Make the first unequal, and all else in life for which men strive will adjust itself to those terms. If, doubtless, the distribution of property were built upon a principle of unquestionable justice so that each man received in proportion to his contribution to the common stock, it would not greatly matter that there were differences of position in society. Inequality would be a function of merit, intelligible and defensible. But this is so demonstrably not the case, that inequality everywhere is the nurse of envy and hate and corruption; and of these, everywhere as well, the outcome is revolution. So that states which seek the postponement of equality have always within themselves a festering sore which is bound to break out sooner or later. They lack the essential condition of stable government, which is a widespread sense of allegiance to the constitution as the protector of the equal rights of men.

"The surest way to prevent seditions," said Bacon, "is to take away the matter of them." Where we have a state in which no man is so rich that he can buy his neighbor and none so poor that he must sell himself, we have present the fundamental condition of security. For men who can purchase others are free only at the cost of these; and men who are driven to sell themselves turn naturally to revolution as the alternative to slavery. In an equal state we confer upon all citizens the effective hope of bettering their conditions. We elevate the quality of their effort by giving them the right to aspire. We prevent that persistent frustration of impulse which is the major consequence of inequality. The divisions of society build themselves on the actual service they perform. Upon any other basis this is not the case. Intrust, as we intrust, the governance of the state to an aristocracy, whether of wealth or birth, and it is bound, in the end, to govern badly. For it cannot escape temptation and flattery. It is unacquainted with the realities of life as these are experienced by those over whom it rules. It is driven to elevate its own sense of superiority to the position of a social axiom; and it entirely fails to observe that the axiom is in fact the narrowest of indications from the most partial of evidence, the substance of its own desires. The proof of this is simple enough. Confront any aristocracy with novelty, and it is patently incapable of its rational examination. The nobility of the *ancien régime* in France, the Romanoff dynasty in Russia, the English landowner in Ireland, the Austrian conqueror in Italy — these had before their eyes the evidence of a new and inescapable temper with which terms had to be made; and they could only equate it with original sin. Yet great agitations are not marks of popular crime; popular crime is only a mark of great agitation born of some suffering too grievous to be endured. And the root of great passions is the unchanging passion for equality.

The skeptic, of course, is horrified at a panegyric of this sort. All that we know, he argues, teaches us that men are different in taste and different in talent; to treat them as equals is to fly in the face of elementary principles of nature. But this is to mistake equality with identity. Equality does not mean that the differences of men are to be neglected; it means only that those differences are to be selected for emphasis which are deliberately relevant to the common good. It refuses to recognize the legitimacy of barriers which are born, not of the nature of things, but of accident illegitimate in its social consequence. It does not mean that the Heaven-sent painter shall be compelled to the study of advanced mathematics; but merely that the Heaven-sent painter shall not be driven to waste his talent through the absence of organized opportunity. It means a shift in the emphasis of social action from the few to the many. It implies the utilization, of set purpose, of the national resources to the elevation of quality in the ordinary man. It is built upon a belief that when the ordinary man is trained to coöperate in the government of society, his powers are quickened, his self-respect increased. He is something more than a passive spectator of the social process. His individuality becomes articulate; he contributes his little stock of experience and wisdom to the common store. The tradition he inherits is widened and quickened by his knowledge and opinion. The power of social adaptation is strengthened by the wider induction that can be made.

We need not doubt, with the skeptic, that a single individual of outstanding ability will often perform better the functions of government than the members of a democratic state. Caesar, Cromwell, Napoleon, Lenin had, doubtless, more energy, more perseverance, more capacity to plan in a wholesale way, and more art to perfect the details of their planning. But the answer to this is at least twofold. The energy, the perseverance, the capacity of the great dictators are almost always from the outset, and in the end invariably, purchased at the expense of the growth of those qualities in those over whom they rule. Democracy is not the most efficient form of government; neither is it the most capable of conceiving the greatest ideas. But a democratic government provokes in its citizens that which no other political system is able to secure. There flows from its equality in citizenship a restless energy, a pervasive vitality, more favorable to individuality than any other qualities. The knowledge there that the road lies open to power is a spur and an incentive which neither the favors of a dictatorship nor the prestige of an aristocracy can evoke. And the equalization of citizenship in the political field is itself a safe-guard of the public interest. The political leader in a democratic state may be, often enough, less able or less honorable than the leader of an aristocracy. But his tenure of power is subject always to the condition that he must, in the end, submit himself to the will of the majority. His interest is in the democratic system more securely merged with the interest of the whole than is the case in any alternative scheme. The government of an aristocracy is, at its best, always in some sort a conspiracy against the nation. The very fact that it is protecting the privileged interest of a minority tends to make it shape institutions to its own ends and to protect them against invasion for the benefit of the whole. That has been, of course, unconsciously the history of the interpretation of the American Constitution by the Supreme Court; and, still more notably and again unconsciously, the history of the interpretation of trade-union law by English judges. Minority government always narrows public policy to mean the perpetuation of its own power.

Nor, finally, must we forget the significance of the historical aspect of the problem. Englishmen, to whom equality is still a strange ideal, Americans, who rarely observe the growth of a privileged aristocracy among themselves, too often forget that the history of society is supremely the history of the abolition of differences which reason cannot explain and justice cannot excuse. That has been the case in the sphere of religion; it has been, in Western civilization, predominantly the case in politics. Everyone has read the half-dozen remarkable pages in which Tocqueville explained how the movement of French history has been the evolution of an irresistible tendency to equalization of conditions. "Those who have knowingly labored in its cause," he wrote, "and those who have served it unwittingly; those who have fought for it and those who have announced themselves its opponents; all have been driven along the same track; . . . the gradual development of equal conditions . . . possesses all the characteristics of a divine decree; it is universal; it is desirable; it constantly eludes all human interference; and all events as well as all men contribute to its progress."

Certainly it does not appear likely that a democracy which has established equality in religion and politics, which has overthrown the power of churches and kings and aristocracies, will leave untouched the economic and the social field. Yet nothing is more dangerous in social philosophy than the postulation of inevitable victories. The power of inequality is still immense, the interests it protects gigantic. To be optimistic about the prospect of its abdication is folly; to believe that it is certain of defeat is overconfidence. It is the tragedy of modern society that science has made social conflict the parent of social disaster; for the forces of democracy in this new realm to try their strength with the forces of privilege may well make the second state worse than what they seek to overthrow. We must rather have faith in the power of reason to direct the human spirit to the prospects of concession and sacrifice. We must rather seek to persuade our masters that our equality is their freedom.

THE IDEA OF EQUALITY[1]

Aldous Huxley

ALDOUS HUXLEY, whose father was a son of the great scientist and whose mother was a niece of Matthew Arnold, was born in 1894. On graduating from Oxford he spent some time in journalism as a member of the editorial staff of the *Athenaeum*, 1919–1920, and dramatic critic of the *Westminster Gazette*, 1920–1921. After publishing some excellent poetry, he began his success as a writer of prose fiction with *Crome Yellow* in 1921 and *Mortal Coils* in 1922. It may be doubted whether any novel he has thus far written (the most ambitious being *Point Counter-Point*, 1928) will long survive; but several of his short stories bid fair to become classic. In addition to fiction he has written essays, collected in *Texts and Pretexts* (1932), and travels, notably *Beyond the Mexique Bay* (1934). A satirical and unpleasant picture of the future of mankind, *O Brave New World* (1932), is not among his happiest efforts.

SUNDAY FAITH AND WEEKDAY FAITH

That all men are created equal is a proposition to which, at ordinary times, no sane human being has ever given his assent. A man who has to undergo a dangerous operation does not act on the assumption that one doctor is just as good as another. Editors do not print every contribution that reaches them. And when they require civil servants, even the most democratic governments make a careful selection among their theoretically equal subjects. At ordinary times, then, we are perfectly certain that men are not equal. But when, in a democratic country, we think or act politically, we are no less certain that men are equal. Or at any rate — which comes to the same thing in practice — we behave as though we were certain of men's equality. Similarly, the pious mediaeval nobleman who, in church, believed in forgiving enemies and turning the other cheek was ready, as soon as he had emerged again into the light of day, to draw his sword at the slightest provocation. The human mind has an almost infinite capacity for being inconsistent.

The amount of time during which men are engaged in thinking or acting politically is very small when compared with the whole period of their lives; but the brief activities of man the politician exercise a disproportionate influence on the daily life of man the worker, man at

[1] From *Proper Studies*, by Aldous Huxley, copyright 1927 by Doubleday, Doran & Company, Inc.

play, man the father and husband, man the owner of property. Hence the importance of knowing what he thinks in his political capacity and why he thinks it.

THE EQUALITARIAN AXIOM

Politicians and political philosophers have often talked about the equality of man as though it were a necessary and unavoidable idea, an idea which human beings must believe in, just as they must, from the very nature of their physical and mental constitution, believe in such notions as weight, heat, and light. Man is "by nature free, equal, and independent," says Locke, with the calm assurance of one who knows he is saying something that cannot be contradicted. It would be possible to quote literally thousands of similar pronouncements. One must be mad, says Babeuf, to deny so manifest a truth.

EQUALITY AND CHRISTIANITY

In point of historical fact, however, the notion of human equality is of recent growth, and, so far from being a directly apprehended and necessary truth, is a conclusion logically drawn from preëxisting metaphysical assumptions. In modern times the Christian doctrines of the brotherhood of men and of their equality before God have been invoked in support of political democracy. Quite illogically, however. For the brotherhood of men does not imply their equality. Families have their fools and their men of genius, their black sheep and their saints, their worldly successes and their worldly failures. A man should treat his brothers lovingly and with justice, according to the deserts of each. But the deserts of every brother are not the same. Neither does men's equality before God imply their equality as among themselves. Compared with an infinite quantity, all finite quantities may be regarded as equal. There is no difference, where infinity is concerned, between one and a thousand. But leave infinity out of the question, and a thousand is very different from one. Our world is a series of finite quantities, and where worldly matters are concerned, the fact that all men are equal in relation to the infinite quantity which is God is entirely irrelevant. The church has at all times conducted its worldly policy on the assumption that it was irrelevant. It is only recently that the theorists of democracy have appealed to Christian doctrine for a confirmation of their equalitarian principles. Christian doctrine, as I have shown, gives no such support.

EQUALITY AND THE PHILOSOPHER

The writers who in the course of the eighteenth century supplied our modern political democracy with its philosophical basis did not turn to Christianity to find the doctrine of human equality. They were, to begin with, almost without exception anticlerical writers, to whom the idea of accepting any assistance from the church would have been extremely repugnant. Moreover, the church, as organized for its worldly activities, offered them no assistance, but a frank hostility. It represented, even more clearly than the monarchical and feudal state, that mediaeval principle of hierarchical, aristocratic government against which, precisely, the equalitarians were protesting.

The origin of our modern idea of human equality is to be found in the philosophy of Aristotle. The tutor of Alexander the Great was not, it is true, a democrat. Living as he did in a slaveholding society, he regarded slavery as a necessary state of affairs. Whatever is, is right; the familiar is the reasonable; and Aristotle was an owner of slaves, not a slave himself; he had no cause to complain. In his political philosophy he rationalized his satisfaction with the existing state of things, and affirmed that some men are born to be masters (himself, it went without saying, among them) and others to be slaves. But in saying this he was committing an inconsistency. For it was a fundamental tenet of his metaphysical system that specific qualities are the same in every member of a species. Individuals of one species are the same in essence or substance. Two human beings differ from one another in matter, but are the same in essence, as being both rational animals. The essential human quality which distinguishes the species Man from all other species is identical in both.

INCONSISTENCIES

How are we to reconcile this doctrine with Aristotle's statement that some men are born to be masters and others slaves? Clearly, no reconciliation is possible; the doctrines are contradictory. Aristotle said one thing when he was discussing the abstract problems of metaphysics and another when, as a slave-owner, he was discussing politics. Such inconsistencies are extremely common, and are generally made in perfectly good faith. In cases where material interests are at stake, where social and religious traditions, inculcated in childhood, and consequently incorporated into the very structure of the mind, can exercise their influence, men will naturally think in one way; in other cases, where their interests and their early-acquired beliefs are not concerned, they will naturally and inevitably think in quite a different way. A man who thinks and behaves as an open-minded, unprejudiced scientist so long as he is repairing his automobile will be outraged if asked to think about the creation of the world or the future life except in terms of the mythology current among the barbarous Semites three thousand years ago; and though quite ready to admit that the present system of wireless telegraphy might be improved, he will regard anyone who desires to alter the existing economic and political system as either a madman or a criminal. The greatest men of genius have not been exempt from these curious inconsistencies. Newton created the science of celestial mechanics; but he was also the author of *Observations on the Prophecies of Daniel and the Apocalypse of Saint John*, of a *Lexicon Propheticum* and a *History of the Creation*. With one part of his mind he believed in the miracles and prophecies about which he had been taught in childhood; with another part he believed that the universe is a scene of order and uniformity. The two parts were impenetrably divided one from the other. The mathematical physicist never interfered with the commentator on the Apocalypse; the believer in miracles had no share in formulating the laws of gravitation. Similarly, Aristotle the slave-owner believed that some men are born to command and others to serve; Aristotle the metaphysician, thinking in the abstract, and unaffected by the social prejudices which influenced the slave-owner, expounded a doctrine of specific essences, which entailed belief in the real and substantial equality of all human beings. The opinion of the slave-owner was probably nearer the truth than that of the metaphysician. But it is by the metaphysician's doctrine that our lives are influenced today.

APPLIED METAPHYSICS

That all members of a species are identical in essence was still, in the Middle Ages, a purely metaphysical doctrine. No attempt was made to apply it practically in politics. So long as the feudal and ecclesiastical hierarchies served their purpose of government, they seemed, to all but a very few,. necessary and unquestionable. Whatever is, is right; feudalism and Catholicism *were*. It was only after what we call the Reformation and the Renaissance, when, under the stress of new economic and intellectual forces, the old system had largely broken down, that men began to think of applying the metaphysical doctrine of Aristotle and his mediaeval disciples to politics. Feudalism and ecclesiastical authority lingered on, but as the merest ghosts of themselves. They had, to all intents and purposes, ceased to be, and not being, they were wrong.

It was not necessary, however, for the political thinkers of the eighteenth century to go back directly to Aristotle and the School-men. They had what was for them a better authority nearer home. Descartes, the most influential philosopher of his age, had reaffirmed the Aristotelian and Scholastic doctrine in the most positive terms. At the beginning of his *Discourse on Method* we read that "what is called good sense or reason is equal in all men," and a little later he says, "I am disposed to believe that [reason] is to be found complete in each individual; and on this point to adopt the opinion of philoso-phers who say that the difference of greater or less holds only among the accidents, and not among the forms or natures of individuals of the same species." Descartes took not the slightest interest in politics, and was concerned only with physical science and the theory of knowl-edge. It remained for others to draw the obvious political conclusions from what was for him, as it had been for Aristotle and the Schoolmen, a purely abstract metaphysical principle. These conclusions might have been drawn at any time during the preceding two thousand years. But it was only in the two centuries immediately following Descartes's death that political circumstances in Europe, especially in France, were favorable to such conclusions being drawn. The forms of government current during classical antiquity and the Middle Ages had been efficient and well adapted to the circumstances of the times. They seemed, accordingly, right and reasonable. In the eighteenth century, on the other hand, particularly on the continent of Europe, the existing form of government was not adapted to the social circum-stances of the age. At a period when the middle classes were already rich and well educated, absolute monarchy and the ineffectual remains of feudalism were unsuitable as forms of government. Being unsuit-able, they therefore seemed utterly unreasonable and wrong. Middle class Frenchmen wanted a share in the government. But men are not content merely to desire; they like to have a logical or a pseudo-logical justification for their desires; they like to believe that when they want something, it is not merely for their own personal advantage, but that their desires are dictated by pure reason, by nature, by God Himself. The greater part of the world's philosophy and theology is merely an intellectual justification for the wishes and the daydreams of philosophers and theologians. And practically all political theories are elaborated, after the fact, to justify the interests and desires of certain individuals, classes, or nations. In the eighteenth century, middle class Frenchmen justified their very natural wish to participate in the government of the country by elaborating a new political philosophy from the metaphysical doctrine of Aristotle, the Schoolmen, and Descartes. These philosophers had taught that the specific essence is the same in all individuals of a species. In the case of *Homo Sapiens* this specific essence is reason. All men are equally reasonable. It follows that all men have an equal capacity, and therefore an equal right, to govern; there are no born slaves nor masters. Hence, monarchy and hereditary aristocracy are inadmissible. Nature herself demands that government shall be organized on democratic principles. Thus middle class Frenchmen had the satisfaction of discovering that their desires were indorsed as right and reasonable, not only by Aristotle, St. Thomas, and Descartes, but also by the Creator of the Universe in person.

MAKING THE FACTS FIT

Even metaphysicians cannot entirely ignore the obvious facts of the world in which they live. Having committed themselves to a belief in this fundamental equality of all men, the eighteenth century political philosophers had to invent an explanation for the manifest inequalities which they could not fail to observe on every side. If Jones, they argued, is an imbecile and Smith a man of genius, that is due, not to any inherent and congenital differences between the two men, but to purely external and accidental differences in their upbringing, their education, and the ways in which circumstances have compelled them to use their minds. Give Jones the right sort of training, and you can turn him into a Newton, a St. Francis, or a Caesar according to taste. "The diversity of opinions," says Descartes, "does not arise from some being endowed with a larger share of reason than others, but solely from this, that we conduct our thoughts along different ways, and do not fix our attention on the same objects." "Intelligence, genius, and virtue," says Helvétius, whose work, *De l'Esprit*, was published in 1758, and exercised an enormous contemporary influence, "are the products of education." And again (*De l'Esprit*, Discours III, Ch. 26): "*La grande inégalité d'esprit qu'on aperçoit entre les hommes dépend donc uniquement et de la différente éducation qu'ils reçoivent, et de l'enchaînement inconnu et divers dans lesquels ils se trouvent placés,*"[1] and so on.

[1] "The great inequality of intelligence which one perceives among men results, then, only from the different education which they receive and from the unknown and varied environment in which they are placed."

The political and philosophical literature of the eighteenth century teems with such notions. It was only to be expected; for such notions, it is obvious, are the necessary corollaries of the Cartesian axiom that reason is the same and entire in all men. They followed no less necessarily from the *tabula rasa* theory of mind elaborated by Locke. Both philosophers regarded men as originally and in essence equal, the one in possessing the same specific faculties and innate ideas, the other in possessing no innate ideas. It followed from either assumption that men are made or marred exclusively by environment and education. Followers whether of Locke or of Descartes, the eighteenth century philosophers were all agreed in attributing the observed inequalities of intelligence and virtue to inequalities of instruction. Men were naturally reasonable and therefore good; but they lived in the midst of vice and abject superstition. Why? Because evil-minded legislators — kings and priests — had created a social environment calculated to warp the native reason and corrupt the morals of the human race. Why priests and kings, who, as human beings, were themselves naturally reasonable and therefore virtuous, should have conspired against their fellows, or why their reasonable fellows should have allowed themselves to be put upon by these crafty corrupters, was never adequately explained. The democratic religion, like all other religions, is founded on faith as much as on reason. The king-priest theory in its wildest and most extravagant form is the inspiration and subject of much of Shelley's finest poetry. Poor Shelley, together with large numbers of his less talented predecessors and contemporaries, seems seriously to have believed that by getting rid of priests and kings you could inaugurate the golden age.[1]

THE TESTS OF EXPERIMENT

The historical and psychological researches of the past century have rendered the theory which lies behind the practice of modern democracy entirely untenable. Reason is not the same in all men; human beings belong to a variety of psychological types separated one from another by irreducible differences. Men are not the exclusive products of their environments. A century of growing democracy has shown that the reform of institutions and the spread of education are by no means necessarily followed by improvements in individual virtue and intelligence. At the same time biologists have accumulated an enormous mass of evidence tending to show that physical peculiarities

[1] For a magnificent expression of this idea, read the final speech of the Spirit of the Hour, in Act III of Shelley's *Prometheus Unbound*.

are inherited in a perfectly regular and necessary fashion. Body being indissolubly connected with mind, this evidence would almost be enough in itself to prove that mental peculiarities are similarly heritable. Direct observation on the history of families reinforces this evidence, and makes it certain that mental idiosyncrasies are inherited in exactly the same way as physical idiosyncrasies. Indeed, mind being in some sort a function of brain, a mental idiosyncrasy is also a physical one, just as much as red hair or blue eyes. Faculties are heritable: we are born more or less intelligent, more or less musical, mathematical, and so on. From this it follows that men are not essentially equal, and that human beings are at least as much the product of their heredity as of their education.

THE BEHAVIORIST REACTION

Recently, it is true, Helvétius's doctrine of the all-effectiveness of nurture and the unimportance of nature and heredity has been revived by psychologists of the Behaviorist School. Unlike the philosophers of the eighteenth century, the Behaviorists have no political axe to grind and are not metaphysicians. If they agree with Helvétius, it is not because they want the vote (they have it), nor, presumably, because they accept the authority of Aristotle, the Schoolmen, and Descartes on the one hand, or of Locke on the other. They agree with Helvétius on what they affirm to be scientific grounds. Helvétius's theory, according to the Behaviorists, is in accordance with the observed facts. Before going further, let us briefly examine their claims.

"The Behaviorist," writes Mr. J. B. Watson, the leader of the school, "no longer finds support for hereditary patterns of behavior nor for special abilities (musical, art, etc.), which are supposed to run in families. He believes that, given the relatively simple list of embryological responses which are fairly uniform in infants, he can build (granting that both internal and external environment can be controlled) any infant along any specified line — into rich man, poor man, beggar man, thief." Taken literally, this last statement is merely silly. No one was ever such a fool as to suggest that riches and poverty were heritable in the sense that a Roman nose or a talent for music may be said to be heritable. Opulent fathers have long anticipated this great discovery of the Behaviorists, and have "built their children into rich men" by placing large cheques to their account at the bank. We must presume, in charity to Mr. Watson, that he does not mean what he says, and that when he says "rich man, poor man, beggar man, thief," he really means something like intelligent man, imbecile, mathematician and non-mathematician, musical person and unmusical person, etc. Presuming that this is what he does mean, let us examine the Behaviorists' hypothesis, which is identical with that of the philosophers who, in the eighteenth century, elaborated the theory of modern democracy. The first thing that strikes one about the Behaviorists' hypothesis is that the observations on which it is based are almost exclusively observations on small children, not on fully grown men and women. It is on the ground that all infants are very much alike that the Behaviorists deny the hereditary transmission of special aptitudes, attributing the enormous differences of mental capacity observable among grown human beings exclusively to differences in environment, internal and external. Now it is an obvious and familiar fact that the younger a child, the less individually differentiated it is. Physically, all newborn children are very much alike: there are few fathers who, after seeing their newborn infant once, could recognize it again among a group of other infants. Mr. Watson will not, I suppose, venture to deny that physical peculiarities may be inherited. Yet the son who at twenty will have his father's aquiline nose and his mother's dark, straight hair may be as snubnosed and golden at two as another child whose father is pugfaced and his mother blonde, and who will grow up to be like them. If the Behaviorists had made their observations on children a few months before they were born, they would have been able to affirm not only the psychological identity of all men and women, but also their physical identity. Three days after their respective conceptions, Pocahontas, Shakespeare, and a Negro congenital idiot would probably be indistinguishable from one another, even under the most powerful microscope. According to Behaviorist notions, this should be regarded as a conclusive proof of the omnipotence of nurture. Since they are indistinguishable at conception, it must be environment that turns the fertilized ova into respectively a Red Indian woman, an English man of genius, and a Negro idiot.

Mind and body are closely interdependent: they come to maturity more or less simultaneously. A mind is not fully grown until the body with which it is connected through the brain has passed the age of puberty. The mind of a young child is as much undifferentiated and unindividualized as its body. It does not become completely itself until the body is more or less fully grown. A child of two has neither his father's nose nor his maternal grandfather's talent for mathematics. But that is no argument against his developing both when he is a few years older. A young child looks and thinks like other children of the same age and not like his parents. Later on he will certainly look like his parents. What reason is there to suppose that his mind will not also be like theirs? If he has his father's nose, why not his father's brain, and with it his father's mentality? The Behaviorists give us no answers to these questions. They merely state, what we already knew, that small children are very much alike. But this is entirely beside the point. Two fertilized ova may be indistinguishable; but if one belongs to a Negress and the other to a Japanese, no amount of nurture will make the Japanese egg develop into a Negro, or vice versa. There is no more valid reason for supposing the two very similar infants who were to become Shakespeare and Stratford's village idiot could have been educated into exchanging their adult parts. To study human psychology exclusively in babies is like studying the anatomy of frogs exclusively in tadpoles. That environment may profoundly influence the course of mental development is obvious. But it is no less obvious that there is a hereditarily conditioned development to be modified. Environment no more creates a mental aptitude in a grown boy than it creates the shape of his nose.

EQUALITY OF VIRTUE

We have dealt so far with the primary assumption from which the whole theory and practice of democracy flows: that all men are substantially equal; and with one of its corollaries: that the observed differences between human beings are due to environment, and that education, in the widest sense of the term, is all-powerful. It is now necessary to touch briefly on one or two other corollaries. Men being in essence equally reasonable, it follows that they are also in essence equally moral. For morality (according to the philosophers who formulated the theory of democracy) is absolute and exists in itself, apart from any actual society of right- or wrong-doing individuals. The truths of morality can be apprehended by reason. All men are equally reasonable: therefore all are equally capable of grasping the absolute truths of moral science. They are therefore, in essence, equally virtuous, and if, in practice, they behave badly, that is merely an accident, due to corrupting surroundings. Man must be delivered from his corrupting surroundings (and for the most ardent and ruthlessly logical spirits all government, all law, and organized religion are corrupting influences). Finding himself once more in that idyllic "state of nature" from which he should never have tried to rise, man

will become, automatically, perfectly virtuous.   There are few people
now, I suppose, who take the theories of Rousseau very seriously.
But though our intellect may reject them, our emotions are still
largely influenced by them.   Many people still cherish a vague sentimental belief that the poor and uncultivated, who are nearer to the
"state of nature" than the cultured and the rich, are for that reason
more virtuous.

DEMOCRATIC POT AND CATHOLIC KETTLE

Pots have a diverting way of calling kettles black, and the prophets
of the democratic-humanitarian religion have at all times, from the
eighteenth century down to the present day, denounced the upholders
of Christian orthodoxy as anti-scientific.   In certain important respects, however, the dogmas and the practice of orthodox Catholic
Christianity were and are more nearly in accordance with the facts
than the dogmas and practice of democratic-humanitarianism.   The
doctrine of original sin is, scientifically, much truer than the doctrine
of natural reasonableness and virtue.   Original sin, in the shape of
antisocial tendencies inherited from our animal ancestors, is a familiar
and observable fact.   Primitively, and in a state of nature, human
beings were not, as the eighteenth century philosophers supposed, wise
and virtuous: they were apes.

Practically, the wisdom of the church displays itself in a recognition
among human beings of different psychological types.   It is not every
Tom, Dick, or Harry who is allowed to study the intricacies of
theology.   What may strengthen the faith of one may bewilder or
perhaps even disgust another.   Moreover, not all are called upon to
rule; there must be discipline, a hierarchy, the subjection of many and
the dominion of few.   In these matters the theory and practice of the
church is based on observation and long experience.   The humanitarian democrats who affirm that men are equal, and who on the
strength of their belief distribute votes to everybody, can claim no
experimental justification for their beliefs and actions.   They are men
who have a faith, and who act on it, without attempting to discover
whether the faith corresponds with objective reality.

THE RELATION OF THEORY TO ACTION

It is in the theory of human equality that modern democracy finds
its philosophic justification and some part, at any rate, of its motive
force.   It would not be true to say that the democratic movement took

its rise in the theories propounded by Helvétius and his fellows.   The origin of any widespread social disturbance is never merely a theory. It is only in pursuit of their interests, or under the influence of powerful emotions, that large masses of men are moved to action.   When we analyze any of the historical movements in favor of democracy and self-determination, we find that they derive their original impetus from considerations of self-interest on the part of the whole or a part of the population.   Autocracy and the rule of foreigners are often (though by no means invariably) inefficient, cruel, and corrupt. Large masses of the subjects of despots or strangers find their interests adversely affected by the activities of their rulers.   They desire to change the form of government, so that it shall be more favorable to their particular national or class interests.   But the discontented are never satisfied with mere discontent and desire for change.   They like, as I have already pointed out, to justify their discontent, to find exalted and philosophical excuses for their desires, to feel that the state of affairs most agreeable to them is also the state of affairs most agreeable to Pure Reason, Nature, and the Deity.   Violent oppression begets violent and desperate reaction.   But if their grievances are only moderate, men will not fight whole-heartedly for their redress, unless they can persuade themselves of the absolute rightness, the essential reasonableness of what they desire.   Nor will they be able, without some kind of intellectual rationalization of these desires, to persuade other men, with less immediate cause for discontent, to join them.   Emotion cannot be communicated by a direct contagion. It must be passed from man to man by means of a verbal medium. Now words, unless they are mere onomatopoeic exclamations, appeal to the emotions through the understanding.   Feelings are communicated by means of ideas, which are their intellectual equivalent; at the sound of the words conveying the ideas the appropriate emotion is evoked.   Thus, theory is seen to be doubly important: first, as providing a higher, philosophical justification for feelings and wishes; and second, as making possible the communication of feeling from one man to another.   "The equality of all men" and "natural rights" are examples of simple intellectual generalizations which have justified emotions of discontent and hatred, and at the same time have rendered them easily communicable.   The rise and progress of any democratic movement may be schematically represented in some such way as this: Power is in the hands of a government that injures the material interests, or in some way outrages the feelings, of all, or at least an influential fraction of its subjects.   The subjects are discontented and desire to change the existing government for one which shall be, for their purposes, better. But discontent and desire for change are not in themselves enough to drive men to action. They require a cause which they can believe to be absolutely, and not merely relatively and personally, good. By postulating (quite gratuitously) the congenital equality of all men, by assuming the existence of certain "natural rights" (the term is entirely meaningless), existing absolutely, in themselves and apart from any society in which such rights might be exercised, the discontented are able to justify their discontent, and at the same time to communicate it by means of easily remembered intellectual formulas to their less discontented fellows.

THEORY GETS OUT OF HAND

The invention of transcendental reasons to justify actions dictated by self-interest, instinct, or prejudice would be harmless enough if the justificatory philosophy ceased to exist with the accomplishment of the particular action it was designed to justify. But once it has been called into existence, a metaphysic is difficult to kill. Men will not let it go, but persist in elaborating the system, in drawing with a perfect logic ever fresh conclusions from the original assumptions. These assumptions, which are accepted as axiomatic, may be demonstrably false. But the arguments by which conclusions are reached may be logically flawless. In that case, the conclusions will be what the logicians call "hypothetically necessary." That is to say that, granted the truth of the assumptions, the conclusions are necessarily true. If the assumptions are false, the conclusions are necessarily false. It may be remarked, in passing, that the hypothetical necessity of the conclusions of a logically correct argument has often and quite unjustifiably been regarded as implying the absolute necessity of the assumptions from which the argument starts.

In the case of the theory of democracy the original assumptions are these: that reason is the same and entire in all men, and that all men are naturally equal. To these assumptions are attached several corollaries: that men are naturally good as well as naturally reasonable; that they are the product of their environment; that they are indefinitely educable. The main conclusions derivable from these assumptions are the following: that the state ought to be organized on democratic lines; that the governors should be chosen by universal suffrage; that the opinion of the majority on all subjects is the best opinion; that education should be universal, and the same for all citizens. The primary assumptions, as we have seen, are almost certainly false; but the logic by which the metaphysicians of democracy deduced the conclusions was sound enough. Given the assumptions, the conclusions were necessary.

In the early stages of that great movement which has made the whole of the West democratic, there were only discontent and a desire for such relatively small changes in the mode of government as would increase its efficiency and make it serve the interests of the discontented. A philosophy was invented to justify the malcontents in their demand for change; the philosophy was elaborated; conclusions were relentlessly drawn; and it was found that, granted the assumptions on which the philosophy was based, logic demanded that the changes in the existing institutions should be, not small, but vast, sweeping, and comprehensive. Those who rationalize their desires for the purpose of persuading themselves and others that these desires are in accord with nature and reason find themselves persuading the world of the rightness and reasonableness of many ideas and plans of action of which they had, originally, never dreamed. Whatever is, is right. Becoming familiar, a dogma automatically becomes right. Notions which for one generation are dubious novelties become for the next absolute truths, which it is criminal to deny and a duty to uphold. The malcontents of the first generation invent a justifying philosophy. The philosophy is elaborated, conclusions are logically drawn. Their children are brought up with the whole philosophy (remote conclusion as well as primary assumption), which becomes, by familiarity, not a reasonable hypothesis, but actually a part of the mind, conditioning and, so to speak, canalizing all rational thought. For most people, nothing which is contrary to any system of ideas with which they have been brought up since childhood can possibly be reasonable. New ideas are reasonable if they can be fitted into an already familiar scheme, unreasonable if they cannot be made to fit. Our intellectual prejudices determine the channels along which our reason shall flow.

Of such systems of intellectual prejudices some seem merely reasonable, and some are sacred as well as reasonable. It depends on the kind of entity to which the prejudices refer. In general it may be said that intellectual prejudices about non-human entities appear to the holder of them as merely reasonable, while prejudices about human entities strike him as being sacred as well as reasonable. Thus, we all believe that the earth moves round the sun, and that the sun is at a distance of some ninety million miles from our planet. We believe, even though we may be quite incapable of demonstrating the truth of either of these propositions — and the vast majority of those who believe in the findings of modern astronomy do so as an act of blind faith, and would be completely at a loss if asked to show reasons for their belief. We have a prejudice in favor of modern astronomy. Having been brought up with it, we find it reasonable, and any new idea which contradicts the findings of contemporary astronomy strikes us as absurd. But it does not strike us as morally reprehensible. Our complex of what may be called astronomy-prejudices is only reasonable, not sacred.

THE NEARER, THE MORE SACRED

There was a time, however, when men's astronomy-prejudices were bound up with a great human activity — religion. For their contemporaries the ideas of Copernicus and Galileo were not merely absurd, as contradicting the established intellectual prejudices; they were also immoral. The established prejudices were supported by high religious authority. For its devotees, the local and contemporary brand of religion is "good," "sacred," "right," as well as reasonable and true. Anything which contradicts any part of the cult is therefore not only false and unreasonable, but also bad, unholy, and wrong. As the Copernican ideas became more familiar, they seemed less frightful. Brought up in a heliocentric system, the religious folk of ensuing generations accepted without demur the propositions which to their fathers had seemed absurd and wicked. History repeated itself when, in the middle of the nineteenth century, Darwin published his *Origin of Species*. The uproar was enormous. The theory of natural selection seemed much more criminal than the Copernican theory of planetary motion. Wickedness in these matters is proportionate to the distance from ourselves. Copernicus and Galileo had propounded unorthodox views about the stars. It was a crime, but not a very grave one; the stars are very remote. Darwin and the Darwinians propounded unorthodox views about man himself. Their crime was therefore enormous. The dislike of the Darwinian hypothesis is by no means confined to those who believe in the literal truth of the Book of Genesis. One does not have to be an orthodox Christian to object to what seems an assault on human dignity, uniqueness, and superiority.

DEMOCRACY AS A RELIGION

The prejudices in favor of democracy belong to the second class; they seem, to those who cherish them, sacred as well as reasonable,

morally right as well as true.   Democracy is natural, good, just, progressive, and so forth.   The opponents of it are reactionary, bad,
unjust, antinatural, etc.   For vast numbers of people the idea of
democracy has become a religious idea, which it is a duty to try to
carry into practice in all circumstances, regardless of the practical
requirements of each particular case.   The metaphysic of democracy
which was in origin the rationalization of certain French and English
men's desires for the improvement of their governments, has become
a universally and absolutely true theology which it is all humanity's
highest duty to put into practice.   Thus, India must have democracy,
not because democratic government would be better than the existing
undemocratic government — it would almost certainly be incomparably worse — but because democracy is everywhere and in all circumstances right.   The transformation of the theory of democracy
into theology has had another curious result: it has created a desire
for progress in the direction of more democracy among numbers of
people whose material interests are in no way harmed, and are even
actively advanced, by the existing form of government which they
desire to change.   This spread of socialism among the middle classes,
the spontaneous granting of humanitarian reforms by power-holders
to whose material advantages it would have been to wield their power
ruthlessly and give none of it away — these are phenomena which
have become so familiar that we have almost ceased to comment on
them.   They show how great the influence of a theory can be when by
familiarity it has become a part of the mind of those who believe in it.
In the beginning is desire; desire is rationalized; logic works on the
rationalization and draws conclusions; the rationalization, with all
these conclusions, undreamed of in many cases by those who first
desired and rationalized, becomes one of the prejudices of men in the
succeeding generations; the prejudice determines their judgment of
what is right and wrong, true and false; it gives direction to their
thoughts and desires; it drives them into action.   The result is that a
man whose interests are bound up with the existing order of things will
desire to make changes in that order much more sweeping than those
desired by his grandfather, though the latter's material interests were
genuinely injured by it.   Man shall not live by bread alone.   The
divine injunction was unnecessary.   Man never has lived by bread
alone, but by every word that proceeded out of the mouth of every
conceivable God.   There are occasions when it would be greatly to
man's advantage if he did confine himself for a little exclusively to
bread.

SOCIALISM[1]

G. D. H. Cole

GEORGE DOUGLAS HOWARD COLE is one of the most industrious and voluminous of writers. Born in England in 1889, he was educated at Oxford, where he is now university reader in economics and fellow of University College. He has given much work to various phases of the labor movement, and is vice-president of the Workers Educational Association. With his wife, Margaret Cole, he has written a considerable shelf of detective stories. But it is for his other work, his serious volumes on economics, that he is most noted. Some of these volumes are in defense of guild socialism, notably *Guild Socialism Restated* (1920). Some are on the labor question: *Labour in the Commonwealth* (1918), and *Organized Labour* (1924). Others are efforts to inform the plain man about the ceaseless flux in contemporaneous politics and economics. Mr. Cole is a theorist, an expositor, and a propagandist rolled into one. It is as an expositor that he is most successful, for his style is delightfully lucid, and what he writes is always well documented and completely up to date. For example, it would be hard to find a better introduction to European politics than his and Margaret Cole's book *The Intelligent Man's Review of Europe Today* (1934). But he is seldom able to keep his theories out of his book, and they usually lead him into propagandist conclusions. As Alfred Zimmern says: in his writing, three-fourths of the volume is likely to be a scrupulously fair account of what *is*, followed in the final quarter by a rather apocalyptic statement of what *ought to be*. "One has the sensation of being borne peacefully along upon the stream of knowledge and then suddenly being precipitated over Niagara."

"Socialism" is the name given both to a widespread body of doctrines and to a world-wide movement taking many different forms. It has a long history behind it; and the word has been used in shifting senses as the ideas behind it have developed and the situations facing it changed. A short and comprehensive definition is therefore impossible. We can only say that socialism is essentially a doctrine and a movement aiming at the collective organization of the community in the interests of the mass of the people by means of the common ownership and collective control of the means of production and exchange.

It is well to begin by ruling altogether out from the scope of this article certain popular uses of the term "socialism" which were current, especially during the past generation. The well-known phrase "We are all socialists now," and the constant references to "socialistic legislation," only serve to obscure the real meaning of the word. "We are all socialists now" only means that everybody in these days,

[1] From *Encyclopædia Britannica* (14th ed.). Reprinted by permission.

whatever his politics, is ready to agree to a greater amount of government intervention both in industry and in the affairs of society generally than most people even conceived as possible a generation ago. And "socialistic legislation" is, as a rule, only a phrase indicating disapproval of any measure which increases this collective intervention or seeks in any way to promote a more equal distribution of income among the members of the community.

Again, almost any extension of local government activity, such as the taking over of a tramway system or an electric supply station, or the establishment of a municipal bank, is liable to be referred to as "municipal socialism," even if the public body which does it consists mainly of persons who are strongly opposed to socialism. Socialists certainly urge the extension of municipal trading; but so do many persons who are not in any sense socialists. These and similar uses of the word are accordingly left out of consideration in this article.

We must, however, try to make our initial attempt at a definition somewhat more precise. Socialism, we have said, is the name given at once to a doctrine and to a movement. In its early days, before there existed any widespread or clearly defined socialist movement, it was used chiefly as the name of a doctrine, or body of doctrines, and thus tended to be applied very widely to all social theories which stressed the need for collective political or economic action in opposition to the dominant individualist doctrines. The so-called "socialism of the chair," which had a vogue in Germany during the second quarter of the nineteenth century, was called "socialism" mainly in the broad philosophical sense; and "Christian socialism," in many of its manifestations, is socialist only in the sense that it stresses, in opposition to individualism, the corporate nature of society and the need for social solidarity based on the fatherhood of God and the brotherhood of man. In more recent times, as distinctively socialist ideas have become embodied in a number of organized movements, national and international, the tendency has been to think of socialism more as a movement than as a doctrine, and to sum it up rather as what the socialists want than as a definite body of theoretical dogma. For there exists no canon of socialist doctrines on which all socialists would agree. Karl Marx came nearest to providing such a canon in his formulation of "scientific socialism" as contrasted with the "Utopianism" of his predecessors. But, while most of the Continental socialist parties profess to base their policy on Marxism, and employ Marxian phrases and ideas for its expression, there are many different interpretations of Marxism, and, in any case, the fundamental doctrines of Marx himself form rather a philosophy of history and a critique of capitalist industrialism and orthodox political economy than a positive policy for socialism today. Moreover, there are many socialists, including the majority in Great Britain, who do not profess to be Marxists at all.

From the Marxian standpoint, socialism is the struggle of the working class, or proletariat, to free itself from the domination of capitalism, and establish a new classless society collectively controlled in the interest of the whole people. Marx nowhere formulates clearly either the nature of this new society or the detailed steps by which it is to be approached. He is far more interested in the struggle than in the goal to which it tends; and any attempt to forecast in detail the structure of a socialist community would have seemed to him mere Utopianism. The parties based on Marxism follow the master's lead, and tend to define their policy in terms rather of the class struggle between capitalists and laborers than of the positive ends sought in the struggle. The non-Marxist British socialists, for their part, have usually been more concerned with the early stages in a gradual evolution toward socialism than with the completed process. Only the "guild socialists," of modern socialist groups, have attempted to forecast in detail the structure of the new society they are seeking; and even their attempt is confined, in the main, to an outline of the structure of industry under a system of "workers' control" or "industrial self-government."

We have, then, in attempting to make more precise our definition of socialism, to avoid relating it in our minds to any utopian picture of the future. We can say that socialists seek the common ownership and collective control of the means of production and exchange; but we cannot say that this involves either the "nationalization" of all industries or some particular way of managing them. There are many possible forms of common ownership — nationally by the state, locally by municipalities or similar bodies, and locally or nationally by quasi-public trusts, guilds or corporations acting on behalf of the public. There are also many possible forms of administration — directly by state or municipal departments, by specially constituted boards or commissions of experts, or by representative bodies of producers or consumers or of both. All these forms of ownership and administration have had advocates among socialists, and many socialist plans embody features from several of them, or allow for diversity of experiment in different cases. Nor can it even be assumed that socialists wish all the means of production to be publicly owned. If the vital and basic industries and services were under public control, many socialists would be ready to leave smaller enterprises largely in private hands.

It is, however, clear that, whatever might be the precise form of social organization desired, all socialists would wish the vital aspects of the economic life of society to be brought under collective control. This applies to production and distribution alike. One aspect of socialism is the collective control of the productive forces; another, certainly no less important, is the collective control of the distribution of the social income. For, fundamentally, the object of the control of production is the abolition of poverty, unemployment, and social classes, and the sharing out of all the wealth that the community is able to produce on more equitable lines than capitalism allows.

All socialists would agree that a more equitable distribution of the social income means a less unequal distribution. But, while some regard absolute equality of income as the only socialist solution of the problem, others reject this view, and seek only to insure an adequate minimum for all, and to limit within reasonable bounds the degree of inequality above this minimum. "To each according to his needs" has been a frequent cry among socialists as well as anarchists, and many socialists have regarded complete "communism," in the sense of unlimited free distribution, as desirable for as many goods as can be produced in the necessary abundance. William Morris's socialist Utopia, *News from Nowhere*, is purely communistic in this sense of the term. But the conception of distribution according to need has commonly, as a practical policy, been either restated as a conception of complete equality, on the ground that equality is, in face of the limitation of human resources, the nearest workable equivalent, or limited to a demand for an assured minimum standard of living. A desire to lessen inequality of incomes, and to use the state and taxation as the means of achieving this, is all that can be safely assumed as the common doctrine of all schools of socialists.

The socialist desire for a nearer approach to equality is not, however, confined to the region of incomes. It implies also the desire both for equality of political rights and for equality of economic and social status. Political democracy, socialists often contend, can never be made a reality as long as gross inequalities of wealth and status are allowed to persist. Wealth, for example, gives its possessor the means of exerting an exceptional influence on political opinion, and often neutralizes the effects of formally democratic political institutions. Socialists, therefore, stand for political democracy completed and made workable by the abolition of class distinctions and of dangerous inequalities of wealth. This does not imply that they believe the means of transition to socialism must conform to orthodox democratic ideas; for the communists, for example, repudiate existing political democracy as a sham, and insist that socialism can be introduced only by a revolutionary "dictatorship of the proletariat." This view is repudiated by the majority of socialists outside Russia; and the socialist parties usually attempt to work toward socialism by using the methods of parliamentary democracy. This, however, is a matter of expediency rather than of principle; whereas all socialists, including communists, believe that socialism, once securely established, will organize its collective control of society on democratic lines. The "dictatorship" of the communists is regarded only as a necessary instrument of the transition to a really democratic system.

The differences of view among socialists, and the difficulty of formulating any precise definition of the policy of socialism, do not mean that socialism does not constitute a clearly recognizable movement and body of tendencies in economic and social policy. It is indeed sometimes difficult to say whether a particular organization can properly be described as socialist or not. The British Labor Party, for example, founded originally in 1900 as the Labor Representation Committee, on a basis of an alliance between the socialist societies and the trade unions, had at the outset no definite policy, and only adopted socialist views gradually. There was, in its early years, a dispute at the International Socialist Conference on the question whether its delegates ought to be admitted. Even today, though its policy is, in general, clearly socialist, it is quite possible for non-socialists who agree with its immediate program to be actively associated with it. The Continental parties, having for the most part a definitely Marxian basis, are, in words, far more fully committed to socialism; but it does not appear that the verbal difference exerts any important influence on their policy. Broadly speaking, the political labor movement is everywhere socialist, in that its declared policy conforms with the definition given at the beginning of this article. *Labor and the New Social Order*, the famous manifesto issued by the British Labor Party in 1918, is perhaps the best and clearest short exposition of moderate and evolutionary socialist policy that has yet been produced. . . .

Socialist Policy. The distinction between socialism, as represented by the various socialist and labor parties of Europe and the New World, and communism, as represented by the Russians and the minority groups in other countries, is one of tactics and strategy rather than of objective. Communism is indeed only socialism pursued by revolutionary means and making its revolutionary method a canon of faith. Communists, like other socialists, believe in the collective control and ownership of the vital means of production, and seek to achieve, through state action, the coördinated control of the economic forces of society. They differ from other socialists in believing that this control can be secured, and its use in the interests of the workers insured, only by revolutionary action leading to the "dictatorship of the proletariat" and the creation of a new proletarian state as the instrument of change. The existing states and parliaments, which the orthodox socialists seek to capture and use as the agents of social transformation, the communists denounce as purely capitalist institutions, which must be forcibly overthrown before the constructive work of socialism can even begin. This doctrine, derived from Marx's *Communist Manifesto* of 1848, is forcibly developed by Lenin in his book, *The State and Revolution* (1917), which gives the clearest account of the underlying political theories of the Communist Party. It follows from this view that the orthodox socialists, who seek to use the existing institutions of state and parliament as the agents of gradual socialization, are regarded by communists as the worst enemies of the workers, and denounced with a vigor far exceeding that which is meted out to the defenders of capitalist society.

Apart from this fundamental cleavage, socialist ideas have undergone considerable transformation in recent years. All schools of socialists still urge the transference of large-scale industry from private to public ownership; but mere state socialism, or nationalization of the old type, is no longer a satisfying conception to socialists of any school. Partly under guild socialist influence, and partly as a result of changes in the economic situation, all socialist programs now insist that the socialist state must create special economic organs for the administration of industries under public control, and that the workers must be given some participation in the management of these services. For example, whereas before the war the British miners urged merely the nationalization of the coal industry by its transference to a state department, they now, in conjunction with the Labor Party, propose that it should be administered by a representative commission, and its policy coördinated with that of allied services by an expert power and transport board holding a largely independent position. Similarly, the French unions have put forward a new plan of "industrial nationalization," and the problem of "workers' control" has appeared largely in German schemes of socialization since the war. Guild socialism, influential during and after the war in drawing attention to these problems of the control of industry, appears now to have made its distinctive contribution to socialist thought and policy, and to have become merged in the general body of revised socialist doctrine.

The war and its aftermath have everywhere brought socialism far nearer to the tests of practical experience and responsibility. Naturally, under these conditions, difficulties are more clearly seen, new problems come to the front, and differences previously latent tend to become more pronounced. It would take a bold man to prophesy what will be the outcome of the present disputes between communists and orthodox socialists. It may be that the need for unity in pursuit of economic ends will, in the long run, reunite the warring factions in the European movement, and compel them to arrive at some basis of political agreement. For the existence of two contending working-class parties, each claiming to stand for socialism, but seeking its end by distinctive means, has manifest disadvantages for the workers, especially if the quarrel is pushed into the industrial field, and results in a disruption of trade unionism in accordance with the political cleavage. This situation has not arisen in Great Britain in any grave form; but where it has arisen, as in France and Germany, it has weakened trade unionism even more seriously than political socialism.

The forces making for unity are: first, that the ultimate aims proclaimed by the rival groups are largely the same; and secondly, that socialism is essentially not so much a theoretical plan of social reorganization as a class movement arising directly out of the economic divisions in society. It is an attempt to formulate, primarily for the working class, or proletariat, a policy designed to promote at once a larger and more balanced production and a more equal distribution of wealth, and to abolish class distinction based on inequalities of wealth or social opportunity, or on property laws which encourage the accumulation of the means of production in private hands. Its forms and policies differ from place to place, and vary with the movement of events and economic forces; but through all its changes it retains the fundamental character proclaimed for it in the *Communist Manifesto* of 1848, as a movement based primarily on working-class organization and solidarity. By no means all socialists, especially in Great Britain, call themselves Marxists; but to this extent, at least, modern socialism bases itself firmly upon Marx's diagnosis of the social and economic problem.

Socialism has thus necessarily an economic foundation in the working-class movement; but it is important at the same time to realize that much of its driving force comes from its possession of a certain body of principles shared by socialists of all schools and scarcely subject to change with changes in the concrete political and economic situation.

Thus, all socialists agree that the conduct of industry for private profit produces antisocial results, and challenge the view that the pursuit by each citizen of his private economic interests works out for the good of society on a whole. All socialists, whatever their different views of the best forms of administration for socialist undertakings, agree in holding that the major industries and services should pass under some form of coördinated public control, whether in the hands of the state, of local authorities, of self-governing guilds or coöperative societies, or of new forms of organization specially developed for the purpose. They agree in denouncing private control of the vital means of production, and in holding that both the form and the extent of the national output should be determined by considerations of social need.

Moreover, all socialists insist that with a change in the control of industry will go a change in the motives which operate in the industrial system and that the motive of public service, at present thwarted and inhibited by private capitalism, will be brought rapidly into play by the change from private to social ownership and control. Within this common ground there is room for wide differences of opinion and of practical policy; but, through all the changes and chances of the socialistic movements of the world, these unifying conceptions give a common meaning to the vast variety of organizations and policies to which the term "socialist" is habitually applied.

A REBUTTAL OF SOCIALIST ARGUMENTS[1]

Oscar D. Skelton

OSCAR DOUGLAS SKELTON, born in Orangeville, Ontario, in 1878, but educated in part at the University of Chicago, is one of the best-known of Canadian historical writers. After newspaper and magazine work in the United States, he was for many years a professor in Queen's University at Kingston, Ontario. Since 1925 he has been Under-Secretary of State for External Affairs in the Canadian government. Dr. Skelton won the Hart, Schaffner, & Marx prize in economics by his volume of 1910 called *Socialism: A Critical Analysis*.

"Socialism" is of course a vague term. One of the merits of Dr. Skelton's compact volume is that it gives definiteness to the subject. Without granting excessive space to the distinctions between different schools of socialism — Owenite, Fourierite, Saint-Simonian, Marxian, Fabian, and so on — he makes their several characters clear, and then treats them all in their relation to the existing capitalist order. That is, he considers socialism first as an indictment of capitalism; next as an analysis of capitalism; third as a campaign against capitalism; and finally as a substitute for capitalism. It is from his consideration of socialism as an indictment of the evils of capitalistic society that the selection here presented is taken. Those who can find time will also do well to read his three chapters on "The Marxian Analysis," an incisive critical presentation of the ideas of one of the most influential thinkers of modern times. Dr. Skelton gives due weight to the environments out of which socialism has sprung: "Every country gets the socialists it deserves, from the bomb-throwing revolutionaries of autocratic Russia to the gas-and-water Fabians of democratic Britain." For reasons not hard to understand, the great literary exponents of socialism (William Morris, Bernard Shaw, Ramsay MacDonald, Sidney Webb, Bertrand Russell, H. N. Brailsford, to mention Englishmen alone) have usually been more eloquent and persuasive than their opponents. But vigorous presentations of the other side may be found in Hartley Withers' *The Case for Capitalism* and in Arthur Shadwell's *The Breakdown of Socialism* as well as in this volume.

The socialist has painted too black a picture. It is not merely that he has contrasted the dreamed ideals of socialism with the actualities of the competitive order; he has viewed those actualities out of all perspective. In his survey of society the one instance of failure is ever present to his gaze, the nine of success do not come within the range of his misery-focused lens. He cannot see the woods for the few decaying branches on the trees. His ear is attuned only to inharmonies. He sees the reeking fester of the slum, but is blind to the

[1] From *Socialism: A Critical Analysis* (Hart Schaffner & Marx Prize Essays No. 6; Houghton Mifflin Company). Reprinted by permission of Hart Schaffner & Marx.

millions of homes in city and town and country where hard work brings forth its fruits of modest comfort and life is held well worth the living. He is alert to the occasional failure in adjustment of supply and demand, but passes over the continuous miracle by which the products of the ends of the earth are brought to each man's door and the world's markets made one. He culls industriously the instances of graft and dishonesty in contemporary business life — no difficult task — and presents them as typical of current practice, forgetting the sound honesty of the majority that provides the drab background for the scarlet sins, forgetting that no enduring commercial structure can be built on fraud, that general honesty and fair dealing are absolutely indispensable to the working of our complicated and inter-dependent industrial system, that the fabric of credit that the past few generations have reared posits a general high standard of business ethics — not the perfect standard of the closet moralist, but a pretty presentable workday approximation; that, in short, unless there existed a general expectation of squareness, born of experience, the operations of the exceptional crook would be impossible. He is like the yellow journal which mirrors, not life, but the exceptional sensation and crime that mar life; leaves John Smith in obscurity if for a lifetime he does honest work and devotes himself to his home interests, and exalts him to front-page publicity if on a day he loses himself in drink and murders half the family.

The socialist indictment gives but grudging recognition or none to the proved and tried efficiency of the existing order. Under an industrial system based on private property and individual competition, the most powerful and abiding force in human nature, self-interest, which includes the interest in the wider self, the family, is harnessed in society's service. The prizes in the struggle — not mere heaped up and hoarded dollars, but the prestige of success, the power that money gives, the opportunities of enjoyment or of service it opens — fall in the main to those who most widely and most efficiently have met the economic needs of their fellows. The price of success is alertness to seize on every uncatered opportunity; courage to break new trails; ability to make the process of production more efficient, the integration and adjustment of industry more thorough, the fitting of ability to task more complete; keenness to stop all leakages and wastes, unremitting striving to outbid one's fellows by offering most for least. "The stimulus of private property," wrote Arthur Young a century ago, "turns the sands to gold." It is not implied that personal interest is the sole force at the disposal of a society based on private property. Altruistic motives find ever wider scope. More and more under the existing order men are animated by the desire to serve their fellows, both in the day's work and out of the wealth a life of work has garnered. Never was the social conscience so keen, never was the sense of the trusteeship of wealth so widespread, never was the organization of philanthropy and public service so complete. But the effectiveness of the altruistic motive is no reason for disregarding the self-seeking spur to action. Both must be utilized. The task of meeting the needs of the millions who every day grow more ambitious in their standards and more insistent in their demands is too tremendous to make it possible to discard the instrument which has been found of most effective service. Individual ambition will always keep men's demands on life high. Individual ambition must be harnessed to keep the supply as high.

Individual initiative does not involve individual isolation. Its complement is voluntary coöperation. Stockholders in a corporation, artisans in a trade union, farmers in a purchasing or selling syndicate, seek the strength that comes from union. Mutual aid knits up the otherwise scattered and incoherent forces. Society must not be confused with the state. Compulsory coöperation is not the only alternative to individualist anarchy. Society is inexhaustibly fertile in its spontaneous groupings: religious, political, scientific, charitable, commercial interest draw men together in countless associations. We are caught in a thousand strands.

Nor does individual initiative in meeting economic wants involve a serious lack of adjustment between demand and supply. It might seem at first glance that without central supervision harmonious cooperation would be impossible; that the competitive system, faced for example with the task of the daily provisioning of New York or London, would break down under the task, alternating between unforeseen glut and unforeseen famine. But the miracle is every day performed. The fact is that in great totals chance is self-canceled; a defection here offsets an accession there. There is really nothing less arbitrary, less unpredictable than the sequences of social phenomena. Births and deaths, marriages and divorces, suicides and murders, the posting of letters without any address, occur year in and year out with remarkable regularity. And so with the affairs of trade and industry: without any conscious, centralized compulsion demand and supply approximate, not with exact precision, it is true, but without serious gaps in normal times. Even if we adopt the favorite socialist conception of society as an organism, it is to be remembered that the chief organic movements of the human body are carried on without conscious volition or reflection. If every breath, every heart-beat, had to be consciously and separately willed, neither the bodily nor the mental functions would be performed with much success.

The mechanism by which equilibrium is secured between the de-mand of widely scattered consumers and the supply forthcoming from independent producers is simply price variation. The oscillations of the money price of commodities act as a barometer for the producers' guidance. If an insufficient proportion of the productive forces of a country is engaged in cotton manufacture, the rise of price of cotton goods, or rather the increase of the margin between cost and sale price, indicates an opportunity for more than average gain, and new capital pours in until the equilibrium is restored. If too large a share is turned into the channel of boot and shoe production, the fall of price or profit effects the same adjustment. The purchasing power of the consuming public may not be fairly distributed, judged by some abstract principle of justice, may not be rationally directed, judged by some sociological canon of expenditure, but distributed and directed as it is, it secures in marvelous fashion, through the price oscillations of a competitive economy, the most efficient disposition of the pro-ductive forces. It is the very simplicity and familiarity of the mechanism of price variation which leads superficial critics of social institutions to overlook its remarkably efficient services.

The institutions of private property and individual competition are based, not on blind traditionalism or class oppression, but on the experience which all the progressive races of mankind have attained of their social utility and their flexible adaptability to changing social needs. Private property has ousted the primitive communism which preceded it simply because it has been found to be the property form most conducive to industrial progress and efficiency. . . . Doubtless private property has its drawbacks, its wastes and its failures, but the test of efficiency in any social institution is not the impossible one of unqualified perfection but the degree of service over cost, the net balance of advantage. So incalculably great is the driving force which the stimulus of private interest supplies that even such a thoroughgoing critic as Professor Veblen sums up his indictment of the social waste of much competitive effort by declaring: "While it is in the nature of things unavoidable that the management of industry by modern business methods should involve a large misdirection of effort and a large waste of goods and services, it is also true that the aims and ideals to which this manner of economic life gives effect act

forcibly to offset all this incidental futility.   These pecuniary aims and
ideals have a very great effect, for instance, in making men work hard
and unremittingly, so that on this ground alone the business system
probably compensates for any waste involved in its working.   There
seems, therefore, to be no tenable ground for thinking that the working
of the modern system involves a curtailment of the community's
livelihood."

The socialist indictment errs, therefore, in ignoring the strong
features of a competitive system, its positive advantages, and stressing
out of all proportion the weak points, the negative deductions.   Yet
what of these weak points, these unsocial tendencies charged against
competition, the poisonous adulteration, the young children stunted
at the loom, the careless waste of human life in the pursuit of material
wealth?   In or out of proportion, they are none the less real.   No
impartial observer of contemporary conditions can maintain that
individual and social interests invariably coincide, that in the race
for wealth only those succeed who have best served their fellows.
The frequently dangerous and unwholesome tendencies of unregulated
competition are a patent fact.   The socialist error here lies not in any
misstatement of these tendencies but in the failure to recognize the
counteracting forces at work.   In many cases the self-interest of one
section or group suffices to thwart the injurious tendencies of the self-
interest of another group.   And where this recourse fails, the power
of the state may be invoked to hold the balance fair.

If our existing industrial organization were committed to a *laissez
faire* acceptance of the results, good and bad alike, of unregulated
competition, the position of its socialist opponent would be a strong
one.   But fortunately for society such an extreme doctrinaire attitude
does not prevail.   Our existing society is not of individualism all
compact.   In it, as in every other society since time began, there have
been combined the complementary forces of individual initiative and
social control.   They have been combined in varying proportions,
now the one force dominating, now the other.   Following the excess
of state regulation in the early stages of modern industrial development, there came the excessive license of the early nineteenth century.
The manufacturer was led by unenlightened selfishness to resist all
restraint; the public was blinded to the human cost by the tremendous
increase in material productivity; the economist, in his more doctrinaire moods, assumed a harmony of social and individual interest
providential in its completeness.   Yet the complacency was short-
lived.   The public came to realize that individualism pure and un-

defiled was at one with socialism in requiring for its successful working a perfected human nature. A new system of regulation aiming at raising competition to a higher level began to take shape long before the destruction of the old system of regulation, aiming at the repression of competition, approached completion. The first factory act, regulating the employment of apprentices, was passed in Great Britain in 1802, over fifty years before the protective tariff was completely overthrown. The pendulum still swings in the same direction. More and more the modern state is realizing its true function of raising the ethical level of competition, retaining the struggle while insisting that it shall not be carried on at the expense of the weak and helpless. While it declines to follow the advice of the socialist and play the whole game itself, the state gives inestimable service by acting as referee.

The socialist complaint that under a régime of individual enterprise important utilities will fail to be provided because yielding no profit that may be privately appropriated would hold good against the mythical *laissez faire* bogey it attacks, but has little application in the case of the actual state. Even Adam Smith's statement of the irreducible minimum of state functions included "the duty of erecting and maintaining certain public works and certain public institutions, which it can never be for the interest of any individual, or small number of individuals, to erect and maintain; because the profit would never repay the expense to any individual or small number of individuals, though it may frequently do much more than repay it to a great society." The principle is a far-reaching one, and has guided and justified a wide program of governmental encouragement to production and commerce as well as of social reform, from the provision of lighthouses to the provision of supervised playgrounds. Especially important has been the rôle of the state as the conservator of society's permanent interests. It is a rôle which has not always been assumed as promptly and played as whole-heartedly as might be desired; the tardiness of American governments in following European example in preserving the forests is a case in point, due in part, it is true, to the shortsighted hostility of private interest, but in part also to the difficulty of readjusting conceptions formed in the days of seemingly illimitable resources to the needs of a less sanguine and more thrifty time, and in part to the characteristic and crippling lack of initiative in state administration. Even where governmental intervention has been invoked to supply the lack of individual profit-making enterprise, it has as a rule been made possible only by long agitation and pressure from without by individuals or voluntary associations.

The socialist complains that in the competitive struggle the weaklings are trampled on, and hastily cries out for the abolition of competition and the assumption of industrial functions by the all-wise and all-kindly state. The remedy actually applied has been the saner one of preserving competition while endeavoring to make the weaklings fit for the fray, training all to take a manful and intelligent part in the struggle for existence. In nearly every industrial state, though in greatly varying degree, the government supplements the efforts of the family and of individual and organized philanthropy to insure that every child grows up in sanitary surroundings, that he is given the cultural and vocational education to equip him for living as well as for making a living, that wholesome recreational facilities are brought within his reach, and that he is not prematurely swept into the industrial struggle, before, on its lowest terms, his full economic efficiency has been developed. Much yet remains to be done even in the most advanced countries; much to bring the more backward to their level; the very benevolence of modern society tends to complicate its problems by preserving many halt and weak who would otherwise have gone down in the fray; the immigration of countless hordes of peoples from the countries not yet organized on a competitive industrial basis — the factoryless paradises of southeastern Europe and of Asia, where the "blight of capitalism" has not yet seriously entered — into the capitalistic countries which they unaccountably prefer, makes the task of training never ending. But it is a task which a competitive society must face or perish, and it is being manfully faced and encouragingly accomplished.

Competition, the socialist charges, may be carried on at the expense of the consumer, increasing the price he must pay for his wares and debasing their quality. The paradoxical assertion of increased prices is based on the assumption that the middleman is merely a parasite on industry, or, if his potential productive service is recognized, that too great a number of middlemen are engaged in commerce, with resultant expense for the consumers on whom they are quartered. The attitude is of long standing. In mediaeval times the socialist's ancestor passed strict laws against the evil machinations of the forestaller and the engrosser who came between the producer and the ultimate consumer. The socialist of today suffers from the same inability to grasp the elementary fact that the utilities of time and space may be as real as the utilities of form and content. The merchant who brings the cloth to the consumer's town, and stores it until the demand arises, performs as essential service as the rancher who grew the wool or the weaver who wove the yarn into cloth. When, again, it is charged that free competition inevitably lures into commerce more merchants than are needed, the question turns on the measure of need, on the degree of specialization of function desired. Doubtless in any city it would be possible to exist with only half the present number of stores, possible even to concentrate custom on a single central establishment in each line, but it would be possible only by sacrificing the time and convenience of the thousands of customers, by throwing on the consumer part of the burden of storage and distribution which in a fully organized division of labor is assumed by the merchant. The gain would be as illusory as the gain of the busy professional man who would seek to economize by making his own shoes or typewriting his own correspondence.

Or it is from adulteration and scamping of work that the consumer is said to suffer. Rivalry in price-cutting leads the more unscrupulous to sand the sugar and paper-sole the shoe; the anonymity and the continental scale of modern production, far afield from the conditions of handicraft days, when producer and consumer lived side by side and a care for reputation safeguarded quality, make it impossible to detect the fraud. The indictment has only too much truth, but here again it ignores the possibilities of remedy inherent in the existing system. To an increasing extent the self-interest of the producer effects a cure. Competition is at work not merely in price but in quality, wherever the credit for quality may be secured. The employment of distinctive labels and trademarks, the growing use of package goods, brought to the consumer's attention by advertising, do away with the anonymity of production and protect the consumer by locating the responsibility. Of narrower range, but still important, is the allied protection which the union label affords in some lines, particularly against the danger of infection by commodities produced in unsanitary surroundings. Yet a third remedy is afforded by government inspection, analysis, and publicity, particularly adaptable to the cases where the average buyer is not qualified to make the necessary tests.

Or it is financial rather than commercial fraud which is emphasized. The investor, it is claimed, is as much at the mercy of the unscrupulous promoter as the consumer is at the mercy of the unscrupulous manufacturer; the anonymity of the joint-stock company cloaks as much rascality as the anonymity of consumption goods. The case is not so hopeless as is alleged. For the untrained investor there are always available safe, if not highly remunerative, opportunities for deposit or investment, whether in chartered or postal savings-banks, or in the bonds of the more stable governments or industrial enterprises. In the more precarious undertakings, so far as the risk is due to fraudulent promotion or speculative management, it is as much the duty of the state to provide safeguard and punishment as in the case of highway robbery. It is a duty which every state has recognized and endeavored to fulfill, though with varying degrees of success. . . .

The workingman, it is further charged, suffers even more seriously than the consumer and the investor under a competitive system based on private property in the instruments of production. We are given a harrowing picture of the present-day wage slave cowering under the lash of the tyrannical capitalist, forced to accept long hours, low wages, and unsanitary working and housing surroundings, and condemned to lifelong monotony of toil. The picture suffers from that lack of perspective and proportion which results from the habitual socialist preoccupation with the failures rather than the successes of modern industrialism. It ignores the forces actively at work in our existing society to repress abuse of power on the part of the capitalist and to secure to the workingman his full share of the fruits of progress. The strength of the working class is threefold; in the employer's realization of the trusteeship his power imposes, in the intervention of the state to see that the game is fairly played, and in the self-help of trade-union organization.

In the first place no one who surveys the situation calmly would agree with the current socialist contention that every employer of labor grinds the faces of the poor, oblivious of the claims of his fellow men to fair treatment. A striking feature of contemporary social development is the growth of industrial betterment activities, whether taking the form of model villages, attractive factory surroundings, recreational and educational facilities, or profit-sharing. The social secretary restores the intimate personal touch lost with the expansion of the workshop into the factory and the transformation of individual into joint-stock ownership. Hard-headed business men make once more the old discovery that decency pays even in dollars and cents. It is true that these welfare activities cannot, even if universally adopted, of themselves provide a solution of the relations between capital and labor satisfactory to our democratic age; they may even make matters worse, if inspired by fussy paternalism and the condescending charity of Lady Bountifuls, or if designed to take the place of wage concessions due or to break up labor organizations. Prompted, however, by a sympathetic recognition of the human needs and potentialities of the men and women employed, buttressed by experience of their financial expediency, and democratized by entrusting their operation as far as possible to the employees themselves, they hold high promise of social service.

Of more widespread importance is the intervention of the state. In country after country, as industrial development proceeds and experience of the evils that come with its gains compels action, codes of factory legislation have been formed which are virtually workingmen's charters. A national minimum of sanitation and of light and space is prescribed, the labor of children of tender years prohibited, the hours of work of older children, women, and in many instances, men, regulated, safeguards against accidents and occupational disease demanded, the time and manner of payment of wages strictly stipulated. The stand is firmly taken that competition must not be carried on at the expense of the worker's health and vitality.

Yet neither the good will of the better type of employers nor the intervention of the state does more than supplement the workingman's own efforts. Collective self-help is the most indispensable weapon in his arsenal. Under the existing industrial order it has become ever surer and more efficient. The typical modern workingman, labeled "wage slave" in the heated rhetoric of socialist denunciation, is well equipped for the struggle to secure the largest possible share of the national dividend. Education has widened his horizon, the training and companionship of the factory or railroad have sharpened his perceptions, improved working and housing conditions have increased his stamina. Union with his fellow workers in local, national, and even international organizations has given to each man's labor something of the indispensableness of labor as a whole, has pooled scanty individual resources to provide reserves for strike or unemployment, and has placed at the service of all the bargaining ability and shrewder tactics of the few who forge to the front as leaders. Collective bargaining steadily makes its way; trade agreements between the representatives of organized capital and organized labor witness the coming of "the constitutional factory," the gradual democratization of industry by giving the workers a direct share in settling the conditions of their labor. Not even grafting or dishonoring of contracts by occasional labor leaders, nor the militant anti-unionism of belated reactionaries of the Parry and Kirby type, nor the eighteenth century interpretations of freedom of contract still lurking in some judicial quarters, can permanently hinder or obscure the movement.

The rapid development of insurance to cover the principal contingencies to which the workman is exposed further arms him for his life struggle. The isolated individual deprived of the support of the old kinship groups or ecclesiastical organizations which would once have given succor in time of crisis is liable to be crushed by sudden misfortune. Accident or prolonged sickness may incapacitate him for further work, unemployment may result from a general trade crisis or shift in fashion, his death may leave his family unprepared to grapple with the world. Fortunately, through the coöperative device of insurance, it has been found possible to redress the flukes of fate and to ease the burden by distributing it over a wide group.

Such are the main agencies actually at work to enable the working-man to obtain and to hold his share of the wealth which the progress of science and the opening up of new lands are producing in ever greater abundance. In face of the growing enlightenment of the em-ployers, the state's insistence on refereeing the game, the trade union's unending pressure, the joint insurance against the crises of the in-dividual's life, the socialist contention that the workers of today are but wage slaves is seen to be the emptiest rhetoric. The employer and the workingman, each equally dependent, in the long run, on the other's coöperation, meet face to face as equal bargainers, now the one, now the other reaping advantage in the bargaining as the condi-tions of industrial activity vary. It is true that large-scale production makes uniformity of rules and regulations inevitable: it is, in fact, the impossibility of each workman individually dickering as to the hours of beginning or ceasing work or the number of cubic feet of air space allowed — an impossibility which would remain even in Mr. Keir Hardie's socialistic factory — that affords the justification of collective bargaining. To confuse individual conformity to rule with slavery, however, is utterly to misconceive the relation between law and liberty.

Nor do the further specific counts in this section of the socialist indictment possess any greater validity than the charge that the factory system spells slavery. It is undeniable that under the influ-ence of the various agencies noted, long hours and unsanitary and dangerous working surroundings are rapidly becoming isolated ex-ceptions. As for the monotony and the narrowing effect of machine labor, it should be borne in mind that if for the former artisan the machine sometimes means a cramping and paralyzing of skill, for the unskilled laborer it opens up fields hitherto unattainable. Even for the artisan, it is a tenable position that within the factory the com-panionship and social interests developed quite offset the loss in ver-

satility and all-round activity involved in the passing of the autonomous but solitary handicraft, while the greater leisure afforded by the
steady shortening of hours gives opportunity for the cultivation of
outside interests. Again, the difficulty experienced by handicraftsmen, on the first extensive introduction of machinery, in adapting
themselves to the new conditions, was a real and serious one, entailing
untold misery. Today, however, new inventions rarely produce such
serious effects, since the similarity of the machinery used in many
allied fields of industry, together with the growth of technical education, makes it possible for workingmen to change from one line to
another, the more easily because not isolated, as the handicraftsmen
often were, in the country districts. The adjustment of supply and
demand is effected not so much by actual displacement as by turning
the new recruits into the growing industries and away from the
decaying ones. . . . There is no greater proportion of women and
children employed today than in our great-grandfathers' day; they
have merely shifted the scene of their activities as one occupation
after another, spinning, weaving, clothes-making, baking, butter-
making, jam-making, has been sheared away from the primitive all-
comprehensive functions of the home and converted into a specialized
factory industry. . . .

Turning from the problems of wage-earning to the problems of
wage-spending, we are faced with serious presentations of the poverty
of the mass of the people. There is necessity here for discrimination.
The poverty which is merely lesser wealth is not greatly to be deplored. Inequality in wealth is not in itself an evil. Great fortunes
may be open to attack on exactly the same ground as small fortunes,
wherever, that is, they have been heaped up by fraud, by the financial
magnate's manipulation of the corporate properties under his control
or by the small tradesman's use of his thirty-five-inch yardstick. Inequalities in wealth which correspond to differences in enterprise, in
industry, in thrift, can be leveled only at the cost of paralyzing production and plunging the whole of society into an equality of misery.
It is otherwise with the poverty that means positive degradation, the
poverty in whose train follow overcrowding and disease, starvation
of body and soul. Of such poverty there is only too much, especially
in older lands. But, as has been pointed out above, the pictures of
poverty presented err grievously in perspective, an error which may
be excused when the object is to rouse the careless to attention, but
inexcusable when a calm estimate of the good and evil of the existing
industrial system as a whole is being sought. The possibilities of

decent living are increasingly brought within the reach of the vast majority. The stimulus of private enterprise has so perfected production as to lower prices of goods and services in nearly every line, and to bring within the reach of the many of today what were the luxuries of the few of yesterday. Private benevolence and public intervention have provided for all comers the school, the library, and the museum, the park, the playground, and the bathing beach. If, with these facilities for meeting the most necessary wants, ends do not always meet, the responsibility is not wholly to be thrown on the insufficiency of wage resources.

Nor should attention be confined solely to the material goods whose unequal sharing has been the burden of socialist complaint. The overemphasis which socialism has placed on the material outcome of the competitive struggle is radically unsound. It is not merely dollars, many or few, that a man wins in life's battle. The struggle calls for and develops qualities of character of immensely greater significance. It is not implied that financial success is an unfailing index of moral strength; few Pittsburgh millionaires have been canonized. Yet by and large it is true that the industrial organization which makes each tub stand on its own bottom has by its disciplinary and selective action developed the homely virtues of industry and thrift, the qualities of insight and initiative which compel success. There is no monopoly in these goods of character. One man's more does not mean another's less.

It is also true that life's choicest gifts, love and honor and consecration to others' service, the glory of the sunset and the peace of the midnight stars, are goods not bought with a price, and goods as close within the reach of the cottage as of the mansion. Not that material goods may be dispensed with: it is necessary to live before it is possible to live well, and to offer to a man who asks for bread, free access to a gallery of old masters, is empty mockery. Starvation is as fatal to aspiration as surfeit. But once this minimum is secured, it rests with the individual to determine whether he will live for his neighbor's eyes or by his own; whether he will devote his means to competitive display and conspicuous waste, or will seek to develop his own personality. By all means let us strive to insure for every man and woman the possibility of making an adequate living, but do not let us forget, as the socialist, like the multi-millionaire, is prone to forget, that making a living is not living.

A final source of error in the socialist arraignment is the disregard of the outstanding facts in the relation of men to their tools. Neither the weaknesses nor the strength of human nature will ever permit this earth to harbor a flawless social order. The weaknesses of human nature will not permit it; however cunningly devised the institutions, the Old Adam will break through and wreak havoc. The utopian fallacy dies hard, that hidden in some undiscovered Atlantis or shrouded in the mists of the future there may be found an ideal social organization which man, naturally perfect, will be able to work without creak or friction. It is true of course that human nature is not an unvarying quantity, and that the reflex action of institutions on men is as important as the action of men on institutions. The current stress on the responsibility of society for individual ills marks a wholesome reaction from the atomistic attitude which threw on the pauper or the criminal the whole responsibility for his shortcoming. Yet, as is the way with reactions, it has already gone to an extreme, and at present we are in danger of losing sight of the responsibility of the individual by shouldering all the blame on that intangible and ungrieving entity Society, absolving A by holding B and C at fault, and B by A's and C's neglect.

Nor will the strength of human nature, the ceaseless striving for betterment, any more than its weaknesses, ever permit this faultily faultless perfection. In the future as in the past progress must be rooted in divine discontent. The goal ever fades into the distance; every step upward opens new horizons; achievement always lags behind conception. If ever the voice of the critic is hushed, it will mean that society has attained not perfection but stagnation. That finality is impossible is no reason for folding the hands and acquiescing in the present ills, but it is a reason for disregarding the factious criticism which would have us scrapheap civilization because with all our progress there yet remain many a blot to be removed and many a manful fight to be waged.

IV

WAR AND WORLD ORDER

BEFORE the cataclysm of 1914 several broad factors seemed to be strengthening the cause of world peace. One was the growing interdependence of nations both financially and commercially; the economic life of the Great Powers was being knit together in increasing degree, and each stood to lose heavily from any breach of world peace. Another factor was the increasing power of organized labor. It, like capital, had become a force of international character, and it threw its strength on the side of the older forces, cultural and legal, which emphasized the fraternity of man. A third great factor was the tendency in most Occidental nations toward a stationary level of population, which at once reduced the principal incentive of warlike expansion, and cut down the supply of "gun-fodder." A fourth, though more dubious, element was the enormous increase in the quantity and the destructiveness of armaments, transforming the character of war and making it a far more terrible risk. The outbreak of the World War showed that these and other restraints were less effective than many had hoped; but the close of the conflict brought an unprecedented new effort to organize against the repetition of such a calamity. It is obvious that as yet little hope of an assured peace can be based upon the League and the supplementary treaties (Locarno, the Kellogg-Briand Pact, and so on) designed to prevent war. These are useful, but it is necessary to strike at the root causes of war. Some see the best means of doing this in a mighty effort of education; some in governmental changes to reduce nationalism and imperialism; some in socialistic or communistic attacks upon capitalism as the prime cause of conflict and aggression; and so on. In the pages which follow, Graham Wallas presents an acute general statement of the problem; Stephen Graham and C. E. Montague offer eloquent indictments of war; William James deals with the subject in more philosophical vein; and in the papers by John Bassett Moore and Newton D. Baker we have a debate upon the practical course which Americans should follow.

NATIONALITY AND HUMANITY[1]

Graham Wallas

"GRAHAM WALLAS touched the cause of the trouble when he pointed out that political science today discusses institutions and ignores the nature of the men who make and live under them. I have heard professors reply that it wasn't their business to discuss human nature but to record and interpret economic and political facts. Yet if you probe those 'interpretations' there is no escaping the conclusion that they rest upon some notion of what man is like. 'The student of politics,' writes Mr. Wallas, 'must, consciously or unconsciously, form a conception of human nature, and the less conscious he is of his conception the more likely he is to be dominated by it.' For politics is an interest of men — a tool which they fabricate and use — and no comment has much value if it tries to get along without mankind. You might as well try to describe food by ignoring the digestion.

"Mr. Wallas has called a halt. I think we may say that his is the distinction of having turned the study of politics back to the humane tradition of Plato and Machiavelli — of having made man the center of political investigation. The very title of his book — *Human Nature in Politics* — is significant. Now in making that statement, I am aware that it is a sweeping one, and I do not mean to imply that Mr. Wallas is the only modern man who has tried to think about politics psychologically. Here in America alone we have two splendid critics, a man and a woman, whose thought flows from an interpretation of human character. Thorstein Veblen's brilliant descriptions penetrate deeply into our mental life, and Jane Addams has given new hope to many of us by her capacity for making ideals the goal of natural desire."

To this statement by one of the editors of this volume (in *A Preface to Politics*) it is necessary only to add a few biographical facts. Graham Wallas was born at Sunderland, England, in 1858, and educated at Oxford. At first a schoolmaster, he joined the Fabian Society, was one of the authors of *Fabian Essays*, and became a close friend of Bernard Shaw. Indeed, for several years he, Shaw, Sidney Olivier, and Sidney Webb were inseparable — "the bravoes of advanced economics" in England. His first important book was a life of Francis Place, the English reformer, published in 1897, two years after he became a lecturer in the London School of Economics; it offers a lucid exposition of the way in which British politics were "wire-pulled" from behind the scenes, early in the nineteenth century, by a gifted tailor. In 1908 he published *Human Nature in Politics* and in 1914 his most famous work, *The Great Society*. These were followed by *Our Social Heritage* (1921) and *The Art of Thought* (1926). All his books showed marked originality, great insight into modern social and political forces, and unusual literary charm. He was for some years (1914–1923) professor of political science in London University, and was well known in the United States as teacher and lecturer, appearing at Harvard, giving the Lowell Lectures in Boston in 1914, and being Dodge Lecturer at Yale in 1919. As a public speaker he had marked fluency and force, for his Fabian days had given him good training. He died in 1932.

[1] From *Human Nature in Politics*, by Graham Wallas. Reprinted by permission of F. S. Crofts & Company, publishers.

Aristotle, writing under the conditions of the Ancient World, laid it down that a community whose population extended to a hundred thousand would no more be a state than would one whose population was confined to ten. He based his argument on measurable facts as to the human senses and the human memory. The territory of a state must be "visible as a whole" by one man's eye, and the assembly attended by all the full citizens must be able to hear one voice — which must be that of an actual man and not of the legendary Stentor. The governing officials must be able to remember the faces and characters of all their fellow citizens. He did not ignore the fact that nearly all the world's surface as he knew it was occupied by states enormously larger than his rule allowed. But he denied that the great barbarian monarchies were in the truest sense "states" at all.

We ourselves are apt to forget that the facts on which Aristotle relied were both real and important. The history of the Greek and mediaeval city-states shows how effective a stimulus may be given to some of the highest activities and emotions of mankind when the whole environment of each citizen comes within the first-hand range of his senses and memory. It is now only here and there, in villages outside the main stream of civilization, that men know the faces of their neighbors, and see daily as part of one whole the fields and cottages in which they work and rest. Yet, even now, when a village is absorbed by a sprawling suburb or overwhelmed by the influx of a new industrial population, some of the older inhabitants feel that they are losing touch with the deeper realities of life.

A year ago I stood with a hard-walking and hard-thinking old Yorkshire schoolmaster on the high moorland edge of Airedale. Opposite to us was the country-house where Charlotte Brontë was governess, and below us ran the railway, linking a string of manufacturing villages which already were beginning to stretch out toward each other, and threatened soon to extend through the valley an unbroken succession of tall chimneys and slate roofs. He told me how, within his memory, the old affection for place and home had disappeared from the district. I asked whether he thought that a new affection was possible; whether, now that men lived in the larger world of knowledge and inference, rather than in the narrower world of sight and hearing, a patriotism of books and maps might not appear which should be a better guide to life than the patriotism of the village street.

This he strongly denied; as the older feeling went, nothing, he said, had taken its place, or would take its place, but a naked and restless individualism, always seeking for personal satisfaction, and always missing it. And then, almost in the words of Morris and Ruskin, he began to urge that we should pay a cheap price if we could regain the true riches of life by forgetting steam and electricity, and returning to the agriculture of the mediaeval village and the handicrafts of the mediaeval town.

He knew and I knew that his plea was hopeless. Even under the old conditions the Greek and Italian and Flemish city-states perished, because they were too small to protect themselves against larger though less closely organized communities; and industrial progress is an invader even more irresistible than the armies of Macedon or Spain. For a constantly increasing proportion of the inhabitants of modern England there is now no place where in the old sense they "live." Nearly the whole of the class engaged in the direction of English industry, and a rapidly increasing proportion of the manual workers, pass daily, in tram or train, between sleeping-place and working-place, a hundred times more sights than their eyes can take in or their memory retain. They are, to use Mr. Wells's phrase, "delocalized."

But now that we can no longer take the range of our senses as a basis for calculating the possible area of the civilized state, there might seem to be no facts at all which can be used for such a calculation. How can we fix the limits of effective intercommunication by steam or electricity, or the area which can be covered by such political expedients as representation and federalism? . . . If once we assume that a state may be larger than the field of vision of a single man, then the merely mechanical difficulty of bringing the whole earth under a government as effective as that of the United States or the British Empire has already been overcome. If such a government is impossible, its impossibility must be due to the limits not of our senses and muscles but of our powers of imagination and sympathy.

I have already pointed out that the modern state must exist for the thoughts and feelings of its citizens, not as a fact of direct observation but as an entity of the mind, a symbol, a personification or an abstraction. The possible area of the state will depend, therefore, mainly on the facts which limit our creation and use of such entities. Fifty years ago the statesmen who were reconstructing Europe on the basis of nationality thought that they had found the relevant facts in the causes which limit the physical and mental homogeneity of nations. A state, they thought, if it is to be effectively governed, must be a homogeneous "nation," because no citizen can imagine his state or make it the object of his political affection unless he believes in the existence of a national type to which the individual inhabitants of the state are assimilated; and he cannot continue to believe in the existence of such a type unless in fact his fellow citizens are like each other and like himself in certain important respects. Bismarck deliberately limited the area of his intended German Empire by a quantitative calculation as to the possibility of assimilating other Germans to the Prussian type. He always opposed the inclusion of Austria, and for a long time the inclusion of Bavaria, on the ground that while the Prussian type was strong enough to assimilate the Saxons and Hanoverians to itself, it would fail to assimilate Austrians and Bavarians. He said, for instance, in 1866: "We cannot use these Ultramontanes, and we must not swallow more than we can digest."

Mazzini believed, with Bismarck, that no state could be well governed unless it consisted of a homogeneous nation. But Bismarck's policy of the artificial assimilation of the weaker by the stronger type seemed to him the vilest form of tyranny; and he based his own plans for the reconstruction of Europe upon the purpose of God, as revealed by the existing correspondence of national uniformities with geographical facts. "God," he said, "divided humanity into distinct groups or nuclei upon the face of the earth. . . . Evil governments have disfigured the divine design. Nevertheless you may still trace it, distinctly marked out — at least as far as Europe is concerned — by the course of the great rivers, the direction of the higher mountains, and other geographical conditions."

Both Mazzini and Bismarck, therefore, opposed with all their strength the humanitarianism of the French Revolution, the philosophy which, as Canning said, "reduced the nation into individuals in order afterwards to congregate them into mobs." Mazzini attacked the "cosmopolitans," who preached that all men should love each other without distinction of nationality, on the ground that they were asking for a psychological impossibility. No man, he argued, can imagine, and therefore no one can love, mankind, if mankind means to him all the millions of individual human beings. Already in 1836 he denounced the original Carbonari for this reason: "The cosmopolitan," he then said, "alone in the midst of the immense circle by which he is surrounded, whose boundaries extend beyond the limits of his vision; possessed of no other weapons than the consciousness of his rights (often misconceived) and his individual faculties — which, however powerful, are incapable of extending their activity over the whole sphere of application constituting the aim . . . has but two paths before him. He is compelled to choose between despotism and inertia." He quotes the Breton fisherman who, as he puts out to sea, prays to God, "Help me, my God! My boat is so small and Thy ocean so wide."

For Mazzini the divinely indicated nation stood therefore between the individual man and the unimaginable multitude of the human race. A man could comprehend and love his nation because it consisted of beings like himself "speaking the same language, gifted with the same tendencies, and educated by the same historical tradition" and could be thought of as a single national entity. The nation was "the intermediate term between humanity and the individual," and man could only attain to the conception of humanity by picturing it to himself as a mosaic of homogeneous nations. "Nations are the citizens of humanity as individuals are the citizens of the nation"; and again, "The pact of humanity cannot be signed by individuals, but only by free and equal peoples, possessing a name, a banner, and the consciousness of a distinct existence."

Nationalism, as interpreted either by Bismarck or by Mazzini, played a great and valuable part in the development of the political consciousness of Europe during the nineteenth century. But it is becoming less and less possible to accept it as a solution for the problems of the twentieth century. We cannot now assert with Mazzini that the "indisputable tendency of our epoch" is toward a reconstitution of Europe into a certain number of homogeneous national states "as nearly as possible equal in population and extent." Mazzini, indeed, unconsciously but enormously exaggerated the simplicity of the question even in his own time. National types throughout the greater part of southeastern Europe were not even then divided into homogeneous units by "the course of the great rivers and the direction of the high mountains," but were intermingled from village to village; and events have since forced us to admit that fact. We no longer, for instance, can believe, as Mr. Swinburne and the other English disciples of Mazzini and of Kossuth seem to have believed in the 1860's, that Hungary is inhabited only by a homogeneous population of patriotic Magyars. We can see that Mazzini was already straining his principle to the breaking point when he said in 1852: "It is in the power of Greece . . . to become, by extending itself to Constantinople, a powerful barrier against the European encroachments of Russia." In Macedonia today bands of Bulgarian and Greek patriots, both educated in the pure tradition of Mazzinism, are attempting to exterminate the rival populations in order to estab-

lish their own claim to represent the purposes of God as indicated by
the position of the Balkan mountains. Mazzini himself would,
perhaps, were he living now, admit that, if the Bismarckian policy
of artificial assimilation is to be rejected, there must continue to be
some states in Europe which contain inhabitants belonging to widely
different national types.

Bismarck's conception of an artificial uniformity created by "blood
and iron" corresponded more closely than did Mazzini's to the facts
of the nineteenth century. But its practicability depended upon the
assumption that the members of the dominant nationality would
always vehemently desire to impose their own type on the rest. Now
that the Social Democrats, who are a not inconsiderable proportion
of the Prussian population, apparently admire their Polish or Ba-
varian or Danish fellow subjects all the more because they cling to
their own national characteristics, Prince Bülow's Bismarckian dictum
the other day, that the strength of Germany depends on the existence
and dominance of an intensely national Prussia, seemed a mere political survival. The same change of feeling has also shown itself in
the United Kingdom, and both the English parties have now tacitly
abandoned the Anglicization of Ireland and Wales, which all parties
once accepted as a necessary part of English policy.

A still more important difficulty in applying the principle that the
area of the state should be based on homogeneity of national type,
whether natural or artificial, has been created by the rapid extension
during the last twenty-five years of all the larger European states
into non-European territory. Neither Mazzini, till his death in 1872,
nor Bismarck, till the colonial adventure of 1884, was compelled to
take into his calculations the inclusion of territories and peoples outside Europe. Neither of them, therefore, made any effective intellectual preparation for those problems which have been raised in our
time by "the scramble for the world." Mazzini seems, indeed, to
have vaguely expected that nationality would spread from Europe
into Asia and Africa, and that the "pact of humanity" would ultimately be "signed" by homogeneous and independent "nations,"
who would cover the whole land surface of the globe. But he never
indicated the political forces by which that result was to be brought
about. The Italian invasion of Abyssinia in 1896 might have been
represented either as a necessary stage in the Mazzinian policy of
spreading the idea of nationality to Africa, or as a direct contradiction
of that idea itself.

Bismarck, with his narrower and more practical intellect, never looked forward, as Mazzini did, to a "pact of humanity," which should include even the nations of Europe, and, indeed, always protested against the attempt to conceive of any relation whatsoever, moral or political, as existing between any state and the states or populations outside its boundaries. "The only sound principle of action," he said, "for a great state is political egoism." When, therefore, after Bismarck's death German sailors and soldiers found themselves in contact with the defenseless inhabitants of China or East Africa, they were, as the Social Democrats quickly pointed out, provided with no conception of the situation more highly developed than that which was acted upon in the fifth century A.D., by Attila and his Huns.

The modern English imperialists tried for some time to apply the idea of national homogeneity to the facts of the British Empire. From the publication of Seeley's *Expansion of England* in 1883 till the Peace of Vereeniging in 1902 they strove to believe in the existence of a "Blood," an "Island Race," consisting of homogeneous English-speaking individuals, among whom were to be reckoned not only the whole population of the United Kingdom, but all the reasonably white inhabitants of our colonies and dependencies; while they thought of the other of the Empire as "the white man's burden" — the necessary material for the exercise of the white man's virtues. The idealists among them, when they were forced to realize that such a homogeneity of the whites did not yet exist, persuaded themselves that it would come peacefully and inevitably as a result of the reading of imperial poems and the summoning of an imperial council. The Bismarckian realists among them believed that it would be brought about, in South Africa and elsewhere, by "blood and iron." Lord Milner, who is perhaps the most loyal adherent of the Bismarckian tradition to be found out of Germany, contended even at Vereeniging against peace with the Boers on any terms except such an unconditional surrender as would involve the ultimate Anglicization of the South African colonies. He still dreams of a British Empire whose egoism shall be as complete as that of Bismarck's Prussia, and warns us in 1907, in the style of 1887, against those "ideas of our youth" which were "at once too insular and too cosmopolitan."

But in the minds of most of our present imperialists, imperial egoism is now deprived of its only possible psychological basis. It is to be based not upon national homogeneity but upon the consciousness of national variation. The French in Canada are to remain intensely French, and the Dutch in South Africa intensely Dutch; though both are to be divided from the world outside the British

Empire by an unbridgeable moral chasm. To imperialism so conceived facts lend no support. The loyal acceptance of British Imperial citizenship by Sir Wilfred Laurier or General Botha constitutes something more subtle, something, to adapt Lord Milner's phrase, less insular but more cosmopolitan than imperial egoism. It does not, for instance, involve an absolute indifference to the question whether France or Holland shall be swallowed up by the sea.

At the same time the non-white races within the Empire show no signs of enthusiastic contentment at the prospect of existing, like the English "poor" during the eighteenth century, as the mere material of other men's virtues. They too have their own vague ideas of nationality; and if those ideas do not ultimately break up our Empire, it will be because they are enlarged and held in check, not by the sentiment of imperial egoism, but by those wider religious and ethical conceptions which pay little heed to imperial or national frontiers. . . .

If the policy of imperial egoism is a successful one it will be adopted by all empires alike, and whether we desire it or not, the victor in each inter-imperial war will take over the territory of the loser. After centuries of warfare and the steady retrogression, in the waste of blood and treasure and loyalty, of modern civilization, two empires, England and Germany, or America and China, may remain. Both will possess an armament which represents the whole "surplus value," beyond mere subsistence, created by its inhabitants. Both will contain white and yellow and brown and black men hating each other across a wavering line of the map of the world. But the struggle will go on, and, as the result of a naval Armageddon in the Pacific, only one empire will exist. "Imperial egoism," having worked itself out to its logical conclusion, will have no further meaning, and the inhabitants of the globe, diminished to half their number, will be compelled to consider the problems of race and of the organized exploitation of the globe from the point of view of mere humanitarianism.

Is the suggestion completely wanting in practicability that we might begin that consideration before the struggle goes any further? Fifteen hundred years ago, in southeastern Europe, men who held the Homoousian opinion of the Trinity were gathered in arms against the Homoiousians. The generals and other *Realpolitiker* on both sides may have feared, like Lord Milner, lest their followers should become "too cosmopolitan," too ready to extend their sympathies across the frontiers of theology. "This," a Homoousian may have said, "is a practical matter. Unless our side learn by training themselves in theological egoism to hate the other side, we shall be beaten in the nest battle." And yet we can now see that the practical interests of Europe were very little concerned with the question whether "we" or "they" won, but very seriously concerned with the question whether the division itself into "we" or "they" could not be obliterated by the discovery either of a less clumsy metaphysic, or of a way of thinking about humanity which made the continued existence of those who disagreed with one in theology no longer intolerable. May the Germans and ourselves be now marching toward the horrors of a world war merely because "nation" and "empire" like "Homoousia" and "Homoiousia" are the best that we can do in making entities of the mind to stand between us and an unintelligible universe, and because having made such entities our sympathies are shut up within them?

I have already urged, when considering the conditions of political reasoning, that many of the logical difficulties arising from our tendency to divide the infinite stream of our thoughts and sensations into homogeneous classes and species are now unnecessary and have been avoided in our time by the students of the natural sciences. Just as the modern artist substitutes without mental confusion his ever-varying curves and surfaces for the straight and simple lines of the savage, so the scientific imagination has learned to deal with the varying facts of nature without thinking of them as separate groups, each composed of identical individuals and represented to us by a single type.

Can we learn so to think of the varying individuals of the whole human race? Can we do, that is to say, what Mazzini declared to be impossible? And if we can, shall we be able to love the fifteen hundred million different human beings of whom we are thus enabled to think?

To the first question the publication of the *Origin of Species* in 1859 offered an answer. Since then we have in fact been able to represent the human race to our imagination, neither as a chaos of arbitrarily varying individuals, nor as a mosaic of homogeneous nations, but as a biological group, every individual in which differs from every other not arbitrarily but according to an intelligible process of organic evolution. And, since that which exists for the imagination can exist also for the emotions, it might have been hoped that the second question would also have been answered by evolution, and that the warring egoisms of nations and empires might henceforth have been dissolved by love for that infinitely varying multitude whom we can watch as they work their way through so much pain and confusion toward a more harmonious relation to the universe.

But it was the intellectual tragedy of the nineteenth century that the discovery of organic evolution, instead of stimulating such a general love of humanity, seemed at first to show that it was forever impossible. Progress, it appeared, had been always due to a ruthless struggle for life, which must still continue unless progress was to cease. Pity and love would lead inevitably to the degeneration of the species.

This grim conception of an internecine conflict, inevitable and unending, in which all races must play their part, hung for a generation after 1859 over the study of world politics as the fear of a cooling sun hung over physics, and the fear of a population to be checked only by famine and war hung over the century of political economy. Before Darwin wrote, it had been possible for philanthropists to think of the non-white races as "men and brothers" who, after a short process of education, would become in all respects except color identical with themselves. Darwin made it clear that the difficulty could not be so glossed over. Racial variations were shown to be unaffected by education, to have existed for millions of years, and to be tending perhaps toward divergence rather than assimilation.

The practical problem also of race relationship has, by a coincidence, presented itself since Darwin wrote in a sterner form. During the first half of the nineteenth century the European colonists who were in daily contact with non-European races, although their impulses and their knowledge alike revolted from the optimistic ethnology of Exeter Hall, yet could escape all thought about their own position by assuming that the problem would settle itself. To the natives of Australia or Canada or the Hottentots of South Africa trade automatically brought disease, and disease cleared the land for a stronger population. But the weakest races and individuals have now died out, the surviving populations are showing unexpected powers of resisting the white man's epidemics, and we are adding every year to our knowledge of, and therefore our responsibility for, the causation of infection. We are nearing the time when the extermination of races, if it is done at all, must be done deliberately.

But if the extermination is to be both inevitable and deliberate, how can there exist a community either of affection or purpose between the killers and the killed? No one at this moment professes, as far as I know, to have an easy and perfect answer to this question. The point of ethics lies within the region claimed by religion. But Christianity, which at present is the religion chiefly concerned, has conspicuously failed even to produce a tolerable working compromise. The official Christian theory is, apparently, that all human souls are of equal value, and that it ought to be a matter of indifference to us whether a given territory is inhabited a thousand years hence by a million converted Central African pigmies or a million equally converted Europeans or Hindus. On the practical point, however, whether the stronger race should base its plans of extension on the extermination of the weaker race, or on an attempt, within the limits of racial possibility, to improve it, Christians have, during the nineteenth century, been infinitely more ruthless than Mohammedans, though their ruthlessness has often been disguised by more or less conscious hypocrisy.

But the most immediately dangerous result of political "Darwinism" was not its effect in justifying the extermination of African aborigines by European colonists, but the fact that the conception of the "struggle for life" could be used as a proof that that conflict among the European nations for the control of the trade routes of the world which has been threatening for the last quarter of a century is for each of the nations concerned both a scientific necessity and a moral duty. Lord Ampthill, for instance, the athletic ex-governor of Madras, said the other day: "From an individual struggle, a struggle of families, of communities, and nations, the struggle for existence has now advanced to a struggle of empires." . . .

Any such identification of the biological advantage arising from the "struggle for life" among individuals with that which is to be expected from a "struggle of empires," is, of course, thoroughly unscientific. The "struggle of empires" must either be fought out between European troops alone, or between Europeans in combination with their non-European allies and subjects. If it takes the first form, and if we assume, as Lord Ampthill probably does, that the North European racial type is "higher" than any other, then the slaughter of half a million selected Englishmen and half a million selected Germans will clearly be an act of biological retrogression. Even if the non-European races are brought in, and a corresponding number of selected Turks and Arabs and Tartars, or of Gurkhas and Pathans and Soudanese, are slaughtered, the biological loss to the world, as measured by the percentage of surviving "higher" or "lower" individuals, will only be slightly diminished.

Nor is that form of the argument much better founded which contends that the evolutionary advantage to be expected from the "struggle of empires" is the "survival" not of races but of political and cultural types. Our victory over the German Empire, for instance, would mean, it is said, a victory for the idea of political liberty. This argument, which, when urged by the rulers of India, sounds somewhat temerarious, requires the assumption that types of culture are in the modern world most successfully spread by military occupation. But in the Ancient World, Greek culture spread most rapidly after the fall of the Greek Empire; Japan in our own time adopted Western culture more readily as an independent nation than she would have done as a dependency of Russia or France; and India is perhaps more likely today to learn from Japan than from England.

Lord Ampthill's phrase, however, represents not so much an argument as a habit of feeling shared by many who have forgotten or never known the biological doctrine which it echoes. The first followers of Darwin believed that the human species had been raised above its prehuman ancestors because, and in so far as, it had surrendered itself to a blind instinct of conflict. It seemed, therefore, as if the old moral precept that men should control their more violent impulses by reflection had been founded upon a mistake. Unreflecting instinct was, after all, the best guide, and nations who acted instinctively toward their neighbors might justify themselves, like the Parisian ruffians of ten years ago, by claiming to be "strugforlifeurs."

If this habit of mind is to be destroyed it must be opposed, not merely by a new argument, but by a conception of man's relation to the universe which creates emotional force as well as intellectual conviction.

And the change that has already shown itself in our conception of the struggle for life among individuals indicates that, by some divine chance, a corresponding change may come in our conception of the struggle between peoples. The evolutionists of our own time tell us that the improvement of the biological inheritance of any community is to be hoped for, not from the encouragement of individual conflict, but from the stimulation of the higher social impulses under the guidance of the science of eugenics; and the emotional effect of this new conception is already seen in the almost complete disappearance from industrial politics of that unwillingly brutal "individualism" which afflicted kindly Englishmen in the 1860's.

An international science of eugenics might in the same way indicate that the various races should aim, not at exterminating each other, but at encouraging the improvement by each of its own racial type. Such an idea would not appeal to those for whom the whole species arranges itself in definite and obvious grades of "higher" and "lower," from the northern Europeans downward, and who are as certain of the ultimate necessity of a "white world" as the Sydney politicians are of the necessity of a "white Australia." But in this respect during the last few years the inhabitants of Europe have shown signs of a new humility, due partly to widespread intellectual causes and partly to the hard facts of the Russo-Japanese War and the arming of China. The "spheres of influence" into which we divided the Far East eight years ago seem to us now a rather stupid joke, and those who read history are already bitterly ashamed that we destroyed, by the sack of the Summer Palace in 1859, the products of a thousand years of such art as we can never hope to emulate. We are coming honestly to believe that the world is richer for the existence both of other civilizations and of other racial types than our own. We have been compelled by the study of the Christian documents to think of our religion as one only among the religions of the world, and to acknowledge that it has owed much and may owe much again to the longer philosophic tradition and the subtler and more patient brains of Hindustan and Persia. Even if we look at the future of the species as a matter of pure biology, we are warned by men of science that it is not safe to depend only on one family or one variety for the whole breeding-stock of the world. For the moment we shrink from the interbreeding of races, but we do so in spite of some conspicuous examples of successful interbreeding in the past, and largely because of our complete ignorance of the conditions on which success depends.

Already, therefore, it is possible without intellectual dishonesty to look forward to a future for the race which need not be reached through a welter of blood and hatred. We can imagine the nations settling the racial allocation of the temperate or tropical breeding-grounds, or even deliberately placing the males and females of the few hopelessly backward tribes on different islands, without the necessity that the most violent passions of mankind should be stimulated in preparation for a general war. No one now expects an immediate, or prophesies with certainty an ultimate, Federation of the Globe; but the consciousness of a common purpose in mankind, or even the acknowledgment that such a common purpose is possible, would alter the face of world politics at once. The discussion at The Hague of a halt in the race of armaments would no longer seem utopian, and the strenuous profession by the colonizing powers that they have no selfish ends in view might be transformed from a sordid and useless hypocrisy into a fact to which each nation might adjust its policy. The irrational race hatred which breaks out from time to time on the fringes of empire would have little effect in world politics when opposed by a consistent conception of the future of human progress.

Meanwhile, it is true, the military preparations for a death struggle of empires still go on, and the problem even of peaceful immigration becomes yearly more threatening, now that shipping companies can land tens of thousands of Chinese or Indian laborers for a pound or two a head at any port in the world. But when we think of such things we need no longer feel ourselves in the grip of a Fate that laughs at human purpose and human kindliness. An idea of the whole existence of our species is at last a possible background to our individual experience. Its emotional effect may prove to be not less than that of the visible temples and walls of the Greek cities, although it is formed not from the testimony of our eyesight, but from the knowledge which we acquire in our childhood and confirm by the half-conscious corroboration of our daily life.

We all of us, plain folk and learned alike, now make a picture for ourselves of the globe with its hemispheres of light and shadow, from every point of which the telegraph brings us hourly news, and which may already be more real to us than the fields and houses past which we hurry in the train. We can see it, hanging and turning in the monstrous emptiness of the skies, and obedient to forces whose action we can watch hundreds of light-years away and feel in the beating of our hearts. The sharp new evidence of the camera brings every year nearer to us its surface of ice and rock and plain, and the wondering eyes of alien peoples.

It may be that we shall long continue to differ as to the full significance of this vision. But now that we can look at it without helpless pain it may stir the deepest impulses of our being. To some of us it may bring confidence in that Love that Dante saw, "which moves the Sun and the other Stars." To each of us it may suggest a kinder pity for all the bewildered beings who hand on from generation to generation the torch of conscious life.

THE MORAL EQUIVALENT OF WAR[1]

William James

WILLIAM JAMES, the greatest of American psychologists and with Jonathan Edwards and Emerson one of the three greatest American philosophers, may be credited with a striking series of achievements. His first book, *Principles of Psychology* (1890), which he was twelve years in writing, was notable for its assertion of the right of psychology to all the privileges and dignities of a special science, for its felicity of style, its humor and its picturesque illustrations, and for its original ideas. Two of these ideas — that of the continuity of the stream of consciousness, and the James-Lange theory of the emotions — at once became famous. His second important book, *The Will to Believe and Other Essays* (1897), was a brilliant exposition of certain moral ideas. The title-paper, which he later said should have been called "The Right to Believe," set forth the principle that when men pass the bounds of demonstrable fact or logic and enter upon philosophy and religion, they do quite right to let their "passional nature" fix their beliefs. No one had previously explained the rôle of will and emotion in belief so clearly or persuasively. Another essay in the same volume, "The Dilemma of Determinism," expounded James's quite Puritan belief in the superiority of moral over aesthetic standards, while a paper called "Is Life Worth Living?" taught his doctrine of strenuous effort and heroism. In a third volume, *Talks to Teachers on Psychology* (1899), James did much to define and popularize the new theories of educational psychology. This was followed by his impressive work on *The Varieties of Religious Experience* (1902), a scientific and empirical study of all religious states of mind — despair, conversion, mysticism, saintliness, and so on. It drove home to students the fact that ecclesiastical history and the dogmas and outward trappings of religion are actually a less fruitful field of study than the mental and emotional states produced by religion. For a time the author collected material for a proposed volume on varieties of military experience, and from this sprang his essay on "The Moral Equivalent of War." As throughout his earlier career he had been deeply interested in philosophy, so during his later career he remained true to his early delight in psychological studies; but after 1905 his publications were all definitely in the metaphysical field. The principal works in which he defended the idealist position from an empirical standpoint were *Pragmatism* (1907), *The Meaning of Truth* (1909), *A Pluralistic Universe* (1909), and *Essays in Radical Empiricism* (1912).

James, who was born in New York in 1842 and educated in the Harvard Medical School, spent most of his life — he died in 1910 — teaching at Harvard, first in anatomy and physiology, and later in psychology and philosophy. The son of a brilliant man and the brother of the eminent novelist Henry James, he enjoyed a cosmopolitan training, moved in the most cultivated circles of Europe and America, and made a host of friends in England and on the Continent. His personality had a power which is best understood through the two volumes of his *Letters*. Associ-

[1] From *Memories and Studies*, by William James. Reprinted by permission of Longmans, Green & Company, publishers.

ates felt a central mystical fire in him, apart from his fine intellect, which was always throwing off sparks. He was unconventional, fearless, masculine. "He was a sage and a holy man," writes John Jay Chapman, "and yet in conjunction with this he was a sportive, wayward, Gothic sort of spirit, who was apt, on meeting a friend, to burst into foolery, and whose wit was always three parts poetry." And Santayana pictures him as constantly puzzling his classes (he used to ask them "What *was* I talking about?") and often startling them: "In the midst of this routine of the classroom the spirit would sometimes come upon him, and leaning his head on his hand, he would let fall golden words, picturesque, fresh from the heart, full of the knowledge of good and evil . . .; radicalisms plunging sometimes into the sub-soil of all human philosophies; and, on occasion, thoughts of simple wisdom and wistful piety, the most unfeigned and manly that anybody ever had."

The war against war is going to be no holiday excursion or camping party. The military feelings are too deeply grounded to abdicate their place among our ideals until better substitutes are offered than the glory and shame that come to nations as well as to individuals from the ups and downs of politics and the vicissitudes of trade. There is something highly paradoxical in the modern man's relation to war. Ask all our millions, north and south, whether they would vote now (were such a thing possible) to have our war for the Union expunged from history, and the record of a peaceful transition to the present time substituted for that of its marches and battles, and probably hardly a handful of eccentrics would say yes. Those ancestors, those efforts, those memories and legends, are the most ideal part of what we now own together, a sacred spiritual possession worth more than all the blood poured out. Yet ask those same people whether they would be willing in cold blood to start another civil war now to gain another similar possession, and not one man or woman would vote for the proposition. In modern eyes, precious though wars may be, they must not be waged solely for the sake of the ideal harvest. Only when forced upon one, only when an enemy's injustice leaves us no alternative, is a war now thought permissible.

It was not thus in ancient times. The earlier men were hunting men, and to hunt a neighboring tribe, kill the males, loot the village and possess the females, was the most profitable, as well as the most exciting, way of living. Thus were the more martial tribes selected, and in chiefs and peoples a pure pugnacity and love of glory came to mingle with the more fundamental appetite for plunder.

Modern war is so expensive that we feel trade to be a better avenue to plunder; but modern man inherits all the innate pugnacity and all the love of glory of his ancestors. Showing war's irrationality and horror is of no effect upon him. The horrors make the fascination.

War is the *strong* life; it is life *in extremis;* war taxes are the only ones men never hesitate to pay, as the budgets of all nations show us.

History is a bath of blood. The *Iliad* is one long recital of how Diomedes and Ajax, Sarpedon and Hector, *killed.* No detail of the wounds they made is spared us, and the Greek mind fed upon the story. Greek history is a panorama of jingoism and imperialism — war for war's sake, all the citizens being warriors. It is horrible reading, because of the irrationality of it all — save for the purpose of making "history" — and the history is that of the utter ruin of a civilization in intellectual respects perhaps the highest the earth has ever seen.

Those wars were purely piratical. Pride, gold, women, slaves, excitement, were their only motives. In the Peloponnesian War, for example, the Athenians asked the inhabitants of Melos (the island where the "Venus of Milo" was found), hitherto neutral, to own their lordship. The envoys meet, and hold a debate which Thucydides gives in full, and which, for sweet reasonableness of form, would have satisfied Matthew Arnold. "The powerful exact what they can," said the Athenians, "and the weak grant what they must." When the Meleans say that sooner than be slaves they will appeal to the gods, the Athenians reply: "Of the gods we believe and of men we know that, by a law of their nature, wherever they can rule they will. This law was not made by us, and we are not the first to have acted upon it; we did but inherit it, and we know that you and all mankind, if you were as strong as we are, would do as we do. So much for the gods; we have told you why we expect to stand as high in their good opinion as you." Well, the Meleans still refused, and their town was taken. "The Athenians," Thucydides quietly says, "thereupon put to death all who were of military age and made slaves of the women and children. They then colonized the island, sending thither five hundred settlers of their own."

Alexander's career was piracy pure and simple, nothing but an orgy of power and plunder, made romantic by the character of the hero. There was no rational principle in it, and the moment he died his generals and governors attacked one another. The cruelty of those times is incredible. When Rome finally conquered Greece, Paulus Aemilius was told by the Roman Senate to reward his soldiers for their toil by "giving" them the old kingdom of Epirus. They sacked seventy cities and carried off a hundred and fifty thousand inhabitants as slaves. How many they killed I know not; but in Etolia they killed all the senators, five hundred and fifty in number. Brutus was "the noblest Roman of them all," but to reanimate his soldiers on the eve of Philippi he similarly promises to give them the cities of Sparta and Thessalonica to ravage, if they win the fight.

Such was the gory nurse that trained societies to cohesiveness. We inherit the warlike type; and for most of the capacities of heroism that the human race is full of we have to thank this cruel history. Dead men tell no tales, and if there were any tribes of other type than this they have left no survivors. Our ancestors have bred pugnacity into our bone and marrow, and thousands of years of peace won't breed it out of us. The popular imagination fairly fattens on the thought of wars. Let public opinion once reach a certain fighting pitch, and no ruler can withstand it. In the Boer War both governments began with bluff, but couldn't stay there; the military tension was too much for them. In 1898 our people had read the word WAR in letters three inches high for three months in every newspaper. The pliant politician McKinley was swept away by their eagerness, and our squalid war with Spain became a necessity.

At the present day, civilized opinion is a curious mental mixture. The military instincts and ideals are as strong as ever, but are confronted by reflective criticisms which sorely curb their ancient freedom. Innumerable writers are showing up the bestial side of military service. Pure loot and mastery seem no longer morally avowable motives, and pretexts must be found for attributing them solely to the enemy. England and we, our army and navy authorities repeat without ceasing, arm solely for "peace"; Germany and Japan it is who are bent on loot and glory. "Peace" in military mouths today is a synonym for "war expected." The word has become a pure provocative, and no government wishing peace sincerely should allow it ever to be printed in a newspaper. Every up-to-date dictionary should say that "peace" and "war" mean the same thing, now *in posse*, now *in actu*. It may even reasonably be said that the intensely sharp competitive *preparation* for war by the nations *is the real war*, permanent, unceasing; and that the battles are only a sort of public verification of the mastery gained during the "peace" interval.

It is plain that on this subject civilized man has developed a sort of double personality. If we take European nations, no legitimate interest of any one of them would seem to justify the tremendous destructions which a war to compass it would necessarily entail. It would seem as though common sense and reason ought to find a way to reach agreement in every conflict of honest interests. I myself think it our bounden duty to believe in such international rationality as possible. But, as things stand, I see how desperately hard it is to bring the peace party and the war party together, and I believe that the difficulty is due to certain deficiencies in the program of pacificism which set the militarist imagination strongly, and to a certain extent justifiably, against it. In the whole discussion both sides are on imaginative and sentimental ground. It is but one utopia against another, and everything one says must be abstract and hypothetical. Subject to this criticism and caution, I will try to characterize in abstract strokes the opposite imaginative forces, and point out what to my own very fallible mind seems the best utopian hypothesis, the most promising line of conciliation.

In my remarks, pacificist though I am, I will refuse to speak of the bestial side of the war régime (already done justice to by many writers) and consider only the higher aspects of militaristic sentiment. Patriotism no one thinks discreditable; nor does anyone deny that war is the romance of history. But inordinate ambitions are the soul of every patriotism, and the possibility of violent death the soul of all romance. The militarily patriotic and romantic-minded every- where, and especially the professional military class, refuse to admit for a moment that war may be a transitory phenomenon in social evolution. The notion of a sheep's paradise like that revolts, they say, our higher imagination. Where then would be the steeps of life? If war had ever stopped, we should have to reinvent it, on this view, to redeem life from flat degeneration.

Reflective apologists for war at the present day all take it religiously. It is a sort of sacrament. Its profits are to the vanquished as well as to the victor; and quite apart from any question of profit, it is an absolute good, we are told, for it is human nature at its highest dynamic. Its "horrors" are a cheap price to pay for rescue from the only alternative supposed, of a world of clerks and teachers, of co- education and zoöphily, of "consumer's leagues" and "associated charities," of industrialism unlimited and feminism unabashed. No scorn, no hardness, no valor any more! Fie upon such a cattleyard of a planet!

So far as the central essence of this feeling goes, no healthy-minded person, it seems to me, can help to some degree partaking of it. Militarism is the great preserver of our ideals of hardihood, and human life with no use for hardihood would be contemptible. With- out risks or prizes for the darer, history would be insipid indeed; and there is a type of military character which everyone feels that the race should never cease to breed, for everyone is sensitive to its superiority. The duty is incumbent on mankind, of keeping military characters in stock — of keeping them, if not for use, then as ends in themselves and as pure pieces of perfection — so that Roosevelt's weaklings and mollycoddles may not end by making everything else disappear from the face of nature.

This natural sort of feeling forms, I think, the innermost soul of army writings. Without any exception known to me, militarist authors take a highly mystical view of their subject, and regard war as a biological or sociological necessity, uncontrolled by ordinary psychological checks and motives. When the time of development is ripe the war must come, reason or no reason, for the justifications pleaded are invariably fictitious. War is, in short, a permanent human *obligation*. General Homer Lea, in his recent book, *The Valor of Ignorance*, plants himself squarely on this ground. Readiness for war is for him the essence of nationality, and ability in it the supreme measure of the health of nations.

Nations, General Lea says, are never stationary — they must necessarily expand or shrink, according to their vitality or decrepitude. Japan now is culminating; and by the fatal law in question it is impossible that her statesmen should not long since have entered, with extraordinary foresight, upon a vast policy of conquest — the game in which the first moves were her wars with China and Russia and her treaty with England, and of which the final objective is the capture of the Philippines, the Hawaiian Islands, Alaska, and the whole of our coast west of the Sierra Passes. This will give Japan what her ineluctable vocation as a state absolutely forces her to claim, the possession of the entire Pacific Ocean; and to oppose these deep designs we Americans have, according to our author, nothing but our conceit, our ignorance, our commercialism, our corruption, and our feminism. General Lea makes a minute technical comparison of the military strength which we at present could oppose to the strength of Japan, and concludes that the islands, Alaska, Oregon, and Southern California, would fall almost without resistance, that San Francisco must surrender in a fortnight to a Japanese investment; that in three or four months the war would be over, and our Republic, unable to regain what it had heedlessly neglected to protect sufficiently, would then "disintegrate," until perhaps some Caesar should arise to weld us again into a nation.

A dismal forecast indeed! Yet not unplausible, if the mentality of Japan's statesmen be of the Caesarian type of which history shows so many examples, and which is all that General Lea seems able to imagine. But there is no reason to think that women can no longer be the mothers of Napoleonic or Alexandrian characters; and if these come in Japan and find their opportunity, just such surprises as *The Valor of Ignorance* paints may lurk in ambush for us. Ignorant as we still are of the innermost recesses of Japanese mentality, we may be foolhardy to disregard such possibilities.

Other militarists are more complex and more moral in their considerations. The *Philosophie des Krieges*, by S. R. Steinmetz, is a good example. War, according to this author, is an ordeal instituted by God, who weighs the nations in its balance. It is the essential form of the state, and the only function in which peoples can employ all their powers at once and convergently. No victory is possible save as the resultant of a totality of virtues, no defeat for which some vice or weakness is not responsible. Fidelity, cohesiveness, tenacity, heroism, conscience, education, inventiveness, economy, wealth, physical health and vigor — there isn't a moral or intellectual point of superiority that doesn't tell, when God holds his assizes and hurls the peoples upon one another. *Die Weltgeschichte ist das Weltgericht*[1]*;* and Dr. Steinmetz does not believe that in the long run chance and luck play any part in apportioning the issues.

The virtues that prevail, it must be noted, are virtues anyhow, superiorities that count in peaceful as well as in military competition; but the strain on them, being infinitely intenser in the latter case, makes war infinitely more searching as a trial. No ordeal is comparable to its winnowings. Its dread hammer is the welder of men into cohesive states, and nowhere but in such states can human nature adequately develop its capacity. The only alternative is "degeneration."

Dr. Steinmetz is a conscientious thinker, and his book, short as it is, takes much into account. Its upshot can, it seems to me, be summed up in Simon Patten's word, that mankind was nursed in pain and fear, and that the transition to a "pleasure economy" may be fatal to a being wielding no powers of defense against its disintegrative influences. If we speak of the *fear of emancipation from the fear régime*, we put the whole situation into a single phrase; fear regarding ourselves now taking the place of the ancient fear of the enemy.

Turn the fear over as I will in my mind, it all seems to lead back to two unwillingnesses of the imagination, one aesthetic, and the

---

[1] "The history of the world is the judgment of the world."

other moral: unwillingness, first to envisage a future in which army
life, with its many elements of charm, shall be forever impossible, and
in which the destinies of peoples shall nevermore be decided quickly,
thrillingly, and tragically, by force, but only gradually and insipidly
by "evolution"; and, secondly, unwillingness to see the supreme
theatre of human strenuousness closed, and the splendid military
aptitudes of men doomed to keep always in a state of latency and
never show themselves in action. These insistent unwillingnesses,
no less than other aesthetic and ethical insistencies, have, it seems to
me, to be listened to and respected. One cannot meet them effectively by mere counter-insistency on war's expensiveness and horror.
The horror makes the thrill; and when the question is of getting the
extremest and supremest out of human nature, talk of expense sounds
ignominious. The weakness of so much merely negative criticism
is evident — pacifism makes no converts from the military party.
The military party denies neither the bestiality nor the horror, nor the
expense; it only says that these things tell but half the story. It only
says that war is *worth* them; that, taking human nature as a whole,
its wars are its best protection against its weaker and more cowardly
self, and that mankind cannot *afford* to adopt a peace economy.

Pacifists ought to enter more deeply into the aesthetical and ethical
point of view of their opponents. Do that first in any controversy,
says J. J. Chapman; *then move the point*, and your opponent will follow.
So long as anti-militarists propose no substitute for war's disciplinary
function, no *moral equivalent* of war, analogous, as one might say, to
the mechanical equivalent of heat, so long they fail to realize the full
inwardness of the situation. And as a rule they do fail. The duties,
penalties, and sanctions pictured in the utopias they paint are all too
weak and tame to touch the military-minded. Tolstoi's pacificism
is the only exception to this rule, for it is profoundly pessimistic as regards all this world's values, and makes the fear of the Lord furnish
the moral spur provided elsewhere by the fear of the enemy. But
our socialistic peace advocates all believe absolutely in this world's
values; and instead of the fear of the Lord and the fear of the enemy,
the only fear they reckon with is the fear of poverty if one be lazy.
This weakness pervades all the socialistic literature with which I am
acquainted. Even in Lowes Dickinson's exquisite dialogue,[1] high
wages and short hours are the only forces invoked for overcoming
man's distaste for repulsive kinds of labor. Meanwhile men at large
still live as they always have lived, under a pain-and-fear economy —

[1] *Justice and Liberty*, New York, 1909.

for those of us who live in an ease economy are but an island in the
stormy ocean — and the whole atmosphere of present-day utopian
literature tastes mawkish and dishwatery to people who still keep a
sense for life's more bitter flavors.   It suggests, in truth, ubiquitous
inferiority.

Inferiority is always with us, and merciless scorn of it is the keynote
of the military temper.   "Dogs, would you live forever?" shouted
Frederick the Great.   "Yes," say our utopians, "let us live forever,
and raise our level gradually."   The best thing about our "inferiors"
today is that they are as tough as nails, and physically and morally
almost as insensitive.   Utopianism would see them soft and squeam-
ish, while militarism would keep their callousness, but transfigure it
into a meritorious characteristic, needed by "the service," and redeemed by that from the suspicion of inferiority.   All the qualities
of a man acquire dignity when he knows that the service of the collectivity that owns him needs them.   If proud of the collectivity, his
own pride rises in proportion.   No collectivity is like an army for
nourishing such pride; but it has to be confessed that the only sentiment which the image of pacific cosmopolitan industrialism is capable
of arousing in countless worthy breasts is shame at the idea of belonging to *such* a collectivity.   It is obvious that the United States
of America as they exist today impress a mind like General Lea's
as so much human blubber.   Where is the sharpness and precipitous-
ness, the contempt for life, whether one's own or another's?   Where
is the savage "yes" and "no," the unconditional duty?   Where is
the conscription?   Where is the blood tax?   Where is anything that
one feels honored by belonging to?

Having said thus much in preparation, I will now confess my own
utopia.   I devoutly believe in the reign of peace and in the gradual
advent of some sort of socialistic equilibrium.   The fatalistic view
of the war function is to me nonsense, for I know that war-making
is due to definite motives and subject to prudential checks and reasonable criticisms, just like any other form of enterprise.   And when
whole nations are the armies, and the science of destruction vies in
intellectual refinement with the sciences of production, I see that war
becomes absurd and impossible from its own monstrosity.   Extravagant ambitions will have to be replaced by reasonable claims, and
nations must make common cause against them.   I see no reason
why all this should not apply to yellow as well as to white countries,
and I look forward to a future when acts of war shall be formally
outlawed as between civilized peoples.

All these beliefs of mine put me squarely into the anti-militarist party. But I do not believe that peace either ought to be or will be permanent on this globe, unless the states pacifically organized preserve some of the old elements of army discipline. A permanently successful peace economy cannot be a simple pleasure economy. In the more or less socialistic future toward which mankind seems drifting we must still subject ourselves collectively to these severities which answer to our real position upon this only partly hospitable globe. We must make new energies and hardihoods continue the manliness to which the military mind so faithfully clings. Martial virtues must be the enduring cement; intrepidity, contempt of softness, surrender of private interest, obedience to command, must still remain the rock upon which states are built — unless, indeed, we wish for dangerous reactions against commonwealths fit only for contempt, and liable to invite attack whenever a center of crystallization for military-minded enterprise gets formed anywhere in their neighborhood.

The war party is assuredly right in affirming and reaffirming that the martial virtues, although originally gained by the race through war, are absolute and permanent human goods. Patriotic pride and ambition in their military form are, after all, only specifications of a more general competitive passion. They are its first form, but that is no reason for supposing them to be its last form. Men now are proud of belonging to a conquering nation, and without a murmur they lay down their persons and their wealth, if by so doing they may fend off subjection. But who can be sure that *other aspects of one's country* may not, with time and education and suggestion enough, come to be regarded with similarly effective feelings of pride and shame? Why should men not some day feel that it is worth a blood tax to belong to a collectivity superior in *any* ideal respect? Why should they not blush with indignant shame if the community that owns them is vile in any way whatsoever? Individuals, daily more numerous, now feel this civic passion. It is only a question of blowing on the spark till the whole population gets incandescent, and on the ruins of the old morals of military honor, a stable system of morals of civic honor builds itself up. What the whole community comes to believe in grasps the individual as in a vise. The war function has grasped us so far; but constructive interests may some day seem no less imperative, and impose on the individual a hardly lighter burden.

Let me illustrate my idea more concretely. There is nothing to make one indignant in the mere fact that life is hard, that men should toil and suffer pain.   The planetary conditions once for all are such, and we can stand it.   But that so many men, by mere accidents of birth and opportunity, should have a life of *nothing else* but toil and pain and hardness and inferiority imposed upon them, should have *no* vacation, while others natively no more deserving never get any taste of this campaigning life at all — *this* is capable of arousing indignation in reflective minds.   It may end by seeming shameful to all of us that some of us have nothing but campaigning, and others nothing but unmanly ease.   If now — and this is my idea — there were, instead of military conscription, a conscription of the whole youthful popula- tion to form for a certain number of years a part of the army enlisted against *Nature*, the injustice would tend to be evened out, and numer- ous other goods to the commonwealth would follow.   The military ideals of hardihood and discipline would be wrought into the growing fiber of the people; no one would remain blind as the luxurious classes now are blind, to man's real relations to the globe he lives on, and to the permanently sour and hard foundations of his higher life. To coal and iron mines, to freight trains, to fishing fleets in December, to dish-washing, clothes-washing, and window-washing, to road- building and tunnel-making, to foundries and stokeholes, and to the frames of skyscrapers, would our gilded youths be drafted off, accord- ing to their choice, to get the childishness knocked out of them, and to come back into society with healthier sympathies and soberer ideas.   They would have paid their blood tax, done their own part in the immemorial human warfare against nature, they would tread the earth more proudly, the women would value them more highly, they would be better fathers and teachers of the following generation.

Such a conscription, with the state of public opinion that would have required it, and the many moral fruits it would bear, would preserve in the midst of a pacific civilization the manly virtues which the military party is so afraid of seeing disappear in peace.   We should get toughness without callousness, authority with as little criminal cruelty as possible, and painful work done cheerily because the duty is temporary, and threatens not, as now, to degrade the whole remainder of one's life.   I spoke of the "moral equivalent" of war.   So far, war has been the only force that can discipline a whole community, and until an equivalent discipline is organized, I believe that war must have its way.   But I have no serious doubt that the ordinary prides and shames of social man, once developed to a certain intensity, are capable of organizing such a moral equivalent as I have sketched, or some other just as effective for preserving manliness of type.   It is but a question of time, of skillful propagandism, and of opinion-making men seizing historic opportunities.

The martial type of character can be bred without war.   Strenuous honor and disinterestedness abound elsewhere.   Priests and medical men are in a fashion educated to it, and we should all feel some degree of it imperative if we were conscious of our work as an obligatory service to the state.   We should be *owned*, as soldiers are by the army, and our pride would rise accordingly.   We could be poor, then, without humiliation, as army officers now are.   The only thing needed henceforward is to inflame the civic temper as past history has inflamed the military temper.   H. G. Wells, as usual, sees the center of the situation.   "In many ways," he says, "military organization is the most peaceful of activities.   When the contemporary man steps from the street, of clamorous insincere advertisement, push, adulteration, underselling and intermittent employment, into the barrack yard, he steps on to a higher social plane, into an atmosphere of service and coöperation and of infinitely more honorable emulations.   Here at least men are not flung out of employment to degenerate because there is no immediate work for them to do.   They are fed and drilled and trained for better services.   Here at least a man is supposed to win promotion by self-forgetfulness and not by self-seeking."[1] . . .

Wells adds that he thinks that the conceptions of order and discipline, the tradition of service and devotion, of physical fitness, unstinted exertion, and universal responsibility, which universal military duty is now teaching European nations, will remain a permanent acquisition, when the last ammunition has been used in the fireworks that celebrate the final peace.   I believe as he does.   It would be simply preposterous if the only force that could work ideals of honor and standards of efficiency into English or American natures should be the fear of being killed by the Germans or the Japanese.   Great indeed is Fear; but it is not, as our military enthusiasts believe and try to make us believe, the only stimulus known for awakening the higher ranges of men's spiritual energy.   The amount of alteration in public opinion which my utopia postulates is vastly less than the difference between the mentality of those black warriors who pursued Stanley's party on the Congo with their cannibal war cry of "Meat! Meat!" and that of the General Staff of any civilized nation.   History has seen the latter interval bridged over: the former one can be bridged over much more easily.

[1] *First and Last Things*, 1908, p. 215.

THE DEAD[1]

Stephen Graham

"Attracted to Russia by the spirit in Russian literature, (he) gave up life in London and took his chances with Russian peasants and students" — so STEPHEN GRAHAM summarizes the beginning of his career. Born in England in 1884, the son of the editor of *Country Life*, he was gifted with a powerful body and a keen desire to see plain people and rough places at first hand. He had something of the spirit of George Borrow, tramping through Spain with a Bible in one hand and a protecting cudgel in the other. Graham first covered a great part of Russia on foot: the Caucasus, the Crimea, the Urals, the Far North. Still unsatisfied, he accompanied the Russian peasant pilgrims to Jerusalem, and went with a body of steerage passengers, Jews and Gentiles, across the Atlantic from Russia to New York. With a beautiful simplicity, reporting precisely what he had seen, he recorded his observations — *Undiscovered Russia, With the Russian Pilgrims to Jerusalem*, and so on. The war found him a private in the Scots Guards. But in 1919 he was back on the open road again, this time covering the route of Sherman to the sea, to discover what tales and traditions of the Union army remained and what kind of folk dwelt in Georgia and the Carolinas. A little later, Christopher Morley introduced him at the Brevoort Hotel in New York to another literary tramp, Vachel Lindsay. They resolved on a new set of "adventures while preaching the gospel of beauty"; the *Evening Post* partly financed the expedition by publishing Graham's letters from the Far West; and the result was a captivating book, *Tramping with a Poet in the Rockies*. Later Graham and his wife traveled from Spain to the West Indies, and with the history of the conquistadores in mind, he trudged across the Isthmus of Panama to glimpse the Pacific from "a peak in Darien." His later books, in a world where international tramping offers some difficulty, have been more prosaic. Turning to biography, he has written lives of Peter the Great, Ivan the Terrible, Boris Godunov, and other Russians. But it is by his graphic, poetic, and very human travels that he will be remembered.

"We were fighting in a rose garden which was strewn with men who had been dead for some days. The pink roses and the green corpses were a strange combination," said L——, the young poet who wrote charming lyrics and had such a taste in art. He was fresh to the work and looked on the dead for the first time. The memory was distasteful, and yet it inevitably recurred to his mind. He strove to banish it as an elegant person in civil life would naturally banish from the mind something evil and repulsive, such as, for instance, say, some beggar woman's face that his eyes by chance had seen. I met the same L—— a month later; we were discussing impressions of

[1] From *A Private in the Guards*, by Stephen Graham. Reprinted by permission of The Macmillan Company, publishers.

the war, and he confessed that he felt no interest in the dead as such; they were just so many old cases of what had once been men. He had seen so many dead that already the instinctive horror had gone.

"They say Madame Tussaud offered a reward to anyone who would sleep a night in the Chamber of Horrors, but I think I could do it," said Dusty one night by a campfire. "I've slept in dugouts with dead men and been too tired to throw them out, and I've wakened to feel rats' breath on my cheeks. I think no waxworks could have terrors for me."

The greatest number of the soldiers had become indifferent to the horror of death, even if more intensely alive than before to the horror of dying themselves. In many an extraordinary callousness toward dead bodies was bred. They could kick a dead body, rifle the pockets of the dead, strip off clothing, make jokes about facial expressions, see wagon wheels go over corpses, and never be haunted by a further thought of it. Only if the dead were British, or if it were known to you, the dead body of someone in the same regiment, there seemed to be a sadness and a coldness, a sort of presentiment that you yourself would perish before the end and lie thus in trench or battlefield, cold and inanimate, soaked with rain, uncared for, lost to home and dear ones.

But the German dead had no interest. They lay about everywhere unburied, for our own dead had precedence with the burying parties. All along the devastated village streets the Germans lay dead as they had been shot down in action of flight, the look of running in fear was still on the brown faces, and the open mouth and white teeth seemed to betoken calls to their comrades as they ran. In the debris of the houses to which men rushed for souvenirs the dead lay too, with gentle empty faces, and ever so shabby, shoddy tunics, and their little round caps beside the subdued and thoughtless heads. Germans lay in the dusty gutters like old parcels, and men would turn them over to see the face that was biting the dust. When we were in the long ravine of Noreuil and Vaux-Vraucourt, the ridges, and indeed the hollows of the ravine itself for miles round, were strewn with dead. The air was heavy with putrefaction, and on either hand extended the battlefield, covered with wreckage and dug out with huge shell-holes. Discarded rifles, equipments, ration tins, clothes, moldy loaves of German bread, tins of corned beef, drums of ammunition lay everywhere. Unexploded German bombs lay about in scores, and likewise packages of explosives for mining. The roads were scattered with unexploded cartridges, with hundreds of thousands of them, and shells of many calibers lay about in extraordinary promiscuity, and amid all these the miserable dead lay where they fell, British and German, friend and foe. The long trenches that traversed the green fields were inhabited by corpses, and it was a pity to think of them lying long unburied, and of the souvenir-hunters handling them day by day and leaving them ever more bare.

I lived at that time for a fortnight in the midst of this wreckage of war. The dugout which I had appropriated had been used by a German before me, and there was a half-finished, sodden letter in it to a German mother, and there was a box of revolver ammunition. It was eight feet in length and a little deeper than a grave, and it was dug out of bright yellow clay at the side of a sunken road. Parties of men went to and fro all the day along the way, and the way was one of running mud. The roof was made of planks thrown across, two German blankets, and a waterproof cape detached from a set of equipment lying on the moorland above. There were five steps in the mud of the bank leading up to the dugout, and these were made of German ammunition boxes full of machine-gun ammunition. There was a shelf which was an iron sleeper from the German light railway, a fireplace made of a provision tin; for table a German stool, and for seat two petrol tins filled with dirt. Outside there were hundreds of strands of loose telegraph wire which were wandering from their shattered posts, and on one of these, pegged down by two "buckshee" bayonets, a soldier's washing could be hung out to dry. Every morning there was enough water in the sagging waterproof cape on the roof to wash in, and sometimes for a regimental shave. The sense of being surrounded on all sides by the dead never left one, and as I sat and looked out on the scene I saw displayed on a hillside a hundred yards distant the red and gray silhouettes of the ruins of Noreuil looking like some village in Palestine.

From this point I used the privilege of liberty which I had, and made expeditions to Queant and the Drocourt switch and to Bourlon Wood and Bourlon village, pulsating with the life of the British and French-Canadians who had just taken it, to Pronville and Moeuvres, and to the trenches known as P and Q and R where our battalion lay. The fascination of going from dead to dead and looking at each, and of going to every derelict tank, abandoned gun, and shattered aeroplane, was so great that inevitably one went on further and further from home, seeking and looking with a strange intensity in the heart. I saw a great number of the dead, those blue bundles and green bundles strewn far and wide over the autumn fields. The story of each man's death was plainly shown in the circumstances in which he lay. The brave machine-gunners, with resolute look in shoulders and face, lay scarcely relaxed beside their oiled machines, which if you understood you could still use, and beside piles of littered brass, the empty cartridge cases of hundreds of rounds which they had fired away before being bayoneted at their posts. Never to be forgotten was the sight of the dead defenders of Ecoust lying there with all their gear about them. On the other hand, facing those machine-gunners, one saw how our men, rushing forward in extended formation, each man a good distance from his neighbor, had fallen, one here, another there, one directly he had started forward to the attack, and then others, one, two, three, four, five, all in a sort of sequence, here, here, here, here, here; one poor wretch had got far but had got tangled in the wire, had pulled and pulled and at last been shot to rags; another had got near enough to strike the foe and been shot with a revolver. Down at the bottom of deep trenches many dead men lay, flat in the mud, sprawling along the duckboards or in the act of creeping cautiously out of holes in the side. In other parts of the field one saw the balance of battle and the Germans evidently attacking, not extended, but in groups, and now in groups together dead. One saw Germans taking cover and British taking cover in shell-holes inadequately deep, and now the men stiff as they crouched. I remember especially two of our fellows in a shell-hole; fear was in their faces, they were crouching unnaturally, and one had evidently been saying to the other, "Keep your head down!" Now in both men's heads was a dent, the sort of dent that appears in the side of a rubber ball when not fully expanded by air. There were those who had thought their cover inadequate and had run for something better and been caught by a shell on the way — hideous butcheries of men; and there were men whose pink bodies lay stripped to the waist and someone had been endeavoring to save them and had abandoned them in death — men with all their kit about them, men without kit, men with their greatcoats on and men without greatcoats.

The nearer one approached to the battle lines the less touched the dead appeared. But those near our encampment at Noreuil all lay with the whites of their pockets turned out and their tunics and shirts undone by the souvenir-hunters — which brings me once more to the general relationship of the average living soldier to the dead. I remarked that though those in the battle line were very swift in the pursuit of the so-called souvenir, in other words, in pursuit of the loot, it was those behind, such as the artillerymen and labor corps, who were the authentic human crows. I used to walk a mile or so every evening to the five derelict tanks which lay on the skyline on the way toward Queant and I got to know the dead on the way, and I watched them daily grow more and more naked as successive waves of souvenir-hunters went over them. There was a handsome German some six feet three, very well clothed, and the first time I saw him he was as he had fallen. Then his boots went — he had a good pair of boots. Then his tunic had been taken off. A few days later he was lying in his pants with many parts of the dead body exposed.

I came home late one evening and fell in with a man from one of the sixty-pounder batteries at Queant. He was grubbily but methodically examining the corpses of the German machine-gunners and hoping to pick up a revolver. I watched him examine one without success and he gave the dead body a kick. "The dirty barsted," said he, as if he were accusing the corpse, "somebody's bin 'ere before me."

The revolver or automatic pistol was the best prize of the souvenir-hunter. Money was sought, and watches and rings. There is something gruesome in the act of taking a marriage ring or even an ordinary ring from a dead man's hand and then wearing it or giving it to be worn in England. But very few German dead were left with rings, and the Roman Catholics were despoiled of their crosses. The legitimate tokens to take were the brightly colored numerals from the shoulders of tunic or greatcoat, the officers' helmets (not the saucepans but the Alexander-the-Greats), field glasses, pocketbooks, etc. But the hope of each seeker was the pistol.

I was wandering through a shattered and deserted military camp one morning and a questing major burst upon me. I saluted, but he brushed formality aside. "Hullo, hullo," says he, "is it true that your regiment has a special privilege to look for automatic pistols?"

I looked demure in the presence of such exalted rank and the major regarded me searchingly.

"I'm out to give fifty francs for every automatic pistol I can pick up," said he. And that was a plain hint to me that if I could sell he would buy.

He was a major in a regiment impolitely referred to by our haughty Spartans as a "grabby mob."

There must have been many men who were not as lacking in imagination and impressionableness as the majority who ranged o'er the battlefield seeking for treasures. But I did not myself meet these. Even the best saw nothing in taking away any property which might remain with the dead. Such property was no good to corpses. It was curious what a great number of letters, both British and German, lay on the battlefield. These had been taken out of the pockets and pocketbooks of the dead and since they were no use had been thrown to the winds — literally to the winds, for when the wind rose they blew about like dead leaves. There were photographs, too, prints of wife or sweetheart, of mother, or perchance of baby born while father was at the war — the priceless, worthless possessions of those whose bodies lay on the altar.

It never seemed to me worth while to collect lurid mementoes such as helmets or bombs, but I often designed to make a representative collection of the letters, both German and British, which were lying about one's feet. I read many of them; though there was something almost intolerably tragic in the hopes and fears and boasts and pre- sentiments of those who had written to men who were in truth des- tined to be killed. Many, many of the letters said someone was sorry that letters had not been written, but promised to write longer and oftener. Many letters were full of admonitions to be careful, not to take risks. Others promised "leave soon," "home for Christmas," "the war over." Some old stories of the air raids on London; others were full of domestic details and never mentioned the war. Some obviously endeavored to keep cheery because it had been said the men needed cheerful letters, but others refused to be reconciled to the separation which the soldier's going to the Front had meant. Perhaps they might have sounded trite and ordinary, but as being written to those who were about to die, it seemed as if Fate read them also and smiled in malice.

I had a suspicion that many of the dead who lay unburied for so long were not reported dead — but simply as "missing." So in one case where several letters lay strewn round a corpse whose pockets were inside out, I took one crumpled missive and sent it to the writer of it with a carefully written note about the young lad's fate. In answer I received a letter from the father asking for definite news of his son if I had any, as he had not been heard of for a long while. Whatever reply I sent, would I please send it to his business address, not to his home, as the mother was so anxious. By that time, how- ever, the boy's body with seven others had been put into one hastily dug grave; the names but not the units nor the numbers had been printed on the one cross. I then informed the father of his son's death and of the exact locality of the grave. In due course of time the father replied that I must be mistaken, for his son had been reported as wounded and missing. I wrote no more, but I formed the opinion, which was afterward completely confirmed, that "missing" very often meant *dead and unburied,* and that an unburied British soldier if he belonged to a unit which had passed on was almost inevitably reported "missing." Burying was such a tedious job, when it had to be done as a fatigue by a party not really responsible for burying, that it was done in the most rough-and-ready way.

War robs the individual soldier of reverence, of care except for himself, of tenderness, of the hush of awe which should silence and restrain. War and the army have their own atmosphere in which someone else being dead, as much as killing someone else, succeeds in being trivial and even upon occasion jocular. Two sergeants going out for a stroll came upon a German corpse with the steel helmet right down over the eyes. One of them lifted up the helmet in order to see the face properly. A saturnine gloom was on the lips and this had been intensified by the masking of the eyes. When the sergeant lifted the helmet it pulled up the flesh with it, and the upper lip rose from over the ivory teeth with a ghastly grin. "Take that smile off your face," said the sergeant, and let the helmet drop back over the eyes again. And they laughed. In these and in so many, imagination and sensitiveness were swallowed up by war. . . .

The greatest and perhaps the only consoling truth which can be learned from the expression of the dead is that a corpse has very little to do with a living body. The dead body is sacred, but it is not the person who died. That person has mysteriously disappeared. The look of the dead body, its shrunken individuality as compared with that of a live man, must have partly caused the great vogue of spiritualism — that look might be taken as part of the evidence of immortality. That was the chief positive impression which I obtained. For the rest, the whole matter was infinitely pathetic. There were one or two of us who felt there would always, ever after, be a cast of sadness in us because of what we had seen. I felt how inhuman we had been to one another. How could we come at last to Our Father with all this brothers' blood upon our hands?

"Europe, Europe!" I thought; "what a picture might be painted of Europe, the tragic woman, with bare breasts, anguished eyes, but no children. — *Oh, Europe, where are thy children?*"

AUTUMN TINTS IN CHIVALRY[1]

C. E. Montague

"We," writes C. E. MONTAGUE in an autobiographical passage, "that grew up by the Thames among roses and apples, and walked home from school of an evening down the nave of St. Paul's and through the courts of the Temple, and heard the chimes from Oxford towers at midnight and lived elately in the rhythms of her jocund choruses and racing oars! We that have failed and thriven and been rich and poor, on our little scale, and have been happy in our love and found work after our hearts and rambled in sun and mist over Pennine and Cambrian hills and seen sunset and dawn from great peaks of the Alps and across several seas and over lost battles and victories." In these few lines of musical prose the English journalist has summed up his intrepid life. For many years he and C. P. Scott and a few other men made the Manchester *Guardian* what it still is, one of the world's greatest journals. As a writer of leaders — editorials — he had few equals, and among newspapermen his fame went round the world. He also wrote novels, *A Hind Let Loose* (1910) and *The Morning's War* (1913), which were too intellectual in content to find favor except with a select body of admirers. Then, though long past age — he was born in 1867 — he forced his way into the British army in 1915, beginning as a private. He fought through the war, and in two books, one sober fact and the other fiction (*Disenchantment* in 1922 and *Fiery Particles* in 1923), gave a memorable picture of its horrors and heroisms. Later he wrote other books, of which one, *The Right Place*, deserves special mention. It is a book of travel essays, and captures the poetic flavor of places while it re-captures all the elation of sightseeing. Montague, educated at Oxford, had a rich fund of scholarship, but his was an adventurous temperament and he loved the outdoors more than books. He was a bold Alpinist, and won a medal for saving life from drowning. Active as journalist, novelist, and traveler to the last, he died in 1931.

I

In either of two opposite tempers you may carry on war. In one of the two you will want to rate your enemy, all round, as high as you can. You may pursue him down a trench, or he you; but in neither case do you care to have him described by somebody far, far away as a fat little shortsighted scrub. Better let him pass for a paladin. This may at bottom be vanity, sentimentality, all sort of contemptible things. Let him who knows the heart of man be dogmatic about it. Anyhow, this temper comes, as they would say in Ireland, of decent people. It spoke in Porsena of Clusium's whimsical prayer that

[1] From *Disenchantment*, by C. E. Montague. Reprinted by permission of Peter Smith, publisher.

Horatius might swim the Tiber safely; it animates Velasquez' knightly "Surrender of Breda"; it prompted Lord Roberts' first words to Cronje when Paardeberg fell — "Sir, you have made a very gallant defense"; it is avowed in a popular descant of Newbolt's —

> To honor, while you strike him down,
> The foe who comes with eager eyes.

The other temper has its niche in letters, too. There was the man that "wore his dagger in his mouth." And there was Little Flanigan, the bailiff's man in Goldsmith's play. During one of our old wars with France he was always "damning the French, the parle-vous, and all that belonged to them." "What," he would ask the company, "makes the bread rising? The parle-vous that devour us. What makes the mutton fivepence a pound? The parle-vous that eat it up. What makes the beer threepence-halfpenny a pot?"

Well, your first aim in war is to hit your enemy hard, and the question may well be quite open — in which of these tempers can he be hit hardest? If, as we hear, a man's strength be "as the strength of ten because his heart is pure," possibly it may add a few foot-pounds to his momentum in an attack if he has kept a clean tongue in his head. And yet the production of heavy woolens in the West Riding, for War Office use, may, for all that we know, have been accelerated by yarns about crucified Canadians and naked bodies of women found in German trenches. There is always so much, so bewilderingly much, to be said on both sides. All I can tell is that during the war the Newbolt spirit seemed, on the whole, to have its chief seat in and near our front line, and thence to die down westward all the way to London. There Little Flanigan was enthroned, and, like Montrose, would bear no rival near his throne, so that a man on leave from our trench system stood in some danger of being regarded as little better than one of the wicked. Anyhow, he was a kind of provincial. Not his will, but that of Flanigan, had to be done. For Flanigan was the center of things; he had leisure, or else volu-bility was his trade; and he had got hold of the megaphones.

II

In the first months of the war there was any amount of good sportsmanship going; most, of course, among men who had seen already the whites of enemy eyes. I remember the potent emetic effect of Flaniganism upon a little blond Regular subaltern maimed at the first battles of Ypres. "Pretty measly sample of the sin against the Holy Ghost!" the one-legged child grunted savagely, showing a London paper's comic sketch of a corpulent German running away. The first words I ever heard uttered in palliation of German misdoings in Belgium came from a Regular N.C.O., a Dragoon Guards sergeant, holding forth to a sergeants' mess behind our line. "We'd have done every damn thing they did," he averred, "if it had been we." I thought him rather extravagant, then. Later on, when the long row of hut hospitals, jammed between the Calais-Paris Railway at Etaples and the great reinforcement camp on the sandhills above it, was badly bombed from the air, even the wrath of the R.A.M.C. against those who had wedged in its wounded and nurses between two staple targets scarcely exceeded that of our Royal Air Force against war correspondents who said the enemy must have done it on purpose.

Airmen, no doubt, or some of them, went to much greater lengths in the chivalrous line than the rest of us. Many things helped them to do it. Combatant flying was still new enough to be almost wholly an officer's job; the knight took the knocks, and the squire stayed behind and looked after his gear. Air fighting came to be pretty well the old duel, or else the mediaeval mêlée between little picked teams. The clean element, too, may have counted — it always looked a clean job from below, where your airy notions got mixed with trench mud, while the airman seemed like Sylvia in the song, who so excelled "each mortal thing upon the dull earth dwelling." Whatever the cause, he excelled in his bearing toward enemies, dead or alive. The funeral that he gave to Richthofen in France was one of the few handsome gestures exchanged in the war. And whenever Little Flanigan at home began squealing aloud that we ought to take some of our airmen off fighting and make them bomb German women and children instead, our airmen's scorn for these ethics of the dirt helped to keep up the flickering hope that the post-war world might not be ignoble.

Even on the dull earth it takes time and pains to get a cleanrun boy or young man into a mean frame of mind. A fine N.C.O. of the Grenadier Guards was killed near Laventie — no one knows how — while going over to shake hands with the Germans on Christmas morning. "What! not shake on Christmas Day?" He would have thought it poor, sulky fighting. Near Armentières at the Christmas of 1914 an incident happened which seemed quite the natural thing to most soldiers then. On Christmas Eve the Germans lit up their front line with Chinese lanterns. Two British officers thereupon walked some way across No Man's Land, hailed the enemy's sentries, and asked for an officer. The German sentries said, "Go back, or we shall have to shoot." The Englishmen said "Not likely!" advanced to the German wire, and asked again for an officer. The sentries held their fire and sent for an officer. With him the Englishmen made a one-day truce, and on Christmas Day the two sides exchanged cigarettes and played football together. The English intended the truce to end with the day, as agreed, but decided not to shoot next day till the enemy did. Next morning the Germans were still to be seen washing and breakfasting outside their wire; so our men, too, got out of the trench and sat about in the open. One of them, cleaning his rifle, loosed a shot by accident, and an English subaltern went to tell the Germans it had not been fired to kill. The ones he spoke to understood, but as he was walking back a German somewhere wide on a flank fired and hit him in the knee, and he has walked lame ever since. Our men took it that some German sentry had misunderstood our fluke shot. They did not impute dishonor. The air in such places was strangely clean in those distant days. During one of the very few months of open warfare a cavalry private of ours brought in a captive, a gorgeous specimen of the terrific Prussian Uhlan of tradition. "But why didn't you put your sword through him?" an officer asked, who belonged to the school of Froissart less obviously than the private. "Well, sir," the captor replied, "the gentleman wasn't looking."

III

At no seat of war will you find it quite easy to live up to Flanigan's standards of hatred toward an enemy. Reaching a front, you find that all you want is just to win the war. Soon you are so taken up with the pursuit of this aim that you are always forgetting to burn with the gem-like flame of pure fury that fires the lion-hearted publicist at home.

A soldier might have had the Athanasian ecstasy all right till he reached the firing line. Every individual German had sunk the *Lusitania;* there was none righteous, none. And yet at a front the holy passion began to ooze out at the ends of his fingers. The bottom trouble is that you cannot fight a man in the physical way without somehow touching him. The relation of actual combatants is a personal one — no doubt, a rude, primitive one, but still quite advanced as compared with that between a learned man at Berlin who keeps on saying *Delenda est Britannia!* at the top of his voice and a learned man in London who keeps on saying that every German must have a black heart because Caesar did not conquer Germany as he did Gaul and Britain. Just let the round head of a German appear for a passing second, at long intervals, above a hummock of clay in the middle distance. Before you had made half a dozen sincere efforts to shoot him the fatal germ of human relationship had begun to find a nidus again: he had acquired in your mind the rudiments of a personal individuality. You would go on trying to shoot him with zest — indeed, with a diminished likelihood of missing, for mere hatred is a flustering emotion. And yet the hatred business had started crumbling. There had begun the insidious change that was to send you home, on your first leave, talking unguardedly of "old Fritz" or of "the good old Boche" to the pain of your friends, as if he were a stout dog fox or a real stag or a hare.

The deadliest solvent of your exalted hatreds is laughter. And you can never wholly suppress laughter between two crowds of millions of men standing within earshot of each other along a line of hundreds of miles. There was, in the Loos salient in 1916, a German who, after his meals, would halloo across to an English unit taunts about certain accidents of its birth. None of his British hearers could help laughing at his mistakes, his knowledge, and his English. Nor could the least humorous priest of ill-will have kept his countenance at a relief when the enemy shouted: "We know you are relieving," "No good hiding it," "Good-by, Ox and Bucks," "Who's coming in?" and some hurried humorist in the obscure English battalion relieving shouted back, with a terrific assumption of accent, "Furrst Black Watch!" or "Th' Oirish Gyards!" and a hush fell at the sound of these great names. Comedy, expelled with a fork by the dignified figure of Quenchless Hate, had begun to steal back of herself.

At home that tragedy queen might do very well; she did not have these tenpenny nails scattered about on her road to puncture the nobly inflated tires of her chariot. The heroes who spoke up for shooing all the old German governesses into the barbed wire compounds were not exposed to the moral danger of actually hustling, *propria persona*, these formidable ancients. But while Hamilcar at home was swearing Hannibal and all the other little Hamilcars to undying hatred of the foe, an enemy dog might be trotting across to the British front line to sample its rats, and its owner be losing in some British company's eyes his proper quality as an incarnation of all the Satanism of Potsdam and becoming simply "him that lost the dog." If you took his trench it might be no better; perhaps Incarnate

Evil had left its bit of food half-cooked, and the muddy straw, where it lay last, was pressed into a hollow by Incarnate Evil's back as by a cat's. Incarnate Evil should not do these things that other people in trenches do. It ought to be more strange and beastly and keep on making *beaux gestes* with its talons and tail, like the proper dragon slain by St. George. Perhaps Incarnate Evil was extinct and you went over its pockets. They never contained the right things — no poison to put in our wells, no practical hints for crucifying Canadians; only the usual stuffing of all soldiers' pockets — photographs and tobacco and bits of string and the wife's letters, all about how tramps were always stealing potatoes out of the garden, and how the baby was worse, and was his leave never coming? No good to look at such things.

IV

With this guilty weakness gaining upon them our troops drove the Germans from Albert to Mons. There were scandalous scenes on the way. Imagine two hundred German prisoners grinning inside a wire cage while a little Cockney corporal chaffs them in half the dialects of Germany! His father, he says, was a slop tailor in Whitechapel; most of his journeymen came from somewhere or other in Germany — "Ah! and my dad sweated 'em proper," he says proudly; so the boy learned all their kinds of talk. He convulses Bavarians now with his flow of Silesian. He fraternizes grossly and jubilantly. Other British soldiers laugh when one of the Germans sings, in return for favors received, the British ballad "Knocked 'em in the Ol' Kent Road." By the time our men had marched to the Rhine there was little hatred left in them. How can you hate the small boy who stands at the farm door visibly torn between dread of the invader and deep delight in all soldiers, as soldiers? How shall a man not offer a drink to the first disbanded German soldier who sits next to him in a public house at Cologne, and try to find out if he was ever in the line at the Brickstacks or near the Big Crater? Why, that might have been his dog!

The billeted soldier's immemorial claim on "a place by the fire" carried on the fell work. It is hopelessly bad for your grand Byronic hates if you sit through whole winter evenings in the abhorred foe's kitchen and the abhorred foe grants you the uncovenanted mercy of hot coffee and discusses without rancor the relative daily yields of the British and the German milch cow. And then comes into play the British soldier's incorrigible propensity, wherever he be, to form virtuous attachments. "Love, unfoiled in the war," as Sophocles says. The broad road has a terribly easy gradient. When all the great and wise at Paris were making peace, as somebody said, with a vengeance, our command on the Rhine had to send a wire to say that unless something was done to feed the Germans starving in the slums it could not answer for discipline in its army; the men were giving their rations away, and no orders would stop them. Rank "Pro-Germanism," you see — the heresy of Edith Cavell; "Patriotism is not enough; I must have no hatred or bitterness in my heart." While these men fought on, year after year, they had mostly been growing more void of mere spite all the time, feeling always more and more sure that the average German was just a decent poor devil like everyone else. One trembles to think what the really first-class haters at home would have said of our army if they had known at the time.

V

Even at places less distant than home the survival of old English standards of fighting had given some scandal. In that autumn of the war when our generalship seemed to have explored all its own talents and found only the means to stage in an orderly way the greatest possible number of combats of pure attrition, the crying up of unknightliness became a kind of fashion among a good many staff officers of the higher grades. "I fancy our fellows were not taking many prisoners this morning," a corps commander would say with a complacent grin, on the evening after a battle. Jocose stories of comic things said by privates when getting rid of undesired captives became current in messes far in the rear. The other day I saw in a history of one of the most gallant of all British divisions an illustration given by the officer who wrote it of what he believed to be the true martial spirit. It was the case of a wounded Highlander who had received with a bomb a German Red Cross orderly who was coming to help him. A general of some consequence during part of the war gave a lecture, toward its end, to a body of officers and others on what he called "the fighting spirit." He told with enthusiasm an anecdote of a captured trench in which some of our men had been killing off German appellants for quarter. Another German appearing and putting his hands up, one of our men — so the story went — called out, " 'Ere! Where's 'Arry? 'E ain't 'ad one yet." Probably someone had pulled the good general's leg, and the thing never happened. But he believed it, and deeply approved the "blooding" of 'Arry. That, he explained, was "the fighting spirit." Men more

versed than he in the actual hand-to-hand business of fighting this
war knew that he was mistaken, and that the spirit of trial by combat
and that of pork-butchery are distinct. But that is of course. The
notable thing was that such things should be said by anyone wearing
our uniform. Twenty years before, if it had been rumored, you would,
without waiting, have called the rumor a lie invented by some de-
tractor of England or of her army. Now it passed quite unhissed.
It was the latter-day wisdom. Scrofulous minds at home had long
been itching, publicly and in print, to bomb German women and
children from aeroplanes, and to "take it out of" German prisoners of
war. Now the disease had even affected some parts of the non-
combatant staff of our army.

VI

You know the most often quoted of all passages of Burke. Indeed, it is only through quotations of it that most of us know Burke
at all —

But the age of chivalry is gone . . . the unbought grace of life, the
cheap defense of nations, the nurse of manly sentiment and heroic enterprise is gone! It is gone, that sensibility of principle, that chastity of honor,
which felt a stain like a wound, which inspired courage whilst it mitigated
ferocity, which ennobled whatever it touched, and under which vice itself
lost half its evil by losing all its grossness.

Burke would never say a thing by halves. And as truth goes by
halves, and declines to be sweeping like rhetoric, Burke made sure of
being wrong to the tune of some fifty per cent. The French Revolution did not, as his beautiful language implies, confine mankind for
the rest of its days to the procreation of curs. And yet his words do
give you, in their own lush, Corinthian way, a notion of something
that probably did happen, a certain limited shifting of the center of
gravity of West European morals or manners.

One would be talking like Burke — talking, perhaps you might say,
through Burke's hat — if one were to say that the war found chivalry
alive and left it dead. Chivalry is about as likely to perish as brown
eyes or the moon. Yet something did happen, during the war, to
which these wild words would have some sort of relation. We were
not all Bayards in 1914; even then a great part of our press could
not tell indignation from spite, nor uphold the best cause in the world
without turpitude. Nor were we all, after the Armistice, rods of the
houses of Thersites and Cleon. But something had happened:
the chivalrous temper had had a setback.

AN APPEAL TO REASON[1]

John Bassett Moore

The greatest living authority upon international arbitrations, and one of the greatest authorities upon international law, JOHN BASSETT MOORE was born at Smyrna, Delaware, in 1860, and educated at the University of Virginia. He served his novitiate in the State Department under the cautious and conciliatory Thomas F. Bayard, also of Delaware, and retained the Third Assistant Secretary-ship for a time under Secretary Blaine. In 1891 he took the chair of international law and diplomacy at Columbia. Thereafter he combined teaching with intervals of public service. During the Spanish-American War he was Assistant Secretary of State, and at the close of the fighting accompanied the Peace Commission to Paris as secretary and counsel. President Taft appointed him a delegate to the fourth Pan-American Conference at Buenos Aires in 1910. He was counselor of the State Department under Bryan in 1913–1914 and exercised no little influence on its policies. On the organization of the so-called World Court — the Permanent Court of International Justice — he was selected as one of its judges. The publication for which he was long best known was his eight-volume *Digest of International Law* (1906), a monumental work which embodies much historical research in the provision of accurate illustrations of the development of legal principles. He also is the author of some distinctively technical works, as on extradition, and books on the history and principles of American diplomacy. Of recent years, having become professor-emeritus at Columbia, he has been engaged upon a massive compilation of *International Adjudications, Ancient and Modern,* with historical and legal commentaries.

OUR BIRTHRIGHT

Washington, in his Farewell Address, said:

Against the insidious wiles of foreign influence, I conjure you to believe me, fellow citizens, the jealousy of a free people ought to be *constantly* awake, since history and experience prove that foreign influence is one of the most baneful foes of republican government. . . . The great rule of conduct for us, in regard to foreign nations, is, in extending our commercial relations, to have with them as little *political* connection as possible. . . . Europe has a set of primary interests which to us have none or a very remote relation. Hence she must be engaged in frequent controversies, the causes of which are essentially foreign to our interests. . . . Why quit our own to stand upon foreign ground? Why, by interweaving our destiny with that of any part of Europe, entangle our peace and prosperity in the toils of European ambition, rivalship, interest, humor, or caprice?

[1] From *Foreign Affairs,* July, 1933. Reprinted by permission.

The original draft of this admonition was made by Alexander Hamilton, who, like Washington himself, was born a British subject; but their minds embraced the entire world.

Jefferson, not forgetting the Declaration of Independence which he drew, warned his countrymen that their form of government exposed them more than any other to "the insidious intrigues and pestilent influences of foreign nations," and that nothing but an inflexible neutrality could preserve us. Their mutual jealousies and their complicated alliances were, he said, all foreign to us. They were nations of eternal war. His motto therefore was: "Peace, commerce, and honest friendship with all nations — entangling alliances with none."

Sagacious John Adams, who spent many years in Europe and signed our first treaty with Holland as well as the treaty with Great Britain acknowledging our independence, when a European diplomatist remarked that he seemed to be afraid of being made the tool of the Powers of Europe, exclaimed, "Indeed I am"; and when asked "What Powers?" replied "All of them." And he added:

It is obvious that all the Powers of Europe will be continually manoeuvring with us to work us into their real or imaginary balances of power. They will all wish to make of us a make-weight candle, when they are weighing out their pounds. Indeed, it is not surprising; for we shall very often, if not always, be able to turn the scale. But I think it ought to be our rule not to meddle; and that of all the Powers of Europe, not to desire us, or, perhaps, even to permit us, to interfere, if they can help it.

Nothing more profoundly true was ever said; and this was fully recognized by all our national administrations and by our greatest statesmen down to twenty years ago, when, to the disturbance of our interests and our happiness, we began to swing on the trapeze at international political performances and even to pay for the privilege of so doing.

Not long ago a callow stripling, when I mentioned the name of George Washington, curtly remarked that his ideas were out of date and unsuited to the modern world. This is an essential postulate of the shallow dupes who, prating of our having lately become a "World Power," urge that we blindly don an imported livery of "world service," to be paid for, on demand, in unestimated installments of blood and treasure. But it is a sad day when the children of a nation are taught to prattle ignorant and perverted slights of the men who, with steady and skillful hands, laid the foundations of its greatness and prosperity; men to whom, by reason of their exemplary valor, integrity, and wisdom, an understanding world has awarded the highest place among the immortals. Thomas Jefferson, who spoke with the authority of an intimate official association, and with an intelligence that embraced all times and all climes, declared that in elevation of character, in sureness of judgment, in firmness of purpose, in inflexible justice, and in scrupulous obedience to the laws, civil and military, throughout his whole career, Washington furnished an example unparalleled in history. Jefferson himself stands before the world as a great political genius, whose ideas still stir men's minds. Alexander Hamilton, soldier, jurist, great administrator, of whom Webster said that "he touched the dead corpse of Public Credit, and it sprung upon its feet," is still studied as a profound political theorist, at home and abroad. And what of Benjamin Franklin, discoverer, inventor, philosopher, consummate diplomatist, at home in all lands, of whom Charles Phillips eloquently said that his fame would revive the hopes of men in ages yet to come?

Such are the men whom our vaporers of current sublimities would shelve as fossils in our museums of natural history, on the hasty supposition that by various modern devices, by which men may more rapidly and more frequently communicate, and more quickly hurt or help one another, discordant races and peoples have been harmoniously united in thought and in action and in brotherly love. Where congeniality is lacking, propinquity does not tend to create affection; on the contrary, it tends to breed hatreds. Where are today the danger spots of the world? They are coterminous countries. The French and the Germans have for centuries lived side by side. No artificial device is needed to enable them quickly to come into contact. The thin line of their common frontier can instantly be strided. For ages they have crossed and recrossed it in peace and in war; and yet, how much have they learned to love one another? Their recent fierce and desperate conflict, and the unappeased sorrows and resentments by which it was followed, will be accepted as a conclusive answer, except by those who would employ processes of peace that would cause the echoes of war daily to haunt the fireside. The times must be out of joint when a warlike ardor for peace depreciates the glory that was Greece and the grandeur that was Rome; when new and untried visions are held superior to the proved philosophies of Plato and Aristotle, of Cicero and Seneca, of Bacon and John Locke; and when the wisdom of great statesmen, heard with reverence only twenty years ago, is suddenly rejected as having no current value.

We hear much today of the duties of the United States as a "World Power," and the supposition seems widely to prevail that we have only lately reached that eminence. But the United States has always been a World Power. It acted as a World Power when, on the outbreak of the wars growing out of the French Revolution, its first President, George Washington, with Thomas Jefferson as his Secretary of State, proclaimed our neutrality. It acted as a World Power when, some years later, it suppressed the activities of the Barbary pirates. It acted as a World Power when, in 1812, it went to war in defense of neutral rights and the freedom of the seas. It acted as a World Power when it proclaimed the Monroe Doctrine. It acted as a World Power in extending its trade and opening up foreign countries to its commerce, as it so effectually did by peaceful processes during the presidency of General Andrew Jackson. It acted as a World Power when it refused to permit the intervention of foreign nations in our Civil War. It acted as a World Power when it forbade the further maintenance of the European empire set up in Mexico by French arms during our Civil War. It acted as a World Power when, in the administration of President Grant, with Hamilton Fish as his Secretary of State, it brought about, through the greatest of all international arbitrations, the amicable settlement of the Alabama Claims, and in so doing made a signal contribution to the further development of the law of neutrality.

It is useless to continue the specification of instances. Nations, like individuals, may increase their power by combining with a due attention to their own business the extension of their friendly offices to brethren in trouble, and by conserving their militant resources for occasions when their vital interests are at stake. A nation that undertakes to meddle with every foreign disturbance is bound to become an international nuisance, to its own detriment as well as to the annoyance of other countries. Power is neither gained nor kept by such methods. Although megalomania may be sincere, it is noted for its mistakes.

In the French National Convention which met on September 21, 1792, the dominant factor was called the Mountain. This group, comprising the most radical Jacobin element, of which Marat and Robespierre were the chief spokesmen, was always in a state of more or less delirious eruption. During the Reign of Terror, with which the group is identified, the French government instructed its minister in the United States to bring about "a national agreement, in which two great peoples shall suspend their commercial and political interests, and establish a mutual understanding to defend the empire of liberty, wherever it can be embraced." This appeal is similar to that which is constantly heard in the United States today, but it did not move the unfeeling statesmen who then guided our destinies.

Those who oppose our intermeddling with what does not properly concern us are dubbed "isolationists." We should not resent this; we have good ancestral justification. All through her history Great Britain has held aloof from Continental alliances except so far as they might seem to be temporarily necessary for her safety. In the Thirty Years' War which convulsed the entire Continent she took no part. At the close of the Wars of the Spanish Succession she dropped her alliances and made her own peace. As is pointed out by Lord Loreburn, every single Great Power on the Continent was, during the sixty years preceding 1914, repeatedly engaged in Continental war; France thrice, Germany thrice, Russia twice, Austria three times and Italy four times. During the same sixty years Great Britain was involved in Continental war only once, in 1854, when in alliance with France she backed Turkey against Russia and committed the mistake later described by Lord Salisbury as "putting her money on the wrong horse." One of Great Britain's reasons for abstention as declared by her statesmen was the prevalence of deadly animosities and conflicts of interest that still survived among the Continental Powers. The British policy was to maintain good relations with all her Continental neighbors not only with a view to exerting a friendly influence in composing their differences but also to avoid commitments which might compel a participation in foreign wars and deprive the country of its independent control of its own policy. But there was yet another reason; all the great Continental Powers had adopted universal compulsory service. Great Britain's cardinal principle was to rely upon an overwhelming superiority at sea. It was these things that led Lord Salisbury, when Secretary for Foreign Affairs at the close of the last century, to boast of England's "splendid isolation." When an inheritor of the name of Elizabeth's great minister used this phrase it did not occur to Englishmen to reproach him for an abandonment of their "world leadership," or to wail over their neglect of their international duties. On the contrary, when Lord Salisbury spoke of "isolation," Great Britain was still tingling with memories of the Diamond Jubilee, when statesmen coming from the ends of the earth to pay homage to the Great Queen saw without dread the vast fleet that confidently rode the inviolate sea that washes England's shores. Here, the victims of the new psychology use the word "isolation" as a term of opprobrium. It would be as sensible to condemn as an "isolationist" a man who did not tie himself up with unnecessary contracts, and especially of the kind that were likely to impoverish or to ruin him, without benefit to himself and perhaps with injury to others. Such epithets serve only to exemplify the want of knowledge and of understanding of those who employ them.

Conspicuous in the lingo of the past decade is the plea for the continuance of the kind of "leadership" with which we began to bless the world less than twenty years ago. Some of our very eminent men have urged this plea. But I have often wished that those who use such language would reflect on how it may strike other peoples, in Europe and elsewhere. Why, for instance, should the British, the Dutch, the French, or the Italian people pant for our spiritual, our moral, or our political guidance? Why should they regard as superior to them a people whom they benevolently associate with mass production, skyscrapers, and prohibition? If they were to express their inmost thoughts would they not confess that such utterances sound to them somewhat boastful, somewhat neglectful of their great historic tradition? How should we ourselves now feel if the eminent foreign statesmen who lately responded to President Roosevelt's invitation to visit him had, before leaving the United States, intimated that we needed their "leadership," and that any counsels or conditions they suggested should be accepted in that sense? Perhaps it is unfortunate for us that they did not say so. But, having had long experience in leadership, they can well afford to pay a polite deference to those who ingenuously profess to have usurped their ancient prerogative.

We also hear much of the "international mind." Would to God that we had more of it! But in devoutly expressing this wish I do not confine it to my own country, nor do I lack a definite conception of what an international mind ought to be. Having for many years been connected with the administration of foreign affairs, I can truthfully affirm that there is no nation toward which I cherish a feeling of enmity. I have always been a peacemaker; and, as an international judge, I am willing to stand on my record as one who strove to act without fear or favor. But I confess that of all countries I love my own the best. No international mind is, in my opinion, to be desired or to be trusted that is not built on a national foundation. The man who cannot sing his national anthem with a whole heart is not fit to be entrusted with negotiations with foreign Powers. No experienced diplomatist would trust out of his sight an adversary who did not seek to obtain for his own country a square deal. Only those who are disposed to maintain the rights and interests of their respective countries can treat with one another on the basis of mutual self-respect. The best diplomatists are those who are willing to give as well as to take; who can grasp and apply the equitable solution that assures to each that which is justly due; who, in leaving behind them no heartburnings and resentments, conserve the interests of all. It is a pleasure to remember the men of this type with whom I have dealt.

We are told that invention and trade and industrial organization cannot be reversed. But nobody wishes or proposes to reverse them. We are told that the world has become too dependent on comforts to be willing to give them up; but, although dependence on comforts is not a sign of strength, either physical or mental, no one is specially advocating their abandonment. But the culmination is reached when we are told that we cannot "retire within our own borders" and lead a life of "isolation." When have we ever done such a thing, or proposed to do it? The late Grand Duke Alexander of Russia, on revisiting the United States in 1928 after an absence of thirteen years, said that on his return the impression he got was that what he had admired as the robustness of American life "had given place to the sickening self-consciousness of an hysterical idealism," and had been superseded by the "same hodgepodge of badly digested ideas" as had characterized the Guards Barracks in St. Petersburg thirty years back. "So this," he exclaimed, "was the American share of the Versailles spoils! It seemed bewildering that any nation should send two million men across the ocean, fight for something that did not concern it in the least, tear up the map of the world, and lend billions of dollars to its competitors — all for the purpose of acquiring the worst traits of pre-war Europe."

And for what is our birthright to be thrown away? Among other things, for membership in an association which, although established in the name of peace, is in the present state of the popular mind chiefly characterized by warlike devices. I am not opposed to an association of nations for the purposes of peace, and would not disparage any useful work the League has done. But the League, in dealing with political matters, suffers from the radical defects of its charter. My first and consistent opinion of the Covenant fully accords with that so thoughtfully and prophetically expressed by Mr. Elihu Root as early as March 13, 1919, in these words: "The more I study it, the more satisfied I am that it has some very useful provisions, some very bad ones, some glaring deficiencies, and that if it is not very materially amended not merely in form but in substance, the world will before very long wake up to realize that a great opportunity has been wasted in the doing of a futile thing." Most fully has this profoundly prescient comment been justified by the recent and too frequent occasions on which loose, excited, and unfulfilled threats of employing the warlike devices of the Covenant have exposed the League to reproach if not to contempt. Nor do I hesitate to mention as an example the unhappy conflict between China and Japan in which, while warlike words were heard from Geneva, the Ministers for Foreign Affairs of powerful members of the League were disavowing in their capitals any intention to intervene in the armed strife in Manchuria.

Originally, the League had the character of a political club which nations could enter only by invitation. To this phase Argentina long ago intelligently objected. There was a list of original members and a list of states invited to accede. No recent enemy state was on either list, although President Wilson, before going abroad, had declared that Germany would necessarily be admitted, for the purpose of controlling her if for nothing else. Mexico, although never an enemy state, was, because the United States did not then approve her, unbidden to the banquet of peace. Russia, in spite of her vast contribution in blood and in treasure to the Allied cause, had fallen from grace and entered upon courses that were not approved. With absences such as these it could not, even had the United States been present, have been truly said that the voice of the world was heard at Geneva.

But the most fundamental defect of the plan was the creation of the warlike devices on the fantastic assumption that the members of the League would, in making use of those devices, divest themselves of their individual interests and prepossessions, of their historic and instinctive antagonisms, and altruistically unite in enforcing the ideal of impartial justice. In the ordinary administration of the law, persons who have formed prejudgments are peremptorily excluded from the jury as being presumptively incapable of weighing the proofs and rendering a fair and just verdict. The members of the Council of the League of Nations are the delegates of governments; the members of the Assembly also represent governments. It cannot either justly or rationally be expected of such bodies to divest themselves of all prepossessions or consciousness of national interests, to say nothing of the fact that they must inevitably differ in opinion. It is for reasons such as these that where a conflict between nations occurs and the warlike devices of the Covenant are invoked they so readily excite apprehension and distrust. It is very significant that the professed friends of the League are the readiest to censure it for not hastening to employ the warlike devices. On the assumption that such persons accurately represent the spirit of Geneva and are influential in its deliberations, those who do not believe in war as the prime, or as the natural and appropriate, creator of peace cannot help reflecting upon the demonstrated fact that war may as readily be used for unjust as for just ends, for oppression as well as for liberty, for the crushing of some and the exaltation of others, and for evil as well as for good. No wonder that the League is visibly rocked and rent and the world disturbed and divided whenever an agitation arises for the use of the warlike devices which visionary men in an excited and unsettled time foisted upon those who were wiser and more modest in the estimation of what was practicable and desirable. It was on this rock that the great Confederation of Europe, based on the treaties that ended the Napoleonic War and the Holy Alliance, eventually was wrecked. Although it contained no elaboration of warlike devices for the preservation of peace, the attempt of subsequent conferences to employ united military action divided the Powers and brought to an end their association. Such a result may be regarded as inevitable.

Esau, thinking that he was about to die, sold his birthright for a mess of pottage; but the Bible censures him for having despised his birthright. What would have been the nature of the censure if he had thrown his birthright wantonly away, or had allowed himself to be cheated out of it? Europe is the victim of history, a seething mass of hereditary feuds. They exist in the western part as well as in the eastern, and they are peculiarly bitter in the southeastern, where the war in 1914 originated. The Balkan Peninsula may be likened to a Vesuvius, always in danger of an eruption. Once, when I asked an Albanian to meet a Serbian he did not know, he hissed in reply: "He i-s-s my en-ne-my!" The United States may, if it should unhappily see fit to do so, associate itself with these feuds and henceforth help to fight them out. It may embitter and help to perpetuate them, but it cannot end them.

In my early days I learned from great teachers the unity of human history. Human nature has not changed. Human propensities, human appetites, and human passions have not changed. We come into the world in the same way, and our necessities are the same.

The struggle for existence still continues and it will go on. As one long and intimately acquainted with men of arms, I may say that they do not share the new view that peace and tranquillity on earth may be promoted and stabilized by boycotts, by playing fast and loose with the law of neutrality, and by the extension of the area of wars. Wars are not brought about by the officers of our army and our navy; but wars have often been fomented by agitations recklessly conducted by persons who professed a special abhorrence of war. The motives and objects of war have been various; but, as war is a contention by force, it is waged for victory. The struggle, as it progresses, becomes more and more intense. Each day brings its tale of death and of desolation. Griefs accumulate; the passions burn more fiercely; the hoarse cry of vengeance grows louder and more insistent; and the cases are rare in which the peace that is extorted does not by humiliating conditions sow the seeds of future wars.

The true and only foundation of peace among men is the concession to each of that which is due. No doubt perfect justice is unattainable in this world. But there is an ideal of justice toward which every nation, every people, every individual should aspire. This ideal can be attained only through the reconciliation of our conflicting views and our conflicting interests. We are not all alike. No two men and no two women are alike. No two nations are alike. We differ in race, we differ in creed, we differ in color; and all differences tend to provoke antagonism. If we would keep men and nations at peace, we must remove the causes of their discontent, elevate their moral sentiments, inculcate a spirit of justice and toleration, and compose and settle their differences.

Such is my message, on which I am prepared to stand before any future Seat of Judgment, in all confidence that no sudden reversal during the past twenty years of the ways of God to man will exclude me from the reward promised to good and faithful servants.

THE "NEW SPIRIT" AND ITS CRITICS[1]

Newton D. Baker

The United States has had more than fifty Secretaries of War, and in the list are famous names — Monroe, Calhoun, Jefferson Davis, Stanton, Elihu Root, Taft. With the possible exception of Stanton, none had so difficult a work to perform as that given NEWTON D. BAKER between 1916 and 1921. The burden was novel in character; never before had we mobilized the whole nation for war, never before had we sent a great army overseas. It was unprecedented in size. "His is really an impossible task," wrote his associate, Secretary Houston, at the time; "he is meeting it with rare courage and intelligence; . . . I am impressed with the quickness and soundness of his decisions." And Mr. Baker himself wrote later, "Every day of twenty-four hours had a week's work packed into it." A partial history of that achievement is offered in Frederick Palmer's two volumes on *Newton D. Baker: America at War;* only a partial history, for it will be years before the debt owed Mr. Baker is fully appreciated. But he will be remembered as more than a rarely effective administrator — as one of the finest personalities and in some respects most progressive spirits of his time. Born at Martinsburg, West Virginia, in 1871, and educated at Johns Hopkins and Washington and Lee, he had the good fortune to fall under the influence of West Virginia's greatest leader, William L. Wilson. In the stirring days of the second Cleveland Administration he was Mr. Wilson's private secretary in the Post Office Department, and from him as from his teachers at Johns Hopkins imbibed a strong Manchester liberalism. An assiduous reader, a careful thinker, he too became a "scholar in politics." Going to Cleveland to practice law, he at once plunged into city affairs, first as city solicitor and chief lieutenant of Tom L. Johnson in the latter's fight for lower traction fares and more direct instrumentalities of government, and later as mayor in succession to Johnson. When Woodrow Wilson offered Mr. Baker the Secretaryship of the Interior in 1913, he refused because he still had important municipal reforms to achieve. An avowed pacifist, his energy as Secretary of War quickly conquered all distrust; and he was able to say at the close of the conflict that "no army of similar size has ever been raised, equipped, or trained so quickly." Five million men had been enlisted and two million men sent to France. Partisan and hostile investigations into his work at the close of the war simply revealed more fully how enormous had been his task and how admirable his achievement. Almost a penniless man after sixteen years in public office, he returned in 1921 to a small rented apartment in Cleveland and his law practice. But he continued to give much time to public activities. He had been a devoted believer in world organization for peace, and a zealous champion of the League in 1919–1920, and in 1924 made a gallant but losing fight for a strong League plank in the Democratic platform. In recognition of his zeal for world peace President Coolidge appointed him in 1929 a member of the Permanent Court of Arbitration at The Hague.

[1] From *Foreign Affairs*, October, 1933. Reprinted by permission.

In 1754 the long-heralded philosophical works of Lord Bolingbroke were published. To Edmund Burke they constituted an effort to exclude God from his universe as a wholly unnecessary phenomenon, and he composed "A Vindication of Natural Society" as an indignant protest. The form of this protest was a seriously argued examination of all merely human institutions, with a view to demonstrating "that every endeavor which the art and policy of mankind has used from the beginning of the world until this day, in order to relieve or cure natural ills, has only served to introduce new mischiefs or to aggravate or inflame the old." This thesis, set forth with stately logic and illustrated by critical examinations in all the fields of political activity, leads the reader, with solemn power, to the conviction that all human efforts to improve the world in which we live are necessarily fruitless and that the only true state of happiness for mankind is that Edenic condition in which our first parents were before wisdom, in the form of a serpent, had beguiled them into a reliance upon mere human powers for improvement.

But, of course, Burke was playful and was imposing upon us with sham artillery. By using Bolingbroke's method, he destroys his conclusion and then proves that man, too, is worse than useless in the universe in which Bolingbroke had sought to place him as the dominant and supreme if not solitary figure. Burke knew, as we know when we read his paper, that he was exemplifying one of those common states of mind which make progress difficult. The fact is that all efforts to solve human problems are beset by unidentic twin evils. On the one hand, we have the enthusiast who declines to see difficulties, is indifferent to the lessons of history, takes no account of the deep ruts worn by mental habit, and, by expecting too much, either in speed or achievement, takes a flight from reality and accomplishes less than the possible. On the other, we have the pessimist, his ranks all too often recruited by disillusioned enthusiasts. Starting with an assumption of human incorrigibility, he soon despairs of any progress in a tough and obdurate world and looks with sour disfavor upon those who would disturb any arrangement which has been found to ease the galling of a burden which it is the inescapable lot of mankind to carry. This acceptance of failure as a guide for future conduct is easily fortified by a selective reading of history, and Burke's "Vindication of Natural Society," if read without the humor which underlies it, is a classical illustration of how fiercely learned and at the same time unwise this temper can be.

Somewhere between these temperamental extremes lies the great

mass of mankind; neither credulous nor incredulous, neither foolishly hopeful nor foolishly hopeless, aware of the fact that progress
is not a steadily ascending spiral but a jagged thing on a chart, with
peaks and valleys and yet constantly rising, as is shown by the median
line in the diagram which marks increasing comfort, security, beauty,
and nobility in the life of man.   This great mass of people, unnumbed
by learning, are yet aware that old abuses have been swept away,
tyrannies over the body and spirit of man abolished, superstitions and
fears dissipated, and that all this has come about by experimental
processes, many of which were failures, all of which were assailed, and
only some of which fruited in lasting good.   It may well be, therefore,
that "the new spirit" has been greeted with too much enthusiasm by
some of its proponents; but it is certainly true that the emanations
of that new spirit, in practical efforts to establish a better order in international relations, have been too quickly distrusted and condemned
by those who stand at the other extreme in philosophical outlook.

In the course of his "Vindication of Natural Society," Burke
examines war as one of the results of man's effort at political organization.   He says: "The first accounts we have of mankind are but
so many accounts of their butcheries.   All empires have been cemented in blood, and in these early periods when the races of mankind first began to form themselves into parties and combinations,
the first effect of the combination and, indeed, the thing for which it
seems purposely formed and best calculated, was their mutual
destruction."   Following this, he makes what he calls "a small
calculation" of the number of people done to death by war as a political institution, from the earliest times to the middle of the eighteenth century, and comes to the serious conclusion that the number is
not less than thirty-five billion human beings.   To this number no
doubt would have to be added indirect losses from epidemics and
famines resulting from wars.   These ragings of the heathen and more
refined slaughterings among the civilized had taken place with undiminished ferocity, in spite of diplomacy, resident ambassadorial
representation, and all manner of other efforts, by way of offensive
and defensive alliances and bargains, which from time to time constituted the mechanism of international relations.   Since Burke made
this estimate the world has gone steadily on, increasing the possibility
of large-scale mobilization and wholesale destruction, until in our own
day we have had actual world war with losses counted in tens of
millions and dislocations of normal life world-wide in extent and
covering decades — how many we do not know — in their duration.

Thus war has presented historically, and still presents, the major catastrophe in human relations. In its modern forms it challenges the very continuance of organized society. It is no longer fought by selected champions but engages the energies of whole peoples. Its stage is no longer some remote and confined battlefield but the whole area of the combatant nations. It is fought in three dimensions and with weapons which, like Satan's dart, seize us with "strange terrors, pangs unfelt before." The consequences of modern wars, we have now learned, threaten an integrated world with the complete dissolution of the foundations upon which organized and expanding life must rest. Whether history is encouraging or discouraging, we cannot contemplate the World War, and the world which has resulted from it, without realizing that no spirit can be too bold which refuses to accept war as a constantly recurring menace and that no experiment can be too rash, however much the books on international law and history may creak on their shelves, if its intention is to rescue the race from this threat of destruction. The time has come for somebody to be "a fool in Christ" if necessary.

Clearly, if there is any substitute for war it must lie in the pacific settlement of controversies out of which wars grow. Throughout the long period of recorded history, efforts of one sort or another to establish the means of such pacific settlements have been made. They have, however, been sporadic rather than consecutive, and for the most part were responses to war weariness, religious enthusiasm, the brief ascendency of a philosophical spirit, or a change in political policy in a dominant state. Writers on international law have, since Vattel, given the subject some attention. But until recent years the discussion of pacific settlements usually revolved around the possibility of a substitution of arbitration or adjudication for an appeal to arms; and, of course, both of these agencies take hold of a full-grown conflict, and the likelihood of their being used is diminished by the fact that passion has already been engendered before they can be appealed to. They are envisaged, frankly, as alternatives to war rather than as anticipatory adjusters of incipient controversies in which the seeds of conflict have only begun to germinate. For the most part, statesmen have preferred to try one or the other of two policies to preserve the peace of the world: either a Roman Peace, dictated by a single authoritative state, strong enough to impose its will upon the rest of the world, or a balance of power, which seeks to divide the world into an equipoise by systems of alliances and understandings. Both of these types of effort, repeated under every variation of time and circumstance, have failed. The spirit of nationality has always been too strong to endure an imposed peace. Balances of power, being organized with war in mind, become unstable as one side or the other feels that it has acquired a momentary supremacy or has detached from the other side and annexed to itself an ally, thus putting itself in a position to overpower its adversaries and accomplish certain long-cherished political objectives of its own group.

As against these policies, based frankly upon power, the intermittent suggestion of securing pacific settlement by using among nations the agencies worked out in the domestic policy of civilized states, secured a hearing with difficulty. One obvious reason for this lies in the fact that the people who made wars and resorted to them to accomplish their political objectives were not the people who suffered in wars, while the people who did suffer and pay the price had no voice in the councils where the extent of their sacrifices might be weighed against the advantage of a political policy which the governing class sought to pursue. King William of Prussia had a violent quarrel with Bismarck, after the humiliation of Austria, because of Bismarck's unwillingness to annex Austrian territory from the defeated enemy. The King said to him that it had been the policy of his House to enlarge Prussia and that each of his ancestors had annexed territory as the result of his conquests. The whole diplomatic history of the world has revolved around the dreams of empire-builders; and the historic policies of states, lying buried in the archives of their Foreign Offices, have contemplated conquest and acquisitions based on opportunities, as they might arise, for advantageous wars. Sometimes these policies have been purely defensive, as for instance the interest of England in Persia and Afghanistan to protect the Indian frontier. Sometimes they are aggressive, like the policy which has for centuries dictated to the Russian mind the dominance of Asia and an outlet through the Bosporus to the Mediterranean. Under the old order, each new Foreign Minister came to his task with orders to follow the chart. Necessity might require gestures, opportunity might have to be waited for; but all concessions and all combinations looked to the ultimate accomplishment of objectives which, though often undeclared and unexposed, were the final and supreme concern of the state. As these policies were hopelessly irreconcilable, the relations of the nations which entertained them were necessarily transitory and unstable. That this picture is not fanciful is illustrated by any realistic view of the relations of modern Europe. Bismarck's Reinsurance Treaty,

Caprivi's failure to renew it, the hesitance of Germany as between friendship with England and friendship with Russia, the effort to build a European anti-English alliance, these and a hundred other episodes in modern European diplomatic history evidence the uneasy tension of nationalistic policies against the restraints of world order and world peace. Even the United States was captured by "manifest destiny" and made overnight into an Asiatic power by exactly the sort of impulse which has led Russia and Japan through a long period of years to look with acquiring eyes on Manchuria and Chosen.

The existence of these forces, controlled only by considerations of national advantage, has always been perfectly well known, but the cost of leaving them so controlled has only gradually come to be realized. The scientific spirit, which has given us in the realm of material things the courage to look unpleasant facts in the face and to follow truth wherever it may lead, has in recent years begun increasingly to make itself felt in considerations of the social and political relations of men, and this has given both new dignity to the speculations of philosophers and new hopefulness to the efforts of statesmen in the international field. If wider knowledge and franker thinking have bred a new spirit which by searching has found common interests in the preservation of peace that are of higher value than the ruthless pursuit of national objectives, we may be permitted to hope that the moral equivalent of war, if not at hand, is at least not so remote as it was when these matters of life and death were held to be games for princes to play at and, like the wills of princes, not subject to moral restraint. Surely, too, the triumphs of science in the material world encourage us to do some laboratory work with the human spirit. A peaceful world would have been less amazing to George Washington than wireless telegraphy. We must not think too well of atoms at the expense of thinking too ill of men.

From its beginnings the United States has had an attitude favoring the pacific settlement of international controversies. This has been manifested particularly in our attitude toward arbitration. But we early began to advocate the addition of adjudication to the means of settlement. Long before the World War, American public opinion had reached the settled conviction that coöperative international action was necessary for the preservation of peace, and but for the controversy of prestige between the Senate and the President it seems likely that an enlightened sentiment against war would have made the United States a partner, if not the leader, in widespread arrangements — perhaps compulsory in character — for pacific settlements.

Theodore Roosevelt was certainly one of the most combative and valiant of modern Americans. Yet, in accepting the Nobel Peace Prize, he said in 1910:

Finally, it would be a master stroke if those Great Powers honestly bent on peace would form a league of peace, not only to keep the peace among themselves, but to prevent, by force if necessary, its being broken by others. The supreme difficulty in connection with developing the peace work of The Hague arises from the lack of any executive power, of any police power to enforce the decrees of the court. In any community of any size the authority of the courts rests upon actual or potential force; on the existence of a police, or on the knowledge that the able-bodied men of the country are both ready and willing to see that the decrees of judicial and legislative bodies are put into effect. In new and wild communities where there is violence, an honest man must protect himself; and until other means of securing his safety are devised, it is both foolish and wicked to persuade him to surrender his arms while the men who are dangerous to the community retain theirs. He should not renounce the right to protect himself by his own efforts until the community is so organized that it can effectively relieve the individual of the duty of putting down violence. So it is with nations. Each nation must keep well prepared to defend itself until the establishment of some form of international police power, competent and willing to prevent violence as between nations. As things are now, such power to command peace throughout the world could best be assured by some combination between those great nations which sincerely desire peace and have no thought themselves of committing aggressions. The combination might at first be only to secure peace within certain definite limits and certain definite conditions; but the ruler or statesman who should bring about such a combination would have earned his place in history for all time and his title to the gratitude of all mankind.

That this was not a mere rhetorical flourish by a retired President was shortly made manifest, for about a month later, by joint resolution, the Congress of the United States authorized the President to appoint a commission in relation to universal peace, its duty being to consider the expediency of utilizing existing international agencies for the purpose of limiting the armaments of the nations of the world by international agreement; and it was especially charged to consider and report upon any other means "to lessen the probabilities of war."

After the Great War had broken upon the world, the League to Enforce Peace enlisted in support of its program the highest types of

Americans, men trained in the practical administration of affairs, and the idea of the League was universally acclaimed as perhaps the greatest gift of the American spirit to a world forced to admit the complete breakdown of its system of international relations. It was not a plan to deal with the existing war, but to deal with the future after that war.

Later, of course, we ourselves became involved in the conflict. But America's attitude toward war remained unchanged and is best illustrated by the fact that the two slogans which most profoundly affected the American mind in all those years were first, "He kept us out of war"; and second, "This is a war to end war." It has become the fashion nowadays to be cynical about the latter of these slogans and to say that America's participation was in fact no crusade in behalf of peace, but rather the pursuit of any one of a half-dozen sordid objectives which have come as afterthoughts of partisan rancor; but no one who lived through the days of America's participation can fail still to feel the thrill and exaltation which we had then from the belief that we were unselfish and fought both for a just and a permanent peace. And the soldiers of a country which had not denied knowledge to its citizens died on French battlefields believing that they were contributing their lives to the cause of peace. Since the end of the war, the world has been seeking with quickened zeal the means of pacific settlement. If some of these means in the future turn out to be frail reliances, America's background requires that we should exercise toward them, in their hour of trial, a great charity of judgment and extend to the effort to improve them and use them a spirit of sympathetic coöperation.

What, then, is the new spirit, what is its approach to the problem of pacific settlement, and what agencies has it established, experimental or otherwise, to accomplish its purpose? Perhaps it is enough to say that the new spirit is an awakened conscience, chastened by experience, informed by research, and driven by the necessity of finding a solution for the problem presented by man's most destructive enemy. The principles underlying the agencies so far established or suggested are principally four — adjudication, arbitration, conciliation, and conference.

The World Court is the embodiment of the first of these. As we have already seen, it is equipped to deal only with matured controversies, and of these, only those which lie within the field of legal rights. It can interpret and apply treaties which define, by contract, the obligations which the high contracting parties are willing to assume toward each other. To a more limited extent it can determine rights upon generally accepted principles of law, and it may be expected that, as time goes on, larger areas of jurisdiction will be conceded to it as confidence in its wisdom and disinterestedness grows. It has not been and ought not now to be given any jurisdiction over political questions. Whether it should ever be given such jurisdiction is a profitless speculation. Our own Supreme Court at the beginning moved with hesitant steps and slow, and in an early case its judgment was flouted by a state in the Union, so that its contemporary critics foresaw its early dissolution. It was in that spirit that the judgment of the World Court in the *Anschluss* case was assailed until John W. Davis, in a dispassionate and irresistible paper,[1] demonstrated that the Court had acted judicially upon questions of intricacy and difficulty, and had reached a judgment about which conflict of opinion was possible but with the weight of argument strongly with the judgment of the Court. But with the years our Supreme Court has been tried in the fire of fierce contests and has acquired finality for its judgments based upon unshakable confidence in its wisdom and integrity. The controversies which our Supreme Court now decides are such as in Europe cause general mobilizations and marching armies. In the so-called Chicago Drainage Canal case, the plaintiff state, Wisconsin, and the states associated with it in interest aggregated a population of thirty-nine millions, while on the other side were arrayed Illinois and the states of the Mississippi Valley with an aggregate population of twenty-two millions. The issue was believed on both sides to have vital economic implications. Yet it was argued, determined, and the judgment accepted, without any emotional outburst due to wounded pride or loss of prestige. In like manner the judgments of the World Court will come to have authority in great matters. This precedent of our own Supreme Court in adjudicating controversies among forty-eight sovereign states makes the idea of a world court peculiarly congenial to our mode of thought, as is evidenced by the practically unanimous judgment of the American people outside of the Senate in favor of adhesion to its protocol. Even in the Senate, where the appetite for reservations and interpretations is as yet unsatisfied, the sentiment is practically unanimous for a court, even on the part of those who are critical of this one.

It would be idle to set out again the extent to which the World Court as now constituted is an American institution, but it is difficult

[1] *Atlantic Monthly*, January, 1932.

for an American lawyer to check an expression of his pride that at The Hague Conference and elsewhere this great idea was exploited as an expression of American confidence in the supremacy of law and the efficacy of justice, and even more difficult for him to restrain an exclamation of grateful admiration for his countryman, Elihu Root, whose services in connection with the Court dignify the profession of which he is the leader as they nobly express the political philosophy of the people for whom he spoke.

But useful as is the function of the Court, its limitations are obvious. It must sit at the door of its tent until the controversy is brought to it. It may not anticipate controversies, and especially it may not deal with political and economic questions. And it is out of these latter that wars are likely to arise. As a part of the modern peace machinery the World Court is indispensable, but it is probable that the very nature of adjudication has retarded the acceptance of the other agencies which have been suggested for use in the field which the Court cannot cover. Conciliation and conference are more remote and less tangible in their operation. When they succeed, they are not known to have averted tragedies, and, like the undisclosed charities of the really benevolent, they are recorded in no books except those of the Guardian Angel. Everything about our modern life makes us thirst for the dramatic. Conciliation and conference administer no knock-out blows, and yet, if we are to find modes of pacific settlement, they will have to be based upon long-range wisdom which must see the cloud of controversy while it is still no larger than a man's hand. The process must afford no opportunity for diplomatic triumphs and either the gaining or losing of face.

These considerations have perhaps tended to make very practical people impatient and cause them to point out that the world always has enough real and threatening troubles to make it unnecessary to go poking about to see if there are any merely possible future troubles to be borrowed. To this is to be added a difficulty which arises from the fact that international conferences in the past have rather served the purpose of dramatically registering conclusions arrived at before the conference was held than actually reaching and adopting conclusions as the result of the conference itself. But when all of these difficulties are recognized, it must still be admitted that conference belongs in the scheme of pacific settlement. Great international conferences, with agenda prepared long in advance, serve a useful purpose even when they collapse without apparent result. The mere fact that nations are willing to meet and discuss their problems in public is a gain. They will continue to afford opportunities for the making of nationalistic speeches for home consumption and the adoption of intransigent attitudes upon questions which engage popular passion; but, even in such an atmosphere, agreements are often reached upon questions of real significance while the conferees maintain unyielding attitudes on others, and the ground is laid for future consideration, in a cleared atmosphere, of contentious and for the moment intractable differences. Nor is it to be forgotten that with each such conference the technique improves. A more patient and scholarly research, a more sympathetic comprehension of the facts in issue, a longer view of the history of the questions in controversy, and a more sobered realization of the value of agreement can be expected as the novelty of international conference wears off and the value of frank discussion becomes more apparent. We have a long way to go before we can feel that we have given conference a fair trial. It is to be hoped that we will more and more move away from the selection of personages as delegates and to an increasing degree give scholarship and character first consideration in the selection of conferees. If we can acquire the habit of appointing, not politicians with an eye on retaining or obtaining an office, but men who are willing to play for the long verdict of history, and surround them with knowledge dispassionately collected by men who work in the scientific spirit, the possibilities of conference are unlimited. If such improvements in the make-up and technique of conferences be regarded as fanciful, I can only reply that I write this paper in the deep conviction that the natural tendency of man is upward, that what is good will ultimately come to pass, and without the least impatience at not being able instantly to accomplish the best if I can but be sure that our aim is constantly toward the good.

The League of Nations is, of course, the visible and ultimate embodiment of all these principles of pacific settlement. Established in the peace treaty which ended the World War, it has always been beset by difficulties growing out of territorial and political arrangements made by other parts of the treaty in which the Covenant is contained, which it has no power *suo motu* to revise. Nations prostrated by their losses, paupered by their expenditures, and eager both for revenge for the past and security for the future, wrote their triumphant passions in the treaty and then said their prayers in the Covenant. The League of Nations is neither so authoritative nor so dentate as the Roosevelt-Taft-Lodge proposal for a League to Enforce Peace. Both its nature and its machinery rely on research, consultation, and conciliation; and the restraint of its deliberations and actions from the day of its organization has been in accordance with this theory of its functions. America's relationship to the League was at the outset confused by a wholly shabby, domestic, partisan controversy. As the years have gone by, however, a graver question has arisen, and while the United States no longer denies the existence of the League and does increasingly coöperate with it, we are far from having settled upon any practical basis by which a democracy like ours can so combine and delegate its power in foreign affairs, which is distributed by the Constitution between the executive and the Senate, as to make full participation on our part helpful. Indeed, as the world comes to be more and more governed by democracies, in the sense of being ultimately controlled by popular opinion, the whole problem of foreign affairs becomes infinitely more complicated, for democracies will brook no check upon their emotions and yet, in the very nature of the case, must operate under inescapable limitations upon their information, thus making the agitation of demagogues and the appeal of super-nationalists peculiarly effective. The absence of the United States from the League has caused difficulties too well known to need recital. Without, for the moment, considering the possible use of force or even sanctions, the moral authority of the League is diminished by the absence from its composite voice of the disinterested and detached note which, in many controversies, the United States alone can strike. The League has, therefore, like the children in Maeterlinck's *Blue Bird*, had certain infirmities handed to it before its birth, and to these have been added the grave misfortune of abstention by the United States, together with a third difficulty, arising out of exaggerated expectations on the one side and exaggerated fears on the other, according to the temperament of the particular critics who have watched its proceedings.

To me it has always seemed irrational to expect instant *ad hoc* solutions of age-old difficulties and to criticize the League because there is still abroad in some parts of the world the spirit of Jenghiz Khan. It has seemed to me equally irrational to criticize the League as envisioning war as the ultimate recourse. It may be possible to dispute whether the good offices of the League, to date, have prevented this or that threatened outbreak of hostility; the "ifs" and "ands" of an event which has not happened are always numerous. But it is certainly impossible to assert that any action of the League has in the slightest degree tended to cause or increase the likelihood of hostility. To a dispassionate view, the offices of the League seem to have been wholly conciliatory in the post-war agitations, and the labors of the devoted scholars and statesmen who have worked in and for the League have developed a new and sounder technique of international inquiry and promoted a broad basis of understanding and sympathy among the nations whose delegates, sitting in the Council and Assembly, have discussed international problems and policies with thoughts of understanding and peace always uppermost in their minds. Of the League as an institution we may say that Paul has planted, Apollos has watered, and all sincere lovers of their kind pray that God will give the increase.

The things which have grown out of the League, the fruit of its spirit as well as the developments of its experience, form the great body of mechanisms which now constitute the agencies for pacific settlement. The League has developed the principles underlying the Bryan Treaties of Arbitration: it promoted the Locarno Treaty and its congeners. In 1925 it created a preparatory commission to study the possibilities of world disarmament. On the basis of its work the present Disarmament Conference is still laboring, and whatever formal treaties it may or may not achieve, an immense gain has already been had from its frank discussions and disclosures. In 1928 the Assembly prepared and promulgated a series of model conventions, many of which have been adopted as bilateral arrangements, for pacific settlements by definite provision for arbitration and conciliation. Ultimately there came out of the troubled waters the healing influence of the Pact of Paris, which was opened to general accession in 1928 and has since been adhered to by practically all the nations of the world, including, *mirabile dictu*, the United States.

I suppose when Moses brought down the Tables of the Law from Mount Sinai there was an immediate division of opinion about them. The sage but weary fathers in Israel doubtless asked on the one side, "Where are the sanctions?" and on the other, "Why all these innovations? Is not the old law, which was good enough for our fathers, good enough for us?" But truth has its own sanctions and so the Pact of Paris, enunciating a great moral datum, will continue to stand, as the Tables of the Law have stood, violated by casual lawbreakers but avenged in the consequences as the moral sense of mankind unites to rebuke the transgressor. In a world which has throughout its history treated war as an instrument of policy, a moral revolution is manifest when the nations of that world unite in a declaration condemning recourse to war for the solution of international controversies, and renouncing it as an instrument of national policy in their relations with one another. A new standard of judgment is set up. This is a thing around which world opinion can gather; and in the future of the world, so far as we can foresee it, the controlling force is going to be the slow-moving but irresistible tide of public opinion.

Whether, and by what means, and how fast the Pact of Paris should be implemented, the evolutions of time alone can determine. To criticize the Pact because the right of self-defense is reserved, or because nations retained freedom of action in special areas, or because certain Senators of the United States made slighting remarks about it when they voted for it, is all beside the point. For thousands of years the right to make war has been regarded as an attribute of sovereignty and it was inconceivable that anybody should question the discretion of a sovereign in resorting to it. Under that theory, war always lay in the field of normal expectation. Under this new theory, the normal expectation is pacific settlement. The burden of proof has shifted. The irrebuttable presumption of the right of the sovereign to go to war for political objectives has been abolished and the war-maker is put upon the defensive. How important this is any soldier will testify. Big guns are important, but a defensible cause is indispensable to ultimate success in war. Some of the criticism of the Briand-Kellogg Pact, and indeed of all this pacific settlement machinery, proceeds on the theory that when the world goes mad it pays no attention to previously enacted self-denying ordinances; and it must be conceded that the world has gone mad occasionally and ruthlessly disregarded prudential checks set upon its own behavior. But I fancy the best we can do is to legislate for a sane world and, so far as we can, set up standards of conduct so that departures from the normal will be recognized and all possible restraints exerted. The whole of mankind's conventional morality has grown by that process and there would seem to be no reason why the growth of an international morality might not be similarly fostered.

Particularly since the adoption of the Briand-Kellogg Pact, there has grown up the practice of multilateral treaties dealing with special circumstances and regional situations. These treaties include provisions for consultation upon the occasion of alleged violation by one of the high contracting parties, and among the critics of modern peace machinery this provision causes special concern. The fear, apparently, is that if ten nations make a treaty and one of them appears to have violated it, if the other nine get together and consult about what ought to be done, their propensity will be to declare war at once or at least to make among themselves such commitments as may ultimately carry them into a war which they might otherwise avoid. This entirely overlooks the fact that both the purpose and spirit of such proposed consultation is to find a peaceful solution. So far as the United States is concerned, it would seem adequate to reply that the power to declare war rests with Congress, and any consultation in which the United States was a party would necessarily be subject to that final safeguard. But the only alternative to consultations is not to consult, and the consequences of not consulting are either that the treaty will be violated with impunity, in which case it might as well not have been made, or the alleged violation will go unanalyzed and unredressed, breeding ill-will and suspicion and war if the point of the violation is of sufficient interest to justify war by any one or more of the contracting parties which feel themselves sufficiently powerful to enforce the treaty. After all, it ought to be easy to prevent consultations from automatically becoming conspiracies, and if such consultations are conducted in the spirit of the modern devices for pacific settlement the danger from improper commitments would seem to be far less than that from a failure to consult. But consultation is not a novelty. Under the old procedure, consultation *ad hoc* was common. When war threatened, hurriedly gathered groups of Ambassadors or Foreign Ministers got together to consult with a view to averting the outbreak. There are not wanting those who feel that if there had been some standing machinery for consultation in Europe in August, 1914, the World War could have been averted. Sir Edward Grey's noble but pathetic effort to secure consultation is an excellent illustration of the point under consideration. If Russia, Austria, Germany, France, and England had been under a treaty arrangement which required consultation, his fatal race against the limitations of time might not have been in vain.

But the chief flutter in the dovecote of all this criticism of arrangements for pacific settlement seems to grow out of the possible effect it may have upon the doctrine of neutrality.

When the World War broke out, President Wilson, issuing a proclamation of neutrality, called upon the American people not merely to be neutral within the restraints of legal definitions of that status, but to be neutral "in thought as well as action." This was in August, 1914. In April, 1917, President Wilson declared "neutrality is no longer feasible or desirable where the peace of the world is involved and the freedom of its peoples." And it must be admitted that Article 16 of the Covenant of the League of Nations, in effect, recognizes

that resort to war by a member of the League in disregard of the restraints of the Covenant is an act of war against all other members
of the League, to the extent at least of justifying immediate severance
of all trade or financial relations between them and the aggressor
and ultimate coöperative action, by force if necessary. It ought to
be admitted that while the machinery for pacific settlement counts
heavily — or perhaps it ought to be said, hopes fervently — for success through peaceful agencies, it does not and cannot close its eyes
to the possibility of failure and the ultimate necessity of resort to
force. But surely advocates of the doctrine of neutrality offer no
more attractive prospect; for the rights of neutrals are, and always
have been, no stronger than the power of the neutral to enforce them
against the interest of a belligerent to break them. I am not here
speaking of the status of perpetual neutrality accorded to certain
areas of the world by the concerted action of surrounding states,
like that of Switzerland, although in this connection it is wise to remember that Belgium had such a status and that Germany was a
co-guarantor.

Temporary neutrality has had a long and varied history. Its
periods of success have been largely those in which there were many
strong nations neutral as to a particular conflict. Its periods of
failure have been those when the dominant nations of the world
were at war and their interest led them to disregard so-called neutral
rights. Grotius considered the subject in the third book of his
treatise *On the Law of War and Peace* and suggested that neutrals
should form an opinion upon the justice or injustice of the hostility
and then do nothing which would further the cause of the one in the
wrong or hamper the movements of the one in the right. Vattel
dissented from this view, holding that the neutral should not constitute himself a judge but that his greater safety lay in equal treatment of the belligerents. Modern statesmen and international
lawyers have sought to build around the idea of neutrality a system of
principles, with a view to restricting the extent of the conflict by
defining the limits of conduct permissible to a neutral state and its
nationals.

In its essence neutrality is a sort of indifferentism based on the
theory that one is not obliged to imperil one's interests by espousing
the cause of another, however innocent the victim or vicious his
assailant. It has always been conceded that the doctrine of neutrality does not prevent a state from going to war when it has a sufficient interest to justify its intervention. It would seem, therefore,

that the doctrine is really a system of rules of conduct for a state which has no interest justifying intervention and hopes to have, either alone or in concert with other states like-minded, the power to stay out of the conflict. Undoubtedly the doctrine has been highly useful to small states with warlike neighbors, but its dignity as a principle has often been marred by the fact that it has been used as a counter in bargains made in anticipation of aggression. A single example will suffice. Germany's neutrality in the Russo-Japanese War was the equivalent of an alliance. It protected Russia on her western frontier and at Constantinople and thus freed her to exert her entire power in Manchuria. A somewhat different case was presented when Germany in 1875 and 1887 contemplated fresh aggressions upon France to retard her recovery from the Franco-Prussian War. Bismarck inquired whether England would be neutral, and being unable to secure a promise of neutrality refrained from a fresh war upon France. In this aspect, neutrality is in effect intervention. The assumption of British neutrality in 1914 was Bethmann-Hollweg's fatal mistake. On the basis of its history, therefore, the doctrine of neutrality can hardly claim to be an adequate safeguard, or indeed to be a basis which, however extended and developed, will sustain peace even to the peaceful.

The World War experience with the doctrine of neutrality was disastrous. Not only were solemn obligations to respect neutrality disregarded, but a world situation was created in which neutrality was impossible. How can an integrated world, in which finance and commerce are thoroughly internationalized, be neutral when the high seas are marked out into lanes of permitted but limited travel and the list of contraband is extended beyond all the categories of arms and munitions so as to include, not the subsistence of armies alone, but the raw materials and manufactured products which sustain civilian life? If the doctrine of neutrality ever had a friend, it was President Wilson. He hoped with passionate fervor that the United States might remain neutral. He prayed that the United States might "speak the counsels of peace and accommodation not as a partisan but as a friend," and he struggled with all the belligerent governments to protect some vestige of America's right as a neutral, to remain at peace and store up a great reservoir of good will with which to bind up the wounds of the belligerents and make possible the restoration of peace and ultimate understanding among them. There were times when it was thought that we might be forced into the war to defend the definition of neutral goods. By 1917 he had come to realize that under the conditions of modern war neutrality had become impossible and, in the presence of so devastating a spectacle, that it was undesirable. After all, there is no reflection upon the soldier who lives up to the exact letter of the bond of his military obligation; but Congressional Medals of Honor are awarded for heroism above and beyond the call of duty. The law of neutrality and the rights of neutrals are brands plucked from the burning. They ought to be preserved, made more definite and certain, and every effort made to secure for them wider usefulness and more general acceptance. But there are situations, and the world has just faced one of them, where neutrality is not enough and where the thing needed is the sword of righteousness and not the mere security of a bomb-proof while our common civilization is being destroyed.

This was, to be sure, a special case, and no general way of defining aggression or determining the aggressor can be easily formulated. Even if we had a formula, the facts can rarely be gathered, in the midst of conflict, with final completeness. Don Quixote's procedures are not to be recommended for international action. But can we abandon the problem because it is difficult? There are both moral responsibilities and practical difficulties about being indifferent to the distinction between right and wrong. To insist on the right to sell pistols both to the highwaymen and to the occupants of the stagecoach is bad morals and, when we have occasion to use the stagecoach, may prove inconvenient if not fatal. But if this be a dilemma it is a very old one, and one which, for all practical purposes, has long been solved in all domestic matters. We let the community decide. We have determined that the chances of a wrong decision are immeasurably less serious than either not having it decided at all or letting each man decide for himself. The analogy is persuasive. The nations of the world are coming more and more to be a family or a community of nations, and the new mechanisms seek its judgments. The neutrality which merely refuses to decide has a hard case to make against an international consciousness which coöperates to decide and so to prevent the conflict. Even if a war, prevented by joint international action, would have been "a good war" the loss is not irreparable. The result may still be worked out by some other means, or the war started later, with a better chance for the side now known to be in the right.

Within its limited sphere neutrality is a useful doctrine, but its defense does not require an attack upon measures conceived in a bolder spirit and designed to avert catastrophes of a kind where neutrality is, as we have seen, impossible or undesirable. Indeed we should remember that neutrality does not even aim to prevent war. Its more modest and local object is to restrain its extension.

The world is cursed by its common fears. It is made better by its great faiths. The new spirit is the evidence of such a fighting faith. The agencies it has so far devised have in them the seeds of growth. Lawyers with their doubts and statesmen with their policies may encumber this spirit and delay its achievements. Its progress by trial and error may be slow and its course may sometimes seem to be inviting new perils. Some of the steps it eagerly takes may have to be retraced and fresh starts made, but if this is ever to be a world in which nations, like civilized men, are governed by moral restraints, and from which licensed war for the private objectives of ambitious states will disappear, it must be fought for in this spirit. Those who share this faith and work in this hope have no apology to make to their own or future generations.

V

SCIENCE AND THE MODERN WORLD

THE twentieth century already has many specific scientific achievements to its credit. In medicine the World War produced important practical discoveries, the chief being connected with the name of Alexis Carrel; Dr. F. G. Banting's discovery of insulin has brought diabetes under control; the study of vitamines has rendered possible a new attack on problems of nutrition; work on the endocrine glands and hormones has turned a new page in physiology; under Freud and others psychoanalysis has made great progress. In biology Mendel's work, which goes back to 1865 but was almost unknown till after 1900, has drastically modified our ideas of evolution. In physics we have arrived, through study of the atom, at wholly new ideas of the constitution of matter. Knowledge of radioactivity, thanks to Moseley, Planck, Bohr, Millikan, and others, has advanced along new lines. Much has often been achieved by copartnership between two different sciences; thus biochemistry has been rapidly developed, and biophysics has made promising beginnings. Astronomy has not only enhanced our knowledge of the universe but greatly enlarged our appreciation of the number of unsolved (and perhaps insoluble) problems in that field. But the principal scientific event of recent times has been Einstein's work on the doctrine of relativity, which, involving questions of space-time and a new conception of the general nature of the universe, has had a many-sided effect upon human thought. The idea that space possesses other properties than extension alone, that time has other properties than duration alone, that neither is infinite as the Newtonian physics assumed they were, obviously gives us a new cosmology; and already broad new philosophical concepts are appearing in response to Einstein's doctrines. In the section which follows, no effort is made to present a summary of the great scientific advances of recent times. The attempt is rather to furnish a few typical glimpses of a field in which multiplicity of effort has been accompanied by revolutionary changes; and these are preceded by a definition of principles by such older writers as Tyndall, Spencer, and Huxley.

THE BELFAST ADDRESS

John Tyndall

Few brief autobiographies are more striking than that which JOHN TYNDALL prepared as an address at the Birkbeck Institution in London in 1884, and published in his *New Fragments*. A poor Irish boy, born in County Carlow in 1820; largely self-taught, attending mechanics' institute lectures in Lancashire while employed by the British Ordnance Survey; working night and day as a railway engineer in Yorkshire, so that he later recalled "the refreshment derived occasionally from five minutes' sleep on a deal table, with Babbage and Callet's Logarithms under my head for a pillow"; gradually saving up enough money to go to the University of Marburg for his doctorate; coming back to England to lecture on physics at Queenwood College; becoming about 1851 a warm friend of Faraday and Huxley — such is the story. Readers of Thomas Carlyle's letters will gain from them some impression of the robust strength, the strong, vigorous gusto, which marked Tyndall's activities; always "kind, cheery, inventive, helpful," as Carlyle says. In 1853 he became professor of natural philosophy at the Royal Institution, and in 1867 he succeeded Faraday, whom he revered to the point of worship, as its superintendent. His researches into heat and light were of great scientific value. But he was distinguished rather as a personality than as a discoverer. No scientist of the day, not even Huxley, was so effective as a public speaker, and the lecture tour he made in the United States in 1872–1873 is still remembered. He was humorous, fluent, vehement, and of irresistible earnestness in discourse, and he had a gift for presenting scientific facts in picturesque form. Devoted to pure science for its own sake, he set an example of fine indifference to sordid considerations; for example, he gave every penny of the large sums derived from his American lectures to scientific advancement. His books on heat, light, and sound are now of course outdated. But his memoir of Faraday, his *Belfast Address* of 1874 on science and religion, and his interesting occasional papers in *Fragments of Science* and *New Fragments* are still of value; while his *Hours of Exercise in the Alps* is a classic record of the enjoyments of mountain-climbing.

In our day great generalizations have been reached. The theory of the origin of species is but one of them. Another, of still wider grasp and more radical significance, is the doctrine of the conservation of energy, the ultimate philosophical issues of which are as yet but dimly seen — that doctrine which "binds nature fast in fate" to an extent not hitherto recognized, exacting from every antecedent its equivalent consequent, from every consequent its equivalent antecedent, and bringing vital as well as physical phenomena under the dominion of that law of causal connection which, as far as the human understanding has yet pierced, asserts itself everywhere in nature. Long in advance of all definite experiment upon the subject, the con-

stancy and indestructibility of matter had been affirmed; and all
subsequent experience justified the affirmation.   Later researches extended the attribute of indestructibility to force.   This idea, applied
in the first instance to inorganic, rapidly embraced organic nature.
The vegetable world, though drawing almost all its nutriment from
invisible sources, was proved incompetent to generate anew either
matter or force.   Its matter is for the most part transmuted air; its
force, transformed solar force.   The animal world was proved to be
equally uncreative, all its motive energies being referred to the combustion of its food.   The activity of each animal as a whole was proved
to be the transferred activities of its molecules.   The muscles were
shown to be stores of mechanical force, potential until unlocked by the
nerves, and then resulting in muscular contractions.   The speed at
which messages fly to and fro along the nerves was determined, and
found to be, not, as had been previously supposed, equal to that of
light or electricity, but less than the speed of a flying eagle.

This was the work of the physicist; then came the conquests of the
comparative anatomist and physiologist, revealing the structure of
every animal, and the function of every organ in the whole biological
series, from the lowest zoöphyte up to man.   The nervous system had
been made the object of profound and continued study, the wonderful,
and at bottom entirely mysterious, controlling power which it exercises over the whole organism, physical and mental, being recognized
more and more.   Thought could not be kept back from a subject so
profoundly suggestive.   Besides the physical life dealt with by Mr.
Darwin, there is a psychical life presenting similar gradations, and
asking equally for a solution.   How are the different grades and
orders of mind to be accounted for?   What is the principle of growth
of that mysterious power which on our planet culminates in reason?
These are questions which, though not thrusting themselves so
forcibly upon the attention of the general public, had not only occupied many reflecting minds, but had been formally broached by one
of them before the *Origin of Species* appeared.

With the mass of materials furnished by the physicist and physiologist in his hands, Mr. Herbert Spencer, twenty years ago, sought
to graft upon this basis a system of psychology; and two years ago a
second and greatly amplified edition of his work appeared.   Those
who have occupied themselves with the beautiful experiments of
Plateau will remember that when two spherules of olive oil, suspended
in a mixture of alcohol and water of the same density as the oil, are
brought together, they do not immediately unite.   Something like a

pellicle appears to be formed around the drops, the rupture of which is immediately followed by the coalescence of the globules into one. There are organisms whose vital actions are almost as purely physical as that of these drops of oil. They come into contact and fuse themselves thus together. From such organisms to others a shade higher, and from these to others a shade higher still, and on through an ever-ascending series, Mr. Spencer conducts his argument. There are two obvious factors to be here taken into account — the creature and the medium in which it lives, or, as it is often expressed, the organism and its environment. Mr. Spencer's fundamental principle is that between these two factors there is incessant interaction. The organism is played upon by the environment, and is modified to meet the requirements of the environment. Life he defines to be "a continuous adjustment of internal relations to external relations."

In the lowest organisms we have a kind of tactual sense diffused over the entire body; then, through impressions from without and their corresponding adjustments, special portions of the surface become more responsive to stimuli than others. The senses are nascent, the basis of all of them being that simple tactual sense which the sage Democritus recognized twenty-three hundred years ago as their common progenitor. The action of light, in the first instance, appears to be a mere disturbance of the chemical processes in the animal organism, similar to that which occurs in the leaves of plants. By degrees the action becomes localized in a few pigment cells, more sensitive to light than the surrounding tissue. The eye is here incipient. At first it is merely capable of revealing differences of light and shade produced by bodies close at hand. Followed, as the interception of the light is in almost all cases, by the contact of the closely adjacent opaque body, sight in this condition becomes a kind of "anticipatory touch." The adjustment continues; a slight bulging out of the epidermis over the pigment granules supervenes. A lens is incipient, and, through the operation of infinite adjustments, at length reaches the perfection that it displays in the hawk and the eagle. So of the other senses; they are special differentiations of a tissue which was originally vaguely sensitive all over.

With the development of the senses the adjustments between the organism and its environment gradually extend in *space*, a multiplication of experiences and a corresponding modification of conduct being the result. The adjustments also extend in *time*, covering continually greater intervals. Along with this extension in space and time, the adjustments also increase in specialty and complexity, passing through the various grades of brute life and prolonging themselves into the domain of reason.   Very striking are Mr. Spencer's remarks regarding the influence of the sense of touch upon the development of intelligence.   This is, so to say, the mother tongue of all the senses, into which they must be translated to be of service to the organism.   Hence its importance.   The parrot is the most intelligent of birds, and its tactual power is also greatest.   From this sense it gets knowledge unattainable by birds which cannot employ their feet as hands.   The elephant is the most sagacious of quadrupeds — its tactual range and skill, and the consequent multiplication of experiences, which it owes to its wonderfully adaptable trunk being the basis of its sagacity. Feline animals, for a similar cause, are more sagacious than hoofed animals — atonement being to some extent made in the case of the horse by the possession of sensitive prehensile lips.   In the primates the evolution of intellect and the evolution of tactual appendages go hand in hand.   In the most intelligent anthropoid apes we find the tactual range and delicacy greatly augmented, new avenues of knowledge being thus opened to the animal.   Man crowns the edifice here, not only in virtue of his own manipulatory power, but through the enormous extension of his range of experience by the invention of instruments of precision, which serve as supplemental senses and supplemental limbs.   The reciprocal action of these is finely described and illustrated.   That chastened intellectual emotion to which I have referred in connection with Mr. Darwin is, I should say, not absent in Mr. Spencer.   His illustrations possess at times exceeding vividness and force, and from his style on such occasions it is to be inferred that the ganglia of this apostle of the understanding are sometimes the seat of a nascent poetic thrill.

It is a fact of supreme importance that actions the performance of which at first requires even painful effort and deliberation may by habit be rendered automatic.   Witness the slow learning of its letters by a child, and the subsequent facility of reading in a man, when each group of letters which forms a word is instantly and without effort fused to a single perception.   Instance the billiard player, whose muscles of hand and eye, when he reaches the perfection of his art, are unconsciously coördinated.   Instance the musician, who by practice is enabled to fuse a multitude of arrangements — auditory, tactual, and muscular — into a process of automatic manipulation.   Combining such facts with the doctrine of hereditary transmission, we reach a theory of instinct.   A chick, after coming out of the egg, balances itself correctly, runs about, picks up food, thus showing that it possesses a power of directing its movements to definite ends. How did the chick learn this very complex coördination of eye, muscles, and beak? It has not been individually taught; its personal experience is nil; but it has the benefit of ancestral experience. In its inherited organization are registered all the powers which it displays at birth. So also as regards the instinct of the hive bee. The distance at which the insects stand apart when they sweep their hemispheres and build their cells is "organically remembered." Man also carries with him the physical texture of his ancestry, as well as the inherited intellect bound up with it. The defects of intelligence during infancy and youth are probably less due to a lack of individual experience than to the fact that in early life the cerebral organization is still incomplete. The period necessary for completion varies with the race and with the individual. As a round shot outstrips a rifled one on quitting the muzzle of the gun, so the lower race in childhood may outstrip the higher. But the higher eventually overtakes the lower, and surpasses it in range. As regards individuals, we do not always find the precocity of youth prolonged to mental power in maturity, while the dullness of boyhood is sometimes strikingly contrasted with the intellectual energy of after years. Newton, when a boy, was weakly, and he showed no particular aptitude at school; but in his eighteenth year he went to Cambridge, and soon afterward astonished his teachers by his power of dealing with geometrical problems. During his quiet youth his brain was slowly preparing itself to be the organ of those energies which he subsequently displayed.

By myriad blows (to use a Lucretian phrase) the image and superscription of the external world are stamped as states of consciousness upon the organism, the depth of the impression depending upon the number of the blows. When two or more phenomena occur in the environment invariably together, they are stamped to the same depth or to the same relief, and are indissolubly connected. And here we come to the threshold of a great question. Seeing that he could in no way rid himself of the consciousness of space and time, Kant assumed them to be necessary "forms of thought," the molds and shapes into which our intuitions are thrown, belonging to ourselves solely and without objective existence. With unexpected power and success Mr. Spencer brings the hereditary experience theory, as he holds it, to bear upon this question. "If there exist certain external relations which are experienced by all organisms at all instants of their waking lives — relations which are absolutely constant and universal — there will be established answering internal relations that are absolutely constant and universal. Such relations we have in those of space and time. As the substratum of all other relations of the Non-Ego, they must be responded to by conceptions that are the substrata of all other relations in the Ego. Being the constant and infinitely repeated elements of thought, they must become the automatic elements of thought — the elements of thought which it is impossible to get rid of — the 'forms of intuition.'"

Throughout this application and extension of the "law of inseparable association," Mr. Spencer stands on totally different ground from Mr. John Stuart Mill, invoking the registered experiences of the race instead of the experiences of the individual. His overthrow of Mr. Mill's restriction of experience is, I think, complete. That restriction ignores the power of organizing experience furnished at the outset to each individual; it ignores the different degrees of this power possessed by different races and by different individuals of the same race. Were there not in the human brain a potency antecedent to all experience, a dog or cat ought to be as capable of education as a man. These predetermined internal relations are independent of the experiences of the individual. The human brain is the "organized register of infinitely numerous experiences received during the evolution of life, or rather during the evolution of that series of organisms through which the human organism has been reached. The effects of the most uniform and frequent of these experiences have been successfully bequeathed, principal and interest, and have slowly mounted to that high intelligence which lies latent in the brain of the infant. Thus it happens that the European inherits from twenty to thirty cubic inches more of brain than the Papuan. Thus it happens that faculties, as of music, which scarcely exist in some inferior races, become congenital in superior ones. Thus it happens that out of savages unable to count up to the number of their fingers, and speaking a language containing only nouns and verbs, arise at length our Newtons and Shakespeares."

At the outset of this address it was stated that physical theories which lie beyond experience are derived by a process of abstraction from experience. It is instructive to note from this point of view the successive introduction of new conceptions. The idea of the attraction of gravitation was preceded by the observation of the attraction of iron by a magnet, and of light bodies by rubbed amber. The polarity of magnetism and electricity appealed to the senses and thus became the substratum of the conception that atoms and molecules are endowed with definite, attractive, and repellent poles, by the play of which definite forms of crystalline architecture are produced. This molecular force becomes *structural*. It required no great boldness of thought to extend its play into organic nature, and to recognize in molecular force the agency by which both plants and animals are built up. In this way, out of experience arise conceptions which are wholly ultra-experiential.

The *origination* of life is a point lightly touched upon, if at all, by Mr. Darwin and Mr. Spencer. Diminishing gradually the number of progenitors, Mr. Darwin comes at length to one "primordial form"; but he does not say, as far as I remember, how he supposes this form to have been introduced. He quotes with satisfaction the words of a celebrated author and divine who had "gradually learned to see that it is just as noble a conception of the Deity to believe He created a few original forms, capable of self-development into other and needful forms, as to believe that He required a fresh act of creation to supply the voids caused by the action of his laws." What Mr. Darwin thinks of this view of the introduction of life I do not know. Whether he does or does not introduce his "primordial form" by a creative act, I do not know. But the question will inevitably be asked: How came the form there? With regard to the diminution of the number of created forms, one does not see that much advantage is gained by it. The anthropomorphism, which it seemed the object of Mr. Darwin to set aside, is as firmly associated with the creation of a few forms as with the creation of a multitude. We need clearness and thoroughness here. Two courses, and two only, are possible. Either let us open our doors freely to the conception of creative acts, or, abandoning them, let us radically change our notions of matter. If we look at matter as pictured by Democritus, and as defined for generations in our scientific textbooks, the absolute impossibility of any form of life coming out of it would be sufficient to render any other hypothesis preferable; but the definitions of matter given in our textbooks were intended to cover its purely physical and mechanical properties. And taught as we have been to regard these definitions as complete, we naturally and rightly reject the monstrous notion that out of *such* matter any form of life could possibly arise. But are the definitions complete? Everything depends on the answer to be given to this question. Trace the line of life backward, and see it approaching more and more to what we call the purely physical condition. We reach at length those organisms which I have compared to drops of oil suspended in a mixture of alcohol and water. We reach the *protogenes* of Haeckel, in which we have "a type distinguishable from a fragment of albumen only by its finely granular character." Can we pause here? We break a magnet and find two poles in each of its fragments. We continue the process of breaking, but however small the parts, each carries with it, though enfeebled, the polarity of the whole. And when we can break no longer, we prolong the intellectual vision to the polar molecules. Are we not urged to do *something* similar in the case of life? Is there not a temptation to close to some extent with Lucretius, when he affirms that "Nature is seen to do all things spontaneously of herself without the meddling of the gods," or with Bruno, when he declares that matter is not "that mere empty *capacity* which philosophers have pictured her to be, but the universal mother who brings forth all things as the fruit of her own womb"? The questions here raised are inevitable. They are approaching us with accelerated speed, and it is not a matter of indifference whether they are introduced with reverence or irreverence. Abandoning all disguise, the confession that I feel bound to make before you is that I prolong the vision backward across the boundary of the experimental evidence, and discern in that matter, which we in our ignorance, and notwithstanding our professed reverence for its Creator, have hitherto covered with opprobrium, the promise and potency of every form and quality of life.

The "materialism" here enunciated may be different from what you suppose, and I therefore crave your gracious patience to the end. "The question of an external world," says Mr. J. S. Mill, "is the great battle ground of metaphysics."[1] Mr. Mill himself reduces external phenomena to "possibilities of sensation." Kant, as we have seen, made time and space "forms" of our own intuitions. Fichte, having first by the inexorable logic of his understanding proved himself to be a mere link in that chain of external causation which holds so rigidly in nature, violently broke the chain by making nature, and all that it inherits, an apparition of his own mind.[2] And it is by no means easy to combat such notions. For when I say I see you, and that I have not the least doubt about it, the reply is that what I am really conscious of is an affection of my own retina. And if I urge that I can check my sight of you by touching you, the retort would be that I am equally transgressing the limits of fact; for what I am really conscious of is, not that you are there, but that the nerves of my hand have undergone a change. All we hear, and see, and touch, and taste, and smell are, it would be urged, mere variations of our own condition, beyond

[1] *Examination of Hamilton*, p. 154.
[2] *Bestimmung des Menschen.*

which, even to the extent of a hair's breadth, we cannot go. That anything answering to our impressions exists outside of ourselves is not a *fact*, but an *inference*, to which all validity would be denied by an idealist like Berkeley, or by a skeptic like Hume. Mr. Spencer takes another line. With him, as with the uneducated man, there is no doubt or question as to the existence of an external world. But he differs from the uneducated, who think that the world really *is* what consciousness represents it to be. Our states of consciousness are mere *symbols* of an outside entity which produces them and determines the order of their succession, but the real nature of which we can never know.[1] In fact, the whole process of evolution is the manifestation of a Power absolutely inscrutable to the intellect of man. As little in our day as in the days of Job can man, by searching, find this Power out. Considered fundamentally, it is by the operation of an insoluble mystery that life is evolved, species differentiated, and mind unfolded from their prepotent elements in the immeasurable past. There is, you will observe, no very rank materialism here.

The strength of the doctrine of evolution consists, not in an experimental demonstration (for the subject is hardly accessible to this mode of proof), but in its general harmony with the method of nature as hitherto known. From contrast, moreover, it derives enormous relative strength. On the one side we have a theory (if it could with any propriety be so called) derived, as were the theories referred to at the beginning of this address, not from the study of nature, but from the observation of men — a theory which converts the Power whose garment is seen in the visible universe into an artificer, fashioned after the human model, and acting by broken efforts as man is seen to act. On the other side we have the conception that all we see around us, and all we feel within us — the phenomena of physical nature as well as those of the human mind — have their unsearchable roots in a

[1] In a paper, at once popular and profound, entitled "Recent Progress in the Theory of Vision," contained in the volume of lectures by Helmholtz published by Longmans [*Popular Lectures on Scientific Subjects*], this symbolism of our states of consciousness is also dwelt upon. The impressions of sense are the mere *signs* of external things. In this paper Helmholtz contends strongly against the view that the consciousness of space is inborn; and he evidently doubts the power of the chick to pick up grains of corn without some preliminary lessons. On this point, he says, further experiments are needed. Such experiments have been since made by Mr. Spalding, aided, I believe, in some of his observations by the accomplished and deeply lamented Lady Amberley; and they seem to prove conclusively that the chick does not need a single moment's tuition to teach it to stand, run, govern the muscles of its eyes, and peck. Helmholtz, however, is contending against the notion of preëstablished harmony; and I am not aware of his views as to the organization of experiences of race or breed.

cosmical life, if I dare apply the term, an infinitesimal span of which only is offered to the investigation of man. And even this span is only knowable in part. We can trace the development of a nervous system, and correlate with it the parallel phenomena of sensation and thought. We see with undoubting certainty that they go hand in hand. But we try to soar in a vacuum the moment we seek to comprehend the connection between them. An Archimedean fulcrum is here required which the human mind cannot command; and the effort to solve the problem, to borrow an illustration from an illustrious friend of mine, is like the effort of a man trying to lift himself by his own waistband. All that has been here said is to be taken in connection with this fundamental truth. When "nascent senses" are spoken of, when "the differentiation of a tissue at first vaguely sensitive all over" is spoken of, and when these processes are associated with "the modification of an organism by its environment," the same parallelism without contact, or even approach to contact, is implied. There is no fusion possible between the two classes of facts — no motor energy in the intellect of man to carry it without logical rupture from the one to the other.

Further, the doctrine of evolution derives man, in his totality, from the interaction of organism and environment through countless ages past. The human understanding, for example — the faculty which Mr. Spencer has turned so skillfully round upon its own antecedents — is itself a result of the play between organism and environment through cosmic ranges of time. Never surely did prescription plead so irresistible a claim. But then it comes to pass that, over and above his understanding, there are many other things appertaining to man whose prescriptive rights are quite as strong as that of the understanding itself. It is a result, for example, of the play of organism and environment that sugar is sweet and that aloes are bitter, that the smell of henbane differs from the perfume of a rose. Such facts of consciousness (for which, by the way, no adequate reason has ever yet been rendered) are quite as old as the understanding itself; and many other things can boast an equally ancient origin. Mr. Spencer at one place refers to that most powerful of passions — the amatory passion — as one which, when it first occurs, is antecedent to all relative experience whatever; and we may pass its claim as being at least as ancient and as valid as that of the understanding itself. Then there are such things woven into the texture of man as the feeling of awe, reverence, wonder — and not alone the sexual love just referred to, but the love of the beautiful, physical and moral, in nature, poetry, and art.

There is also that deep-set feeling which, since the earliest dawn of history, and probably for ages prior to all history, incorporated itself in the religions of the world. You who have escaped from these religions in the high and dry light of the understanding may deride them; but in so doing you deride accidents of form merely, and fail to touch the immovable basis of the religious sentiment in the emotional nature of man. To yield this sentiment reasonable satisfaction is the problem of problems at the present hour. And grotesque in relation to scientific culture as many of the religions of the world have been and are — dangerous, nay, destructive, to the dearest privileges of freemen as some of them undoubtedly have been, and would, if they could, be again — it will be wise to recognize them as the forms of force, mischievous, if permitted to intrude on the region of *knowledge*, over which it holds no command, but capable of being guided by liberal thought to noble issues in the region of *emotion*, which is its proper sphere. It is vain to oppose this force with a view to its extirpation. What we should oppose, to the death if necessary, if every attempt to found upon this elemental bias of man's nature a system which should exercise despotic sway over his intellect. I do not fear any such consummation. Science has already to some extent leavened the world, and it will leaven it more and more. I should look upon the mild light of science breaking in upon the minds of the youth of Ireland, and strengthening gradually to the perfect day, as a surer check to any intellectual or spiritual tyranny which might threaten this island than the laws of princes or the swords of emperors. Where is the cause of fear? We fought and won our battle even in the Middle Ages: why should we doubt the issue of a conflict now?

The impregnable position of science may be described in a few words. All religious theories, schemes, and systems which embrace notions of cosmogony, or which otherwise reach into its domain, must, in so far as they do this, submit to the control of science and relinquish all thought of controlling it. Acting otherwise proved disastrous in the past, and it is simply fatuous today. Every system which would escape the fate of an organism too rigid to adjust itself to its environment must be plastic to the extent that the growth of knowledge demands. When this truth has been thoroughly taken in, rigidity will be relaxed, exclusiveness diminished, things now deemed essential will be dropped, and elements now rejected will be assimilated. The lifting of the life is the essential point; and as long as dogmatism, fanaticism, and intolerance are kept out, various modes of leverage may be employed to raise life to a higher level. Science itself not infrequently derives motive power from an ultra-scientific source. Whewell speaks of enthusiasm of temper as a hindrance to science; but he means the enthusiasm of weak heads. There is a strong and resolute enthusiasm in which science finds an ally; and it is to the lowering of this fire, rather than to a diminution of intellectual insight, that the lessening productiveness of men of science in their mature years is to be ascribed. Mr. Buckle sought to detach intellectual achievement from moral force. He gravely erred; for without moral force to whip it into action, the achievements of the intellect would be poor indeed.

It has been said that science divorces itself from literature. The statement, like so many others, arises from lack of knowledge. A glance at the less technical writings of its leaders — of its Helmholtz, its Huxley, and its Du Bois-Reymond — would show what breadth of literary culture they command. Where among modern writers can you find their superiors in clearness and vigor of literary style? Science desires no isolation, but freely combines with every effort toward the bettering of man's estate. Single-handed, and supported not by outward sympathy but by inward force, it has built at least one great wing of the many-mansioned home which man in his totality demands. And if rough walls and protruding rafter ends indicate that on one side the edifice is still incomplete, it is only by wise combination of the parts required with those already irrevocably built that we can hope for completeness. There is no necessary incongruity between what has been accomplished and what remains to be done. The moral glow of Socrates, which we all feel by ignition, has in it nothing incompatible with the physics of Anaxagoras which he so much scorned, but which he would hardly scorn today. And here I am reminded of one among us, hoary, but still strong, whose prophet voice some thirty years ago, far more than any other of this age, unlocked whatever of life and nobleness lay latent in its most gifted minds — one fit to stand beside Socrates or the Maccabean Eleazar, and to dare and suffer all that they suffered and dared — fit, as he once said of Fichte, "to have been the teacher of the Stoa, and to have discoursed of beauty and virtue in the groves of Academe." With a capacity to grasp physical principles which his friend Goethe did not possess, and which even total lack of exercise has not been able to reduce to atrophy, it is the world's loss that he, in the vigor of his years, did not open his mind and sympathies to science and make its conclusions a portion of his message to mankind. Marvelously endowed as he was — equally equipped on the side of the heart and of the understanding — he might have done much toward teaching us how to reconcile the claims of both, and to enable them in coming times to dwell together in unity of spirit and in the bond of peace.[1]

And now the end is come. With more time, or greater strength and knowledge, what has been here said might have been better said, while worthy matters here omitted might have received fit expression. But there would have been no material deviation from the views set forth. As regards myself, they are not the growth of a day; and as regards you, I thought you ought to know the environment which, with or without your consent, is rapidly surrounding you, and in relation to which some adjustment on your part may be necessary. A hint of Hamlet's however, teaches us all how the troubles of common life may be ended; and it is perfectly possible for you and me to purchase intellectual peace at the price of intellectual death. The world is not without refuges of this description; nor is it wanting in persons who seek their shelter and try to persuade others to do the same. I would exhort you to refuse such shelter, and to scorn such base repose — to accept, if the choice be forced upon you, commotion before stagnation, the leap of the torrent before the stillness of the swamp. In the one there is at all events life, and therefore hope; in the other, none. I have touched on debatable questions, and led you over dangerous ground; and this partly with the view of telling you, and through you the world, that as regards these questions science claims unrestricted right of search. It is not to the point to say that the views of Lucretius and Bruno, of Darwin and Spencer, may be wrong. Here I should agree with you, deeming it indeed certain that these views will undergo modification. But the point is that, whether right or wrong, we claim the freedom to discuss them. The ground which they cover is scientific ground; and the right claimed is one made good through tribulation and anguish, inflicted and endured in darker times than ours, but resulting in the immortal victories which science has won for the human race. I would set forth equally the inexorable advance of man's understanding in the path of knowledge, and the unquenchable claims of his emotional nature which the understanding can never satisfy. The world embraces not only a Newton, but a Shakespeare; not only a Boyle, but a Raphael; not only a Kant, but a Beethoven; not only a Darwin, but a Carlyle. Not in each of these, but in all, is human nature whole. They are not opposed, but supplementary; not mutually exclusive, but reconcilable. And if,

[1] Tyndall refers here to Carlyle. — *Editors.*

still unsatisfied, the human mind, with the yearning of a pilgrim for his distant home, will turn to the mystery from which it has emerged, seeking so to fashion it as to give unity to thought and faith — so long as this is done, not only without intolerance or bigotry of any kind, but with the enlightened recognition that ultimate fixity of conception is here unattainable, and that each succeeding age must be held free to fashion the mystery in accordance with its own needs, then, in opposition to all the restrictions of materialism, I would affirm this to be a field for the noblest exercise of what, in contrast with the *knowing* faculties, may be called the *creative* faculties of man. Here, however, I must quit a theme too great for me to handle, but which will be handled by the loftiest minds ages after you and I, like streaks of morning cloud, shall have melted into the infinite azure of the past.

THE RELATIVITY OF ALL KNOWLEDGE

Herbert Spencer

HERBERT SPENCER was born at Derby, England, in 1820. Refusing to go to Cambridge, he was practically self-educated. In the years 1837–1846 he was an engineer on the London and Birmingham Railway; in 1848–1853 he was one of the editors of the *Economist*. Thereafter his life was devoted to writing. For a time he had a hard struggle with poverty. But just after the Civil War, American admirers presented him with $7,000 in a form which could not be refused, and his books soon began to pay. No one has ever devoted himself with more single-mindedness to scientific thought and writing. An attractive picture of the man may be found in Beatrice Webb's autobiography. He died in 1903.

Though Spencer was one of the true molders of the nineteenth century, though in America his successive works (thanks largely to John Fiske and E. L. Youmans) had enormous influence, though in Europe he was so highly regarded that the Italian Chamber adjourned on hearing of his death, he is no longer widely read. In part this is because much of his teaching has been absorbed into the general atmosphere of our day. His ideas upon evolution, education, psychology, sociology, were in his own time often arrestingly novel. Some have since been rejected, but the larger number have become part of the common stock-in-trade, an element in the foundations of present-day thought. He has paid the penalty, also, for attempting too ambitious a structure. Beginning with his *Social Statics* (1850) he essayed to incorporate in a single synthesis the fundamental principles of every branch of knowledge. Though he combined vast learning, a scientific temper, prodigious industry, and a marvelous grasp of abstract ideas, the task was impossible in his time, and perhaps will be so in any time. We can say that he was one of the chief educators of a long generation; we can still pronounce his *First Principles* a metaphysical epic, which awes the reader by its vastness of conception while it charms him by its nobility of spirit. But the currents of thought have moved past Spencer.

Nevertheless, there is much in Spencer that remains highly stimulating. His books are even yet one of the principal armories of those who wish weapons against the advance of the state. It is interesting to note that he first popularized the word "regimentation" as an argument against the excessive encroachments of government upon the individual. His essays, again, still offer some of the most powerful arguments against imperialism, militarism, and war. He has much that is pointed and pregnant to say upon social reform, its aims and methods; upon education — his essay bearing that title is classic; upon morals and ethics; upon the arts, from music to writing. In everything that he touched the originality and power of his mind are evident. Though he grew highly dogmatic, the total effect of his writing is to stimulate contempt for authority, to encourage the free expression of honest individual views. Readers will find his *Man and the State* still cogently applicable to present-day affairs. They will find the three volumes of *Essays, Scientific, Political, and Speculative*, full of pungent entertainment. In *Facts and Comments*, his last book, they will find that the last essay, "Ultimate Questions," strikes a philosophic and religious chord with an eloquence that is literally unforgettable.

If, when walking through the fields some day in September, you hear a rustle a few yards in advance and, on observing the ditch side where it occurs, see the herbage agitated, you will probably turn toward the spot to learn by what this sound and motion are produced. As you approach there flutters into the ditch a partridge; on seeing which your curiosity is satisfied — you have what you call an *explanation* of the appearances. The explanation, mark, amounts to this: that whereas throughout life you have had countless experiences of disturbance among small stationary bodies, accompanying the movement of other bodies among them, and have generalized the relation between such disturbances and such movements, you consider this particular disturbance explained, on finding it to present an instance of the like relation. Suppose you catch the partridge and, wishing to ascertain why it did not escape, examine it, and find at one spot a slight trace of blood upon its feathers. You now *understand*, as you say, what has disabled the partridge. It has been wounded by a sportsman — adds another case to the many cases already seen by you, of birds being killed or injured by the shot discharged at them from fowling pieces. And in assimilating this case to other such cases consists your understanding of it. But now, on consideration, a difficulty suggests itself. Only a single shot has struck the partridge, and that not in a vital place: the wings are uninjured, as are also those muscles which move them; and the creature proves by its struggles that it has abundant strength. Why then, you inquire of yourself, does it not fly? Occasion favoring, you put the question to an anatomist, who furnishes you with a *solution*. He points out that this solitary shot has passed close to the place at which the nerve supplying the wing muscles of one side diverges from the spine; and that a slight injury to this nerve, extending even to the rupture of a few fibers, may, by preventing a perfect coördination in the actions of the two wings, destroy the power of flight. You are no longer puzzled. But what has happened? What has changed your state from one of perplexity to one of *comprehension?* Simply the disclosure of a class of previously known cases, along with which you can include this case. The connection between lesions of the nervous system and paralysis of the limbs has been already many times brought under your notice, and you here find a relation of cause and effect that is essentially similar.

Let us suppose you are led on to make further inquiries concerning organic actions, which, conspicuous and remarkable as they are, you had not before cared to understand. How is respiration effected? you ask. Why does air periodically rush into the lungs? The answer is that in the higher vertebrata, as in ourselves, influx of air is caused by an enlargement of the thoracic cavity, due partly to depression of the diaphragm, partly to elevation of the ribs. But how does elevation of the ribs enlarge the cavity? In reply the anatomist shows you that the plane of each pair of ribs makes an acute angle with the spine; that this angle widens when the movable ends of the ribs are raised; and he makes you realize the consequent dilatation of the cavity by pointing out how the area of a parallelogram increases as its angles approach to right angles — you understand this special fact when you see it to be an instance of a general geometrical fact. There still arises, however, the question: Why does the air rush into this enlarged cavity? To which comes the answer that, when the thoracic cavity is enlarged, the contained air, partially relieved from pressure, expands, and so loses some of its resisting power; that hence it opposes to the pressure of the external air a less pressure; and that as air, like every other fluid, presses equally in all directions, motion must result along any line in which the resistance is less than elsewhere; whence follows an inward current. And this *interpretation* you recognize as one, when a few facts of like kind, exhibited more plainly in a visible fluid such as water, are cited in illustration. Again, when it was pointed out that the limbs are compound levers acting in essentially the same way as levers of iron or wood, you might consider yourself as having obtained a partial *rationale* of animal movements. The contraction of a muscle, seeming before utterly unaccountable, would seem less unaccountable were you shown how, by a galvanic current, a series of soft iron magnets could be made to shorten itself, through the attraction of each magnet for its neighbors — an alleged analogy which especially answers the purpose of our argument, since, whether real or fancied, it equally illustrates the mental illumination that results on finding a class of cases within which a particular case may possibly be included. And it may be further noted how, in the instance here named, an additional feeling of comprehension arises on remembering that the influence conveyed through the nerves to the muscles is, though not positively electric, yet a form of force nearly allied to the electric. Similarly when you learn that animal heat arises from chemical combinations; when you learn that the absorption of nutrient fluids through the coats of the intestines is an instance of osmotic action; . . . you regard yourself as *knowing* something about the natures of these phenomena.

Observe now what we have been doing. Turning to the general question, let us note where these successive interpretations have carried us. We began with quite special and concrete facts. In explaining each, and afterward explaining the more general facts of which they are instances, we have got down to certain highly general facts: to a geometrical principle or property of space, to a simple law of mechanical action, to a law of fluid equilibrium — to truths in physics, in chemistry, in thermology, in electricity. The particular phenomena with which we set out have been merged in larger and larger groups of phenomena; and as they have been so merged, we have arrived at solutions that we consider profound in proportion as this process has been carried far. Still deeper explanations are simply further steps in the same direction. When, for instance, it is asked why the law of the lever is what it is, or why fluid equilibrium and fluid motion exhibit the relations which they do, the answer furnished by mathematicians consists in the disclosure of the principle of virtual velocities — a principle holding true alike in fluids and solids — a principle under which the others are comprehended. And similarly, the insight obtained into the phenomena of chemical combination, heat, electricity, etc., implies that a rationale of them, when found, will be the exposition of some highly general fact respecting the constitution of matter, of which chemical, electrical, and thermal facts are merely different manifestations.

Is this process limited or unlimited? Can we go on forever explaining classes of facts by including them in larger classes, or must we eventually come to a largest class? The supposition that the process is unlimited, were anyone absurd enough to espouse it, would still imply that an ultimate explanation could not be reached, since infinite time would be required to reach it. While the unavoidable conclusion that it is limited (proved not only by the finite sphere of observation open to us, but also by the diminution in the number of generalizations that necessarily accompanies increase of their breadth) equally implies that the ultimate fact cannot be understood. For if the successively deeper interpretations of nature which constitute advancing knowledge are merely successive inclusions of special truths in general truths, and of general truths in truths still more general, it obviously follows that the most general truth, not admitting of inclusion in any other, does not admit of interpretation. Manifestly, as the *most* general cognition at which we arrive cannot be reduced to a *more* general one, it cannot be understood. Of necessity, therefore, explanation must eventually bring us down to the inexplicable. The deepest truth which we can get at must be unaccountable. Comprehension must become something other than comprehension before the ultimate fact can be comprehended.

THE METHOD OF SCIENTIFIC INVESTIGATION

Thomas Henry Huxley

THOMAS HENRY HUXLEY was born in 1825 at Ealing, England; studied medicine at Charing Cross Hospital, London; and immediately afterward was appointed surgeon to H. M. S. *Rattlesnake,* bound on an exploring voyage. This marked the beginning of a long career devoted to scientific research and writing. He held numerous teaching and governmental posts, and in 1881–1885 was president of the Royal Society. In 1895 he died.

Huxley was the great fighter among the evolutionists of Mid-Victorian England. His master Darwin had no taste or talents for controversy, and little concern for the rapid diffusion of his doctrines; he cared only to pursue his researches, recognized by the expert few. But Huxley gladly became his "bulldog," gladly gave his life to the popularization of new scientific ideas and the endless battles and skirmishes over evolution. His mission was to make knowledge human, to defeat the narrow clericalism that was trying to stifle science, and to set an inspiring example of a life full of resolution, of battle, of unselfish activity. He hated all forms of humbug, superstition, and cant. As a research scientist (at nineteen he discovered a tissue in the human body still known as Huxley's membrane), as a lecturer, as an administrator, above all as a writer, he labored until he was worn out; and he helped evolution to invade every branch of science, ethics, philosophy, and sociology. He was one of the clearest of thinkers, and as profound as he was clear. "When I read Huxley," wrote Hooker, "I feel quite infantine in intellect." Some of his conflicts with ecclesiastics, notably his duel with Bishop Samuel Wilberforce in 1860, are matter for legend. But it was in no hostility to religion that he invented for himself and his followers the term "agnostic." He wished to make it plain that he was not a materialist — that he admitted the possibility that scientific phenomena may be related to some hidden reality of a spiritual nature, but he simply did not know. It was this significance which Leslie Stephen also tried to fix upon the word by his beautiful essay called *An Agnostic's Apology.* Attentive readers of Huxley's principal works will perceive that he held a religion of truth that at some points clashed with the religion of the church, but at others agreed with it. Hence it is that this sturdy, generous, clear-headed Englishman may, for all that he was an "agnostic," be called one of the masters of modern faith. His labors hastened a great scientific transformation in thought. But as his books — *Man's Place in Nature, Lay Sermons, Collected Essays* — show, he wished science to lift men's souls as well as liberate their minds. He liked a robust faith. "Add to prophetic Judaism something from the best Stoics, and something from Spinoza, and something from Goethe," he wrote, "and there is a religion for *men.*" Huxley did not accept Darwinian ideas without qualifications of his own. He anticipated later scientific views by stating that in his opinion "transmutation may take place without transition." But it is as Darwin's greatest lieutenant that he will be remembered.

Students who are interested in Huxley as a controversialist upon religious topics will find him in his most redoubtable form in *Science and Christian Tradition,* which includes a lusty attack upon Gladstone.

The method of scientific investigation is nothing but the expression of the necessary mode of working of the human mind. It is simply the mode at which all phenomena are reasoned about, rendered precise and exact. There is no more difference, but there is just the same kind of difference, between the mental operations of a man of science and those of an ordinary person, as there is between the operations and methods of a baker or of a butcher weighing out his goods in common scales, and the operations of a chemist in performing a difficult and complex analysis by means of his balance and finely graduated weights. It is not that the action of the scales in the one case, and the balance in the other, differ in the principles of their construction or manner of working; but the beam of one is set on an infinitely finer axis than the other, and of course turns by the addition of a much smaller weight.

You will understand this better, perhaps, if I give you some familiar example. You have all heard it repeated, I dare say, that men of science work by means of *induction* and *deduction*, and that by the help of these operations they, in a sort of sense, wring from nature certain other things, which are called *natural laws*, and *causes*, and that out of these, by some cunning skill of their own, they build up *hypotheses* and *theories*. And it is imagined by many that the operations of the common mind can be by no means compared with these processes, and that they have to be acquired by a sort of special apprenticeship to the craft. To hear all these large words, you would think that the mind of a man of science must be constituted differently from that of his fellow men; but if you will not be frightened by terms, you will discover that you are quite wrong, and that all these terrible apparatus are being used by yourselves every day and every hour of your lives. . . .

A very trivial circumstance will serve to exemplify this. Suppose you go into a fruiterer's shop, wanting an apple — you take up one, and, on biting it, you find it sour; you look at it, and see that it is hard and green. You take up another one, and that too is hard, green, and sour. The shopman offers you a third; but before biting it you examine it, and find that it is hard and green, and you immediately say that you will not have it, as it must be sour, like those that you have already tried.

Nothing can be more simple than that, you think; but if you will take the trouble to analyze and trace out into its logical elements what has been done by the mind, you will be greatly surprised. In the first place, you have performed the operation of induction. You found that, in two experiences, hardness and greenness in apples went together with sourness. It was so in the first case, and it was confirmed by the second. True, it is a very small basis, but still it is enough to make an induction from; you generalize the facts, and you expect to find sourness in apples where you get hardness and greenness. You found upon that a general law, that all hard and green apples are sour; and that, so far as it goes, is a perfect induction. Well, having got your natural law in this way, when you are offered another apple which you find is hard and green, you say, "All hard and green apples are sour; this apple is hard and green, therefore this apple is sour." That train of reasoning is what logicians call a syllogism, and has all its various parts and terms — its major premise, its minor premise, and its conclusion. And by the help of further reasoning, which, if drawn out, would have to be exhibited in two or three other syllogisms, you arrive at your final determination, "I will not have that apple." So that, you see, you have, in the first place, established a law by induction, and upon that you have founded a deduction, and reasoned out the special conclusion of the particular case. Well now, suppose, having got your law, that at some time afterward you are discussing the qualities of apples with a friend: you will say to him, "It is a very curious thing — but I find that all hard and green apples are sour!" Your friend says to you, "But how do you know that?" You at once reply, "Oh, because I have tried them over and over again, and have always found them to be so." Well, if we were talking science instead of common sense, we should call that an experimental verification. And, if still opposed, you go further, and say, "I have heard from the people in Somersetshire and Devonshire, where a large number of apples are grown, that they have observed the same thing. It is also found to be the case in Normandy, and in North America. In short, I find it to be the universal experience of mankind wherever attention has been directed to the subject." Whereupon, your friend, unless he is a very unreasonable man, agrees with you, and is convinced that you are quite right in the conclusion you have drawn. He believes, although perhaps he does not know he believes it, that the more extensive verifications are — that the more frequently experiments have been made, and results of the same kind arrived at — that the more varied the conditions under which the same results are attained, the more certain is the ultimate conclusion, and he disputes the question no further. He sees that the experiment has been tried under all sorts of conditions, as to time, place, and people, with the same result; and he says with you, therefore, that the law you have laid down must be a good one, and he must believe it.

In science we do the same thing — the philosopher exercises precisely the same faculties, though in a much more delicate manner. In scientific inquiry it becomes a matter of duty to expose a supposed law to every possible kind of verification, and to take care, moreover, that this is done intentionally, and not left to a mere accident, as in the case of the apples. And in science, as in common life, our confidence in a law is in exact proportion to the absence of variation in the result of our experimental verifications. For instance, if you let go your grasp of an article you may have in your hand, it will immediately fall to the ground. That is a very common verification of one of the best established laws of nature — that of gravitation. The method by which men of science establish the existence of that law is exactly the same as that by which we have established the trivial proposition about the sourness of hard and green apples. But we believe it in such an extensive, thorough, and unhesitating manner because the universal experience of mankind verifies it, and we can verify it ourselves at any time; and that is the strongest possible foundation on which any natural law can rest.

So much, then, by way of proof that the method of establishing laws in science is exactly the same as that pursued in common life. Let us now turn to another matter (though really it is but another phase of the same question), and that is, the method by which, from the relations of certain phenomena, we prove that some stand in the position of causes toward the others.

I want to put the case clearly before you, and I will therefore show you what I mean by another familiar example. I will suppose that one of you, on coming down in the morning to the parlor of your house, finds that a teapot and some spoons which had been left in the room on the previous evening are gone — the window is open, and you observe the mark of a dirty hand on the window frame, and perhaps, in addition to that, you notice the impress of a hobnailed shoe on the gravel outside. All these phenomena have struck your attention instantly, and before two seconds have passed you say, "Oh, somebody has broken open the window, entered the room, and run off with the spoons and the teapot!" That speech is out of your mouth in a moment. And you will probably add, "I know there has; I am quite sure of it!" You mean to say exactly what you know; but in reality you are giving expression to what is, in all essential particulars, an hypothesis. You do not *know* it at all; it is nothing but an hypothesis rapidly framed in your own mind. And it is an hypothesis founded on a long train of inductions and deductions.

What are those inductions and deductions, and how have you got at this hypothesis? You have observed, in the first place, that the window is open; but by a train of reasoning involving many inductions and deductions, you have probably arrived long before at the general law — and a very good one it is — that windows do not open of themselves; and you therefore conclude that something has opened the window. A second general law that you have arrived at in the same way is that teapots and spoons do not go out of a window spontaneously, and you are satisfied that, as they are not now where you left them, they have been removed. In the third place, you look at the marks on the window sill, and the shoe marks outside, and you say that in all previous experience the former kind of mark has never been produced by anything else but the hand of a human being; and the same experience shows that no other animal but man at present wears shoes with hobnails in them such as would produce the marks in the gravel. I do not know, even if we could discover any of those "missing links" that are talked about, that they would help us to any other conclusion! At any rate the law which states our present experience is strong enough for my present purpose. You next reach the conclusion that as these kinds of marks have not been left by any other animals than men, nor are liable to be formed in any other way than by a man's hand and shoe, the marks in question have been formed by a man in that way. You have, further, a general law, founded on observation and experience — and that, too, is, I am sorry to say, a very universal and unimpeachable one — that some men are thieves; and you assume at once from all these premises — and that is what constitutes your hypothesis — that the man who made the marks outside and on the window sill opened the window, got in the room, and stole your teapot and spoons. You have now arrived at a *vera causa;* you have assumed a cause which it is plain is competent to produce all the phenomena you have observed. You can explain all these phenomena only by the hypothesis of a thief. But that is a hypothetical conclusion, of the justice of which you have no absolute proof at all; it is only rendered highly probable by a series of inductive and deductive reasonings.

I suppose your first action, assuming that you are a man of ordinary common sense, and that you have established this hypothesis to your own satisfaction, will very likely be to go off for the police, and set them on the track of the burglar, with the view to the recovery of your property. But just as you are starting with this object, some person comes in, and on learning what you are about, says, "My good friend, you are going on a great deal too fast. How do you know that the man who really made the marks took the spoons? It might have been a monkey that took them, and the man may have merely looked in afterward." You would probably reply, "Well, that is all very well, but you see it is contrary to all experience of the way teapots and spoons are abstracted; so that, at any rate, your hypothesis is less probable than mine." While you are talking the thing over in this way, another friend arrives, one of that good kind of people that I was talking of a little while ago. And he might say, "Oh, my dear sir, you are certainly going on a great deal too fast. You are most presumptuous. You admit that all these occurrences took place when you were fast asleep, at a time when you could not possibly have known anything about what was taking place. How do you know that the laws of nature were not suspended during the night? It may be that there has been some kind of supernatural interference in this case." In point of fact, he declares that your hypothesis is one of which you cannot at all demonstrate the truth, and that you are by no means sure that the laws of nature are the same when you are asleep as when you are awake.

Well, now, you cannot at the moment answer that kind of reasoning. You feel that your worthy friend has you somewhat at a disadvantage. You will feel perfectly convinced in your own mind, however, that you are quite right, and you say to him, "My good friend, I can only be guided by the natural probabilities of the case, and if you will be kind enough to stand aside and permit me to pass, I will go and fetch the police." Well, we will suppose that your journey is successful, and that by good luck you meet with a policeman; that eventually the burglar is found with your property on his person, and the marks correspond to his hand and of the shoes. Probably any jury would consider those facts a very good experimental verification of your hypothesis, touching the cause of the abnormal phenomena observed in your parlor, and would act accordingly.

Now, in this supposititious case, I have taken phenomena of a very common kind, in order that you might see what are the different steps in an ordinary process of reasoning, if you will only take the trouble to analyze it carefully. All the operations I have described, you will see, are involved in the mind of any man of sense in leading him to a conclusion as to the course he should take in order to make good a robbery and punish the offender. I say that you are led, in that case, to your conclusion by exactly the same train of reasoning as that which a man of science pursues when he is endeavoring to discover the origin and laws of the most occult phenomena.   The process is, and always must be, the same; and precisely the same mode of reasoning was employed by Newton and Laplace in their endeavors to discover and define the causes of the movements of the heavenly bodies, as you, with your own common sense, would employ to detect a burglar.   The only difference is that, the nature of the inquiry being more abstruse, every step has to be most carefully watched, so that there may not be a single crack or flaw in your hypothesis.   A flaw or crack in many of the hypotheses of daily life may be of little or no moment as affecting the general correctness of the conclusions at which we may arrive; but in a scientific inquiry a fallacy, great or small, is always of importance, and is sure to be in the long run constantly productive of mischievous, if not fatal results.

Do not allow yourselves to be misled by the common notion that an hypothesis is untrustworthy simply because it is an hypothesis.   It is often urged, in respect to some scientific conclusion, that, after all, it is only an hypothesis.   But what more have we to guide us in nine-tenths of the most important affairs of daily life than hypotheses, and often very ill-based ones?   So that in science, where the evidence of an hypothesis is subjected to the most rigid examination, we may rightly pursue the same course.   You may have hypotheses and hypotheses.   A man may say, if he likes, that the moon is made of green cheese: that is an hypothesis.   But another man, who has devoted a great deal of time and attention to the subject, and availed himself of the most powerful telescopes and the results of the observations of others, declares that in his opinion it is probably composed of materials very similar to those of which our own earth is made up — and that is also only an hypothesis.   But I need not tell you that there is an enormous difference in the value of the two hypotheses.   That one which is based on sound scientific knowledge is sure to have a corresponding value; and that which is a mere hasty, random guess is likely to have but little value.   Every great step in our progress in discovering causes has been made in exactly the same way as that which I have detailed to you.   A person observing the occurrence of certain facts and phenomena asks, naturally enough: What process, what kind of operation known to occur in nature applied to the particular case, will unravel and explain the mystery?   Hence you have the scientific hypothesis; and its value will be proportionate to the care and completeness with which its basis had been tested and verified. . . .

INTRODUCTION TO *THE NATURE OF THE PHYSICAL WORLD*[1]

Sir Arthur Stanley Eddington

SIR ARTHUR STANLEY EDDINGTON was born at Kendal, England, in 1882, and educated at Owens College (now Manchester University) and Cambridge. In 1913 he was made professor of astronomy in Cambridge University, and the following year became director of the observatory there. His first writings were rigidly scientific. But in a series of luminously written books for general readers — *The Nature of the Physical World* (1928), *Science and the Unseen World* (1929), *The Expanding Universe* (1933), and *New Pathways in Science* (1934) — he has dealt in popular exposition of new concepts in astronomy and physics, and has won a wide following. The need for such books as his and Sir James Jeans's had in fact become imperative. The revolutionary theories of Einstein, as epochal as those of Newton and far more difficult to understand; the discoveries of Rutherford, Planck, Bohr, and others upon the atom and the constitution of matter; the truths revealed by the larger telescopes and vastly improved techniques of present-day astronomy — the discussion of all this in scientific circles had created by 1925 a public eager for expert information, but knowing not where to find it. In Sir Arthur Eddington we have a first-rate scientific mind that is sufficiently flexible to bring the results of expert research and abstruse thinking to ordinary minds, and yet that never, in the task of popular illustration and demonstration, detracts from the dignity of the subject. Sprung from a Quaker family, and deeply, even mystically religious in temperament, Eddington in some of his writings has given great encouragement to those who find the newer scientific theories a chilly background for the religious tenets to which they cling.

I have settled down to the task of writing these lectures and have drawn up my chairs to my two tables. Two tables! Yes; there are duplicates of every object about me — two tables, two chairs, two pens.

This is not a very profound beginning to a course which ought to reach transcendent levels of scientific philosophy. But we cannot touch bedrock immediately; we must scratch a bit at the surface of things first. And whenever I begin to scratch the first thing I strike is — my two tables.

One of them has been familiar to me from earliest years. It is a commonplace object of that environment which I call the world. How shall I describe it? It has extension; it is comparatively permanent; it is colored; above all it is *substantial*. By "substantial" I do not

[1] From *The Nature of the Physical World*, by Sir Arthur Stanley Eddington. By permission of The Macmillan Company, publishers.

merely mean that it does not collapse when I lean upon it; I mean that it is constituted of "substance," and by that word I am trying to convey to you some conception of its intrinsic nature. It is a *thing;* not like space, which is a mere negation; nor like time, which is — Heaven knows what! But that will not help you to my meaning because it is the distinctive characteristic of a "thing" to have this substantiality, and I do not think substantiality can be described better than by saying that it is the kind of nature exemplified by an ordinary table. And so we go round in circles. After all, if you are a plain common-sense man, not too much worried with scientific scruples, you will be confident that you understand the nature of an ordinary table. I have even heard of plain men who had the idea that they could better understand the mystery of their own nature if scientists would discover a way of explaining it in terms of the easily comprehensible nature of a table.

Table No. 2 is my scientific table. It is a more recent acquaintance and I do not feel so familiar with it. It does not belong to the world previously mentioned — that world which spontaneously appears around me when I open my eyes, though how much of it is objective and how much subjective I do not here consider. It is part of a world which in more devious ways has forced itself on my attention. My scientific table is mostly emptiness. Sparsely scattered in that emptiness are numerous electric charges rushing about with great speed; but their combined bulk amounts to less than a billionth of the bulk of the table itself. Notwithstanding its strange construction it turns out to be an entirely efficient table. It supports my writing paper as satisfactorily as Table No. 1; for when I lay the paper on it the little electric particles with their headlong speed keep on hitting the underside, so that the paper is maintained in shuttlecock fashion at a nearly steady level. If I lean upon this table I shall not go through; or, to be strictly accurate, the chance of my scientific elbow going through my scientific table is so excessively small that it can be neglected in practical life. Reviewing their properties one by one, there seems to be nothing to choose between the two tables for ordinary purposes; but when abnormal circumstances befall, then my scientific table shows to advantage. If the house catches fire my scientific table will dissolve quite naturally into scientific smoke, whereas my familiar table undergoes a metamorphosis of its substantial nature which I can only regard as miraculous.

There is nothing *substantial* about my second table. It is nearly all empty space — space pervaded, it is true, by fields of force, but these are assigned to the category of "influences," not of "things." Even in the minute part which is not empty we must not transfer the old notion of substance. In dissecting matter into electric charges we have traveled far from that picture of it which first gave rise to the conception of substance, and the meaning of that conception — if it ever had any — has been lost by the way. The whole trend of modern scientific views is to break down the separate categories of "things," "influences," "forms," etc., and to substitute a common background of all experience. Whether we are studying a material object, a magnetic field, a geometrical figure, or a duration of time, our scientific information is summed up in measures; neither the apparatus of measurement nor the mode of using it suggests that there is anything essentially different in these problems. The measures themselves afford no ground for a classification by categories. We feel it necessary to concede some background to the measures — an external world; but the attributes of this world, except in so far as they are reflected in the measures, are outside scientific scrutiny. Science has at last revolted against attaching the exact knowledge contained in these measurements to a traditional picture gallery of conceptions which convey no authentic information of the background and obtrude irrelevancies into the scheme of knowledge.

I will not here stress further the non-substantiality of electrons, since it is scarcely necessary to the present line of thought. Conceive them as substantially as you will, there is a vast difference between my scientific table, with its substance (if any) thinly scattered in specks in a region mostly empty, and the table of everyday conception which we regard as the type of solid reality — an incarnate protest against Berkeleian subjectivism. It makes all the difference in the world whether the paper before me is poised as it were on a swarm of flies and sustained in shuttlecock fashion by a series of tiny blows from the swarm underneath, or whether it is supported because there is substance below it, it being the intrinsic nature of substance to occupy space to the exclusion of other substance; all the difference in conception at least, but no difference to my practical task of writing on the paper.

I need not tell you that modern physics has by delicate test and remorseless logic assured me that my second scientific table is the only one which is really there — wherever "there" may be. On the other hand I need not tell you that modern physics will never succeed in exorcising that first table — strange compound of external nature, mental imagery, and inherited prejudice — which lies visible to my eyes and tangible to my grasp. We must bid good-bye to it for the present, for we are about to turn from the familiar world to the scientific world revealed by physics. This is, or is intended to be, a wholly external world.

"You speak paradoxically of two worlds. Are they not really two aspects or two interpretations of one and the same world?"

Yes, no doubt they are ultimately to be identified after some fashion. But the process by which the external world of physics is transformed into a world of familiar acquaintance in human consciousness is outside the scope of physics. And so the world studied according to the methods of physics remains detached from the world familiar to consciousness, until after the physicist has finished his labors upon it. Provisionally, therefore, we regard the table which is the subject of physical research as altogether separate from the familiar table, without prejudging the question of their ultimate identification. It is true that the whole scientific inquiry starts from the familiar world and in the end it must return to the familiar world; but the part of the journey over which the physicist has charge is in foreign territory.

Until recently there was a much closer linkage; the physicist used to borrow the raw material of his world from the familiar world, but he does so no longer. His raw materials are ether, electrons, quanta, potentials, Hamiltonian functions, etc., and he is nowadays scrupulously careful to guard these from contamination by conceptions borrowed from the other world. There is a familiar table parallel to the scientific table, but there is no familiar electron, quantum, or potential parallel to the scientific electron, quantum, or potential. We do not even desire to manufacture a familiar counterpart to these things or, as we should commonly say, to "explain" the electron. After the physicist has quite finished his world-building a linkage or identification is allowed; but premature attempts at linkage have been found to be entirely mischievous.

Science aims at constructing a world which shall be symbolic of the world of commonplace experience. It is not at all necessary that every individual symbol that is used should represent something in common experience or even something explicable in terms of common experience. The man in the street is always making this demand for concrete explanation of the things referred to in science; but of necessity he must be disappointed. It is like our experience in learning to read. That which is written in a book is symbolic of a story in real life. The whole intention of the book is that ultimately a reader will identify some symbol, say BREAD, with one of the conceptions of familiar life. But it is mischievous to attempt such identifications prematurely, before the letters are strung into words and the words into sentences. The symbol A is not the counterpart of anything in familiar life. To the child the letter A would seem horribly abstract; so we give him a familiar conception along with it. "A was an Archer who shot at a frog." This tides over his immediate difficulty; but he cannot make serious progress with word-building so long as Archers, Butchers, Captains, dance round the letters. The letters are abstract, and sooner or later he has to realize it. In physics we have outgrown archer and apple pie definitions of the fundamental symbols. To a request to explain what an electron really is supposed to be we can only answer, "It is part of the A B C of physics."

The external world of physics has thus become a world of shadows. In removing our illusions we have removed the substance, for indeed we have seen that substance is one of the greatest of our illusions. Later perhaps we may inquire whether in our zeal to cut out all that is unreal we may not have used the knife too ruthlessly. Perhaps, indeed, reality is a child which cannot survive without its nurse illusion. But if so, that is of little concern to the scientist, who has good and sufficient reasons for pursuing his investigations in the world of shadows and is content to leave to the philosopher the determination of its exact status in regard to reality. In the world of physics we watch a shadowgraph performance of the drama of familiar life. The shadow of my elbow rests on the shadow table as the shadow ink flows over the shadow paper. It is all symbolic, and as a symbol the physicist leaves it. Then comes the alchemist Mind who transmutes the symbols. The sparsely spread nuclei of electric force become a tangible solid; their restless agitation becomes the warmth of summer; the octave of ethereal vibrations becomes a gorgeous rainbow. Nor does the alchemy stop here. In the transmuted world new significances arise which are scarcely to be traced in the world of symbols; so that it becomes a world of beauty and purpose — and, alas, suffering and evil.

The frank realization that physical science is concerned with a world of shadows is one of the most significant of recent advances. I do not mean that physicists are to any extent preoccupied with the philosophical implications of this. From their point of view it is not so much a withdrawal of untenable claims as an assertion of freedom for autonomous development. At the moment I am not insisting on the shadowy and symbolic character of the world of physics because of its bearing on philosophy, but because the aloofness from familiar conceptions will be apparent in the scientific theories I have to describe. If you are not prepared for this aloofness you are likely to be out of sympathy with modern scientific theories, and may even think them ridiculous — as, I daresay, many people do.

It is difficult to school ourselves to treat the physical world as purely symbolic. We are always relapsing and mixing with the symbols incongruous conceptions taken from the world of consciousness. Untaught by long experience we stretch a hand to grasp the shadow, instead of accepting its shadow nature. Indeed, unless we confine ourselves altogether to mathematical symbolism it is hard to avoid dressing our symbols in deceitful clothing. When I think of an electron there rises to my mind a hard, red, tiny ball; the proton similarly is neutral grey. Of course the color is absurd — perhaps not more absurd than the rest of the conception — but I am incorrigible. I can well understand that the younger minds are finding these pictures too concrete and are striving to construct the world out of Hamiltonian functions and symbols so far removed from human preconception that they do not even obey the laws of orthodox arithmetic. For myself I find some difficulty in rising to that plane of thought; but I am convinced that it has got to come.

In these lectures I propose to discuss some of the results of modern study of the physical world which give most food for philosophic thought. This will include new conceptions in science and also new knowledge. In both respects we are led to think of the material universe in a way very different from that prevailing at the end of the last century. I shall not leave out of sight the ulterior object which must be in the mind of a Gifford Lecturer, the problem of relating these purely physical discoveries to the wider aspects and interests of our human nature. These relations cannot but have undergone change, since our whole conception of the physical world has radically changed. I am convinced that a just appreciation of the physical world as it is understood today carries with it a feeling of open-mindedness toward a wider significance transcending scientific measurement, which might have seemed illogical a generation ago; and in the latter lectures I shall try to focus that feeling and make inexpert efforts to find where it leads. But I should be untrue to science if I did not insist that its study is an end in itself. The path of science must be pursued for its own sake, irrespective of the views it may afford of a wider landscape; in this spirit we must follow the path whether it leads to the hill of vision or the tunnel of obscurity. . . .

THE NEW WORLD OF MODERN PHYSICS[1]

Sir James Jeans

SIR JAMES HOPWOOD JEANS, born in London in 1877, was educated at Cambridge, and became first fellow and then lecturer there. He was professor of applied mathematics at Princeton from 1905 to 1909, and later became research associate at the Mt. Wilson Observatory. But most of his work has been done in England, where he was secretary of the Royal Society 1919–1929, and has held other important positions. Like Eddington, he turned to the popular exposition of scientific ideas late in the last decade. In a series of books published between 1929 and 1935 — *The Universe around Us*, *The Mysterious Universe*, *The New Background of Science*, *Through Space and Time* — he has presented the cosmos as revealed by both the most powerful telescopes and the most powerful microscopes. But as he states, the word "cosmos" evokes an idea of order and beauty which hardly fits the present-day cosmogony. This cosmogony shows us "vast spaces of unthinkable extent and terrifying desolation, redeemed from utter emptiness only at rare intervals by small particles of cold, lifeless matter, and at still rarer intervals by those vivid balls of flaming gas we call stars"; and as he states, its incomprehensible vastness, its uncountable multiplicity of stars even in our own universe, without going to the extra-galactic nebulae, and the terrifying idea of its steady explosive expansion which many scientists now accept, are sufficient to justify philosophic pessimism of the deepest order. From this pessimism he takes refuge in a thesis expressed to the British Association in 1934. "Our minds," he said, "can only be acquainted with things inside themselves — never with things outside. . . . There is in fact no clear-cut division between the subject and the object; they form an indivisible whole which now becomes nature. . . . It may seem strange, and almost too good to be true, that nature should in the last resort consist of something we can really understand; but there is always the simplest solution available — that the external world is essentially of the same nature as mental ideas."

Primitive man must have found nature singularly puzzling and intricate. The simplest phenomena could be trusted to recur indefinitely; an unsupported body invariably fell, a stone thrown into water sank, while a piece of wood floated. Yet other more complicated phenomena showed no such uniformity — the lightning struck one tree in the grove while its neighbor of similar growth and equal size escaped unharmed; one month the new moon brought fair weather, the next month foul.

Confronted with a natural world which was to all appearances as capricious as himself, man's first impulse was to create nature in his own image; he attributed the seemingly erratic and unordered course

[1] From *The Mysterious Universe*, by Sir James Jeans. By permission of The Macmillan Company, publishers.

352

of the universe to the whims and passions of gods, or of benevolent or malevolent lesser spirits. Only after much study did the great principle of causation emerge. In time it was found to dominate the whole of inanimate nature: a cause which could be completely isolated in its action was found invariably to produce the same effect. What happened at any instant did not depend on the volitions of extraneous beings, but followed inevitably by inexorable laws from the state of things at the preceding instant. And this state of things had in turn been inevitably determined by an earlier state, and so on indefinitely, so that the whole course of events had been unalterably determined by the state in which the world found itself at the first instant of its history; once this had been fixed, nature could move only along one road to a predestined end. In brief, the act of creation had created not only the universe but its whole future history. Man, it is true, still believed that he himself was able to affect the course of events by his own volition, although in this he was guided by instinct rather than by logic, science, or experience, but henceforth the law of causation took charge of all such events as he had previously assigned to the actions of supernatural beings.

The final establishment of this law as the primary guiding principle in nature was the triumph of the seventeenth century, the great century of Galileo and Newton. Apparitions in the sky were shown to result merely from the universal laws of optics; comets, which had hitherto been regarded as portents of the fall of empires or the death of kings, were proved to have their motions prescribed by the universal law of gravitation. "And," wrote Newton, "would that the rest of the phenomena of nature could be deduced by a like kind of reasoning from mechanical principles."

Out of this resulted a movement to interpret the whole material universe as a machine, a movement which steadily gained force until its culmination in the latter half of the nineteenth century. It was then that Helmholtz declared that "the final aim of all natural science is to resolve itself into mechanics," and Lord Kelvin confessed that he could understand nothing of which he could not make a mechanical model. He, like many of the great scientists of the nineteenth century, stood high in the engineering profession; many others could have done so had they tried. It was the age of the engineer-scientist, whose primary ambition was to make mechanical models of the whole of nature. Waterston, Maxwell, and others had explained the properties of a gas as machine-like properties with great success; the machine consisted of a vast multitude of tiny, round, smooth spheres, harder than the hardest steel, flying about like a hail of bullets on a battlefield. The pressure of a gas, for instance, was caused by the impact of the speedily flying bullets; it was like the pressure which a hailstorm exerts on the roof of a tent. When sound was transmitted through a gas, these bullets were the messengers. Similar attempts were made to explain the properties of liquids and solids as machine-like properties, although with considerably less success, and also on light and gravitation — with no success at all. Yet this want of success failed to shake the belief that the universe must in the last resort admit of a purely mechanical interpretation. It was felt that only greater efforts were needed, and the whole of inanimate nature would at last stand revealed as a perfectly acting machine.

All this had an obvious bearing on the interpretation of human life. Each extension of the law of causation, and each success of the mechanical interpretation of nature, made the belief in free will more difficult. For if all nature obeyed the law of causation, why should life be exempt? Out of such considerations arose the mechanistic philosophies of the seventeenth and eighteenth centuries, and their natural reactions, the idealist philosophies which succeeded them. Science appeared to favor a mechanistic view which saw the whole material world as a vast machine. By contrast, the idealistic view attempted to regard the world as the creation of thought and so as consisting of thought.

Until early in the nineteenth century it was still compatible with scientific knowledge to regard life as something standing entirely apart from inanimate nature. Then came the discovery that living cells were formed of precisely the same chemical atoms as non-living matter, and so were presumably governed by the same natural laws. This led to the question why the particular atoms of which our bodies and brains were formed should be exempt from the laws of causation. It began to be not only conjectured, but even fiercely maintained, that life itself must, in the last resort, prove to be purely mechanical in its nature. The mind of a Newton, a Bach, or a Michelangelo, it was said, differed only in complexity from a printing press, a whistle, or a steam saw; their whole function was to respond exactly to the stimuli they received from without. Because such a creed left no room for the operation of choice and free will, it removed all basis for morality. Paul did not choose to be different from Saul; he could not help being different; he was affected by a different set of external stimuli.

An almost kaleidoscopic rearrangement of scientific thought came with the change of century. The early scientists were only able to study matter in chunks large enough to be directly apprehended by the unaided senses; the tiniest piece of matter with which they could experiment contained millions of millions of molecules. Pieces of this size undoubtedly behaved in a mechanical way, but this provided no guarantee that single molecules would behave in the same way; everyone knows the vast difference between the behavior of a crowd and that of the individuals that compose it.

At the end of the nineteenth century it first became possible to study the behavior of single molecules, atoms, and electrons. The century had lasted just long enough for science to discover that certain phenomena, radiation and gravitation in particular, defied all attempts at a purely mechanical explanation. While philosophers were still debating whether a machine could be constructed to reproduce the thoughts of Newton, the emotions of Bach, or the inspiration of Michelangelo, the average man of science was rapidly becoming convinced that no machine could be constructed to reproduce the light of a candle or the fall of an apple. Then, in the closing months of the century, Professor Max Planck of Berlin brought forward a tentative explanation of certain phenomena of radiation which had so far completely defied interpretation. Not only was his explanation non-mechanical in its nature; it seemed impossible to connect it up with any mechanical line of thought. Largely for this reason, it was criticized, attacked, and even ridiculed. But it proved brilliantly successful, and ultimately developed into the modern "quantum theory," which forms one of the great dominating principles of modern physics. Also, although this was not apparent at the time, it marked the end of the mechanical age in science, and the opening of a new era.

In its earliest form, Planck's theory hardly went beyond suggesting that the course of nature proceeded by tiny jumps and jerks, like the hands of a clock. Yet, although it does not advance continuously, a clock is purely mechanical in its ultimate nature, and follows the law of causation absolutely. Einstein showed in 1917 that the theory founded by Planck appeared, at first sight at least, to entail consequences far more revolutionary than mere discontinuity. It appeared to dethrone the law of causation from the position it had heretofore held as guiding the course of the natural world. The old science had confidently proclaimed that nature could follow only one road, the road which was mapped out from the beginning of time to its end by the continuous chain of cause and effect; state A was inevitably succeeded by state *B*. So far the new science has only been able to say that state *A* may be followed by state *B* or *C* or *D* or by innumerable other states. It can, it is true, say that *B* is more likely than *C*, *C* than *D*, and so on; it can even specify the relative probabilities of states *B*, *C*, and *D*. But, just because it has to speak in terms of probabilities, it cannot predict with certainty which state will follow which; this is a matter which lies on the knees of the gods — whatever gods there be.

A concrete example will explain this more clearly. It is known that the atoms of radium, and of other radio-active substances, disintegrate into atoms of lead and helium with the mere passage of time, so that a mass of radium continually diminishes in amount, being replaced by lead and helium. The law which governs the rate of diminution is very remarkable. The amount of radium decreases in precisely the same way as a population would if there were no births and a uniform death rate which was the same for every individual *regardless of his age*. Or again, it decreases in the same way as the numbers of a battalion of soldiers who are exposed to absolutely random undirected fire. In brief, old age appears to mean nothing to the individual radium atom; it does not die because it has lived its life, but rather because in some way fate knocks at the door.

To take a concrete illustration, suppose that our room contains two thousand atoms of radium. Science cannot say how many of these will survive after a year's time; it can only tell us the relative odds in favor of the number being 2,000, 1,999, 1,998, and so on. Actually the most likely event is that the number will be 1,999; the probabilities are in favor of one, and only one, of the 2,000 atoms breaking up within the next year.

We do not know in what way this particular atom is selected out of the 2,000. We may at first feel tempted to conjecture it will be the atom that gets knocked about most or gets into the hottest places, or what not, in the coming year. Yet this cannot be, for if blows or heat could disintegrate one atom, they could disintegrate the other 1,999, and we should be able to expedite the disintegration of radium merely by compressing it or heating it up. Every physicist believes this to be impossible; he rather believes that every year fate knocks at the door of one radium atom in every 2,000, and compels it to break up. This is the hypothesis of "spontaneous disintegration" advanced by Rutherford and Soddy in 1903.

History of course may repeat itself, and once again an apparent capriciousness in nature may be found, in the light of fuller knowledge, to arise out of the inevitable operation of the law of cause and effect. When we speak in terms of probabilities in ordinary life, we merely show that our knowledge is incomplete; we may say it appears probable that it will rain tomorrow, while the meterological expert, knowing that a deep depression is coming eastward from the Atlantic, can say with confidence that it will be wet. We may speak of the odds on a horse, while the owner knows it has broken its leg. In the same way, the appeal of the new physics to probabilities may merely cloak its ignorance of the true mechanism of nature.

An illustration will suggest how this might be. Early in the present century, McLennan, Rutherford, and others detected in the earth's atmosphere a new type of radiation, distinguished by its extremely high powers of penetrating solid matter. Ordinary light will penetrate only a fraction of an inch through opaque matter; we can shield our faces from the rays of the sun with a sheet of paper, or an even thinner screen of metal. The X-rays have a far greater penetrating power; they can be made to pass through our hands, or even our whole bodies, so that the surgeon can photograph our bones. Yet metal of the thickness of a coin stops them completely. But the radiation discovered by McLennan and Rutherford could penetrate through several yards of lead or other dense metal.

We now know that a large part of this radiation, generally described as "cosmic radiation," has its origin in outer space. It falls on the earth in large quantities, and its powers of destruction are immense. Every second it breaks up about twenty atoms in every cubic inch of our atmosphere, and millions of atoms in each of our bodies. It has been suggested that this radiation, falling on germ plasm, may produce the spasmodic biological variations which the modern theory of evolution demands; it may have been cosmic radiation that turned monkeys into men.

In the same way, it was at one time conjectured that the falling of cosmic radiation on radio-active atoms might be the cause of their disintegration. The rays fell like fate, striking now one atom and now another, so that the atoms succumbed like soldiers exposed to random fire, and the law which governed their rate of disappearance was explained. This conjecture was disproved by the simple device of taking radio-active matter down a coal mine. It was now completely shielded from the cosmic rays, but continued to disintegrate at the same rate as before.

This hypothesis failed, but probably many physicists expect that some other physical agency may yet be found to act the rôle of fate in radio-active disintegration. The death rate of atoms would obviously then be proportional to the strength of this agency. But other similar phenomena present far greater difficulties.

Among these is the familiar phenomenon of the emission of light by an ordinary electric light bulb. The essentials are that a hot filament receives energy from a dynamo and discharges it as radiation. Inside the filament, the electrons of millions of atoms are whirling round in their orbits, every now and then jumping, suddenly and almost discontinuously, from one orbit to another, sometimes emitting, and sometimes absorbing, radiation in the process. In 1917, Einstein investigated what may be described as the statistics of these jumps. Some are of course caused by the radiation itself and the heat of the filament. But these are not enough to account for the whole of the radiation emitted by the filament. Einstein found that there must be other jumps as well, and that these must occur spontaneously, like the disintegration of the radium atom. In brief, it appears as though fate must be invoked here also. Now if some ordinary physical agency played the part of fate in this case, its strength ought to affect the intensity of the emission of radiation by the filament. But, so far as we know, the intensity of the radiation depends only on known constants of nature, which are the same here as in the remotest stars. And this seems to leave no room for the intervention of an external agency.

We can perhaps form some sort of picture of the nature of these spontaneous disintegrations or jumps, by comparing the atom to a party of four card-players who agree to break up as soon as a hand is dealt in which each player receives just one complete suit. A room containing millions of such parties may be taken to represent a mass of radio-active substance. Then it can be shown that the number of card parties will decrease according to the exact law of radio-active decay on one condition — *that the cards are well shuffled between each deal*. If there is adequate shuffling of the cards, the passage of time and the past will mean nothing to the card-players, for the situation is born afresh each time the cards are shuffled. Thus the death rate per thousand will be constant, as with atoms of radium. But if the cards are merely taken up after each deal, without shuffling, each deal follows inevitable from the preceding, and we have the analogue of the old law of causation. Here the rate of diminution in the number of players would be different from that actually observed in radio-active disintegration. We can only reproduce this by supposing the cards to be continually shuffled, and the shuffler is he whom we have called fate.

Thus, although we are still far from any positive knowledge, it seems possible that there may be some factor, for which we have so far found no better name than fate, operating in nature to neutralize the cast-iron inevitability of the old law of causation. The future may not be as unalterably determined by the past as we used to think; in part at least it may rest on the knees of whatever gods there be.

Many other considerations point in the same direction. For instance, Professor Heisenberg has shown that the concepts of the modern quantum theory involve what he calls a "principle of indeterminacy." We have long thought of the workings of nature as exemplifying the acme of precision. Our man-made machines are, we know, imperfect and inaccurate, but we have cherished a belief that the innermost workings of the atom would exemplify absolute accuracy and precision. Yet Heisenberg now makes it appear that nature abhors accuracy and precision above all things.

According to the old science, the state of a particle, such as an electron, was completely specified when we knew its position in space at a single instant and its speed of motion through space at the same instant. These data, together with a knowledge of any forces which might act on it from outside, determined the whole future of the electron. If these data were given for all the particles in the universe, the whole future of the universe could be predicted.

The new science, as interpreted by Heisenberg, asserts that these data are, from the nature of things, unprocurable. If we know that an electron is at a certain point in space, we cannot specify exactly the speed with which it is moving — nature permits a certain "margin of error," and if we try to get within this margin, nature will give us no help: she knows nothing, apparently, of absolutely exact measurements. In the same way, if we know the exact speed of motion of an electron, nature refuses to let us discover its exact position in space. It is as though the position and motion of the electron had been marked on the two different faces of a lantern slide. If we put the slide in a bad lantern, we can focus halfway between the two faces, and shall see both position and motion of the electron tolerably clearly. With a perfect lantern, we could not do this; the more we focused on one, the more blurred the other would become.

The imperfect lantern is the old science. It gave us the illusion that, if only we had a perfect lantern, we should be able to determine both the position and motion of a particle at a given instant with perfect sharpness, and it was this illusion that introduced determinism into science. But now that we have the more perfect lantern in the new science, it merely shows us that the specifications of position and motion lie in two different planes of reality, which cannot be brought simultaneously into sharp focus. In so doing, it cuts away the ground on which the old determinism was based.

Or again, to take another analogy, it is almost as though the joints of the universe had somehow worked loose, as though its mechanism had developed a certain amount of "play," such as we find in a well-worn engine. Yet the analogy is misleading if it suggests that the universe is in any way worn out or imperfect. In an old or worn engine, the degree of "play" or "loose-jointedness" varies from point to point; in the natural world it is measured by the mysterious quantity known as "Planck's constant h," which proves to be absolutely uniform throughout the universe. Its value, both in the laboratory and in the stars, can be measured in innumerable ways, and always proves to be precisely the same. Yet the fact that "loose-jointedness," of any type whatever, pervades the whole universe destroys the case for absolutely strict causation, this latter being the characteristic of perfectly fitting machinery.

The uncertainty to which Heisenberg has called attention is partially, but not wholly, of a subjective nature. The fact that we cannot specify the position and speed of an electron with absolute precision arises in part from the clumsiness of the apparatus with which we work — just as a man cannot weigh himself with absolute accuracy if he has no weight less than a pound at his disposal. The smallest unit known to science is an electron, so that no smaller unit can possibly be at the disposal of the physicist. In actual fact, it is not the finite size of this unit that is the immediate cause of the trouble, so much as that of the mysterious unit h introduced by Planck's quantum theory. This measures the size of the "jerks" by which nature moves, and so long as these jerks are of finite size, it is as impossible to make exact measurements as to weigh oneself exactly on a balance which can only move by jerks.

This subjective uncertainty has, however, no bearing on the problems of radio-activity and radiation previously discussed. And there are many other phenomena of nature, too numerous even to enumerate here, which cannot be included in any consistent scheme unless the conception of indeterminacy is introduced somewhere and somehow.

These and other considerations have led many physicists to suppose that there is no determinism in events in which atoms and electrons are involved singly, and that the apparent determinism in large-scale events is only of a statistical nature.   Dirac describes the situation as follows:

When an observation is made on any atomic system . . . in a given state, the result will not in general be determinate; i.e., if the experiment is repeated several times under identical conditions, several different results may be obtained.   If the experiment is repeated a large number of times, it will be found that each particular result will be obtained a definite fraction of the total number of times, so that one can say there is a definite probability of its being obtained any time the experiment is performed. This probability the theory enables one to calculate.   In special cases, the probability may be unity, and the result of the experiment is then quite determinate.

In other words, when we are dealing with atoms and electrons in crowds, the mathematical law of averages imposes the determinism which physical laws have failed to provide.

We can illustrate the concept by an analogous situation in the large-scale world.   If we spin a halfpenny, nothing within our knowledge may be able to decide whether it will come down heads or tails, yet if we throw up a million tons of halfpence, we know there will be 500,000 tons of heads and 500,000 tons of tails.   The experiment may be repeated time after time, and will always give the same result.   We may be tempted to instance it as evidence of the uniformity of nature, and to infer the action of an underlying law of causation: in actual fact it is an instance only of the operation of the purely mathematical laws of chance.

Yet the number of halfpence in a million tons is nothing in comparison with the number of atoms in even the smallest piece of matter with which the earlier physicists could experiment.   It is easy to see how the illusion of determinacy — if it is an illusion — crept into science.

We have still no definite knowledge on any of these problems. A number, although I think a rapidly diminishing number, of physicists still expect that in some way the law of strict causation will in the end be restored to its old place in the natural world, but the recent trend of scientific progress gives them no encouragement.   At any rate, the concept of strict causation finds no place in the picture of the universe which the new physics presents to us, with the result that this picture contains more room than did the old mechanical picture for life and consciousness to exist within the picture itself, together with the attributes which we commonly associate with them, such as free will, and the capacity to make the universe in some small degree different by our presence. For, for aught we know, or for aught that the new science can say to the contrary, the gods which play the part of fate to the atoms of our brains may be our minds. Through these atoms our minds may perchance affect the motions of our bodies and so the state of the world around us. Today science can no longer shut the door on this possibility; she has no longer any unanswerable arguments to bring against our innate conviction of free will. On the other hand, she gives no hint as to what absence of determinism or causation may mean. If we, and nature in general, do not respond in a unique way to external stimuli, what determines the course of events? If anything at all, we are thrown back on determinism and causation; if nothing at all, how can anything ever occur?

As I see it, we are unlikely to reach any definite conclusions on these questions until we have a better understanding of the true nature of time. The fundamental laws of nature, in so far as we are at present acquainted with them, give no reason why time should flow steadily on: they are equally prepared to consider the possibility of time standing still or flowing backward. The steady onward flow of time, which is the essence of the cause-effect relation, is something which we superpose on to the ascertained laws of nature out of our own experience; whether or not it is inherent in the nature of time, we simply do not know, although the theory of relativity goes at any rate some distance towards stigmatizing this steady onward flow of time and the cause-effect relation as illusions; it regards time merely as a fourth dimension to be added to the three dimensions of space, so that *post hoc ergo propter hoc* may be no more true of a sequence of happenings in time than it is of the sequence of telegraph poles along the Great North Road.

It is always the puzzle of the nature of time that brings our thoughts to a standstill. And if time is so fundamental that an understanding of its true nature is forever beyond our reach, then so also in all probability is a decision in the age-long controversy between determinism and free will.

THE FUTURE OF BIOLOGY [1]

J. B. S. Haldane

JOHN BURDON SANDERSON HALDANE may be called a combination of journalist and scientist. He has had a varied experience. Born in England in 1892, educated at Oxford, serving with the Black Watch in France and Iraq during the World War and twice wounded, he has taught in succession at Oxford, Cambridge, the Royal Institution, and in the University of London, where he has been professor of genetics since 1933. He is an experimental scientist of standing. But it is as a popular essayist upon scientific topics, especially in the field of biology, that he is best known. He first attracted attention by a slender volume on the future of science — a deliberately audacious venture in prophecy — called *Daedalus* (1924). Indeed, in all his writings the element of audacity is strong; a good illustration is what he says in the essay "Meroz" in *Possible Worlds* (1927) upon the practical record of the various religious sects with regard to war. He also remains fond of prophecy, as his essay on the end of the world in the same volume shows. His other books include *Science and Ethics* (1928); *The Inequality of Man* (1932); *The Causes of Evolution* (1933); and *Fact and Faith* (1934) — all pungent, full of new facts and ideas, and decidedly stimulating.

In forecasting the future of scientific research there is one quite general law to be noted. The unexpected always happens. So one can be quite sure that the future will make any detailed predictions look rather silly. Yet an actual research worker can perhaps see a little further than the most intelligent onlooker. Even so, it may seem presumptuous for any one man, especially one who is almost completely ignorant of botany, to attempt to cover, however inadequately, the whole field of biological investigation.

Every science begins with the observation of striking events like thunderstorms or fevers, and soon establishes rough connections between them and other events, such as hot weather or infection. The next stage is a stage of exact observation and measurement, and it is often very difficult to know what we should measure in order best to explain the events we are investigating. In the case of both thunderstorms and fever the clue came from measuring the lengths of mercury columns in glass tubes, but what prophet could have predicted this? Then comes a stage of innumerable graphs and tables of figures, the despair of the student, the laughing-stock of the man in the street. And out of this intellectual mess there suddenly crystal-

[1] From *Possible Worlds*, by J. B. S. Haldane. Reprinted by permission of Harper & Brothers, publishers.

lizes a new and easily grasped idea, the idea of a cyclone or an electron, a bacillus or an antitoxin, and everybody wonders why it had not been thought of before.

At present much of biology is in the stage of measuring and waiting for the idea. One man is measuring the lengths of the feelers of two thousand beetles; another the amount of cholesterol in one hundred samples of human blood; each in the hope, but not the certainty, that his series of numbers will lead him to some definite law. Another is designing a large and complicated apparatus to measure the electrical currents produced by a single nerve fiber when excited, and does not even look beyond the stage of the column of figures. If I were writing this article for biologists it would be largely a review of present and future methods; to a wider public I shall try to point out some of the results now emerging, and their possible application.

Let us begin with what used to be called natural history; the study of the behavior of animals and plants in their wild or normal condition. Apart from animal psychology this has split up into two sciences, ecology and animal sociology. Extraordinary progress has recently been made in the latter. Wheeler of Harvard has made it very probable that the behavior of social insects such as ants, instead of being based on a complicated series of special instincts, rests largely on an economic foundation not so very unlike our own. The ant that brings back a seed to the nest gets paid for it by a sweet juice secreted by those that stayed at home. Others, again, have been tackling the problem of how much one bee can tell another, and how it does it. Tomorrow it looks as if we should be overhearing the conversation of bees, and the day after tomorrow joining in it. We may be able to tell our bees that there is a tin of treacle for them if they will fertilize those apple trees five minutes' fly to the southeast; Mr. Johnson's tree over the wall can wait! To do this we should presumably need a model bee to make the right movements, and perhaps the right noise and smell. It would probably not be a paying proposition, but there is no reason to regard it as an impossible one. Even now, if we take a piece of wasps' comb and hum the right note, the grubs put out their heads; if we then stroke them with a very fine brush they will give us a drop of sweet liquid just as they do to their nurses. Why should we wait to see if there are "men" on Mars when we have on our own planet highly social and perhaps fairly intelligent beings with a means of communication? Talking with bees will be a tough job, but easier than a voyage to another planet.

In ecology, where we deal with animal and plant communities which consist of many different species, each eaten by others from inside and outside, each living in amity with some of its neighbors, in competition with others, we are at present often lost in detail.   But we are constantly finding that some hitherto unexpected but often easily modifiable factor, such as the acidity of the soil or the presence of some single parasite on an important species, will make a whole new fauna and flora appear, say an oak forest with wild pigs instead of a pine forest with ants.

We apply these principles in agriculture by using chemical manures and insects parasitic on those that attack our crops.   But as we find the key chemical or key organism in a given association, we may be able vastly to increase the utility to man of forests, lakes, and even the sea.   Besides this, however, one gets the very strong impression that from the quantitative study of animal and plant associations some laws of a very unsuspected and fundamental character are emerging; laws of which much that we know of human history and economics only constitute special and rather complicated cases.   When we can see human history and sociology against a background of such simpler phenomena, it is hard to doubt that we shall understand ourselves and one another more clearly.

In the domain of classificatory zoölogy our ideal is to establish a family tree of plants and animals: to be able to say definitely, let us say, that the latest common ancestor of both man and dog was a certain definite type of animal living, for example, in what is now the North Atlantic 51,400,000 years ago, under the shade of the latest common ancestor of the palm and beech trees, while the last common ancestor of the dog and bear lived only 5,200,000 years back.   We are still thousands of years from this ideal, but we are now attacking the problem of relationships between living forms by a number of new methods, especially chemical methods.   For example, we find that man agrees with the chimpanzee and other tailless apes, and differs from the tailed monkeys, in being unable to oxidize uric acid to allantoin in his tissues, as well as in many anatomical characters.   This merely confirms our view that these apes are man's nearest relations. But the same kind of method will be applied to solving problems of relationship in which the anatomical evidence is less clear;   for example, what group of four-footed animals is most nearly related to the whale.   Animals have a chemical as well as a physical anatomy, and it will have to be taken into account in their classification.

But the most important evidence about evolution is coming from the study of genetics.   We take any animal or plant, and with sufficient time and money at our disposal should be able to answer the following questions (though if it is a slow-breeding animal like a cow it is more likely that our great-great-grandchildren will have to wait for the answer):

1. What inheritable variations or mutations arise in it and how are they inherited?
2. Why do they arise?
3. Do they show any sign of being mainly in any one direction, or of advantage to their possessor?
4. Would natural selection acting on such, if any, as are advantageous, account for evolution at a reasonable speed, and for the kind of differences which are found between species (e.g. that which causes sterility in hybrids)?

The first question can often be answered, the second rarely. Occasionally we can provoke mutations, as with radium or X-rays. There is no indubitable evidence that they ever arise in children in sympathy with bodily changes in their parents (the alleged transmission of acquired characters), and plenty of well-established cases where they do not. Now, we know how the genes, or units which determine heredity, are arranged in the nucleus of the cell, and also about how big they are. If we magnified a hen's egg to the size of the world (which would make atoms rather larger than eggs and electrons barely visible) we could still get a gene into a room and probably on to a small table. But such magnification being impossible, the question how to alter a single gene without interfering with the others becomes serious, and some men have already spent their lives vainly on it; many more will. The two most hopeful methods seem to be to find chemical substances which will attack one gene and not another; and to focus ultra-violet rays on a fraction of a chromosome, the microscopic constituent of the nucleus in which the genes are packed. One can focus ultra-violet rays far more exactly than ordinary light, but even under the best conditions imaginable they would probably stimulate or destroy several hundreds of genes at a time.

Until we can force mutations in some such way as this we can only alter the hereditary composition of ourselves, plants, and animals by combining in one organism genes present in several, and so getting their combined effect. A great deal may thus be done with man. We know very little about human heredity as yet, though about hardly any subject are more confident assertions made by the half-educated; and many of the deeds done in America in the name of eugenics are about as much justified by science as were the proceedings of the Inquisition by the Gospels.

The first thing to do in the study of human heredity is to find characters which vary sharply so as to divide mankind definitely into classes. Most ordinary characters are no good for this purpose. We find every gradation of height, weight, hair, and skin color. A few characters have been found, such as two which determine whether it is safe to transfuse blood from one man into another, which are definitely present or absent, and admit of no doubt. These are inherited in a very simple manner, and divide mankind into four classes.

Now, if we had about fifty such characters, instead of two, we could use them, by a method worked out on flies by Morgan of New York and his associates, as landmarks for the study of such characters as musical ability, obesity, and bad temper. When a baby arrived we should have a physical examination and a blood analysis done on him, and say something like this: "He has got iso-agglutinin B and tyrosinase inhibitor J from his father, so it's twenty to one that he will get the main gene that determined his father's mathematical powers; but he's got Q4 from his mother, to judge from the bit of hair you gave me (it wasn't really enough), so it looks as if her father's inability to keep away from alcohol would crop up in him again; you must look out for that."

When that day comes intelligent people will certainly consider their future spouses' hereditary make-up, and the possibility of bringing off a really brilliant combination in one of their future children, just as now we consider his or her health and education, before deciding on marriage. It is as certain that voluntary adoption of this kind of eugenics will come, as it is doubtful that the world will be converted into a human stud-farm.

The third question can be answered in the negative for certain forms at any rate. Out of over four hundred mutations observed in one fly, all but two seemed to be disadvantageous; and they showed no definite tendency in any one direction. But, of course, mutation may be biased in other species. The fourth question is largely a matter of mathematics. No competent biologist doubts that evolution and natural selection are taking place, but we do not yet know whether natural selection alone, acting on chance variations, will account for the whole of evolution. If it will, we shall have made a big step toward understanding the world; if it will no more account for all evolution than, for example, gravitation will account for chemical affinity, as was once believed, then biologists have a bigger job before them than many of them think.   But a decision of this question one way or the other will greatly affect our whole philosophy and probably our religious outlook.

To turn now to the study of the single animal or plant, physiological researches fall into several classes according to the methods used. Some of us measure the production of small amounts of heat or electrical energy with complicated apparatus, others hunt down unknown chemical substances, or measure accurately the amount of already known ones in the tissues.   Taking the biophysicists first, a whole new field has been opened up by recent work on radiation. When X-rays were first applied to living tissues, it was very difficult to get the same result twice running.   But now, thanks to the work of our physical colleagues, we can get X-rays of a definite wave-length and intensity, and our results are correspondingly more intelligible. In the same animal one tissue is more sensitive than another to rays of a given wave-length.   Moreover, cells are generally more easily upset when engaged in division than at other times.   These facts account for our occasional success with X-rays against cancer, and our hope for greater things in the future.   It is quite possible that some combinations of invisible wave-lengths may be found to have special properties, just as a mixture of red and violet spectral lights gives us the sensation of purple, which intermediate wave-lengths do not.

Similarly, sunlight, besides warming us and enabling us to see, gives us bronzed skin, blisters us, wards off rickets, and cures many cases of tuberculosis.   But are all these effects due to the same group of rays acting in the same way?   We treat skin tuberculosis with ultra-violet light.   Can we increase the curative effect without increasing the danger of severe sunburn?   These questions are being answered as I write.   The application of rays will gradually be taken out of the doctor's hands.   He will write out a prescription, and we will go round to the radiologist's shop next door to the chemist's and ask for the prescribed treatment in his back-parlor.   The next man at the counter will be after an apparatus to radiate the buds of his rose bushes during the winter, and kill off insect eggs which are out of reach of chemicals, without hurting the plants.   The quack is already in the market with lamps producing radiation to cure rheumatism and make your hair grow.   These are mostly harmless, though a few may be of value; but probably the sale of X-ray tubes, which may cause cancer, will some day be as carefully regulated as that of strychnine.

Physical methods are also being applied in the study of the nervous system. We have by now gone most of the way in the localization of function there, for although a given area of the brain is always concerned in moving the hand, yet a given point in it may cause different movements at different times; just as any one telephonist in an exchange can only ring up certain subscribers, but yet has a fairly wide choice. So we have now got to work out the detail of the processes of excitation and inhibition, as calling up and ringing off are technically called. This involves very accurate measurement of the electrical changes in nerve fibers under different circumstances. Here we are still in the graph and table stage, but probably only about ten years off a fairly comprehensive theory of how the different parts of the nervous system act on one another. This will at once react on psychology, and more slowly on normal life and practical medicine. A great deal that passes as psychology is really rather bad physiology dressed in long words, and the alleged physiology in psychological textbooks is their worst part. We shall alter that. Until, however, we have got a sounder neurology, scientific psychology, except of a fragmentary character, is no more possible than was physiology until chemistry and physics had reached a certain point. And until psychology is a science, scientific method cannot be applied in politics.

In chemical physiology we are after two rather different things. The first is to trace out the chemical processes in the cells, the nature, origin, and destiny of each substance in them. The second, which is much easier, is to trace the effect on cell life of various chemical substances; including those in which they are normally found in the body, and unusual ones, such as drugs and poisons. The first, if pushed to its logical conclusion, would give us a synthetic cell, and later a synthetic man, or "robot." The second would give us a complete system of medicine, which is more immediately required. But, of course, the two react on one another and are not wholly separable.

At the moment the study of cell chemistry is leading to the most interesting results in the case of simple organisms such as yeasts and bacteria. For example, Neuberg of Berlin worked out a number of the steps in the transformation of sugar into alcohol and carbon dioxide by yeast; and was able, by appropriate chemical methods, to sidetrack the process so that it yielded other products. One of these is glycerine. During the war the Germans were unable to import the fats and oils from which glycerine is generally made. They needed glycerine for their propellant explosives, which contain nitro-glycerine.

By getting yeast to make it from sugar they were able, in spite of the blockade, to produce all the nitro-glycerine they wanted.

This special process does not pay in peace-time, but there are others which do; and every day molds and bacteria are playing a more important part in industrial chemistry. Similarly, we are now studying the chemical processes in bacteria as carefully as we do those in our own bodies. There is generally a weak link in such a chain; for example, in human beings the links whose breaking gives us diabetes or rickets. If we study the tubercle bacillus carefully we may find his weak point. The relatively direct methods which gave us the cure for syphilis are here no use, for the tubercle bacillus is a far tougher organism than the spirochaete, and we cannot yet kill him without killing his host. Similarly, we are trying to find out how the chemical processes in normal and cancerous cells differ.

In man the study of what our body cells can and cannot do is gradually leading us to the perfect diet. It is becoming quite clear that faulty diet gives us some diseases, including most of our bad teeth, and predisposes us to others; and that nothing out of a tin or package so far comes up to natural foodstuffs. On the other hand, as the population of large cities cannot get these, we have got to determine what can be done to improve a diet based largely on milled cereals and tinned milk and meat. It is a tough problem, and for every pound we can spend on research and publicity put together the food-faking firms have a thousand for advertising of "scientific" foods.

To turn now to the chemical coördination of the body, we know that various organs secrete into the blood substances (often called hormones) which profoundly affect the rest of the tissues. A number of these have been obtained in a fairly concentrated form — that is to say, mixed with perhaps only ten or a hundred times their weight of other substances. Only two have been obtained entirely pure, though presumably all will be. Now, if we take one of the most widely popularized of recent therapeutic methods, the grafting of apes' testicles into old or prematurely senile men, this is just an attempt to get a hitherto unisolated hormone into the blood stream. The operation is expensive, the idea unpleasant, and the graft generally dies in a few years at most. The problem is to isolate the hormone free from other poisonous substances found in most tissue extracts, and later to find its chemical formula and synthesize it. One of the corresponding substances found in the female sex has been obtained free from harmful companions by Allen and Doisy in America.

When we have these substances available in the pure state we ought to be able to deal with many departures from the normal sexual life, ranging from gross perversion to a woman's inability to suckle her children; since lactation, as well as the normal instincts, appears to depend on the presence of definite substances in the blood. We shall also probably be able, if we desire, to stave off the sudden ending of woman's sexual life between the ages of forty and fifty. It is worth pointing out that there is no serious reason to believe that any of the rather expensive products of the sex glands now on the market, and often prescribed by doctors, are of any value except as faith cures.

A much more ambitious attempt to deal with old age is being started by Carrel. Cultures from individual cells from a chicken can be kept alive in suitable media for twenty years, and as far as we know forever. To live they must have certain extracts of chicken embryo. The blood of a young fowl contains substances (which can be separated by suitable methods) that both stimulate and check their growth. The former is absent in very old fowls. The problem of perpetual youth has, therefore, been solved for one kind of cell. But to make a pullet immortal we should have to solve it for all the different cells of its body at once. We do not know if this is possible, or whether it is like trying to design a society which is ideal alike for cowboys, automobile manufacturers, and symbolist poets, all of whom can hardly flourish side by side. Fifty years hence we shall probably know whether it is worth seriously trying to obtain perpetual youth for man by this method. A hundred years hence our great-grand-children may be seeing the first results of such attempts.

Besides these rather sensational substances which were first detected by their effects on organs, the proper working of the organism depends on the amount of quite well-known bodies, such as sugar, oxygen, and lime in the blood. We are gradually getting to know the amounts of these required for health, but it is much harder to estimate the amount needed of such a substance as, say, insulin. We can now kill an animal and produce a fluid from inorganic constituents that will keep its heart or liver alive for a day or more. Soon it will be a matter of months or years. To keep tissues alive for a time comparable with the life of their owner we shall have to have about one hundred substances, but perhaps not very many more, present in the normal amounts in the fluid perfusing them. At present we only know the correct quantity of some twenty, if that. Given this knowledge and the means of applying it, we could make good the deficiency of any organ but the nervous system. We could grow human embryos in such a solution, for their connection with their mother seems to be purely chemical. We could cut our beefsteak from a tissue culture of muscle with no nervous system to make it waste food in doing work, and a supply of hormones to make it grow as fast as that of an embryo calf.

In pharmacology our knowledge rests mainly on a series of lucky accidents. A few of the complicated substances made by plants have a striking effect on animals, but why a molecule of a given build has a given physiological effect we are only beginning to discover. When we know, we should be able to make as great an advance on plant products as we did with dyes when the relations between color and chemical composition were discovered. If we had a drug that was as good a pain-killer as morphine, but one-tenth as poisonous and not a habit-former, we could use it indiscriminately, and wipe out a good half of the physical pain in human life at one stroke.

Such are a few of the possibilities of our science. It is easy enough to say what we would do if we had a method to measure A or isolate B. But it is in inventing and applying these methods that our biggest problems often arise.

VI

RELIGION AND MORALS

IN the great and impinging spheres of religion and ethics the multiplicity of voices has for more than a century been confusing and dismaying. There are rationalists and mystics, utilitarians and idealists, positivists and transcendentalists, individualists and authoritarians. Most Americans are introduced to religion and morals on the authoritarian principle. It is in reading English literature that they first become vividly aware of the great conflict or rather mèlée that has long been raging: there they meet with Coleridge's opposition of intuitive understanding to reason, and Carlyle's counter-exaltation of reason over understanding; with Emerson's exposition of transcendentalism, and Santayana's condemnation of it; with William James's defense of the will to believe, and Huxley's or Leslie Stephen's scornful condemnation of any such attitude of mind; with Newman's acceptance of dogma and Matthew Arnold's revolt against it; with the conflicting conceptions of ethics as set forth by Mill, by Herbert Spencer, and many others down to Shaw and Bertrand Russell; and with the never-ending battle between some forms of theology and some forms of science — a battle in which the "Victorian compromise," condemned from opposing points of view by G. K. Chesterton and by H. G. Wells, is now sadly out of date. Today a sound understanding of the principal issues in religion and ethics requires no inconsiderable technical equipment. The inquirer must be grounded in anthropology, in psychology, in philosophy. But the subject must first be approached on a more popular level, and in the essays which follow an effort is made to provide a general *coup d'oeil* of the field. One great Catholic thinker, Lord Acton, sets forth certain historical considerations from his church's point of view. One scientific view of religion (others have already been partially suggested in the section on science) is provided by Professor Joad. Dean Inge presents a mystic's opinions; Bertrand Russell the opposing views of a logician. And finally ethics are discussed on a philosophical basis by Dr. Cohen, and on a more practical and concrete basis by Mr. Lippmann.

THE HISTORY OF FREEDOM IN CHRISTIANITY[1]
Lord Acton

LORD ACTON, the son of Sir Richard Acton, was born in Naples in 1834. He was educated under Dr. (later Cardinal) Wiseman in England and the great German theologian J. J. I. von Döllinger at Munich, and devoted his life to journalism and history. He succeeded Newman as editor of a Catholic magazine, *The Rambler;* he wrote much for British reviews; and in 1895 Lord Rosebery appointed him Regius Professor of Modern History at Cambridge. He died in 1902. For a long generation he was one of the influential liberals of Europe, and in English Catholic circles the outstanding liberal. A warm friend of De Tocqueville, Bluntschli, and Gladstone, a traveler who spent much time in the chief European centers and the United States, he united a cosmopolitan outlook to great independence of thought and a passionate love of freedom in all its forms.

Lord Action unfortunately never wrote the great *History of Liberty* for which early in life he had formed a plan. He mastered a vast erudition, historical, theological, and political; he collected a magnificent historical library — the library that Carnegie later acquired for Lord Morley; but he never penned a sustained work. His influence was largely personal. By his tremendous scholarship, his devotion to truth, his grasp of the forces of history, he vitalized the work of a whole generation of British historians. His inaugural lecture at Cambridge on *The Study of History* remains perhaps the best brief expression available anywhere of the opportunities, difficulties, and duties of students of history in modern times. The plan he drew up for the great *Cambridge Modern History* exhibits the range of his ideas upon history, and the spirit in which he believed that historical data should be criticized and cast into narrative. His historical as well as political and religious ideals were of the highest. Men should exact much of modern historians, he thought, because "we have the power to be more rigidly impersonal, disinterested, and just" than older writers. Though always a devout communicant of the Catholic Church, his liberalism led him to combat the doctrine of papal infallibility and other Ultramontane principles. The fragments which he has left upon liberty show that he conceived of it as "the assurance that every man should be protected in doing what he believed to be his duty against the influence of authority and majorities, custom and opinion"; and he believed liberty to be as sacred in affairs of church as of state. Hence his writings upon ecclesiastical questions, and especially upon toleration, have as refreshingly liberal a quality as his writings upon politics. The Catholic point of view, somewhat more narrowly if more eloquently presented by Cardinal Newman, found in him a broad and wise interpreter. His principal publications were brief but masterly essays upon *Democracy in Europe, The History of Freedom in Antiquity,* and *The History of Freedom in Christianity,* all related to his projected work on liberty, and a critique upon modern German historians contributed to the first issue of the *English Historical Review,* which he was instrumental in founding.

[1] From *The History of Freedom and Other Essays,* by Lord Acton. By permission of The Macmillan Company, publishers.

When Constantine the Great carried the seat of empire from Rome to Constantinople he set up in the market place of the new capital a porphyry pillar which had come from Egypt, and of which a strange tale is told. In a vault beneath he secretly buried the seven sacred emblems of the Roman state, which were guarded by the virgins in the temple of Vesta, with the fire that might never be quenched. On the summit he raised a statue of Apollo, representing himself, and enclosing a fragment of the Cross; and he crowned it with a diadem of rays consisting of the nails employed at the Crucifixion, which his mother was believed to have found at Jerusalem.

The pillar still stands, the most significant monument that exists of the converted empire; for the notion that the nails which had pierced the body of Christ became a fit ornament for a heathen idol as soon as it was called by the name of a living emperor indicates the position designed for Christianity in the imperial structure of Constantine. Diocletian's attempt to transform the Roman government into a despotism of the Eastern type had brought on the last and most serious persecution of the Christians; and Constantine, in adopting their faith, intended neither to abandon his predecessor's scheme of policy nor to renounce the fascinations of arbitrary authority, but to strengthen his throne with the support of a religion which had astonished the world by its power of resistance; and to obtain that support absolutely and without a drawback, he fixed the seat of his government in the East, with a patriarch of his own creation.

Nobody warned him that by promoting the Christian religion he was tying one of his hands and surrendering the prerogative of the Caesars. As the acknowledged author of the liberty and superiority of the church, he was appealed to as the guardian of her unity. He admitted the obligation; he accepted the trust; and the divisions that prevailed among the Christians supplied his successors with many opportunities of extending that protectorate, and preventing any reduction of the claims or of the resources of imperialism.

Constantine declared his own will equivalent to a canon of the church. According to Justinian, the Roman people had formally transferred to the emperors the entire plenitude of its authority, and therefore the emperor's pleasure, expressed by edict or by letter, had force of law. Even in the fervent age of its conversion the Empire employed its refined civilization, the accumulated wisdom of ancient sages, the reasonableness and subtlety of Roman law, and the entire inheritance of the Jewish, the pagan, and the Christian world, to make the church serve as a gilded crutch of absolutism. Neither an enlightened philosophy, nor all the political wisdom of Rome, nor even the faith and virtue of the Christians availed against the incorrigible tradition of antiquity. Something was wanted beyond all the gifts of reflection and experience — a faculty of self-government and self-control, developed like its language in the fiber of a nation, and growing with its growth. This vital element, which many centuries of warfare, of anarchy, of oppression had extinguished in the countries that were still draped in the pomp of ancient civilization, was deposited on the soil of Christendom by the fertilizing stream of migration that overthrew the empire of the West.

In the height of their power the Romans became aware of a race of men that had not abdicated freedom in the hands of a monarch; and the ablest writer of the Empire pointed to them with a vague and bitter feeling that, to the institutions of these barbarians, not yet crushed by despotism, the future of the world belonged. Their kings, when they had kings, did not preside at their councils; they were sometimes elective; they were sometimes deposed; and they were bound by oath to act in obedience with the general wish. They enjoyed real authority only in war. This primitive republicanism, which admits monarchy as an occasional incident, but holds fast to collective supremacy of all free men, of the constituent authority over all constituted authorities, is the remote germ of parliamentary government. The action of the state was confined to narrow limits; but, besides his position as head of the state, the king was surrounded by a body of followers attached to him by personal or political ties. In these, his immediate dependents, disobedience or resistance to orders was no more tolerated than in a wife, a child, or a soldier; and a man was expected to murder his own father if his chieftain required it. Thus these Teutonic communities admitted an independence of government that threatened to dissolve society; and a dependence on persons that was dangerous to freedom. It was a system very favorable to corporations, but offering no security to individuals. The state was not likely to oppress its subjects, and was not able to protect them.

The first effect of the great Teutonic migration into the regions civilized by Rome was to throw back Europe many centuries to a condition scarcely more advanced than that from which the institutions of Solon had rescued Athens. While the Greeks preserved the literature, the arts, and the science of antiquity and all the sacred monuments of early Christianity with a completeness of which the rended fragments that have come down to us give no commensurate idea, and even the peasants of Bulgaria knew the New Testament by heart, Western Europe lay under the grasp of masters the ablest of whom could not write their names. The faculty of exact reasoning, of accurate observation, became extinct for five hundred years, and even the sciences most needful to society, medicine and geometry, fell into decay until the teachers of the West went to school at the feet of Arabian masters. To bring order out of chaotic ruin, to rear a new civilization and blend hostile and unequal races into a nation, the thing wanted was not liberty but force. And for centuries all progress is attached to the action of men like Clovis, Charlemagne, ⚹ and William the Norman, who were resolute and peremptory, and prompt to be obeyed.

The spirit of immemorial paganism which had saturated ancient society could not be exercised except by the combined influence of church and state; and the universal sense that their union was necessary created the Byzantine despotism. The divines of the Empire, who could not fancy Christianity flourishing beyond its borders, insisted that the state is not in the church, but the church in the state. This doctrine had scarcely been uttered when the rapid collapse of the Western Empire opened a wider horizon; and Salvianus, a priest at Marseilles, proclaimed that the social virtues, which were decaying amid the civilized Romans, existed in greater purity and promise among the pagan invaders. They were converted with ease and rapidity; and their conversion was generally brought about by their kings.

Christianity, which in earlier times had addressed itself to the masses, and relied on the principle of liberty, now made its appeal to the rulers and threw its mighty influence into the scale of authority. The barbarians, who possessed no books, no secular knowledge, no education, except in the schools of the clergy, and who had scarcely acquired the rudiments of religious instruction, turned with childlike attachment to men whose minds were stored with the knowledge of Scripture, of Cicero, of St. Augustine; and in the scanty world of their ideas the church was felt to be something infinitely vaster, stronger, holier than their newly founded states. The clergy supplied the means of conducting the new governments, and were made exempt from taxation, from the jurisdiction of the civil magistrate, and of the political administrator. They taught that power ought to be conferred by election; and the Councils of Toledo furnished the framework of the parliamentary system of Spain, which is, by a long interval, the oldest in the world. But the monarchy of the Goths in Spain, as well as that of the Saxons in England, in both of which the nobles and the prelates surrounded the throne with the semblance of free institutions, passed away; and the people that prospered and over-shadowed the rest were the Franks, who had no native nobility, whose law of succession to the Crown became for one thousand years the fixed object of an unchanging superstition, and under whom the feudal system was developed to excess.

Feudalism made land the measure and the master of all things. Having no other source of wealth than the produce of the soil, men depended on the landlord for the means of escaping starvation; and thus his power became paramount over the liberty of the subject and the authority of the state. Every baron, said the French maxim, is sovereign in his own domain. The nations of the West lay between the competing tyrannies of local magnates and of absolute monarchs, when a force was brought upon the scene which proved for a time superior alike to the vassal and his lord.

In the days of the Conquest, when the Normans destroyed the liberties of England, the rude institutions which had come with the Saxons, the Goths, and the Franks from the forests of Germany were suffering decay, and the new element of popular government after-ward supplied by the rise of towns and the formation of a middle class was not yet active. The only influence capable of resisting the feudal hierarchy was the ecclesiastical hierarchy; and they came into collision, when the process of feudalism threatened the independence of the church by subjecting the prelates severally to that form of personal dependence on the kings which was peculiar to the Teutonic state.

To that conflict of four hundred years we owe the rise of civil liberty. If the church had continued to buttress the thrones of the king whom it anointed, or if the struggle had terminated speedily in an undivided victory, all Europe would have sunk down under a Byzantine or Muscovite despotism. For the aim of both contending parties was absolute authority. But although liberty was not the end for which they strove, it was the means by which the temporal and spiritual power called the nations to their aid. The towns of Italy and Ger-many won their franchises, France got her States-General, and Eng-land her Parliament out of the alternate phases of the contest; and as long as it lasted it prevented the rise of divine right. A disposition existed to regard the crown as an estate descending under the law of real property in the family that possessed it. But the authority of religion, and especially of the papacy, was thrown on the side that denied the indefeasible title of kings. In France what was afterward called the Gallican theory maintained that the reigning house was above the law, and that the scepter was not to pass away from it as long as there should be princes of the royal blood of St. Louis. But in other countries the oath of fidelity itself attested that it was conditional, and should be kept only during good behavior; and it was in conformity with the public law to which all monarchs were held subject that King John was declared a rebel against the barons, and that the men who raised Edward III to the throne from which they had deposed his father invoked the maxim *Vox populi vox Dei*.

And this doctrine of the divine right of the people to raise up and pull down princes, after obtaining the sanctions of religion, was made to stand on broader grounds, and was strong enough to resist both church and king. In the struggle between the House of Bruce and the House of Plantagenet for the possession of Scotland and Ireland, the English claim was backed by the censures of Rome. But the Irish and the Scots refused it, and the address in which the Scottish Parliament informed the Pope of their resolution shows how firmly the popular doctrine had taken root. Speaking of Robert Bruce, they say: "Divine Providence, the laws and customs of the country, which we will defend till death, and the choice of the people, have made him our king. If he should ever betray his principles, and consent that we should be subjects of the English king, then we shall treat him as an enemy, as the subverter of our rights and his own, and shall elect another in his place. We care not for glory or for wealth, but for that liberty which no true man will give up but with his life." This estimate of royalty was natural among men accustomed to see those whom they most respected in constant strife with their rulers. Gregory VII had begun the disparagement of civil authorities by saying that they are the work of the Devil; and already in his time both parties were driven to acknowledge the sovereignty of the people, and appealed to it as the immediate source of power.

Two centuries later this political theory had gained both in definiteness and in force among the Guelphs, who were the church party, and among the Ghibellines, or imperialists. Here are the sentiments of the most celebrated of all the Guelphic writers: "A king who is unfaithful to his duty forfeits his claim to obedience. It is not rebellion to depose him, for he is himself a rebel whom the nation has a right to put down. But it is better to abridge his power, that he may be unable to abuse it. For this purpose, the whole nation ought to have a share in governing itself; the Constitution ought to combine a limited and elective monarchy, with an aristocracy of merit, and such an admixture of democracy as shall admit all classes to office by popular election. No government has a right to levy taxes beyond the limit determined by the people. All political authority is derived from popular suffrage, and all laws must be made by the people or their representatives. There is no security for us as long as we depend on the will of another man." This language which contains the earliest exposition of the Whig theory of the revolution is taken from the works of St. Thomas Aquinas, of whom Lord Bacon says that he had the largest heart of the school divines. And it is worth while to observe that he wrote at the very moment when Simon de Montfort summoned the Commons; and that the politics of the Neapolitan friar are centuries in advance of the English statesman's.

The ablest writer of the Ghibelline party was Marsilius of Padua. "Laws," he said, "derive their authority from the nation, and are invalid without its assent. As the whole is greater than any part, it is wrong that any part should legislate for the whole; and as men are equal, it is wrong that one should be bound by laws made by another. But in obeying laws to which all men have agreed, all men in reality govern themselves. The monarch, who is instituted by the legislature to execute its will, ought to be armed with a force sufficient to coerce individuals, but not sufficient to control the majority of the people. He is responsible to the nation, and subject to the law; and the nation that appoints him, and assigns him his duties, has to see that he obeys the Constitution, and has to dismiss him if he breaks it. The rights of citizens are independent of the faith they profess; and no man may be punished for his religion." This writer, who saw in some respects farther than Locke or Montesquieu, who, in regard to the sovereignty of the nation, representative government, the superiority of the legislature over the executive, and the liberty of conscience, had so firm a grasp of the principles that were to sway the modern world, lived in the reign of Edward II, five hundred and fifty years ago.

It is significant that these two writers should agree on so many of the fundamental points which have been, ever since, the topic of controversy; for they belonged to hostile schools, and one of them would have thought the other worthy of death. St. Thomas would have made the papacy control all Christian governments. Marsilius would have had the clergy submit to the law of the land, and would have put them under restrictions both as to property and numbers. As the great debate went on, many things gradually made themselves clear, and grew into settled convictions. For these were not only the thoughts of prophetic minds that surpassed the level of contemporaries; there was some prospect that they would master the practical world. The ancient reign of the barons was seriously threatened. The opening of the East by the Crusades had imported a great stimulus to industry. A stream set in from the country to the towns, and there was no room for the government of towns in the feudal machinery. When men found a way of earning a livelihood without depending for it on the good will of the class that owned the land, the landowner lost much of his importance, and it began to pass to the possessors of movable wealth. The townspeople not only made themselves free from the control of prelates and barons, but endeavored to obtain for their own class and interest the command of the state.

The fourteenth century was filled with the tumult of this struggle between democracy and chivalry. The Italian towns, foremost in intelligence and civilization, led the way with democratic constitutions of an ideal and generally an impracticable type. The Swiss cast off the yoke of Austria. Two long chains of free cities arose, along the valley of the Rhine, and across the heart of Germany. The citizens of Paris got possession of the king, reformed the state, and began their tremendous career of experiments to govern France. But the most healthy and vigorous growth of municipal liberties was in Belgium, of all countries on the Continent, that which has been from immemorial ages the most stubborn in its fidelity to the principle of self-government. So vast were the resources concentrated in the Flemish towns, so widespread was the movement of democracy, that it was long doubtful whether the new interest would not prevail, and whether the ascendency of the military aristocracy would not pass over to the wealth and intelligence of the men that lived by trade. But Rienzi, Marcel, Artevelde, and the other champions of the unripe democracy of those days, lived and died in vain. The upheaval of the middle class had disclosed the need, the passions, the aspirations of the suffering poor below; ferocious insurrections in France and England caused a reaction that retarded for centuries the readjustment of power and the red specter of social revolution arose in the track of democracy. The armed citizens of Ghent were crushed by the French chivalry; and monarchy alone reaped the fruit of the change that was going on in the position of classes, and stirred the minds of men.

Looking back over the space of a thousand years, which we call the Middle Ages, to get an estimate of the work they had done, if not toward perfection in their institutions, at least toward attaining the knowledge of political truth, this is what we find: Representative government, which was unknown to the ancients, was almost universal. The methods of election were crude; but the principle that no tax was lawful that was not granted by the class that paid it — that is, that taxation was inseparable from representation — was recognized, not as the privilege of certain countries, but as the right of all. Not a prince in the world, said Philip de Commines, can levy a penny without the consent of the people. Slavery was almost everywhere extinct; and absolute power was deemed more intolerable and more criminal than slavery. The right of insurrection was not only admitted but defined as a duty sanctioned by religion. Even the principles of the Habeas Corpus Act, and the method of the income tax, were already known. The issue of ancient politics was an absolute state planted on slavery. The political produce of the Middle Ages was a system of states in which authority was restricted by the representation of powerful classes, by privileged associations, and by the acknowledgment of duties superior to those which are imposed by man.

As regards the realization in practice of what was seen to be good, there was almost everything to do. But the great problems of principle had been solved. . . .

THE ORIGIN AND EVOLUTION OF RELIGION[1]

C. E. M. Joad

Boldness, amounting frequently to audacity, has thus far been the principal trait of the philosophical writing of CYRIL EDWIN MITCHISON JOAD. Born in England in 1891 and educated at Oxford, he spent a number of years in the civil service, first under the Board of Trade and then in the Ministry of Labor. But since 1930 he has been head of the department of philosophy and psychology at Birkbeck College, the University of London. He has written a volume upon the United States, *The Babbitt Warren*, which is far from a happy effort. Among his other books are *Common Sense Ethics; Common Sense Theology; A Guide to Modern Thought;* and *Is Christianity True?* His views upon the evolution of religion may usefully be compared with the writings of the more impressive English rationalists of an older generation, Leslie Stephen and Henry Sidgwick. In especial they offer a parallel, so far as they go, with Sidgwick's great work on the evolution of ethics (*Outlines of the History of Ethics*), which after forty years is still full of interest.

In discussing the need for religion, I use the words "origin and nature" deliberately, because the conjunction of these two words seems to me to mask a fallacy which it is important to bring to light. The fallacy is to assume that to lay bare the origins of a thing is tantamount to describing its present nature.

That this is very far from being the case, I shall try to show; yet we more often assume that it is, especially if we are of a scientific turn, than we are commonly aware, and the assumption is nowhere more prevalent than in regard to religion. By most of us, indeed, it is not even realized that an assumption is involved. We take it for granted that to demonstrate that religion began as witchcraft, totemism, or exogamy is to prove that it is in essence no more than witchcraft, totemism, and exogamy now, although we should never dream of asserting that the fact that the savage can only count on the fingers of one hand, coupled with the demonstration that arithmetic began with and developed from such counting, invalidates the multiplication table. To show how a belief arises is not to describe, still less to discredit it, and, unless we are to deny to religion the kind of growth which we are prepared to concede to other expressions of the human spirit, it is obvious that there must be more in the religious consciousness today than in the savage fears and flatteries from which it may

[1] From *The Present and Future of Religion*, by C. E. M. Joad. By permission of The Macmillan Company, publishers.

384

be shown to have arisen.   And, if there is, it will be for just that "more" that an account of religion in terms of its origin and history will fail to make provision.   The point is of importance because the interpretation of religion in terms of its origin is often used to prove that religion is not a permanent and necessary need of the human spirit; savage in inception, it will, it is urged, disappear when we have finally left our savagery behind us.   Religion, it is often said, belongs to the childhood of the race, and will one day be outgrown, together with war and other savage habits, such as the habit of imprisoning men for punishment and animals for show, or the habit of decking the bodies of women with fragments of stone, lumps of metal, and portions of dead birds.

For myself, I do not hold this view, and I shall try to show the fallacy latent in the mode of reasoning upon which it rests.   For the present, let us see what the explanations of religions in terms of origin involve.

They are advanced chiefly by anthropologists, who visit remote Melanesian islands for the purpose of observing the religious practices of the natives.   Recording them, they conclude that primitive religion is the offspring of human fear and human conceit; it springs from the desire to propitiate the alien forces of nature, to invest human life with significance in face of the vast indifference of the universe, and to secure the support of an immensely powerful and ferocious personage for the individual, the tribe, or the nation.   This general attitude to religion, by ascribing it to a subjective need of human nature, robs it of objective validity.   Religion, if this account is correct, is not a revelation of reality, but a symptom of a state of mind; it is an expression of what man is like.   To say that there is God is not to say anything more than that we need to think that there is, and the need is in no sense a guarantee of the existence of that which satisfies it.   Thus the great religions of the world are not theology, but psychology; witnesses, not to the attributes of God, but to the inventive faculty of man.   God is not a real being; He is the image of man, projected, enlarged, upon the empty canvas of the universe.

This view of religion as subjective expresses itself in different forms, according to the nature of the primitive feelings upon which it lays stress.   I will take three as examples.

(1) The argument from man's feeling of loneliness and insecurity may be summarized as follows: Human life is immensely insignificant. It is an accidental development of matter, the chance product of

forces, an accident unplanned and unforeseen in the history of the planet. A casual and unwanted passenger, it struggles across a fundamentally alien and hostile environment, in which the material and the brutal on all sides condition and determine the spiritual and the vital. One day it will finish its pointless journey with as little noise and significance as, in the person of the amoeba, it began it. Until this consummation occurs, man will fare naked and forlorn through an indifferent universe, a puppet twitched into love and war by an indifferent showman who pulls the strings. His destiny is swayed by an inescapable fate; his fortunes are at the mercy of an irresponsible chance. He is a mere target for the shafts of doom.

These things we know; yet the knowledge is intolerable to us. We cannot bear to be without significance in the universe; we long to feel that we count, that somehow and to something we matter. And so we invent an immensely powerful and important personage called God, to whom we matter enormously.

By making ourselves important to a person who is Himself so enormously important, we achieve the desired significance, and the more powerful God is conceived to be, the more significant do we, His chief concern, become. So tremendously does He care about us that He has made the material universe for our benefit, this world rightly regarded being merely a school for human nature, in which it is trained and educated for life elsewhere; while by making Him in our own image we secure His special interest in the human race. The creation of the brute beasts to sustain our bodies and obey our orders is a token of that interest.

Interested as He is in the human species as a whole, He is quite specially interested in the particular race, nation, or tribe to which we happen to belong; so that, whatever the quarrel upon which the nation or tribe may happen to be engaged, it may rest assured of His support, since He is guaranteed to take the same view of the rights and wrongs of it as we do ourselves.

Among polytheistic peoples this concept causes no difficulty; each has its own deity or set of deities, and the strongest gods win. But where there is one God, and only one, who sustains the worship and is the repository of the prayers of opposed nations, the zeal of His adherents tends to place the Almighty in a dilemma.

> To God the embattled nations sing and shout,
> "God strafe England" and "God save the King,"
> God this, that, and God the other thing.
> "Good God!" said God, "I've got my work cut out."

But it is easy to provide for God's solution of the difficulty by invoking His omnipotence.

Interested in the nation or tribe to which we happen to belong, He is quite specially interested in ourselves; interested in and favorable toward, assisting us against those who seek to humiliate us, and generally discomfiting our enemies. This is a world in which the good man is notoriously oppressed, while the wicked flourish like a green bay tree. The arrangement offends our sense of justice, and, what is more, since we are good men ourselves, it is unfair to us personally. Very well, then, we invent another world in which the good man flourishes eternally and the bad one is eternally punished. Thus the fundamental rightness of things is vindicated, and we incidentally benefit in the process.

But in order that the system may work, it is necessary that the good man and the bad man should be under continual observation, that neither the unrequited goodness of the one nor the unchastised badness of the other may go unregistered. This function is admirably performed by the vertical or upstairs God. Thoughtfully accommodated with an abode in the skies, a position admirably adapted for purposes of espionage, He keeps a dossier of each individual, recognizing in us the worth that others unaccountably fail to recognize, and observing the wickedness and hypocrisy of those whom the world equally unaccountably exalts. These things are carefully noted, and in the next world all is made right. Immensely important, admired and envied — for are we not the favored children of Omnipotence? — we live happily ever afterward; scorned and hated, our enemies are convincingly humiliated. Assuredly an admirable arrangement! It is difficult to see how it could be improved upon. But God is essential to its proper working, and God flourishes accordingly.

God, then, on this view, is at once the product of human terror and the prop of human pride. He comforts our wretchedness, calms our fears, gives us an assurance of justice, and makes us feel important. "Religious ideas," says Freud, "have sprung from the same need as all the other achievements of culture; from the necessity for defending oneself against the crushing supremacy of nature."

(2) But though Freud recognizes one of the sources of religion in man's subjection to the forces of nature, he finds its chief root in his relationship to society. Hence his main account of the origin of religion is rather different from that just summarized.

This account will be found in Freud's book, *The Future of an Illusion*, which appeared in 1928. It is not very original, but it is typical of a certain attitude to religion, and may be taken as fairly representative of the view of many educated people, especially psychological and scientific workers today. Freud proceeds upon the basis of what is, in effect, a social contract theory of the origin of society. This theory is admirably stated early in the second book of Plato's *Republic*. Essential to it is the conception of primitive man as a completely non-moral animal; as such his natural inclination is to get his own way at all costs, without thought of the consequences to his neighbors. If his neighbor's wife attracts him, he makes off with her; if his neighbor annoys him, he knocks him on the head. Thus every man has, as Glaucon puts it in the *Republic*, a *natural* tendency to do injustice to his fellows. Admirable in theory, this system, or lack of system, has one serious drawback in practice; the right of every man to do injustice to his neighbors carries with it a corresponding right on the part of his neighbors to do injustice to him. He is one, but his neighbors are many, with the result that, where his hand is against every man and every man's hand is against him, he tends to get the worst of the bargain. His existence is intolerably insecure, he must be perpetually on his guard, and he has no secure enjoyment of his possessions. In the days before society was formed man's life, as the philosopher Hobbes puts it, was "nasty, brutish, and short." Finding the situation intolerable, men ended it by making a compact known as the social contract.

The compact was to form society. Consenting to live in society, man surrendered his natural right to do what he pleased to his fellows, on condition that they made a similar concession as regards himself. Social relations were regulated by public opinion, which later crystallized into law, and man for the future restrained his natural instincts lest he incur the social displeasure of his fellows. Thus was society formed, and from its formation springs the system of inhibitions and restraints which men call morality. To act morally is the reverse of acting naturally and implies a victory over the "natural man"; we obey the law, and keep our hands off our neighbor's wife and property, not because we are by nature moral, but in fear of the penalties with which society has prescribed actions which violate the contract upon which it was formed. In other words, we do right only through fear of the consequences of doing wrong. Remove this fear of consequences, as, for example, by endowing the individual with the gift of invisibility at will, and the social man would immediately relapse into the natural man, with the result that no property would be safe, no wife inviolable. The conclusion is that morality, which is simply the habit of acting in a manner of which other people approve, is not natural to man; on the contrary, it runs counter to his natural interests, frustrates his natural desires, and requires him to surrender his natural rights.

Now, man is not born social. He only becomes so at the cost of suffering and repression. Every child is born "natural," endowed with an egotism that bids him tyrannize over his world. Seeking to impose his imperious will upon his environment, he is surprised when his environment fails to respond, pained when it begins to resent. For a creature who starts with this "natural" endowment the business of growing up into a social adult who knows the lawful limits that must be set upon his desires is, it is obvious, a formidable one — so formidable that, according to Freud, it is seldom more than partially achieved, and never achieved without suffering and injury. To assist him in the difficult process of social adjustment the individual invokes the aid of religion. Hence the essence of religion, according to Freud, is compensation. It is compensation for man's loneliness in face of the vast indifference of the universe; it is also, and more importantly, compensation for the renunciations which he must undertake at the bidding of society.

Wherein (asks Freud) lies the peculiar virtue of religious ideas? We have spoken of the hostility to culture produced by the pressure it exercises and the instinctual renunciations that it demands. If one imagined its prohibitions removed, then one could choose any woman who took one's fancy as one's sexual object, one could kill without hesitation one's rival or whoever interfered with one in any other way, and one could seize what one wanted of another man's goods without asking his leave: how splendid, what a succession of delights life would be!

Forgo these delights, we must, if we are to achieve civilization. And, forgoing them we demand that the gods shall reward us for our sacrifice. Hence religion is the force that reconciles man to the burden of civilization. It is the most important of the compensations that civilization offers to its citizens; so important that only by offering it does civilization become possible. When we have learned as by second nature to refrain from incest, murder, torture, and arson, when we "pass right along the car, please," adjust our dress before leaving, and take our places at the end of the queue, without thinking whether we want to do these things or not, the external restrictions which society imposes have become instinctive habits, the primitive child has become the civilized adult, and social adjustment has been achieved. But achieved only by the aid of religion. Had we no God to whom to turn for comfort and consolation, to whom to tell the unfulfilled wishes and thwarted ambitions, to whom to pray for fortitude to suffer and strength to forbear, the task would be too great for us.

With the very dawn of consciousness, the need for a father confessor makes itself felt. ·

Thus little by little I became conscious where I was, and to have a wish to express my wishes to those who could content them; and I could not; for the wishes were within me and they without; nor could they, by any sense of theirs, enter within my spirit.

Thus St. Augustine, who proceeds to tell how he sought and found in God the confidant whom the world denied.

Nor is it only from others that we need a refuge. There is the riot of our desires, there are the prickings of our consciences; there is the sting of remorse. For, though manhood is achieved, the adjustment to society is not yet complete; still, though with decreasing vigor as the individual grows older and society more civilized, the natural man raises his head and rebels. When the rebellion comes into the open, when we refuse to pass down the car, take the head of the queue, or insist upon our inalienable privilege of driving upon the right-hand side of the road, society has little difficulty in quelling us. There are policemen, there are law courts, there are prisons, there are even scaffolds. But sometimes the rebellion stays underground, or, though it comes to the surface, goes undetected.

Against these hidden revolts society must protect itself, and evolves accordingly a system of espionage. There is a spy within the individual citadel itself, a spy in the service of society. This is our old Victorian acquaintance, the conscience, the policeman of society, stationed within the individual to see that social interests are duly observed. Directly we go wrong — directly, that is to say, we cease to act in a way of which society approves — conscience begins to nag. Like a dog that does not stop us from passing, but that we cannot prevent from barking, conscience voices the disapproval of society. The voice of conscience is an unpleasant one, causing us grave discomfort, and in extreme cases driving us to madness. Some refuge from the stings of conscience we must find, and we duly find it — in religion. Stricken by remorse, we demand that our sins be forgiven us. Who can forgive sin but God? Fouled by our sins of wrongdoing, we demand to be made clean. How can we be cleansed save by bathing in the blood of Jesus? And so we come to a new function of religion, a new use for God. Again religion takes the form of an insurance. We deny ourselves the minor luxuries, abstain from the grosser forms of vice, and submit to a little boredom on Sunday, and in return we are guaranteed against discomfort from the stings of conscience in the present and possible discomfort at the hands of the Almighty in the hereafter.

In all these ways and in many others religion seeks to compensate us for the strain and stress of living in society.

Freud traces the gradual evolution of religion to perform this function and the success with which it has, in fact, performed it. He distinguishes various stages in the growth of religion, determined by the nature of the need which at each successive stage it has been chiefly invoked to satisfy. Initially, the chief use of the gods is to protect man from the capriciousness of nature; but, as man progressed, the discoveries of science introduced order into disorder, and substituted law for caprice. At the same time, the growing complexity of civilization increases the strain of social adjustment. Less needed in the physical world, God becomes an indispensable refuge for the harassed soul of man. Thus history records a decline in the physical and a growth in the moral attributes of the gods.

In the course of time the first observations of law and order in natural phenomena are made, and therewith the forces of nature lose their human traits. But men's helplessness remains, and with it their father-longing and the gods. . . . And the more autonomous nature becomes and the more the gods withdraw from her, the more earnestly are all expectations concentrated on the third task assigned to them and the more does morality become their real domain. It now becomes the business of the gods to adjust the defects and evils of culture, to attend to the sufferings that men inflict on each other in their communal life, and to see that the laws of culture, which men obey so ill, are carried out. The laws of culture themselves are claimed to be of divine origin, they are elevated to a position above human society, and they are extended over nature and the universe.

Thus Freud records the progress of religion, and summarizes the different functions which it performs. Nor is his account singular. On the contrary, it is one to which, with minor modifications, most psychologists and anthropologists would subscribe. The more we learn about our mental, the more we learn about our bodily natures, the more, it is said, do we lay bare the roots of religion in the fundamental needs of our natures. Psychologists derive the doctrine of original sin from the sense of man's impotence in the face of chance and destiny; physiologists from the transgressions of his passionate

body against the taboos of society.   From our infancy we walk between a fear and a fear, between ruthless nature and restricting culture, crying, like Bunyan's Pilgrim, "What shall I do to be saved?"
And demanding salvation at all costs, we create God to save us.

Thus religion is the consolation of mankind, and as such its appeal
is universal.

(3) But we now come to a more limited, but scarcely less important,
function which religion has played in the history of man.   To its
successful performance of this function its growth and vigor in more
modern times is mainly attributable.

There are evils which are the common heritage of all men; they are
death, disease, the ingratitude of man to man, the malevolence of
destiny.   These are no respecters of persons, and bear with impartial
severity upon us all.   But there are others which do not belong to the
essential conditions of human life, but are incidental to the way in
which man has chosen collectively to organize his life.   For men, equal
in the eyes of God, are far from equal in the eyes of society.   There are,
and always have been, rulers and ruled, oppressors and oppressed,
rich and poor; according to many authorities, there always will be.
Society, moreover, is based upon force, which its rulers employ to
maintain and perpetuate the inequalities on which they thrive.   To
make their task easier they invoke the assistance of religion.   For
religion is not only a means of reconciling the individual to society;
it is also, and more particularly, a device for inducing the poor and
oppressed to tolerate the particular order of society which impoverishes and oppresses them.   Thus religion becomes the instrument of
the rich and the bridle of the poor.   How is the oracle worked?

It is significant, in the first place, that most religions extol the virtues appropriate to slaves — namely, meekness, humility, unselfish-
ness, and contentment — and censure as the vices of pride and presumption the virtues of courage, originality, and independence, and
that passionate resentment at injustice and wrong which are characteristic of those who aspire to rise above their servitude.   The
Christian religion goes further, and makes a virtue of poverty.   It is
only, we are assured, with the greatest difficulty that the rich man shall
enter the Kingdom of Heaven, which opens its gates to the humble
and needy.   Poverty and insignificance are not, therefore, as they
appear to be, and as the world insists on regarding them, disabilities
to be avoided at all costs; they are passports to celestial bliss. . . .

As it has pleased Him to call ninety-nine out of every hundred of us
to an extremely lowly state, religion, in so far as it is taken seriously,

assists in keeping us where we are. Assists whom? Those who benefit by our remaining where we are — namely, our rulers. For the governing classes have been quick to seize the chance religion has offered them of not only subduing their inferiors, but of representing their subjection as a positive asset to their subjects. Ever since an early governing-class realist slipped the parable about Lazarus into the text of the Gospel of St. Luke, the priest and the parson, seeking to persuade the poor that it was only by remaining poor that they would go to Heaven, have been able to produce good scriptural backing for their propaganda. The poor, on the whole, have been only too ready to agree, and have gladly embraced the promise of celestial bliss in the next world as a compensation for the champagne and cigars they were missing in this one. Since the celestial bliss was known to be of indefinite continuance, while the champagne and cigars could not last at most for more than a beggarly fifty years (as a matter of fact, they often lasted less, God having from time to time seen fit to punish the excesses of the worldly by dulling their palates and depriving them of their appetites in the present as an earnest of His intentions for the future; more recently, of course, He has added cancer to the list of penalties), the poor — it is obvious — have the best of the bargain. If it has ever occurred to them to wonder why the rich and powerful should recklessly jeopardize the chances which they have so freely proffered and warmly recommended to their poorer brethren, they may possibly have comforted themselves with the reflection that *quem deus vult perdere prius dementit*.[1] Possibly, but not probably, for, on the whole, the poor and oppressed have been too much engaged with their poverty and oppression to reflect upon the motives of their betters.

Religion, from this point of view, is a gigantic social hoax, a hoax which has been, on the whole, remarkably successful; so much so, indeed, that from time to time one or another of the rulers of mankind, franker or more secure than the rest, has not scrupled to show how the trick was worked. Thus Napoleon, a notorious skeptic, taxed with the protection which he afforded to a religion in which he did not believe, and stoutly refusing to be drawn into anti-Christian or anti-clerical legislation:

"What is it," he asked his critics, "that makes the poor man think it quite natural that there are fires in my palace while he is dying of cold? that I have ten coats in my wardrobe while he goes naked? that at each of my meals enough is served to feed his family for a week? It is simply

[1] "Whom the gods would destroy, they first make mad."

religion, which tells him that in another life I shall be only his equal, and that he actually has more chance of being happy there than I. Yes, we must see to it that the floors of the churches are open to all, and that it does not cost the poor man much to have prayers said on his tomb."

Napoleon was right. The poor have a need for religion which the rich do not feel, and it is not surprising, therefore, to find that, while skepticism and atheism have on occasion flourished among the rich, religion has uniformly been embraced with eagerness by the poor. The growth of disbelief in governing-class circles, while it may have evoked the censure of society — the rich have always thought it prudent to keep up religious observances — has rarely called down the penalties of the law. Thus governing-class writers of the eighteenth century, Gibbon, Voltaire, or the Encyclopaedists, for example, who were notoriously irreligious or hostile to religion, went comparatively scathless. Naturally, since they wrote for the educated upper, not for the ignorant lower, classes. Most of the early rationalists, again, were academic people whose books were too difficult or too dull to command a popular circulation. Excepting Woolston, they escaped unpunished. But Peter Annett, a schoolmaster who tried to popularize free thought and held forth on the village green, was sentenced to the pillory and hard labor in 1763. "If we take the cases in which the civil authorities have intervened to repress the publication of unorthodox opinions during the last two centuries," says Professor Bury, "we find that the object has always been to prevent the spread of free thought among the masses." . . .

In the nineteenth century, as the danger to society from the new proletariat first made itself felt, the beliefs of the governing classes, it is interesting to note, become more pronounced as their religious example becomes more edifying. It was most important that the wage slaves of the industrial revolution should learn to know God, and in knowing Him to respect their betters. Their betters, then, should show them the way. This they proceeded to do. . . .

That the position remains radically unaltered is shown by the following dialogue between Cusins and Undershaft from Shaw's *Major Barbara*, a dialogue which has become a classic.

CUSINS (*in a white fury*): Do I understand you to imply that you can buy Barbara?

UNDERSHAFT: No; but I can buy the Salvation Army.

CUSINS: Quite impossible.

UNDERSHAFT: You shall see. All religious organizations exist by selling themselves to the rich.

CUSINS: Not the Army. That is the church of the poor.

UNDERSHAFT: All the more reason for buying it.

CUSINS: I don't think you quite know what the Army does for the poor.

UNDERSHAFT: Oh yes, I do. It draws their teeth: that is enough for me —
as a man of business —

CUSINS: Nonsense! It makes them sober —

UNDERSHAFT: I prefer sober workmen. The profits are larger.

CUSINS: — honest —

UNDERSHAFT: Honest workmen are the most economical.

CUSINS: — attached to their homes —

UNDERSHAFT: So much the better: they will put up with anything sooner
than change their shop.

CUSINS: — happy —

UNDERSHAFT: An invaluable safeguard against revolution.

CUSINS: — unselfish —

UNDERSHAFT: Indifferent to their own interests, which suits me exactly.

CUSINS: — with their thoughts on heavenly things —

UNDERSHAFT (*rising*): And not on trade unionism nor socialism. Excellent.

CUSINS (*revolted*): You really are an infernal old rascal.

Summing up, we may note that this conception of the special function of religion as the instrument of the rich and the bridle of the poor
follows logically from its main social function considered above. I
have already summarized Freud's account of religion as man's
compensation for the renunciations which society demands of him.
This may be described as the general social function of religion. It
is the part which religion has been called upon to play in the lives of
tribal and civilized men, because they live in tribes and societies.
But in addition to the general there is a special social function of
religion, which is to render the inequalities of society tolerable to the
masses. Civilization, requiring of the many poor far greater instinctive renunciations than it demands of the rich, has given them far
fewer material compensations. It is essential, therefore, if they are
to acquiesce in a state of society which on the material side demands
so much while giving so little, that they should receive some compensation of the spirit, a compensation which brings comfort in the present
and gives hope for the future. Such compensation is afforded by an
ingeniously devised and richly satisfying religious system, which,
while making a virtue of humility, feeds the fires of self-esteem, lest,
revolting against their insignificance, the poor and the many should
turn against society and destroy it. This, then, is one of the functions which religion, and especially the Christian religion, has performed in civilized societies; it has taken the revolutionary sting from

poverty and blunted the edge of present discontent with promises of future well-being. Performing this function, religion has been sedulously exploited and used by the rich as an instrument of class domination. God, it has been found, is cheaper than a living wage. Very well, then, let us invest in Him! Religion is a show to keep the poor amused. Very well, then, let us build churches in the slums! For this reason socialists have tended to be hostile to religion, and the Bolshevik government veers between reluctant toleration and covert persecution.

I have endeavored briefly to summarize a number of different accounts of the origin, the growth, and the function of religion. These accounts dominate the modern psychological and sociological treatment of the subject, which is, on the whole, markedly hostile to religion. There are, admittedly, differences on points of detail, and different writers put the emphasis differently according to the purposes which their account is intended to serve and the aspect of religion with which it is chiefly concerned. But all the accounts which I have summarized are in fundamental agreement in interpreting religion on subjectivist lines.

On this one fundamental point they concur. When faced with the question, "Why is there religion?" they answer unanimously, "Because man wants it." When asked, "Whence does religion rise?" their reply is, "From the needs of man's nature." Pressed for an explanation of its authority and appeal, they represent it as a "rationalization of his instinctive wishes." Thus all these accounts are in their different ways subjectivist. They affirm that religion enables man to accommodate himself to this world, that it expresses a human need, and that it is, therefore, pleasant and consoling; they do not say that it represents an objective fact, that it points forward to a different world, and that it is therefore true. With most of what they assert I am largely, if not entirely, in agreement. I think that the interpretations they give of the origin of religion in terms of the needs which it fulfills, and of the ground of its appeal in terms of the wishes that it rationalizes, are in the main true. But I do not think that they are complete. They are, that is to say, interpretations in terms of origin only, and they take no account of the conception of end or purpose. They ask how religion began and why it flourished; they do not ask what it may become. Both conceptions are, I am convinced, necessary to an adequate description of the status of religion in the present, and a reasoned estimate of its chance of survival in the future.

Now, I shall consider the reasons for including in our survey an account of religion in terms of what it may become.

If a thing's nature is exhibited only in its complete development, a complete account of its nature can be given only in terms of that development.   Thus, to describe its nature *as it is now*, we must seek to estimate its future; so only can we hope to understand the tentative beginnings and premonitory stirrings that foreshadow it.   A thing reflects its past, no doubt, and to understand it we must know its past; but it also foreshadows its future, and to understand it we must seek to forecast its future; and we must do this not only as a disinterested exercise in prophecy, but because the future in part determines and renders intelligible the present. It follows that, adequately to understand a growing and developing thing, we must take into account not only the origins from which it sprang, but the goal which it may be seeking to achieve.   We must think of it not only as determined from behind by its past, but determined from in front by its future.   We must, in a word, introduce the notion of purpose.

Our conclusion is in accordance with, indeed it is demanded by, the teaching of evolution.   Life, we are agreed, changes; it evolves. If the changes which evolution implies are real changes — and if they are not, everything that exists must have existed always, and time and growth and movement are illusions — then at any given stage in the growth of a living organism the organism must be different from what it was at the preceding stages.   But it not only changes; it develops, and in saying that it develops we are implying that at each stage it is not only different from but also more than it was before. Consider, for example, the case of the growing human body.   The matter of which a living body is composed, beginning as a microscopic speck of protoplasm, ends as a many-millioned colony of cells.   These cells are highly organized, and specialized for the performance of different functions.   Some are marshaled to carry on the work of the nervous system; others to form the engines we call muscles; others, again, serve the comparatively lowly purpose of bone-levers.   Instruments of incredible delicacy, the eye and the ear, are evolved; yet the whole complex mechanism of a living human body is developed from a particle of living matter smaller than the finest pinhead.   Now, either these complex cells and organs were present in the pinhead to begin with, or they were not.   If they were not, then they are literally new; there was, that is to say, a time when they were not, and we are entitled to say that there is more in the present state of the body than there was in its origin.

What is true of the life of the body is true also of that of the mind. Knowledge which is literally new comes into the world. An engineer knows how to build a bridge, a mathematician understands the differential calculus. Either this knowledge and this understanding are new in the sense that there was a time when no mind possessed them, or they are not. If they are not, then they existed in some form when the earth was populated by amoebas. A similar argument may be applied to any other planet upon which life has appeared, the conclusion being that there is nothing new under the sun. Thus change is unreal, since whatever is always has been, and evolution is an illusion. If they are new, then there was a time when the universe knew them not; in other words, they have appeared from nowhere, since there is nowhere outside the universe, and evolved out of nothing. Granted, then, that the fact of growth implies the coming into being of new elements, that there may be more in a thing's present state than there was in its ingredients or its origin; granted further that this is true of the human mind or spirit, why should we deny its application to expressions of the human spirit, to art, for example, to science or to religion? To art and to science, indeed, we apply it readily enough; but what of religion? Why should we arbitrarily exclude religion from the operation of the laws of growth and development? For it is high time to apply these considerations to the subject of this article. Applying them, we assert that religion can no more receive an adequate interpretation in terms of its origin alone than can any other growing and developing thing. This is not to say that the interpretation in terms of origin is inappropriate, but merely that it is not complete; it is not complete because the religious consciousness is more than the ingredients from which it has emerged.

It is also more than the psychological machinery which is involved in its emergence. Psychoanalysts are fond of pointing out that religion is sublimated emotion. Primitive lusts, social maladjustments and misfits, and unacknowledged desires are mixed together in an unholy brew of which the religious consciousness is the distilled essence. The ingredients exposed, it is somehow implied that their outcome is discredited. Erroneously, for to lay bare the assorted and possibly disreputable elements of which the religious consciousness may have been compounded is not to show that they *are* that consciousness; the theory of sublimation, if it means anything at all, means, in fact, that they are not.

I assert that an account of the origin, the history, and the psychology of religion, interesting as it is to the anthropologist, the historian, and the psychologist, is not an account of religion, and that arguments derived from it cannot, therefore, be used to discredit or to dispose of religion. Were it not for the fears of the savage and the social maladjustments of the citizen, religion admittedly would be very different from what it is. But, originating in the stress of human need and flowering on the dunghill of human emotions, the religious consciousness rises above its origins and transcends its machinery. The mechanism, I repeat, is other than its product.

In its account of religion, and not of religion alone, psychoanalysis makes the mistake of identifying, and therefore confusing, the unconscious trends of our nature with their conscious outcrop. Unmasking the malevolence of our unconscious wishes, analysts exhibit the ingenuity with which they are sublimated to appear honorable; they succeed; but they also exhibit the efficiency with which they are sublimated so that they are indeed honorable. One day, no doubt, psychoanalysts will succeed, if they have not done so already, in reducing the sense of duty to something else, probably to something discreditable, but this would not explain away the sense of duty any more than the successful reduction of matter to electricity explains away matter, or of religion to the needs and desires of which it can be shown to be a sublimation explains away religion.

For this reason criticisms of religion urged by psychoanalysts, valid up to a point, are valueless beyond it. It is not that they are not true, but that they are incomplete.

If religion does, in fact, derive from the sources previously mentioned, if it has fulfilled the needs and served the purposes enumerated, then it still fulfills those needs and serves those purposes now. If it is the product of human fear, and the projection of human vanity, then it will still reassure man's nervousness and flatter his egotism. But while it still sustains the rôle which it has sustained through the ages, it will no longer sustain that rôle alone. It will both do more and be more, and the "more" that it does and is will receive adequate interpretation, in so far as it can be interpretated at all, not in terms of the origin and history of religion, but in terms appropriate to its future and its goal. Admittedly, we do not know its future and we can only dimly guess its goal. But of this at least we may be sure: that in the confused complex of tendencies — social and individual, inherited and acquired, instinctive and intellectual — in the vaguely felt aspirations and the scarce acknowledged faith, the sense of spiritual loneliness and the need of spiritual communion, that go to make up what is called religion today, there will always be present an element to which the Freudian, or the anthropological, or the social, or any similar account of the appeal and functions of religion will not only not apply, but which it will completely falsify. I say an element, but there is no need to limit my assertion to one. Religion in the past has been a rope of many strands; it is not likely to grow simple and single in the future. Let us, then, say provisionally that there are two or, perhaps, three aspects or phases of the religious consciousness which none of the subjectivist explanations in terms of the origin and past of religion can explain, and which can be understood only in terms of what religion may become. These aspects we must try to separate from the rest, and, having separated, use as the point of departure for our account of the religion of the future.

To answer the question whether religion is a permanent and necessary growth of the human spirit, and whether as such it will have a future, it is sufficient to point out that there are such aspects. Requiring interpretation in terms of the future rather than the past, it is clear that, as man advances in the path of evolution, they will become more prominent and definite than they are today. Religion, therefore, in so far as it contains them, will not die out. . . .

In conclusion, let us summarize the results at which we have arrived. When we have to deal with growing and developing things, with living organisms, with the institutions in which they are organized, and the activities in which they find expression, the explanation of their present state in terms of their origin is inadequate. This statement is true both of morals and of religion. To say that the moral consciousness arose because it promoted tribal efficiency, or that the religious consciousness arose because it promoted cosmic comfort, tells us something but not everything about the moral or the religious consciousness now. To understand them as they are now we must judge them not only by their roots but by their fruits, looking not only to what they have been, but to what they may become. The mind, in short, is Janus-like; it looks forward as well as backward, bearing upon it at any given moment traces not only of what it has been, but what it may become. . . .

The conclusion is that there is more in a complex product like the religious consciousness than can be adequately explained by a reference to its origin. This "more" will be a pointer to the future, and we must try, therefore, to disentangle it from the rest, in order to estimate the prospects of religion in the future.

THE IDEA OF PROGRESS[1]

Dean W. R. Inge

In the long line of eloquent Anglican preachers at St. Paul's which goes back to Jeremy Taylor, none has won a more intellectual following than the VERY REV. WILLIAM RALPH INGE, Dean of St. Paul's from 1911 to 1934. Part of his popular renown after the World War was traceable to his extremely pessimistic views of contemporaneous social and cultural tendencies, which gave him the title of "the gloomy Dean." But his real reputation rested upon more substantial bases: upon the closeness and penetration of his thought, the rich cultural background which it reflected, and the depth and sincerity of his religious philosophy. This philosophy is essentially mystical in character, and many of Dean Inge's books and essays deal with mysticism in its relations with faith, with personal idealism, and with ecclesiastical history. His thought derives much from the seventeenth century mystics, and especially the Cambridge Platonists who were best represented by Henry More. It may interestingly be compared with the writings of an American, Paul Elmer More, upon Neo-Platonism. Dean Inge, who was born at Crayke, Yorkshire, in 1860, and educated at Cambridge, was for many years a teacher at Eton and Oxford, and became professor of divinity at Cambridge in 1907. During these years his writings upon religion and mysticism appealed to but a narrow public. With the end of the war, however, he turned to the consideration of scientific, literary, and social questions of broad and general interest, and his books sold widely in England and America. The two best-known volumes are *Outspoken Essays* and *More Outspoken Essays*. But they were followed by a series of equally readable and stimulating books — *Lay Thoughts of a Dean; Assessments and Anticipations; Christian Ethics and Modern Problems;* and *Things New and Old*. These represent Dean Inge's ripest thought. But to study the development of this thought some attention must be paid to the earlier works, such as *Studies of English Mystics* and *Personal Idealism and Mysticism*.

The racial life of the species to which we happen to belong is a brief episode even in the brief life of the planet. And what we call civilization or culture, though much older than we used to suppose, is a brief episode in the life of our race. For tens of thousands of years the changes in our habits must have been very slight, and chiefly those which were forced upon our rude ancestors by changes of climate. Then in certain districts man began, as Samuel Butler says, to wish to live beyond his income. This was the beginning of the vast series of inventions which have made our life so complex. And, we used to be told, the "law of all progress is the same, the evolution of the simple into the complex by successive differentiations." This is the gospel

[1] From *Outspoken Essays*, by W. R. Inge. Reprinted by permission of Longmans, Green & Company, publishers.

according to Herbert Spencer. As a universal law of nature, it is ludicrously untrue. Some species have survived by becoming more complex; others, like the whole tribe of parasites, by becoming more simple. On the whole, perhaps the parasites have had the best of it. The progressive species have in many cases flourished for a while and then paid the supreme penalty. The living dreadnoughts of the Saurian age have left us their bones, but no progeny. But the microbes, one of which had the honor of killing Alexander the Great at the age of thirty-two, and so changing the whole course of history, survive and flourish. The microbe illustrates the wisdom of the maxim, λάθε βιώσας.[1] It took thousands of years to find him out. Our own species, being rather poorly provided by nature for offense and defense, had to live by its wits, and so came to the top. It developed many new needs, and set itself many insoluble problems. Physiologists like Metchnikoff have shown how very ill-adapted our bodies are to the tasks which we impose upon them; and in spite of the Spencerian identification of complexity with progress, our surgeons try to simplify our structure by forcibly removing various organs which they assure us that we do not need. If we turn to history for a confirmation of the Spencerian doctrine, we find, on the contrary, that civilization is a disease which is almost invariably fatal, unless its course is checked in time. The Hindus and Chinese, after advancing to a certain point, were content to mark time; and they survive. But the Greeks and Romans are gone; and aristocracies everywhere die out. Do we not see today the complex organization of the ecclesiastic and college don succumbing before the simple squeezing and sucking apparatus of the profiteer and trade unionist? If so-called civilized nations show any protracted vitality, it is because they are only civilized at the top. Ancient civilizations were destroyed by imported barbarians; we breed our own.

It is also an unproved assumption that the domination of the planet by our own species is a desirable thing, which must give satisfaction to its Creator. We have devastated the loveliness of the world; we have exterminated several species more beautiful and less vicious than ourselves; we have enslaved the rest of the animal creation, and have treated our distant cousins in fur and feathers so badly that beyond doubt, if they were able to formulate a religion, they would depict the Devil in human form. If it is progress to turn the fields and woods of Essex into East and West Ham, we may be thankful that progress is a sporadic and transient phenomenon in history.

[1] " Live obscurely."

It is a pity that our biologists, instead of singing paeans to Progress and thereby stultifying their own researches, have not preached us sermons on the sin of racial self-idolatry, a topic which really does arise out of their studies. *L'anthropolatrie, voila l'ennemi*, is the real ethical motto of biological science, and a valuable contribution to morals.

It was impossible that such shallow optimism as that of Herbert Spencer should not arouse protests from other scientific thinkers. Hartmann had already shown how a system of pessimism, resembling that of Schopenhauer, may be built upon the foundation of evolutionary science. And in this place we are not likely to forget the second Romanes Lecture, when Professor Huxley astonished his friends and opponents alike by throwing down the gauntlet in the face of nature, and bidding mankind to find salvation by accepting for itself the position which the early Christian writer Hippolytus gives as a definition of the Devil — "he who resists the cosmic process" (ὁ ἀντιτάττων τοῖς κοσμικοῖς). The revolt was not in reality so sudden as some of Huxley's hearers supposed. He had already realized that "so far from gradual progress forming any necessary part of the Darwinian creed, it appears to us that it is perfectly consistent with indefinite persistence in one state, or with a gradual retrogression. Suppose, e.g., a return of the glacial period or a spread of polar climatical conditions over the whole globe." The alliance between determinism and optimism was thus dissolved; and as time went on, Huxley began to see in the cosmic process something like a power of evil. The natural process, he told us in this place, has no tendency to bring about the good of mankind. Cosmic nature is no school of virtue, but the headquarters of the enemy of ethical nature. Nature is the realm of tiger rights; it has no morals and no ought-to-be; its only rights are brutal powers. Morality exists only in the "artificial" moral world: man is a glorious rebel, a Prometheus defying Zeus. This strange rebound into Manichaeism sounded like a blasphemy against all the gods whom the lecturer was believed to worship, and half-scandalized even the clerics in his audience. It was bound to raise the question whether this titanic revolt against the cosmic process has any chance of success. One recent thinker, who accepts Huxley's view that the nature of things is cruel and immoral, is willing to face the probability that we cannot resist it with any prospect of victory. Mr. Bertrand Russell, in his arresting essay, "A Free Man's Worship," shows us Prometheus again, but Prometheus chained to the rock and still hurling defiance against God. He proclaims the

moral bankruptcy of naturalism, which he yet holds to be forced
upon us:

> That man is the product of causes which had no prevision of the end they
> were achieving; that his origin, his growth, his hopes and fears, his loves
> and his beliefs, are but the outcome of accidental collocations of atoms;
> that no fire, no heroism, no intensity of thought and feeling, can preserve
> an individual life beyond the grave; that all the labors of the ages, all the
> devotion, all the inspiration, all the noonday brightness of human genius,
> are destined to extinction in the vast death of the solar system, and that the
> whole temple of man's achievement must inevitably be buried beneath the
> debris of a universe in ruins — all these things, if not quite beyond dispute,
> are yet so nearly certain, that no philosophy which rejects them can hope
> to stand. Only within the scaffolding of these truths, only on the firm
> foundation of unyielding despair, can the soul's habitation henceforth be
> safely built.

Man belongs to "an alien and inhuman world," alone amid "hostile
forces." What is man to do? The God who exists is evil; the God
whom we can worship is the creation of our own conscience, and has
no existence outside it. The "free man" will worship the latter; and,
like John Stuart Mill, "to hell he will go."

If I wished to criticize this defiant pronouncement, which is not
without a touch of bravado, I should say that so complete a separation
of the real from the ideal is impossible, and that the choice which the
writer offers us, of worshiping a Devil who exists or a God who does
not, is no real choice, since we cannot worship either. But my object
in quoting from this essay is to show how completely naturalism has
severed its alliance with optimism and belief in progress. Professor
Huxley and Mr. Russell have sung their palinode and smashed the old
gods of their creed. No more proof is needed, I think, that the
alleged law of progress has no scientific basis whatever.

But superstition has also invaded and vitiated our history, our
political science, our philosophy, and our religion.

The historian is a natural snob; he sides with the gods against Cato,
and approves the winning side. He lectures the vanquished for their
willfulness and want of foresight, sometimes rather prematurely, as
when Seeley, looking about for an example of perverse refusal to
recognize facts, exclaims "Sedet, aeternumque sedebit unhappy
Poland!" The nineteenth century historian was so loath to admit
retrogression that he liked to fancy the river of progress flowing
underground all through the Dark Ages, and endowed the German
barbarians who overthrew Mediterranean civilization with all the

manly virtues.   If a nation, or a religion, or a school of art dies, the historian explains why it was not worthy to live.

In political science the corruption of the scientific spirit by the superstition of progress has been flagrant.   It enables the disputant to overbear questions of right and wrong by confident prediction, a method which has the double advantage of being peculiarly irritating and incapable of refutation.   On the theory of progress, what is "coming" must be right.   Forms of government and modes of thought which for the time being are not in favor are assumed to have been permanently left behind.   A student of history who believed in cyclical changes and long swings of the pendulum would take a very different and probably much sounder view of contemporary affairs. The votaries of progress mistake the flowing tide for the river of eternity, and when the tide turns they are likely to be left stranded like the corks and scraps of seaweed which mark the high-water line. This has already happened, though few realize it.   The praises of liberty are mainly left to Conservatives, who couple it with property as something to be defended, and to conscientious objectors, who dissociate it from their country, which is not to be defended.   Democracy — the magic ballot-box — has few worshipers any longer except in America, where men will still shout for about two hours — and indeed much longer — that she is "great."   But our pundits will be slow to surrender the useful words "progressive" and "reactionary."   The classification is, however, a little awkward.   If a reactionary is anyone who will not float with the stream, and a progressive anyone who has the flowing tide with him, we must classify the Christian Fathers and the French Encylopaedists as belonging to the same type, the progressive; while the Roman Stoics under the Empire and the Russian bureaucrats under Nicholas II will be placed together under the opposite title, as reactionaries.   Or is the progressive not the supporter of the winning cause for the time being, but the man who thinks, with a distinguished head of a college who, as I remember, affirmed his principles in Convocation, that "any leap in the dark is better than standing still"; and is the reactionary the man whose constitutional timidity would deter him from performing this act of faith when caught by a mist on the Matterhorn?   Machiavelli recognizes fixed types of human character, such as the cautious Fabius and the impetuous Julius II, and observes that these qualities lead sometimes to success and sometimes to failure.   If a reactionary only means an adherent of political opinions which we happen to dislike, there is no reason why a bureaucrat should not call a republican a reactionary, as Maecenas may have applied the name to Brutus and Cassius. Such examples of evolution as that which turned the Roman Republic into a principate, and then into an empire of the Asiatic type, are inconvenient for those who say "It is coming," and think that they have vindicated the superiority of their own theories of government.

We have next to consider the influence of the superstition of progress on the philosophy of the last century. To attempt such a task in this place is a little rash, and to prove the charge in a few minutes would be impossible even for one much better equipped than I am. But something must be said. Hegel and Comte are often held to have been the chief advocates of the doctrine of progress among philosophers. Both of them give definitions of the word — a very necessary thing to do, and I have not yet attempted to do it. Hegel defines progress as spiritual freedom; Comte as true or positive social philosophy. The definitions are peculiar; and neither theory can be made to fit past history. . . . Hegel is perhaps more independent of facts; his predecessor Fichte professes to be entirely indifferent to them. "The philosopher," he says, "follows the *a priori* thread of the world plan which is clear to him without any history; and if he makes use of history, it is not to prove anything, since his theses are already proved independently of all history." Certainly, Hegel's dialectical process cannot easily be recognized in the course of European events; and, what is more fatal to the believers in a law of progress who appeal to him, he does not seem to have contemplated any further marked improvements upon the political system of Prussia in his own time, which he admired so much that his critics have accused him of teaching that the Absolute first attained full self-consciousness at Berlin in the nineteenth century. He undoubtedly believed that there has been progress in the past; but he does not, it appears, look forward to further changes; as a politician, at any rate, he gives us something like a closed system. Comte can only bring his famous "three stages" into history by arguing that the Catholic monotheism of the Middle Ages was an advance upon pagan antiquity. A Catholic might defend such a thesis with success; but for Comte the chief advantage seems to be that the change left the Olympians with only one neck, for Positive Philosophy to cut off. But Comte himself is what his system requires us to call a reactionary; he is back in the "theological stage"; he would like a theocracy, if he could have one without a God. The state is to be subordinate to the Positive Church, and he will allow "no unlimited freedom of thought." The connection of this philosophy with the doctrine of progress seems very slender.   It is not so easy to answer the question in the case of Hegel, because his contentment with the Prussian government may be set down to idiosyncrasy or to prudence; but it is significant that some of his ablest disciples have discarded the belief.   To say that "the world is as it ought to be" does not imply that it goes on getting better, though some would think it was not good if it was not getting better.   It is hard to believe that a great thinker really supposed that the universe as a whole is progressing, a notion which Mr. Bradley has stigmatized as "nonsense, unmeaning or blasphemous."   Mr. Bradley may perhaps be interpreting Hegel rightly when he says that for a philosopher "progress can never have any temporal sense," and explains that a perfect philosopher would see the whole world of appearance as a "progress," by which he seems to mean only a re-arrangement in terms of ascending and descending value and reality. But it might be objected that to use "progress" in this sense is to lay a trap for the unwary.   Mathematicians undoubtedly talk of progress, or rather of progression, without any implication of temporal sequence; but outside this science to speak of "progress without any temporal sense" is to use a phrase which some would call self-contradictory. Be that as it may, popularized Hegelianism has laid hold of the idea of a self-improving universe, of perpetual and universal progress, in a strictly temporal sense.   The notion of an evolving and progressing cosmos, with a Creator who is either improving himself (though we do not put it quite so crudely) or who is gradually coming into his own, has taken strong hold of the popular imagination.   The latter notion leads straight to ethical dualism of the Manichaean type. The theory of a single purpose in the universe seems to me untenable. Such a purpose, being infinite . . . could never be accomplished. The theory condemns both God and man to the doom of Tantalus. Mr. Bradley is quite right in finding this belief incompatible with Christianity.

It would not be possible, without transgressing the limits set for lecturers on this foundation, to show how the belief in a law of progress has prejudicially affected the religious beliefs of our time.   I need only recall to you the discussions whether the perfect man could have lived in the first, and not in the nineteenth or twentieth century — although one would have thought that the ancient Greeks, to take one nation only, have produced many examples of hitherto unsurpassed genius;   the secularization of religion by throwing its ideals into the near future — a new apocalyptism which is doing mischief enough in politics without the help of the clergy; and the unauthorized belief in future probation, which rests on the queer assumption that, if a man is given time enough, he must necessarily become perfect. In fact, the superstition which is the subject of this lecture has distorted Christianity almost beyond recognition. Only one great church, old in worldly wisdom, knows that human nature does not change, and acts on the knowledge. Accordingly, the papal syllabus of 1864 declares: *"Si quis dixerit:* Romanus pontifex potest ac debet cum progressu, cum liberalismo, et cum recenti civilitate sese reconciliare et componere, *anathema sit."* [1]

Our optimists have not made it clear to themselves or others what they mean by progress, and we may suspect that the vagueness of the idea is one of its attractions. There has been no physical progress in our species for many thousands of years. The Cro-Magnon race, which lived perhaps twenty thousand years ago, was at least equal to any modern people in size and strength; the ancient Greeks were, I suppose, handsomer and better formed than we are; and some unprogressive races, such as the Zulus, Samoans, and Tahitians, are envied by Europeans for either strength or beauty. Although it seems not to be true that the sight and hearing of civilized peoples are inferior to those of savages, we have certainly lost our natural weapons, which from one point of view is a mark of degeneracy. Mentally, we are now told that the men of the Old Stone Age, ugly as most of them must have been, had as large brains as ours; and he would be a bold man who should claim that we are intellectually equal to the Athenians or superior to the Romans. The question of moral improvement is much more difficult. Until the Great War few would have disputed that civilized man had become much more humane, much more sensitive to the sufferings of others, and so more just, more self-controlled, and less brutal in his pleasures and in his resentments. The habitual honesty of the Western European might also have been contrasted with the rascality of inferior races in the past and present. It was often forgotten that, if progress means the improvement of human nature itself, the question to be asked is whether the modern civilized man behaves better in the same circumstances than his ancestor would have done. Absence of temptation may produce an appearance of improvement; but this is hardly what we mean by progress, and there is an old saying that the Devil has a clever trick of pretending to be dead. It seems to me very doubtful whether when we are ex-

[1] "It shall be anathema for anyone to say that the head of the Roman Church either could or should reconcile himself with and make concessions to progress, liberalism, and recent political ideas."

posed to the same temptations we are more humane or more sympathetic or juster or less brutal than the ancients.   Even before this war,
the examples of the Congo and Putumayo, and American lynchings,
proved that contact with barbarians reduces many white men to the
moral condition of savages; and the outrages committed on the
Chinese after the Boxer rebellion showed that even a civilized nation
cannot rely on being decently treated by Europeans if its civilization
is different from their own.   During the Great War, even if some
atrocities were magnified with the amiable object of rousing a good-
natured people to violent hatred, it was the well-considered opinion
of Lord Bryce's commission that no such cruelties had been committed
for three hundred years as those which the Germans practiced in
Belgium and France.   It was startling to observe how easily the
blood lust was excited in young men straight from the fields, the
factory, and the counter, many of whom had never before killed anything larger than a wasp, and that in self-defense.   As for the Turks,
we must go back to Jenghiz Khan to find any parallel to their massacres in Armenia;   and the Russian terrorists have reintroduced
torture into Europe, with the help of Chinese experts in the art.
With these examples before our eyes, it is difficult to feel any confidence that either the lapse of time or civilization has made the
bête humaine less ferocious.   On biological grounds there is no reason
to expect it.   No selection in favor of superior types is now going on;
on the contrary, civilization tends now, as always, to an *Ausrottung
der Besten* — a weeding-out of the best; and the new practice of sub-
sidizing the unsuccessful by taxes extorted from the industrious is
cacogenics erected into a principle.   The best hope of stopping this
progressive degeneration is in the science of eugenics. But this
science is still too tentative to be made the basis of legislation, and we
are not yet agreed what we should breed for.   The two ideals, that of
the perfect man and that of the perfectly organized state, would lead
to very different principles of selection.   Do we want a nation of
beautiful and moderately efficient Greek gods, or do we want human
mastiffs for policemen, human greyhounds for postmen, and so on?
However, the opposition which eugenics has now to face is based on
less respectable grounds, such as pure hedonism ("Would the super-
man be any happer?"); indifference to the future welfare of the race
("Posterity has done nothing for me; why should I do anything for
posterity?"); and, in politics, the reflection that the unborn have no
votes.

We have, then, been driven to the conclusion that neither science nor history gives us any warrant for believing that humanity has advanced, except by accumulating knowledge and experience and the instruments of living. The value of these accumulations is not beyond dispute. Attacks upon civilization have been frequent, from Crates, Pherecrates, Antisthenes, and Lucretius in antiquity to Rousseau, Walt Whitman, Thoreau, Ruskin, Morris, and Edward Carpenter in modern times. I cannot myself agree with these extremists. I believe that the accumulated experience of mankind, and his wonderful discoveries, are of great value. I only point out that they do not constitute real progress in human nature itself, and that in the absence of any real progress these gains are external, precarious, and liable to be turned to our own destruction, as new discoveries in chemistry may easily be.

But it is possible to approach the whole question of progress from another side, and from this side the results will not be quite the same, and may be more encouraging. We have said that there can be no progress in the macrocosm, and no single purpose in a universe which has neither beginning nor end in time. But there may be an infinite number of finite purposes, some much greater and others much smaller than the span of an individual life; and within each of these some divine thought may be working itself out, bringing some life or series of lives, some nation or race or species, to that perfection which is natural to it — what the Greeks called its "nature." The Greeks saw no contradiction between this belief and the theory of cosmic cycles, and I do not think that there is any contradiction. It may be that there is an immanent teleology which is shaping the life of the human race toward some completed development which has not yet been reached. To advocate such a theory seems like going back from Darwin to Lamarck; but "vitalism," if it be a heresy, is a very vigorous and obstinate one; we can hardly dismiss it as unscientific. The possibility that such a development is going on is not disproved by the slowness of the change within the historical period. Progress in the recent millennia seems to us to have been external, precarious, and disappointing. But let this last adjective give us pause. By what standard do we pronounce it disappointing, and who gave us this standard? This disappointment has been a constant phenomenon, with a very few exceptions. What does it mean? Have those who reject the law of progress taken it into account? The philosophy of naturalism always makes the mistake of leaving human nature out. The climbing instinct of humanity, and our discontent with things as they are, are facts which have to be accounted for, no less than the stable instincts of nearly all other species. We all desire to make progress, and our ambitions are not limited to our own lives or our lifetimes. It is part of our nature to aspire and hope; even on biological grounds this instinct must be assumed to serve some function. The first Christian poet, Prudentius, quite in the spirit of Robert Browning, names hope as the distinguishing characteristic of mankind.

Nonne hominum et pecudum distantia separat una?
quod bona quadrupedum ante oculos sita sunt, ego contra spero.[1]

We must consider seriously what this instinct of hope means and implies in the scheme of things.

It is of course possible to dismiss it as a fraud. Perhaps this was the view most commonly held in antiquity. Hope was regarded as a gift of dubious value, an illusion which helps us to endure life, and a potent spur to action; but in the last resort an *ignis fatuus*. A Greek could write for his tombstone:

I've entered port. Fortune and Hope, adieu!
Make game of others, for I've done with you.

And Lord Brougham chose this epigram to adorn his villa at Cannes. So for Schopenhauer hope is the bait by which Nature gets her hook in our nose, and induces us to serve her purposes, which are not our own. This is pessimism, which, like optimism, is a mood, not a philosophy. Neither of them needs refutation, except for the adherent of the opposite mood; and these will never convince each other, for the same arguments are fatal to both. If our desires are clearly contrary to the nature of things, of which we are a part, it is our wisdom and our duty to correct our ambitions, and, like the Bostonian Margaret Fuller, to decide to "accept the universe." "Gad! she'd better," was Carlyle's comment on this declaration. The true inference from nature's law of vicarious sacrifice is not that life is a fraud, but that selfishness is unnatural. The pessimist cannot condemn the world except by a standard which he finds somewhere, if only in his own heart; in passing sentence upon it he affirms an optimism which he will not surrender to any appearances.

The ancients were not pessimists; but they distrusted hope. I will not follow those who say that they succumbed to the barbarians because they looked back instead of forward; I do not think it is true. If the Greeks and Romans had studied chemistry and metallurgy

---

[1] " Does not the distinction between man and beast lie in one fact alone? The beast seeks advantages in what is before his eyes, while I rely upon hope."

instead of art, rhetoric, and law, they might have discovered gunpowder and poison gas and kept the Germans north of the Alps. But St. Paul's deliberate verdict on pagan society, that it "had no hope," cannot be lightly set aside. No other religion, before Christianity, ever erected hope into a moral virtue. "We are saved by hope" was a new doctrine when it was pronounced. The later Neoplatonists borrowed St. Paul's triad, Faith, Hope, and Love, adding Truth as a fourth. Hopefulness may have been partly a legacy from Judaism; but it was much more a part of the intense spiritual vitality which was disseminated by the new faith. In an isolated but extremely interesting passage St. Paul extends his hope of "redemption into the glorious liberty of the children of God" to the "whole creation" generally. In the absence of any explanation or parallel passages it is difficult to say what vision of cosmic deliverance was in his mind. Students of early Christian thought must be struck by the vigor of hope in the minds of men, combined with great fluidity in the forms or molds into which it ran. After much fluctuation, it tended to harden as belief in a supramundane future, a compromise between Jewish and Platonic eschatology, since the Jews set their hopes on a terrestrial future, the Platonists on a supramundane present. Christian philosophers still inclined to the Platonic faith, while popular belief retained the apocalyptic Jewish ideas under the form of millenarianism. Religion has oscillated between these two types of belief ever since, and both have suffered considerably by being vulgarized. In times of disorder and decadence, the Platonic ideal world, materialized into a supraterrestrial physics and geography, has tended to prevail: in times of crass prosperity and intellectual confidence the Jewish dream of a kingdom of the saints on earth has been coarsened into promises of "a good time coming." At the time when we were inditing the paeans to Progress which I quoted near the beginning of my lecture, we were evolving a Deuteronomic religion for ourselves even more flattering than the combination of determinism with optimism which science was offering at the same period. We almost persuaded ourselves that the words "the meek-spirited shall possess the earth" were a prophecy of the expansion of England.

It is easy to criticize the forms which hope has assumed. But the hope which has generated them is a solid fact, and we have to recognize its indomitable tenacity and power of taking new shapes. The belief in a law of progress, which I have criticized so unmercifully, is one of these forms; and if I am not mistaken, it is nearly worn out. Disraeli in his detached way said, "The European talks of progress because by the aid of a few scientific discoveries he has established a society which has mistaken comfort for civilization." It would not be easy to sum up better the achievements of the nineteenth century, which will be always remembered as the century of accumulation and expansion. It was one of the great ages of the world; and its greatness was bound up with that very idea of progress which, in the crude forms which it usually assumed, we have seen to be an illusion. It was a strenuous, not a self-indulgent age. The profits of industry were not squandered, but turned into new capital, providing new markets and employment for more labor. The nation, as an aggregate, increased in wealth, numbers, and power every day; and public opinion approved this increase, and the sacrifices which it involved. It was a great century; there were giants in the earth in those days; I have no patience with the pygmies who gird at them. But, as its greatest and most representative poet said: "God fulfills himself in many ways, Lest one good custom should corrupt the world." The mold in which the Victorian age cast its hope is broken. There is no law of progress; and the gains of that age now seem to some of us to have been purchased too high, or even to be themselves of doubtful value. In Clough's fine poem, beginning "Hope evermore and believe, O man," a poem in which the ethics of Puritanism find their perfect expression, the poet exhorts us:

Go! say not in thine heart, And what then, were it accomplished,
Were the wild impulse allayed, what were the use and the good?

But this question, which the blind Puritan asceticism resolutely thrust on one side, has begun to press for an answer. It had begun to press for an answer before the great cataclysm, which shattered the material symbols of the cult which for a century and a half had absorbed the chief energies of mankind. Whether our widespread discontent is mainly caused, as I sometimes think, by the unnatural conditions of life in large towns, or by the decay of the ideal itself, it is not easy to say. In any case, the gods of Queen Victoria's reign are no longer worshiped. And I believe that the dissatisfaction with things as they are is caused not only by the failure of nineteenth century civilization, but partly also by its success. We no longer wish to progress on those lines if we could. Our apocalyptic dream is vanishing into thin air. It may be that the industrial revolution which began in the reign of George III has produced most of its fruits, and has had its day. We may have to look forward to such a change as is imagined by Anatole France at the end of his *Isle of the Penguins*,

when, after an orgy of revolution and destruction, we shall slide back
into the quiet rural life of the early modern period.   If so, the authors
of the revolution will have cut their own throats, for there can be no
great manufacturing towns in such a society.   The race will have
tried a great experiment, and will have rejected it as unsatisfying.
We shall have added something to our experience.   Fontenelle exclaimed, "How many foolish things we should say now, if the ancients
had not said them all before us!"   Fools are not so much afraid of
plagiarism as this Frenchman supposed; but it is true that "Eventu
rerum stolidi didicere magistro."[1]

There is much to support the belief that there is a struggle for existence among ideas, and that those tend to prevail which correspond
with the changing needs of humanity.   It does not necessarily follow
that the ideas which prevail are better morally, or even truer to the
law of nature, than those which fail.   Life is so chaotic, and development so sporadic and one-sided, that a brief and brilliant success may
carry with it the seeds of its own early ruin.   The great triumphs of
humanity have not come all at once.   Architecture reached its climax
in an age otherwise barbarous;   Roman law was perfected in a dismal
age of decline; and the nineteenth century, with its marvels of applied
science, has produced the ugliest of all civilizations.   There have been
notable flowering times of the spirit of man — Ages of Pericles,
Augustan Ages, Renaissances.   The laws which determine these
efflorescences are unknown.   They may depend on undistinguished
periods when force is being stored up.   So in individual greatness, the
wind bloweth where it listeth.   Some of our greatest may have died
unknown, "carent quia vate sacro."[2]   Emerson indeed tells us that
"One accent of the Holy Ghost The careless world has never lost."
But I should like to know how Emerson obtained this information.
The world has not always been "careless" about its inspired prophets;
it has often, as Faust remarks, burned or crucified them, before they
have delivered all their message.   The activities of the race spirit
have been quite unaccountable.   It has stumbled along blindly,
falling into every possible pitfall.

The laws of nature neither promise progress nor forbid it.   We
could do much to determine our own future; but there has been no
consistency about our aspirations, and we have frequently followed
false lights, and been disillusioned as much by success as by failure.
The well-known law that all institutions carry with them the seeds of

---

[1] Freely translated, "The stupid learn from no master but experience."
[2] "Lacking anyone to herald their fame."

their own dissolution is not so much an illustration of the law of cyclical revolution, as a proof that we have been carried to and fro by every wind of doctrine. What we need is a fixed and absolute standard of values, that we may know what we want to get and whither we want to go. It is no answer to say that all values are relative and ought to change. Some values are not relative but absolute. Spiritual progress must be within the sphere of a reality which is not itself progressing, or for which, in Milton's grand words, "progresses the dateless and irrevoluble circle of its own perfection, joining inseparable hands with joy and bliss in over-measure forever." Assuredly there must be advance in our apprehension of the ideal, which can never be fully realized because it belongs to the eternal world. We count not ourselves to have apprehended in aspiration any more than in practice. As Nicholas of Cusa says: "To be able to know ever more and more without end, this is our likeness to the eternal Wisdom. Man always desires to know better what he knows, and to love more what he loves; and the whole world is not sufficient for him, because it does not satisfy his craving for knowledge." But since our object is to enter within the realm of unchanging perfection, finite and relative progress cannot be our ultimate aim, and such progress, like everything else most worth having, must not be aimed at too directly. Our ultimate aim is to live in the knowledge and enjoyment of the absolute values, Truth, Goodness, and Beauty. If the Platonists are right, we shall shape our surroundings more effectively by this kind of idealism than by adopting the creed and the methods of secularism. I have suggested that our disappointments have been very largely due to the unworthiness of our ideals, and to the confused manner in which we have set them before our minds. The best men and women do not seem to be subject to this confusion. So far as they can make their environment, it is a society immensely in advance of anything which has been realized among mankind generally.

If any social amelioration is to be hoped for, its main characteristic will probably be simplification rather than further complexity. This, however, is not a question which can be handled at the end of a lecture.

Plato says of his ideal state that it does not much matter whether it is ever realized on earth or not. The type is laid up in Heaven, and approximations to it will be made from time to time, since all living creatures are drawn upward toward the source of their being. It does not matter very much, if he was right in believing — as we too believe

— in human immortality. And yet it does matter; for unless our communing with the eternal Ideas endows us with some creative virtue, some power which makes itself felt upon our immediate environment, it cannot be that we have made those Ideas in any sense our own. There is no alchemy by which we may get golden conduct out of leaden instincts — so Herbert Spencer told us very truly; but if our ideals are of gold, there is an alchemy which will transmute our external activities, so that our contributions to the spiritual temple may be no longer "wood, hay, and stubble," to be destroyed in the next conflagration, but precious and durable material.

For individuals, then, the path of progress is always open; but as Hesiod told us long before the Sermon on the Mount, it is a narrow path, steep and difficult, especially at first. There will never be a crowd gathered round this gate; "few there be that find it." For this reason, we must cut down our hopes for our nation, for Europe, and for humanity at large, to a very modest and humble aspiration. We have no millennium to look forward to; but neither need we fear any protracted or widespread retrogression. There will be new types of achievement which will enrich the experience of the race; and from time to time, in the long vista which science seems to promise us, there will be new flowering-times of genius and virtue, not less glorious than the Age of Sophocles or the Age of Shakespeare. They will not merely repeat the triumphs of the past, but will add new varieties to the achievements of the human mind.

Whether the human type itself is capable of further physical, intellectual, or moral improvement, we do not know. It is safe to predict that we shall go on hoping, though our recent hopes have ended in disappointment. Our lower ambitions partly succeed and partly fail, and never wholly satisfy us; of our more worthy visions for our race we may perhaps cherish the faith that no pure hope can ever wither, except that a purer may grow out of its roots.

A FREE MAN'S WORSHIP[1]

Bertrand Russell[2]

To Dr. Faustus in his study Mephistopheles told the history of the Creation, saying: "The endless praises of the choirs of angels had begun to grow wearisome; for, after all, did he not deserve their praise? Had he not given them endless joy? Would it not be more amusing to obtain undeserved praise, to be worshiped by beings whom he tortured? He smiled inwardly, and resolved that the great drama should be performed.

"For countless ages the hot nebula whirled aimlessly through space. At length it began to take shape, the central mass threw off planets, the planets cooled, boiling seas and burning mountains heaved and tossed, from black masses of cloud hot sheets of rain deluged the barely solid crust. And now the first germ of life grew in the depths of the ocean, and developed rapidly in the fructifying warmth into vast forest trees, huge ferns springing from the damp mold, sea monsters breeding, fighting, devouring, and passing away. And from the monsters, as the play unfolded itself, Man was born, with the power of thought, the knowledge of good and evil, and the cruel thirst for worship. And Man saw that all is passing in this mad, monstrous world, that all is struggling to snatch, at any cost, a few brief moments of life before Death's inexorable decree. And Man said: 'There is a hidden purpose, could we but fathom it, and the purpose is good; for we must reverence something, and in the visible world there is nothing worthy of reverence.' And Man stood aside from the struggle, resolving that God intended harmony to come out of chaos by human efforts. And when he followed the instincts which God had transmitted to him from his ancestry of beasts of prey, he called it Sin, and asked God to forgive him. But he doubted whether he could be justly forgiven, until he invented a divine Plan by which God's wrath was to have been appeased. And seeing the present was bad, he made it yet worse, that thereby the future might be better. And he gave God thanks for the strength that enabled him to forgo even the joys that were possible. And God smiled; and when he saw that

---

[1] From *Mysticism and Logic*, by Bertrand Russell. By permission of W. W. Norton & Company, publishers.

[2] For biographical note, see page 175.

Man had become perfect in renunciation and worship, he sent another
sun through the sky, which crashed into Man's sun; and all returned
again to nebula.

"'Yes,' he murmured, 'it was a good play; I will have it performed
again.'"

Such, in outline, but even more purposeless, more void of meaning,
is the world which science presents for our belief. Amid such a world,
if anywhere, our ideals henceforward must find a home. That man
is the product of causes which had no prevision of the end they were
achieving; that his origin, his growth, his hopes and fears, his loves
and his beliefs, are but the outcome of accidental collocations of atoms;
that no fire, no heroism, no intensity of thought and feeling, can preserve an individual life beyond the grave; that all the labors of the
ages, all the devotion, all the inspiration, all the noonday brightness
of human genius, are destined to extinction in the vast death of the
solar system, and that the whole temple of man's achievement must
inevitably be buried beneath the debris of a universe in ruins — all
these things, if not quite beyond dispute, are yet so nearly certain,
that no philosophy which rejects them can hope to stand. Only
within the scaffolding of these truths, only on the firm foundation of
unyielding despair, can the soul's habitation henceforth be safely
built.

How, in such an alien and inhuman world, can so powerless a creature as man preserve his aspirations untarnished? A strange mystery
it is that Nature, omnipotent but blind, in the revolutions of her
secular hurryings through the abysses of space, has brought forth at
last a child, subject still to her power, but gifted with sight, with
knowledge of good and evil, with the capacity of judging all the works
of his unthinking mother. In spite of death, the mark and seal of the
parental control, man is yet free, during his brief years, to examine, to
criticize, to know, and in imagination to create. To him alone, in the
world with which he is acquainted, this freedom belongs; and in this
lies his superiority to the resistless forces that control his outward
life.

The savage, like ourselves, feels the oppression of his impotence
before the powers of nature; but having in himself nothing that he
respects more than power, he is willing to prostrate himself before his
gods, without inquiring whether they are worthy of his worship.
Pathetic and very terrible is the long history of cruelty and torture,
of degradation and human sacrifice, endured in the hope of placating
the jealous gods: surely, the trembling believer thinks, when what is

most precious has been freely given, their lust for blood must be appeased, and more will not be required. The religion of Moloch — as such creeds may be generically called — is in essence the cringing submission of the slave, who dare not, even in his heart, allow the thought that his master deserves no adulation. Since the independence of ideals is not yet acknowledged, power may be freely worshiped, and receive an unlimited respect, despite its wanton infliction of pain.

But gradually, as morality grows bolder, the claim of the ideal world begins to be felt; and worship, if it is not to cease, must be given to gods of another kind than those created by the savage. Some, though they feel the demands of the ideal, will still consciously reject them, still urging that naked power is worthy of worship. Such is the attitude inculcated in God's answer to Job out of the whirlwind: the divine power and knowledge are paraded, but of the divine goodness there is no hint. Such also is the attitude of those who, in our own day, base their morality upon the struggle for survival, maintaining that the survivors are necessarily the fittest. But others, not content with an answer so repugnant to the moral sense, will adopt the position which we have become accustomed to regard as specially religious, maintaining that, in some hidden manner, the world of fact is really harmonious with the world of ideals. Thus man creates God, all-powerful and all-good, the mystic unity of what is and what should be.

But the world of fact, after all, is not good; and, in submitting our judgment to it, there is an element of slavishness from which our thoughts must be purged. For in all things it is well to exalt the dignity of man, by freeing him as far as possible from the tyranny of non-human power. When we have realized that power is largely bad, that man, with his knowledge of good and evil, is but a helpless atom in a world which has no such knowledge, the choice is again presented to us: Shall we worship force, or shall we worship goodness? Shall our God exist and be evil, or shall he be recognized as the creation of our own conscience?

The answer to this question is very momentous, and affects profoundly our whole morality. The worship of force, to which Carlyle and Nietzsche and the creed of militarism have accustomed us, is the result of failure to maintain our own ideals against a hostile universe: it is itself a prostrate submission to evil, a sacrifice of our best to Moloch. If strength indeed is to be respected, let us respect rather the strength of those who refuse that false "recognition of facts" which fails to recognize that facts are often bad. Let us admit that, in the world we know, there are many things that would be better otherwise, and that the ideals to which we do and must adhere are not realized in the realm of matter.   Let us preserve our respect for truth, for beauty, for the ideal of perfection which life does not permit us to attain, though none of these things meet with the approval of the unconscious universe.   If power is bad, as it seems to be, let us reject it from our hearts.   In this lies man's true freedom: in determination to worship only the God created by our own love of the good, to respect only the Heaven which inspires the insight of our best moments.   In action, in desire, we must submit perpetually to the tyranny of outside forces; but in thought, in aspiration, we are free, free from our fellow men, free from the petty planet on which our bodies impotently crawl, free even, while we live, from the tyranny of death.   Let us learn, then, that energy of faith which enables us to live constantly in the vision of the good; and let us descend, in action, into the world of fact, with that vision always before us.

When first the opposition of fact and ideal grows fully visible, a spirit of fiery revolt, of fierce hatred of the gods, seems necessary to the assertion of freedom.   To defy with Promethean constancy a hostile universe, to keep its evil always in view, always actively hated, to refuse no pain that the malice of power can invent, appears to be the duty of all who will not bow before the inevitable.   But indignation is still a bondage, for it compels our thoughts to be occupied with an evil world; and in the fierceness of desire from which rebellion springs there is a kind of self-assertion which it is necessary for the wise to overcome.   Indignation is a submission of our thoughts, but not of our desires; the Stoic freedom in which wisdom consists is found in the submission of our desires, but not of our thoughts.   From the submission of our desires springs the virtue of resignation; from the freedom of our thoughts springs the whole world of art and philosophy, and the vision of beauty by which, at last, we half reconquer the reluctant world.   But the vision of beauty is possible only to unfettered contemplation, to thoughts not weighted by the load of eager wishes; and thus freedom comes only to those who no longer ask of life that it shall yield them any of those personal goods that are subject to the mutations of time.

Although the necessity of renunciation is evidence of the existence of evil, yet Christianity, in preaching it, has shown a wisdom exceeding that of the Promethean philosophy of rebellion.   It must be admitted that, of the things we desire, some, though they prove impossible, are yet real goods; others, however, as ardently longed for, do not form part of a fully purified ideal. The belief that what must be renounced is bad, though sometimes false, is far less often false than untamed passion supposes; and the creed of religion, by providing a reason for proving that it is never false, has been the means of purifying our hopes by the discovery of many austere truths.

But there is in resignation a further good element: even real goods, when they are unattainable, ought not to be fretfully desired. To every man comes, sooner or later, the great renunciation. For the young, there is nothing unattainable; a good thing desired with the whole force of a passionate will, and yet impossible, is to them not credible. Yet, by death, by illness, by poverty, or by the voice of duty, we must learn, each one of us, that the world was not made for us, and that, however beautiful may be the things we crave, fate may nevertheless forbid them. It is the part of courage, when misfortune comes, to bear without repining the ruin of our hopes, to turn away our thoughts from vain regrets. This degree of submission to power is not only just and right: it is the very gate of wisdom.

But passive renunciation is not the whole of wisdom; for not by renunciation alone can we build a temple for the worship of our own ideals. Haunting foreshadowings of the temple appear in the realm of.imagination, in music, in architecture, in the untroubled kingdom of reason, and in the golden sunset magic of lyrics, where beauty shines and glows, remote from the touch of sorrow, remote from the fear of change, remote from the failures and disenchantments of the world of fact. In the contemplation of these things the vision of Heaven will shape itself in our hearts, giving at once a touchstone to judge the world about us, and an inspiration by which to fashion to our needs whatever is not incapable of serving as a stone in the sacred temple.

Except for those rare spirits that are born without sin, there is a cavern of darkness to be traversed before that temple can be entered. The gate of the cavern is despair, and its floor is paved with the gravestones of abandoned hopes. There self must die; there the eagerness, the greed of untamed desire must be slain, for only so can the soul be freed from the empire of fate. But out of the cavern the gate of renunciation leads again to the daylight of wisdom, by whose radiance a new insight, a new joy, a new tenderness, shine forth to gladden the pilgrim's heart.

When, without the bitterness of impotent rebellion, we have learned both to resign ourselves to the outward rule of fate and to recognize that the non-human world is unworthy of our worship, it becomes possible at last so to transform and refashion the unconscious universe, so to transmute it in the crucible of imagination, that a new image of shining gold replaces the old idol of clay. In all the multiform facts of the world — in the visual shapes of trees and mountains and clouds, in the events of the life of man, even in the very omnipotence of death — the insight of creative idealism can find the reflection of a beauty which its own thoughts first made. In this way mind asserts its subtle mastery over the thoughtless forces of nature. The more evil the material with which it deals, the more thwarting to untrained desire, the greater is its achievement in inducing the reluctant rock to yield up its hidden treasures, the prouder its victory in compelling the opposing forces to swell the pageant of its triumph. Of all the arts, tragedy is the proudest, the most triumphant; for it builds its shining citadel in the very center of the enemy's country, on the very summit of his highest mountain; from its impregnable watchtowers, his camps and arsenals, his columns and forts, are all revealed; within its walls the free life continues, while the legions of death and pain and despair, and all the servile captains of tyrant fate, afford the burghers of that dauntless city new spectacles of beauty. Happy those sacred ramparts, thrice happy the dwellers on that all-seeing eminence. Honor to those brave warriors who, through countless ages of warfare, have preserved for us the priceless heritage of liberty, and have kept undefiled by sacrilegious invaders the home of the unsubdued.

But the beauty of tragedy does but make visible a quality which, in more or less obvious shapes, is present always and everywhere in life. In the spectacle of death, in the endurance of intolerable pain, and in the irrevocableness of a vanished past, there is a sacredness, an overpowering awe, a feeling of the vastness, the depth, the inexhaustible mystery of existence, in which, as by some strange marriage of pain, the sufferer is bound to the world by bonds of sorrow. In these moments of insight, we lose all eagerness of temporary desire, all struggling and striving for petty ends, all care for the little trivial things that, to a superficial view, make up the common life of day by day; we see, surrounding the narrow raft illumined by the flickering light of human comradeship, the dark ocean on whose rolling waves we toss for a brief hour; from the great night without, a chill blast breaks in upon our refuge; all the loneliness of humanity amid hostile forces is concentrated upon the individual soul, which must struggle alone, with what of courage it can command, against the whole weight of a universe that cares nothing for its hopes and fears. Victory, in this struggle with the powers of darkness, is the true baptism into the glorious company of heroes, the true initiation into the overmastering beauty of human existence. From that awful encounter of the soul with the outer world, enunciation, wisdom, and charity are born; and with their birth a new life begins. To take into the inmost shrine of the soul the irresistible forces whose puppets we seem to be — death and change, the irrevocableness of the past, and the powerlessness of man before the blind hurry of the universe from vanity to vanity — to feel these things and know them is to conquer them.

This is the reason why the past has such magical power. The beauty of its motionless and silent pictures is like the enchanted purity of late autumn, when the leaves, though one breath would make them fall, still glow against the sky in golden glory. The past does not change or strive; like Duncan, after life's fitful fever it sleeps well; what was eager and grasping, what was petty and transitory, has faded away, the things that were beautiful and eternal shine out of it like stars in the night. Its beauty, to a soul not worthy of it, is unendurable; but to a soul which has conquered fate it is the key of religion.

The life of man, viewed outwardly, is but a small thing in comparison with the forces of nature. The slave is doomed to worship time and fate and death, because they are greater than anything he finds in himself, and because all his thoughts are of things which they devour. But, great as they are, to think of them greatly, to feel their passionless splendor, is greater still. And such thought makes us free men; we no longer bow before the inevitable in Oriental subjection, but we absorb it, and make it a part of ourselves. To abandon the struggle for private happiness, to expel all eagerness of temporary desire, to burn with passion for eternal things — this is emancipation, and this is the free man's worship. And this liberation is effected by a contemplation of fate; for fate itself is subdued by the mind which leaves nothing to be purged by the purifying fire of time.

United with his fellow men by the strongest of all ties, the tie of a common doom, the free man finds that a new vision is with him always, shedding over every daily task the light of love. The life of man is a long march through the night, surrounded by invisible foes, tortured by weariness and pain, toward a goal that few can hope to reach, and where none may tarry long. One by one, as they march, our comrades vanish from our sight, seized by the silent orders of omnipotent death. Very brief is the time in which we can help them, in which their happiness or misery is decided. Be it ours to shed sunshine on their path, to lighten their sorrows by the balm of sympathy, to give them the pure joy of a never-tiring affection, to strengthen failing courage, to instill faith in hours of despair.   Let us not weigh in grudging scales their merits and demerits, but let us think only of their need — of the sorrows, the difficulties, perhaps the blindnesses that make the misery of their lives; let us remember that they are fellow sufferers in the same darkness, actors in the same tragedy with ourselves.   And so, when their day is over, when their good and their evil have become eternal by the immortality of the past, be it ours to feel that, where they suffered, where they failed, no deed of ours was the cause; but wherever a spark of the divine fire kindled in their hearts, we were ready with encouragement, with sympathy, with brave words in which high courage glowed.

Brief and powerless is man's life; on him and all his race the slow, sure doom falls pitiless and dark.   Blind to good and evil, reckless of destruction, omnipotent matter rolls on its relentless way; for man, condemned today to lose his dearest, tomorrow himself to pass through the gate of darkness, it remains only to cherish, ere yet the blow falls, the lofty thoughts that ennoble his little day; disdaining the coward terrors of the slave of fate, to worship at the shrine that his own hands have built; undismayed by the empire of chance, to preserve a mind free from the wanton tyranny that rules his outward life; proudly defiant of the irresistible forces that tolerate, for a moment, his knowledge and his condemnation, to sustain alone, a weary but unyielding Atlas, the world that his own ideals have fashioned despite the trampling march of unconscious power.

WHAT IS THE TRUE BASIS OF MORALS?[1]

Morris R. Cohen

MORRIS R. COHEN was born in Minsk, Russia, in 1880, and was brought to the United States at the age of twelve. Reared under many hardships on the New York East Side, he found means to educate himself at the College of the City of New York and at Harvard, attracting attention by his brilliancy of mind. For a decade he taught mathematics at City College. But his primary interest lay in philosophy and political science, and since 1912 he has held the chair of philosophy in that institution. Like John Locke, he deferred the publication of any important work until he was past fifty, imposing upon himself an arduous discipline in the mastery of many fields of thought and knowledge. But in 1931 he achieved an immediate reputation by his weighty treaties on *Reason and Nature*, and in 1932 enlarged it by his volume *Law and the Social Order*.

As law and justice concern large numbers of individuals living in relatively permanent groups, it has proved feasible for courts and jurists to elaborate some more or less definite techniques to answer certain of the questions involved. This, however, is not the case with the more subtle and elusive problems of personal life. Can science be applied to the whole art of living? It is easy to see that the problems of law themselves involve assumptions as to the ultimate good of human life, and ancient Semitic jurists suggested that he who would deal with the law must meditate on life and death.

We cannot, therefore, avoid the question whether there can be a science of ethics covering the whole field of human conduct. Let us, before considering more objective difficulties inherent in the conception of a moral science, review the more important of the human obstacles in the way of adopting a scientific attitude toward the values of life.

The difficulties of social science are intensified in the realm of morals. For moral judgments are deeply rooted in our habitual emotional attitudes and in those of the community of which we are a part. It is thus most difficult to detach ourselves from the roots of our accustomed faith, to question what seems obviously the right, and to devote the necessary patience and intellectual sympathy to the understanding of opposing views that we almost instinctively abhor and despise. This is true not only of the vast majority to whom the ways of respectability are unquestionable and decisive, but also of revolutionists in morals who move in groups that are inflexibly proud of being "up to date," "emancipated," "forward-looking," "amoralist," etc. I remember as a child having great difficulty in realizing that while the dome of heaven had its highest point directly over where I was, others living far off thought that the same was true for them. A similar realization in the moral realm is much more difficult.

Another difficulty in the way of attaining true views as to morals is the fear that these views will be perverted by the unintelligent or will have a bad effect on the young. Logically it might seem that if we believe new or heterodox views of morals to be true we should teach them to our children. But it is easier to change our theoretic views than our socially approved habitual attitudes. Thus many an agnostic sends his children to an orthodox Sunday school, and many confirmed Nietzschean amoralists are shocked when they hear their heterodox morality expressed before children. Some there are who justified this on the theory of vital lies, viz. that the young and the uneducated are not prepared for the truth and that we must keep them in check by convenient lies. Not many years ago a mother had no compunction about saying to her child: Don't tell lies or the bogey-man will get you! But older children are still taught the falsehood that the virtuous will be (financially) prosperous and that the wicked will always be punished either by society or by their own guilty conscience. This disregard of truth in moral education is as old as Plato. Nevertheless I suspect that it prevails largely among those who have not attained full confidence in the truth of their own views. There are many stages between entertaining a heterodox view as to morals, and actually living according to it. And the extent to which a man lives up to a new moral insight depends on his personal situation and courage rather than on the truth of these insights.

Closely connected with the foregoing obstacle is the irrationality of moral theory resulting from the effort to give justifying reasons for the institutions which happen to exist. It is obvious that if the maxim *What is, is right* were true there would be nothing wrong in the world — not even with those who are always complaining of the evil in it — and all distinction between right and wrong would disappear as inapplicable or meaningless. Yet the fact that an institution exists gives arguments in its behalf an irrationally persuasive advantage over arguments against its value. We may illustrate this by a parable. Suppose that some magician came to us and offered us a magic carriage having great convenience, but demanded of us in return the sacrifice of thirty thousand lives every year. Most of us would be morally horrified by such an offer. Yet when the automobile is actually with us we can invent many ingenious arguments against the proposal to abolish it. Certainly an undue amount of moral philosophy is just an exercise in apologetics for what happen to be the prevailing moral institutions. Where the conclusion seems excellent we are not critical as to the supporting arguments.

Against the foregoing difficulties the moral philosopher must arm himself with the ethical neutrality of the scientist. Only by studying propositions about morals with the same detachment as propositions about electrons, caring more for the rules of the scientific game than for any particular result, can he hope to fulfill his function as a builder of sound ethical theory or science. How, indeed, can he promote the good life unless he first finds out what is the meaning of the good life and what are the conditions for attaining it?

In practice, the impetus to free scientific reflection on morality is greatly stimulated by familiarity with, and imaginatively living into, diverse moral systems. By taking note of moral variations, we may free ourselves from the absolute unreflective certainty which comes of not being able to imagine any possibility other than the one to which we are accustomed.

THE ILLUSIONS OF MORALITY

If with the ideal of scientific detachment in mind we approach the task of developing a rational ethics, we find two conflicting ways before us — the way of those who believe in absolute principles and the way of those who think that the needs of life are cruelly crushed by such principles. To explain the persistence of the two parties it is safe to assume that each has some part of the truth in its possession; but the fact of conflict is also presumptive evidence that each party is in the grip of some illusion which prevents it from seeing the whole truth.

1. THE ILLUSIONS OF ABSOLUTISM

Moral rules are most often viewed as absolute. It does not occur to most people that there *can* be any genuine doubt about them. Men generally are surprised and painfully shocked at the suggestion that we need to search for new moral truth or to revise the old. For the most part the absoluteness of these accepted rules is supported by some authority regarded as beyond question, e.g. by some priest, sacred book, or prevailing respectability. When, however, these or other authorities are in fact questioned, any attempted justification must involve an appeal to some "scheme of things entire," of which these moral teachers form a consequence. Otherwise the moral teacher is in the position of the poor pedagogue who, when asked to explain or justify some questionable statement, stamps his foot and shouts, "I tell you so."

The sayings of great moral and religious teachers frequently find a magically responsive echo in our conscience. Yet our deepest moral feelings may seem to others no better than the superstitious taboos of primitive peoples appear to us. Indeed the morality of unreflective people does consist very largely of a series of taboos; you must not do so and so, and it is not proper to ask too insistently, "Why not?" Take one whom no one will lightly accuse of being unenlightened or irrational, to wit, Plato. The moral aversions which affect him most deeply are eating forbidden food (that is set aside for the gods) and incest. Yet not only the former but also the latter aversion depends upon accidental or external traditions. To Biblical heroes like Abraham and David, there seems nothing wrong in anyone's marrying his sister by the same father, provided there are different mothers; and among the Egyptians and others, a marriage between brothers and sisters was considered rather honorable, at least in royalty. Many have shared Hamlet's desperate horror of a man's marrying his brother's widow. Yet that was under certain conditions a pious command of the older Mosaic law.

When we are told that all civilized people are agreed about the immorality of murder, lying, theft, and adultery, we may well raise the doubt whether the agreement (of those who agree with us and are therefore called civilized) is not largely a linguistic phenomenon. We agree to use certain terms in a reprobative sense, but really differ as to what acts are to be so designated. There is certainly great diversity of opinion as to what acts we shall condemn as murder, lying, theft, and adultery.

Consider, for example, the commandment, *Thou shalt not kill*.

If this be viewed absolutely, should it not apply to the killing of animals as well as of humans? Anyone who has played with a dog (moralists are not reputed to be playful), or watched the gambols of lambs, knows how shocking can be the thought of killing them. The conventional argument that animals have not any reason like man need not be taken seriously. Are insane or idiotic men more rational than intelligent dogs? There seems to be no moral objection to killing a domestic pet to save it from suffering; why not justify euthanasia to relieve people of agonizing tortures?

Again, if the rule against killing be regarded as absolute, shall we not say that morally every heroic warrior is a murderer? If *Thou shalt not kill* be an absolute rule, how can it cease to be so because someone orders us to do it? "God will send the bill to you." Can we escape the difficulty by distinguishing between justifiable and unjustifiable wars, and say, for instance, that wars in defense of one's country justify the taking of life? Any such qualification obviously breaks down the absoluteness of our rule in making it depend on the somewhat shadowy distinction between offensive and defensive measures.

Furthermore, does the absoluteness of the rule, *Thou shalt not kill*, apply only to direct or short-range killing? We know perfectly well that unless more safety appliances are introduced into mines, railroads, and factories, tens of thousands of workers will surely be killed. Are those who have the power to make the changes and do not do so guilty of murder? If in economic competition I take away somebody's bread (to increase my own comfort or power), and he dies of undernourishment or of a disease to which undernourishment makes him liable, am I not killing him? If by monopolizing our fertile lands we confine the Chinese to a territory insufficient to keep them above the starvation line, are we or are we not guilty of killing them?

To common sense and to many moralists nothing seems morally so self-evident as the sacredness of human life. Yet there seems good reason to question the rule that life should always and everywhere be increased and prolonged, and that to restrict birth or hasten death is always and everywhere evil.

The sacredness of life is sometimes supported on supernatural grounds, viz. that since it comes from on high we have no right to meddle with it. We must not lay human hands on the gates of life and death. But this cannot possibly be carried out consistently. Disease comes from the same source as life and death; yet few now follow those moralists who denounced efforts to cure diseases sent by God to punish sinners. Does any moralist condemn the martyr who throws away his life to testify to his faith? We characterize as base those who purchase life at the expense of freedom, honor, or convictions. Not life as a biologic fact, but the good life (involving some coördinated plan or pattern) is the object of enlightened endeavor.

We arrive at the same result by considering the false naturalistic conception of self-preservation as a law of nature that leads everyone to seek always to preserve his own existence. In the chapter on biology we have had some indication of how misleading this phraseology is. But in the field of morals it is even less worthy of respect. Men generally have a positive preference or urge to live and want to postpone the pain of death. But they also want certain things for which they willingly shorten their lives by hard work, risks, etc. Of mere living existence we might soon get weary if it did not offer opportunity and hope of fulfilling some of the heart's particular desires.

These doubts do not diminish the horror of murder in the cases where we feel that horror. But they are sufficient to suggest that the absoluteness of our rule is generally saved only by refusing to think of many of its possible applications to life. The rule against murder does express a prevailing moral attitude in a number of clear though not explicitly qualified cases. It claims extension to cases similar in principle. In such extensions, however, we have to introduce so many sorts of qualifications that the rule soon ceases to be categoric and becomes rather dialectical: to the extent that any action involves the destruction of life it is to be condemned — but other principles may supply countervailing considerations. As any definite course of action involves many elements, actual judgment upon it must depend upon some estimate of the relative weights of diverse conflicting moral rules that can be applied to it. What we call a situation involving a conflict of duties is really a case in which different results would follow if we attended to one or another of rival dialectical rules.

A great and noteworthy effort was made by Kant to prove all moral rules absolutely obligatory and to derive them all from one principle, the categoric imperative to so act that the maxim of our acts can be made a principle of universal legislation. To one who asks, "Why should I accept this categorical imperative as the rule of my conduct?" Kant offers no reason except to offer this principle as a formula for the unconditionally obligatory character of all moral rules, such as the absolute prohibition against lying. But why should I regard the latter as absolute? Why may not a lie to save a human being hovering between life and death be justified? There is no logical force at all in the claim that there is some absolute contradiction or inconsistency in telling a lie and wishing to be believed. Nor is there any force in the argument that lying is morally bad because it cannot be made universal. The familiar argument, "If everybody did so and so . . ." applies just as well to baking bread, building houses, and the like. It is just as impossible for everybody to tell lies all the time as to bake bread all the time or to build houses all the time.

Empirically, of course, it is true that lying is subversive of that mutual confidence that is necessary to all social coöperation. And this justifies a general condemnation of lying — but not an absolute prohibition.

One of the consequences of the absolutistic conception of moral rules is the Stoic and Kantian contention that since the moral law demands that sin be punished, it is immoral to pardon any sinner. This appears in the contention that if we know the world is to be destroyed tomorrow we must see to it that the last murderer is executed, else we shall all perish with the blood of his victim on our heads. It shows itself in the orthodox theologic conception of a hell for most of God's creatures; for if God forgave sinners (without an expiating blood sacrifice on His own part which these sinners must accept) He would transgress the moral law. It seems that we have here a glorified development of the primitive idea that honor demands the avenging of insults, and the greater the dignity of the one offended, the greater must be the vengeance.

A scientific ethics certainly cannot accept absolute moral rules of the character indicated by the foregoing examples.

2. The Illusions of Antinomianism

The perception of the variations and inconsistencies of our moral judgments has, since the days of the Greeks, led people to entertain the view that morality is nothing but a matter of opinion or convention. There are many forms of this attitude, of which we may consider: (1) moral anarchism, (2) dogmatic immoralism, and (3) antirational empiricism.

(1) *Moral Anarchism.* By *moral anarchism* I mean the view which denies that there are any moral rules at all, and insists that our moral judgments are mere opinions, having no support in the nature of things. In fact, however, no one of us believes that his own moral opinions are as bad or as absurd as those of others which fill us with repugnance or resentment. If, on the other hand, it is not true that every opinion is as good or as bad as any other, there must be some principle indicating the direction of preferable or more adequate judgment. We may not be always clearly aware of the principle involved in our actual judgments of approval or disapproval, and we may distrust abstract formulations of them, preferring to let tact or the feeling of the situation control us. But we cannot deny that such tact or intuition may involve serious error, and that such error might be corrected by fuller knowledge and reflection.

Skepticism is a natural reaction to the absurd claims of moral absolutism. It is justified in insisting that there is an arbitrary (in the sense of volitional) and indemonstrable assumption in every moral system, since we cannot have an *ought* in our conclusion unless there is an *ought* in one of our initial assumptions or premises. But from this it by no means follows that moral systems contain nothing but assumptions or that all assumptions are equally true or equally false.

(2) *Amoralism.* By the term *amoralism* I mean the attempt to deny validity to the distinctively moral point of view: to wit, that from which we judge that certain human acts ought or ought not to be. It is difficult to formulate without seeming self-contradiction a direct denial of any distinction between such seemingly different considerations as what *is* and what *ought to be.* However, there are many indirect denials of the validity of the moral point of view — by defining it in terms of the non-moral. The classical example of it is expressed by Plato's Thrasymachus when he defines justice as the interest of the stronger. More recently this has been expressed in the formula: Justice is the command of the sovereign, the interest of the dominant class, etc. If this means that we, the weaker or the subjects, *ought* to obey the expressed command of one who has the power to compel obedience, we have here a moral judgment, but of the kind that can rightly be called slave morality. For it is slavish to *respect* brute power, however prudent it may be to obey it, and the free intelligent man refuses to let mere external power confuse his vision of what is *better*.

Those who define justice or *right* exclusively in terms of some sort of *might* generally, however, wish to insist that judgments of right are in fact determined by certain external forces. But that is not a question of the *meaning* of the moral judgment but rather of its *genesis.* It is doubtless true that modern ruling classes do have some power directly or indirectly to mold the moral judgments of the community. But it would be folly to deny the fact that men can and do distinguish between that which they see prevailing about them and that which they think ought to prevail. The facts of moral indignation or the persistent and bitter cry for justice are too vehement to be easily ignored.

It is, of course, true that our moral aspiration can never be realized in this world unless we find an effective machinery for it, and this involves recognition and acceptance of the necessary concatenation between available causes and desired effects. It is thus in a sense true that only by submitting to nature can we control it. But this does not deny the distinction between what is and what is desirable.

Hegel and others have argued that individual judgments as to morality or what *ought* to be must be subordinated to the actually existing social institutions, on the ground that the latter embody a fuller and less capricious world reason. But while it is prudent for any individual to reflect and inform himself more fully before he condemns an existing social institution as immoral, an iniquity cannot cease to be judged an iniquity simply because it exists embodied in the Prussian or in any other state.

It is a significant indication of how far morality is popularly identified with conformity to the established order that Nietzsche calls himself and is called by others an immoralist. True, he attacks the moral value of Christianity, humility, and charity; but he himself is preaching a moral or categorical imperative: Act to obtain power regardless of ease and comfort. Despite his aversion for the Prussian state, this is a hard militaristic morality. Nietzsche's illusion that power is an absolute good is indicative of the uncritical character of his thought. It is rather obvious that power can be exercised only in society. If isolated in a cave or on a mountain man has no power over his fellows and is more dependent on external nature. And a study of social power shows that rulership always involves a heavy sacrifice of freedom on the part of the ruler. Warriors and rulers have to give up their enjoyment and their life in fighting for the protection of their subjects; and in time of peace they may be ruled by priests who are distinguished by slavish obedience to the rules of their orders. In general, rulers are successful to the extent that they recognize the superior power of mass inertia, custom, religion, etc., and do not put themselves in opposition to such forces. The expert ruler must practice the art of flattery and cajolery or else be, like an Oriental despot, a slave to customary law and to the constant fear of losing his life. Stated more broadly, we may say that Nietzsche does not take into account the essentially social nature of man, i.e. his incompleteness by himself and his dependence on his fellow man. The love of power is one element of our nature, but the love of ease and comfort makes most of us shun the arduous labor, responsibility, and risks that are inevitable in the exercise of power. On the whole, government or rulership is possible because the vast majority find it easier to obey and thus be free from responsibility in all except some particular phase of life. The father may rule his children, who rule the mother, who rules the father. The scholar or artist may (and wisely so) care more for his learning or art than for the political governorship of his commonwealth.

There seem to be always moral protestants, who think that by merely breaking the traditional moral rules they will attain freedom and happiness. Alas for the irony of fate! In order to stand strong in each other's esteem and to make up for the disapproval of the multitude, these moral non-conformists must develop a code of their own. The Bohemians of the Quartier Latin or Greenwich Village have their own taboos no less rigid than those of the Philistines.

(3) *Anti-rational Empiricism.* Anti-rational empiricism in ethics generally sets up the claims of what is called "the concrete facts of the situation" against all abstract rules. It refuses to subordinate the actual needs of life to preconceived tags. It rejects all Procrustean rules into which all men must fit themselves regardless of their diverse characters and changing circumstances. All this is a natural reaction to the illusion of absolutism. But it is equally illusory to suppose that a humanly desirable life can be lived without rules to regulate it or without the recognition of invariant laws or relations on which these rules must be based. Changing conditions are not inconsistent with the possibility and serviceableness of a rule of conduct, any more than physical changes preclude the possibility of an invariant law of constant elements or proportions. Against the claim that there can be no moral rules because no two situations are absolutely alike, we may urge that there could be no sort of intelligence as to life, no tact, intuition, or empirical wisdom of any sort, if there were nothing about any situation applicable to another. No two physical situations are ever absolutely identical. Yet this does not preclude the possibility of abstract physical laws that give us control over nature undreamed of by other means. In action as in science, not all that exists is relevant; and neither the fullness of life nor the fullness of knowledge can be attained without scientific organization which ignores or eliminates the irrelevant. What is chaos but a universe in which there is no order or law ruling out certain possibilities? The raving maniac's mind, in which a piece of bread can become a burning volcano, or the ceiling a herd of elephants, points toward, though it falls short of, the absolute chaos in which all things are possible and anything may become anything else.

But if we cannot accept either absolutism or antinomianism, whither shall we turn?

Our previous analyses in the light of the principle of polarity of the issues between absolutism and empiricistic relativism provide a vantage point from which to see the truth at the basis of both contentions. Concretely every issue of life involves a choice. The absolutist is right in insisting that every such choice logically involves a principle of decision, and the empiricist is right in insisting on the primacy of the feeling or perception of the demands in the actual case before us. If it is possible for us to be mistaken in our moral judgments, there must be some ground for the distinction between the true and the false in this as in other fields. Even if we deny that principles are psychologically primary sources of moral truth and view them as only the formulas which give us abstract characteristics of our actual judgments in moral affairs, the errors of the latter can be corrected only by considering our judgments in similar cases, and this means cases alike in principle. Principles express the essence or form of a whole class of individual cases. And they enable us to correct the individual judgment precisely because the recognition of what is essential in many cases helps us to distinguish the relevant from the irrelevant in any one case.

The moral rules whose absolutistic claims we have rejected are useful generalizations of human experience, like the cruder generalizations of popular physics, e.g. that all bodies fall. The existence of exceptions to such generalizations proves that we must either refine their statement so that the exceptions will be included in the rule (just as the law of gravitation accounts for some bodies not falling) or else formulate our principles dialectically, as what would logically prevail if other principles did not offer countervailing considerations.

The imperfection of our generalizations makes the relativist underestimate their importance or reject them outright, while the absolutist falls into the logical error of confusing generalizations of experience subject to exception with truly universal or necessary propositions. We must, therefore, accept empiricism as to the content of moral rules without abandoning logical absolutism in our scientific procedure.

THE MORALIST IN AN UNBELIEVING WORLD[1]

Walter Lippmann[2]

I. THE DECLARATION OF IDEALS

Of all the bewilderments of the present age none is greater than that of the conscientious and candid moralist himself. The very name of moralist seems to have become a term of disparagement and to suggest a somewhat pretentious and a somewhat stupid, perhaps even a somewhat hypocritical, meddler in other men's lives. In the minds of very many in the modern generation moralists are set down as persons who, in the words of Dean Inge, fancy themselves attracted by God when they are really repelled by man.

The disesteem into which moralists have fallen is an historical accident. It so happens that those who administered the affairs of the established churches have, by and large, failed utterly to comprehend how deep and how inexorable was the dissolution of the ancestral order. They imagined either that this change in human affairs was a kind of temporary corruption, or that, like the eighty propositions listed in the Syllabus of Pope Piux IX, it could be regarded as due to "errors" of the human mind. There were, of course, churchmen who knew better, but on the whole those who prevailed in the great ecclesiastical establishments could not believe that the skepticism of mind and the freedom of action which modern men exercise were due to inexorable historic causes. They declined to acknowledge that modern freedom was not merely a willful iconoclasm, but the liquidation of an older order of human life.

Because they could not comprehend the magnitude of the revolution in which they were involved, they set themselves the task of impeding its progress by chastising the rebels and refuting their rationalizations. This was described as a vindication of morals. The effect was to associate morality with the vindication of the habits and dispositions of those who were most thoroughly out of sympathy with the genuine need of modern men.

The difficulties of the new age were much more urgent than those which the orthodox moralists were concerned with. The moralists

---

[1] From *A Preface to Morals*, by Walter Lippmann. By permission of The Macmillan Company, publishers.

[2] For biographical note, see page 73.

436

insisted that conduct must conform to the established code; what really worried men was how to adjust their conduct to the novel circumstances which confronted them. When they discovered that those who professed to be moralists were continuing to deny that the novelty of modern things had any bearing upon human conduct, and that morality was a word signifying a return to usages which it was impossible to follow, even if it were desirable, there was a kind of tacit agreement to let the moralists be moral and to find other language in which to describe the difference between good and bad, right and wrong. Mr. Joad is not unrepresentative of this reaction into contempt when he speaks of "the dowagers, the aunts, the old maids, the parsons, the town councillors, the clerks, the members of vigilance committees and purity leagues, all those who are themselves too old to enjoy sex, too unattractive to obtain what they would wish to enjoy, or too respectable to prefer enjoyment to respectability." Thus for many the name of moralist came to be very nearly synonymous with antipathy to the genius and the vitality of the modern age.

But it is idle for moralists to ascribe the decline of their influence to the perversity of their fellow creatures. The phenomenon is worldwide. Moreover, it is most intensely present at precisely those points where the effect of science and the machine technology have been most thoroughly manifested. The moralists are not confronted with a scandal but with history. They have to come to terms with a process in the life of mankind which is working upon the inner springs of being, and altering inevitably the premises of conduct. They need not suppose that their pews are empty and that their exhortations are ignored because modern men are really as willful as the manners of the younger generation lead them to conclude. Much of what appears to be a tough self-sufficiency is protective: it is a brittle crust covering depths of uncertainty. If the advice of moralists is ignored, it is not because this generation is too proud to listen, or unaware that it has anything to learn. On the contrary, there is such curiosity and questioning as never before engaged so large a number of men. The audience to which a genuine moralist might speak is there. If it is inattentive when the orthodox moralist speaks, it is because he seems to speak irrelevantly.

The trouble with the moralists is in the moralists themselves: they have failed to understand their times. They think they are dealing with a generation that refuses to believe in ancient authority. They are, in fact, dealing with a generation that cannot believe in it. They think they are confronted with men who have an irrational preference for immorality, whereas the men and women about them are ridden by doubts because they do not know what they prefer, nor why. The moralists fancy that they are standing upon the rock of eternal truth, surveying the chaos about them. They are greatly mistaken. Nothing in the modern world is more chaotic — not its politics, its business, or its sexual relations — than the minds of orthodox moralists who suppose that the problem of morals is somehow to find a way of reinforcing the sanctions which are dissolving. How can we, they say in effect, find formulas and rhetoric potent enough to make men behave? How can we revive in them that love and fear of God, that sense of the creature's dependence upon his creator, that obedience to the commands of a heavenly king, which once gave force and effect to the moral code?

They have misconceived the moral problem, and therefore they misconceive the function of the moralist. An authoritative code of morals has force and effect when it expresses the settled customs of a stable society: the pharisee can impose upon the minority only such conventions as the majority find appropriate and necessary. But when customs are unsettled, as they are in the modern world, by continual change in the circumstances of life, the pharisee is helpless. He cannot command with authority because his commands no longer imply the usages of the community: they express the prejudices of the moralist rather than the practices of men. When that happens, it is presumptuous to issue moral commandments, for in fact nobody has authority to command. It is useless to command when nobody has the disposition to obey. It is futile when nobody really knows exactly what to command. In such societies, wherever they have appeared among civilized men, the moralist has ceased to be an administrator of usages and has had to become an interpreter of human needs. For ages when custom is unsettled are necessarily ages of prophecy. The moralist cannot teach what is revealed; he must reveal what can be taught. He has to seek insight rather than to preach.

The disesteem into which moralists have fallen is due at bottom to their failure to see that in an age like this one the function of the moralist is not to exhort men to be good but to elucidate what the good is. The problem of sanctions is secondary. For sanctions cannot be artificially constructed: they are a product of agreement and usage. Where no agreement exists, where no usages are established, where ideals are not clarified, and where conventions are not followed comfortably by the mass of men, there are not, and cannot be, sanctions.

It is possible to command where most men are already obedient. But even the greatest general cannot discipline a whole army at once. It is only when the greater part of his army is with him that he can quell the mutiny of a faction.

The acids of modernity are dissolving the usages and the sanctions to which men once habitually conformed. It is therefore impossible for the moralist to command. He can only persuade. To persuade he must show that the course of conduct he advocates is not an arbitrary pattern to which vitality must submit, but that which vitality itself would choose if it were clearly understood. He must be able to show that goodness is victorious vitality and badness defeated vitality; that sin is the denial and virtue the fulfillment of the promise inherent in the purposes of men. The good, said the Greek moralist, is "that which all things aim at"; we may perhaps take this to mean that the good is that which men would wish to do if they knew what they were doing.

If the morality of the naïve hedonist who blindly seeks the gratification of his instincts is irrational in that he trusts immature desire, disregards intelligence, and damns the consequences, the morality of the pharisee is no less irrational. It reduces itself to the wholly arbitrary proposition that the best life for man would be some other kind of life than that which satisfies his nature. The true function of the moralist in an age when usage is unsettled is what Aristotle, who lived in such an age, described it to be: to promote good conduct by discovering and explaining the mark at which things aim. The moralist is irrelevant, if not meddlesome and dangerous, unless in his teaching he strives to give a true account, imaginatively conceived, of that which experience would show is desirable among the choices that are possible and necessary. If he is to be listened to, and if he is to deserve a hearing among his fellows, he must set himself this task which is so much humbler than to command and so much more difficult than to exhort: he must seek to anticipate and to supplement the insight of his fellow men into the problems of their adjustment to reality. He must find ways to make clear and ordered and expressive those concerns which are latent but overlaid and confused by their preoccupations and misunderstandings.

Could he do that with perfect lucidity he would not need to summon the police nor evoke the fear of Hell: Hell would be what it really is, and what in all inspired moralities it has always been understood to be, the very quality of evil itself. Nor would he find himself in the absurd predicament of seeming to argue that virtue is highly desirable but intensely unpleasant. It would not be necessary to praise goodness, for it would be that which men most ardently desired. Were the nature of good and evil really made plain by moralists, their teachings would appear to the modern listener not like exhortations from without, but as Keats said of poetry: "a wording of his own highest thoughts and . . . almost a remembrance."

2. THE CHOICE OF A WAY

What modernity requires of the moralist is that he should see with an innocent eye how men must reform their wants in a world which is not concerned to make them happy. The problem, as I have tried to show, is not a new one. It has been faced and solved by the masters of wisdom. What is new is the scale on which the problem is presented — in that so many must face it now — and its radical character in that the organic bonds of custom and belief are dissolving. There ensues a continual necessity of adjusting their lives to complex novelty. In such a world simple customs are unsuitable and authoritative commandments incredible. No prescription can now be written which men can naïvely and obediently follow. They have, therefore, to reëducate their wants by an understanding of their own relation to a world which is unconcerned with their hopes and fears. From the moralists they can get only hypotheses — distillations of experience carefully examined — probabilities, that is to say, upon which they may begin to act, but which they themselves must constantly correct by their own insight.

It is difficult for the orthodox moralists to believe that amid the ruins of authority men will ever learn to do this. They can point to the urban crowds and ask whether anyone supposes that such persons are capable of ordering their lives by so subtle an instrument as the human understanding. They can insist with unanswerable force that this is absurd: that the great mass of men must be guided by rules and moved by the symbols of hope and fear. And they can ask what there is in the conception of the moralist as I have outlined it which takes the character of the populace into account.

What I take into account first of all is the fact, which it seems to me is indisputable, that for the modern populace the old rules are becoming progressively unsuitable and the old symbols of hope and fear progressively unreal. I ascribe that to the inherent character of the modern ways of living. I conclude from this that if the populace must be led, if it must have easily comprehended rules, if it must have common symbols of hope and fear, the question is: How are its leaders to be developed, rules to be worked out, symbols created? The ultimate question is not how the populace is to be ruled, but what the teachers are to think. That is the question that has to be settled first: it is the preface to everything else.

For while moralists are at sixes and sevens in their own souls, not much can be done about morality, however high or low may be our estimates of the popular intelligence and character. If it were necessary to assume that ideals are relevant only if they are universally attainable, it would be a waste of time to discuss them. For it is evident enough that many, if not most men, must fail to comprehend what modern morality implies. But to recognize this is not to prophesy that the world is doomed unless men perform the miracle of reverting to their ancestral tradition. This is not the first time in the history of mankind when a revolution in the affairs of men has produced chaos in the human spirit. The world can endure a good deal of chaos. It always has. The ideal inherent in any age is never realized completely: Greece, which we like to idealize as an oasis of rationality, was only in some respects Hellenic; the Ages of Faith were only somewhat Christian. The processes of nature and of society go on somehow none the less. Men are born and they live and die with some happiness and some sorrow though they neither envisage wholly nor nearly approximate the ideals they pursue.

But if civilization is to be coherent and confident it must be *known* in that civilization what its ideals are. There must exist in the form of clearly available ideas an understanding of what the fulfillment of the promise of that civilization might mean, an imaginative conception of the good at which it might and, if it is to flourish, at which it must aim. That knowledge, though no one has it perfectly, and though relatively few have it at all, is the principle of all order and certainty in the life of that people. By it they can clarify the practical conduct of life in some measure, and add immeasurably to its dignity.

To elucidate the ideals with which the modern world is pregnant is the original business of the moralist. In so far as he succeeds in disentangling that which men think they believe from that which it is appropriate for them to believe, he is opening his mind to a true vision of the good life. The vision itself we can discern only faintly, for we have as yet only the occasional and fragmentary testimony of sages and saints and heroes, dim anticipations here and there, a most imperfect science of human behavior, and our own obscure endeavor to make explicit and rational the stresses of the modern world within

our own souls.   But we can begin to see, I think, that the evidence
converges upon the theory that what the sages have prophesied as
high religion, what psychologists delineate as matured personality,
and the disinterestedness which the Great Society requires for its
practical fulfillment, are all of a piece, and are the basic elements of a
modern morality.   I think the truth lies in this theory.

If it does, experience will enrich and refine it, and what is now an
abstract principle arrived at by intuition and dialectic will engender
ideas that marshal, illuminate, and anticipate the subtle and intricate
detail of our actual experience.   That at least can be our belief.
In the meantime, the modern moralist cannot expect soon to construct
a systematic and harmonious moral edifice like that which St. Thomas
Aquinas and Dante constructed to house the aspirations of the mediaeval world.   He is in a much earlier phase in the evolution of his
world, in the phase of inquiry and prophecy rather than of ordering
and harmonizing, and he is under the necessity of remaining close
to the elements of experience in order to apprehend them freshly.
He cannot, therefore, permit the old symbols of faith and the old
formulations of right and wrong to prejudice his insight.   In so far
as they contain wisdom for him or can become its vehicles, he will
return to them.   But he cannot return to them with honor or with
sincerity until he has himself gone and drunk deeply at the sources of
experience from which they originated.

Only when he has done that can he again in any honest sense take
possession of the wisdom which he inherits.   It requires wisdom to
understand wisdom;   the music is nothing if the audience is deaf.
In the great moral systems and the great religions of mankind are
embedded the record of how men have dealt with destiny, and only
the thoughtless will argue that that record is obsolete and insignificant.
But it is overlaid with much that is obsolete and for that reason it is
undeciphered and inexpressive.   The wisdom it contains has to be
discovered anew before the old symbols will yield up their meaning.
That is the only way in which Bacon's aphorism can be fulfilled, that
"a little philosophy inclineth man's mind to atheism, but depth in
philosophy bringeth men's minds about to religion."   The depth in
philosophy which can bring them about is a much deeper and more
poignant experience than complacent churchmen suppose.

It can be no mere settling back into that from which men in the
ardor of their youth escaped.   This man and that may settle back, to
be sure;   he may cease to inquire though his questions are unanswered.
But such conformity is sterile, and due to mere weariness of mind and

body. The inquiry goes on because it has to go on, and while the vitality of our race is unimpaired, there will be men who feel with Mr. Whitehead that "to acquiesce in discrepancy is destructive of candor and of moral cleanliness," and that "it belongs to the self-respect of intellect to pursue every tangle of thought to its final unravelment." The crisis in the religious loyalties of mankind cannot be resolved by weariness and good nature, or by the invention of little intellectual devices for straightening out the dilemmas of biology and Genesis, history and the Gospels, with which so many churchmen busy themselves. Beneath these little conflicts there is a real dilemma which modern men cannot successfully evade. "Where is the way where light dwelleth?" They are compelled to choose consciously, clearly, and with full realization of what the choice implies, between religion as a system of cosmic government and religion as insight into a cleansed and matured personality: between God conceived as the master of that fate, creator, providence, and king, and God conceived as the highest good at which they might aim. For God is the supreme symbol in which man expresses his destiny, and if that symbol is confused, his life is confused.

Men have not, hitherto, had to make that choice, for the historic churches have sheltered both kinds of religious experience, and the same mysteries have been the symbols of both. That confusion is no longer benign because men are no longer unconscious of it. They are aware that it is a confusion, and they are stultified by it. Because the popular religion of supernatural governments is undermined, the symbols of religion do not provide clear channels for religious experience. They are choked with the debris of dead notions in which men are unable to believe and unwilling to disbelieve. The result is a frustration in the inner life which will persist as long as the leaders of thought speak of God in more senses than one, and thus render all faith invalid, insincere, and faltering.

3. THE RELIGION OF THE SPIRIT

The choice is at last a personal one. The decision is rendered not by argument but by feeling. Those who believe that their salvation lies in obedience to, and communion with, the King of Creation can know how whole-hearted their faith is by the confidence of their own hearts. If they are at peace, they need inquire no further. There are, however, those who do not find a principle of order in the belief that they are related to a supernatural power. They cannot be argued into the ancient belief, for it has been dissolved by the circumstances of their lives. They are deeply perplexed. They have learned that the absence of belief is vacancy; they know, from disillusionment and anxiety, that there is no freedom in mere freedom. They must find, then, some other principle which will give coherence and direction to their lives.

If the argument in these pages is sound, they need not look for and, in fact, cannot hope for some new and unexpected revelation. Since they are unable to find a principle of order in the authority of a will outside themselves, there is no place they can find it except in an ideal of the human personality. But they do not have to invent such an ideal out of hand. The ideal way of life for men who must make their own terms with experience and find their own happiness has been stated again and again. It is that only the regenerate, the disinterested, the mature, can make use of freedom. This is the central insight of the teachers of wisdom. We can see now, I think, that it is also the mark at which the modern study of human nature points. We can see, too, that it is the pattern of successful conduct in the most advanced phases of the development of modern civilization. The ideal, then, is an old one, but its confirmation and its practical pertinence are new. The world is able at last to take seriously what its greatest teachers have said. And since all things need a name, if they are to be talked about, devotion to this ideal may properly be called by the name which these greatest teachers gave it; it may be called the religion of the spirit. At the heart of it is the knowledge that the goal of human effort is to be able, in the words I have so often quoted from Confucius, to follow what the heart desires without transgressing what is right.

In an age when custom is dissolved and authority is broken, the religion of the spirit is not merely a possible way of life. In principle it is the only way which transcends the difficulties. It alone is perfectly neutral about the constitution of the universe, in that it has no expectation that the universe will justify naïve desire. Therefore, the progress of science cannot upset it. Its indifference to what the facts may be is indeed the very spirit of scientific inquiry. A religion which rests upon particular conclusions in astronomy, biology, and history may be fatally injured by the discovery of new truths. But the religion of the spirit does not depend upon creeds and cosmologies; it has no vested interest in any particular truth. It is concerned not with the organization of matter, but with the quality of human desire. It alone can endure the variety and complexity of things, for the religion of the spirit has no thesis to defend. It seeks excellence wherever it may appear, and finds it in anything which is inwardly understood; its motive is not acquisition but sympathy. Whatever is completely understood with sympathy for its own logic and purposes ceases to be external and stubborn and is wholly tamed. To understand is not only to pardon, but in the end to love. There is no itch in the religion of the spirit to make men good by bearing down upon them with righteousness and making them conform to a pattern. Its social principle is to live and let live. It has the only tolerable code of manners for a society in which men and women have become freely-moving individuals, no longer held in the grooves of custom by their ancestral ways. It is the only disposition of the soul which meets the moral difficulties of an anarchical age, for its principle is to civilize the passions, not by regulating them imperiously, but by transforming them with a mature understanding of their place in an adult environment. It is the only possible hygiene of the soul for men whose selves have become disjointed by the loss of their central certainties, because it counsels them to draw the sting of possessiveness out of their passions, and thus by removing anxiety to render them harmonious and serene.

The philosophy of the spirit is an almost exact reversal of the worldling's philosophy. The ordinary man believes that he will be blessed if he is virtuous, and therefore virtue seems to him a price he pays now for a blessedness he will some day enjoy. While he is waiting for his reward, therefore, virtue seems to him drab, arbitrary, and meaningless. For the reward is deferred, and there is really no instant proof that virtue really leads to the happiness he has been promised. Because the reward is deferred, it too becomes vague and dubious, for that which we never experience, we cannot truly understand. In the realm of the spirit, blessedness is not deferred: there is no future which is more auspicious than the present; there are no compensations later for evils now. Evil is to be overcome now and happiness is to be achieved now, for the Kingdom of God is within you. The life of the spirit is not a commercial transaction in which the profit has to be anticipated; it is a kind of experience which is inherently profitable.

And so the mature man would take the world as it comes, and within himself remain quite unperturbed. When he acted, he would know that he was only testing an hypothesis, and if he failed, he would know that he had made a mistake. He would be quite prepared for the discovery that he might make mistakes, for his intelligence would be disentangled from his hopes. The failure of his experiment could not, therefore, involve the failure of his life. For the aspect of life which implicated his soul would be his understanding of life, and, to the understanding, defeat is no less interesting than victory. It would be no effort, therefore, for him to be tolerant, and no annoyance to be skeptical. He would face pain with fortitude, for he would have put it away from the inner chambers of his soul. Fear would not haunt him, for he would be without compulsion to seize anything and without anxiety as to its fate. He would be strong, not with the strength of hard resolves, but because he was free of that tension which vain expectations beget. Would his life be uninteresting because he was disinterested? He would have the whole universe, rather than the prison of his own hopes and fears, for his habitation, and in imagination all possible forms of being. How could that be dull unless he brought the dullness with him? He might dwell with all beauty and all knowledge, and they are inexhaustible. Would he, then, dream idle dreams? Only if he chose to. For he might go quite simply about the business of the world, a good deal more effectively perhaps than the worldling, in that he did not place an absolute value upon it, and deceive himself. Would he be hopeful? Not if to be hopeful was to expect the world to submit rather soon to his vanity. Would he be hopeless? Hope is an expectation of favors to come, and he would take his delights here and now. Since nothing gnawed at his vitals, neither doubt nor ambition, nor frustration, nor fear, he would move easily through life. And so whether he saw the thing as comedy, or high tragedy, or plain farce, he would affirm that it is what it is, and that the wise man can enjoy it.

VII

EDUCATION IN ITS MODERN ASPECTS

NUMEROUS and striking as changes in the machinery of education in the United States have been of recent years, they are hardly more remarkable than the changes in its method and spirit. The enormous expansion of the high schools, of which we possessed some 16,000 by 1925; the equally striking physical development of our universities, which were compelled to furnish mass education and which began to boast of registrations ranging from 10,000 to 30,000; the reorganization of the school system in many cities to include two years of "junior college," thus enabling universities to dispense with part of the general training and give more time to professional work — these mechanical changes are familiar. But along with them have come attempts to break sharply with the older traditions of education. In high schools and colleges alike new efforts are being made to reduce the attention to the old disciplines of mathematics, Greek, and Latin. The demand for more attention to the natural sciences is an old one; it is now being supplemented by the demand for fuller teaching of the social sciences. That this is a world-wide change is evident to anyone who studies the newer educational movements in Germany, Russia, and Great Britain. Higher education has meanwhile shown an increasing experimentalism of temper. The English tutorial system, first adopted — or rather adapted — at Princeton, and since widely used; the abolition of formal classes at Rollins College in favor of supervised reading and informal conferences; the experiment of the University of Chicago in dispensing with strict residential requirements for the degree, and granting it to certain students for achievement as ascertained by a general examination; the experiment at Antioch College in alternating study with industrial or professional work outside — these are the most striking. In a society that is more and more thoroughly industrialized, and in a fast-shrinking, ever more specialized world, the old humanistic training seems to many inadequate. The essays here given deal with the fundamental principles of education rather than with the controversial issues of the day. Some principles, at least, must be agreed upon before the issues can be settled.

IN DEFENSE OF THE STUDY OF GREEK[1]

James Russell Lowell

JAMES RUSSELL LOWELL was born in 1819 and died in 1891 in the same house, "Elmwood," in Cambridge, Massachusetts. The son of a Unitarian minister, he read widely from early boyhood, was given a good classical education at Harvard, and graduated in 1840 from the Harvard Law School. He made his literary debut in 1841 with a small volume of poetry, *A Year's Life;* his reputation in 1848 with three important books at once, *A Fable for Critics*, the first volume of *The Biglow Papers*, and *The Vision of Sir Launfal*. Thenceforward until his death he was one of the foremost figures in American literature. From 1857 to 1861 he was editor of the *Atlantic Monthly*. Later he became a teacher at Harvard College, and during this period wrote much more prose than poetry, taking a high — but by no means the highest — rank as a critic. In 1877 he was made Minister to Spain, and in 1880 Minister to England, a post he retained until 1885. Of the large body of his work, it may be predicted that only the *Biglow Papers*, a few of the best essays, and a handful of poems (the best his *Harvard Commemoration Ode*) will long survive; but with these every literate American should be acquainted.

One is sometimes tempted to think that all learning is as repulsive to ingenuous youth as the multiplication table to Scott's little friend Marjorie Fleming, though this is due in great part to mechanical methods of teaching. "I am now going to tell you," she writes, "the horrible and wretched plaege that my multiplication table gives me; you can't conceive it; the most Devilish thing is 8 times 8 and 7 times 7; it is what nature itself can't endure." I know that I am approaching treacherous ashes which cover burning coals, but I must on. Is not Greek, nay, even Latin, yet more unendurable than poor Marjorie's task? How many boys have not sympathized with Heine in hating the Romans because they invented Latin Grammar? And they were quite right, for we begin the study of languages at the wrong end, at the end which nature does not offer us, and are thoroughly tired of them before we arrive at them, if you will pardon the bull. But is that any reason for not studying them in the right way? I am familiar with the arguments for making the study of Greek especially a matter of choice or chance. I admit their plausibility and the honesty of those who urge them. I should be willing also to admit that the study of the ancient languages without the hope or the prospect of going on to what they contain would be useful only as a

[1] "Address on the Two Hundred and Fiftieth Anniversary of Harvard University, November 8, 1886." From *Democracy, and Other Addresses*, 1887.

form of intellectual gymnastics.   Even so they would be as serviceable as the higher mathematics to most of us.   But I think that a wise teacher should adapt his tasks to the highest, and not the lowest, capacities of the taught.   For those lower also they would not be wholly without profit.   When there is a tedious sermon, says George Herbert, "God takes a text and teacheth patience," not the least pregnant of lessons.   One of the arguments against the compulsory study of Greek — namely, that it is wiser to give our time to modern languages and modern history than to dead languages and ancient history — involves, I think, a verbal fallacy.   Only those languages can properly be called dead in which nothing living has been written. If the classic languages are dead, they yet speak to us, and with a clearer voice than that of any living tongue.

> Graiis ingenium, Graiis dedit ore rotundo
> Musa loqui, praeter laudem nullius avaris.[1]

If their language is dead, yet the literature it enshrines is rammed with life as perhaps no other writing, except Shakespeare's, ever was or will be.   It is as contemporary with today as with the ears it first enraptured, for it appeals not to the man of then or now, but to the entire round of human nature itself.   Men are ephemeral or evanescent, but whatever page the authentic soul of man has touched with her immortalizing finger, no matter how long ago, is still young and fair as it was to the world's gray fathers.   Oblivion looks in the face of the Grecian Muse only to forget her errand.   Plato and Aristotle are not names but things.   On a chart that should represent the firm earth and wavering oceans of the human mind, they would be marked as mountain-ranges, forever modifying the temperature, the currents, and the atmosphere of thought, astronomical stations whence the movements of the lamps of heaven might best be observed and predicted.   Even for the mastering of our own tongue, there is no expedient so fruitful as translation out of another; how much more when that other is a language at once so precise and so flexible as the Greek! Greek literature is also the most fruitful comment on our own.   Coleridge has told us with what profit he was made to study Shakespeare and Milton in conjunction with the Greek dramatists. It is no sentimental argument for this study that the most justly balanced, the most serene, and the most fecundating minds since the revival of learning have been steeped in and saturated with Greek

---

[1] "The genius of the Greeks lies in this: the Muse has granted them the power to speak with eloquence, coveting nothing but praise."

literature.   We know not whither other studies will lead us, especially
if dissociated from this; we do know to what summits, far above our
lower region of turmoil, this has led, and what the many-sided outlook
thence.   Will such studies make anachronisms of us, unfit us for the
duties and the business of today?   I can recall no writer more truly
modern than Montaigne, who was almost more at home in Athens and
Rome than in Paris.   Yet he was a thrifty manager of his estate and
a most competent mayor of Bordeaux.   I remember passing once in
London where demolition for a new thoroughfare was going on.
Many houses left standing in the rear of those cleared away bore
signs with the inscription "Ancient Lights."   This was the protest
of their owners against being built out by the new improvements
from such glimpse of heaven as their fathers had, without adequate
equivalent.   I laid the moral to heart.

ON VARIOUS KINDS OF THINKING[1]

James Harvey Robinson

JAMES HARVEY ROBINSON, born at Bloomington, Illinois, in 1863, was educated at Harvard and Freiburg. He had been a teacher of history for thirty years, nearly all of that period in Columbia University, and was well known for a number of standard textbooks in European history, when in 1921 he gained a new reputation by *The Mind in the Making*.

This slender volume, which surprisingly became a best seller, is at once much more and much less than a history of human thought. It is rather a history of freedom of thought, and an exposition of the vital importance of that freedom to the progress, happiness, and nobility of mankind. He showed how late, how slowly, how painfully the free and creative intelligence of mankind developed; how powerfully it has been warred upon by ecclesiastical and political tyrannies; how devotedly certain leaders, Bacon, Descartes, Milton, Locke, Diderot, John Stuart Mill, have labored to emancipate the modern mind from its various forms of bondage. Into his essay, which runs only to 150 pages, is compressed the results of a lifetime of reading and thinking; and as he says, many of its pages could be expanded into a volume. Dr. Robinson, stating that he addressed a generation that was in the midst of a great revolutionary era, pleaded with it to realize that it must free itself from old taboos, outworn assumptions, and the conservatism of selfish interests, or pay a heavy penalty. His work is stimulating as a pungent review of one phase of the whole past history of mankind; it is still more stimulating as a challenge to skepticism, boldness, and experimentalism. H. G. Wells, who shared his conviction that in facing the successive crises of recent times human intelligence "has hitherto been painfully timid and blindly credulous of and confident in the working assumptions of the past," and that it should display a new venturesomeness, hailed the essay as "a cardinal work." For himself, he wrote, "I think James Harvey Robinson is going to be almost as important as was Huxley in my adolescence and William James in later years." Conservatives will take a hostile view of the book, but its arguments they will not find it easy to answer.

Dr. Robinson has also written *The Humanizing of Knowledge* (1923) and *The Ordeal of Civilization* (1926).

We do not think enough about thinking, and much of our confusion is the result of current illusions in regard to it. Let us forget for the moment any impressions we may have derived from the philosophers, and see what seems to happen in ourselves. The first thing that we notice is that our thought moves with such incredible rapidity that it is almost impossible to arrest any specimen of it long enough to have a look at it. When we are offered a penny for our thoughts we always

---

[1] From *The Mind in the Making*, by James Harvey Robinson. Reprinted by permission of Harper & Brothers, publishers.

find that we have recently had so many things in mind that we can easily make a selection which will not compromise us too nakedly. On inspection we shall find that even if we are not downright ashamed of a great part of our spontaneous thinking it is far too intimate, personal, ignoble, or trivial to permit us to reveal more than a small part of it. I believe this must be true of everyone. We do not, of course, know what goes on in other people's heads. They tell us very little and we tell them very little. The spigot of speech, rarely fully opened, could never emit more than driblets of the ever renewed hogshead of thought — *noch grösser wie's Heidelberger Fass.*[1] We find it hard to believe that other people's thoughts are as silly as our own, but they probably are.

We all appear to ourselves to be thinking all the time during our waking hours, and most of us are aware that we go on thinking while we are asleep, even more foolishly than when awake. When uninterrupted by some practical issue we are engaged in what is now known as a *reverie*. This is our spontaneous and favorite kind of thinking. We allow our ideas to take their own course, and this course is determined by our hopes and fears, our spontaneous desires, their fulfillment or frustration; by our likes and dislikes, our loves and hates and resentments. There is nothing else anything like so interesting to ourselves as ourselves. All thought that is not more or less laboriously controlled and directed will inevitably circle about the beloved Ego. It is amusing and pathetic to observe this tendency in ourselves and in others. We learn politely and generously to overlook this truth, but if we dare to think of it, it blazes forth like the noontide sun.

The reverie or "free association of ideas" has of late become the subject of scientific research. While investigators are not yet agreed on the results, or at least on the proper interpretation to be given to them, there can be no doubt that our reveries form the chief index to our fundamental character. They are a reflection of our nature as modified by often hidden and forgotten experiences. We need not go into the matter further here, for it is only necessary to observe that the reverie is at all times a potent and in many cases an omnipotent rival to every other kind of thinking. It doubtless influences all our speculations in its persistent tendency to self-magnification and self-justification, which are its chief preoccupations, but it is the last thing to make directly or indirectly for honest increase of knowl-

[1] "Even larger than the Heidelberg tun " (famous for its size).

edge.[1] Philosophers usually talk as if such thinking did not exist or were in some way negligible. This is what makes their speculations so unreal and often worthless.

The reverie, as any of us can see for himself, is frequently broken and interrupted by the necessity of a second kind of thinking. We have to make practical decisions. Shall we write a letter or no? Shall we take the subway or a bus? Shall we have dinner at seven or half past? Shall we buy U. S. Rubber or a Liberty Bond? Decisions are easily distinguishable from the free flow of the reverie. Sometimes they demand a good deal of careful pondering and the recollection of pertinent facts; often, however, they are made impulsively. They are a more difficult and laborious thing than the reverie, and we resent having to "make up our mind" when we are tired or absorbed in a congenial reverie. Weighing a decision, it should be noted, does not necessarily add anything to our knowledge, although we may, of course, seek further information before making it.

RATIONALIZING

A third kind of thinking is stimulated when anyone questions our belief and opinions. We sometimes find ourselves changing our minds without any resistance or heavy emotion, but if we are told that we are wrong we resent the imputation and harden our hearts. We are incredibly heedless in the formation of our beliefs, but find ourselves filled with an illicit passion for them when anyone proposes to rob us of their companionship. It is obviously not the ideas themselves that are dear to us, but our self-esteem, which is threatened. We are by nature stubbornly pledged to defend our own from attack, whether it be our person, our family, our property, or our opinion. A United States Senator once remarked to a friend of mine that God Almighty could not make him change his mind on our Latin America

[1] The poet-clergyman, John Donne, who lived in the time of James I, has given a beautifully honest picture of the doings of a saint's mind: "I throw myself down in my chamber and call in and invite God and His angels thither, and when they are there I neglect God and His angels for the noise of a fly, for the rattling of a coach, for the whining of a door. I talk on in the same posture of praying, eyes lifted up, knees bowed down, as though I prayed to God, and if God or His angels should ask me when I thought last of God in that prayer I cannot tell. Sometimes I find that I had forgot what I was about, but when I began to forget it I cannot tell. A memory of yesterday's pleasures, a fear of tomorrow's dangers, a straw under my knee, a noise in mine ear, a light in mine eye, an anything, a nothing, a fancy, a chimera in my brain troubles me in my prayer." — Quoted by ROBERT LYND, *The Art of Letters*, pp. 46–47.

policy. We may surrender, but rarely confess ourselves vanquished. In the intellectual world, at least, peace is without victory.

Few of us take the pains to study the origin of our cherished convictions; indeed, we have a natural repugnance to so doing. We like to continue to believe what we have been accustomed to accept as true, and the resentment aroused when doubt is cast upon any of our assumptions leads us to seek every manner of excuse for clinging to them. *The result is that most of our so-called reasoning consists in finding arguments for going on believing as we already do.*

I remember years ago attending a public dinner to which the Governor of the state was bidden. The chairman explained that His Excellency could not be present for certain "good" reasons; what the "real" reasons were the presiding officer said he would leave us to conjecture. This distinction between "good" and "real" reasons is one of the most clarifying and essential in the whole realm of thought. We can readily give what seem to us "good" reasons for being a Catholic or a Mason, a Republican or a Democrat, an adherent or opponent of the League of Nations. But the "real" reasons are usually on quite a different plane. Of course the importance of this distinction is popularly, if somewhat obscurely, recognized. The Baptist missionary is ready enough to see that the Buddhist is not such because his doctrines would bear careful inspection, but because he happened to be born in a Buddhist family in Tokio. But it would be treason to his faith to acknowledge that his own partiality for certain doctrines is due to the fact that his mother was a member of the First Baptist Church of Oak Ridge. A savage can give all sorts of reasons for his belief that it is dangerous to step on a man's shadow, and a newspaper editor can advance plenty of arguments against the Bolsheviki. But neither of them may realize why he happens to be defending his particular opinion.

The "real" reasons for our beliefs are concealed from ourselves as well as from others. As we grow up we simply adopt the ideas presented to us in regard to such matters as religion, family relations, property, business, our country, and the state. We unconsciously absorb them from our environment. They are persistently whispered in our ear by the group in which we happen to live. Moreover, as Mr. Trotter has pointed out, these judgments, being the product of suggestion and not of reasoning, have the quality of perfect obviousness, so that to question them

. . . is to the believer to carry skepticism to an insane degree, and will be met by contempt, disapproval, or condemnation, according to the nature of the belief in question. When, therefore, we find ourselves entertaining an opinion about the basis of which there is a quality of feeling which tells us that to inquire into it would be absurd, obviously unnecessary, unprofitable, undesirable, bad form, or wicked, we may know that that opinion is a nonrational one, and probably, therefore, founded upon inadequate evidence.[1]

Opinions, on the other hand, which are the result of experience or of honest reasoning do not have this quality of "primary certitude." I remember when as a youth I heard a group of business men discussing the question of the immortality of the soul, I was outraged by the sentiment of doubt expressed by one of the party. As I look back now I see that I had at the time no interest in the matter, and certainly no least argument to urge in favor of the belief in which I had been reared. But neither my personal indifference to the issue, nor the fact that I had previously given it no attention, served to prevent an angry resentment when I heard *my* ideas questioned.

This spontaneous and loyal support of our preconceptions — this process of finding "good" reasons to justify our routine beliefs — is known to modern psychologists as "rationalizing" — clearly only a new name for a very ancient thing. Our "good" reasons ordinarily have no value in promoting honest enlightenment, because, no matter how solemnly they may be marshaled, they are at bottom the result of personal preference or prejudice, and not of an honest desire to seek or accept new knowledge.

In our reveries we are frequently engaged in self-justification, for we cannot bear to think ourselves wrong, and yet have constant illustrations of our weaknesses and mistakes. So we spend much time finding fault with circumstances and the conduct of others, and shifting on to them with great ingenuity the onus of our own failures and disappointments. *Rationalizing is the self-exculpation which occurs when we feel ourselves, or our group, accused of misapprehension or error.*

The little word *my* is the most important one in all human affairs, and properly to reckon with it is the beginning of wisdom. It has the same force whether it is *my* dinner, *my* dog, and *my* house, or *my* faith, *my* country, and *my* God. We not only resent the imputation that our watch is wrong, or our car shabby, but that our conception of the canals of Mars, of the pronunciation of "Epictetus," of the medicinal value of salicine, or the date of Sargon I, are subject to revision.

Philosophers, scholars, and men of science exhibit a common sen-

[1] *Instincts of the Herd*, p. 44.

sitiveness in all decisions in which their *amour propre* is involved. Thousands of argumentative works have been written to vent a grudge. However stately their reasoning, it may be nothing but rationalizing, stimulated by the most commonplace of all motives. A history of philosophy and theology could be written in terms of grouches, wounded pride, and aversions, and it would be far more instructive than the usual treatments of these themes. Sometimes, under Providence, the lowly impulse of resentment leads to great achievements. Milton wrote his treatise on divorce as a result of his troubles with his seventeen-year old wife, and when he was accused of being the leading spirit in a new sect, the Divorcers, he wrote his noble *Areopagitica* to prove his right to say what he thought fit, and incidentally to establish the advantage of a free press in the promotion of truth.

All mankind, high and low, thinks in all the ways which have been described. The reverie goes on all the time not only in the mind of the mill hand and the Broadway flapper, but equally in weighty judges and godly bishops. It has gone on in all the philosophers, scientists, poets, and theologians that have ever lived. Aristotle's most abstruse speculations were doubtless tempered by highly irrelevant reflections. He is reported to have had very thin legs and small eyes, for which he doubtless had to find excuses, and he was wont to indulge in very conspicuous dress and rings and was accustomed to arrange his hair carefully.[1] Diogenes the Cynic exhibited the impudence of a touchy soul. His tub was his distinction. Tennyson in beginning his "Maud" could not forget his chagrin over losing his patrimony years before as the result of an unhappy investment in the Patent Decorative Carving Company. These facts are not recalled here as a gratuitous disparagement of the truly great, but to insure a full realization of the tremendous competition which all really exacting thought has to face, even in the minds of the most highly endowed mortals.

And now the astonishing and perturbing suspicion emerges that perhaps almost all that had passed for social science, political economy, politics, and ethics in the past may be brushed aside by future generations as mainly rationalizing. John Dewey has already reached this conclusion in regard to philosophy.[2] Veblen[3] and other writers have revealed the various unperceived presuppositions of the tradi-

[1] Diogenes Lærtius, Book V.
[2] *Reconstruction in Philosophy.*
[3] *The Place of Science in Modern Civilization.*

tional political economy, and now comes an Italian sociologist, Vilfredo Pareto, who, in his huge treatise on general sociology, devotes hundreds of pages to substantiating a similar thesis affecting all the social sciences.[1] This conclusion may be ranked by students of a hundred years hence as one of the several great discoveries of our age. It is by no means fully worked out, and it is so opposed to nature that it will be very slowly accepted by the great mass of those who consider themselves thoughtful. As an historical student I am personally fully reconciled to this newer view. Indeed, it seems to me inevitable that just as the various sciences of nature were, before the opening of the seventeenth century, largely masses of rationalizations to suit the religious sentiments of the period, so the social sciences have continued even to our own day to be rationalizations of uncritically accepted beliefs and customs.

It will become apparent as we proceed that the fact that an idea is ancient and that it has been widely received is no argument in its favor, but should immediately suggest the necessity of carefully testing it as a probable instance of rationalization.

HOW CREATIVE THOUGHT TRANSFORMS THE WORLD

This brings us to another kind of thought which can fairly easily be distinguished from the three kinds described above. It has not the usual qualities of the reverie, for it does not hover about our personal complacencies and humiliations. It is not made up of the homely decisions forced upon us by everyday needs, when we review our little stock of existing information, consult our conventional preferences and obligations, and make a choice of action. It is not the defense of our own cherished beliefs and prejudices just because they are our own — mere plausible excuses for remaining of the same mind. On the contrary, it is that peculiar species of thought which leads us to *change* our mind.

It is this kind of thought that has raised man from his pristine, subsavage ignorance and squalor to the degree of knowledge and comfort which he now possesses. On his capacity to continue and greatly extend this kind of thinking depends his chance of groping his way

---

[1] *Traité de Sociologie Générale, passim.* The author's term *derivations* seems to be his precise way of expressing what we have called the "good" reasons, and his *residus* correspond to the "real" reasons. He well says, *"L'homme éprouve le besoin de raisonner, et en outre d'étendre un voile sur ses instincts et sur ses sentiments"* — hence, rationalization. (P. 788.) His aim is to reduce sociology to the "real" reasons. (P. 791.)

out of the plight in which the most highly civilized peoples of the world now find themselves. In the past this type of thinking has been called reason. But so many misapprehensions have grown up around the word that some of us have become very suspicious of it. I suggest, therefore, that we substitute a recent name and speak of "creative thought" rather than of reason. *For this kind of meditation begets knowledge, and knowledge is really creative inasmuch as it makes things look different from what they seemed before and may indeed work for their reconstruction.*

In certain moods some of us realize that we are observing things or making reflections with a seeming disregard of our personal preoccupations. We are not preening or defending ourselves; we are not faced by the necessity of any practical decision, nor are we apologizing for believing this or that. We are just wondering and looking and mayhap seeing what we never perceived before.

Curiosity is as clear and definite as any of our urges. We wonder what is in a sealed telegram or in a letter in which someone else is absorbed, or what is being said in the telephone booth or in low conversation. This inquisitiveness is vastly stimulated by jealousy, suspicion, or any hint that we ourselves are directly or indirectly involved. But there appears to be a fair amount of personal interest in other people's affairs even when they do not concern us except as a mystery to be unraveled or a tale to be told. The reports of a divorce suit will have "news value" for many weeks. They constitute a story, like a novel or play or moving picture. This is not an example of pure curiosity, however, since we readily identify ourselves with others, and their joys and despair then become our own.

We also take note of, or "observe," as Sherlock Holmes says, things which have nothing to do with our personal interests and make no personal appeal either direct or by way of sympathy. This is what Veblen so well calls "idle curiosity." And it is usually idle enough. Some of us when we face the line of people opposite us in a subway train impulsively consider them in detail and engage in rapid inferences and form theories in regard to them. On entering a room there are those who will perceive at a glance the degree of preciousness of the rugs, the character of the pictures, and the personality revealed by the books. But there are many, it would seem, who are so absorbed in their personal reverie or in some definite purpose that they have no bright-eyed energy for idle curiosity. The tendency to miscellaneous observation we come by honestly enough, for we note it in many of our animal relatives.

Veblen, however, uses the term "idle curiosity" somewhat ironically, as is his wont. It is idle only to those who fail to realize that
it may be a very rare and indispensable thing from which almost all
distinguished human achievement proceeds, since it may lead to
systematic examination and seeking for things hitherto undiscovered.
For research is but diligent search which enjoys the high flavor of
primitive hunting. Occasionally and fitfully idle curiosity thus leads
to creative thought, which alters and broadens our own views and
aspirations and may in turn, under highly favorable circumstances,
affect the views and lives of others, even for generations to follow.
An example or two will make this unique human process clear.

Galileo was a thoughtful youth and doubtless carried on a rich and
varied reverie. He had artistic ability and might have turned out
to be a musician or painter. When he had dwelt among the monks
at Vallombrosa he had been tempted to lead the life of a religious.
As a boy he busied himself with toy machines and he inherited a
fondness for mathematics. All these facts are of record. We may
safely assume also that, along with many other subjects of contemplation, the Pisan maidens found a vivid place in his thoughts.

One day when seventeen years old he wandered into the cathedral
of his native town. In the midst of his reverie he looked up at the
lamps hanging by long chains from the high ceiling of the church.
Then something very difficult to explain occurred. He found himself no longer thinking of the building, worshipers, or the services;
of his artistic or religious interests; of his reluctance to become a
physician as his father wished. He forgot the question of a career
and even the *graziosissime donne*. As he watched the swinging lamps
he was suddenly wondering if mayhap their oscillations, whether long
or short, did not occupy the same time. Then he tested this hypothesis by counting his pulse, for that was the only timepiece he had with
him.

This observation, however remarkable in itself, was not enough to
produce a really creative thought. Others may have noticed the
same thing and yet nothing came of it. Most of our observations
have no assignable results. Galileo may have seen that the warts
on a peasant's face formed a perfect isosceles triangle, or he may have
noticed with boyish glee that just as the officiating priest was uttering
the solemn words, *ecce agnus Dei*, a fly lit on the end of his nose. To
be really creative, ideas have to be worked up and then "put over,"
so that they become a part of man's social heritage. The highly accurate pendulum clock was one of the later results of Galileo's dis-

covery. He himself was led to reconsider and successfully to refute the old notions of falling bodies. It remained for Newton to prove that the moon was falling, and presumably all the heavenly bodies. This quite upset all the consecrated views of the heavens as managed by angelic engineers. The universality of the laws of gravitation stimulated the attempt to seek other and equally important natural laws and cast grave doubts on the miracles in which mankind had hitherto believed. In short, those who dared to include in their thought the discoveries of Galileo and his successors found themselves in a new earth surrounded by new heavens.

On the 28th of October, 1831, three hundred and fifty years after Galileo had noticed the isochronous vibrations of the lamps, creative thought and its currency had so far increased that Faraday was wondering what would happen if he mounted a disk of copper between the poles of a horseshoe magnet. As the disk revolved an electric current was produced. This would doubtless have seemed the idlest kind of experiment to the staunch business men of the time, who, it happened, were just then denouncing the child labor bills in their anxiety to avail themselves to the full of the results of earlier idle curiosity. But should the dynamos and motors which have come into being as the outcome of Faraday's experiment be stopped this evening, the business man of today, agitated over labor troubles, might, as he trudged home past lines of "dead" cars, through dark streets to an unlighted house, engage in a little creative thought of his own and perceive that he and his laborers would have no modern factories and mines to quarrel about had it not been for the strange practical effects of the idle curiosity of scientists, inventors, and engineers.

The examples of creative intelligence given above belong to the realm of modern scientific achievement, which furnishes the most striking instances of the effects of scrupulous, objective thinking. But there are, of course, other great realms in which the recording and embodiment of acute observation and insight have wrought themselves into the higher life of man. The great poets and dramatists and our modern storytellers have found themselves engaged in productive reveries, noting and artistically presenting their discoveries for the delight and instruction of those who have the ability to appreciate them.

The process by which a fresh and original poem or drama comes into being is doubtless analogous to that which originates and elaborates so-called scientific discoveries; but there is clearly a temperamental difference. The genesis and advance of painting, sculpture, and music offer still other problems. We really as yet know shockingly little about these matters, and indeed very few people have the least curiosity about them.[1] Nevertheless, creative intelligence in its various forms and activities is what makes man. Were it not for its slow, painful, and constantly discouraged operations through the ages man would be no more than a species of primate living on seeds, fruit, roots, and uncooked flesh, and wandering naked through the woods and over the plains like a chimpanzee.

The origin and progress and future promotion of civilization are ill-understood and misconceived. These should be made the chief theme of education, but much hard work is necessary before we can reconstruct our ideas of man and his capacities and free ourselves from innumerable persistent misapprehensions. There have been obstructionists in all times, not merely the lethargic masses, but the moralists, the rationalizing theologians, and most of the philosophers, all busily if unconsciously engaged in ratifying existing ignorance and mistakes and discouraging creative thought. Naturally, those who reassure us seem worthy of honor and respect. Equally naturally those who puzzle us with disturbing criticisms and invite us to change our ways are objects of suspicion and readily discredited. Our personal discontent does not ordinarily extend to any critical questioning of the general situation in which we find ourselves. In every age the prevailing conditions of civilization have appeared quite natural and inevitable to those who grew up in them. The cow asks no questions as to how it happens to have a dry stall and a supply of hay. The kitten laps its warm milk from a china saucer, without knowing anything about porcelain; the dog nestles in the corner of a divan with no sense of obligation to the inventors of upholstery and the manufacturers of down pillows. So we humans accept our breakfasts, our trains and telephones and orchestras and movies, our national Constitution, or moral code and standards of manners, with the simplicity and innocence of a pet rabbit. We have absolutely inexhaustible capacities for appropriating what others do for us with no thought of a "thank you." We do not feel called upon to make any least contribution to the merry game ourselves. Indeed, we are usually quite unaware that a game is being played at all.

---

[1] Recently a reëxamination of creative thought has begun as a result of new knowledge which discredits many of the notions formerly held about "reason." See, for example, *Creative Intelligence*, by a group of American philosophic thinkers; John Dewey, *Essays in Experimental Logic* (both pretty hard books); and Veblen, *The Place of Science in Modern Civilization*. Easier than these and very stimulating are Dewey, *Reconstruction in Philosophy*, and Woodworth, *Dynamic Psychology*.

We have now examined the various classes of thinking which we can readily observe in ourselves and which we have plenty of reasons to believe go on, and always have been going on, in our fellow men. We can sometimes get quite pure and sparkling examples of all four kinds, but commonly they are so confused and intermingled in our reverie as not to be readily distinguishable. The reverie is a reflection of our longings, exultations, and complacencies, our fears, suspicions, and disappointments. We are chiefly engaged in struggling to maintain our self-respect and in asserting that supremacy which we all crave and which seems to us our natural prerogative. It is not strange, but rather quite inevitable, that our beliefs about what is true and false, good and bad, right and wrong, should be mixed up with the reverie and be influenced by the same considerations which determine its character and course. We resent criticisms of our views exactly as we do of anything else connected with ourselves. Our notions of life and its ideals seem to us to be *our own* and as such necessarily true and right, to be defended at all costs.

We very rarely consider, however, the process by which we gained our convictions. If we did so, we could hardly fail to see that there was usually little ground for our confidence in them. Here and there, in this department of knowledge or that, some one of us might make a fair claim to have taken some trouble to get correct ideas of, let us say, the situation in Russia, the sources of our food supply, the origin of the Constitution, the revision of the tariff, the policy of the Holy Roman Apostolic Church, modern business organization, trade unions, birth control, socialism, the League of Nations, the excess profits tax, preparedness, advertising in its social bearings; but only a very exceptional person would be entitled to opinions on all of even these few matters. And yet most of us have opinions on all these, and on many other questions of equal importance, of which we may know even less. We feel compelled, as self-respecting persons, to take sides when they come up for discussion. We even surprise ourselves by our omniscience. Without taking thought we see in a flash that it is most righteous and expedient to discourage birth control by legislative enactment, or that one who decries intervention in Mexico is clearly wrong, or that big advertising is essential to big business and that big business is the pride of the land. As godlike beings why should we not rejoice in our omniscience?

It is clear, in any case, that our convictions on important matters are not the result of knowledge or critical thought, nor, it may be added, are they often dictated by supposed self-interest. Most of them are *pure prejudices* in the proper sense of that word. We do not form them ourselves. They are the whisperings of "the voice of the herd." We have in the last analysis no responsibility for them and need assume none. They are not really our own ideas, but those of others no more well-informed or inspired than ourselves, who have got them in the same careless and humiliating manner as we. It should be our pride to revise our ideas and not to adhere to what passes for respectable opinion, for such opinion can frequently be shown to be not respectable at all. We should, in view of the considerations that have been mentioned, resent our supine credulity. As an English writer has remarked:

"If we feared the entertaining of an unverifiable opinion with the warmth with which we fear using the wrong implement at the dinner table, if the thought of holding a prejudice disgusted us as does a foul disease, then the dangers of man's suggestibility would be turned into advantages."[1]

The purpose of this essay is to set forth briefly the way in which the notions of the herd have been accumulated. This seems to me the best, easiest, and least invidious educational device for cultivating a proper distrust for the older notions on which we still continue to rely.

The "real" reasons, which explain how it is we happen to hold a particular belief, are chiefly historical. Our most important opinions — those, for example, having to do with traditional, religious, and moral convictions, property rights, patriotism, national honor, the state, and indeed all the assumed foundations of society — are, as I have already suggested, rarely the result of reasoned consideration, but of unthinking absorption from the social environment in which we live. Consequently, they have about them a quality of "elemental certitude," and we especially resent doubt or criticism cast upon them. So long, however, as we revere the whisperings of the herd, we are obviously unable to examine them dispassionately and to consider to what extent they are suited to the novel conditions and social exigencies in which we find ourselves today.

The "real" reasons for our beliefs, by making clear their origins and history, can do much to dissipate this emotional blockade and rid us of our prejudices and preconceptions. Once this is done and we come critically to examine our traditional beliefs, we may well find some of them sustained by experience and honest reasoning, while

---

[1] Trotter, *op. cit.*, p. 45. The first part of this little volume is excellent.

others must be revised to meet new conditions and our more extended knowledge. But only after we have undertaken such a critical examination in the light of experience and modern knowledge, freed from any feeling of "primary certitude," can we claim that the "good" are also the "real" reasons for our opinions.

I do not flatter myself that this general show-up of man's thought through the ages will cure myself or others of carelessness in adopting ideas, or of unseemly heat in defending them just because we have adopted them. But if the considerations which I propose to recall are really incorporated into our thinking and are permitted to establish our general outlook on human affairs, they will do much to relieve the imaginary obligation we feel in regard to traditional sentiments and ideals. Few of us are capable of engaging in creative thought, but some of us can at least come to distinguish it from other and inferior kinds of thought and accord to it the esteem that it merits as the greatest treasure of the past and the only hope of the future.

HABIT OR EDUCATION[1]

William James[2]

It is very important that teachers should realize the importance of habit, and psychology helps us greatly at this point. We speak, it is true, of good habits and of bad habits; but, when people use the word "habit," in the majority of instances it is a bad habit which they have in mind. They talk of the smoking habit and the swearing habit and the drinking habit, but not of the abstention habit or the moderation habit or the courage habit. But the fact is that our virtues are habits as much as our vices. All our life, so far as it has definite form, is but a mass of habits — practical, emotional, and intellectual — systematically organized for our weal or woe, and bearing us irresistibly toward our destiny, whatever the latter may be.

Since pupils can understand this at a comparatively early age, and since to understand it contributes in no small measure to their feeling of responsibility, it would be well if the teacher were able himself to talk to them of the philosophy of habit in some such abstract terms as I am now about to talk of it to you.

I believe that we are subject to the law of habit in consequence of the fact that we have bodies. The plasticity of the living matter of our nervous system, in short, is the reason why we do a thing with difficulty the first time, but soon do it more and more easily, and finally, with sufficient practice, do it semi-mechanically, or with hardly any consciousness at all. Our nervous systems have (in Dr. Carpenter's words) *grown* to the way in which they have been exercised, just as a sheet of paper or a coat, once creased or folded, tends to fall forever afterward into the same identical folds.

Habit is thus a second nature, or rather, as the Duke of Wellington said, it is "ten times nature" — at any rate as regards its importance in adult life; for the acquired habits of our training have by that time inhibited or strangled most of the natural impulsive tendencies which were originally there. Ninety-nine hundredths or, possibly, nine hundred and ninety-nine thousandths of our activity is purely automatic and habitual, from our rising in the morning to our lying down

[1] From *Talks to Teachers on Psychology*, by William James. Reprinted by permission of Henry Holt and Company, publishers.
[2] For biographical note, see page 263.

each night. Our dressing and undressing, our eating and drinking, our greetings and partings, our hat-raisings and giving way for ladies to precede, nay, even most of the forms of our common speech, are things of a type so fixed by repetition as almost to be classed as reflex actions. To each sort of impression we have an automatic, ready-made response. My very words to you now are an example of what I mean; for, having already lectured upon habit and printed a chapter about it in a book, and read the latter when in print, I find my tongue inevitably falling into its old phrases and repeating almost literally what I said before.

So far as we are thus mere bundles of habit, we are stereotyped creatures, imitators and copiers of our past selves. And since this, under any circumstances, is what we always tend to become, it follows first of all that the teacher's prime concern should be to ingrain into the pupil that assortment of habits that shall be most useful to him throughout life. Education is for behavior, and habits are the stuff of which behavior consists.

To quote my earlier book directly, the great thing in all education is to *make our nervous system our ally instead of our enemy*. It is to fund and capitalize our acquisitions, and live at ease upon the interest of the fund. *For this we must make automatic and habitual, as early as possible, as many useful actions as we can*, and as carefully guard against the growing into ways that are likely to be disadvantageous. The more of the details of our daily life we can hand over to the effortless custody of automatism, the more our higher powers of mind will be set free for their own proper work. There is no more miserable human being than one in whom nothing is habitual but indecision, and for whom the lighting of every cigar, the drinking of every cup, the time of rising and going to bed every day, and the beginning of every bit of work are subjects of express volitional deliberation. Full half the time of such a man goes to the deciding or regretting of matters which ought to be so ingrained in him as practically not to exist for his consciousness at all. If there be such daily duties not yet ingrained in any one of my hearers, let him begin this very hour to set the matter right.

In Professor Bain's chapter on "The Moral Habits" there are some admirable practical remarks laid down. Two great maxims emerge from the treatment. The first is that in the acquisition of a new habit, or the leaving off of an old one, we must take care to *launch ourselves with as strong and decided an initiative as possible.* Accumulate all the possible circumstances which shall reinforce the right motives; put yourself assiduously in conditions that encourage the new way; make engagements incompatible with the old; take a public pledge, if the case allows; in short, envelop your resolution with every aid you know. This will give your new beginning such a momentum that the temptation to break down will not occur as soon as it otherwise might; and every day during which a breakdown is postponed adds to the chances of its not occurring at all.

I remember long ago reading in an Austrian paper the advertisement of a certain Rudolph Somebody, who promised fifty gulden reward to anyone who after that date should find him at the wine shop of Ambrosius So-and-so. "This I do," the advertisement continued, "in consequence of a promise which I have made my wife." With such a wife, and such an understanding of the way in which to start new habits, it would be safe to stake one's money on Rudolph's ultimate success.

The second maxim is: *Never suffer an exception to occur till the new habit is securely rooted in your life.* Each lapse is like the letting fall of a ball of string which one is carefully winding up: a single slip undoes more than a great many turns will wind again. Continuity of training is the great means of making the nervous system act infallibly right. As Professor Bain says:

The peculiarity of the moral habits, contradistinguishing them from the intellectual acquisitions, is the presence of two hostile powers, one to be gradually raised into the ascendant over the other. It is necessary above all things, in such a situation, never to lose a battle. Every gain on the wrong side undoes the effect of many conquests on the right. The essential precaution, therefore, is so to regulate the two opposing powers that the one may have a series of uninterrupted successes, until repetition has fortified it to such a degree as to enable it to cope with the opposition, under any circumstances. This is the theoretically best career of mental progress.

A third maxim may be added to the preceding pair: *Seize the very first possible opportunity to act on every resolution you make, and on every emotional prompting you may experience in the direction of the habits you aspire to gain.* It is not in the moment of their forming, but in the moment of their producing motor effects, that resolves and aspirations communicate the new "set" to the brain.

No matter how full a reservoir of maxims one may possess, and no matter how good one's sentiments may be, if one have not taken advantage of every concrete opportunity to act, one's character may remain entirely unaffected for the better. With good intentions, Hell proverbially is paved. This is an obvious consequence of the principles I have laid down. A "character," as J. S. Mill says, "is a completely fashioned will"; and a will, in the sense in which he means it, is an aggregate of tendencies to act in a firm and prompt and definite way upon all the principal emergencies of life. A tendency to act only becomes effectively ingrained in us in proportion to the uninterrupted frequency with which the actions actually occur, and the brain "grows" to their use. When a resolve or a fine glow of feeling is allowed to evaporate without bearing practical fruit, it is worse than a chance lost: it works so as positively to hinder future resolutions and emotions from taking the normal path of discharge. There is no more contemptible type of human character than that of the nerveless sentimentalist and dreamer, who spends his life in a weltering sea of sensibility, but never does a concrete manly deed.

This leads to a fourth maxim. *Don't preach too much to your pupils or abound in good talk in the abstract.* Lie in wait rather for the practical opportunities, be prompt to seize those as they pass, and thus at one operation get your pupils both to think, to feel, and to do. The strokes of *behavior* are what give the new set to the character, and work the good habits into its organic tissue. Preaching and talking too soon become an ineffectual bore.

There is a passage in Darwin's short autobiography which has been often quoted, and which, for the sake of its bearing on our subject of habit, I must now quote again. Darwin says:

Up to the age of thirty or beyond it, poetry of many kinds gave me great pleasure; and even as a schoolboy I took intense delight in Shakespeare, especially in the historical plays. I have also said that pictures formerly gave me considerable, and music very great delight. But now for many years I cannot endure to read a line of poetry. I have tried lately to read Shakespeare, and found it so intolerably dull that it nauseated me. I have also almost lost my taste for pictures or music. . . . My mind seems to have become a kind of machine for grinding general laws out of large collections of facts; but why this should have caused the atrophy of that part of the brain alone, on which the higher tastes depend, I cannot conceive. . . . If I had to live my life again, I would have made a rule to read some poetry and listen to some music at least once every week; for perhaps the parts of my brain now atrophied would thus have been kept alive through use. The loss of these tastes is a loss of happiness, and may possibly be injurious to the intellect, and more probably to the moral character, by enfeebling the emotional part of our nature.

We all intend when young to be all that may become a man, before the destroyer cuts us down. We wish and expect to enjoy poetry always, to grow more and more intelligent about pictures and music, to keep in touch with spiritual and religious ideas, and even not to let the greater philosophic thoughts of our time develop quite beyond our view. We mean all this in youth, I say; and yet in how many middle-aged men and women is such an honest and sanguine expectation fulfilled? Surely, in comparatively few; and the laws of habit show us why. Some interest in each of these things arises in everybody at the proper age; but, if not persistently fed with the appropriate matter, instead of growing into a powerful and necessary habit, it atrophies and dies, choked by the rival interests to which the daily food is given. We make ourselves into Darwins in this negative respect by persistently ignoring the essential practical conditions of our case. We say abstractly: "I mean to enjoy poetry, and to absorb a lot of it, of course. I fully intend to keep up my love of music, to read the books that shall give new turns to the thought of my time, to keep my higher spiritual side alive," etc. But we do not attack these things concretely, and we do not begin *today*. We forget that every good that is worth possessing must be paid for in strokes of daily effort. We postpone and postpone, until those smiling possibilities are dead. Whereas ten minutes a day of poetry, of spiritual reading or meditation, and an hour or two a week at music, pictures, or philosophy, provided we began *now* and suffered no remission, would infallibly give us in due time the fullness of all we desire. By neglecting the necessary concrete labor, by sparing ourselves the little daily tax, we are positively digging the graves of our higher possibilities. This is a point concerning which you teachers might well give a little timely information to your older and more aspiring pupils.

According as a function receives daily exercise or not, the man becomes a different kind of being in later life. We have lately had a number of accomplished Hindu visitors at Cambridge, who talked freely of life and philosophy. More than one of them has confided to me that the sight of our faces, all contracted as they are with the habitual American over-intensity and anxiety of expression, and our ungraceful and distorted attitudes when sitting, made on him a very painful impression. "I do not see," said one, "how it is possible for you to live as you do, without a single minute in your day deliberately given to tranquillity and meditation. It is an invariable part of our Hindu life to retire for at least half an hour daily into silence, to relax our muscles, govern our breathing, and meditate on eternal things. Every Hindu child is trained to this from a very early age." The good fruits of such a discipline were obvious in the physical repose and lack of tension, and the wonderful smoothness and calmness of facial expression, and imperturbability of manner of these Orientals. I felt that my countrymen were depriving themselves of an essential grace of character. How many American children ever hear it said, by parent or teacher, that they should moderate their piercing voices, that they should relax their unused muscles, and as far as possible, when sitting, sit quite still? Not one in a thousand, not one in five thousand! Yet, from its reflex influence on the inner mental states, this ceaseless over-tension, over-motion, and over-expression are working on us grievous national harm.

I beg you teachers to think a little seriously of this matter. Perhaps you can help our rising generation of Americans toward the beginning of a better set of personal ideals.

To go back now to our general maxims, I may at last, as a fifth and final practical maxim about habits, offer something like this: *Keep the faculty of effort alive in you by a little gratuitous exercise every day.* That is, be systematically heroic in little unnecessary points, do every day or two something for no other reason than its difficulty, so that, when the hour of dire need draws nigh, it may find you not unnerved and untrained to stand the test. Asceticism of this sort is like the insurance which a man pays on his house and goods. The tax does him no good at the time, and possibly may never bring him a return. But, if the fire *does* come, his having paid it will be his salvation from ruin. So with the man who has daily inured himself to habits of concentrated attention, energetic volition, and self-denial in unnecessary things. He will stand like a tower when everything rocks around him, and his softer fellow mortals are winnowed like chaff in the blast.

I have been accused, when talking of the subject of habit, of making old habits appear so strong that the acquiring of new ones, and particularly anything like a sudden reform or conversion, would be made impossible by my doctrine. Of course, this would suffice to condemn the latter; for sudden conversions, however infrequent they may be, unquestionably do occur. But there is no incompatibility between the general laws I have laid down and the most startling sudden alterations in the way of character. New habits *can* be launched, I have expressly said, on conditions of there being new stimuli and new excitements. Now life abounds in these, and sometimes they are such critical and revolutionary experiences that they change a man's whole scale of values and system of ideas. In such cases, the old order of his habits will be ruptured; and, if the new motives are lasting, new habits will be formed, and build up in him a new or re-generate "nature."

All this kind of fact I fully allow. But the general laws of habit are no wise altered thereby, and the physiological study of mental conditions still remains on the whole the most powerful ally of hortatory ethics. The Hell to be endured hereafter, of which theology tells, is no worse than the Hell we make for ourselves in this world by habitually fashioning our characters in the wrong way. Could the young but realize how soon they will become mere walking bundles of habits, they would give more heed to their conduct while in the plastic state. We are spinning our own fates, good or evil, and never to be undone. Every smallest stroke of virtue or of vice leaves its never-so-little scar. The drunken Rip Van Winkle, in Jefferson's play, excuses himself for every fresh dereliction by saying, "I won't count this time!" Well, he may not count it, and a kind Heaven may not count it, but it is being counted none the less. Down among his nerve cells and fibers the molecules are counting it, registering and storing it up to be used against him when the next temptation comes. Nothing we ever do is, in strict scientific literalness, wiped out.

Of course, this has its good side as well as its bad one. As we become permanent drunkards by so many separate drinks, so we become saints in the moral, and authorities and experts in the practical scientific spheres, by so many separate acts and hours of work. Let no youth have any anxiety about the upshot of his education, whatever the line of it may be. If he keep faithfully busy each hour of the working day, he may safely leave the final result to itself. He can with perfect certainty count on waking up some fine morning to find himself one of the competent ones of his generation, in whatever pursuit he may have singled out. Silently, between all the details of his business, the *power of judging* in all that class of matter will have built itself up within him as a possession that will never pass away. Young people should know this truth in advance. The ignorance of it has probably engendered more discouragement and faint-heartedness in youths embarking on arduous careers than all other causes put together.

WHAT SHALL WE EDUCATE FOR?[1]

Bertrand Russell[2]

I

Before considering how to educate, it is well to be clear as to the sort of result which we wish to achieve. Doctor Arnold of Rugby wanted "humbleness of mind" — a quality not possessed by Aristotle's "magnanimous man." Nietzsche's ideal is not that of Christianity. No more is Kant's: for while Christ enjoins love, Kant teaches that no action of which love is the motive can be truly virtuous. And even people who agree as to the ingredients of a good character may differ as to their relative importance. One man will emphasize courage, another learning, another kindliness, and another rectitude. One man, like the elder Brutus, will put duty to the state above family affection; another, like Confucius, will put family affection first. All these divergences will produce differences as to education. We must have some conception of the kind of person we wish to produce before we can have any definite opinion as to the education which we consider best.

Of course an educator may be foolish, in the sense that he produces results other than those at which he was aiming. Uriah Heep was the outcome of lessons in humility at a Charity School, which had had an effect quite different from what was intended. But in the main the ablest educators have been fairly successful. Take as examples the Chinese literati, the modern Japanese, Doctor Arnold, and the men who direct the policy of the American public schools. All these, in their various ways, have been highly successful. The results aimed at in the different cases were utterly different, but in the main the results were achieved. It may be worth while to spend a few moments on these different systems before attempting to decide what we ourselves should regard as the aims which education should have in view.

Traditional Chinese education was, in some respects, very similar to that of Athens in its best days. Athenian boys were made to learn Homer by heart from beginning to end; Chinese boys were made to

---

[1] From *Education and the Good Life*, by Bertrand Russell. By permission of Liveright Publishing Corporation, publishers.

[2] For biographical note, see page 175.

473

learn the Confucian classics with similar thoroughness. Athenians were taught a kind of reverence for the gods which consisted in outward observances and placed no barrier in the way of free intellectual speculation. Similarly, the Chinese were taught certain rites connected with ancestor-worship, but were by no means obliged to have the beliefs which the rites would seem to imply. An easy and elegant skepticism was the attitude expected of an educated adult; anything might be discussed, but it was a trifle vulgar to reach very positive conclusions. Opinions should be such as could be discussed pleasantly at dinner, not such as man would fight for. Carlyle calls Plato "a lordly Athenian gentleman, very much at his ease in Zion." This characteristic of being "at his ease in Zion" is found also in Chinese sages, and is, as a rule, absent from the sages produced by Christian civilizations, except when, like Goethe, they have deeply imbibed the spirit of Hellenism. The Athenians and the Chinese alike wished to enjoy life, and had a conception of enjoyment which was refined by an exquisite sense of beauty.

There were, however, great differences between the two civilizations, owing to the fact that, broadly speaking, the Greeks were energetic and the Chinese were lazy. The Greeks devoted their energies to art and science and mutual extermination — in all of which they achieved unprecedented success. Politics and patriotism afforded practical outlets for Greek energy: when a politician was ousted he led a band of exiles to attack his native city. When a Chinese official was disgraced he retired to the hills and wrote poems on the pleasures of country life. Accordingly, the Greek civilization destroyed itself, but the Chinese civilization could be destroyed only from without. These differences, however, seem not wholly attributable to education, since Confucianism in Japan never produced the indolent cultured skepticism which characterized the Chinese literati, except in the Kyoto nobility, who formed a kind of Faubourg Saint Germain.

Chinese education produced stability and art; it failed to produce progress or science. Perhaps this may be taken as what is to be expected of skepticism. Passionate beliefs produce either progress or disaster, not stability. Science, even when it attacks traditional beliefs, has beliefs of its own, and can scarcely flourish in an atmosphere of literary skepticism. In a pugnacious world, which has been unified by modern invention, energy is needed for national self-preservation. And without science democracy is impossible: the Chinese civilization was confined to the small percentage of educated men and the Greek civilization was based on slavery. For these reasons the traditional education of China is not suited to the modern world, and has been abandoned by the Chinese themselves. Cultivated eighteenth century gentlemen, who in some respects resembled Chinese literati, have become impossible for the same reasons.

Modern Japan affords the clearest illustration of a tendency which is prominent among all the Great Powers — the tendency to make national greatness the supreme purpose of education. The aim of Japanese education is to produce citizens who shall be devoted to the state through the training of their passions, and useful to it through the knowledge they have acquired. I cannot sufficiently praise the skill with which this double purpose has been pursued. Ever since the advent of Commodore Perry's squadron the Japanese have been in a situation in which self-preservation was very difficult; their success affords a justification of their methods, unless we are to hold that self-preservation itself may be culpable. But only a desperate situation could have justified their educational methods, which would have been culpable in any nation not in imminent peril. The Shinto religion, which must not be called in question even by university professors, involves history just as dubious as Genesis; the Dayton trial pales into insignificance beside the theological tyranny in Japan. There is an equal ethical tyranny; nationalism, filial piety, Mikado-worship, etc., must not be called in question, and, therefore, many kinds of progress are scarcely possible. The great danger of a cast-iron system of this sort is that it may provoke revolution as the sole method of progress. This danger is real, though not immediate, and is largely caused by the educational system.

We have thus in modern Japan a defect opposite to that of ancient China. Whereas the Chinese literati were too skeptical and lazy, the products of Japanese education are likely to be too dogmatic and energetic. Neither acquiescence in skepticism nor acquiescence in dogma is what education should produce. What it should produce is a belief that knowledge is attainable in a measure, though with difficulty; that much of what passes for knowledge at any given time is likely to be more or less mistaken, but that the mistakes can be rectified by care and industry. In acting upon our beliefs, we should be very cautious where a small error would mean disaster; nevertheless, it is upon our beliefs that we must act. This state of mind is rather difficult: it requires a high degree of intellectual culture without emotional atrophy. But though difficult, it is not impossible; it is in fact the scientific temper. Knowledge, like other good things, is difficult, but not impossible; the dogmatist forgets the difficulty, the skeptic denies the possibility. Both are mistaken, and their errors, when widespread, produce social disaster.

Doctor Arnold's system, which has remained in force in English public schools to the present day, had another defect: namely, that it was aristocratic. The aim was to train men for positions of authority and power, whether at home or in distant parts of the Empire. An aristocracy, if it is to survive, needs certain virtues; these were to be imparted at school. The product was to be energetic, stoical, physically fit, possessed of certain unalterable beliefs, with high standards of rectitude, and convinced that it had an important mission in the world. To a surprising extent, these results were achieved. Intellect was sacrificed to them, because intellect might produce doubt. Sympathy was sacrificed, because it might interfere with governing "inferior" races or classes. Kindliness was sacrificed for the sake of toughness; imagination, for the sake of firmness.

In an unchanging world the result might have been a permanent aristocracy, possessing the merits and defects of the Spartans. But aristocracy is out of date, and subject populations will no longer obey even the most wise and virtuous rulers. The rulers are driven into brutality, and brutality further encourages revolt. The complexity of the modern world increasingly requires intelligence, and Doctor Arnold sacrificed intelligence to "virtue." The battle of Waterloo may have been won on the playing fields of Eton, but the British Empire is being lost there. The modern world needs a different type, with more imaginative sympathy, more intellectual suppleness, less belief in bulldog courage and more belief in technical knowledge. The administrator of the future must be the servant of free citizens, not the benevolent ruler of admiring subjects. The aristocratic tradition embedded in British higher education is its bane. Perhaps this tradition can be eliminated gradually; perhaps the older educational institutions will be found incapable of adapting themselves. As to that, I do not venture an opinion.

The American public schools achieve successfully a task never before attempted on a large scale: the task of transforming a heterogeneous selection of mankind into a homogeneous nation. This is done so ably, and is, on the whole, such a beneficent work, that on the balance great praise is due to those who accomplish it. But America, like Japan, is placed in a peculiar situation, and what the special circumstances justify is not necessarily an ideal to be followed everywhere and always. America has had certain advantages and certain difficulties. Among the advantages were: a higher standard of wealth; freedom from the danger of defeat in war; comparative absence of cramping traditions inherited from the Middle Ages. Immigrants found in America a generally diffused sentiment of democracy and an advanced stage of industrial technique. These, I think, are the two chief reasons why almost all of them came to admire America more than their native countries. But actual immigrants, as a rule, retain a dual patriotism: in European struggles they continue to take passionately the side of the nation to which they originally belonged. Their children, on the contrary, lose all loyalty to the country from which their parents have come and become merely and simply Americans. The attitude of the parents is attributable to the general merits of America; that of the children is very largely determined by their school education. It is only the contribution of the school that concerns us.

In so far as the school can rely upon the genuine merits of America, there is no need to associate the teaching of American patriotism with the inculcation of false standards. But where the Old World is superior to the New, it becomes necessary to instill a contempt for genuine excellences. The intellectual level in Western Europe and the artistic level in Eastern Europe are, on the whole, higher than in America. Throughout Western Europe, except in Spain and Portugal, there is less theological superstition than in America. In almost all European countries the individual is less subject to herd domination than in America: his inner freedom is greater even where his political freedom is less. In these respects the American public schools do harm. The harm is essential to the teaching of an exclusive American patriotism. The harm, as with the Japanese, comes from regarding the pupils as means to an end, not as ends in themselves. The teacher should love his children better than his state; otherwise he is not an ideal teacher.

II

When I say that pupils should be regarded as ends, not as means, I may be met by the retort that, after all, everybody is more important as a means than as an end. What a man is as an end perishes when he dies; what he produces as a means continues to the end of time. We cannot deny this, but we can deny the consequences deduced from it. A man's importance as a means may be for good or for evil; the remote effects of human actions are so uncertain that a wise man will tend to dismiss them from his calculations. Broadly speaking, good men have good effects, and bad men bad effects. This, of course, is not an invariable law of nature. A bad man may murder a tyrant because he has committed crimes which the tyrant intends to punish; the effects of his act may be good, though he and his act are bad. Nevertheless, as a broad general rule, a community of men and women who are intrinsically excellent would have better effects than one composed of people who are ignorant and malevolent. Apart from such considerations, children and young people feel instinctively the difference between those who genuinely wish them well and those who regard them merely as raw material for some scheme. Neither character nor intelligence will develop as well or as freely where the teacher is deficient in love; and love of this kind consists essentially in *feeling* the child as an end. We all have this feeling about ourselves: we desire good things for ourselves without first demanding a proof that some great purpose will be furthered by our obtaining them. Every ordinarily affectionate parent feels the same sort of thing about his or her children. Parents want their children to grow, to be strong and healthy, to do well at school, and so on, in just the same way in which they want things for themselves; no effort of self-denial and no abstract principle of justice is involved in taking trouble about such matters. This parental feeling is not always strictly confined to one's own children. In its diffused form it must exist in anyone who is to be a good teacher of little boys and girls. And as the pupils grow older it grows less important. But only those who possess it can be trusted to draw up schemes of education. Those who regard it as one of the purposes of male education to produce men willing to kill and be killed for frivolous reasons are clearly deficient in diffused parental feeling; yet they control education in all civilized countries except Denmark and China.

But it is not enough that the educator should love the young; it is necessary also that he should have a right conception of human excellence. Even those who love all mankind may err through a wrong conception of the good life. I shall try, therefore, to give an idea of what I consider excellent in men and women, quite without regard to practicality, or to educational methods by which it might be brought into being.

We must first make a distinction: some qualities are desirable in a certain proportion of mankind, others are desirable universally. We want artists, but we want also men of science. We want great administrators, but we want also plowmen and millers and bakers. The qualities which produce a man of great eminence in some one

direction are often such as might be undesirable if they were universal.
Shelley describes the day's work of a poet as follows:

> He will watch from dawn to gloom
> The lake-reflected sun illume
> The honey-bees in the ivy bloom
> Nor heed nor see what things they be.

These habits are praiseworthy in a poet, but not — shall we say — in
a postman. We cannot therefore frame our education with a view to
giving everyone the temperament of a poet. But some characteristics
are universally desirable, and it is these alone that I shall consider.

I make no distinction whatever between male and female excellence. A certain amount of occupational training is desirable for a
woman who is to have the care of babies, but that only involves the
same sort of difference as there is between a farmer and a miller. It
is in no degree fundamental, and does not demand consideration at
our present level.

I will take four characteristics which seem to me jointly to form
the basis of an ideal character: vitality, courage, sensitiveness, and
intelligence. I do not suggest that this list is complete, but I think
it carries us a good way. Moreover, I firmly believe that, by proper
physical, emotional, and intellectual care of the young, these qualities
could all be made very common. I shall consider each in turn.

III

Vitality is rather a physiological than a mental characteristic;
it is presumably always present where there is perfect health, but it
tends to ebb with advancing years, and gradually dwindles to nothing
in old age. In vigorous children it quickly rises to a maximum before
they reach school age, and then tends to be diminished by education.
Where it exists there is pleasure in feeling alive, quite apart from any
specific pleasant circumstance. It heightens pleasures and diminishes
pains. It makes it easy to take an interest in whatever occurs, and
thus promotes objectivity, which is an essential of sanity. Human
beings are prone to become absorbed in themselves, unable to be
interested in what they see and hear or in anything outside their
own skins. This is a great misfortune to themselves, since it entails
at best boredom and at worst melancholia; it is also a fatal barrier
to usefulness, except in very exceptional cases. Vitality promotes
interest in the outside world; it also promotes the power of hard work.
Moreover, it is a safeguard against envy, because it makes one's

own existence pleasant.   As envy is one of the great sources of human misery, this is a very important merit in vitality.   Many bad qualities are of course compatible with vitality — for example, those of a healthy tiger.   And many of the best qualities are compatible with its absence: Newton and Locke, for example, had very little.   Both these men, however, had irritabilities and envies from which better health would have set them free.   Probably the whole of Newton's controversy with Leibnitz, which ruined English mathematics for over a hundred years, would have been avoided if Newton had been robust and able to enjoy ordinary pleasures.   In spite of its limitations, therefore, I reckon vitality among the qualities which it is important that all men should possess.

IV

Courage — the second quality on our list — has several forms, and all of them are complex.   Absence of fear is one thing, and the power of controlling fear is another.   And absence of fear, in turn, is one thing when the fear is rational, another when it is irrational.   Absence of irrational fear is clearly good; so is the power of controlling fear.   But absence of rational fear is a matter as to which debate is possible.   However, I shall postpone this question until I have said something about the other forms of courage.

Irrational fear plays an extraordinarily large part in the instinctive emotional life of most people.   In its pathological forms, as persecution mania, anxiety complex, or what not, it is treated by alienists.   But in milder forms it is common among those who are considered sane.   It may be a general feeling that there are dangers about, more correctly termed "anxiety," or a specific dread of things that are not dangerous, such as mice or spiders.   It used to be supposed that many fears were instinctive, but this is now questioned by most investigators.   There are apparently a few instinctive fears — for instance, of loud noises — but the great majority arise either from experience or from suggestion.   Fear of the dark, for example, seems to be entirely due to suggestion.   Vertebrates, there is reason to think, do not feel instinctive fear of their natural enemies, but catch this emotion from their elders.   When human beings bring them up by hand the fears usually among the species are found to be absent.   But fear is exceedingly infectious: children catch it from their elders even when their elders are not aware of having shown it.   Timidity in mothers or nurses is very quickly imitated by children through suggestion. Hitherto, men have thought it attractive in women to be full of irrational terrors, because it gave men a chance to seem protective without incurring any real danger. But the sons of these men have acquired the terrors from their mothers, and have had to be afterward trained to regain a courage which they need never have lost if their fathers had not desired to despise their mothers. The harm that has been done by the subjection of women is incalculable; this matter of fear affords only one incidental illustration.

I am not at the moment discussing the methods by which fear and anxiety may be minimized; that is a matter which I shall consider later. There is, however, one question which arises at this stage, namely: Can we be content to deal with fear by means of repression, or must we find some more radical cure? Traditionally, aristocracies have been trained not to show fear, while subject nations, classes, and sexes have been encouraged to remain cowardly. The test of courage has been crudely behavioristic; a man must not run away in battle; he must be proficient in "manly" sports; he must retain self-command in fires, shipwrecks, earthquakes, etc. He must not merely do the right thing, but he must avoid turning pale, or trembling, or gasping for breath, or giving any other easily observed sign of fear. All this I regard as of great importance; I should wish to see courage cultivated in all nations, in all classes, and in both sexes. But when the method adopted is repressive, it entails the evils always associated with that practice. Shame and disgrace have always been potent weapons in producing the appearance of courage; but in fact they merely cause a conflict of terrors, in which it is hoped that the dread of public condemnation will be the stronger. Fear should be overcome not only in action, but in feeling; and not only in conscious feeling but in the unconscious as well. The purely external victory over fear, which satisfies the aristocratic code, leaves the impulse operative underground and produces evil twisted reactions which are not recognized as the offspring of terror. . . . When recently, in Shanghai, a British officer ordered a number of unarmed Chinese students to be shot in the back without warning, he was obviously actuated by terror just as much as a soldier who runs away in battle. But military aristocracies are not sufficiently intelligent to trace such actions to their psychological source; they regard them rather as showing firmness and a proper spirit.

From the point of view of psychology and physiology, fear and rage are closely analogous emotions: the man who feels rage is not possessed of the highest kind of courage. The cruelty invariably displayed in suppressing Negro insurrections, communist rebellions, and other threats to aristocracy, is an offshoot of cowardice, and deserves the same contempt as is bestowed upon the more obvious forms of that vice. I believe that it is possible so to educate ordinary men and women that they shall be able to live without fear. Hitherto, only a few heroes and saints have achieved such a life; but what they have done others could do if they were shown the way.

For the kind of courage which does not consist in repression, a number of factors must be combined. To begin with the humblest: health and vitality are very helpful, though not indispensable. Practice and skill in dangerous situations are very desirable. But when we come to consider, not courage in this and that respect, but universal courage, something more fundamental is wanted. What is wanted is a combination of self-respect with an impersonal outlook on life. To begin with self-respect: some men live from within, while others are mere mirrors of what is felt and said by their neighbors. The latter can never have true courage: they must have admiration, and are haunted by the fear of losing it. The teaching of "humility" which used to be thought desirable was the means of producing a perverted form of this same vice. "Humility" suppressed self-respect, but not the desire for the respect of others; it merely made nominal self-abasement the means of acquiring credit. Thus it produced hypocrisy and falsification of instinct. Children were taught unreasoning submission, and proceeded to exact it when they grew up; it was said that only those who have learned to obey know how to command. What I suggest is that no one should learn how to obey and no one should attempt to command. I do not mean, of course, that there should not be leaders in coöperative enterprises; but their authority should be like that of a captain of a football team, which is suffered voluntarily in order to achieve a common purpose. Our purposes should be our own, not the result of external authority; and our purposes should never be forcibly imposed upon others. . . .

There is one thing more required for the highest courage, and that is what I called just now an impersonal outlook on life. The man whose hopes and fears are all centered upon himself can hardly view death with equanimity, since it extinguishes his whole emotional universe. Here, again, we are met by a tradition urging the cheap and easy way of repression: the saint must learn to renounce self, must mortify the flesh and forgo instinctive joys. This can be done, but its consequences are bad. Having renounced pleasure for himself, the ascetic saint renounces it for others also — which is easier. Envy persists underground and leads him to the view that suffering is ennobling, and may therefore be legitimately inflicted. Hence arises a complete inversion of values; what is good is thought bad, and what is bad is thought good. The source of all the harm is that the good life has been sought in obedience to a negative imperative, not in broadening and developing natural desires and instincts. There are certain things in human nature which take us beyond self without effort. The commonest of these is love, more particularly parental love, which in some is so generalized as to embrace the whole human race. Another is knowledge. There is no reason to suppose that Galileo was particularly benevolent; yet he lived for an end which was not defeated by his death. Another is art. But in fact every interest in something outside a man's own body makes his life to that degree impersonal. For this reason, paradoxical as it may seem, a man of wide and vivid interests finds less difficulty in leaving life than is experienced by some miserable hypochondriac whose interests are bounded by his own ailments. Thus the perfection of courage is found in the man of many interests, who *feels* his ego to be but a small part of the world, not through despising himself, but through valuing much that is not himself. This can hardly happen except where instinct is free and intelligence is active. From this union of the two grows a comprehensiveness of outlook unknown both to the voluptuary and to the ascetic; and to such an outlook personal death appears a trivial matter. Such courage is positive and instinctive, not negative and repressive. It is courage in this positive sense that I regard as one of the major ingredients in a perfect character.

V

Sensitiveness, the third quality in our list, is in a sense a corrective of mere courage. Courageous behavior is easier for a man who fails to apprehend dangers, but such courage may often be foolish. We cannot regard as satisfactory any way of acting which is dependent upon ignorance or forgetfulness: the fullest possible knowledge and realization are an essential part of what is desirable. The cognitive aspect, however, comes under the head of intelligence; sensitiveness, in the sense in which I am using the term, belongs to the emotions. A purely theoretical definition would be that a person is emotionally sensitive when many stimuli produce emotions in him; but taken thus broadly the quality is not necessarily a good one. If sensitiveness is to be good, the emotional reaction must be in some sense *appropriate:* mere intensity is not what is needed. The quality I have in mind is that of being affected pleasurably or the reverse by many things, and by the right things. What are the right things, I shall try to explain.

The first step, which most children take at the age of about five months, is to pass beyond mere pleasures of sensation, such as food and warmth, to the pleasure of social approbation. This pleasure, as soon as it has arisen, develops very rapidly: every child loves praise and hates blame. Usually the wish to be thought well of remains one of the dominant motives throughout life. It is certainly very valuable as a stimulus to pleasant behavior, and as a restraint upon impulses of greed. If we were wiser in our admirations, it might be much more valuable. But so long as the most admired heroes are those who have killed the greatest number of people, love of admiration cannot alone be adequate to the good life.

The next stage in the development of a desirable form of sensitiveness is sympathy. There is a purely physical sympathy: a very young child will cry because a brother or sister is crying. This, I suppose, affords the basis for the further developments. The two enlargements that are needed are: first, to feel sympathy even when the sufferer is not an object of special affection; secondly, to feel it when the suffering is merely known to be occurring, not sensibly present. The second of these enlargements depends largely upon intelligence. It may go only so far as sympathy with suffering which is portrayed vividly and touchingly, as in a good novel; it may, on the other hand, go so far as to enable a man to be moved emotionally by statistics. This capacity for abstract sympathy is as rare as it is important. Almost everybody is deeply affected when someone he loves suffers from cancer. Most people are moved when they see the sufferings of unknown patients in hospitals. Yet when they read that the death rate from cancer is such and such, they are as a rule moved only to momentary personal fear lest they or someone dear to them should acquire the disease. The same is true of war: people think it dreadful when their son or brother is mutilated, but they do not think it a million times as dreadful that a million people should be mutilated. A man full of kindliness in all personal dealings may derive his income from incitement to war or from the torture of children in "backward" countries. All these familiar phenomena are due to the fact that sympathy is not stirred, in most people, by a merely abstract stimulus. A large proportion of the evils in the modern world would cease if this could be remedied. Science has greatly increased our power of affecting the lives of distant people, without increasing our sympathy for them. Suppose you are a shareholder in a company which manufactures cotton in Shanghai. You may be a busy man, who has merely followed financial advice in making the investment; neither Shanghai nor cotton interests you, but only your dividends. Yet you become part of the force leading to massacres of innocent people, and your dividends would disappear if little children were not forced into unnatural and dangerous toil. You do not mind, because you have never seen the children, and an abstract stimulus cannot move you. That is the fundamental reason why large-scale industrialism is so cruel, and why oppression of subject races is tolerated. An education producing sensitiveness to abstract stimuli would make such things impossible.

VI

I will now pass on to the last of the four qualities we enumerated: namely, intelligence.

One of the great defects of traditional morality has been the low estimate it placed upon intelligence. The Greeks did not err in this respect, but the church led men to think that nothing matters except virtue, and virtue consists in abstinence from a certain list of actions arbitrarily labeled "sin." So long as this attitude persists, it is impossible to make men realize that intelligence does more good than an artificial conventional "virtue." When I speak of intelligence I include both actual knowledge and receptivity to knowledge. The two are, in fact, closely connected. Ignorant adults are unteachable; on such matters as hygiene or diet, for example, they are totally incapable of believing what science has to say. The more a man has learned, the easier it is for him to learn still more — always assuming that he has not been taught in a spirit of dogmatism. Ignorant people have never been compelled to change their mental habits, and have stiffened into an unchangeable attitude. It is not only that they are credulous where they should be skeptical; it is just as much that they are incredulous where they should be receptive. No doubt the word "intelligence" properly signifies rather an aptitude for acquiring knowledge than knowledge already acquired; but I do not think this aptitude is acquired except by exercise, any more than the aptitude of a pianist or an acrobat. It is, of course, possible to impart information in ways that do not train intelligence; it is not only possible, but easy, and frequently done. But I do not believe that it is possible to train intelligence without imparting information, or at any rate causing knowledge to be acquired. And without intelligence our complex modern world cannot subsist; still less can it make progress.

I regard the cultivation of intelligence, therefore, as one of the major purposes of education. This might seem a commonplace, but in fact it is not. The desire to instill what are regarded as correct beliefs has made educationists too often indifferent to the training of intelligence. To make this clear, it is necessary to define intelligence a little more closely, so as to discover the mental habits which it requires.

The instinctive foundation of the intellectual life is curiosity, which is found among animals in its elementary forms. Intelligence demands an alert curiosity, but it must be of a certain kind. The sort that leads village neighbors to try to peer through curtains after dark has no very high value. The widespread interest in gossip is inspired, not by a love of knowledge, but by malice; no one gossips about other people's secret virtues, but only about their secret vices. Accordingly, most gossip is untrue, but care is taken not to verify it. Our neighbor's sins, like the consolations of religion, are so agreeable that we do not stop to scrutinize the evidence closely. Curiosity properly so called, on the other hand, is inspired by a genuine love of knowledge. You may see this impulse, in a moderately pure form, at work in a cat which has been brought to a strange room, and proceeds to smell every corner and every piece of furniture. You will see it also in children, who are passionately interested when a drawer or cupboard, usually closed, is opened for their inspection. Animals, machines, thunderstorms, and all forms of manual work arouse the curiosity of children, whose thirst for knowledge puts the most intelligent adult to shame. This impulse grows weaker with advancing years, until at last what is unfamiliar inspires only disgust, with no desire for a closer acquaintance. This is the stage at which people announce that the country is going to the dogs, and that "things are not what they were in my young days." The thing which is not the same as it was in that far-off time is the speaker's curiosity. And with the death of curiosity we may reckon that active intelligence, also, has died.

But although curiosity lessens in intensity and in extent after childhood, it may for a long time improve in quality. Curiosity about general propositions shows a higher level of intelligence than curiosity about particular facts; broadly speaking, the higher the order of generality the greater is the intelligence involved. Curiosity dissociated from personal advantage shows a higher development than curiosity connected, say, with a chance of food. The cat that sniffs in a new room is not a wholly disinterested scientific inquirer, but probably also wants to find out whether there are mice about.

If curiosity is to be fruitful it must be associated with a certain technique for the acquisition of knowledge. There must be habits of observation, belief in the possibility of knowledge, patience, and industry. These things will develop of themselves, given the original fund of curiosity and the proper intellectual education. But since our intellectual life is only a part of our activity, and since curiosity is perpetually coming into conflict with other passions, there is need of certain intellectual virtues, such as open-mindedness. We become impervious to new truth both from habit and from desire: we find it hard to disbelieve what we have emphatically believed for a number of years, and also what ministers to self-esteem or any other fundamental passion. Open-mindedness should therefore be one of the qualities that education aims at producing.

Courage is essential to intellectual probity, as well as to physical heroism. The real world is more unknown than we like to think; from the first day of life we practice precarious inductions, and confound our mental habits with laws of external nature. All sorts of intellectual systems — Christianity, Socialism, Patriotism, etc. — are ready, like orphan asylums, to give safety in return for servitude. A free mental life cannot be as warm and comfortable and sociable as a life enveloped in a creed: only a creed can give the feeling of a cosy fireside while the winter storms are raging without.

This brings us to a somewhat difficult question: To what extent should the good life be emancipated from the herd? I hesitate to use the phrase "herd instinct," because there are controversies as to its correctness. But, however interpreted, the phenomena which it describes are familiar. We like to stand well with those whom we feel to be the group with which we wish to coöperate — our family, our neighbors, our colleagues, our political party, or our nation. This is natural, because we cannot obtain any of the pleasures of life without coöperation. Moreover, emotions are infectious, especially when they are felt by many people at once. Very few people can be present at an excited meeting without getting excited: if they are opponents, their opposition becomes excited. And to most people such opposition is possible only if they can derive support from the thought of a different crowd in which they will win approbation. That is why the Communion of Saints has afforded such comfort to the persecuted. Are we to acquiesce in this desire for coöperation with the crowd, or shall our education try to weaken it? There are arguments on both sides, and the right answer must consist in finding a just proportion, not in a whole-hearted decision for either party.

I think myself that the desire to please and to coöperate should be strong and normal, but should be capable of being overcome by other desires on certain important occasions. The desirability of a wish to please has already been considered in connection with sensitiveness. Without it we should all be boors, and all social groups, from the family upward, would be impossible. Education of young children would be very difficult if they did not desire the good opinion of their parents. The contagious character of emotions also has its uses, when the contagion is from a wiser person to a more foolish one. But in the case of panic fear and panic rage it is, of course, the very reverse of useful. Thus the question of emotional receptivity is by no means simple. Even in purely intellectual matters the issue is not clear. The great discoverers have had to withstand the herd and incur hostility by their independence. But the average man's opinions are much less foolish than they would be if he thought for himself: in science, at least, his respect for authority is on the whole beneficial.

I think that in the life of a man whose circumstances and talents are not very exceptional there should be a large sphere where what is vaguely termed herd instinct dominates, and a small sphere into which it does not penetrate. The small sphere should contain the region of his special competence. We think ill of a man who cannot admire a woman unless everybody else also admires her: we think that in the choice of a wife a man should be guided by his own independent feelings, not by a reflection of the feelings of his society. It is no matter if his judgments of people in general agree with those of his neighbors, but when he falls in love he ought to be guided by his own independent feelings. Much the same thing applies in other directions. A farmer should follow his own judgment as to the capacities of his fields which he cultivates himself, though his judgment should be formed after acquiring a knowledge of scientific agriculture. An economist should form an independent judgment on currency questions, but an ordinary mortal had better follow authority. Wherever there is special competence there should be independence. But a man should not make himself into a kind of hedgehog, all bristles to keep the world at a distance. The bulk of our ordinary activities must be coöperative, and coöperation must have an instinctive basis. Nevertheless, we should all learn to be able to think for ourselves about matters that are particularly well known to us, and we ought all to have acquired the courage to proclaim unpopular opinions when we believe them to be important.

The application of these broad principles in special cases may, of course, be difficult. But it will be less difficult than it is at present in a world where men commonly have the virtues we have been considering. The persecuted saint, for instance, would not exist in such a world. The good man would have no occasion to bristle and become self-conscious; his goodness would result from following his impulses and would be combined with instinctive happiness. His neighbors would not hate him because they would not fear him: the hatred of pioneers is due to the terror they inspire, and this terror would not exist among men who had acquired courage. Only a man dominated by fear would join the Ku Klux Klan or the Fascisti. In a world of brave men such persecuting organizations could not exist, and the good life would involve far less resistance to instinct than it does at present. The good world can be created and sustained only by fearless men, but the more they succeed in their task, the fewer occasions there will be for the exercise of their courage.

A community of men and women possessing vitality, courage, sensitiveness, and intelligence in the highest degree that education can produce would be very different from anything that has hitherto existed. Very few people would be unhappy. The main causes of unhappiness at present are ill-health, poverty, and an unsatisfactory sex life. All of these would become very rare. Good health could be almost universal, and even old age could be postponed. Poverty, since the industrial revolution, is due only to collective stupidity. Sensitiveness would make people wish to abolish it, intelligence would show them the way, and courage would lead them to adopt it. (A timid person would rather remain miserable than do anything unusual.) Most people's sex life at present is more or less unsatisfactory. This is partly due to bad education, partly to persecution by the authorities and Mrs. Grundy. A generation of women brought up without irrational sex fears would soon make an end of this. Fear has been thought the only way to make women "virtuous," and they have been deliberately taught to be cowards, both physically and mentally. Women in whom love is cramped encourage brutality and hypocrisy in their husbands and distort the instinct of their children. One generation of fearless women could transform the world by bringing into it a generation of fearless children, not contorted into unnatural shapes, but straight and candid, generous, affectionate, and free. Their ardor would sweep away the cruelty and pain which we endure because we are lazy, cowardly, hard-hearted, and stupid. It is education that gives us these bad qualities, and education that must give us the opposite virtues. Education is the key to the new world.

THE DISADVANTAGES OF BEING EDUCATED[1]

Albert Jay Nock

ALBERT JAY NOCK, who in earlier years had been a clergyman, gave vitality and sparkle to that erratic weekly *The Freeman* during its short life in New York, 1920–1924. Though it had a brilliant staff, his was the informing spirit of the sophisticated and cynical journal, and any examination of the entertaining compilation which B. W. Huebsch made from its files, *The Freeman Book*, will show that his was its most gifted and mature pen. Politically it was too perverse to make much impression or be missed when it died; to economic subjects it gave the scantiest attention. But on literary, artistic, and other cultural topics its comment and its long "middle articles" were extremely valuable; the United States never had anything quite of its kind, the old-time *Nation* having been more scholarly and less catholic and cosmopolitan altogether. Since the demise of *The Freeman* Mr. Nock, living chiefly in Belgium, has distilled his varied learning, which he uses jauntily and somewhat eccentrically, into a few books and many magazine articles. Of the books his highly individual estimate of *Thomas Jefferson* (1926), his *Francis Rabelais, The Man and His Work* (1929), and his edition of Rabelais, with a long and admirably written introduction (1931), are the most notable. But he is at his best in shorter critiques and essays, of which the selection here given is a good example.

I

My interest in education had been comfortably asleep since my late youth, when circumstances waked it up again about six years ago. I then discovered that in the meantime our educational system had changed its aim. It was no longer driving at the same thing as formerly and no longer contemplated the same kind of product. When I examined it I was as far "out" on what I expected to find as if I had gone back to one of the sawmills familiar to my boyhood in Michigan, and found it turning out boots and shoes.

The difference seemed to be that while education was still spoken of as a "preparation for life," the preparation was of a kind which bore less directly on intellect and character than in former times, and more directly on proficiency. It aimed at what we used to call training rather than education; and it not only did very little with education, but seemed to assume that training *was* education, thus overriding a distinction that formerly was quite clear. Forty years ago a man trained to proficiency in anything was respected accordingly, but was not regarded as an educated man, or "just as good,"

[1] From *Harper's Magazine*, September, 1932. Reprinted by permission.

on the strength of it.   A trained mechanic, banker, dentist, or man of business got all due credit for his proficiency, but his education, if he had any, lay behind that and was not confused with it.   His training, in a word, bore directly upon what he could do or get, while his education bore directly on neither; it bore upon what he could become and be.

Curiosity led me to look into the matter a little more closely, and my observations confirmed the impression that the distinction between training and education was practically wiped out.   I noticed, too, that there was a good deal of complaint about this: even professional educators, many of them, were dissatisfied with it.   Their complaints when boiled down seemed to be that education is too little regarded as an end in itself, and that most of the country's student population take a too strictly vocational view of what they are doing, while the remainder look at it as a social experience, encouraged largely in order to keep the cubs from being underfoot at home, and reciprocally appreciated mostly because it puts off the evil day when they must go to work; and that our institutions show too much complacency in accommodating themselves to these views.

These complaints, I observed, were not confined to educators; one heard them from laymen as well, and the laymen seemed to be as clear in their minds about the difference between education and training as the professional educators were.   For example, one of America's most distinguished artists (whom I am not authorized to quote, and I therefore call him Richard Roe) told a friend of mine that when his ship came in he proposed to give magnificent endowments to Columbia, Harvard, Princeton, and Yale on the sole condition that they should shut up shop and go out of business forever.   Then he proposed to put up a bronze plate over the main entrance to each of these institutions, bearing this legend:

CLOSED

THROUGH THE BENEFACTION

OF

RICHARD ROE

AN HUMBLE PAINTER

IN BEHALF OF EDUCATION

As I saw the situation at the moment, these complaints seemed reasonable.   Training is excellent, it cannot be too well done, and opportunity for it cannot be too cheap and abundant.   Probably a glorified *crèche* for delayed adolescents here and there is a good thing, too; no great harm in it anyway. Yet it struck me as apparently it struck others, that there should also be a little education going on. Something should be done to mature the national resources of intellect and character as well as the resources of proficiency; and, moreover, something should be done to rehabilitate a respect for these resources as a social asset. Full of this idea, I rushed into print with the suggestion that in addition to our present system of schools, colleges, and universities which are doing first-class work as training schools, we ought to have a few educational institutions. My notion was that the educable person ought to have something like an even chance with the ineducable, because he is socially useful. I thought that even a society composed of well-trained ineducables might be improved by having a handful of educated persons sifted around in it every now and then. I therefore offered the suggestion, which did not seem exorbitant, that in a population of a hundred and twenty-odd million there should be at least one set of institutions, consisting of a grade school, a secondary school, and an undergraduate college, which should be strictly and rigorously educational, kept in perpetual quarantine against the contagion of training.

II

This was five years ago. My modest proposal was hardly in print before I received a letter from a friend in the University of Oxford, propounding a point which — believe it or not — had never occurred to me.

But think of the poor devils who shall have gone through your mill! It seems a cold-blooded thing . . . to turn out a lot of people who simply can't live at home. Vivisection is nothing to it. As I understand your scheme, you are planning to breed a batch of cultivated, sensitive beings who would all die six months after they were exposed to your actual civilization. This is not Oxford's superciliousness, I assure you, for things nowadays are precious little better with us. I agree that such people are the salt of the earth, and England used to make some kind of place for them. . . . But now — well, I hardly know. It seems as though some parts of the earth were jolly well salt-proof. The salt melts and disappears, and nothing comes of it.

As I say, I had never thought of that. It had never occurred to me that there might be disadvantages in being educated. I saw at once where my mistake lay. I had been looking at the matter from the point of view of an elderly person to whom such education as he had was just so much clear gain, not from the point of view of a youth who

is about to make his start in the world.   I saw at once that circumstances, which had been more or less in favor of my educated contemporaries, were all dead against the educated youngster of today.
Therefore, last year, when I was appointed to deal again with the
subject in a public way, I went back on all I had said, and ate my
ration of humble pie with the best grace I could muster.

Every shift in the social order, however slight, puts certain classes
irrevocably out of luck, as our vulgarism goes.   At the beginning of
the sixteenth century the French feudal nobility were out of luck.
They could do nothing about it, nobody could do anything about it,
they were simply out of luck.   Since the middle of the last century,
monarchs and a hereditary aristocracy are out of luck.   The *Zeitgeist*
seems always arbitrarily to be picking out one or another social institution, breathing on it with the devouring breath of a dragon; it
decays and dissolves, and those who represent it are out of luck.   Up
to a few years ago an educated person, even in the United States, was
not wholly out of luck; since then, however, an educated young man's
chance, or an educated young woman's, is slim.   I do not here refer
exclusively to the mere matter of picking up a living, although, as I
shall show, education is a good bit of hindrance even to that; but also
to conditions which make any sort of living enjoyable and worth
while.

So in regard to my championship of education it turned out again
that everybody is wiser than anybody, at least from the short-time
point of view, which is the one that human society invariably takes.
Some philosophers think that society is an organism, moving instinctively always toward the immediate good thing, as certain blind worms
of a very low order of sensibility move toward food.   From the long-
time point of view, this may often be a bad thing for the worm; it
may get itself stepped on or run over or picked up by a boy looking for
fish-bait.   Nothing can be done about it, however, for the worm's
instinct works that way and, according to these philosophers, so does
society's, and the individual member of society has little practical
choice but to go along.

Hence our institutions which profess and call themselves educational
have probably done the right thing — the immediate right thing, at
any rate — in converting themselves, as our drug stores have done,
into something that corresponds only very loosely to their profession.
No doubt the lay and professional complaint against this tendency
is wrong; no doubt the artist Richard Roe's proposal to close up our
four great training schools is wrong.   No doubt, too, our young

people are right in instinctively going at education, in the traditional sense of the term, with very long teeth. If I were in their place, I now think I should do as they do; and since I am in the way of recantation, as an old offender who has at last seen the light of grace, I may be allowed to say why I should do so — to show what I now plainly see to be the disadvantages of being educated.

III

Education deprives a young person of one of his most precious possessions, the sense of coöperation with his fellows. He is like a pacifist in 1917, alone in spirit — a depressing situation, and especially, almost unbearably, depressing to youth. "After all," says Dumas's hero, "man is man's brother," and youth especially needs a free play of the fraternal sense; it needs the stimulus and support of association in common endeavor. The survivor of an older generation in America has had these benefits in some degree; he is more or less established and matured and can rub along fairly comfortably on his spiritual accumulations; and besides, as age comes on, emotions weaken and sensitiveness is dulled. In his day, from the spiritual and social point of view, one could afford to be educated — barely and with difficulty afford it perhaps, but education was not a flat liability. It netted enough to be worth its price. At present one can afford only to be trained. The young person's fellows are turning all their energy into a single narrow channel of interest; they have set the whole current of their being in one direction. Education is all against his doing that, while training is all for it; hence training puts him in step with his fellows, while education tends to leave him a solitary figure, spiritually disqualified.

For these reasons: education, in the first place, discloses other channels of interest and makes them look inviting. In the second place, it gives rise to the view that the interest which absorbs his fellows is not worth mortgaging one's whole self, body, mind, and spirit, to carry on. In the third place, it shows what sort of people one's fellows inevitably become, through their exclusive absorption in this one interest, and makes it hard to reconcile oneself to the thought of becoming like them. Training, on the other hand, raises no such disturbances; it lets one go on one's chosen way, with no uncertainty, no loss of confidence, as a man of the crowd. Education is divisive, separatist; training induces the exhilarating sense that one is doing with others what others do and thinking the thoughts that others think.

Education, in a word, leads a person on to ask a great deal more from life than life, as at present organized, is willing to give him; and it begets dissatisfaction with the rewards that life holds out. Training tends to satisfy him with very moderate and simple returns. A good income, a home and family, the usual run of comforts and conveniences, diversions addressed only to the competitive or sporting spirit or else to raw sensation — training not only makes directly for getting these, but also for an inert and comfortable contentment with them. Well, these are all that our present society has to offer; so it is undeniably the best thing all round to keep people satisfied with them, which training does, and not to inject a subversive influence, like education, into this easy complacency. Politicians understand this — it is their business to understand it — and hence they hold up "a chicken in every pot and two cars in every garage" as a satisfying social ideal. But the mischief of education is its exorbitance. The educated lad may like stewed chicken and motor cars as well as anybody, but his education has bred a liking for other things too, things that the society around him does not care for and will not countenance. It has bred tastes which society resents as culpably luxurious and will not connive at gratifying. Paraphrasing the old saying, education sends him out to shift for himself with a champagne appetite amid a gin-guzzling society.

Training, on the other hand, breeds no such tastes; it keeps him so well content with synthetic gin that a mention of champagne merely causes him to make a wry face. Not long ago I met a young acquaintance from the Middle West who has done well by himself in a business way and is fairly rich. He looked jaded and seedy, evidently from overwork, and as I was headed for Munich at the moment I suggested he should take a holiday and go along. He replied, "Why, I couldn't sell anything in Munich — I'm a business man." For a moment or two I was rather taken aback by his attitude, but I presently recognized it as the characteristic attitude of trained proficiency, and I saw that as things are it was right. Training had kept his demands on life down to a strictly rudimentary order and never tended to muddle up their clear simplicity or shift their direction. Education would have done both; he was lucky to have had none.

It may be plainly seen, I think, that in speaking as he did, my friend enjoyed the sustaining sense of coöperation with his fellows. In his intense concentration, his singleness of purpose, and in the extremely primitive simplicity of his desires and satisfactions he was completely in the essential movement of the society surrounding him; indeed, if his health and strength hold out, he may yet become one of those representative men like Mr. Ford, the late Mr. Eastman, or Mr. Hoover, who take their tone from society in the first instance and in turn give back that tone with interest. Ever since the first westward emigration from the Atlantic seaboard, American civilization may be summed up as a free-for-all scuffle to get rich quickly and by any means. In so far as a person was prepared to accept the terms of this free-for-all and engage in it, so far he was sustained by the exhilaration of what Mr. Dooley called "th' common impulse f'r th' same money." In so far as he was not so prepared, he was deprived of this encouragement.

To mark the tendency of education in these circumstances, we need consider but one piece of testimony. The late Charles Francis Adams was an educated man who overlived the very fag-end of the period when an American youth could afford, more or less hardly, to be educated. He was a man of large affairs, in close relations with those whom the clear consenting voice of American society acclaimed as its representative men, and whose ideals of life were acclaimed as adequate and satisfying; they were the Fords, Eastmans, Owen Youngs, Hoovers of the period. At the close of his career he wrote this:

As I approach the end, I am more than a little puzzled to account for the instances I have seen of business success — money-getting. It comes from rather a low instinct. Certainly, as far as my observation goes, it is rarely met in combination with the finer or more interesting traits of character. I have known, and known tolerably well, a good many "successful" men — "big" financially — men famous during the last half-century; and a less interesting crowd I do not care to encounter. Not one that I have ever known would I care to meet again, either in this world or in the next; nor is one of them associated in my mind with the idea of humor, thought, or refinement. A set of mere money-getters and traders, they were essentially unattractive and uninteresting. The fact is that money-getting, like everything else, calls for a special aptitude and great concentration; and for it I did not have the first to any marked degree, and to it I never gave the last. So, in now summing up, I may account myself fortunate in having got out of my ventures as well as I did.

This is by no means the language of a man who, like my acquaintance from the Middle West, is sustained and emboldened by the consciousness of being in coöperation with his fellows — far from it. It will be enough, I think, to intimate pretty clearly the divisive and separatist tendency of education, and to show the serious risk that a young person of the present day incurs in acquiring an education. As matters now stand, I believe that he should not take that risk, and that anyone advising or tempting him to take it is doing him a great disservice.

IV

An educated young man likes to think; he likes ideas for their own sake and likes to deal with them disinterestedly and objectively.   He will find this taste an expensive one, much beyond his means, because the society around him is thoroughly indisposed toward anything of the kind.   It is preëminently a society, as John Stuart Mill said, in which "the test of a great mind is agreeing in the opinions of small minds."   In any department of American life this is indeed the only final test; and this fact is in turn a fair measure of the extent to which our society is inimical to thought.   The president of Columbia University is reported in the press as having said the other day that "thinking is one of the most unpopular amusements of the human race.   Men hate it largely because they cannot do it.   They hate it because if they enter upon it as a vocation or avocation it is likely to interfere with what they are doing."   This is an interesting admission for the president of Columbia to make — interesting and striking. Circumstances have enabled our society to get along rather prosperously, though by no means creditably, without thought and without regard for thought, proceeding merely by a series of improvisations; hence it has always instinctively resented thought, as likely to interfere with what it was doing.   Therefore, the young person who has cultivated the ability to think and the taste for thinking is at a decided disadvantage, for this resentment is now stronger and more heavily concentrated than it ever was.   Any doubt on this point may be easily resolved by an examination of our current literature, especially our journalistic and periodical literature.

The educated lad also likes to cultivate a sense of history.   He likes to know how the human mind has worked in the past, and upon this knowledge he instinctively bases his expectations of its present and future workings.   This tends automatically to withdraw him from many popular movements and associations because he knows their like of old, and knows to a certainty how they will turn out.   In the realm of public affairs, for instance, it shapes his judgment of this or that humbugging political nostrum that the crowd is running eagerly to swallow; he can match it all the way back to the politics of Rome and Athens, and knows it for precisely what it is.   He cannot get into a ferment over this or that exposure of the almost incredible degradation of our political, social, and cultural character; over an investigation of Tammany's misdoings; over the federal government's flagitious employment of the income tax law to establish a sleeping partnership in the enterprises of gamblers, gangsters, assassins, and racketeers; over the wholesale looting of public property through official connivance; over the crushing burden which an ever-increasing bureaucratic rapicity puts upon production. He knows too much about the origin and nature of government not to know that all these matters are representative, and that nothing significant can be done about them except by a self-sprung change of character in the people represented. He is aware, with Edmund Burke, that "there never was for any long time a corrupt representation of a virtuous people, or a mean, sluggish, careless people that ever had a good government of any form." He perceives, with Ibsen, that "men still call for special revolutions, for revolutions in politics, in externals. But all that sort of thing is trumpery. It is the soul of man that must revolt."

Thus in these important directions, and in others more or less like them, the educated youth starts under disadvantages from which the trained youth is free. The trained youth has no incentive to regard these matters except as one or another of them may bear upon his immediate personal interest. Again, while education does not make a gentleman it tends to inculcate certain partialities and repugnances which training does not tend to inculcate, and which are often embarrassing and retarding. They set up a sense of self-respect and dignity as an arbiter of conduct, with a jurisdiction far outreaching that of law and morals; and this is most disadvantageous. Formerly this disadvantage was not so pressing, but now it is of grave weight. At the close of Mr. Jefferson's first term, some of his political advisers thought it would be a good move for him to make a little tour in the North and let the people see him. He replied, with what now seems an incomprehensible austerity, that he was "not reconciled to the idea of a chief magistrate parading himself through the several states as an object of public gaze, and in quest of an applause which, to be valuable, should be purely voluntary." In his day a chief magistrate could say that and not lose by it; Mr. Jefferson carried every northern state except Connecticut and every southern state except Maryland. At the present time, as we have lately been reminded, the exigencies of politics have converted candidacy for public office into an exact synonym for obscene and repulsive exhibitionism.

Again education tends toward a certain reluctance about pushing oneself forward; and in a society so notoriously based on the principle of each man for himself, this is a disadvantage. Charles Francis Adams's younger brother Henry, in his remarkable book called *The Education of Henry Adams,* makes some striking observations on this point. Henry Adams was no doubt the most accomplished man in America, probably the ablest member of the family which as a whole has been the most notable in American public service since 1776. His youth was spent in acquiring an uncommonly large experience of men and affairs. Yet he says that his native land never offered him but one opportunity in the whole course of his life, and that was an assistant professorship of history at Harvard, at four dollars a day; and he says further that he "could have wept on President Eliot's shoulder in hysterics, so grateful was he for the rare good-will that inspired the compliment." He recalls that at the age of thirty:

No young man had a larger acquaintance and relationship than Henry Adams, yet he knew no one who could help him. He was for sale, in the open market. So were many of his friends. All the world knew it, and knew too that they were cheap; to be bought at the price of a mechanic. There was no concealment, no delicacy, and no illusion about it. Neither he nor his friends complained; but he felt sometimes a little surprised that, as far as he knew, no one seeking in the labor market even so much as inquired about their fitness. . . . The young man was required to impose himself, by the usual business methods, as a necessity on his elders, in order to compel them to buy him as an investment. As Adams felt it, he was in a manner expected to blackmail.

Such were the disabilities imposed upon the educated person fifty years ago, when, as Adams says, "the American character showed singular limitations which sometimes drove the student of civilized man to despair." Owing to increased tension of the economic system, they are now much heavier. Even more than then, the educated youth emerges, as Adams and his friends did, to find himself "jostled of a sudden by a crowd of men who seem to him ignorant that there is a thing called ignorance; who have forgotten how to amuse themselves; who cannot even understand that they are bored."

One might add a few more items to the foregoing, chiefly in the way of spiritual wear and tear — specific discouragements, irritations, disappointments — which in these days fall to the lot of the educated youth, and which the trained youth escapes; but I have mentioned enough for the purpose. Now, it is quite proper to say that the joys and satisfactions of being educated should be brought out as an offset. One cannot get something for nothing, nor can one "have it going and

coming." If an education is in itself as rewarding a thing as it is
supposed to be, it is worth some sacrifice. It is unreasonable to court
the joy of making oneself at home in the world's culture, and at the
same time expect to get Standard Oil dividends out of it. Granted
that your educated lad is out of step, lonesome, short on business
acumen and concentration, and all the rest of it — well, he has his
education; nobody can get it away from him; his treasure is of the
sort that moth and rust do not corrupt, and stock market operators
cannot break through and mark down quotations on it. Agreed that
if Charles Francis Adams had not been an educated gentleman he
might have become another Gould, Fisk, Harriman, Rockefeller,
Huntington, Morgan; but given his choice, would he have swapped
off his education and its satisfactions for the chance to change places
with any of them? Certainly not.

Certainly not; but times have changed. If economic opportunity were now what it was even in Henry Adams's day, a young
person just starting out might think twice about balancing the advantages of an education against its disadvantages. In that day, by
a little stretching and with a little luck, a young person might come to
some sort of compromise with society, but the chance of this is now so
remote that no one should take it. Since the closing of the frontier,
in or about 1890, economic exploitation has tightened up at such a
rate that compromise is hardly possible. It takes every jot of a
young person's attention and energy merely to catch on and hang on;
and as we have been noticing these last two years, he does not keep
going any too well, even at that. The question is not one of being
willing to make reasonable sacrifices; it is one of accepting every
reasonable prospect of utter destitution. The joys and satisfactions
of an education are all that Commencement orators say they are, and
more; yet there is force in the Irishman's question, "What's the world
to a man when his wife's a widdy?"

V

Things may change for the better, in time; no doubt they will.
Economic opportunity may, by some means unforeseen at present,
be released from the hold of its present close monopoly. The social
value of intellect and character may some day be rediscovered, and the
means of their development may be rehabilitated. Were I to be alive
when all this happens, I should take up my parable of five years ago,
and speak as strongly for education as I did then. But I shall not be
alive, and I suspect also that none of the young persons now going

out into the world from our training schools will be alive; so there is no practical point to considering this prospect at present. Hence I can only raise my voice in recantation from the mourner's bench, a convert by force of expediency if not precisely in principle — rice-Christian style, perhaps, and yet, what is one to say? I belong to an earlier time, and for one reason or another the matter of rice does not present itself as an overimportunate problem, but nevertheless I see that the Christians have now "cornered" all the rice; so I cannot advise young persons to do as I and my contemporaries did. No, they are right, their training schools are right; Richard Roe and I are wrong. Let them be honest Christians if they can possibly manage the will to believe — one can make astonishing successes with that sometimes by hard trying — but if not, let them be rice-Christians; they can do no better.

RÔLE OF INVENTION AND CHANGE[1]

Charles E. Merriam

No American has done more than CHARLES E. MERRIAM to study the psychological and sociological background of political methods in the United States. His work deals in large part with the field which Graham Wallas treated more philosophically in his volume on *Human Nature in Politics*. Dr. Merriam was fortunate in his environment; the city of Chicago has offered a rich panorama of machine politics, the exploitation of racial and national prejudices, and the interrelation between crooked business and crooked government. All this Dr. Merriam has been able to study at close range, for he has served as an alderman, acted as head of a commission on city expenditures, and run for mayor (1911) on the Republican ticket. His primary occupation is of course teaching. Born at Hopkinton, Iowa, in 1874, he was educated at the University of Iowa and Columbia University. Since 1900 he has taught political science at the University of Chicago, rising to the head of the department. Among his books are *The American Party System* (1922); *New Aspects of Politics* (1925); *Four American Party Leaders* (1926); *The Making of Citizens* (1931); and *The Written Constitution* (1931).

Modern systems of civic education are fundamentally defective in their overemphasis on the rôle of the inflexible elements in the state and in their failure to recognize adequately the rôle of invention and adaptation. It is, of course, true that great areas of human behavior lie in the domain of the automatic or unconscious, or that of unreflecting habit developed by constant repetition to a point where no conscious effort is required. The values of habit are, everyone must recognize, very great, and no one would venture to suggest the abandonment of the advantages they bring with them. "Habit," said William James, "is the enormous fly wheel of society, its most conservative agent. . . . The great thing then in all our education is to make our nervous system our ally instead of our enemy."

The margin of adaptability and change, however small, is nevertheless of incalculable consequence in the organization of human relations, and contains survival values of the very greatest importance for individuals and societies. The strange stereotypes of behavior found among ants and bees illustrate the seemingly blind alleys in the development of progressive evolution of human types.

A fundamental problem in the field of civic education is that of the relation of tradition to invention and adaptation in the development

[1] From *The Making of Citizens*, by Charles E. Merriam. Reprinted by permission of the University of Chicago Press, publishers.

of types of political behavior.   It is of course possible that tradition may include invention, but in another and in the more common sense traditional is used as if contrasted with the changing and the new. The traditional way is the old way; the new method is opposed to the ancient tradition which it supplants or attempts to supplant.

Historically, civic education has been chiefly a training in the traditional, the transmission of what the group has done, with the veneration of the past, sometimes even its deification, and usually with the presupposition that what has been done should be literally done again and that what has been is a model for future situations. It may even be true that the primitive initiations laid less emphasis upon this than the later, for they stressed alertness and readiness in war and chase, although they of course sanctified the stereotyped ways of their ancestors.

The classic systems were built upon the theory that change is an evil in the political world, and that if our intelligence were keen enough and adroit enough in inventing the necessary devices, the ideal state would remain static.   This conception was unfolded by Plato and Aristotle, both of whom regarded the avoidance of change as the triumph of the political scientist, and advocated all manner of practical preventives against it.   The ideal state must be set back from the sea to avoid contacts with roving sailors who might bring in new and contraband ideas; only the adult may be allowed to go abroad and then must teach the superiority of the local system of government on his return; even new dances and new tunes must not be introduced lest they might start a new rhythm, even in the field of recreation.   Nothing must come in to upset the established harmonies of the state. This continued to be the ideal of political savants until the sixteenth century, when Bodin declared the task of politics was not that of preventing change, but of recognizing its necessity and of making the necessary transitions as easy as possible, with as little loss as might be to the community.

Most modern systems provide for the inculcation of the traditional without recognition of the inevitability and the desirability of change in institutions or mores themselves.   It may be said, moreover, that they are often more concerned with elements of the state where change is threatened than with those of a more permanent character.   Thus the special form of political order in the given state, and the special territorial ethnic pattern, must be more carefully guarded than the general principles of political behavior.   The maintenance of monarchy and the particular holders of power is much more in need of buttressing than the more commonly accepted axiom of the necessity of some form of command and obedience. The supreme court must be made more sacred than the principle of adjudication of differences as it has come down historically in all tribes and groups everywhere. National boundaries must not change, although all systems permit of their enlargement, it seems. Italy is Italy centuries after, and its rulers wear the crown of the Caesars; and England is England and its kings still kings long after the substance of power has died away.

Under modern conditions, however, survival values are found in mobility and adaptability as well as in routine, conformity, and tradition. In the industrial world and in the scientific world tradition has been almost discarded, and progress and profit too depend upon quick adjustment to swiftly altering situations. No one feels himself bound by the previous studies of the atom; no one in modern production adheres consciously to the methods of his ancestors. No one anywhere insists upon driving an ox team because his forefathers did so. The religious revolution of the sixteenth century, the political revolution that followed, and the industrial revolution have shattered the old traditions and have produced a modern world in which change is the watchword of the time. Science has added to the tendency toward mutability in social arrangements.

The uncritical use of tradition and of indoctrination in the ideologies of a special order is usually hostile to the quality of adaptability. They set up as the ideal type of political behavior adherence to a form of theory or a historical character, and tend to regard these type forms as sacréd and unchangeable. In this way the critic and the rebel are inhibited, but also the inventor and the constructive genius. A true view of national heroes and of national doctrines becomes difficult and is placed under the ban of the law or of public opinion.

The chief task, however, of a modern citizen is that of intelligent discrimination between competing types of persons as leaders and between competing types of policies in a changing world. Assuming a degree of interest in and attachment to the community of which he is a part, the value of the citizen to his group depends upon the intelligence and discernment with which he makes necessary choices and adjusts himself to changing situations. In fact, the differences in ability to make readjustments is ordinarily the margin between survival and destruction in political as well as in economic and social life. It is precisely here that we find the danger of excessive use of uncritical tradition.

Stefansson in his interesting description of his Arctic explorations tells of groups of Indians who would not make use of heather grass as a means of cooking their meals because they had always been accustomed to willows.   They therefore insisted upon searching for willow stems and roots while other members of the party gathered the grass, cooked their meals, and went to sleep before the searchers for the willows returned.   The willow searchers, however, were not willing to give up the traditions of their fathers, for this they felt would bring upon them the odium of their group, and as Stefansson said, they held out for a month before they were willing to adopt a new method.

Traditions have unquestionably a definite value, but they are useful only as long as they are applicable.   In some situations they may become harmful patterns of conduct instead of wise and sound precedents.   There is in tradition an element of reason and unreason, an element of ceremonialism and sentimentalism, and an element of intelligence and discrimination.   There are circumstances in which a line of conduct may lead to life; there are other circumstances in which the same line of conduct would lead to death or at least to difficulty.   It is a curious paradox of modern life that, while nationalistic hatreds frequently lead to wars of the most destructive type, ostensibly to preserve the traditional, when these wars are once precipitated, the bitterest foes do not hesitate to borrow from each other in the field of war whatever new device may insure success.   If the enemy uses poison gas, the other quickly adopts it.   If the enemy uses airplanes or tanks, the other quickly follows, but not the other's language, or religion, or culture.

If traditional education is carried through completely, it endangers its own purposes, for, if every citizen were convinced that every technique used by his ancestors was perfect and unalterable, that type of technique would be continued to the destruction of the group itself.   If we insisted on using exactly the same weapons as our forefathers, we would lose all modern wars; if we insisted upon acting upon their complete patterns of ideas, we should find ourselves ill-adapted to a modern world.   Uncritical tradition and rigid indoctrination, in other words, tend to make rigid and inflexible types of attitudes which in a changed and shifting world are inapplicable.   Tradition tends to produce fossilization and crystallization where flexibility and adaptability may be of prime importance.

When I was in Czechoslovakia in 1924, there was an interesting struggle still raging.   The defenders of John Huss insisted that the trial of Huss, in 1415, should be reopened, that he should be retried, vindicated, and absolved from judgment and penalty inflicted upon him over five hundred years ago. This question did not actually become a political issue, but it was by way of becoming an issue — a troublesome factor in the maintenance of a working majority in the Czech government.

In the United States, if we followed the Fathers' example literally, we would disfranchise over three-fourths of our voters, reëstablish human slavery, set up property and religious qualifications for office, reëstablish religions, set up penal and reformatory institutions of the most primitive type, and rebuild a whole series of institutions which we should find absolutely intolerable and impossible.

The past may readily be made a defense for vested wrongs as well as for vested rights. Probably the most common defense of a notoriously selfish interest is to cover itself with an alleged group or unselfish interest. In this case, all the teachings of tradition are capitalized against the group itself.

The significance of fidelity to the past in any group is very great, but beyond a certain point what was originally meat becomes poison. The distortion of loyalty may, in effect, be disloyalty. Or, from another point of view, the exaggeration of loyalty may become intolerance, bigotry, and oppressiveness of the most odious form, designed, however, to protect the interests of some selfish individual or group. In no atmosphere does the demagogue thrive more freely than in that of excited intolerance and overinflamed civic enthusiasm built upon overemphasized tradition.

The citizen trained in hero-worship alone finds himself in a strangely different world when the time comes for real action. His texts and dates and biographical narratives do not seem sufficient. His book heroes made no mistakes; their lives were never gray but always either white or black; their policies were always wholly right and never wrong, or partly right and partly wrong. Their decisions seem to have been made under conditions strangely unlike those puzzling situations confronting the modern citizen and consequently of little help to him.

In practical life the citizen finds that he must frequently decide between two persons as leaders neither of whom exactly measures up to his standards; or must decide between two mixed sets of politics neither of which he fully approves. Perhaps one of these men may be a hero later on, or one of the policies a sound national ideal later on, but not now. What he has before him is not a heroic situation but a practical case in which discernment, discrimination, and judgment are of the highest value.   But the traditionally educated citizen has not been taught this, if he has been taught solely in terms of hero-worship and tradition.   Apparently Washington had no problems; apparently Bismarck had an open field at all times; apparently Clemenceau had only to tread the simple path of duty.   The citizens of Washington's, Bismarck's, and Clemenceau's day had only to follow their great men, of whose qualities there was no doubt, and those clear ways which nobody could mistake; and apparently every-one was always with them, applauding their every act.   From this peaceful atmosphere of high Olympus it seems a long way to the average municipal or state or national election.   Here the puzzled citizen finds that many difficult choices must be made.   He can, of course, follow his impulses or his emotions or the beating of the ready tom-toms, but these may not be satisfactory guides, either for him or for the community.   What he must really do in cases where the com-munity is usefully served is to distinguish between the genuine and the sham, between the sound and the unsound, between types of behavior that are useful for his group and those that are dangerous.

The watchword of modern life is change and adjustment, even to the point of restlessness and dissatisfaction.   Unquestionably, re-adjustment is, and for some time will continue to be, a larger part of the life of our time, at least in the Western world.   Politics cannot continue to live upon tradition and force, two of its great allies in the past, but must rely upon invention, adaptation, adjustment, if it is to continue as a useful part of that modern life in which conscious control over human evolution looms up larger and larger.

I attended, in 1926, in Vienna an International Conference of Town Planners in which the characteristics of the modern political world seemed to me to be most clearly emphasized.   Some 1,100 delegates from many countries came together for the purpose of considering how the city of the future should be built, and how the modern city could be progressively changed and adapted to new conditions.   They were not worshiping the old mansions in Vienna or elsewhere.   On the contrary, they took great pride in exhibiting to us the new struc-tures just erected.   There was not much interest in the early types of street structure or the rich moldiness of ancient city outlines.   The planners were primarily concerned with adjusting old structures to modern conditions of communication developed by the street railway and by the automobile.   For them the test of value was utility in the present and in the future, rather than the past.   They were builders, inventors, adapters of an old to a changed and changing new world.

Their proceedings were not enlivened by emotional appeals or traditional harangues, or ancestral worship, but their discussions turned upon questions of engineering, of finances, and of human health, comfort, and conveniences in our own day. Their civic training had been in large part in invention and adjustment rather than in uncritical hero-worship and rigid indoctrination of ideas, or belief in the immutability of a particular political or economic system. It is in groups such as this that we may find the clue to the type of civic training most useful to the coming generation; and on the other hand it is precisely this type of attitude that seems to me most commonly neglected in what we call civic education.

Modern governments now approach a severe test. Now for the first time everyone is made a citizen and a responsible citizen; now everyone is given the elements of an education; now everyone begins to have a measure of leisure; and equally important, the world begins to change at a rate never before equaled in human history. Magic and myth of earlier days are outdone every decade by modern science with its unexampled power over nature and man. This is the age of advance and adjustment — the period of new patterns of conduct in every walk of life. Traditions still survive, but never in the world's history were they weaker than now in business, in education, in mores, whatever way we turn. The surviving types of life and conduct are those that are able to adjust themselves to this changing world, and raise new temples on the ruins of the old.

It would be a supreme tragedy if government alone still worshiped at the shrine of the past, satisfying itself with the symbols and ceremonials of outlived situations. For this can only mean that the new masters of mob psychology weave out of the patterns of traditionalism the cloaks for their own daring enterprises in popular confusion and control. The demagogue and the rogue will not fail to utilize the prejudices, the hates, and the bigotries of mankind for their own purposes, and with their tongues in their cheeks take over the government of mankind in the name of the supreme order of the charlatan.

Another statesmanship might not be so misled. It could recognize the rôle of political invention and adjustment in the new world, and the part they must play in the life of the coming citizen. It could provide for the cultivation of discernment and discrimination, for the forward look as well as the backward sweep, for tests of adaptability and inventiveness as well as memory, for appreciation of the inventor and the social technician in the present as well as in the past. It could unfold the political world as a shifting scene with constantly changing situations rather than as a closed book left only to be revered. It could picture the ideal citizen not as a devotee of the past but himself as father and founder, joint creator of a new world. The great values to be drawn from the illustrious past need not be lost, but may be placed in their true light, not as magic or mystery, but as preliminary to the understanding of the possibilities of the greater future.

In a sense there is more danger from unwise indoctrination with various ideologies than from the earlier inculcation of the hero-worship of the tribe; for the latter were often depicted as brave, strong, resourceful types of men, hunters, warriors, wise men, meeting a variety of new situations with unexpected and unusual ability. But a modern set of theories may be set down with dogmatic certitude and without possibility of contradiction, whether it be the ideology of communism in Russia, or Fascism in Italy, or democracy in France, or the perpetuation of the peculiarly French national ideology or other national ideology as if it were fixed and unchangeable.

It may again be observed in nationalistic systems of civic education that the tendency is to apply the doctrine of immutability most persistently to those elements of the state which are most likely to change rather than to the fundamentals of government which are not threatened. Thus a particular form of political order, such as communism or Fascism or democracy or capitalism, becomes sacrosanct, and criticism of it in the educational system at least tends to be tabooed. Or the boundaries of a particular state or its *irredenta* are more inflexibly laid down than are the essentials of political behavior upon which group cohesion and power really rest in last analysis. In other words the greatest hardness of political dogma may be found at the weakest part of the structure of civic education, even from an objective, outside point of view favorable to group maintenance. When some group like the Holy Roman Empire, or, at the opposite pole, some localism, feudalism, or federalism, goes down before the sweep of events, we recognize the social value of this movement, and even the advocates of the lost cause will do so, although at the time of conflict they could not, or would not.

The emerging struggle then, in the development of civic training, is that between the older system of traditional indoctrination and one in which much greater stress is laid upon the elements of invention, adaptability, and adjustment in a changing world. Thus far the fixed and rigid systems have been triumphant almost everywhere, but there is growing recognition of the unsatisfactory nature of this method, and it is likely that students of the educational process will observe notable changes at this point. The older systems, resting upon a type of political flexibility, will long and tenaciously resist the new tendencies, but it seems improbable that they can maintain their position in a world of dynamic change.

It may well be that these new elements will come at first through traditionalism itself, which might recognize the qualities of adaptiveness in ancient heroes in the crises of the life of the state, and emphasize the desirability of these very elements in political character. There may be a tradition of flexibility as well as one of absolutism and inflexibility, and the old medium may be used to enforce the importance of the new, paradoxical as it may seem. But later it is likely that the open recognition of the inventive and adaptive quality will emerge and be made an integral part of the civic equipment which is sought.

It is precisely in this field that there is opportunity for the reorientation of the individual personality in his relations with the state of which he is a part. For here it becomes clear that authority may stand in its own light by too great emphasis upon obedience and conformity. Automatism and discipline are important and indispensable factors in the political society as in other organizations, but independence, initiative, inventiveness, are of equal value; and this becomes especially clear in the great tension moments of the body politic, when blind obedience is not enough to save the life of the community or to carry through its purpose. Nonconformity may be one of the qualities tending to insure survival, even in war. Mobility as well as weight is an important element in any contest between human beings, and in the life of the state mental mobility on the part of its citizens is of prime importance. Overemphasis on authority tends to repress the free growth of the personality and to inhibit those types of inventiveness and resourcefulness which are often the decisive factors in times of stress. The wise state-builder will take pains to leave free field for the play of individual criticism and construction in the face of authority. There may be levels or tensions of civilization in which this is undesirable, although this may be questioned even in the primitive stage, where fear, force, and routine are the staple methods of control. But in the modern period of intense mobility and widespread mechanization, there is every reason to encourage the growth of the richest and finest types of personalities. Eccentricity and variability must be encouraged, artificially if necessary.

VIII

LITERATURE AND THE MODERN SCENE

"IT is not without hope," writes Vernon L. Parrington in the final volume of his *Main Currents in American Thought*, "that intelligent America is in revolt. The artist is in revolt, the intellectual is in revolt, the conscience of America is in revolt." The expression of this revolt lies in American literature, and the many changes in form, aim, and mood which its different branches have of late years undergone certainly express a more thoroughly critical temper than ever before. Novelists like Dreiser and Sinclair Lewis, essayists like H. L. Mencken, dramatists like Eugene O'Neill, historians like James Harvey Robinson and Charles A. Beard, represent in various ways a sharp break with the past. The "genteel tradition," as Santayana called it, the complacency and innocence that frequently stamp even so strong a writer as Howells, have been definitely discarded. While skepticism and pessimism have thus become more powerful as intellectual undercurrents, the techniques of the novelist, dramatist, and poet have been changed in important respects; a new experimentalism has been permitted. The essays which follow are intended to serve two objects: to define some of the fundamental verities in literature, and at the same time to indicate some of the fresh ideas which have been entering it. The first two writers represented, George Edward Woodberry and Stuart P. Sherman, are among the ablest latter-day exponents of the older literary tradition in America. Such writers as Ludwig Lewisohn, Wilson Follett, and André Maurois, on the other hand, definitely represent the newer tendencies in letters. It is unfortunate that limitations of space forbid treatment of two important forms, the essay and the history. But the general question of style cannot be neglected, and the diverting paper by Sir Arthur Quiller-Couch has been included as a stimulating discussion of one of its aspects.

THE LANGUAGE OF ALL THE WORLD[1]

George Edward Woodberry

GEORGE EDWARD WOODBERRY, one of the greatest American scholars and critics of his generation, died at the beginning of 1930 in his seventy-fifth year. Born at Beverly, Massachusetts, he was an heir to the New England tradition, falling under the influence of Charles Eliot Norton at Harvard, graduating there in 1877, and coming for several years under the personal sway of James Russell Lowell. In Norton's letters are a number of references to Woodberry's fast-growing literary power as he contributed to the *Atlantic* and the *Nation*, while teaching at the University of Nebraska. A few years later he was at Columbia University, one of the first men in the country to teach comparative literature. He held the chair in that subject until 1904, meanwhile writing many essays, a two-volume life of Poe that is still the standard critical if not biographical work, a life of Hawthorne, and much verse. Students sat at the feet of the slightly stooping figure, with the walrus mustache, with keen appreciation of the spiritual refreshment which he offered. One who attended his classes for several years testified that "he had never heard Mr. Woodberry give the same lecture twice, and he had never gone away from any lecture without new appreciations and ideas." Year after year the students in Columbia College voted him their favorite teacher, and after his resignation a number of them kept alive the Woodberry Society in his honor. His essays on literary topics, first gathered into book form under such titles as *Heart of Man, Makers of Literature, The Torch, Appreciation of Literature,* and *Great Writers,* have been collected into six volumes. A polished style, a rich culture, a sane discrimination, were combined in these essays, and in such books as *The Inspiration of Poetry,* with much originality of thought and nobility of feeling.

The language of literature is the language of all the world. It is necessary to divest ourselves at once of the notion of diversified vocal and grammatical speech which constitutes the various tongues of the earth and conceals the identity of image and logic in the minds of all men. Words are intermediary between thought and things. We express ourselves really not through words, which are only signs, but through what they signify — through things. Literature is the expression of life. The question, then, is: What things has literature found most effectual to express life, and has therefore habitually preferred; and what tradition in consequence of this habit of preference has been built up in all literatures, and obtained currency and authority in this province of the wider realm of all art? It is an interesting question, and fundamental for anyone who desires to appreciate

[1] From *The Torch and Other Lectures,* by George Edward Woodberry. Reprinted by permission of Harcourt, Brace and Company, publishers.

literature understandingly. Perhaps you will permit me to approach it somewhat indirectly.

You are all familiar with something that is called poetic diction — that is, a selected language specially fitted for the uses of poetry; and you are, perhaps, not quite so familiar with the analogous feature in prose, which is now usually termed preciosity, preciousness of language — that is, a highly refined and aesthetic diction, such as Walter Pater employs. The two are constant products of language that receives any literary cultivation, and they are sometimes called diseases of language. Thus, in both early and late Greek there sprang up literary styles of expression, involving the preference of certain words, constructions, and even cadences, and the teaching of art in these matters was the business of the Greek rhetorician; so in Italy, Spain, and France, in the Renaissance, similar styles, each departing from the common and habitual speech of the time, grew up, and in England you identify this mood of language in Elizabeth's day as Euphuism. The phenomenon is common, and belongs to the nature of language. Poetic diction, however, you perhaps associate most clearly with the mannerism in language of the eighteenth century in England, when common and so-called vulgar words were exiled from poetry, and Gray, for example, could not speak of the Eton schoolboys as playing hoop, but only as "chasing the rolling circles' speed," and when, to use the stock example, all green things were "verdant." This is fixed in our memory because Wordsworth has the credit of leading an attack on the poetic diction of that period, both critically in his prefaces and practically in his verse; he went to the other extreme, and introduced into his poetry such homely words as "tub," for example; he held that the proper language of poetry is the language of common life. So Emerson in his addresses, you remember, had recourse to the humblest objects for illustration, and shocked the formalism of his time by speaking of "the meal in the firkin, the milk in the pan." He was applying in prose the rule of Wordsworth in poetry. Walt Whitman represents the extreme of this use of the actual language of men. But if you consider the matter, you will see that this choice of the homely word only sets up at last a fashion of homeliness in the place of a fashion of refinement, and breeds, for instance, dialect poets in shoals; and often the choice is really not of the word, but of the homely thing itself as the object of thought and expressive image of it; and in men so great as Emerson and Wordsworth the practice is a proof of that sympathy with common life which made them both great democrats. But in addition to the diction that characterizes an age, you must have observed that in every original writer there grows up a particular vocabulary, structure, and rhythm that he affects and that in the end become his mannerism, or distinctive style, so marked that you recognize his work by its stamp alone, as in Keats, Browning, and Swinburne in poetry, and in Arnold in prose. In other words there is at work in the language of a man, or of an age even, a constant principle of selection which tends to prefer certain ways and forms of speech to others, and in the end develops a language characteristic of the age or of the man.

This principle of selection, whether it works toward refinement or homeliness, operates in the same way. It must be remembered — and it is too often forgotten — that the problem of any artistic work is a problem of economy. How to get into the two hours' traffic of the stage the significance of a whole life, of a group of lives; how to pack into a sixteen-line lyric a dramatic situation and there sphere it in its own emotion; how to rouse passion and pour it in a three-minute poem, like Shelley's "Indian Air" — all these are problems in economy, by which speed, condensation, intensity are gained. Now words in themselves are colorless, except so far as their musical quality is concerned; but the thing that a word stands for has a meaning of its own and usually a meaning charged with associations, and often this associative meaning is the primary and important one in its use. A rose, for example, is but the most beautiful of flowers in itself, but it is so charged with association in men's lives, and still more heavily charged with long use of emotion in literature, that the very word and mere name of it awakes the heart and sets a thousand memories unconsciously vibrating. This added meaning is what I am accustomed to term an overtone in words; and it is manifest that, in view of the necessity for economy in poetic art, those words which are the richest and deepest in overtone will be preferred, because of the speed, certainty, and fullness they contain. The question will be what overtones in life appeal most to this or that poet; he will reproduce them in his verse; Pope will use the overtones of a polished society, Wordsworth and Emerson those of humble life. Now our larger question is: What overtones are characteristically preferred in great literature, in what objects do they most inhere, and in what way is the authoritative tradition of literature, as respects its means of expression, thus built up?

It goes without saying that all overtones are either of thought or feeling. What modes of expression, then, what material objects, what forms of imagination, what abstract principles of thought, are

most deeply charged with ideas and emotions?   It will be agreed that,
as a mere medium, music expresses pure emotion most directly and
richly; music seems to enter the physical frame of the body itself,
and move there with the warmth and instancy of blood.   The sound
of words, therefore, cannot be neglected, and in the melody and echo
of poetry, sound is a cardinal element; yet it is here only the veining
of the marble, it is not the material itself.   In the objects which words
summon up, there is sometimes an emotional power as direct and
immediate as that of music itself, as, for example, in the great features
of nature, the mountains, the plains, the ocean, which awe even the
savage mind.   But, in general, the emotional power of material objects is lent to them by association — that is, by the human use that
has been made of them — as on the plain of Marathon, to use Dr.
Johnson's old illustration, it is the thought of what happened there
that makes the spectator's patriotism "gain force" as he surveys the
scene.   This human use of the world is the fountain of significance
in all imaginative and poetic speech; and in the broad sense history
is the story of this human use of the world.

History is so much of past experience as abides in race memory,
and underlies race literature in the same way that a poet's own experience underlies his expression of life.   I do not mean that when a poet
unlocks his heart, as Shakespeare did in his sonnets, he necessarily
writes his own biography; in the poems he writes there may be much
of actual event as in Burns's love songs, or little as in Dante's *New
Life*.   Much of a poet's experience takes place in imagination only;
the life he tells is oftenest the life that he strongly desires to live, and
the power, the purity and height of his utterance may not seldom be
the greater because experience here uses the voices of desire.   "All I
could never be," in Browning's plangent line, has been the mounting
strain of the sublimest and the tenderest songs of men.   All Ireland
could never be, thrills and sorrows on her harp's most resonant string,
and is the master note to which her sweetest music ever returns.   All
man could never be, makes the sad majesty of Virgil's verse.   As with
a man, what a nation strongly desires is no small part of its life, and is
the mark of destiny upon it, whether for failure or success. . . .
History, then, must be thought of, in its relation to literature, as including the desire as well as the performance of the race.   History,
however, in the narrowest sense, lies close to the roots of imaginative
literature.   The great place of history and its inspirational power in
the literature of the last century I have already referred to; it is one
of the most important elements in the extraordinary reach and

range of that splendid outburst of imagination throughout Europe. Aristotle recognized the value of history as an aid to the imagination, at the very moment that he elevated poetry above history. In that necessary economy of art, of which I spoke, it is a great gain to have well-known characters and familiar events, such as Agamemnon and the Trojan War, in which much is already done for the spectator before the play begins. So our present historical novelists have their stories half-written for them in the minds of their readers, and especially avail themselves of an emotional element there, a patriotism, which they do not have to create. The use of history to the imagination, however, goes farther than merely to spare it the pains of creating character and incident and evoking emotion. It assists a literary movement to begin with race power much as a poet's or — as in Dickens's case — a novelist's own experience aids him to develop his work, however much that experience may be finally transformed in the work. Thus the novel of the last age really started its great career from Scott's historic sense working out into imaginative expression, and in a lesser degree from so minor a writer as Miss Edgeworth, in whose Irish stories — which were contemporary history — Scott courteously professed to find his own starting point. It is worth noting, also, that the Elizabethan drama had the same course. Shakespeare, following Marlowe's example, developed from the historical English plays, in which he worked in Scott's manner, into his full control of imagination in the purely ideal sphere. History has thus often been the handmaid of imagination, and the foster mother of great literary ages. Yet, to vary Aristotle's phrase, poetry is all history could never be.

It appears to me, nevertheless, that history underlies race literature in a far more profound and universal way. History is mortal: it dies. Yet it does not altogether die. Elements, features, fragments of it survive and enter into the eternal memory of the race, and are there transformed and, as we say, spiritualized. Literature is the abiding-place of this transforming power, and most profits by it. And to come to the heart of the matter, there have been at least three such cardinal transformations in the past.

The first transformation of history is mythology. I do not mean to enter on the vexed question of the origin of mythologies; and, of course, in referring to history as its ground, I include much more than that hero-worship such as you will find elaborated or invented in Carlyle's essay on Odin, and especially I include all that experience of nature and her association with human toil and moods that you will find delineated with such marvelous subtleness and fullness in Walter Pater's essay on Dionysus. In mythology, mankind preserved from his primitive experience of nature, and his own heroic past therein, all that had any lasting significance; and, although all mythologies have specific features and a particular value of their own, yet the race, coming to its best, as I have said, bore here its perfect blossom in Greek mythology. I know not by what grace of Heaven, by what felicity of blend in climate, blood, and the fortune of mortal life, but so it was that the human soul put forth the bud of beauty in the Greek race; and there, at the dawn of our own intellectual civilization and in the first sunrise of our poetry in Homer, was found a world filled with divine, with majestic and lovely figures, which had absorbed into their celestial being and forms the power of nature, the splendor and charm of the material sphere, the fructifying and beneficent operations of the external universe, the providence of the state and the inspiration of all arts and crafts, of games and wars and song; each of these deities was a flashing center of human energy, aspiration, reliance — with a realm and servants of its own; and mingling with them in fair companionship was a company of demi-gods and heroes, of kings and princes, and of golden youths, significant of the fate of all young life — Adonis, Hippolytus, Orestes. This mythologic world was near to earth, and it mixed with legendary history, such history as the *Iliad* contained, and also with the private and public life of the citizens, being the ceremonial religion of the state. It was all, nevertheless, the transformation that man had accomplished of his own past, his joys and sorrows, his labors, his insights and desires, the deeds of his ancestors — the human use that he had made of the world. This was the body of idea and emotion to which the poet appealed in that age, precisely as our historical novelists now appeal to our own knowledge of history and pre-established emotion with regard to it, our patriotism. Here they found a language already full charged with emotion and intelligence, of which they could avail themselves, and speaking which they spoke with the voices of a thousand years. Nevertheless, it was at best a language like others, and subject to change and decay in expressive power. The time came when, the creative impulse in mythology having ceased and its forms being fixed, the mythic world lay behind the mind of the advancing race which had now attained conceptions of the physical universe, and especially ideas of the moral life, which were no longer capable of being held in and expressed by the mythic world, but exceeded the bounds of earlier thought and feeling and broke the ancient molds.

Then it was that Plato desired to exile the poets and their mythology from the state. He could not be content, either, with a certain change that had occurred; for the creative power in mythology having long ceased, as I have said, the imagination put forth a new function — a meditative power — and brooding over the old fables of the world of the gods discovered in them, not a record of fact, but an allegorical meaning, a higher truth which the fable contained. Mythology passed thus into an emblematic stage, in which it was again long used by mankind, as a language of universal power. Plato, however, could not free himself from the mythologic habit of imagination so planted in his race, and found the most effective expression for his ideas in the myths of his own invention which he made up by a dexterous and poetic adaptation of the old elements; and others later than Plato have found it hard to disuse the mythologic language; for, although the old religion as a thing of faith and practice died away, it survived as a thing of form and feature in art, as a phase of natural symbolism and of inward loveliness of action and passion in poetry, as a chapter of romance in the history of the race; and the modern literatures of Europe are, in large measure, unintelligible without this key.

The second great transformation of history is chivalry. Here the phenomenon is nearer in time and lies more within the field of observation and knowledge; it is possible to trace the stages of the growth of the story of Roland with some detail and precision; but, on the other hand, the Arthur myth reaches far back into the beginnings of Celtic imagination, and all such race myths tend to appropriate and embody in themselves the characteristic features both of one another and of whatever is held to be precious and significant in history or even in classical and Eastern legend. The true growth, however, is that feudal culture, which we know as knighthood, working out its own ideal of action and character and sentiment on a basis of bravery, courtesy, and piety, and thereby generating patterns of knighthood, typical careers, and in the end an imaginative interpretation of the purest spiritual life itself in the various legends of the Holy Grail. As in the pagan world the forms and fables of mythology and their interaction downward with the human world furnished the imaginative interpretation of life as it then was, so for the mediaeval age, the figures and tales of chivalry and their interaction upward with the spiritual world of Christianity, and also with the magic diabolism round about, furnished the imaginative interpretation of that later life. It was this new body of ideas and emotion in the minds of men that the mediaeval poets appealed to, availed themselves of, and so spoke a language of imagery and passion that was a world language, charged as I have said with the thought and feeling, the tradition, of a long age. What happened to the language of mythology happened also to this language; it lost the power of reality, and men arose who, being in advance of its conceptions of life, desired to exile it, denounce it or laugh it out of existence, like Ascham in England, and Cervantes in Spain. It also suffered that late change into an allegorical or emblematic meaning, and had a second life in that form as in the notable instance of Spenser's "Faerie Queene." It also could not die, but — just as mythology revived in the Alexandrian poets for a season, and fed Theocritus and Virgil — chivalry was reborn in the last century, and in Tennyson's "Arthur" and Wagner's *Parsifal* lived again in two great expressions of ideal life.

The third great transformation of history is contained in the Scriptures. The Bible is, in itself, a singularly complete expression of the whole life of a race in one volume — its faith and history blending in one body of poetry, thought, and imaginative chronicle. It contains a celestial world in association with human events; its patriarchs are like demi-gods, and it has heroes, legends, tales in good numbers, and much romantic and passionate life, on the human side, besides its great stores of spirituality. In literary power it achieves the highest in the kinds of composition that it uses. It is as a whole, regarded purely from the human point of view, not unfairly to be compared, in mass, variety, and scope of expression, with mythology and chivalry as constituting a third great form of imaginative language; nor has its history been dissimilar in the Christian world to which it came with something of that same remoteness in time and reality that belonged equally to mythology and chivalry. It was first used in a positive manner, as a thing of fact and solid belief; but there soon grew up, you remember, in the Christian world that habit of finding a hidden meaning in its historical record, of turning it to a parable, of extracting from it an allegorical signification. It became, not only in parts but as a whole, emblematic, and its interpretation as such was the labor of centuries. This is commonly stated as the source of that universal mood of allegorizing which characterized the mediaeval world, and was as strongly felt in secular as in religious writers. Its historical tales, its theories of the universe, its cruder morals in the Jewish ages, have been scoffed at, just as was the case with the Greek myth, from the Apostate to Voltaire and later; but how great are its powers as a language is seen in the completeness with which it tyrannized over the

Puritan life in England and made its history, its ideas, its emotions the habitual and almost exclusive speech of that strong Cromwellian age. In our country here in New England it gave the mold of imagination to our ancestors for two whole centuries. A book which contains such power that it can make itself the language of life through so many centuries and in such various peoples is to be reckoned as one of the greatest instruments of race expression that man possesses.

Mythology, chivalry, the Scriptures are the tongues of the imagination. It is far more important to know them than to learn French or German or Italian, or Latin or Greek; they are three branches of that universal language which though vainly sought on the lips of men is found in their minds and hearts. To omit these in education is to defraud youth of its inheritance; it is like destroying a long-developed organ of the body, like putting out the eye or silencing the nerves of hearing. Nor is it enough to look them up in encyclopaedias and notes, and so obtain a piecemeal information; one must grow familiar with these forms of beauty, forms of honor, forms of righteousness, have something of the same sense of their reality as that felt by Homer and Virgil, by the singer of *Roland* and the chronicler of the *Mort d'Arthur*, by St. Augustine and St. Thomas. He must form his imagination upon these idealities, and load his heart with them; else many a masterpiece of the human spirit will be lost to him, and most of the rest will be impaired. If one must know vocabulary and grammar before he can understand the speech of the mouth, much more must he know well mythology, chivalry, and Bible lore before he can take possession of the wisdom that the race mind has spoken, the beauty it has molded life into, as a thing of passion and action, the economy of lucid power it has achieved for perfect human utterance, in these three fundamental forms of a true world language. The literature of the last century is permeated with mythology, chivalry, and to a less degree with Scripture, and no one can hope to assimilate it, to receive its message, unless his mind is drenched with these same things; and the further back his tastes and desires lead him into the literature of earlier times, the greater will be his need of this education in the material, the modes, and the forms of past imagination.

It may be that a fourth great tongue of the imagination is now being shaped upon the living lips of men in the present and succeeding ages. If it be so, this will be the work of the democratic idea, which is now still at the beginning of its career; but since mythology and chivalry had their development in living men, it is natural to suppose that the human force is still operative in our own generation as it once was in those of Hellenic and mediaeval years. The characteristic literature of democracy is that of its ideas, spiritualized in Shelley, and that of the common lot as represented in the sphere of the novel, spiritualized most notably in Victor Hugo. In our own country it is singular to observe that the democratic idea, though efficient in politics, does not yet establish itself in imaginative literature with any great power of brilliancy, does not create great democratic types, or in any way express itself adequately. This democratic idea, in Dickens for example, uses the experience of daily life — that is, contemporary history — or at least it uses an artistic arrangement of such experience; but the novel as a whole has given us, in regard to the common lot, rather a description of life in its variety than that concentrated and essential significance of life which we call typical. If democracy in its future course should evolve such a typical and spiritualized embodiment of itself as chivalry found in Arthur and the Round Table, or as the heroic age of Greece found in Achilles and the Trojan War, or as the genius of Rome found in Aeneas and his fortunes, then imagination — race imagination — will be enriched by this fourth great instrument; but this is to cast the horoscope of too distant an hour. I introduce the thought only for the sake of including in this broad survey of race imagination that experience of the present day, that history in the contemporary process of being transformed, out of which the mass of the books of the day are now made.

Let me recur now to that principle of selection which through the cumulative action of repeated preference of phrase and image fixes a habit of choice which at last stamps the diction of a man, a school, or an age. It is plain that in what I have called the transformation of history, of which literature is the express image, there is the same principle of selection which, working through long periods of race life, results at last in those idealities of persons and events in which inhere most powerfully those overtones of beauty, honor, and righteousness that the race has found most precious both for idea and emotion; and to these are to be added what I have had no time to include and discuss; the idealities of persons and events found outside mythology, chivalry, and Scripture, in the work of individual genius like Shakespeare, which nevertheless have the same ground in history, in experience, that in them is similarly transformed. Life experience spiritualized is the formula of all great literature; it may range from the experience of a single life, like Sidney's in his sonnets to that of an empire in Virgil's *Aeneid*, or of a religion in Dante's *Comedy*. In either case the formula which makes it literature is the same. I have illustrated the point by the obvious spiritualizations of history. Race life, from the point of view of literature, results at last in these molds of imagination, and all else though slowly, yet surely, drops away into oblivion. In truth, it is only by being thus spiritualized that anything human survives from the past. The rose, I said, has been so dipped in human experience that it is less a thing of nature than a thing of passion. In the same way Adonis, Jason and Achilles, Roland and Arthur, Lancelot, Percival and Galahad, Romeo and Hamlet, have drawn into themselves such myriads of human lives by admiration and love that from them everything material, contemporary, and mortal has been refined away, and they seem to all of us like figures moving in an immortal air. They have achieved the eternal world. To do this is the work of art. It may seem a fantastic idea, but I will venture the saying of it, since to me it is the truth. Art, I suppose, you think of as the realm and privilege of selected men, of sculptors, painters, musicians, poets, men of genius and having something that has always been called divine in their faculty; but it appears to me that art, like genius, is something that all men share, that it is the stamp of the soul in everyone, and constitutes their true and immaterial life. The soul of the race, as it is seen in history and disclosed by history, is an artist soul; its career is an artistic career; its unerring selective power expels from its memory every mortal element and preserves only the essential spirit, and thereof builds its ideal imaginative world through which it finds its true expression; its more perfect comprehension of the world is science, its more perfect comprehension of its own nature is love, its more perfect expression of its remembered life is art. Mankind is the grandest and surest artist of all, and history as it clarifies is, in pure fact, an artistic process, a creation in its fullness of the beautiful soul.

It appears, then, that the language of literature in the race is a perfected nature and a perfected manhood and a perfected divinity, so far as the race at the moment can see toward perfection. The life which literature builds up ideally out of the material of experience is not wholly a past life, but there mingles with it and at last controls it the life that man desires to live. Fullness of life — that fullness of action which is poured in the drama, that fullness of desire that is poured in the lyric — the life of which man knows himself capable and realizes as the opportunity and hope of life — this is the life that literature enthrones in its dream. You have heard much of the will to believe and of the desire to live: literature is made of these two, warp and woof. Race after race believes in the gods it has come to know and in the heroes it has borne, and in what it wishes to believe of divine and human experience; and the life it thus ascribes to its gods and to its own past is the life it most ardently desires to live. Literature, which records this, is thus the chief witness to the nobility, the constancy and instancy of man's effort for perfection. What wonder, then, if in his sublimest and tenderest song there steals that note of melancholy so often struck by the greatest masters in the crisis and climax of their works, and which, when so struck, has more of the infinite in it, more of the human in it, than any other in the slowly triumphant theme!

To sum up — the language of literature is experience; the language of race literature is race experience, or history, the human use that the race has made of the world. The law appears to be that history in this sense is slowly transformed by a refining and spiritualizing process into an imaginative world, such as the world of mythology, chivalry, or the Scriptures, and that this world in turn becomes emblematic and fades away into an expression of abstract truth. The crude beginning of the process is seen in our historical fiction; the height of it in Arthur or in Odin; the end of it in the symbolic or allegoric interpretation of even so human a book as Virgil's *Aeneid*. Human desire for the best enters into this process with such force that the record of the past slowly changes into the prophecy of the future, and out of the passing away of what was is built the dream of what shall be; so arises in race life the creed of what man wishes to believe and the dream of the life he desires to live; this human desire for belief and for life is, in the final analysis, the principle of selection whose operation has been sketched, and on its validity rests the validity and truth of all literature.

TRADITION[1]

Stuart P. Sherman

STUART P. SHERMAN was not yet forty-five when he died in Michigan in the summer of 1926; but he had already achieved a place with Paul Elmer More and W. C. Brownell as one of the three greatest American critics since Lowell. After taking his doctorate at Harvard, he began his critical writing in the spirit of More's and Irving Babbitt's very conservative Humanism, and he always shared their general moral standpoint, their insistence on fixed and considered critical standards, their deep scholarliness. His first book, *On Contemporary Literature* (1916), was made up of essays he had contributed to the *Nation* under Paul Elmer More's editorship, and was dedicated to More. But as his views matured he followed an increasingly independent path, until in the end the more radical critics — the supporters of literary innovation, who dissented from More's condemnation of romanticism and realism and his exaltation of classicism — felt that Sherman had come into their camp. He believed, as he wrote in a letter of 1923, that More and Babbitt "keep too far from the scene of action"; that "they interest themselves in too restricted aspects of literature"; that "they are too remorselessly negative"; and that "in their ultimate position they are both dogmatic and mystical." His own position was expounded in a distinguished series of books, close-packed with thought, reflecting an enormous reading, pungently phrased, and irradiated by a shrewd, biting humor. These showed a singularly catholic range of interests, a vigorous concern with all kinds of contemporary American problems, and a warm appreciation for what Matthew Arnold called "the admirable riches of human nature." Some of the volumes — *Matthew Arnold, Points of View, Critical Woodcuts*, for example — deal wholly or almost wholly with literature. But he was at his best in those books — *Americans, The Genius of America, Shaping Men and Women*, for example — which treated a broader range of subjects. It would be difficult to find a better introduction to the American spirit than the papers on Franklin, Emerson, Whitman, the Adams family, Joaquin Miller, Andrew Carnegie, and Theodore Roosevelt in the first of these three volumes.

Apart from his books, Sherman's life fell into three periods. The first was made up of his boyhood in Iowa, the Southwest, and New England, and his education at Williams College and Harvard. The second comprised his long years as teacher of English literature, 1907-1924, at the University of Illinois. The third began when in 1924 he came to New York as literary editor of the *Herald Tribune*. To successive classes of students at the University of Illinois he furnished both intellectual stimulation and spiritual inspiration of the rarest kind, and he gave unselfishly of his time to the more promising long after they had gone out into the world. His rank as a university teacher is with Lowell, Norton, Woodberry, and Spingarn. As literary editor, contributing long essays almost weekly to *Herald Tribune Books*, he had begun to do for America what Sainte-Beuve did for France when death prematurely cut short his labors.

[1] From *Americans*, by Stuart P. Sherman. Reprinted by permission of Charles Scribner's Sons, publishers.

To lengthen the childhood of the individual, at the same time bringing to bear upon it the influences of tradition, is the obvious way to shorten the childhood of races, nations, classes, and so to quicken the general processes of civilization. Yet in the busy hum of self-approbation which accompanies the critical activities of our young people, perhaps the dominant note is their satisfaction at having emancipated themselves from the fetters of tradition, the oppression of classical precedent, the burden of an inherited culture. By detaching the new literature from its learned past they are confident that they are assuring it a popular future. Turn to any one of half a dozen books which discuss the present movement, and you will learn that people are now discovering, for example, "often to their own surprise," that they can read and enjoy poetry. That is because poetry has been subjected to "democratization." The elder writers, such as Shakespeare, Milton, Emerson, and Longfellow, constantly graveled them with strange and obsolete phrases, like "multitudinous seas incarnadine," and like "tumultuous privacy of storm." The ancient writers sent them to out-of-the-way reference books to look up obscure legends about Troy, not the city where collars are made, and old stuff about war in Heaven, and the landing at Plymouth Rock. It is therefore a relief to countless eager young souls that Mr. Mencken has dismissed all this as "the fossil literature taught in colleges," and that Mary Austin insists that native verse rhythms must be "within the capacity of the democratically bred." It is a joy to hear from Mr. Untermeyer that modern readers of poetry may now come out from the "lifeless and literary storehouse" and use life itself for their glossary, as indeed they may — or the morning's newspaper.

Those who encourage us to hope for crops without tillage, learning without study, and literary birth without gestation or travail are doubtless animated by a desire to augment the sum of human felicity; but one recalls Burke's passionate ejaculation: "Oh! no, sir, no. Those things which are not practicable are not desirable." To the new mode of procuring a literary renascence there may be raised one objection, which, to minds of a certain temper, will seem rather grave: all experience is against it. Such is the thesis recently argued by an English critic, Mr. H. J. Massingham, who reviews with mingled amusement and alarm the present "self-conscious rebellion against tradition." In the eyes of our excited young "cosmopolitans," whose culture has a geographic rather than an historical extension, Mr. Massingham's opinions will of course appear to be hopelessly prejudiced by his Oxford breeding, his acquaintance with the classics, his saturation in Elizabethan literature, and his avowed passion for old books in early editions, drilled by the bibliomaniac worm, "prehistoric" things, like Nares' *Glossary* and Camden's *Remains*. But it is not merely the opinion of our critic that is formidable: "The restoration of the traditional link with the art of the past is a conservative and revolutionary necessity." It is not the supporting opinion of Sir Joshua Reynolds: "The only food and nourishment of the mind of an artist is the great works of his predecessors." Sir Joshua, too, was prejudiced by his position as a pillar of the robust English classicism of George III's time. It is not even the opinion of Henry James, whom Mr. Massingham proclaims the profoundest critic since Coleridge, and who even our own irreverent youth seem to suspect should be mentioned respectfully: "It takes an endless amount of history to make even a little tradition, and an endless amount of tradition to make even a little taste, and an endless amount of taste, by the same token, to make even a little tranquillity."

The formidable arguments against the radical engineers of renascence are just the notorious facts of literary history. The fact that a bit of the "fossil literature taught in colleges," the story of Arthur, written in Latin by a Welsh monk in the twelfth century, has flowered and fruited in poetry, painting, and music generation after generation pretty much over the civilized world. The fact that Chaucer and his contemporaries, in whom poetry had a glorious rebirth, had previously devoured everything in what Mr. Untermeyer would call the "lifeless and literary storehouse" of the Middle Ages. The fact that the Elizabethans, to quote Mr. Massingham's vigorous phrase, flung themselves on tradition "like a hungry wolf, not only upon the classics, but upon all the tradition open to them." The fact that Restoration comedy is simply a revival of late Caroline in the hands of men who had studied Molière. The fact that the leaders of the new movement in the eighteenth century, when they wished to break from the stereotyped classicism, did not urge young people to slam the door on the past, but, on the contrary, harked back over the heads of Pope and Dryden to the elder and more central tradition of Milton, Shakespeare, and Spenser; and sluiced into the arid fields of common sense, grown platitudinous, the long-dammed or subterranean currents of mediaeval romance. The fact that "Childe Harold," "Adonais," "The Eve of St. Agnes," "The Cotter's Saturday Night," and "The Castle of Indolence" were all written by imitators of Spenser or by imitators of his imitators. The fact, to omit the Victorians, that

Mr. W. B. Yeats, the most skillful living engineer of literary renascence, set all his collaborators to digging around the roots of the ancient Celtic tree before we enjoyed the blossoming of the new spring in Ireland. The fact that John Masefield, freshest and most tuneful voice in England, is obviously steeped to the lips in the poetry of Byron, Shakespeare, Spenser, and Chaucer.

Why is it that the great poets, novelists, and critics, with few exceptions, have been, in the more liberal sense of the word, scholars — masters of several languages, students of history and philosophy, antiquarians? First of all because the great writer conceives of his vocation as the most magnificent and the most complex of crafts. He is to be his own architect, master builder, carpenter, painter, singer, orator, poet, and dramatist. His materials, his tools, his methods are, or may be, infinite. To him, then, the written tradition is a school and a museum in which, if he has a critical and inventive mind, he learns, from both the successes and the failures of his predecessors, how to set to work upon his own problems of expression. As Mr. Yeats is fond of pointing out, the young poet may find Herbert and Vaughan more helpful to him than the work of his own contemporaries, because the faults in the elder poets, the purple patches that failed to hold their color, will not attract and mislead him.

But tradition is more than a school of crafts. It is a school of mood and manners. The artist who is also a scholar cannot fail to discover that what distinguishes all the golden periods of art, what constitutes the perpetual appeal of the masters, is a kind of innermost poise and serenity, tragic in Sophocles, heroic in Michelangelo, skeptical in Montaigne, idyllic in Sidney, ironic in Fielding. This enviable tranquillity reigns only in a mind that, looking before and after, feels itself the representative of something outlasting time, some national ideal, some religious faith, some permanent human experience, some endless human quest. Nothing begets this mood and manner, the sovereign mark of good breeding in letters, like habitual association with those who have it, the majority of whom are, in the vulgar sense of the word, dead. Izaak Walton, a minor writer in whose work there is a golden afterglow of the great age, calls, in one of his Angler's Dialogues, for "that smooth song which was made by Kit Marlowe, now at least fifty years ago," and for the answer to it "which was made by Sir Walter Raleigh in his younger days." If some of our modern imitators of the auctioneer and the steam calliope would now and then, instead of reading one another, step into the "lifeless and literary storehouse" and compare these "fossils" conscientiously with their own recent efforts to make verse popular! "They were old-fashioned poetry," says Piscator apologetically, "but choicely good, I think much better than the strong lines that are now in fashion in this critical age."

Out of the tranquillity induced by working in a good literary tradition develops form. The clever theorists who insist that form alone matters, that form is the only preservative element in literature, forget that form is not "self-begotten" but a product of the formative spirit. Mr. Massingham is a bit fastidious in his use of this word. He denies form, for example, to Pope and to Swinburne. Though both have technique, that is another matter. "Form," he declares, "is a vision contained and made manifest." He attributes the unproductiveness of our age in the field of satire to a vision without a traditional base, reeling and shifting in the choppy waters of contemporary opinion. His remarks on the deficiencies of Gilbert Cannan as a satirist and novelist further elucidate his idea; and they may serve also as a comment upon many of the younger writers in America.

The works of Mr. Cannan seem to say, "That is what life is — a surge of base and beautiful forces, intensified in the consciousness of man." But that is a fallacy. Life is like that to the layman, but it is the business of the artist to see a clue in it, to give it shape and order, to weld its particles into congruity. Here is where his lack of a constructive or satiric purpose growing out of and controlling the material tells to his hurt. He knows life in the raw, but the satirist would put it in the oven and dish it up. So he wanders in the dark, and we blunder after him. But we want light, if it be only from a tallow candle.

Now, many of the young writers in America are disposed to reject the English tradition as unserviceable lumber. They scorn equally the greater part of the American tradition as puritanical, effeminate, or over-intellectualized. If they seek foreign allies, it is with those who help them forget our national characteristics, our native bent and purposes, our discovered special American "genius." In what measure is the revolt due to the conduct of the movement by writers whose blood and breeding are as hostile to the English strain as a cat to water? Whatever the answer, I suspect that the young people who are being congratulated right and left on their emancipation from tradition are rather open to condolence than to felicitation. They have broken away from so much that was formative, and they suffer so obviously in consequence of the break. Their poets have lost a skill which Poe had: though they paint a little, and chant a little, and speak a great deal of faintly rhythmical prose, they have not learned how to sing. Their novelists have lost a vision which Howells had:

though they have shaken off the "moralistic incubus" and have released their "suppressed desires," they have not learned how to conceive or to present a coherent picture of civilized society. Their
leaders have lost a constructiveness which a critic so laden with
explosives as Emerson exhibited: though they have blown up the old
highways they have not made new roads.

Am I doing the "young people" an injustice? I turn from their
anthologies of verse, where I keep searching in vain for such music as
the angler's milkmaid sang; and from the novels of Mr. Cabell, in
whom I have not discovered that ascending sun heralded by the look-
outs; to *A Modern Book of Criticism*, recently collected and put forth
by Mr. Ludwig Lewisohn. The editor's desire is to show us that
"a group of critics, young men or men who do not grow old, are at
work upon the creation of a civilized cultural atmosphere in America."
The idea resembles that — does it not? — of Mr. Waldo Frank, who recently informed us that literature began in America in 1900 — or was
it 1910? — at Mr. Stieglitz's place in New York. . . . The implication is clearly that the country which developed Bradford, Franklin,
Emerson, Lincoln, Thoreau, Whitman, Mark Twain, here and there in
villages and backwoods, had no "civilized cultural atmosphere" worth
mentioning. It does not seem quite plausible.

But let us proceed with Mr. Lewisohn. His critics: "Like a group
of shivering young Davids — slim and frail but with a glimpse of
morning sunshine on their foreheads — they face an army of Goliaths."
The slim and shivering young Davids turn out on investigation to be
Mr. Huneker, Mr. Spingarn, Mr. Mencken, Mr. Lewisohn, Mr.
Hackett, Mr. Van Wyck Brooks, and Randolph Bourne. It is not a
group, taken as a whole, however it may be connected with the house
of Jesse, which should be expected to hear any profound murmuring of
ancestral voices or to experience any mysterious inflowing of national
experience in meditating on the names of Mark Twain, Whitman,
Thoreau, Lincoln, Emerson, Franklin, and Bradford. One doesn't
blame our Davids for their inability to connect themselves vitally with
this line of Americans, for their inability to receive its tradition or to
carry it on. But one cannot help asking whether this inability does
not largely account for the fact that Mr. Lewisohn's group of critics
are restless impressionists, almost destitute of doctrine, and with no
discoverable unifying tendency except to let themselves out into a
homeless happy land where they may enjoy the "colorful" cosmic
weather, untroubled by business men, or middle class Americans, or
Congressmen, or moralists, or humanists, or philosophers, or pro-

fessors, or Victorians, or Puritans, or New Englanders, or Messrs. Tarkington and Churchill. A jolly lot of Goliaths to slay before we get that "civilized cultural atmosphere."

By faithfully studying the writing of Mr. Mencken, Mr. Lewisohn, and other "shivering young Davids," I have obtained a fairly clear conception of what a "civilized cultural atmosphere" is not. It consists of none of those heart-remembered things — our own revenue officers probing our old shoes for diamond necklaces, our own New York newspapers, and Maryland chicken on the Albany boat — which cause a native American returning from a year in Europe to exclaim as he sails up the tranquil bosom of the Hudson and rushes, by a standard steel Pullman, back to the great warm embrace of his own land, "Thank Heaven, we are home again." No, it is none of these things. If, without going to Munich, you wish to know what a "civilized cultural atmosphere" really is, you must let Mr. Lewisohn describe it for you as it existed, till the passage of the Volstead Act, in one or two odd corners of old New York: "The lamps of the tavern had orange-colored shades, the wainscotting was black with age. The place was filled with a soothing dusk and the blended odor of beer and tobacco and Wiener Schnitzel. *I was, at least, back in civilization.* That tavern is gone now, swept away by the barbarism of the Neo-Puritans."

To the book from which this quotation is made, Mr. Lewisohn's recently published autobiographical record, *Up Stream*, students of contemporary critical currents and eddies are much indebted. The author, like many of the other belligerent young writers who have shown in recent years a grave concern for the state of civilization in America, has ostensibly been directing his attack against our national culture from a very elevated position. He has professed himself one of the enlightened spirits who from time to time rise above the narrowing prejudices of nationality into the free air of the republic of letters, the grand cosmopolis of the true humanist. From his watchtower — apparently "in the skies" — he has launched lightnings of derision at those who still weave garlands for their Lares and Penates, at the nationalist with his "selective sympathies," at the traditionalist with his sentimental fondness for folkways. Those who feel strongly attracted, as I do myself, to the Ciceronian and Stoic conception of a universal humanity and by the Christian and Augustinian vision of a universal City of God, may easily have mistaken Mr. Lewisohn for a "sharpshooter" of the next age, an outpost from the land of their heart's desire. But in *Up Stream*, Mr. Lewisohn drops the mask and reveals himself, for all his Jewish radicalism, as essentially a sentimental and homesick German, longing in exile for a Germany which exists only in his imagination.

Even the purified and liberated mind of a Child of Light, living according to nature and reason, is unable to rid itself wholly of "selective sympathies." It betrays under provocation a merely "traditional emotion" for a cultural atmosphere compounded of the odors of beer, tobacco, and Wiener Schnitzel, with perhaps a whiff of Kant and a strain of Hungarian music floating through it, while two or three high philosophical spirits discuss what a poet can do when his wife grows old and stringy. I do not think it necessary to remonstrate with a man merely because his affective nature responds powerfully to a vision of felicity thus composed; but I think it a bit impractical to ask "a nation of prohibitionists and Puritans" to accept this vision as the goal of cultural efforts in America. It is a help to fruitful controversy, however, when a man abandons his absurdly insincere professions of "universal sympathy" — his purring protestation that he desires "neither to judge nor to condemn" — and frankly admits that he likes the German life, what he knows of it, and that he regards American life, what he knows of it, as "ugly and mean."

The militant hostility of alien-minded critics toward what they conceive to be the dominant traits of the national character is, on the whole, to be welcomed as provocative of reflection and as a corrective to national conceit. But the amendment of that which is really ugly and mean and basely repressive in our contemporary society is less likely to be achieved by listening to the counsels of exiled emancipators from Munich than by harking back to our own liberative tradition, which long antedates the efforts of these bewildered impressionists.

When we grow dull and inadventurous and slothfully content with our present conditions and our old habits, it is not because we are "traditionalists"; it is, on the contrary, because we have ceased to feel the formative spirit of our own traditions. It is not much in the American vein, to be sure, to construct private little anarchies in the haze of a smoking-room; but practical revolt, on a large scale and sagaciously conducted, is an American tradition, which we should continue to view with courage and the tranquillity which is related to courage. America was born because it revolted. It revolted because it condemned. It condemned because its sympathies were not universal but selective. Its sympathies were selective because it had a vision of a better life, pressing for fulfillment. That vision, and not a conception of life as a meaningless "surge of base and beautiful forces," liberated its chief men of letters.   Thence their serenity, in place of that "gentle but chronic dizziness" which a critic of Young Germany, Hugo von Hofmannsthal, says "vibrated among us." Thence, too, their freedom from ancestor-worship and bondage to the letter.   Listen to Emerson:

> Ask not me, as Muftis can,
> To recite the Alcoran;
> Well I love the meaning sweet;
> I tread the book beneath my feet.

Thence, too, the traditional bent of the American spirit toward modernity, toward realism.   It was nearly a hundred years ago that our then leading critic wrote in his journal: "You must exercise your genius in some form that has essential life now; do something which is proper to the hour and cannot but be done."   Did he not recognize what was to be done?   I quote once more from him a finer sentence than any of our impressionists has ever written: "A wife, a babe, a brother, poverty, and a country, which the Greeks had, I have." The grip and the beauty of that simple sentence are due to a union in it of an Athenian vision with Yankee self-reliance.   It is the kind of feeling that comes to a man who has lived in a great tradition.

FIGURES IN A DREAM[1]

Chauncey Brewster Tinker

CHAUNCEY B. TINKER was born at Auburn, Maine, in 1876, and educated at Yale University. After teaching for a time at Bryn Mawr, he returned to Yale in 1903 to teach English literature. Since 1924 he has been Sterling Professor of English. His writings, which are chiefly in the field of the eighteenth century, include *Dr. Johnson and Fanny Burney* (1911); *The Salon and English Letters* (1915); *Young Boswell* (1922); and *Nature's Simple Plan* (1922). He has also edited the letters of James Boswell.

POETRY AND THE FASHIONS

How doth the city sit solitary, that was full of people! how is she become as a widow! she that was great among the nations, and princess among the provinces, how is she become tributary!
— LAMENTATIONS OF JEREMIAH

When, toward the end of May, 1770, "The Deserted Village" issued from the press, its author was, with but a single exception, the best known of living English poets. Thomas Gray, indeed, was still alive, but no longer productive, and was, moreover, at the threshold of the last year of his life. Gray read the poem and praised its author — Gray was chary of praise — and may well have detected in it that rare union of high literary distinction and wide popular appeal that marked his own "Elegy." The "Elegy" had appeared twenty years before, and had been at once received into the hearts of men. "The Deserted Village," like its great predecessor, has kept its place in the esteem of critics and in the affection of readers in a way that may properly challenge the attention of all persons who are seriously concerned for the welfare of poetry.

Evidences of its popularity and influence appeared at once. So many editions of it were issued that they have constituted ever since a bibliographical problem. It begot, soon after its appearance, an imitation by one "A.K." of the Middle Temple, who inscribed his verses "with much respect" to "Dr. Oliver Goldsmith (in whose acquaintance he [the author] is personally honored)," and entitled them, rather presumptuously, "The Frequented Village." This of

---

[1] From *The Good Estate of Poetry*, by Chauncey Brewster Tinker. Reprinted by permission of Little, Brown & Company, publishers.

course is a mere literary curiosity; but the influence of Goldsmith's poem is writ large elsewhere. It exerted an influence truly creative on the Romantic movement, not only in England but on the Continent. This is not the place to dwell on the indebtedness of German literature to Oliver Goldsmith; but we may mention two interesting events which occurred within two years of the publication of the poem in England. In the first place, in 1771 the youthful Goethe translated the poem into German — a work which has unfortunately disappeared. Secondly, in the next year, probably in the month of May, he had the original English text published at Darmstadt, "printed for a friend of the Vicar." In the same year there appeared a French imitation of the poem at Brussels, entitled, "Le Retour du Philosophe, ou le Village abandonné." A long line of translations and imitations followed this.

Among the careful students of the poem was Robert Burns, whose "Cotter's Saturday Night" and a dozen other poems exist to show that the "pastoral simplicity" of rural life, though it may have departed from England, is still to be found in Scotland. When George Crabbe, in revolt from the warm pastoral romanticism of his time, attacked the idealization of rural life, he called his bitter exposé "The Village," in obvious reminiscence of Goldsmith's poem, and summed up his views in the line —

Auburn and Eden can be found no more.

But the poet would certainly not have been content with a merely literary influence. He aspired to draw effective attention to an alarming evidence of national decay. He was disturbed, and he might well be disturbed, by the condition of the English countryside. As a result of the vast accumulation of wealth, he saw an increasing number of great estates with large tracts "improved" by the new art of landscape gardening, and exhibiting long, picturesque prospects, which were often enriched with a glimpse of a Gothic ruin, sometimes genuine, sometimes an imitation of the antique in lath and plaster. It was all got up to look very fine; but cottages formerly occupied by peasants and busy tillers of the soil had at times to be swept away wholesale in order to open out the fine views.[1] Still other tracts of land had to be "preserved" for game.

[1] "It is too much the interest of a parish, both landlords and tenants, to decrease the cottages in it — and, above all, to prevent their increase, that, in a process of time, habitations are extremely difficult to be procured." A. Young, *Farmer's Letters* (1767), p. 173. (Author's note.)

Yet count our gains.   This wealth is but a name
That leaves our useful products still the same.
Not so the loss.   The man of wealth and pride,
Takes up a space that many poor supplied;
Space for his lake, his park's extended bounds,
Space for his horses, equipage, and hounds.

This criticism of the rapidly developing luxury of the middle classes
was not new in the poet's work.   He had written essays on the
menace of luxury.   He had even deplored the decay of villages in
verse before:

Have we not seen, at pleasure's lordly call,
The smiling long-frequented village fall;
Beheld the duteous son, the sire decay'd,
The modest matron, and the blushing maid,
Forc'd from their homes, a melancholy train,
To traverse climes beyond the western main;
Where wild Oswego spreads her swamps around,
And Niagara stuns with thund'ring sound?

"The Deserted Village," therefore, had made its first appearance in
verse near the end of "The Traveler," and had been developing ever
since in the mind of the poet.   It is the result of long meditation on
the change in British life which we have since learned to call the
beginning of the industrial era, with its coal and machinery and factory
hands.

How odd to find a poem germinating from such meditation as that!
What has poetry, we instinctively inquire today, to do with local,
economic conditions such as these?   We feel an irrepressible tendency
to apologize for Goldsmith's sentimentality and ignorance of economic law — "The Deserted Village" antedates Smith's *Wealth of
Nations* by six years — and defend the poem as a cento of beautiful
descriptions such as those of the parson, the schoolmaster, the village
inn, the broken soldier, the peasants at play.   I must confess that I
myself long regarded the poem as saved by the excellence of such details; but of late I have come to feel the inadequacy of such a view.
It concedes too much.   A poem which has exhibited such vitality
must be sound at the core.   There must be something universal in the
central theme to explain the enduring appeal of the poem.   And such
a universality of theme may, I believe, be found.   What we love in
the poem is not merely the beauty of the lines about the parson,
passing rich with forty pounds a year, who allured to brighter worlds
and led the way; not the schoolmaster, though he is as true to type

as one of Chaucer's pilgrims — whose pupils laughed "with counter-feited glee at all his jokes, for many a joke had he." These and the rest we hold in memory with their peculiar warmth of affection which Goldsmith always elicits; but the touching beauty of these and the other descriptions is derived from the central theme, out of which the poem rose. These persons and all the dear simplicity of their lives are no more. The beauty of the deserted village is that pensive grace which clings in memory to blessings lost long since. There is a sadness inseparable from the changes, inevitable though they be, which are wrought by time; and in particular is such regret stimulated by the recollection of the house which we loved at another period of life. Who that has spark of affection for the home of his boyhood can conquer a bitter dismay at its alterations? Such change seems always the work of vandals. And now if our emotions can be kindled by so simple a thing as the recollection of our old home, why should not pro-founder depths of being stir into life as we meditate with the poet upon the sad beauty of a whole village in decay, fallen into ruin under the triumphant wheels of luxury and progress?

It is not essential to think ourselves back into the eighteenth century in order to appreciate all this. The conditions lie about us still. If we could produce a Goldsmith in Connecticut, he would find material ready to his hand in the abandoned farms. Do you fancy that Auburn was more beautiful — or more deserted — than Old Lyme or Hadley, Massachusetts? One given over to artists, the other abandoned to the Poles. It may well be irrational to bewail such changes; but Goldsmith was irrational. Poets often are. Poetry is seldom the handmaid of rationalism. In the pleasant valleys of Connecticut, abandoned by our grandfathers only to be rediscovered by Italian market gardeners and millionaires, who would fain retire from the ugliness which their factories have created — in such phe-nomena, no doubt, there is much to inspire confidence in the future of such a nation as ours; but they do not still the longings of the New England heart for the tender grace of a day that is dead. Do you recall that day? The day of the village before it was quite deserted? The simple white dwelling with green shutters and syringa bushes on either side of the plain front porch — a house wholly unaware that it was in any way picturesque or worthy of being painted by Mr. Childe Hassam. "The decent church that topped the neighboring hill," where simple folk prayed to a God who seemed to be very near them. The fields beyond, with straggling stone walls over which a boy could scramble to pick raspberries, or even escape for a run in the patch of

woods beyond.   Do you recall the half-patriarchal life that centered
in the village?   The aristocracy of the minister, the easy association,
acquaintance with almost everybody in the place.   Quaint figures
like Miss Fanny who lived down by the river and was "Aunt Fanny"
to every boy in town.   The village idiot and the philosophic tramp
and the wise old shoemaker;   the myths and the feuds and the
haunted house!   And above all, the faith in New England, her poets
and her railroads and her destiny in this new world of ours.   Do you,
I ask, remember it?   If you accuse me of idealizing, I shall reply that
I have done so deliberately, for I am speaking of poetry, and what is
poetry without it?   I am confident that I have not heightened and
colored the picture more than did Goldsmith when he drew his
Auburn, "loveliest village of the plain, where health and plenty
cheered the laboring swain."

As long as there are poets, they will lament the passing of earth's
loveliness, inevitable though that passing may be.   But there is, in
the poem, evidence of something else that has disappeared, the departure of which it is not fashionable to deplore.   The subject of Goldsmith's poem is, I have tried to show, deathless, but not so the form in
which he embodied it.   "The Deserted Village" is a kind of essay, or
discussion in verse, sometimes placid, sometimes passionate, but
never heedless of the main theme;   never disdaining argument, and
never forgetful of the necessity of an orderly progression to a conclusion;   always mindful of the reader, and eagerly concerned to
persuade him, point by point.   The essayist aspires to clarity and
order, and has nothing occult or queer in his verses.   If he found a
trace of such mannerism, he would be concerned to erase it, for he has
no wish to tease the reader's emotions or bewilder his mind.   As a
matter of fact, Goldsmith disliked the new "romantic" poetry of his
day, and described it thus:

A parcel of gaudy images pass on before his [the reader's] imagination
like the figures in a dream; but curiosity, induction, reason, and the whole
train of affections, are fast asleep.

Strange words these would seem to Mr. De la Mare or Mr. Edwin
Arlington Robinson, if ever their eye fell upon them.   Poetry, you
see, eschewing vagueness and the evanescent phantasma of dreams,
should stimulate the reader's curiosity and proceed inductively to a
conclusion, awakening meanwhile all the "affections" of the human
heart.   Hence the poet, far from "striking the poem out" in an ecstasy, labored over it tirelessly and doggedly.   He sketched his ideas

in prose, versified them, polished and repolished the lines, and then submitted them to friends for criticism. He aspired to make the verses live in our memory as happy summaries of the truth, *multum in parvo*, "what oft was thought, but ne'er so well expressed"; and knew that, if he was successful in a high degree, his work would at moments have the ring of a proverb, and would enter into the living speech of men.

Now this was a type of poetry that had summoned forth the best efforts of poets since the days of Dryden, or, may we not say, of Horace. Pope's "Essay on Man," Johnson's "Vanity of Human Wishes," and Goldsmith's "Traveler," to mention only three, were all of this species. Each poem had a thesis to propound, to illustrate, to prove, and to recommend. Lesser poets, as though to show to what strange use the type might be put, wrote on all subjects from "The Art of Preserving the Health" to the "Philosophy of Melancholy." Time has buried thousands and thousands of them, but the best remain, as the best of any type will always do. By the nineteenth century the style had begun to fail. No supreme examples of it were produced unless we reckon in Wordsworth's "Prelude, or Growth of the Poet's Mind," which, as a spiritual autobiography in verse, would, I imagine, display nothing which, to an eighteenth century mind, would seem inappropriate to that species of poem. It was, however, in New England that it was to make its last appearance and bid adieu — perhaps only a temporary farewell — to the literary stage. I refer to Dr. Holmes's poems, "Urania: a Rhymed Lesson" (1846) and "Astraea, or the Balance of Illusions" (1850), the latter a typically eighteenth century theme. It was written for the Phi Beta Kappa Society of Yale College, and remains a readable poem today, though Dr. Holmes, for some reason which he never seems to have divulged, did not care to include it in his collected works, but broke it up into a number of fragmentary poems, with no obvious connections. His act is symbolic of the passing of the species.

Now, however ardent we may be in our loyalty to modern poets, we cannot witness the disappearance of a great type of poetry without regret. No such type, which has had a noble history and summoned forth the full power of great poets, can disappear from literature without grave misfortune to us. In the disuse of this polished clarity, this discussion, now urbane, now passionate, of matters that concern all mankind, we are all the poorer. The poets, however much they may congratulate themselves upon their superior subtleties and the finer discernment of modern readers, are, in particular, the losers, for their readers are few and ever fewer. A whole class of men who once read verse, using their minds as they read and finding themselves presently stirred to unsuspected depths of emotion, now read verse no longer. Occasionally they may be caught unaware, as by the *Spoon River Anthology;* but they find themselves uneasy in reading poetry which, for aught that they can see, is addressed to connoisseurs, intended exclusively for the initiate. Such men are not to be thought of as turning from poetry in contempt, for they are generally willing enough to concede that poetry is very fine, only "beyond them." They fancy that they have no power of assimilating such ethereal food. And so they keep away from the poet, and the work that he might have wrought upon their spirit is not even begun. Goldsmith would have won them all.

More serious still is the loss to the reading world of any literary type in which a poet may pass from grave meditation to passionate argument and glowing dream. Even the prose essay, in which exposition may mingle with "appreciation" of a highly individual sort, is no proper medium for the intenser moments of personal expression. Yet all these moods and many more find a natural channel of expression in the kind of verse here discussed. In "The Deserted Village," for instance, a poem which begins as a description of "Sweet Auburn" develops into a dissertation on the evils of luxury, touches on the problem of emigration, laments the depopulation of villages, and ends with the author's impassioned farewell to poetry, which is conceived of as departing with the peasants to America. This touching and eloquent adieu to the Muse, like the less successful appeal to the throne in "The Traveler," could hardly have been introduced into a prose essay, of however intimate a character:

> And thou, sweet Poetry, thou loveliest maid,
> Still first to fly where sensual joys invade;
> Unfit in these degenerate times of shame,
> To catch the heart, or strike for honest fame;
> Dear charming nymph, neglected and decried,
> My shame in crowds, my solitary pride,
> Thou source of all my bliss and all my woe,
> That found'st me poor at first, and keep'st me so;
> Thou guide by which the nobler arts excel,
> Thou nurse of every virtue, fare thee well.

There are subjects, no longer considered "poetical," but which may one day reclaim their right to the poet's attention, which require for their adequate treatment just such a medium as "The Deserted Village." At the present stage of our poetical development they go unhonored and unsung. Out of a thousand that might be specified, I select one, Democracy. Here is a theme of universal interest and appeal. For the past twelve or fifteen years we have been asking ourselves if the ideal of our forefathers has been tried and found wanting, whether government of the people, by the people, and for the people is destined to perish. No newspaper has failed to discuss the question — however inconclusively. Cartoons have been suggested by the query, Has civilization gone wrong? And we have asked ourselves so often whether democracy is safe for the world or the world safe for democracy that the question has become a byword and a jest.

In the eighteenth century the theme would have been seized upon by a poet as a noble subject worthy of that exalted treatment which is possible in poetry alone. He would have sketched in rapid outline the history of democracy, its career in Greece and Rome, in the Italian cities of the Middle Ages, and in the mountains of Switzerland. He would have described its dark hours during the French Revolution, and would have hailed the young republic of the New World. Such a poet, had he known the history of the past fifteen years, would have blazed into what the eighteenth century called "generous indignation" at the mention of Russia, where a new tyranny has again arrayed class against class, lifted the standard of hatred, ignorance, and atheism, and promised to return civilization to the chaos out of which it rose. He would have ended all with a passionate appeal to the hearts of his countrymen with such fervor as Lowell breathed into his fine stanzas beginning —

Oh beautiful, my country!

We do not encourage ourselves to be emotional about such matters nowadays, and unexpressed emotion tends to disappear altogether, or finds an outlet in channels perverse and strange. A degree of poetic eloquence, addressed to the hearts of men, was once permitted to oratory, but oratory, as conceived by Burke and by Webster, has disappeared along with the kind of verse here considered. Under the influence of the scientific specialist and the deterministic philosopher, we have opened a rift between our reason and our other faculties, as though it were possible to discharge all the functions of living with our minds alone, to the exclusion of such emotion as brings the glow of pride to the cheek and the tear of sensibility to the eye. Such stimulus has been at best confined to our hours of relaxation and amusement. Poetry has been increasingly confined to our bosoms and excluded from our business.

As an example of the increasing involution of romantic poetry and the increasing subtlety demanded of the reader, it will be sufficient to cite examples of the modern treatment of the theme of ruin or desolation which may fairly be contrasted with Goldsmith's. It is not necessary to dwell on the popularity of this *motif* among the poets of the Romantic school. What poem of Shelley's is more popular than "Ozymandias"?

> Nothing beside remains. Round the decay
> Of that colossal wreck, boundless and bare
> The lone and level sands stretch far away!

What stanza in the "Rubáiyát" lovelier than this?

> They say the Lion and the Lizard keep
> The Courts where Jamshyd gloried and drank deep,
> And Bahrám, that great Hunter, the Wild Ass
> Stamps o'er his Head, but cannot break his Sleep.

None of the poets is more insistent (for obvious reasons) upon the theme of desolation than is Byron. The fourth canto of "Childe Harold" is a very epic of ruin. Rome herself is, in one aspect, a Titanic image of the desolation of the poet's soul.

> Oh Rome! my country! city of the soul!
> The orphans of the heart must turn to thee,
> Lone mother of dead empires! and control
> In their shut breasts their petty misery.
> What are our woes and sufferance?   Come and see
> The cypress, hear the owl, and plod your way
> O'er steps of broken thrones and temples, Ye!
> Whose agonies are evils of a day —
> A world is at our feet as fragile as our clay.

Here is a typically romantic exaltation of the "sufferance" of a great capital as compared with the petty misery of a mere man, whose years are brief. The woes of Rome are eternal, like her years. Despite what may be deemed a somewhat exaggerated emotionalism, the stanza is yet perfectly intelligible. The ordinary reader may not care to indulge so intense an emotion for the majestic past, but there is nothing to elude his understanding or even to make him feel that the poet is "beyond him." He may reject the stanza and the canto of which it is a part as deficient in thought, but he will never contend that it is unintelligible.

When we pass on to Browning's "Love among the Ruins," which was the introductory poem in *Men and Women* (1855), we encounter a poem so sublimated that the reader's problem is now to bring his emotion to a state where he may be worthy of communion with the poet. If he attempt to use his reason, he will discover that he is confronted with an asseveration which may very likely require a shift in all the standards which he has hitherto instinctively accepted. Browning, having selected the familiar scene of peasant lovers amid the ruins of ancient grandeur, proceeds to the interesting conclusion that the love of the two is somehow the answer to "whole centuries of folly, noise and sin." So eloquently does he set the shepherd boy's passion before us that the sympathetic reader experiences a temporary "suspension of disbelief" in the validity of the contrast emphasized. To the communication of the mood Browning summons a wealth of color and a lilting sweetness of melody to which his readers were hardly accustomed.

> Where the quiet-colored end of evening smiles
>   Miles and miles
> On the solitary pastures where our sheep
>   Half asleep
> Tinkle homeward through the twilight, stray or stop
>   As they crop —
> Was the site once of a city great and gay,
>   (So they say)
> Of our country's very capital, its prince
>   Ages since
> Held his court in, gathered councils, wielding far
>   Peace or war. . . .
>
> Now — the single little turret that remains
>   On the plains,
> By the caper overrooted, by the gourd
>   Overscored,
> While the patching houseleek's head of blossom winks
>   Through the chinks —
> Marks the basement whence a tower in ancient time
>   Sprang sublime.
> And a burning ring, all round, the chariots traced,
>   As they raced,
> And the monarch and his minions and his dames
>   Viewed the games.

There is certainly no loss here in picturesqueness or intensity since the day when a poet could write —

> Amidst thy towers the tyrant's hand is seen,
> And desolation saddens all thy green.

Browning's poem is as brilliant as a painting of Hubert Robert, scores of whose pictures might be entitled "Love among the Ruins," or that famous canvas of Nicolas Poussin's in which three shepherds are spelling out the inscription on an ancient tomb, "Et ego in Arcadia." But Browning is more than a painter of pictures:

> And I know, while thus the quiet-colored eve
> Smiles to leave
> To their folding, all our many-tinkling fleece
> In such peace,
> And the slopes and rills in undistinguished gray
> Melt away —
> That a girl with eager eyes and yellow hair
> Waits me there
> In the turret whence the charioteers caught soil
> For the goal,
> Where the king looked, where she looks now, breathless, dumb
> Till I come. . . .

> In one year they sent a million fighters forth
> South and North,
> And they built their gods a brazen pillar high
> As the sky,
> Yet reserved a thousand chariots in full force,
> Gold, of course.
> Oh heart! oh blood that freezes, blood that burns!
> Earth's returns
> For whole centuries of folly, noise and sin!
> Shut them in,
> With their triumphs and their glories and the rest.
> Love is best!

Now of course there can be no such general agreement in the interpretation of this poem as there most certainly will be in the interpretation of a poem by Oliver Goldsmith or John Dryden or Alexander Pope. Their poems may become rusty of surface, but the rust is easily cleared away when the contemporary allusions are understood, and unanimity among readers follows. There can be no violent disagreements regarding the meaning of Pope's "Essay on Criticism," though there may be the widest divergence of view regarding its beauty and value. But there will be no such unanimity among Browning's readers. To some of them the poem will be a lovely picture. The heart of love (a violet by a mossy stone), created under the ribs and stones of Death, is a sufficient "interpretation" for

many. Others will contend that the poem, and in particular the conclusion, "Love is best," is dramatic, and that the shepherd boy's
ardent love is naturally expressed in the paradox that the emotion of
two peasant lovers is greater than the busy life of a city. But other
and not less intelligent readers will find here a thought highly characteristic of Robert Browning, who insists on the supreme value of the
present moment. The lines in *Parleyings* ("With Gerard de Lairesse,"
xiv) are typical:

> Let things be — not seem,
> I counsel rather — do, and nowise dream!
> Earth's young significance is all to learn:
> The dead Greek lore lies buried in the urn
> Where who seeks fire finds ashes.

The shepherd boy of the Campagna and the yellow-haired girl are
Earth's young significance — its fire — the city about them is ashes.
In this sense the reader, like the more devoted among the commenta-
tors on Browning, may be prevailed on to accept not only the summary,
"Love is best," but also the rather exacting belief that the particular
passion here exhibiting itself is Nature's act of reparation for "whole
centuries of folly, noise and sin." Browning would probably tell us
that the poem is suceptible of many interpretations, and that it is our
function to make what we can of it; but such austere demeanor is
fairly certain to offend the simple reader for whom I am pleading,
and who is bewildered not only by the astonishing opinions to which
he is invited to give assent, but also by the diversity and even antagonism among the poet's readers. After a number of such experiences he will perhaps not unnaturally reach the conclusion that poetry
is beyond his comprehension, and therefore beyond his interests and
his needs. Now if it be retorted that Browning's poem is nevertheless
better than Goldsmith's, I may perhaps be not unwilling to agree.
If left to a free choice I should, I think, be more likely to read "Love
among the Ruins" than "The Deserted Village." I loved the poem
long before I had learned to esteem "The Deserted Village," and
should be the last to belittle it. I am not asking for less poetry of a
subtle kind, but for more poetry of the simple sort, in order that
readers who might have been won by Gray and Burns and Cowper
may not come to feel that the atmosphere of Parnassus is too rarefied
for them to breathe.

If we leap suddenly forward now to the poetry of our own day, we
shall perhaps be startled by the prevailing atmosphere of exoticism.

Art is subtle enough today in all its branches — so subtle, in fact, that many young revolutionists prefer to be crude, ugly, and unintelligible. The reader is derided by the artist (if he may be so called), who has his tongue in his cheek. In music dissonance blares at us. In painting we are invited to admire crooked scrawls and cross-eyed portraits because they are not "Victorian." I have been told of a painter who says that nobody is fit to understand his pictures except himself — as the poetry of the Sitwells can be fully appreciated only by the Sitwells — and that the views of the critic are an impertinence. Well, here, in all conscience, is a limited audience, an audience of one. Art as an expression of universals will have difficulty in surviving such a climax; and the congregation of simple souls who feel that poetry is not for them must soon be increased by the addition of all the rest of us. . . .

We return once more to our own theme of desolation, and send our emotions roaming. Meditate upon the vacancy and stillness of a deserted village or a deserted house until the place becomes in very truth a haunted scene, where phantoms flit at twilight and ghostly echoes of the departed seem to reach the ear. Into the very substance of these stained and broken walls, these oft-trodden floors, something of the human passions that once surged about them has been stamped. To the seeing eye and the feeling heart they are dimly eloquent, vague memorials of folk who seem to be watching us and listening sadly, a little ironically, to the busy hum of our life. Soon we shall join them in the silence. As our emotions flee ever farther from the norm, the simple, practical man, who may know by heart Goldsmith's lines about the clergyman and the village schoolmaster, leaves us to our solitary task of reading modern verse. It may well be that he is a Philistine, but it may also be that he might have been won to poetry if he could have found sustenance there. I understand his impatience with dreams and sentimentalists, but there is much that I should like to say to him if he were still within earshot. I would fain point out to him that if he spent a day and a night in the ruins of Paestum or the rock tombs of Persepolis — alone — he would before the end of his twenty-four hours have experienced some very unusual emotions indeed, for which he might even be the better, the wider-thoughted; and that he might thus conceivably learn a degree of grateful respect for any poet who could put those emotions into words for him. But I can accomplish little if there be no simple poetry by which to hold him while he is being wooed, perhaps without knowing it, to subtler poetry that he ought also to love. I should like to bring him acquainted with the beauty of Mr. De la Mare's rather tenuous poetry, for there is beauty in it. Moreover, it is Mr. De la Mare who can express the very themes of which we have been speaking. He, like Goldsmith, is caught by the eloquence of the deserted scene, the passing of earth's loveliness into the dark backward and abysm of time. But, unlike Goldsmith, he hears far within the chambers of his mind thin voices from the past striving to speak to us.

> See this house, how dark it is
> Beneath its vast-boughed trees!
> Not one trembling leaflet cries
> To that watcher in the skies —
> "Remove, remove thy searching gaze,
> Innocent, of heaven's ways,
> Brood not, Moon, so wildly bright,
> On secrets hidden from sight."

It is significant of the whole change that has come over poetry and our approach to poetry that the deserted village has become "Sunk Lyonesse." In Lyonesse, sunk below the Cornish sea, there is a vaster symbol of desolation than any on which Goldsmith pondered. Sea nymphs hourly ring its knell.

> In sea-cold Lyonesse,
> When the Sabbath eve shafts down
> On the roofs, walls, belfries
> Of the foundered town,
> The Nereids pluck their lyres
> Where the green translucency beats,
> And with motionless eyes at gaze
> Make minstrelsy in the streets.
>
> And the ocean water stirs
> In salt-worn casemate and porch.
> Plies the blunt-snouted fish
> With fire in his skull for torch.
> And the ringing wires resound;
> And the unearthly lovely weep
> In lament of the music they make
> In the sullen courts of sleep:
>
> Whose marble flowers bloom for aye:
> And — lapped by the moon-guiled tide —
> Mock their carber with heart of stone,
> Caged in his stone-ribbed side.

DESIGN IN THE NOVEL[1]

Wilson Follett

WILSON FOLLETT's studies of the novel include *The Modern Novel* (1918), from which the following essay is taken, and *Some Modern Novelists* (1918), a volume of appreciations and estimates written in collaboration with Helen Thomas Follett. He published his first novel, *No More Sea*, a dramatic and unusual piece of fiction, in 1933. Mr. Follett is also the editor of the definitive edition of Stephen Crane's *Works* and *Collected Poems*.

I

If I have succeeded in making a just account of the place which properly belongs to philosophy in fiction, I have brought out at the same time the most cogent of the reasons why the shape of fiction as an art has undergone certain marked changes during the past half-century. Up to 1859 roughly — the year of the first novel of George Eliot, and a date which has in the history of fiction something of the momentousness which we ascribe to it in that of science — the philosophy in fiction is felt either as an intruder or as a guest whose presence is hardly suspected at all; though, as I tried to show, that unsuspected presence is more advantage than disadvantage. Probably all of us do, whether we know it or not, have a philosophy, even if only a philosophy of negations; and, having it, we perforce look at the world through it. This unawareness is the attitude of the drama and of the novel before George Eliot — except, of course, in homiletic, allegorical, or symbolistic pieces such as *The Life and Death of Mr. Badman* or *Rasselas*. But from the time of George Eliot the philosophy in fiction is intensely aware of itself, determined to make the most of itself as an opportunity, not merely put up with itself as a necessity. And from the moment of this conscious acceptance and welcome of philosophy, an entirely new set of considerations begins to govern the shape of fiction. The novel, whenever it deserved its hold on us, has always combined truth with pleasure; but when the emphasis shifted from pleasure to truth, there appeared a new determining principle of inclusion and exclusion, a new standard of criticism for the devices and expedients which fiction had evolved during its vassalage to pleasure.

[1] Reprinted from *The Modern Novel*, by Wilson Follett, by permission of and special arrangement with Alfred A. Knopf, Inc., authorized publishers.

548

I can best state the change as an enormous decrease of the accidental and arbitrary, and a corresponding increase of the causal. The shortest name for the transition is George Eliot, who was doing perhaps her best work during the life of Thackeray, and nearly all of her work during the life of Dickens, but who is animated by a more modern spirit than either. George Eliot represents the universe naturally conceived as an organism; man as a subordinated unit of its evolution and not, philosophically, the pivot of the whole; the intricate dovetailing of cause and effect everywhere; the facts of good and evil as products of remote and invisible causes in heredity and environment; the ungovernable sway of chance in human lives, reducing them, whether it destroy or fulfill, to mere pawns in an inscrutable game — in fine, the character which is fate and the fate which is above character. To express with any fullness this duality of the world and the individual, she must abandon the worn machinery of coincidence and mystery, the various wires and levers by which the novelist himself remains palpably in control of his spectacle; she must substitute for these the machinery of human will and natural forces. To begin with, she must have a narrow scene, where nature itself reduces life to a manageable simplicity; and hence she follows the provincial ideal by which Jane Austen so unconsciously profited — how wondrously we know when we stop to think that we are now only just learning how high, even if how small, is the place rightfully hers. Then, she must study not merely the actions of men and women: she must study the *directions* of their lives, the corrosion of character by its worst or weakest, all the implications of her accustomed theme, "the idealist in search of a vocation"; and hence she must reduce the number of events until none remain except those which have profound importance as illustrating the direction of the lives concerned — the episodes are reduced in number, and mean individually more. Finally, she must investigate not only the physical realities of actions and the emotions that underlie them, but the moral principles that underlie emotion and choice; she must go more deeply than the novel has been wont to go into the moral and intellectual life of her protagonists, in order to bring forth by reflection and analysis those realities which can be expressed but imperfectly, or not at all, in action; whence Savonarola in his cell, Bulstrode on his knees. This patient and fruitful search for the causality in life is the distinguishing contribution of George Eliot to the novel.

In her we see, then, at least three significant changes in the shape of the novel, changes which it has mostly retained and intensified since the conclusion of her work: first, the narrow scene, appointed for rigorous specialization in a few personae; secondly, the elimination of deliberate artifice in the manufacture of plots, and the attempt instead to bring the action out of the personae and the clash of their wills and personalities; thirdly, enlargement of the scope and importance of analysis of motives and feelings.

That such are indeed the chief traits of George Eliot as a novelist is shown by our instinctive objection to her few lapses into the factitious and the accidental. Sir Leslie Stephen says of a certain episode in *Romola:* "Poor Romola, in her despair, gets into a miscellaneous boat lying ashore; and the boat drifts away in a manner rarely practiced by boats in real life, and spontaneously lands her in a place where everybody is dying of the plague, and she can therefore make herself useful to her fellow creatures. She clearly ought to have been drowned, like Maggie, and we feel that Providence is made to interfere rather awkwardly."[1] We all share the feeling; but it is a feeling which we should never experience with the same force in connection with Dickens or Thackeray — writers from whom we expect a full measure of everything that can by any possibility be put into the work of fiction. That we should have the feeling in connection with such palpable contrivances in George Eliot as this extraordinary boat of Romola's, shows in itself how essentially the novel had altered its shape by 1864 — how unmistakably the philosophical point of view had even then brought about the modern change from the casual to the causal.

II

This general change that has come over the form of the novel is, then, the substitution of a higher unity for a lower. The effect of naturalistic philosophy in the novel is to reopen the whole question of the devices and subterfuges of the novel in their relation to the integrity of the whole; to reopen it as a subordinate phase of our other inclusive question, the relation of art to life. Only with the ascendancy of naturalism did the novel attain any philosophy of art to speak of; and it is only with the attainment of a philosophy of art that the novel makes its transition from artifice to truth — stops asking "What will be effective, how can the attention be won and stimulated?" and begins to ask "How best can truth be served, the nature of things unraveled?" I do not mean of course that the matter

[1] *George Eliot* (English Men of Letters Series). By Leslie Stephen. New York: The Macmillan Company. P. 138.

of pure strategy in the novel can be ignored, for if the story does not
capture our interest it can certainly do nothing to us at all: but the
emphasis becomes transferred from one of these questions to the other,
and the question of technique in the novel is being elevated along with
the purpose and meaning of the novel as a whole.

In one way it may even be said that questions of technique become
all the while more important and more exacting; for the modern
notion of truth-telling cuts off all those resources of palpable contrivance in technique upon which so much of the plot interest depends
in Fielding and Dickens. And the result is that the modern practitioner must have, in one particular at least, a fuller equipment than
these; for he must know how to win and hold the interest without
such aids through the historical, the conventional, and simply by the
amount and value of the truth he finds to tell. This elevation of the
whole problem of expedients and devices in the novel means, as I
have said, the substitution of a higher unity for a lower. Unity of
purpose takes the place once held by the unity of trickery and elaborate
organization. It would hardly be an exaggeration to say that naturalism makes the same difference in the novel as in our conception of the
world: it replaces arbitrary creation by the organic evolution of a thing
which grows into certain forms by its own inward nature, as it were
by a kind of self-compulsion.

It would be interesting but futile to speculate how far and with
what consistency these changes could have been followed out in the
novel without Continental influences. The history of these changes
since George Eliot is, as a fact, largely an affair of comparative literature; for it is evident that the novel in France and, presently, the
novel in Russia did incalculably much to furnish both the ideal and
the means.

So far as I can express the difference between these two influences,
it lies in the more fundamental simplicity and naïveté of the Russian
masters, the more sophisticated and more technical proficiency of the
French. It is as though the French had achieved unity as a purely
artistic triumph, because of a compulsion to exhaust the possibilities
of order, symmetry, and austere perfection as things desirable and
matchless in themselves; whereas the Russians achieved it through a
compelling need of reducing everything to an elemental simplicity,
for the sake of getting outside it, mastering it: one feels the Russian
temperament as less various and more strong, more tenacious and less
nimble. While Flaubert and Maupassant were achieving unity by
whittling down their subject to essentials, ruling out all that failed to

contribute to its predetermined harmony, Turgenev and Dostoevski were achieving unity by relating their larger masses of data to some central and magnetic principle of truth. The French temper is to pick and choose, and then weave carefully the chosen elements together into a pattern; the Russian temper is to take everything there is to take, and put it into a single basket large and strong enough to carry it all. And so, while the 'seventies and 'eighties saw British novelists learning something of their technique in France, it also saw them learning perhaps even more of the rationale of technique in Russia. Mr. Howells and Henry James, greatly as they were soon to differ in their use of what they learned, did beyond question learn much, and derive a permanent impetus in certain modern directions, first from Balzac, and then from Turgenev — to name only the most representative of influences.

The distinction between French and Russian art is perhaps not so absolute as I have made it sound: what distinction ever is so absolute as one's account of it? But there is, I think, a measurable truth in my general point, that the Russian character has the greater capacity for obsession, the greater need to see all reality for the time being through a single pair of spectacles, the greater capacity to be interested in everything. And what I wish mainly to point out is this: that by the middle 'nineties, when one of these Continental influences was at its culmination and the other was at least beginning to exert its leverage, then, in the decade when the names now most accredited were just beginning to appear on title-pages, the modern novel in English had pretty well determined its present bent toward the Russian largeness, the Russian inclusiveness. Our younger novelists had learned from France certain of the fine fitnesses of treatment, of order; they had learned from Russia, *through* France, to practice these upon larger and more specialized pieces of subject matter than the French masters since Victor Hugo have commonly treated.

That, on the whole, this choice of emphasis between two influences has resulted to the advantage of the novel, I may perhaps suggest by bare statement of two considerations: first, that the Russian inclusiveness of matter and of event is most like the Victorian inclusiveness which is our chief tradition in the novel, so that full adoption of the French method and ideal might have meant, relatively, the impoverishment of the novel; secondly, that the largest possible interpretation of what is relevant to the subject of a novel best serves our modern notion of life's complexity, and gives the novelist his best chance of seeing life steadily and whole. In 1895 British fiction had its choice of whether it should see highly specialized specimens of life and make of each a perfect picture, or consider highly representative and typical specimens of life and see them with a single eye. The problem was unity by selection versus unity by interpretation. Our novelists mainly chose to interpret large segments of the typical; and on the whole the developments in the form of the novel during the twenty years since that choice crystallized have shown that they did well.

III

Suppose we consider separately, for a moment, these two lessons which the English novel was trying to learn in the last quarter-century of Victoria's reign — the French lesson of unity through internal fitness or congruity, the Russian lesson of unity through the insistence upon a centralizing and directing purpose. Of the details of that first lesson learned in Paris, we can name and illustrate three of some technical importance.

The first is oneness of *tone* or pitch — the necessity of keying all the parts of a given subject within an emotional gamut which does no violence to the reader's sensibilities. If we desire an interesting example of work performed under the most conscientious and single-minded zeal for such oneness, we have it in Sir Arthur Quiller-Couch's completion of Stevenson's unfinished *St. Ives* — a task executed with such loving circumspection that one cannot tell, by internal evidence, where the break occurs. That Stevenson would have appreciated this beautiful competence shown in imitation of his style is proved by his sensitiveness to every one of his own failures adequately to imitate himself. Speaking of an earlier and slighter work, *Prince Otto*, he says in a letter to C. W. Stoddard:

How does your class get along? If you like to touch on *Otto*, any day in a by-hour, you may tell them — as the author's last dying confession — that it is a strange example of the difficulty of being ideal in an age of realism; that the unpleasant giddy-mindedness, which spoils the book and often gives it a wanton air of unreality and juggling with air-bells, comes from unsteadiness of key; from the too great realism of some chapters and passages — some of which I have now spotted, others I dare say I shall never spot — which disprepares the imagination for the cast of the remainder.

Any story can be made *true* in its own key; any story can be made *false* by the choice of a wrong key of detail or style: Otto is made to reel like a drunken — I was going to say man, but let us substitute cipher — by the variations of the key.[1]

[1] *The Letters of Robert Louis Stevenson*, Vol. II, p. 321. New York: Charles Scribner's Sons. 1911.

In this informal comment Stevenson, a Scott with a French artistic conscience, proves how unquestioningly he assumed that the modern sense for unity of texture is necessary, not only to realism, but also to work done in a romantic tradition. There is a kind of story which, if it is to exist at all, demands that the hero shall be invulnerable; there is a kind of modern costume romance in which it is strictly proper that the last chapter shall show the hero converted to the religion of the majority. Perhaps one does better not to write that kind of romance; but if one does write it one must keep it in tune with itself, even at the cost of admitting conventions which are in themselves silly. In their own irresponsible realm, the coincidences and mystifications of Wilkie Collins are not only justifiable but inevitable; *The Woman in White* and *The Moonstone* may not be fiction of a high order, but they are at least consistent with themselves, and works of art in so far as they are of their own kind. In short, there is no art without form; and, for modern purposes, form is fusion.

This general truth becomes still more manifest as I approach a second and more specific agent of unity, the single point of view. It is not enough that the material reported upon be consonant with itself: it must harmonize with the person who reports it, whether that person be the author himself reporting omnisciently — a method which obviously suffers from lack of verisimilitude, since no one can reasonably be expected to know *all* the facts or be everywhere at once — or an observer created by the author expressly to observe, or a character in the story. The omniscient method tends to disappear, as we should expect it to in a period when the novelist finds his reward in the meanings of facts rather than in knowledge of the facts themselves. We no longer see the novelist "stand about in his scene, talking it over with his hands in his pockets, interrupting the action, and spoiling the illusion in which alone the truth of art resides,"[1] as Mr. Howells said of Thackeray's and Trollope's habit of personally conducting the story. The novelist who can be in all places at once and follow simultaneous actions going on apart from each other is too palpably the inventor of his facts; and, as a result of this feeling about him, we see the subplot practically disappear from modern fiction, and the action reduce itself to so much as can be comprehended from a single human point of view working under the ordinary human limitations. We are interested, not in the mechanism of complex actions, but in the moral causes and effects of actions as shown in a life or a few lives followed continuously. The culmination of this

[1] *Criticism and Fiction*, p. 76. New York: Harper & Bros. MDCCCXCIII.

interest thus far appears in the later novels and tales of Henry James, all of which are interpreted for us through the observing consciousness of some person, not the author, who is present in the story. To these we may add the more recent practice of the direct colloquial method in some of the best work of Joseph Conrad.

Thirdly, the modern craftsman has learned that there must be fusion among the various agents of the narrative process — the talk and action, the portrait-painting and characterization, which go to make up the actual written story. We have learned that the one of these elements which predominated in the earlier Victorians and in Scott, and which has latterly threatened to reduce our magazine fiction to a bare skeleton of dialogue — we have learned that the element of talk is the thinnest, most meager of all in real and lasting communicativeness. Even when talk is sifted down to the printable economy and compactness, we require a bushel of it to convey what the novelist's own interpretation of his facts can give us in a tenth of the room; and the narrator whose dialogue is his principal stock-in-trade is not only copying the merits of the drama in conditions where they become positive defects, but he is also crowding out "the golden blocks themselves of the structure" — his own weighed, condensed, and reflective analysis. This complaint is one that Henry James, whose sense for such things was of the most subtly critical, had often to urge as his principal criticism of Mr. Howell's technique; and in one of his *London Notes* he urged it with even more force against the decidedly inferior dialogue of Gissing.

This third point is interestingly argued by Scott in his Preface to *The Bride of Lammermoor*, in an imaginary conversation between Pattieson the novelist and Dick Tinto the painter. Scott inclined on the whole to Pattieson's view of talk as against description; but the modern artist, who has more reasons than Scott had for wishing to weave a firm pattern, and no reasons for wishing to weave one of loose ends, agrees almost completely with Tinto.

" 'Your characters,' he said, 'my dear Pattieson, make too much use of the *gob box;* they *patter* too much' — an elegant phraseology, which Dick had learned while painting the scenes of an itinerant company of players — 'there is nothing in whole pages but mere chat and dialogue.'

" 'The ancient philosopher,' said I in reply, 'was wont to say, "Speak, that I may know thee"; and how is it possible for an author to introduce his *personae dramatis* to his readers in a more interesting and effectual manner than by the dialogue in which each is represented as supporting his own appropriate character?'

" 'It is a false conclusion,' said Tinto; 'I hate it, Peter, as I hate an un-
filled cann.   I will grant you, indeed, that speech is a faculty of some value
in the intercourse of human affairs, and I will not even insist on the doctrine
of that Pythagorean toper, who was of opinion that, over a bottle, speaking
spoiled conversation.   But I will not allow that a professor of the fine arts
has occasion to embody the idea of his scene in language, in order to impress
upon the reader its reality and its effect.   On the contrary, I will be judged
by most of your readers, Peter, should these tales ever become public,
whether you have not given us a page of talk for every single idea which
two words might have communicated, while the posture, and manner, and
incident, accurately drawn, and brought out by appropriate coloring, would
have preserved all that was worthy of preservation, and saved these everlasting "said he's" and "said she's," with which it has been your pleasure
to encumber your pages.'

"I replied that he confounded the operations of the pencil and the pen;
that the serene and silent art, as painting has been called by one of our first
living poets, necessarily appealed to the eye, because it had not the organs
for addressing the ear; whereas poetry, or that species of composition which
approached to it, lay under the necessity of doing absolutely the reverse,
and addressed itself to the ear, for the purpose of exciting that interest
which it could not attain through the medium of the eye.

"Dick was not a whit staggered by my argument, which he contended
was founded on misrepresentation.   'Description,' said he, 'was to the
author of a romance exactly what drawing and tinting were to a painter;
words were his colors, and, if properly employed, they could not fail to place
the scene, which he wished to conjure up, as effectually before the mind's
eye as the tablet or canvas presents it to the bodily organ.   The same rules,'
he contended, 'applied to both, and an exuberance of dialogue, in the
former case, was a verbose and laborious mode of composition which went
to confound the proper art of fictitious narrative with that of the drama, a
widely different species of composition, of which dialogue was the very
essence, because all, excepting the language to be made use of, was presented
to the eye by the dresses, and persons, and actions of the performers upon
the stage.   But as nothing,' said Dick, 'can be more dull than a long narrative written upon the plan of a drama, so where you have approached
most near to that species of composition, by indulging in prolonged scenes
of mere conversation, the course of your story has become chill and con-
strained, and you have lost the power of arresting the attention and exciting
the imagination, in which upon other occasions you may be considered as
having succeeded tolerably well.'

"I made my bow in requital of the compliment, which was probably
thrown in by way of *placebo*, and expressed myself willing at least to make
one trial of a more straightforward style of composition, in which my actors
should do more, and say less, than in my former attempts of this kind. . . ."[1]

[1] From the "Preliminary" of the Introduction to *The Bride of Lammermoor*.

Scott's use of this last concession in *The Bride of Lammermoor*, where he seems really to make a conscious attempt at repairing the proportions of his earlier work, may go farther than is commonly perceived toward accounting for the peculiar distinction of this most lyrical of his tales; though it still remains odd that Scott could be on the whole so indifferent a practitioner of that which he so shrewdly perceived and argued.

IV

So far I speak of a general ideal of craftsmanship which is more French than English, and of some of its practical effects on English fiction. Now let us see what was the general effect of the Russians. We shall find it to have been sweeping; for it resulted in the creation of a strikingly new form in fiction, a form which we may take the risk of calling the novel of the future. At all events it is the novel of the present, and decidedly *not* the novel of the past. It is a form which has evolved, not from the novel alone, but from the novel and the short story — both assimilated in a certain way under the mediation of some modern ideas, and under the intervention, as it seems to me, of direct influences from Russia.

The novel of the past, as we know, formed itself by an ideal of dramatic structure, with a crisis at or after the middle — at all events far enough from the end so that there could be a definite change of direction in the plot. That is, the crisis, served as a new initial impulse, from which the action proceeded under changed conditions to its end. *Romola*, which I have named already in a different connection, is an orthodox example of the dramatic structure carried out on a vast scale. Romola's life of struggle proceeds in a certain direction and toward certain ends until the events which involve the deaths of her husband and her godfather and her flight from the city; then it proceeds in an entirely different direction through the stages of her effort to replan her life and make a new place for herself. This is the general contour of the older conventional novel, as of the drama; and the short story differs from it chiefly in that it has no change of direction, but follows its theme straightforwardly to a crisis which is also the end. The older novel was two stories, or a story and its sequel; the short story is one story, cumulative in its effect.

The new novel is a sublimated short story. It avails itself of the novel's fullness of treatment; it may run to any length, even the inordinate length of the Victorian novels; but its theme is single, and it aims at rigid unity of effect — the unity which comes of one direction inexorably followed, and the use of all the material to illustrate a single principle. It replaces contrast and suspense with intensive thoroughness and the strict logic of causal succession. It is the short story under a microscope, the short story on a vastly enlarged scale. Henry James, an avowed disciple of Turgenev, was the first to practice this form in English; Mrs. Wharton, his disciple, has continued it; Conrad, whose literary kinships are of the Continent, has given it enlargement and several new characteristics; and our bookshelves are being filled with new works of extraordinary formal merit, and in length from 40,000 to 200,000 words, which prove on analysis to be, not novels of the older dramatic figuration, but short stories or *novelle* of the most rigid specialization in a single phase of life or character. The material of a novel may be present; but the purpose is to exhaust the meaning of a single issue, not to range freely over the whole complexity of life.

Howells, whose mind always turned with interest toward the arts as practiced in Europe, despite the strong and sane — slightly too sane — provincialism of his own creative work, recognized these tendencies more than a quarter of a century ago, and was pretty directly writing of them when he said:

. . . each man is a microcosm, and the writer who is able to acquaint us intimately with half a dozen people, or the conditions of a neighborhood or a class, has done something which cannot in any bad sense be called narrow; his breadth is vertical instead of lateral, that is all; and this depth is more desirable than horizontal expansion in a civilization like ours, where the differences are not of classes, but of types, and not of types either so much as of characters. A new method was necessary in dealing with the new conditions, and the new method is world-wide, because the whole world is more or less Americanized. Tolstoi is exceptionally voluminous among modern writers, even Russian writers; and it might be said that the forte of Tolstoi himself is not in his breadth sidewise, but in his breadth upward and downward. *The Death of Ivan Illitch* leaves as vast an impression on the reader's soul as any episode of *War and Peace*, which, indeed, can be recalled only in episodes, and not as a whole. I think that our writers may be safely counseled to continue their work in the modern way, because it is the best way yet known. If they make it true, it will be large, no matter what its superficies are; and it would be the greatest mistake to try to make it big. A big book is necessarily a group of episodes more or less loosely connected by a thread of narrative, and there seems no reason why this thread must always be supplied. Each episode may be quite distinct, or it may be one of a connected group; the final effect will be from the truth of each episode, not from the size of the group.[1]

[1] *Criticism and Fiction*, 142–43. New York: Harper & Bros. MDCCCXCIII.

The effect of this kind of intensive specialization is a singular and most amazing rebirth in imaginative literature of something very like the classical unities of time, place, and action. The unities as they were observed in classic drama and in neo-classic imitations justified themselves in aesthetics and were employed primarily for aesthetic reasons; they served the work which obeyed them, not as agents of a closer contact with the real life of men and women, but as agents of an inward and self-sufficient harmony in the work itself. Marlowe and Shakespeare, when they cast aside the unities in order to get nearer to life, were freeing art from the shackles of convention. But the modern artist has got round to the beginning of the cycle; we see in him the unities recovered and reconstituted, though for different reasons and in a new spirit. He tells one story and one only because he wants to get to the bottom of something, not because of any fancied ideal of artistic symmetry; he takes a short and continuous stretch of time because he wants to preserve unbroken the chain of causality in his action, not because he thinks the flight of time in the work of art should match the flight of time in real events; he keeps his scene narrowed and single because he wants to correlate man causally with his environment, not because he considers a change of scene inherently inartistic. The reasons are different; but the result, in concentration, in focus, is strikingly the same. This change in the shape of the novel, a change brought about by new ideas and a new purpose, constitutes the superiority of the modern novel as a form over any other large unit of imaginative expression whatever; and it is one of the principal reasons for hoping that genius of the future will find more to facilitate, and less to impede, its utterance than it has ever found.

V

Have I seemed thus far to be slighting the purpose and meaning of fiction in favor of its subordinate means and methods? To do so has been far from my intention: I have wanted to speak of these lesser things just in so far as they are governed by the greater, and to treat the form of the novel only as it is ruled by the spirit. If I have not succeeded before this point in showing that our modern way of writing novels is a natural outcome of our modern way of looking at life, I shall have done so when I have noted once more that the service of design or technique is to help fiction represent life — not to copy it, or idealize it, or prove something about it, or make a substitute for it, but to represent it. Just as the details of an artist's subject are chosen to represent the whole subject, to stand for more than they are, so the whole subject is chosen to represent as much as may be of life. Other things equal, the worth of a piece of fiction is proportioned to its wideness or wealth of reference. The more it stands for, the more it *is*, even though it be slight in itself. And shall we not say that the purpose of modern technique, which has on the whole the effect of curtailing the subject matter of the individual story, is to extend and amplify the *meaning* of the story, and, through thoroughness of treatment, to make the artist's little stand for more than ever? That economy of means and material should have led to enlargement of the representational power of the novel seems to me to be the most significant of recent general results in fiction.

It is worth while, I think, to make room here for three examples of that result. Let the first be Mr. Hardy's *Return of the Native*, one of the most powerful novels of localized "atmosphere" in any language. The motif is set in an opening chapter, "A Face on Which Time Makes but Little Impression," a description of Egdon Heath, the barren waste in which the action takes place. This motif dominates the whole tale. As on the heath, so in the souls of the characters, and especially in the soul of the heroine, Eustacia Vye Yeobright, night and day wrestle together in a sort of interminable twilight. The inscrutable face of nature throughout the book is used to symbolize Mr. Hardy's view of the inscrutable way of the cosmos with the whole human species; man's daily life in a natural scene which is and must remain a riddle to him is subtly suggestive of our common life in an immensity which we can neither understand nor change; and the changelessness of that indifferent and mocking face of nature, which neither smiles nor frowns while men and women play for a moment their puny parts under its fixed gaze before they are swallowed into it, is an image of the eternal futility which Hardy saw as perhaps the one unifying reality of our common life. This is not symbolism, and it is not allegory: it is suggestion used to the end of representation on the grandest scale. It weaves a philosophy of the whole into the patterned history of a handful of lives.

My other two examples, both preëminent novels of the first decade of this century, bring us to the threshold of the present. As unlike as possible from each other in substance and in minor points of technique, they are alike in that the masses of subject matter of each are invoked by a single principle and dedicated to its illustration. In each instance, the principle is a large truth about life. Mr. Arnold Bennett's *Old Wives' Tale* has on the surface as defiant a breach of unity as a novel could well contain; for there are two heroines of widely different and widely sundered lives, in large part separately observed and recorded. But there is a unity which comes out of this disjunction, and it is this: the life of Constance and the life of Sophia, separate and unlike as they are, arrive ultimately at an equal and a similar understanding of what life is. Life is something that we never understand until we have lived it; and when we have lived it we see that it is something which we could never have lived at all if we had understood it first. That, says Mr. Bennett, is our common lot and the ultimate wisdom; and it is a triumphant illustration of the modern kind of unity in purpose and effect that he should have brought so large a sense of community out of material inherently so scattered, so little subjected to the other and lesser modern practices of economy.

Mr. Conrad's *Nostromo* is likewise a vindication of unity through principle and purpose, in defiance of technical regulations which are useful in their place. Here is a story of which, materially speaking, the very mainspring is romance — a story of a misgoverned tropical republic of the New World, with a silver mine and a horde of pirates, with revolution and counter-revolution and any number of violent deeds and thrilling rescues, as its principal machinery. It is the representational use of all this that turns it into realism. For the country of the tale, Costaguana, is the modern world in symbolic miniature; and the triumph of the mine of silver over a group of individuals, some of whom loathe it and some covet, some of whom it drives to perjury, to treason, to murder, others of whom it despoils through its tragic effects on those whom they love — this triumph of the precious metal is the ascendancy of material interests in modern life, the tyranny of the economic, the corrosion of greed, the downfall of the idealist through his personal dependence on those whom material interests can corrupt or destroy. *Nostromo* is a pageant and an epic of a civilization founded on commerce; and if half its greatness is in its mastery of the immediate facts, at least we may say that the other half is in the sweep and clarity of its synthetic representation of a good share of modern existence in a world whose most cherished precept is to buy in the cheapest and sell in the dearest market.

A NOTE ON TRAGEDY[1]

Ludwig Lewisohn

LUDWIG LEWISOHN distinguished himself as one of a group — H. L. Mencken, Randolph Bourne, Van Wyck Brooks, George Jean Nathan, and others — who just before and after the World War delivered a fierce attack upon certain traditional characteristics of American life. The objects of their scorn included the inhibitions and reticences of Puritanism; the optimism and uncritical complacency which they ascribed to American culture; the sentimentalism that since Victorian days had marked much of American fiction and poetry; the religious temper (in their opinion hopelessly naïve) of the middle class folk; and the hard, crass materialism that was the result of the rapid conquest of the continent and the erection of a machine industrialism. Their opponents charged this group with a distorted view of American life, with intellectual arrogance, with a false historical conception of such forces as Puritanism, and other errors. But their attack, full of satire, epigram, and amusing invective, produced a powerful impression. Ludwig Lewisohn's most striking contribution to it was his autobiography, *Up Stream* (1922), a book of vivid style, fine flashes of beauty and insight, and rapid narrative interest, but also of great bitterness. It reflected the post-war mood of a German Jew who had suffered much during the conflict from men suspicious of his origin and race; but its quarrel with American ways and traditions went deeper. He struck out at the "stupidity" of "the average conservative American, pillar of the church, supporter of the Anti-Saloon League, member of defense committees and fraternal orders, proclaimer of America's moral mission." He contrasted German literature with English and American literature greatly to the disadvantage of the latter (!). He confessed a longing for the greater spiritual freedom of Central Europe as compared with "Anglo-American" lands.

Mr. Lewisohn, who was born in Berlin in 1882, and who after study at the College of Charleston and Columbia University taught at the University of Wisconsin and Ohio State University, is also known as the author of a number of books on modern drama; as the translator of Gerhart Hauptmann's works; as a novelist of no inconsiderable gifts; and as the author of one of the most acute and incisive (if in some ways also most irritating) volumes yet written on the history of American literature, *Expression in America* (1932).

It has been said many times, and always with an air of authority, that there is no tragedy in the modern drama. And since tragedy, in the minds of most educated people, is hazily but quite firmly connected with the mishaps of noble and mythical personages, the statement has been widely accepted as true. Thus very tawdry Shakespearean revivals are received with a traditional reverence for the sternest and noblest of all the art forms that is consciously withheld from *Ghosts* or

[1] From *The Drama and the Stage*, by Ludwig Lewisohn. Reprinted by permission of Harcourt, Brace and Company, publishers.

Justice or *The Weavers*. Placid people in college towns consider these plays painful. They hasten to pay their respects to awkward chantings of Gilbert Murray's Swinburnian verse and approve the pleasant mildness of the pity and terror native to the Attic stage. The very innocuousness of these entertainments as well as the pain that Ibsen and Hauptmann inflict should give them pause. Pity and terror are strong words and stand for strong things. But our public replies in the comfortable words of its most respectable critics that tragedy has ceased to be written.

These critics reveal a noteworthy state of mind. They are aware that tragedy cuts to the quick of life and springs from the innermost depth of human thinking because it must always seek to deal in some intelligible way with the problem of evil. But since it is most comfortable to believe that problem to have been solved, they avert their faces from a reopening of the eternal question and declare that the answer of the Greeks and the Elizabethans is final. They are also aware, though more dimly, that all tragedy involves moral judgments. And since they are unaccustomed to make such judgments, except by the light of standards quite rigid and quite antecedent to experience, they are bewildered by a type of tragic drama that transfers its crises from the deeds of men to the very criteria of moral judgment, from guilt under a law to the arraignment of the law itself.

Macbeth represents in art and life their favorite tragic situation. They can understand a gross and open crime meeting a violent punishment. When, as in *King Lear*, the case is not so plain, they dwell long and emphatically on the old man's weaknesses in order to find satisfaction in his doom. In the presence of every tragic protagonist of the modern drama they are tempted to play the part of Job's comforters. They are eager to impute to him an absoluteness of guilt which shall, by implication, justify their own moral world and the doctrine of moral violence by which they live. The identical instinct which in war causes men to blacken the enemy's character, in order to justify their tribal rage and hate, persuades the conventional critic to deny the character of tragedy to every action in which disaster does not follow upon crime. Yet, rightly looked upon, man in every tragic situation is a Job, incapable and unconscious of any degree of voluntary guilt that can justify a suffering as sharp and constant as his own.

Thus modern tragedy does not deal with wrong and just vengeance, which are both, if conceived absolutely, pure fictions of our deep-rooted desire for superiority and violence. It is inspired by compassion. But compassion without complacency is still, alas, a very rare emotion. And it seeks to derive the tragic element in human life from the mistakes and self-imposed compulsions, not from the sins, of men. The central idea of *Ghosts*, for instance, is not concerned with the sin of the father that is visited upon the son. It is concerned, as Ibsen sought to make abundantly clear, with Mrs. Alving's fatal conformity to a social tradition that did not represent the pureness of her will. Her tragic mistake arises from her failure to break the law. The ultimate and absolute guilt is in the blind, collective lust of mankind for the formulation and indiscriminate enforcement of external laws.

To such a conception of the moral world, tragedy has but recently attained. That both the critical and the public intelligence should lag far behind is inevitable. Every morning's paper proclaims a world whose moral pattern is formed of terrible blacks and glaring whites. How should people gladly endure the endless and pain-touched gray of modern tragedy? They understand the Greek conception of men who violated the inscrutable will of gods; they understand the Renaissance conception that a breach of the universal law sanctioned and set forth by God needed to be punished. They can even endure such situations as that of Claudio and Isabella in the terrible third act of *Measure for Measure*. For that unhappy brother and sister never question the right of the arbitrary power that caused so cruel a dilemma, nor doubt the absolute validity of the virtue that is named. These two strike at each other's hearts and never at the bars of the monstrous cage that holds them prisoner. Do they not, therefore, rise almost to the dignity of symbols of that moral world in which the majority of men still live?

But it is precisely with the bars of the cage that modern tragedy is so largely and so necessarily concerned. It cannot deal with guilt in the older sense. For guilt involves an absolute moral judgment. That, in its turn, involves an absolute standard. And a literally absolute standard is unthinkable without a superhuman sanction. Even such a sanction, however, would leave the flexible and enlightened spirit in the lurch. For if it were not constantly self-interpretative by some method of progressive and objectively embodied revelation, its interpretation would again become a mere matter of human opinion, and the absoluteness of moral guilt would again be gravely jeopardized. Not only must God have spoken; He would need to speak anew each day. The war has overwhelmingly illustrated how infinitely alien such obvious reflections still are to the

temper of humanity.   We must have guilt.   Else how, without utter
shame, could we endure punitive prisons and gibbets and battles?   Is
it surprising that audiences are cold to Ibsen and Hauptmann and
Galsworthy, and that good critics who are also righteous and angry
men deny their plays the character of tragedy?

But the bars of the absolutist cage are not so bright and firm
as they were once.   The conception of unrelieved guilt and overwhelming vengeance has just played on the stage of history a part so
monstrous that its very name will ring to future ages with immitigable
contrition and grief.   And thus in the serener realm of art the modern
idea of tragedy is very sure to make its gradual appeal to the hearts of
men.   Guilt and punishment will be definitely banished to melodrama, where they belong.   Tragedy will seek increasingly to understand our failures and our sorrows.   It will excite pity for our common
fate; the terror it inspires will be a terror lest we wrong our brother or
violate his will, not lest we share his guilt and incur his punishment.
It will seek its final note of reconciliation not by delivering another
victim to an outraged God or an angry tribe, but through a profound
sense of that community of human suffering which all force deepens
and all freedom assuages.

A NOTE ON COMEDY[1]

Ludwig Lewisohn [2]

The pleasure that men take in comedy arises from their feeling of superiority to the persons involved in the comic action. The Athenian who laughed with Aristophanes over the predicament of the hungry gods, the contemporary New Yorker who laughs over a comedian blundering into the wrong bedroom, are stirred by an identical emotion. The difference in the intellectual character of the two inheres in the nature of the stimulus by which the emotion is in each case aroused. In the former the pleasure was conditioned in a high and arduous activity of mind; in the latter it arises from a momentary and accidental superiority of situation. High and low comedy are dependent in all ages upon the temper of the auditor whose pleasurable emotions of superiority must be awakened. He who has brought a critical attitude of mind to bear upon the institutions and the ways of men will coöperate with the creative activity of a faculty which he himself possesses and has exercised; he to whom all criticism is alien can evidently find no causes for superiority within himself and must be flattered by the sight of physical mishaps and confusions which, for the moment, are not his own. Pure comedy, in brief, and that comedy of physical intrigue which is commonly called farce, cannot from the nature of things differ in the effect they strive to produce. But they must adapt their methods of attaining this common end to the character of the spectator whose emotions they desire to touch.

It follows that pure comedy is rare. Historically we find it flourishing in small, compact, and like-minded groups: the free citizens of Athens, the fashionables of Paris and London who applauded Molière and Congreve. But in all three instances the reign of pure comedy was brief, and in the latter two precarious and artificial at best. With the loss of Athenian freedom, intrigue took the place of social and moral criticism; no later poet dared, as Aristophanes had done in *The Acharnians*, to deride warlikeness in the midst of war. In the New Comedy public affairs and moral criticism disappeared from the Attic stage. In Rome there was no audience for pure comedy. Its func-

---

[1] From *The Drama and the Stage*, by Ludwig Lewisohn. Reprinted by permission of Harcourt, Brace and Company, publishers.

[2] For biographical note, see page 562.

tion was exercised by the satirists alone, precisely as a larger and nobler comic force lives in the satires of Dryden than in the plays of Congreve. Nor should it be forgotten that Molière himself derives from a tradition of farce which reaches, through its Italian origin, to Latin comedy and the New Comedy of Greece, and that the greater number of his own pieces depends for effectiveness on the accidents and complications of intrigue. When he rose above this subject matter and sought the true sources of comic power and appeal in *L'École des Femmes* and *Tartuffe*, he aroused among the uncritical a hatred which pursued him beyond the grave.

The modern theatre, which must address itself primarily to that bulwark of things as they are, the contented middle classes, is, necessarily, a bleak enough place for the spirit of comedy. These audiences will scarcely experience a pleasurable feeling of superiority at the comic exposure of their favorite delusions. Hence Shaw is not popular on the stage; a strong comic talent, like Henri Lavedan's, begins by directing its arrows at those grosser vices which its audience also abhors and then sinks into melodrama; isolated exceptions, such as the success of Hauptmann's massive satire of bureaucratic tyranny in *The Beaver Coat*, scarcely mitigate the loneliness of comedy on the stage of our time. The comic spirit which once sought refuge in satire now seeks it in the novel — that great, inclusive form of art which can always find the single mind to which its speech is articulate.

But since men still desire to laugh in the theatre, there has arisen out of a long and complicated tradition the sentimental comedy. Here the basic action is pseudo-realistic and emotional. Into it are brought, however, odd and absurd characters whose function is the same as that of Shakespeare's fools in tragedy. They break the tension and release the pleasurable feeling of superiority. More often, however, they encroach largely on the sentimental action, and then we have the most popular form of theatrical entertainment among us — a reckless mixture of melodrama and farce. And this form caters, beyond all others, to its huge audience's will to superiority. Men and women laugh at the fools whom they despise, at the villains whose discomfiture vindicates their peculiar sense of social and moral values; they laugh with the heroes in whom those values are embodied and unfailingly triumphant.

From such facile methods pure comedy averts its face. It, too, arouses laughter; it, too, releases the pleasurable emotion of superiority. But it demands a superiority that is hard won and possessed by few. It is profoundly concerned with the intellect that has in very

truth risen above the common follies and group delusions of mankind;
it seeks its fellowship among those who share its perceptions or are
prepared to share them.   It demands not only moral and intellectual
freedom in its audience; it demands a society in which that freedom
can be exercised.   It cannot flourish, as the central example of Attic
comedy illustrates, except in a polity where art and speech are free.
And anyone who reflects on the shifting panorama of political institutions will realize at once how few have been the times and places in
history in which, even given a critically-minded audience, the comic
dramatist could have spoken to that audience in a public playhouse.

The immediate example in our own period is that of Bernard Shaw.
Whatever the ultimate value of his plays may be, he is to us the truest
representation of the comic spirit.   Some of his plays have, on occasion, quite frankly been removed from the stage by the police power;
none are truly popular except in the study.   The bourgeois audiences
who at times witness their performance have set up between themselves and Shaw the protective fiction that he is a high-class clown.
Since they cannot, in self-defense, laugh with him, they attempt to
laugh at him, and thus save their pleasure and their reputation for
cleverness at once.   True comedy, in a word, is a test both of the inner
freedom of the mind and of the outer freedom of the society in which
men live.   Its life has always been brief and hazardous.   Nor is it
likely to flourish unless the liberties of mankind are achieved in a new
measure and with a new intensity.   For the great comic dramatist,
if he would gain the most modest success, must gather in a single
theatre as many free minds in a free state as Lucian or Swift or Heine
seek out and make their own in a whole generation.

THE MODERN BIOGRAPHER[1]

André Maurois

Brand Whitlock has told us how the world first heard of ANDRÉ MAUROIS. In 1917, while Mr. Whitlock was at Havre, a friend showed him the manuscript of a book written by a young Frenchman who had served as interpreter with a British regiment near Ypres and on the staff of General Sir John Asser. The young man had doubts as to its literary value and wished to know if it were worth publishing. Mr. Whitlock took it home, and that night read the remarkable piece of wartime humor which a year later became famous under the title of *The Silence of Colonel Bramble*. These sketches of an English brigade mess deserve immortality for their keen observation, their delightful humanness, their wit and charm. The sparkling conversations of the younger officers, the padre, and the French interpreter are set off by the silences of the stolid, imperturbable, common-sense British colonel, at once hero and butt. The book is full of good stories, of a delicate irony, of strokes that sometimes recall Daudet and at times some English humorist. As Mr. Whitlock shortly wrote: "One does not read very far in this book before one realizes that one is in the presence of a superior and highly civilized intelligence, with a rich background of culture and tradition, and the poetic pessimism of the wise." And the book, for all its lightness of touch, has depth.

Since this beginning M. Maurois has exhibited his brilliancy of wit, his insight into character, and his rich cultural endowment in a series of volumes, chiefly biographic. He has written upon Shelley (*Ariel*), upon Disraeli, upon Byron, upon Edward VII and his times. Though still comparatively young — he was born in 1885 — he has won an international reputation. He is an acknowledged master of that form of biography which, relying upon information already collected by others, gives special emphasis to interpretation, and tries to paint character by a series of rapid, delicate, and yet firm strokes. Possessing a cosmopolitan acquaintance, he has done much to interpret England, France, and America to one another. Slight and simple as his work often seems to hurried readers, its conciseness and economy represent prolonged study and careful thought.

Is there such a thing as modern biography? Can one name a year in which suddenly the old biography ceased to exist and modern biography came into being? And if so, what is the difference between old and modern biography?

The first question, Is there such a thing as modern biography? can be answered in the affirmative. Read a page of Plutarch or Izaak Walton, of Dr. Johnson, or of a Victorian biographer like Trevelyan or Froude, and read after this a page of Strachey. You will see at once that you have before you two different types of book. You will

[1] Reprinted from the January, 1928, issue of *The Yale Review*, copyright Yale University Press, by permission of the Editors.

find the same difference if you read biographers of other countries. Compare, in America, the traditional life of George Washington, of Abraham Lincoln, with the latest lives written. Compare, in Germany, the biographers of the beginning of the nineteenth century with Ludwig's *Kaiser Wilhelm* or with his *Goethe*. As regards France, the comparison is difficult, because biography with us is a new art, but we seem to be making up for lost opportunities by a period of mass production, and biographies built after the Stracheyan pattern have been turned out by the dozen in the last three or four years.

If now we come to the second question, Can one name a year in which suddenly the old biography ceased to exist and modern biography came into being? we shall perhaps find an answer in a quotation from the great English novelist, Virginia Woolf. She hazards an assertion that "on or about December, 1910, human character changed." "I am not saying," she writes, "that one went out, as one might into a garden, and there saw that a rose had flowered, or that a hen had laid an egg. The change was not sudden and definite like that. But a change there was, nevertheless; . . . let us date it about the year 1910. The first signs of it are recorded in the books of Samuel Butler, in *The Way of All Flesh* in particular; the plays of Bernard Shaw continue to record it. In life one can see the change, if I may use a homely illustration, in the character of one's cook. The Victorian cook lived like a leviathan in the lower depths, formidable, silent, obscure, inscrutable; the Georgian cook is a creature of sunshine and fresh air; in and out of the drawing-room, now to borrow the *Daily Herald*, now to ask advice about a hat. Do you ask for more solemn instances of the power of the human race to change? . . . All human relations have shifted — those between masters and servants, husbands and wives, parents and children. And when human relations change there is at the same time a change in religion, conduct, politics, and literature. Let us agree to place one of these changes about the year 1910."

Making allowance for the conscious exaggerations of a delightful writer, there is a great deal of truth in this paradox. In other countries, the great change took place later, in 1918; but it is, I think, indisputable that the outlook on life of the cultured part of humanity, whether in Europe or in America, has undergone deep transformations in the course of the last decade. Has this change been for better or for worse? This remains to be seen, but the fact cannot be denied by an impartial observer that biography, like the novel — like all forms of literature — has been affected by these changes.

As to the third question, What is the difference between old and modern biography? the differences are of two kinds — difference in motive and difference in method. Let us begin with the motive. Why did the biographers of the old days write? We find an answer in one of them: "Biography sets before us the lives of eminent men that we may imitate their virtues and avoid their vices." The object of Plutarch is to teach morality. The object of Walton is a twofold one — "an honor due to the virtuous dead and the lesson in magnanimity to those who shall succeed them." Walton writes about his friends a few years after their deaths, and his charming lives are nothing but monuments to the memories of those friends.

Sir Sidney Lee, in his *Principles of Biography*, tells us with unconscious humor that biography exists to satisfy a natural instinct in man, the commemorative instinct. The creation of instincts makes psychology an easy science. Nevertheless, it is true that most of the old writers of biographies worked, as Sir Sidney says, to keep alive the memories of those who by character and deeds have distinguished themselves from the mass of humanity.

It must not be forgotten that the old biographer had sometimes another motive, which was simply that such lives had been ordered from him by a publisher. Dr. Johnson, for instance, never considered it as a duty toward humanity to write the lives of the British poets. He was asked to do so, and he did so extremely well, because his was a splendid mind, and he could not help giving life and color to everything he wrote.

In the Victorian era, after the death of any great Englishman, his family and his friends chose with care a writer who, they thought, would give suitable praise to the deceased hero. The process was the same in America. "When any distinguished citizen, lawyer or judge, merchant or writer, died," wrote William Roscoe Thayer, "it was taken for granted that his clergyman, if he had one, would write his life, unless his wife, sister, or cousin were preferred." Prudent men, before their death, appointed a biographer just as they appointed an executor of their will. Such choices were sometimes unfortunate. Thus Carlyle found Froude an intimate and dangerous enemy. Byron was hopelessly misunderstood by Moore. The Prince Consort and Cardinal Manning were made ridiculous by two well-meaning biographers. Other choices were happy; for example, the appointment of Monypenny by the trustees of Lord Beaconsfield; or the appointment of Charles Whibley by the family of Lord John Manners.

But in the old Victorian biographies the quality most appreciated by the families of the heroes was respect of the proprieties. The intimate life of a man, his everyday doings, his weaknesses and follies and mistakes, were not to be mentioned. Even if his life had been notoriously scandalous, this should only be vaguely alluded to. "What business," says Tennyson, "has the public to know about Byron's wildnesses? He has given them fine work, and they ought to be satisfied." The author was given all the information available; letters, even private diaries, were generously put at his disposal; but such generosity forced upon him a loyalty which compelled him to be secretive and laudatory. If there was a widow, she kept a careful eye both on the portrait of her deceased husband and on the figure she herself cut in the book before posterity. The results are too well known — "Books so stuffed with virtue," one writer says of them, "that I began to doubt the existence of any virtue."

Of course, such a hard judgment is unfair to the good books of that period. A great deal could be said in favor of the old type of life and letters in three volumes, with notes and appendix. It was an invaluable mass of material, where the modern biographer is very glad to go and dig for precious metal. It was even sometimes fine work of real literary value. Macaulay's life, by Trevelyan, is a very readable book. The custom is to praise Lockhart's life of Scott and Forster's life of Dickens; these are useful books, full of interesting documents; but shall I confess that I do not admire them unreservedly? They are long and badly constructed. On the other hand, Dowden's life of Shelley seems to me perfect.

Even when the Victorian biographer is a good historian and a good writer, we have a grievance against him, which is his attitude of hero-worship. A public man, whether he is an artist or a statesman, always wears a mask. We find in him two characters; one is the man known to the public, or at least the man he would like the public to believe in; the other is the man as he is known to his friends or to himself, if he is sincere. The Victorian biographer always describes a mask, and refuses to look behind it. Read Moore's life of Byron. It is only a mask of Byron. Nobody has ever dared to write about the real Dickens or the real Thackeray. Who has described the real Herbert Spencer, human, rather comical, as we find him in the unconsciously delightful little book, *Home Life with Herbert Spencer?* The tradition was to glide over the real facts if they spoiled the rigid perfection of the mask. Victorian biographers were sculptors of commemorative monuments. Few of them were good sculptors.

We now come to Strachey, who is, I think, by common agreement to be considered as the father and master of modern biography. At once we perceive a difference. Strachey is no hero-worshiper. On the contrary, he is a hero-wrecker, an idol-breaker. Before him the great Victorians were sacred to an English gentleman of letters. General Gordon, great puritan and great soldier, was treated as a sort of national saint. Queen Victoria had Gordon's Bible placed in one of the corridors at Windsor, enclosed in a crystal case. As to the Queen herself, people knew there might be some faint essence of the comic about her, but they preferred not to think about it, and especially not to talk about it.

Then Strachey wrote *Eminent Victorians*. Nobody could complain about the title of the book. The men and women he spoke about were eminent, and they were Victorians. But as soon as one began to read, one perceived that the title was ironic. With great skill, Strachey described these Victorians giants, Cardinal Manning, Thomas Arnold, General Gordon. He did not say a word against them; he never judged; he remained objective; but he portrayed the men as they had been, without hiding anything. He gave us extracts from their letters, from their diaries, and he grouped such extracts in such a cunning way that the intimate life of his unfortunate models was revealed. For instance, he tells us that Cardinal Manning in his diary notes that, having decided to mortify himself, he determined during Lent "to use no pleasant bread except on Sundays and feasts, such as cake and sweetmeat." "But," says Strachey, "a few days later the Cardinal added in the margin 'I do not include plain biscuits.'" No comments from Strachey, but the shaft has gone home.

In Strachey's *Queen Victoria*, you cannot find a single sentence against the Queen, but the quotations and facts collected evoke the image of a fat and resolute little woman, full of pride, accessible to flattery, at the same time touching and ridiculous. The literary method of Strachey is the method of the great humorists. He does not appear himself in his book; he does not judge his model; he walks behind her, imitates her gestures, remains serious, and obtains by such tricks excellent effects of comedy. The fact that he imitates the habits of the Queen, that he underlines like herself all the words of a sentence, that he writes, like her, "Lord M." instead of Lord Melbourne, "Dear Albert" instead of Prince Albert, all these little details create a very natural and very human image. Even the exact quotation of an official document produces an effect of cruel humor. For instance, when he comes to the construction of the Albert Memorial, the ugliest monument in England, Strachey does not say that it is ugly; he simply describes the thing as it is, and gives us the very words of the sculptor: "I have chosen the sitting posture as best conveying the idea of dignity befitting the royal personage. . . . The aim has been, with the individuality of portraiture, to embody rank, character, and enlightenment, and to convey a sense of that responsive intelligence indicating an active, rather than a passive, interest in those pursuits of civilization illustrated in the surrounding figures, groups, and relieves. . . . To identify the figure with one of the most memorable undertakings of the public life of the Prince — the International Exhibition of 1851 — a catalogue of the works collected in that first gathering of the industry of all nations, is placed in the right hand." "The statue was of bronze gilt," Strachey continues, "and weighed nearly ten tons. It was rightly supposed that the simple word 'Albert,' cast on the base, would be a sufficient means of identification."

But it would be unfair to see nothing in Strachey but an idol-breaker. He is also a very deep psychologist. As a painter, he has a curious method. He begins by designing a rather crude portrait; then he corrects a line, then another, and he keeps on making it more involved, more confused, but at the same time nearer to life. He often uses expressions like "and yet, and yet," or "There was something — what was it? —" which give the reader the impression that he pursues an indefinable character just as he would do in real life.

Remember the wonderful portrait of the Prince Consort:

Albert, certainly, seemed to be everything that Stockmar could have wished — virtuous, industrious, persevering, intelligent. And yet — why was it? — all was not well with him. He was sick at heart.

For in spite of everything he had never reached to happiness. His work, for which at last he came to crave with an almost morbid appetite, was a solace and not a cure. . . . The causes of his melancholy were hidden, mysterious, unanalyzable perhaps — too deeply rooted in the innermost recesses of his temperament for the eye of reason to apprehend. There were contradictions in his nature, which, to some of those who knew him best, made him seem an inexplicable enigma: he was severe and gentle; he was modest and scornful; he longed for affection and he was cold. He was lonely, not merely with the loneliness of exile but with the loneliness of conscious and unrecognized superiority. He had the pride, at once resigned and overweening, of a doctrinaire. And yet to say that he was simply a doctrinaire would be a false description; for the pure doctrinaire rejoices always in an internal contentment, and Albert was very far from doing that. There was something that he wanted and that he could never get. What was it? Some absolute, some ineffable sympathy? Some

extraordinary, some sublime success? Possibly, it was a mixture of both.
To dominate and to be understood! To conquer, by the same triumphant
influence, the submission and the appreciation of men — that would be
worth while indeed! But, to such imaginations, he saw too clearly how
faint were the responses of his actual environment. Who was there who
appreciated him, really and truly? Who *could* appreciate him in England?
And, if the gentle virtue of an inward excellence availed so little, could he
expect more from the hard ways of skill and force? The terrible land of his
exile loomed before him a frigid, an impregnable mass. . . . He believed
that he was a failure and he began to despair.

One cannot admire too much the skill of the artist and the way in
which the description of a mind slowly becomes a monologue of the
mind itself. The stream of consciousness, so often alluded to by the
modern novelist, is described in the work of Strachey and also in the
work of his followers. Nobody, perhaps, has done it better than Harold
Nicolson in his *Byron*. Here we follow the moods of the man, just
as we would in one of James Joyce's novels — and at the same time
every thought attributed to Byron is a thought that Byron really had.
Take, for instance, the . . . impressions of Byron at a time when he
starts on his Greek adventure.

It would be idle to pretend that Byron set out upon this his last journey
with any very spirited enthusiasm. . . . For when it had come to packing
up, and destroying old letters, and explaining to Barry what was to be done
with the books, and toting up the accounts, and sending the horses down to
the harbor, and finding everything at the Casa Saluzzo hourly more disintegrated and uncomfortable, he began, definitely and indignantly, to curse
the whole undertaking. It was always like that: people never left one
alone; there he was, good-natured and kindly, and they came along and
took advantage of him, and extracted promises, and imposed upon him
generally. Once again he had been caught in a chain of circumstances:
there had been his first visit to Greece, and "Childe Harold," and "The
Corsair," and that silly passage about the "hereditary bondsmen"; and
there had been Hobhouse (damn Hobhouse!), and that egregious ass
Trelawny. And as a result here was he, who had never done any harm to
anyone, sitting alone in the Casa Saluzzo, with his household gods once again
dismantled around him, and his bulldog growling now and then at the distant voice of Trelawny thundering orders to the servants.

Of all forms of cant, this cant of romanticism was the most insufferable.
There was Trelawny, for instance, trying to look like Lara, with his sham
eagle eyes, his sham disordered hair, his sham abrupt manners. Why
couldn't Trelawny behave quietly and like a man of decent breeding?
Surely, if they were committed to this Greek scrape it would be better to
take the thing soberly and calmly, instead of all this dust and bustle, of all

this cant about Causes, and Liberty, and Adventure. How he *loathed* adventures! At the mere word he ground his teeth in fury.

In the case of Nicolson, just as in the case of Strachey, there is a curious mixture of irony and tenderness; but such tenderness is rather grim. Even when Strachey pats his heroes on the back, you feel that he is ready to scratch them. To treat a great man as a human being, even if this human being is a lovable one, is to make the great man smaller. The statue is brought down from its pedestal. Yes, it cannot be denied, Strachey and his pupils are idol-breakers.

It seems natural that such a school of biographers should be born in England, because a reaction against the excess of propriety of the Victorians was inevitable. After too much hero-worship, the reaction was even necessary. Strachey, Nicolson, Guedalla, have done in biography what Huxley, Forster, Virginia Woolf, have done in the novel. But though the school was born in England, it was imitated in other countries. In the United States, biographers are now re-writing the lives of most of the illustrious statesmen, and the new lives are more frank, more outspoken, than the old ones. We discover a new Franklin, a new Washington; and as to the men who lend themselves to comic treatment, they are treated without mercy by the new generation. As a good example I may mention the very re-markable life of Brigham Young by Werner.

Is this new type of biography written for the pleasure of destroying heroes? If it were so, it would be a rather despicable art. Humanity has always found a source of consolation in the lives of its great men, and one ought to consider very seriously before one destroys a perhaps useful illusion. It cannot be denied that in some instances the new biographer has overdone it. Strachey himself must be admitted in some instances to be a shade nastier than is really fair. His Disraeli is a courtier without scruples, who dominates through flattery a rather unintelligent old woman. Indeed, Disraeli was apt to pay the Queen hyperbolical compliments; but he also knew how to resist her. On the other hand, the letters of the Queen are not only made of the sentences — of the very amusing sentences — so admirably chosen by Strachey, but also of very wise comments on the political situation and a sort of middle class wisdom that was not without useful effect upon the fate of the British Empire.

Strachey is so good a psychologist that truth in his hands is never in real danger; but some of his disciples, without imitating his deep insight, have only got hold of his familiar tricks. Instead of choosing, as heroes for biographies, "eminent men, so that we may imitate their

virtues," they restrict themselves to individualities which are sus-
ceptible of treatment in their favorite mode of irony. The writer
treats his hero with an unheard-of familiarity. There is a biography
of Longfellow in which the biographer persists in calling the poet
Henry. We have regretted in France during the last years the publication of several books where great writers are treated by much lesser
writers as rather contemptible schoolmates. They even take the
liberty of inventing conversations between well-known men and of
putting in their mouths sentences they never pronounced. Some of
these books would make us regret the three-volume life and letters
which, after all, was an historical and a scholarly work. We sometimes get tired of "the plucking of dead lions by the beard."

But when we judge the modern biographer, we must consider that
he represents a reaction, and that a reaction always goes too far.
It was necessary to remind the last of the Victorians that a mask is not
a man; it is now necessary to remind our contemporaries that a man
is never entirely ridiculous, and that his life is very serious for himself. . . .

Whether they work from the motives of Strachey (reaction) or from
the motives that have just been analyzed (self-expression), modern
biographers have one thing in common; that is their refusal to paint
masks, their desire to get to the real man. Is this a good or a bad
thing? Some critics say, Why do away with hero-worship? It is
quite true, perhaps, that a hero is at the same time a man, but why
say so? Is it not healthier for humanity to keep in view an image of
the better type of man, an image which will help us to climb on our
own shoulders? Do you not fear that the spectacle of the weaknesses
of great men will lead minor men to be easily satisfied with their own
conduct? Plutarch was not, perhaps, quite true to life, but he
produced Montaigne, and Napoleon.

Yes; but the danger of the old type of biography is that nobody
believes in it. We all know that Gladstone was not exactly the man
painted by Morley. Would it not be more inspiring to meet real
human beings and to treat them as such? This man Byron was not
the man Moore makes him out to be; he was full of pride; he was
hard on women; he was a strange mixture of his own Manfred and
a typical English gentleman; but he was a very lovable character
just the same. I wonder if make-believe is ever a good policy, and
if there is any real greatness outside of perfect truth. In spite of his
somewhat brutal sincerity, we must give credit to the modern biographer for his genuine respect of truth.

We shall now try to find out what are the methods of the new biographer. The essential point about him is that his aim is to build a work of art. When historians accumulated masses of documents without choice or discrimination, the result might be an interesting book, but the works produced were of considerable length, unreadable for the average man, and certainly they were not works of art. The question will be raised, Should a biography be a work of art?

"Art is essentially," Bacon said, "man added to nature"; that is, facts ordered by a human mind. The novel is constructed; the idea of symmetry, of rhythm, plays an important part in the building of any good novel. But how can symmetry and form be achieved when the author deals with real life? Real life is what it is. We cannot alter it. How shall we give shape to this monster? The author finds himself confronted with long periods in the life of his hero when nothing happens, and then suddenly in the space of a few months events crowd in. Also it may happen that the real life ends where the story begins. Once, in London, an old bookseller said to me, "Well, sir, your life of Shelley — it isn't such a bad book; but I'll give you some advice. Next time, don't make your hero die so young. The public doesn't like it." The sentence sounds absurd, but there is something in it. The real subject of any novel is conflict between man and the universe — what Goethe called the Years of Learning; but the real conclusion of the Years of Learning is reached only in the maturity of man. For Shelley, one does not know what the conclusion might have been had he lived through this maturity.

However, consider the portrait-painter. He also has to deal with a given reality and to build a harmony of colors and lines with this given material. How does he do it? He selects; he leaves out a great many things; he does not add to the face of his model lines that are not there, but he builds by suppression, by concentrating the interest of the onlooker on the important features of the face. This is exactly what the biographer should do. He must not invent anything, but his art is to forget. If he has at his disposal two hundred letters and a long diary, he must know how to extract the few sentences that will convey a general impression.

In any life, there is always a well-hidden harmony; the historian has to discover the mysterious rhythm in that existence. He can give an impression of unity by repeating certain themes, as Wagner does in music. In the biography of Shelley, for instance, there must be a theme of water; water plays a great part in Shelley's life. As a boy he is attracted by it; as a man he spends his life in fragile boats.

From the beginning, you feel that he will die by drowning. The writer should give this impression of impending fate. In the life of Disraeli, rain is a poetical element. Implacable, steady rain is a symbol of the universe fighting the romantic. Peacocks also play a curious part in this life. By a careful handling of such themes, the biographer can hope to achieve some sort of musical construction.

Such construction must, of course, coincide with a respect for facts. A strict adherence to historical truth is necessary to the biographer, but after he has collected his facts, he has a right to eliminate some of them.

Now, there are certain rules which practice has proved useful. The first is that one should follow a chronological order. Ancient biographers like Plutarch had no idea of chronology. They started with a recital of facts, and, after they had told us about the death of their hero, they began again with anecdotes and analysis of character. Then came an ethical judgment. This method gave a painful impression of repetition. It was copied from Plutarch by Walton and also by Johnson; they all tell you from the first that their hero was a great man. The Victorian biographer writes: "This great poet was born in 1788." This, I think, is wrong. A man is not born a great poet, and he will not interest us if he is shown as a great man from his babyhood. What is interesting is to see the child Byron, the young man at Harrow, at Cambridge, and to discover slowly how he became Manfred and Don Juan.

Of course, this idea of chronological development is new. It comes from the fact that we now believe in the evolution of an individual mind as well as of a race. A biographer like Walton did not feel the need of chronology because he did not believe that a man's nature could change very much. All arts react one upon another. In the last twenty years, Marcel Proust has taught us how to avoid drawing static characters. Some of his heroes are unpleasant at the beginning of the novel and delightful at the end. In the case of other characters, the process is reversed. We want the biographer to be as true to life as the novelist. "My object," says Miss Lowell, "has been to make the reader feel as though he were living with Keats, subject to the same influences that surround him, moving in his circle, watching the advent of poems as from day to day they sprang into being." In biography, as in the novel, it is important that the minor characters should be seen from the point of view of the central figure. They should not even be allowed to appear until the very moment when the hero discovers them.

The second rule is to avoid pronouncing moral judgments. The essential difference between art and action is that art builds a world where no real events occur, and where, therefore, man feels that he has no moral decision to make. The characters in *Hamlet* would be painful to meet in real life, because something would have to be done about them, but we accept them on the stage because no moral problem arises for us. If an artist gives the impression that the world he describes is a world where we must act and decide, he may be a great moralist, but he is no more a great artist. A biographer must tell his story in objective and impartial style.

The third rule is to read every word that has ever been written on the subject and to collect all available testimony. What the modern historian wants to describe is not the statue but the man. In official documents, very often he finds nothing but the statue. It may be in the letters or the journal of an unknown woman that he will come across the anecdote that will suddenly reveal a character. He must hunt for details if he wants truth. Of course, the question arises, What is truth? Is there indeed a truth about character? You remember Walt Whitman's —

> When I read the book, biography famous,
> And is this, then (said I), what the author calls a man's life?
> And so will some one, when I am dead and gone, write my life?
> As if any man really knew aught of my life;
> Why, even I myself, I often think, know little or nothing of my real life.

Whitman is partly right. If we think of our own lives, we realize that some of our most important acts have been accomplished by us without any real motivation. Perhaps we have said words which meant more than we thought; and a few months later we found ourselves involved in actions which did not coincide with our real wishes. This is true of Byron. Byron never meant to die in Greece, or even to go to Greece. He had played with the idea because he was bored, because he thought it would relieve him of the tedium of his Italian life. Then the moment came when words were turned into acts and Byron lived up to them.

The writer should be careful not to make the life of his hero appear too well constructed. A human life is very rarely the conscious accomplishment of the will. It is that partly, but you must always leave a certain margin for the action of circumstance. A "tale told by an idiot," says Shakespeare. There is always something of that madness in the lives of great men of action. If you leave out the strange atmosphere of fate, you miss all the real poetry of human life.

Of course, one of the best technical rules to follow in order to avoid showing the life of the hero as too squarely built is to allow the reader to see him through the eyes of friends and enemies who judge him differently. There the biographer can learn much from the modern novelist. Read a novel like Forster's *Passage to India;* there you see the English as they appear to a Hindu, the Hindu as seen by the English, and the Hindu as seen by himself. In the same way, I have attempted as well as I could to show Disraeli as seen by Gladstone, and Gladstone as seen by Disraeli. You cannot say that there was one Gladstone; there were as many Gladstones as there were people who knew him, and it is the sum of these portraits which enables the reader to form an idea of the average Gladstone.

There is one more question to deal with, How is one to select the subject of a biography? Sir Sidney Lee says that the theme should be of a certain magnitude. This has been contradicted. Many writers contend that if you could know every thought that crosses the mind of a beggar, you could write a better book than any life of Caesar. Perhaps; but a great life makes better food for a human soul. Moreover, the life of the beggar leaves very few traces. It may be written by the novelist, not by the biographer, who needs documents, letters, diaries. The man who leaves behind him an historical record is either the great man of thought or the great man of action. In some cases, the theme may be of sufficient magnitude though the man himself is not a great man. This happens when the chosen hero has been the center of important events. A good example is Mr. Shane Leslie's *George the Fourth.* In such cases, the poetical element might be found in the contrast between the magnitude of the tragedy and the misery of the tragedians.

At the end of his biography of his wife, Alice Freeman Palmer, Mr. Palmer says: "If my portrait of her is correct, invigoration will go forth from it and disheartened souls be cheered." This should apply to any biography worth writing. Such books should help us to bear the difficulties of life. They should help us to understand them. Carlyle said that "a well-written life is almost as rare as a well-spent one." This is true, but "great men, taken up in any way, are profitable company."

ON JARGON[1]

Sir A. T. Quiller-Couch

ARTHUR QUILLER-COUCH was born in Cornwall, England, in 1863, and educated at Oxford, where for a time he lectured on the classics. After a period devoted to journalism in London, he settled down at Fowey in Cornwall as a writer. In 1910 he was knighted, and in 1912 he was appointed King Edward VII Professor of English Literature at Cambridge.

The versatile Sir Arthur unites to the talents of a poet, an essayist, and a prolific writer of tales of adventure those of a scholar deeply versed in the whole realm of English literature. He is best known as a romancer, a gifted follower of Robert Louis Stevenson, whose tale *St. Ives* he completed. Those who have not read his *Dead Man's Rock* (1887), which narrates in Stevensonian vein the search for a great ruby in Ceylon, or *The Splendid Spur* (1889), a novel of Cromwell's time, or *Hetty Wesley* (1903), a character study in romance form of the gifted and misunderstood sister of John Wesley, have missed much pleasure. "Q" has also written stirring ballads. His *Oxford Book of English Verse* is the best anthology in the language since Palgrave's *Golden Treasury*, and he followed it by a number of other excellent anthologies. But not least among his productions are his numerous literary papers. At first as a journalist, writing for *The Speaker* and other British weeklies, and later as a professor at Cambridge, he poured out a long and charming series of essays on authors great and small, on the art of reading, and on the art of writing. Readers looking for a guide to introduce them to good books, with discrimination, with acuteness, and always with gusto and charm, will find no one better than Sir Arthur Quiller-Couch. In his *Adventures in Criticism* (1896), and his two series of *Studies in Literature* (1918; 1927) he displays a catholic taste, turning from Ibsen to *Trilby*, from the penny-dreadful to Shakespeare, and from George Moore to Laurence Sterne, and finding something diverting and shrewd to say about each. His book on reading deals with an art too seldom recognized as such, while his book on writing expresses much sound sense with pungency and force.

We parted, gentlemen, upon a promise to discuss the capital difficulty of Prose, as we have discussed the capital difficulty of Verse. But, although we shall come to it, on second thoughts I ask leave to break the order of my argument and to interpose some words upon a kind of writing which, from a superficial likeness, commonly passes for prose in these days, and by lazy folk is commonly written for prose, yet actually is not prose at all; my excuse being the simple practical one that, by first clearing this sham prose out of the way, we shall the better deal with honest prose when we come to it. The proper difficulties of prose will remain; but we shall be agreed in understanding

---

[1] From *On the Art of Writing*, by A. T. Quiller-Couch. Reprinted by permission of G. P. Putnam's Sons, publishers.

what it is, or at any rate what it is not, that we talk about. I remember to have heard somewhere of a religious body in the United States of America which had reason to suspect one of its churches of accepting spiritual consolation from a colored preacher — an offense against the laws of the synod — and dispatched a disciplinary committee with power to act; and of the committee's returning to report itself unable to take any action under its terms of reference, for that while a person undoubtedly colored had undoubtedly occupied the pulpit and had audibly spoken from it in the committee's presence, the performance could be brought within no definition of preaching known or discoverable. So it is with that infirmity of speech — that flux, that determination of words to the mouth, or to the pen — which, though it be familiar to you in parliamentary debates, in newspapers, and as the staple language of Blue Books, committees, official reports, I take leave to introduce to you as prose which is not prose and under its real name of Jargon.

You must not confuse this Jargon with what is called Journalese. The two overlap, indeed, and have a knack of assimilating each other's vices. But jargon finds, maybe, the most of its votaries among good douce people who have never written to or for a newspaper in their life, who would never talk of "adverse climatic conditions" when they mean "bad weather"; who have never trifled with verbs such as "obsess," "recrudesce," "envisage," "adumbrate," or with phrases such as "the psychological moment," "the true inwardness," "it gives furiously to think." It dallies with Latinity — "sub silentio," "de die in diem," "cui bono?" (always in the sense, unsuspected by Cicero, of "What is the profit?") — but not for the sake of style. Your journalist at the worst is an artist in his way; he daubs paint of this kind upon the lily with a professional zeal; the more flagrant (or, to use his own words, arresting) the pigment, the happier is his soul. Like the Babu, he is trying all the while to embellish our poor language, to make it more floriferous, more poetical — like the Babu, for example, who, reporting his mother's death, wrote, "Regret to inform you, the hand that rocked the cradle has kicked the bucket."

There is metaphor; *there* is ornament; *there* is a sense of poetry, though as yet groping in a world unrealized. No such gusto marks — no such zeal, artistic or professional, animates — the practitioners of jargon, who are, most of them (I repeat), douce respectable persons. Caution is its father; the instinct to save everything and especially trouble; its mother, Indolence. It looks precise, but is not. It is, in these times, *safe:* a thousand men have said it before and not one to your knowledge had been prosecuted for it.   And so, like respectability in Chicago, jargon stalks unchecked in our midst.   It is becoming the language of Parliament; it has become the medium through which Boards of Government, county councils, syndicates, committees, commercial firms, express the processes as well as the conclusions of their thought and so voice the reason of their being.

Has a minister to say "No" in the House of Commons?   Some men are constitutionally incapable of saying "No"; but the minister conveys it thus: "The answer to the question is in the negative."   That means "No."   Can you discover it to mean anything less, or anything more except that the speaker is a pompous person? — which was no part of the information demanded.

That is jargon, and it happens to be accurate.   But as a rule jargon is by no means accurate, its method being to walk circumspectly around its target; and its faith, that having done so it has either hit the bull's-eye or at least achieved something equivalent, and safer.

Thus the clerk of a Board of Guardians will minute that —

In the case of John Jenkins deceased the coffin provided was of the usual character.

Now this is not accurate.   "In the case of John Jenkins deceased," for whom a coffin was supplied, it is wholly superfluous to tell us that he is deceased.   But actually John Jenkins never had more than one case, and that was the coffin.   The clerk says he had two — a coffin in a case; but I suspect the clerk to be mistaken, and I am sure he errs in telling us that the coffin was of the usual character; for coffins have no character, usual or unusual. . . .

Have you begun to detect the two main vices of jargon?   The first is that it uses circumlocution rather than short straight speech.   It says: "In the case of John Jenkins deceased, the coffin" when it means "John Jenkins's coffin"; and its yea is not yea, neither is its nay nay; but its answer is in the affirmative or in the negative, as the foolish and superfluous "case" may be.   The second vice is that it habitually chooses vague woolly abstract nouns rather than concrete ones.   I shall have something to say by-and-by about the concrete noun, and how you should ever be struggling for it whether in prose or in verse. For the moment I content myself with advising you, if you would write masculine English, never to forget the old tag of your Latin Grammar —

Masculine will only be
Things that you can touch and see.

But since these lectures are meant to be a course in First Aid to writing, I will content myself with one or two extremely rough rules; yet I shall be disappointed if you do not find them serviceable.

The first is: Whenever in your reading you come across one of these words, *case, instance, character, nature, condition, persuasion, degree* — whenever in writing your pen betrays you to one or another of them — pull yourself up and take thought. If it be "case" (I choose it as jargon's dearest child — "in Heaven yclept Metonomy") turn to the dictionary, if you will, and seek out what meaning can be derived from *casus*, its Latin ancestor; then try how, with a little trouble, you can extricate yourself from that case. The odds are, you will feel like a butterfly who has discarded his chrysalis.

Here are some specimens to try your hand on:

(1) All those tears which inundated Lord Hugh Cecil's head were dry in the case of Mr. Harold Cox.

Poor Mr. Cox! left gasping in his aquarium!

(2) [From a cigar-merchant.] In any case, let us send you a case on approval.

(3) It is contended that Consols have fallen in consequence: but such is by no means the case.

"*Such*," by the way, is another spoiled child of jargon, especially in Committee's Rules — "Co-opted members may be eligible as such; such members to continue to serve for such time as" — and so on.

(4) Even in the purely Celtic areas only in two or three cases do the Bishops bear Celtic names.

For "cases" read "dioceses."

Instance. In most instances the players were below their form.

But what were they playing at? Instances?

Character — Nature. There can be no doubt that the accident was caused through the dangerous nature of the spot, the hidden character of the by-road, and the utter absence of any warning or danger signal.

Mark the foggy wording of it all! And yet the man hit something and broke his neck! Contrast that explanation with the verdict of a coroner's jury in the west of England on a drowned postman: "We find that deceased met his death by an act of God, caused by sudden overflowing of the river Walkham and helped out by the scandalous neglect of the way-wardens."

The Aintree course is notoriously of a trying nature.

On account of its light character, purity, and age, Usher's whiskey is a whiskey that will agree with you. . . .

Condition. He was conveyed to his place of residence in an intoxicated condition.

"He was carried home drunk." . . .

Degree. A singular degree of rarity prevails in the earlier editions of this romance.

That is jargon. In prose it runs simply "The earlier editions of this romance are rare" — or "are very rare" — or even (if you believe what I take leave to doubt) "are singularly rare"; which should mean that they are rarer than the editions of any other work in the world.

Now what I ask you to consider about these quotations is that in each the writer was using jargon to shirk prose, palming off periphrases upon us when with a little trouble he could have gone straight to the point. "A singular degree of rarity prevails," "the accident was caused through the dangerous nature of the spot," "but such is by no means the case." We may not be capable of much; but we can all write better than that, if we take a little trouble. In place of "the Aintree course is of a trying nature" we can surely say "Aintree is a trying course" or "the Aintree course is a trying one" — just that and nothing more. . . .

Let us turn to another trick of jargon — the trick of Elegant Variation, so rampant in the sporting press that there, without needing to attend these lectures, the undergraduate detects it for laughter:

Hayward and C. B. Fry now faced the bowling, which apparently had no terrors for the Surrey crack. The old Oxonian, however, took some time in settling to work. . . .

Yes, you all recognize it and laugh at it. But why do you practice it in your essays? An undergraduate brings me an essay on Byron. In an essay on Byron, Byron is (or ought to be) mentioned many times. I expect, nay exact, that Byron shall be mentioned again and again. But my undergradute has a blushing sense that to call Byron Byron twice on one page is indelicate. So Byron, after starting bravely as Byron, in the second sentence turns into "that great but unequal poet" and thenceforward I have as much trouble with Byron as ever Telemachus with Proteus to hold and pin him back to his proper self. Halfway down the page he becomes "the gloomy master of Newstead"; overleaf he is reincarnated into "the meteoric darling of society"; and so proceeds through successive avatars — "this arch-rebel," "the author of 'Childe Harold,'" "the apostle of scorn," "the ex-Harrovian, proud, but abnormally sensitive of his club-foot," "the martyr of Missolonghi," "the pageant-monger of a bleeding heart." Now this again is jargon. It does not, as most jargon does, come of laziness; but it comes of timidity, which is worse. In literature as in life he makes himself felt who not only calls a spade a spade but has the pluck to double spades and redouble.

For another rule — just as rough-and-ready, but just as useful: Train your suspicions to bristle up whenever you come upon "as regards," "with regard to," "in respect of," "in connection with," "according as to whether," and the like. They are all dodges of jargon, circumlocutions for evading this or that simple statement; and I say that it is not enough to avoid them nine times out of ten, or nine-and-ninety times out of a hundred. You should never use them. That is positive enough, I hope? Though I cannot admire his style, I admire the man who wrote to me, "*Re* Tennyson — your remarks anent his 'In Memoriam' make me sick"; for though *re* is not a preposition of the first water, and "anent" has enjoyed its day, the finish crowned the work. But here are a few specimens far, very far, worse:

The special difficulty in Professor Minocelsi's case [our old friend "case" again] arose *in connection with* the view he holds *relative to* the historical value of the opening pages of Genesis.

That is jargon. In prose, even taking the miserable sentence as it stands constructed, we should write "the difficulty arose over the views he holds about the historical value," etc.

From a popular novelist:

I was entirely indifferent *as to* the results of the game, caring nothing at all *as to* whether *I had losses or gains* —

Cut out the first "as" in "as to," and the second "as to" altogether, and the sentence begins to be prose — "I was indifferent to the results of the game, caring nothing whether I had losses or gains."

But why, like Dogberry, have "had losses"? Why not simply "lose." Let us try again. "I was entirely indifferent to the results of the game, caring nothing at all whether I won or lost."

Still the sentence remains absurd; for the second clause but repeats the first without adding one jot. For if you care not at all whether you win or lose, you must be entirely indifferent to the results of the game. So why not say, "I was careless if I won or lost," and have done with it? . . .

But let us close our *florilegium* and attempt to illustrate jargon by the converse method of taking a famous piece of English (say Hamlet's soliloquy) and remolding a few lines of it in this fashion:

To be, or the contrary? Whether the former or the latter be preferable would seem to admit of some difference of opinion; the answer in the present case being of an affirmative or of a negative character according as to whether one elects on the one hand to mentally suffer the disfavor of fortune, albeit in an extreme degree, or on the other to boldly envisage adverse conditions in the prospect of eventually bringing them to a conclusion. The condition of sleep is similar to, if not indistinguishable from, that of death; and with the addition of finality the former might be considered identical with the latter: so that in this connection it might be argued with regard to sleep that, could the addition be effected, a termination would be put to the endurance of a multiplicity of inconveniences, not to mention a number of downright evils incidental to our fallen humanity, and thus a consummation achieved of a most gratifying nature.

That is jargon: and to write jargon is to be perpetually shuffling around in the fog and cotton-wool of abstract terms; to be for ever hearkening, like Ibsen's Peer Gynt, to the voice of the Boyg exhorting you to circumvent the difficulty, to beat the air because it is easier than to flesh your sword in the thing. The first virtue, the touchstone of masculine style, is its use of the active verb and the concrete noun. When you write in the active voice, "They gave him a silver teapot," you write as a man. When you write "He was made the recipient of a silver teapot," you write jargon. But at the beginning set even higher store on the concrete noun. Somebody — I think it was Fitz-Gerald — once posited the question, "What would have become of Christianity if Jeremy Bentham had had the writing of the Parables?" Without pursuing that dreadful inquiry I ask you to note how carefully the Parables — those exquisite short stories — speak only of "things which you can touch and see" — "A sower went forth to sow," "The Kingdom of Heaven is like unto leaven, which a woman took" — and not the Parables only, but the Sermon on the Mount and almost every verse of the Gospel. The Gospel does not, like my young essayist, fear to repeat a word, if the word be good. The Gospel says "Render unto Caesar the things that are Caesar's" — not "Render unto Caesar the things that appertain to that potentate." The Gospel does not say "Consider the growth of the lilies," or even "Consider how the lilies grow." It says, "Consider the lilies, how they grow."

Or take Shakespeare. I wager you that no writer of English so constantly chooses the concrete word, in phrase after phrase forcing you to touch and see. No writer so insistently teaches the general through the particular. He does it even in *Venus and Adonis* (as Professor Wendell, of Harvard, pointed out in a brilliant little monograph on Shakespeare, published some ten years ago). Read any page of *Venus and Adonis* side by side with any page of Marlowe's *Hero and Leander* and you cannot but mark the contrast: in Shakespeare the definite, particular, visualized image, in Marlowe the beautiful generalization, the abstract term, the thing seen at a literary remove. Take the two openings, both of which start out with the sunrise. Marlowe begins:

> Now had the Morn espied her lover's steeds:
> Whereat she starts, puts on her purple weeds,
> And, red for anger that he stay'd so long,
> All headlong throws herself the clouds among.

Shakespeare wastes no words on Aurora and her feelings, but gets to his hero and to business without ado:

> Even as the sun with purple-color'd face —

(You have the sun visualized at once)

> Even as the sun with purple-color'd face
> Had ta'en his last leave of the weeping morn,
> Rose-cheek'd Adonis hied him to the chase;
> Hunting he loved, but love he laugh'd to scorn. . . .

Or take, if you will, Marlowe's description of Hero's first meeting Leander:

> It lies not in our power to love or hate,
> For will in us is overruled by fate. . .

and set against it Shakespeare's description of Venus' last meeting with Adonis, as she came on him lying in his blood:

> Or as a snail whose tender horns being hit
> Shrinks backward in his shelly cave with pain,
> And there, all smother'd up, in shade doth sit,
> Long after fearing to creep forth again;
> So, at his bloody view —

I do not deny Marlowe's lines (if you will study the whole passage) to be lovely. You may even judge Shakespeare's to be crude by comparison. But you cannot help noting that whereas Marlowe steadily deals in abstract, nebulous terms, Shakespeare constantly uses concrete ones, which later on he learned to pack into verse, such as:

> Sleep that knits up the ravel'd sleeve of care.

Is it unfair to instance Marlowe, who died young? Then let us take Webster for the comparison; Webster, a man of genius or of something very like it, and commonly praised by the critics for his mastery over definite, detailed, and what I may call *solidified sensation.* Let us take this admired passage from his *Duchess of Malfy:*

> *Ferdinand.*   How doth our sister Duchess bear herself
> In her imprisonment?
> *Basola.*   Nobly: I'll describe her.
> She's sad as one long wed to 't, and she seems
> Rather to welcome the end of misery
> Than shun it: a behavior so noble
> As gives a majesty to adversity.[1]
> You may discern the shape of loveliness
> More perfect in her tears than in her smiles;
> She will muse for hours together;[2] and her silence
> Methinks expresseth more than if she spake.

Now set against this the well-known passage from *Twelfth Night* where the Duke asks and Viola answers a question about someone unknown to him and invented by her — a mere phantasm, in short: yet note how much more definite is the language:

> *Viola.*   My father had a daughter lov'd a man;
> As it might be, perhaps, were I a woman,
> *I* should your lordship.
> *Duke.*   And what's her history?
> *Viola.*   A blank, my lord.   She never told her love,
> But let concealment, like a worm i' the bud,
> Feed on her damask cheek; she pined in thought,
> And with a green and yellow melancholy
> She sat like Patience on a monument
> Smiling at grief.   Was not this love indeed?

Observe (apart from the dramatic skill of it) how, when Shakespeare *has* to use the abstract noun "concealment," on an instant it turns into a visible worm "feeding" on the visible rose; how, having to use a second abstract word, "patience," at once he solidifies it in tangible stone.

Turning to prose, you may easily assure yourselves that men who have written learnedly on the art agree in treating our maxim — to prefer the concrete term to the abstract, the particular to the general, the definite to the vague — as a canon of rhetoric.   Whately has

---

[1] Note the abstract term.
[2] Here we first come on the concrete: and beautiful it is.

much to say on it. The late Mr. E. J. Payne, in one of his admirable prefaces to Burke (prefaces too little known and valued, as too often happens to scholarship hidden away in a schoolbook), illustrated the maxim by setting a passage from Burke's speech *On Conciliation with America* alongside a passage of like purport from Lord Brougham's *Inquiry into the Policy of the European Powers*. Here is the deadly parallel:

BURKE	BROUGHAM
In large bodies the circulation of power must be less vigorous at the extremities. Nature has said it. The Turk cannot govern Egypt and Arabia and Kurdistan as he governs Thrace; nor has he the same dominion in Crimea and Algiers which he has in Brusa and Smyrna. Despotism itself is obliged to truck and huckster. The Sultan gets such obedience as he can. He governs with a loose rein, that he may govern at all; and the whole of the force and vigor of his authority in his center is derived from a prudent relaxation in all his borders.	In all the despotisms of the East, it has been observed that the further any part of the empire is removed from the capital, the more do its inhabitants enjoy some sort of rights and privileges: the more inefficacious is the power of the monarch; and the more feeble and easily decayed is the organization of the government.

You perceive that Brougham has transferred Burke's thought to his own page; but will you not also perceive how pitiably, by dissolving Burke's vivid particulars into smooth generalities, he has enervated its hold on the mind?

"This particularizing style," comments Mr. Payne, "is the essence of poetry; and in prose it is impossible not to be struck with the energy it produces. Brougham's passage is excellent in its way: but it pales before the flashing lights of Burke's sentences." The best instances of this energy of style, he adds, are to be found in the classical writers of the seventeenth century. "When South says, 'An Aristotle was but the rubbish of an Adam, and Athens but the rudiments of Paradise,' he communicates more effectually the notion of the difference between the intellect of fallen and of unfallen humanity than in all the philosophy of his sermons put together."

You may agree with me, or you may not, that South in this passage is expounding trash; but you will agree with Mr. Payne and me that he uttered it vividly.

Let me quote to you, as a final example of this vivid style of writing, a passage from Dr. John Donne far beyond and above anything that ever lay within South's compass:

The ashes of an Oak in the Chimney are no epitaph of that Oak, to tell me how high or how large that was; it tells me not what flocks it sheltered while it stood, nor what men it hurt when it fell. The dust of great persons' graves is speechless, too; it says nothing, it distinguishes nothing. As soon the dust of a wretch whom thou wouldest not, as of a prince whom thou couldest not look upon will trouble thine eyes if the wind blow it thither; and when a whirlewind hath blown the dust of the Churchyard into the Church, and the man sweep out the dust of the Church into the Church-yard, who will undertake to sift those dusts again and to pronounce, This is the Patrician, this is the noble flowre [flour], this is the yeomanly, this the Plebeian bran? So is the death of *Iesabel* (*Iesabel* was a Queen) expressed. They shall not say *This is Iesabel;* not only not wonder that it is, nor pity that it should be; but they shall not say, they shall not know, *This is Iesabel.*

Carlyle noted of Goethe, "his emblematic intellect, his never-failing tendency to transform into *shape*, into *life*, the feeling that may dwell in him. Everything has form, has visual excellence: the poet's imagination bodies forth the forms of things unseen, and his pen turns them into shape."

Perpend this, Gentlemen, and maybe you will not hereafter set it down to my reproach that I wasted an hour of a May morning in a denunciation of jargon, and in exhorting you upon a technical matter at first sight so trivial as the choice between abstract and definite words.

A lesson about writing your language may go deeper than language; for language (as in a former lecture I tried to preach to you) is your reason, your λόγος. So long as you prefer abstract words, which express other men's summarized concepts of things, to concrete ones which lie as near as can be reached to things themselves and are the first-hand material for your thoughts, you will remain, at the best, writers at second-hand. If your language be jargon, your intellect, if not your whole character, will almost certainly correspond. Where your mind should go straight, it will dodge: the difficulties it should approach with a fair front and grip with a firm hand it will be seeking to evade or circumvent. For the style is the man, and where a man's treasure is there his heart, and his brain, and his writing, will be also.

IX

ART AND THE MODERN WORLD

THE fine arts are too large a field to be dealt with thoroughly in any work of less than encyclopaedic scope. To treat of recent tendencies in painting alone — of the rise and decline of the Impressionists in the last third of the nineteenth century, of the dozen different groups of Post-Impressionists, and of the continuing influence of the classical, romantic, and realistic traditions — would require a thick volume. As much may be said of architecture, in which the United States has doubtless made its most distinctive mark, and almost as much of sculpture and of music. In the pages which follow, therefore, little effort is made to do more than to illustrate some of the most influential schools of opinion upon the principles of art. The emphasis, as the names of Ruskin, John Addington Symonds, Edward A. MacDowell, and Paul Elmer More indicate, falls upon the side of tradition and conservatism. An understanding of the ideas of such men as these offers the best basis for an approach to newer and more daring thinkers. But Whistler is represented by one of his strikingly individual essays, some of the new forces at work in art are ably described by Morris Davidson, and at the close of the section Eugen Neuhaus casts an inquiring eye into the future.

ART AND HISTORY[1]

John Ruskin

JOHN RUSKIN, who was born in 1819 in London, the son of a merchant of Scottish blood, was largely self-educated, though he studied for a time at Oxford. His enthusiasm for art was awakened by early travel on the Continent, for his parents had wealth, and by the paintings of J. M. W. Turner. These idealized and imaginative landscapes, with their qualities of mysticism and vision, laid a deep impress upon him at the same time that he came under the influence of the Pre-Raphaelite school, with its emphasis upon clarity and minute accuracy of detail. To justify his tastes, to reconcile the two artistic cults, and to express the religious conception of art which his Puritan upbringing had implanted in him, Ruskin gradually erected an elaborate system of aesthetics. His fine imagination, the rich eloquence of his style, and the depth of his mind have given his volumes on art a classical quality. Even those who reject their basic ideas can read them with delight and frequently with instruction — *Modern Painters; The Seven Lamps of Architecture; The Stones of Venice;* and *Pre-Raphaelitism.* There is no greater master of poetic prose, not even Milton or De Quincey, in the language. He knew art thoroughly, having studied the best models with care; he was himself an artist who did excellent work. Often dogmatic, sometimes self-contradictory, he had fine flashes of perception in all he undertook. And his concept of art, his belief that if worthy of the name it must have inner meaning and serious intent, lifted his criticism always to an elevated plane. To him it was the spiritual significance of art, not its mere material usefulness (though that was not to be ignored), which is important. Art, religion, and true morality are not different matters, but identical — they are different facets of the same truth. The great aim of art is always to satisfy a spiritual want, and the artist can never be great, no matter what his virtuosity, unless he possesses a great spirit.

But Ruskin's work falls into two halves. As he developed his system of aesthetics, his attention turned gradually to the social and economic problems of his time, until in 1862 he grappled vigorously and rebelliously with them in *Unto This Last.* A series of books written in the next thirty years showed him a fierce critic of modern civilization. He attacked the age of machinery, which made workingmen slaves to machines; he attacked the individualistic spirit, which made for a heartless society; he attacked the law of supply and demand, which inculcated selfishness and made the economic world a great battleground. In offering constructive remedies he was at once vague and impractical. Condemning competition, he preached coöperation. He wished to humanize industry by scrapping the more gigantic and efficient forms of machinery, and reëstablishing a régime of small workshops. Many of his views on social and economic topics lack soundness of thought, sobriety of judgment, and practical utility. Yet he was flamingly sincere, and he showed great courage in trying to apply some of his ideas. His style, too, in the later volumes — *Munera Pulveris, Sesame and Lilies, Ethics of the Dust, The Crown of Wild Olive* — retains all its first power; and no one has more eloquently indicted the ugliness and frequent injustice of industrial civilization.

[1] From *The Queen of the Air*, by John Ruskin.

ATHENA ERGANE

In different places of my writings, and through many years of endeavor to define the laws of art, I have insisted on this rightness in work, and on its connection with virtue of character, in so many partial ways, that the impression left on the reader's mind — if, indeed, it was ever impressed at all — has been confused and uncertain. In beginning the series of my corrected works, I wish this principle (in my own mind the foundation of every other) to be made plain, if nothing else is, and will try, therefore, to make it so, so far as, by any effort, I can put it into unmistakable words. And, first, here is a very simple statement of it, given lately in a lecture on the Architecture of the Valley of the Somme,[1] which will be better read in this place than in its incidental connection with my account of the porches of Abbeville.

I had used, in a preceding part of the lecture, the expression, "by what faults" this Gothic architecture fell. We continually speak thus of works of art. We talk of their faults and merits, as of virtues and vices. What do we mean by talking of the faults of a picture, or the merits of a piece of stone?

The faults of a work of art are the faults of its workman, and its virtues his virtues.

Great art is the expression of the mind of a great man, and mean art, that of the want of mind of a weak man. A foolish person builds foolishly, and a wise one, sensibly; a virtuous one, beautifully; and a vicious one, basely. If stone work is well put together, it means that a thoughtful man planned it, and a careful man cut it, and an honest man cemented it. If it has too much ornament, it means that its carver was too greedy of pleasure; if too little, that he was rude, or insensitive, or stupid, and the like. So that when once you have learned how to spell these most precious of all legends — pictures and buildings — you may read the characters of men, and of nations, in their art, as in a mirror. Nay, as in a microscope, and magnified a hundredfold; for the character becomes passionate in the art, and intensifies itself in all its noblest or meanest delights. Nay, not only as in a microscope, but as under a scalpel, and in dissection; for a man may hide himself from you, or misrepresent himself to you, every other way; but he cannot in his work: there, be sure, you have him to the inmost. All that he likes, all that he sees — all that he can do

---

[1] *The Flamboyant Architecture of the Valley of the Somme*, a lecture delivered at the Royal Institution, January 29, 1869.

— his imagination, his affections, his perseverance, his impatience, his clumsiness, cleverness, everything is there. If the work is a cobweb, you know it was made by a spider; if a honeycomb, by a bee; a worm-cast is thrown up by a worm, and a nest wreathed by a bird; and a house built by a man, worthily, if he is worthy, and ignobly, if he is ignoble.

And always, from the least to the greatest, as the made thing is good or bad, so is the maker of it.

You all use this faculty of judgment more or less, whether you theoretically admit the principle or not. Take that floral gable;[1] you don't suppose the man who built Stonehenge could have built that, or that the man who built that, *would* have built Stonehenge? Do you think an old Roman would have liked such a piece of filigree work, or that Michelangelo would have spent his time in twisting these stems of roses in and out? Or, of modern handicraftsmen, do you think a burglar, or a brute, or a pickpocket could have carved it? Could Bill Sykes have done it? Or the Dodger, dexterous with finger and tool? You will find in the end, that *no man could have done it but exactly the man who did it;* and by looking close at it, you may, if you know your letters, read precisely the manner of man he was.

Now I must insist on this matter, for a grave reason. Of all facts concerning art, this is the one most necessary to be known: that, while manufacture is the work of hands only, art is the work of the whole spirit of man; and as that spirit is, so is the deed of it: and by whatever power of vice or virtue any art is produced, the same vice or virtue it reproduces and teaches. That which is born of evil begets evil; and that which is born of valor and honor, teaches valor and honor. All art is either infection or education. It *must* be one or other of these.

This, I repeat, of all truths respecting art, is the one of which understanding is the most precious, and denial the most deadly. And I assert it the more, because it has of late been repeatedly, expressly, and with contumely denied; and that by high authority: and I hold it one of the most sorrowful facts connected with the decline of the arts among us, that English gentlemen, of high standing as scholars and artists, should have been blinded into the acceptance and betrayed into the assertion of a fallacy which only authority such as theirs could have rendered for an instant credible. For the con-

[1] The elaborate pediment above the central porch at the west end of Rouen Cathedral, pierced into a transparent web of tracery, and enriched with a border of "twisted eglantine." [Ruskin.]

trary of it is written in the history of all great nations; it is the one sentence always inscribed on the steps of their thrones; the one concordant voice in which they speak to us out of their dust.

All such nations first manifest themselves as a pure and beautiful animal race, with intense energy and imagination. They live lives of hardship by choice, and by grand instinct of manly discipline: they become fierce and irresistible soldiers; the nation is always its own army, and their king, or chief head of government, is always their first soldier. Pharaoh, or David, or Leonidas, or Valerius, or Barbarossa, or Coeur de Lion, or St. Louis, or Dandolo, or Frederick the Great — Egyptian, Jew, Greek, Roman, German, English, French, Venetian — that is inviolable law for them all; their king must be their first soldier, or they cannot be in progressive power. Then, after their great military period, comes the domestic period; in which, without betraying the discipline of war, they add to their great soldiership the delights and possessions of a delicate and tender home-life: and then, for all nations, is the time of their perfect art, which is the fruit, the evidence, the reward of their national ideal of character, developed by the finished care of the occupations of peace. That is the history of all true art that ever was, or can be: palpably the history of it — unmistakably — written on the forehead of it in letters of light — in tongues of fire, by which the seal of virtue is branded as deep as ever iron burned into a convict's flesh the seal of crime. But always, hitherto, after the great period, has followed the day of luxury, and pursuit of the arts for pleasure only. And all has so ended.

Thus far of Abbeville building. Now I have here asserted two things — first, the foundation of art in moral character; next, the foundation of moral character in war. I must make both these assertions clearer, and prove them.

First, of the foundation of art in moral character. Of course artgift and amiability of disposition are two different things. A good man is not necessarily a painter, nor does an eye for color necessarily imply an honest mind. But great art implies the union of both powers: it is the expression, by an art-gift, of a pure soul. If the gift is not there, we can have no art at all; and if the soul — and a right soul too — is not there, the art is bad, however dexterous.

But also, remember, that the art-gift itself is only the result of the moral character of generations. A bad woman may have a sweet voice; but that sweetness of voice comes of the past morality of her race. That she can sing with it at all, she owes to the determination of laws of music by the morality of the past. Every act, every impulse, of virtue and vice, affects in any creature face, voice, nervous power, and vigor and harmony of invention, at once. Perseverance in rightness of human conduct renders, after a certain number of generations, human art possible; every sin clouds it, be it ever so little a one; and persistent vicious living and following of pleasure render, after a certain number of generations, all art impossible. Men are deceived by the long-suffering of the laws of nature; and mistake, in a nation, the reward of the virtue of its sires for the issue of its own sins. The time of their visitation will come, and that inevitably; for, it is always true, that if the fathers have eaten sour grapes, the children's teeth are set on edge.[1] And for the individual, as soon as you have learned to read, you may, as I have said, know him to the heart's core, through his art. Let his art-gift be never so great, and cultivated to the height by the schools of a great race of men; and it is still but a tapestry thrown over his own being and inner soul; and the bearing of it will show, infallibly, whether it hangs on a man or on a skeleton. If you are dim-eyed, you may not see the difference in the fall of the folds at first, but learn how to look, and the folds themselves will become transparent, and you shall see through them the death's shape, or the divine one, making the tissue above it as a cloud of light, or as a winding-sheet.

Then farther, observe, I have said (and you will find it true, and that to the uttermost) that, as all lovely art is rooted in virtue, so it bears fruit of virtue, and is didactic in its own nature. It is often didactic also in actually expressed thought, as Giotto's, Michelangelo's, Dürer's, and hundreds more; but that is not its special function — it is didactic chiefly by being beautiful; but beautiful with haunting thought, no less than with form, and full of myths that can be read only with the heart.

For instance, at this moment there is open beside me, as I write, a page of Persian manuscript, wrought with wreathed azure and gold, and soft green, and violet, and ruby and scarlet, into one field of pure resplendence. It is wrought to delight the eyes only; and does delight them; and the man who did it assuredly had eyes in his head; but not much more. It is not didactic art, but its author was happy: and it will do the good, and the harm, that mere pleasure can do. But, opposite me, is an early Turner drawing of the lake of Geneva, taken about two miles from Geneva, on the Lausanne road, with Mont Blanc in the distance. The old city is seen lying beyond the waveless waters, veiled with a sweet misty veil of Athena's weaving: a faint

[1] *Jeremiah* xxxi, 29.

light of morning, peaceful exceedingly, and almost colorless, shed from behind the Voirons, increases into soft amber along the slope of the Salève, and is just seen, and no more, on the fair warm fields of its summit, between the folds of a white cloud that rests upon the grass, but rises, high and towerlike, into the zenith of dawn above.

There is not as much color in that low amber light upon the hillside as there is in the palest dead leaf. The lake is not blue, but gray in mist, passing into deep shadow beneath the Voirons' pines; a few dark clusters of leaves, a single white flower — scarcely seen — are all the gladness given to the rocks of the shore. One of the ruby spots of the Eastern manuscript would give color enough for all the red that is in Turner's entire drawing. For the mere pleasure of the eye, there is not so much in all those lines of his, throughout the entire landscape, as in half an inch square of the Persian's page. What made him take pleasure in the low color that is only like the brown of a dead leaf? In the cold gray of dawn — in the one white flower among the rocks — in these — and no more than these?

He took pleasure in them because he had been bred among English fields and hills; because the gentleness of a great race was in his heart, and its power of thought in his brain; because he knew the stories of the Alps, and of the cities at their feet; because he had read the Homeric legends of the clouds, and beheld the gods of dawn, and the givers of dew to the fields; because he knew the faces of the crags, and the imagery of the passionate mountains, as a man knows the face of his friend; because he had in him the wonder and sorrow concerning life and death, which are the inheritance of the Gothic soul from the days of its first sea kings; and also the compassion and the joy that are woven into the innermost fabric of every great imaginative spirit, born now in countries that have lived by the Christian faith with any courage or truth. And the picture contains also, for us, just this which its maker had in him to give; and can convey it to us, just so far as we are of the temper in which it must be received. It is didactic if we are worthy to be taught, no otherwise. The pure heart, it will make more pure; the thoughtful, more thoughtful. It has in it no words for the reckless or the base.

THE BIRTH OF MODERN ART[1]

John Addington Symonds

JOHN ADDINGTON SYMONDS'S history of the *Renaissance in Italy*, which appeared in final form in seven volumes in 1887–1888, is the fullest and most admirably written account in English of one of the most interesting periods in human history. Some parts are antiquated today, but as a whole it remains a classic authority on the subject. The volume on Italian literature, which contains many happy translations by the author, is particularly good. Symonds, who was born at Bristol, England, in 1840, and educated at Oxford, first combined teaching and lecturing with writing. But his health failed in 1877, and from that year until his death in 1893 he virtually made his home at Davos Platz in Switzerland. His other works include studies of the Greek poets, a spirited translation of Benvenuto Cellini's autobiography, and biographies of Shelley, Ben Jonson, and Michelangelo. A discerning study of his books and ideas has been made by the American critic, Van Wyck Brooks.

What, let us ask in the first place, was the task appointed for the fine arts on the threshold of the modern world? They had, before all things, to give form to the ideas evolved by Christianity, and to embody a class of emotions unknown to the ancients. The inheritance of the Middle Ages had to be appropriated and expressed. In the course of performing this work, the painters helped to humanize religion, and revealed the dignity and beauty of the body of man. Next, in the fifteenth century, the riches of classic culture were discovered, and art was called upon to aid in the interpretation of the ancient to the modern mind. The problem was no longer simple. Christian and pagan traditions came into close contact, and contended for the empire of the newly liberated intellect. During this struggle the arts, true to their own principles, eliminated from both traditions the more strictly human elements, and expressed them in beautiful form to the imagination and the senses. The brush of the same painter depicted Bacchus wedding Ariadne and Mary fainting on the hill of Calvary. Careless of any peril to dogmatic orthodoxy, and undeterred by the dread of encouraging pagan sensuality, the artists wrought out their modern ideal of beauty in the double field of Christian and Hellenic legend. Before the force of painting was exhausted, it had thus traversed the whole cycle of thoughts and feelings that form the content of the modern mind. Throughout this

[1] From *Renaissance in Italy: The Fine Arts*, Scribner's (1877).

performance, art proved itself a powerful co-agent in the emancipation of the intellect; the impartiality wherewith its methods were applied to subjects sacred and profane, the emphasis laid upon physical strength and beauty as good things and desirable, the subordination of classical and mediaeval myths to one aesthetic law of loveliness, all tended to withdraw attention from the differences between paganism and Christianity, and to fix it on the goodliness of that humanity wherein both find their harmony.

This being in general the task assigned to art in the Renaissance, we may next inquire what constituted the specific quality of modern as distinguished from antique feeling, and why painting could not fail to take the first place among modern arts. In other words, how was it that, while sculpture was the characteristic fine art of antiquity, painting became the distinguishing fine art of the modern era? No true form of figurative art intervened between Greek sculpture and Italian painting. The latter took up the work of investing thought with sensible shape from the dead hands of the former. Nor had the tradition that connected art with religion been interrupted, although a new cycle of religious ideas had been substituted for the old ones. The late Roman and Byzantine manners, through which the vital energies of the Athenian genius dwindled into barren formalism, still lingered, giving crude and lifeless form to Christian conceptions. But the thinking and feeling subjects meanwhile had undergone a change so all-important that it now imperatively required fresh channels for its self-expression. It was destined to find these, not as of old in sculpture, but in painting.

During the interval between the closing of the ancient and opening of the modern age, the faith of Christians had attached itself to symbols and material objects little better than fetishes. The host, the relic, the wonder-working shrine, things endowed with a mysterious potency, evoked the yearning and the awe of mediaeval multitudes. To such concrete actualities the worshipers referred their sense of the invisible divinity. The earth of Jerusalem, the Holy Sepulchre, the House of Loreto, the Sudarium of Saint Veronica, aroused their deepest sentiments of aweful adoration. Like Thomas, they could not be contented with believing; they must also touch and handle. At the same time, in apparent contradistinction to this demand for things of sense as signs of supersensual power, the claims of dogma on the intellect grew more imperious, and mysticism opened for the dreaming soul a realm of spiritual rapture. For the figurative arts there was no true place in either of these regions. Painting and sculpture were alike alien to the grosser superstitions, the scholastic subtleties, and the ecstatic trances of the Middle Ages; nor had they anything in common with the logic of theology. Votaries who kissed a fragment of the cross with passion could have found but little to satisfy their ardor in pictures painted by a man of genius. A formless wooden idol, endowed with the virtue of curing disease, charmed the pilgrim more than a statue noticeable only for its beauty or its truth to life. We all know that *wundertätige Bilder sind meist nur schlechte Gemälde.*[1] In architecture alone, the mysticism of the Middle Ages, their vague but potent feelings of infinity, their yearning toward a deity invisible, but localized in holy things and places, found artistic outlet. Therefore architecture was essentially a mediaeval art. The rise of sculpture and painting indicated the quickening to life of new faculties, fresh intellectual interests, and a novel way of apprehending the old substance of religious feeling; for comprehension of these arts implies delight in things of beauty for their own sake, a sympathetic attitude toward the world of sense, a new freedom of the mind produced by the regeneration of society through love.

The mediaeval faiths were still vivid when the first Italian painters began their work, and the sincere endeavor of these men was to set forth in beautiful and worthy form the truths of Christianity. The eyes of the worshiper should no longer have a mere stock or stone to contemplate: his imagination should be helped by the dramatic presentation of the scenes of sacred history, and his devotion be quickened by lively images of the passion of our Lord. Spirit should converse with spirit, through no veil of symbol, but through the transparent medium of art, itself instinct with inbreathed life and radiant with ideal beauty. The body and the soul, moreover, should be reconciled; and God's likeness should be once more acknowledged in the features and the limbs of man. Such was the promise of art; and this promise was in a great measure fulfilled by the painting of the fourteenth century. Men ceased to worship their God in the holiness of ugliness; and a great city called its street Glad on the birthday festival of the first picture investing religious emotion with aesthetic charm. But in making good the promise they had given, it was needful for the arts on the one hand to enter a region not wholly their own — the region of abstractions and of mystical conceptions; and on the other to create a world of sensuous delightfulness, wherein the spiritual element was materialized to the injury of its own essential quality. Spirit, indeed, spake to spirit, so far as the religious content

[1] "Wonder-working pictures are for the most part only inferior pictures."

was concerned; but flesh spake also to flesh in the aesthetic form. The incarnation promised by the arts involved a corresponding sensuousness. Heaven was brought down to earth, but at the cost of making men believe that earth itself was heavenly.

At this point the subject of our inquiry naturally divides into two main questions. The first concerns the form of figurative art specially adapted to the requirements of religious thought in the fourteenth century. The second treats of the effect resulting both to art and religion from the expression of mystical and theological conceptions in plastic form.

When we consider the nature of the ideas assimilated in the Middle Ages by the human mind, it is clear that art, in order to set them forth, demanded a language the Greeks had never greatly needed, and had therefore never fully learned. To overestimate the difference from an aesthetic point of view between the religious notions of the Greeks and those which Christianity had made essential would be difficult. Faith, hope, and charity, humility, endurance, suffering; the Resurrection and the Judgment; the Fall and the Redemption; Heaven and Hell; the height and depth of man's mixed nature; the drama of human destiny before the throne of God: into the sphere of thoughts like these, vivid and solemn, transcending the region of sense and corporeity, carrying the mind away to an ideal world, where the things of this earth obtained a new reality by virtue of their relation to an invisible and infinite Beyond, the modern arts in their infancy were thrust. There was nothing finite here or tangible, no gladness in the beauty of girlish foreheads or the swiftness of a young man's limbs, no simple idealization of natural delightfulness. The human body, which the figurative arts must needs use as the vehicle of their expression, had ceased to have a value in and for itself, had ceased to be the true and adequate investiture of thoughts demanded from the artist. At best it could be taken only as the symbol of some inner meaning, the shrine of an indwelling spirit nobler than itself; just as a lamp of alabaster owes its beauty and its worth to the flame it more than half conceals, the light transmitted through its scarce transparent walls.

In ancient art those moral and spiritual qualities which the Greeks recognized as truly human, and therefore divine, allowed themselves to be incarnated in well-selected types of physical perfection. The deities of the Greek mythology were limited to the conditions of natural existence; they were men and women of a larger mold and freer personality; less complex, inasmuch as each completed some one attribute; less thwarted in activity, inasmuch as no limit was assigned to exercise of power. The passions and the faculties of man, analyzed by unconscious psychology, and deified by religious fancy, were invested by sculpture with appropriate forms, the tact of the artist selecting corporeal qualities fitted to impersonate the special character of each divinity. Nor was it possible that, the gods and goddesses being what they were, exact analogues should not be found for them in idealized humanity. In a Greek statue there was enough soul to characterize the beauty of the body, to render her due need of wisdom to Pallas, to distinguish the swiftness of Hermes from the strength of Heracles, or to contrast the virginal grace of Artemis with the abundance of Aphrodite's charms. At the same time the spirituality that gave its character to each Greek deity was not such that, even in thought, it could be dissociated from corporeal form. The Greeks thought their gods as incarnate persons; and all the artist had to see to, was that this incarnate personality should be impressive in his marble.

Christianity, on the other hand, made the moral and spiritual nature of man all-essential. It sprang from an earlier religion, that judged it impious to give any form of God. The body and its terrestrial activity occupied but a subordinate position in its system. It was the life of the soul, separable from this frame of flesh, and destined to endure when earth and all that it contains had ended — a life that upon this planet was continued conflict and aspiring struggle — which the arts, in so far as they became its instrument, were called upon to illustrate. It was the worship of a deity, all spirit, to be sought on no one sacred hill, to be adored in no transcendent shape, that they were bound to heighten. The most highly prized among the Christian virtues had no necessary connection with beauty of feature or strength of limb. Such beauty and such strength at any rate were accidental, not essential. A Greek faun could not but be graceful: a Greek hero was of necessity vigorous. But St. Stephen might be steadfast to the death without physical charm; St. Anthony might put to flight the devils of the flesh without muscular force. It is clear that the radiant physical perfection proper to the deities of Greek sculpture was not sufficient in this sphere.

Again, the most stirring episodes of the Christian mythology involved pain and perturbation of the spirit; the victories of the Christian athletes were won in conflicts carried on within their hearts and souls — "For we wrestle not against flesh and blood, but against principalities and powers," demoniac leaders of spiritual legions. It is, therefore, no less clear that the tranquillity and serenity of the Hellenic ideal, so necessary to consummate sculpture, was here out of place. How could the Last Judgment, that day of wrath, when every soul, however insignificant on earth, will play the first part for one moment in an awful tragedy, be properly expressed in plastic form, harmonious and pleasing? And supposing that the artist should abandon the attempt to exclude ugliness and discord, pain and confusion, from his representation of the *Dies Irae,* how could he succeed in setting forth by the sole medium of the human body the anxiety and anguish of the soul at such a time? The physical form, instead of being adequate to the ideas expressed, and therefore helpful to the artist, is a positive embarrassment, a source of weakness. The most powerful pictorial or sculpturesque delineation of the Judgment, when compared with the pangs inflicted on the spirit by a guilty conscience, pangs whereof words may render some account, but which can find no analogue in writhings of the limbs or face, must of necessity be found a failure. Still more impossible, if we pursue this train of thought into another region, is it for the figurative arts to approach the Christian conception of God in his omnipotence and unity. Christ Himself, the central figure of the Christian universe, the desired of all nations, in whom the Deity assumed a human form and dwelled with men, is no fit subject for such art at any rate as the Greeks had perfected. The fact of His incarnation brought Him indeed within the proper sphere of the fine arts; but the religious idea which He represents removed Him beyond the reach of sculpture. This is an all-important consideration. It is to this that our whole argument is tending. Therefore to enlarge upon this point will not be useless.

Christ is specially adored in His last act of love on Calvary; and how impossible it is to set that forth consistently with the requirements of strictly plastic art may be gathered by comparing the passion of St. Bernard's Hymn to our Lord upon the Cross with all that Winckelmann and Hegal have so truly said about the restrained expression, dignified generality, and harmonious beauty essential to sculpture. It is the negation of tranquillity, the excess of feeling, the absence of comeliness, the contrast between visible weakness and invisible omnipotence, the physical humiliation voluntarily suffered by Him that "ruled over all the angels, that walked on the pavements of heaven, whose feet were clothed with stars." . . .

We have never heard that Pheidias or Praxiteles chose Prometheus upon Caucasus for the supreme display of his artistic skill; and even the anguish expressed in the group of the Laocoön is justly thought to violate the laws of antique sculpture. Yet here was a greater than Prometheus — one who had suffered more, and on whose suffering the salvation of the human race depended, to exclude whom from the sphere of representation in art was the same as confessing the utter impotence of art to grasp the vital thought of modern faith. It is clear that the muses of the new age had to haunt Calvary instead of Helicon, slaking their thirst at no Castalian spring, but at the fount of tears outpoured by all creation for a stricken God. What Hellas had achieved supplied no norm or method for the arts in this new service.

From what has hitherto been advanced, we may assert with confidence that, if the arts were to play an important part in Christian culture, an art was imperatively demanded that should be at home in the sphere of intense feeling, that should treat the body as the interpreter and symbol of the soul, and should not shrink from pain and passion. How far the fine arts were at all qualified to express the essential thoughts of Christianity — a doubt suggested in the foregoing paragraphs — and how far, through their proved inadequacy to perform this task completely, they weakened the hold of mediaeval faiths upon the modern mind, are questions to be raised hereafter. For the present it is enough to affirm that, least of all the arts, could sculpture, with its essential repose and its dependence on corporeal conditions, solve the problem. Sculpture had suited the requirements of Greek thought. It belonged by right to men who not unwillingly accepted the life of this world as final, and who worshiped in their deities the incarnate personality of men made perfect. But it could not express the cycle of Christian ideas. The desire of a better world, the fear of a worse; the sense of sin referred to physical appetites, and the corresponding mortification of the flesh; hope, ecstasy, and penitence and prayer; all these imply contempt or hatred for the body, suggest notions too spiritual to be conveyed by the rounded contours of beautiful limbs, too full of struggle for statuesque tranquillity. The new element needed a more elastic medium of expression. Motives more varied, gradations of sentiment more delicate, the fugitive and transient phases of emotion, the inner depths of consciousness, had somehow to be seized. It was here that painting asserted its supremacy. Painting is many degrees further removed than sculpture from dependence on the body in the fullness of its physical proportions. It touches our sensibilities by suggestions more indirect, more mobile, and more multiform. Color and shadow, aerial perspective and complicated grouping denied to sculpture, but within the proper realm of painting, have their own significance, their real relation to feelings vaguer, but not less potent, than those which find expression in the simple human form. To painting, again, belongs the play of feature, indicative of internal movement, through a whole gamut of modulations inapprehensible by sculpture. All that drapery by its partial concealment of the form it clothes, and landscape by its sympathies with human sentiment, may supply to enhance the passion of the spectator, pertains to painting. This art, therefore, owing to the greater variety of means at its disposal, and its greater adequacy to express emotion, became the paramount Italian art.

To sculpture in the Renaissance, shorn of the divine right to create gods and heroes, was left the narrower field of decoration, portraiture, and sepulchral monuments. In the last of these departments it found the noblest scope for its activity; for beyond the grave, according to Christian belief, the account of the striving, hoping, and resisting soul is settled. The corpse upon the bier may bear the stamp of spiritual character impressed on it in life; but the spirit, with its struggle and its passion, has escaped as from a prison-house, and flown elsewhither. The body of the dead man, for whom this world is over, and who sleeps in peace, awaiting resurrection, and thereby not wholly dead, around whose tomb watch sympathizing angels or contemplative genii, was, therefore, the proper subject for the highest Christian sculpture. Here, if anywhere, the right emotion could be adequately expressed in stone, and the molded form be made the symbol of repose, expectant of restored activity. The greatest sculptor of the modern age was essentially a poet of death.

Painting, then, for the reasons already assigned and insisted on, was the art demanded by the modern intellect upon its emergence from the stillness of the Middle Ages. The problem, however, even for the art of painting was not simple. The painters, following the masters of mosaic, began by setting forth the history, mythology, and legends of the Christian Church in imagery freer and more beautiful than lay within the scope of treatment by Romanesque or Byzantine art. So far their task was comparatively easy; for the idyllic grace of maternal love in the Madonna, the pathetic incidents of martyrdom, the courage of confessors, the ecstasies of celestial joy in redeemed souls, the loveliness of a pure life in modest virgins, and the dramatic episodes of sacred story, furnish a multitude of motives admirably pictorial. There was, therefore, no great obstacle upon the threshold, so long as artists gave their willing service to the

Church. Yet, looking back upon this phase of painting, we are able to perceive that already the adaptation of art to Christian dogma entailed concessions on both sides. Much, on the one hand, had to be omitted from the program offered to artistic treatment, for the reason that the fine arts could not deal with it at all. Much, on the other hand, had to be expressed by means which painting in a state of perfect freedom would repudiate. Allegorical symbols, like Prudence with two faces, and painful episodes of agony and anguish, marred her work of beauty. There was consequently a double compromise, involving a double sacrifice of something precious. The faith suffered by having its mysteries brought into the light of day, incarnated in form, and humanized. Art suffered by being forced to render intellectual abstractions to the eye through figured symbols.

As technical skill increased, and as beauty, the proper end of art, became more rightly understood, the painters found that their craft was worthy of being made an end in itself, and that the actualities of life observed around them had claims upon their genius no less weighty than dogmatic mysteries. The subjects they had striven at first to realize with all simplicity now became little better than vehicles for the display of sensuous beauty, science, and mundane pageantry. The human body received separate and independent study, as a thing in itself incomparably beautiful, commanding more powerful emotions by its magic than aught else that sways the soul. At the same time the external world, with all its wealth of animal and vegetable life, together with the works of human ingenuity in costly clothing and superb buildings, was seen to be in every detail worthy of most patient imitation. Anatomy and perspective taxed the understanding of the artist, whose whole force was no longer devoted to the task of bringing religious ideas within the limits of the representable. Next, when the classical revival came into play, the arts, in obedience to the spirit of the age, left the sphere of sacred subjects, and employed their full-grown faculties in the domain of myths and pagan fancies. In this way painting may truly be said to have opened the new era of culture, and to have first manifested the freedom of the modern mind. When Luca Signorelli drew naked young men for a background to his picture of Madonna and the infant Christ, he created for the student a symbol of the attitude assumed by fine art in its liberty of outlook over the whole range of human interests. Standing before this picture in the Uffizzi, we feel that the Church, while hoping to adorn her cherished dogmas with aesthetic beauty, had encouraged a power antagonistic to her own, a power that liberated the spirit she sought to enthrall, restoring to mankind the earthly paradise from which monasticism had expelled it.

Not to diverge at this point, and to entertain the difficult problem of the relation of the fine arts to Christianity, would be to shrink from the most throny question offered to the understanding by the history of the Renaissance. On the very threshold of the matter I am bound to affirm my conviction that the spiritual purists of all ages — the Jews, the iconoclasts of Byzantium, Savonarola, and our Puritan ancestors — were justified in their mistrust of plastic art. The spirit of Christianity and the spirit of figurative art are opposed, not because such art is immoral, but because it cannot free itself from sensuous associations. It is always bringing us back to the dear life of earth, from which the faith would sever us. It is always reminding us of the body which piety bids us to forget. Painters and sculptors glorify that which saints and ascetics have mortified. The master-pieces of Titian and Correggio, for example, lead the soul away from compunction, away from penitence, away from worship even, to dwell on the delight of youthful faces, blooming color, graceful move-ment, delicate emotion. Nor is this all: religious motives may be misused for what is worse than merely sensuous suggestiveness. The masterpieces of the Bolognese and Neapolitan painters, while they pretend to quicken compassion for martyrs in their agony, pander to a bestial blood-lust lurking in the darkest chambers of the soul. There-fore it is that piety, whether the piety of monastic Italy or of Puritan England, turns from these aesthetic triumphs as from something alien to itself. When the worshiper would fain ascend on wings of ecstasy to God, the infinite, ineffable, unrealized, how can he endure the contact of those splendid forms in which the lust of the eye and the pride of life, professing to subserve devotion, remind him rudely of the goodliness of sensual existence? Art, by magnifying human beauty, contradicts these Pauline maxims: "For me to live is Christ, and to die is gain"; "Set your affections on things above, not on things on earth"; "Your life is hid with Christ in God." The sublimity and elevation it gives to carnal loveliness are themselves hostile to the spirit that holds no truce or compromise of traffic with the flesh. As displayed in its most perfect phases, in Greek sculpture and Venetian painting, art dignifies the actual mundane life of man; but Christ, in the language of uncompromising piety, means every-thing most alien to this mundane life — self-denial, abstinence from fleshly pleasure, the waiting for true bliss beyond the grave, seclusion even from social and domestic ties. "He that loveth father and mother more than me is not worthy of me." "He that taketh not his cross and followeth me, is not worthy of me." It is needful to insist upon these extremist sentences of the New Testament, because upon them was based the religious practice of the Middle Ages, more sincere in their determination to fulfill the letter and embrace the spirit of the Gospel than any succeeding age has been.

If, then, there really exists this antagonism between fine art glorifying human life and piety contemning it, how came it, we may ask, that even in the Middle Ages the Church hailed art as her coadjutor? The answer lies in this, that the Church has always compromised. The movement of the modern world, upon the close of the Middle Ages, offered the Church a compromise, which it would have been difficult to refuse, and in which she perceived at first no peril to her dogmas. When the conflict of the first few centuries of Christianity had ended in her triumph, she began to mediate between asceticism and the world. Intent on absorbing all existent elements of life and power, she conformed her system to the Roman type, established her service in basilicas and pagan temples, adopted portions of the antique ritual, and converted local genii into saints. At the same time she utilized the spiritual forces of monasticism, and turned the mystic impulse of ecstatics to account. The Orders of the Preachers and the Begging Friars became her militia and police; the mystery of Christ's presence in the Eucharist was made an engine of the priesthood; the dreams of Paradise and Purgatory gave value to her pardons, interdictions, jubilees, indulgences, and curses. In the Church the spirit of the cloister and the spirit of the world found neutral ground, and to the practical accommodation between these hostile elements she owed her wide supremacy. The Christianity she formed and propagated was different from that of the New Testament, inasmuch as it had taken up into itself a mass of mythological anthropomorphic elements. Thus transmuted and materialized, thus accepted by the vivid faith of an unquestioning populace, Christianity offered a proper medium for artistic activity. The whole first period of Italian painting was occupied with the endeavor to set forth in form and color the popular conceptions of a faith at once unphilosophical and unspiritual, beautiful and fit for art by reason of the human elements it had assumed into its substance. It was natural, therefore, that the Church should show herself indulgent to the arts, which were effecting in their own sphere what she had previously accomplished through purists and ascetics, holding fast by the original spirit of their creed, might remain irreconcilably antagonistic to their influence. The Reformation, on the contrary, rejecting the whole mass of compromises sanctioned by the Church, and returning to the elemental principles of the faith, was no less naturally opposed to fine arts, which, after giving sensuous form to Catholic mythology, had recently attained to liberty and brought again the gods of Greece.

A single illustration might be selected from the annals of Italian painting to prove how difficult even the holiest-minded and most earnest painter found it to effect the proper junction between plastic beauty and pious feeling.   Fra Bartolommeo, the disciple of Savona-rola, painted a Sebastian in the cloister of San Marco, where it re-mained until the Dominican confessors became aware, through the avowals of female penitents, that this picture was a stumblingblock and snare to souls.   It was then removed, and what became of it we do not know for certain.   Fra Bartolommeo undoubtedly intended this ideal portrait of the martyr to be edifying.   St. Sebastian was to stand before the world as the young man, strong and beautiful, who endured to the end and won the crown of martyrdom.   No other ideas but those of heroism, constancy, or faith were meant to be expressed; but the painter's art demanded that their expression should be eminently beautiful, and the beautiful body of the young man dis-tracted attention from his spiritual virtues to his physical perfections. A similar maladjustment of the means of plastic art to the purposes of religion would have been impossible in Hellas, where the temples of Erôs and of Phoebus stood side by side; but in Christian Florence the craftsman's skill sowed seeds of discord in the souls of the devout.

This story is but a coarse instance of the separation between piety and plastic art.   In truth, the difficulty of uniting them in such a way that the latter shall enforce the former, lies far deeper than its powers of illustration reach.   Religion has its proper end in contemplation and in conduct.   Art aims at presenting sensuous embodiment of thoughts and feelings with a view to intellectual enjoyment.   Now, many thoughts are incapable of sensuous embodiment; they appear as abstractions to the philosophical intellect or as dogmas to the theological understanding.   To effect an alliance between art and philosophy or art and theology in the specific region of either religion or speculation is, therefore, an impossibility.   In like manner there are many feelings which cannot properly assume a sensuous form; and these are precisely religious feelings, in which the soul abandons sense, and leaves the actual world behind, to seek her freedom in a spiritual region.   Yet, while we recognize the truth of this reasoning, it would be unscientific to maintain that, until they are brought into close and inconvenient contact, there is direct hostility between religion and the arts. The sphere of the two is separate; their aims are distinct; they must be allowed to perfect themselves, each after his own fashion. In the large philosophy of human nature, represented by Goethe's famous motto, there is room for both, because those who embrace it bend their natures neither wholly to the pietism of the cloister nor to the sensuality of art. They find the meeting point of art and of religion in their own humanity, and perceive that the antagonism of the two begins when art is set to do work alien to its nature, and to minister to what it does not naturally serve.

At the risk of repetition I must now resume the points I have attempted to establish in this chapter. As in ancient Greece, so also in Renaissance Italy, the fine arts assumed the first place in the intellectual culture of the nation. But the thought and feeling of the modern world required an aesthetic medium more capable of expressing emotion in its intensity, variety, and subtlety than sculpture. Therefore painting was the art of arts for Italy. Yet even painting, notwithstanding the range and wealth of its resources, could not deal with the motives of Christianity so successfully as sculpture with the myths of paganism. The religion it interpreted transcended the actual conditions of humanity, while art is bound down by its nature to the limitations of the world we live in. The Church imagined art would help her; and within a certain sphere of subjects, by vividly depicting Scripture histories and the lives of saints, by creating new types of serene beauty and pure joy, by giving form to angelic beings, by interpreting Mariolatry in all its charm and pathos, and by rousing deep sympathy with our Lord in His Passion, painting lent efficient aid to piety. Yet painting had to omit the very pith and kernel of Christianity as conceived by the devout, uncompromising purists. Nor did it do what the Church would have desired. Instead of riveting the fetters of ecclesiastical authority, instead of enforcing mysticism and asceticism, it really restored to humanity the sense of its own dignity and beauty, and helped to prove the untenability of the mediaeval standpoint; for art is essentially and uncontrollably free, and what is more, is free precisely in that realm of sensuous delightfulness from which cloistral religion turns aside to seek her own ecstatic liberty of contemplation.

The first step in the emancipation of the modern mind was taken thus by art, proclaiming to men the glad tidings of their goodliness and greatness in a world of manifold enjoyment created for their use. Whatever painting touched, became by that touch human; piety, at the lure of art, folded her soaring wings and rested on the genial earth. This the Church had not foreseen. Because the freedom of the human spirit expressed itself in painting only under visible images, and not, like heresy, in abstract sentences; because this art sufficed for Mariolatry and confirmed the cult of local saints; because its sensuousness was not at variance with a creed that had been deeply sensualized — the painters were allowed to run their course unchecked. Then came a second stage in their development of art. By placing the end of their endeavor in technical excellence and anatomical accuracy, they began to make representation an object in itself, independently of its spiritual significance. Next, under the influence of the classical revival, they brought home again the old powers of the earth — Aphrodite and Galatea and the Loves, Adonis and Narcissus and the Graces, Phoebus and Daphne and Aurora, Pan and the Fauns, and the Nymphs of the woods and the waves.

When these dead deities rose from their sepulchres to sway the hearts of men in the new age, it was found that something had been taken from their ancient bloom of innocence, something had been added of emotional intensity. Italian art recognized their claim to stand beside Madonna and the Saints in the Pantheon of humane culture; but the painters remade them in accordance with the modern spirit. This slight touch of transformation proved that, though they were no longer objects of religious devotion, they still preserved a vital meaning for an altered age. Having personified for the antique world qualities which, though suppressed and ignored by militant and mediaeval Christianity, were strictly human, the Hellenic deities still signified those qualities for modern Europe, now at length refortified by contact with the ancient mind. For it is needful to remember than in all movements of the Renaissance we ever find a return in all sincerity and faith to the glory and gladness of nature, whether in the world without or in the soul of man. To apprehend that glory and that gladness with the pure and primitive perceptions of the early mythopoets, was not given to the men of the new world. Yet they did what in them lay, with senses sophisticated by many centuries of subtlest warping, to replace the first free joy of kinship with primeval things. For the painters, far more than for the poets of the sixteenth century, it was possible to reproduce a thousand forms of beauty, each attesting to the delightfulness of physical existence, to the inalienable rights of natural desire, and to the participation of mankind in pleasures held in common by us with the powers of earth and sea and air.

It is wonderful to watch the blending of elder and of younger forces in this process. The old gods lent a portion of their charm even to Christian mythology, and showered their beauty-bloom on saints who died renouncing them. Sodoma's Sebastian is but Hyacinth or Hylas, transpierced with arrows, so that pain and martyrdom add pathos to his poetry of youthfulness. Lionardo's St. John is a Faun of the forest, ivy-crowned and laughing, on whose lips the word "repent" would be a gleeful paradox. For the painters of the full Renaissance Roman martyrs and Olympian deities — the heroes of the *Acta Sanctorum*, and the heroes of Greek romance — were alike burghers of one spiritual city, the city of the beautiful and human. What exquisite and evanescent fragrance was educed from these apparently diverse blossoms by their interminglement and fusion — how the high-wrought sensibilities of the Christian were added to the clear and radiant fancies of the Greek, and how the frank sensuousness of the pagan gave body and fullness to the floating wraiths of an ascetic faith — remains a miracle for those who, like our master Lionardo, love to scrutinize the secrets of twin natures and of double graces. There are not a few for whom the mystery is repellent, who shrink from it as from Hermaphroditus. These will always find something to pain them in the art of the Renaissance.

Having coördinated the Christian and pagan traditions in its works of beauty, painting could advance no farther. The stock of its sustaining motives was exhausted. A problem that preoccupied the minds of thinking men at this epoch was how to harmonize the two chief moments of human culture, the classical and the ecclesiastical. Without being as conscious of their hostility as we are, men felt that the pagan ideal was opposed to the Christian, and at the same time that a reconciliation had to be effected. Each had been worked out separately; but both were needed for the modern synthesis. All that aesthetic handling, in this region more precocious and more immediately fruitful than pure thought, could do toward mingling them, was done by the impartiality of the fine arts. Painting, in the work of Raphael, accomplished a more vital harmony than philosophy in the writings of Pico and Ficino. A new Catholicity, a cosmopolitan orthodoxy of the beautiful, was manifested in his pictures. It lay outside his power, or that of any other artist, to do more than to extract from both revelations the elements of plastic beauty they contained, and to show how freely he could use them for a common purpose. Nothing but the scientific method can in the long run enable us to reach that further point, outside both Christianity and paganism, at which the classical ideal of a temperate and joyous natural life shall be restored to the conscience educated by the Gospel. This, perchance, is the religion, still unborn or undeveloped, whereof Joachim of Flora dimly prophesied when he said that the kingdom of the Father was past, the kingdom of the Son was passing, and the kingdom of the Spirit was to be. The essence of it is contained in the whole growth to usward of the human mind; and though a creed so highly intellectualized as that will be, can never receive adequate expression from the figurative arts, still the painting of the sixteenth century forms for it, as it were, a not unworthy vestibule. It does so, because it first succeeded in humanizing the religion of the Middle Ages, in proclaiming the true value of antique paganism for the modern mind, and in making both subserve the purposes of free and unimpeded art.

Meanwhile, at the moment when painting was about to be exhausted, a new art had arisen, for which it remained, within the aesthetic sphere, to achieve much that painting could not do. When the cycle of Christian ideas had been accomplished by the painters, and when the first passion for antiquity had been satisfied, it was given at last to music to express the soul in all its manifold feeling and complexity of movement. In music we see the point of departure where art leaves the domain of myths, Christian as well as pagan, and occupies itself with the emotional activity of man alone, and for its own sake. Melody and harmony, disconnected from words, are capable of receiving most varied interpretations, so that the same combinations of sound express the ecstasies of earthly and of heavenly love, conveying to the mind of the hearer only that element of pure passion which is the primitive and natural ground-material of either. They give distinct form to moods of feeling as yet undetermined; or, as the Italians put it, *la musica è il lamento dell' amore o la preghiera a gli dei.*[1] This, combined with its independence of all corporeal conditions, renders music the true exponent of the spirit in its freedom, and therefore the essentially modern art.

For painting, after the great work accomplished during the Renaissance, when the painters ran through the whole domain of thought within the scope of that age, there only remained portraiture, history, dramatic incident, landscape genre, still life and animals. In these spheres the art is still exercised, and much good work, undoubtedly, is annually produced by European painters. But painting has lost its hold upon the center of our intellectual activity. It can no longer

[1] "Music is the lament of love, or prayer to the gods."

give form to the ideas that at the present epoch rule the modern world. These ideas are too abstract, too much a matter of the understanding, to be successfully handled by the figurative arts; and it cannot be too often or too emphatically stated that these arts produce nothing really great and universal in relation to the spirit of their century, except by a process analogous to the mythopoetic. With conceptions incapable of being sensuously apprehended, with ideas that lose their value when they are incarnated, they have no power to deal. As meteors become luminous by traversing the grosser element of our terrestrial atmosphere, so the thoughts that art employs must needs immerse themselves in sensuousness. They must be of a nature to gain rather than to suffer by such immersion; and they must make a direct appeal to minds habitually apt to think in metaphors and myths. Of this sort are all religious ideas at a certain stage of their development, and this attitude at certain moments of history is adopted by the popular consciousness. We have so far outgrown it, have so completely exchanged mythology for curiosity, and metaphor for science, that the necessary conditions for great art are wanting. Our deepest thoughts about the world and God are incapable of personification by any aesthetic process; they never enter that atmosphere wherein alone they could become through fine art luminous. For the painter, who is the form-giver, they have ceased to be shining stars and are seen as opaque stones; and though divinity be in them, it is a deity that refuses the investiture of form.

THE FEUD BETWEEN PHILOSOPHY AND ART[1]

Paul Elmer More

It was in 1904, at the age of forty, that PAUL ELMER MORE published his first volume of *Shelburne Essays*, making it clear that a new literary critic of the first rank had arisen in the United States. One volume of beautifully chiseled prose followed another till in 1921 the eleventh and last of the *Shelburne* series was issued. In these essays he presents humane, witty, incisive estimates of a wide range of British and American authors, from Sir Thomas Browne to Kipling and Whitman; he ranges into foreign literatures — Tolstoi, Nietzsche, Sainte-Beuve; he treats of movements and problems in the history of thought — pragmatism, humanitarianism, the Forest philosophy of India. But he also does much more. The *Shelburne Essays* are the expression not only of a remarkable erudition and a fine critical perception, but of a rich personality and of a spirit that has quested for truth from New England Cambridge to India and to ancient Athens. "What is a Shelburne essay?" asks Stuart P. Sherman. "It is criticism, it is history, it is philosophy, it is morality, it is religion, it is, above all, a singularly moving poetry, gushing up from deep intellectual and moral substrata, pure, cold, and refreshing, as water of a spring from the rocks in some high mountain hollow. . . . By its compression of serious thought and deep feeling it produces an effect as of one speaking between life and death, as the *Apology* of Socrates does. There is a pulse in the still flow of it, as if it had been stirred once and forever at the bottom of the human heart." No body of literary criticism comparable in the union of both depth and scope has been produced by any other man in the United States, not even Lowell. Those who lack time to go to the entire shelf of the essays (of which the sixth and eighth volumes give the best insight into Mr. More's special vein of thought, while the first and eleventh contain the largest number of essays on American figures) will find an excellent selection by Mr. More himself in the Oxford Press series of World Classics. The best brief statement of Mr. More's philosophical and critical position is in the preface to the eighth volume, which is entitled *The Drift of Romanticism*. Here he explains his belief in "the inner check," superior to instinct or reason, which preserves man from " the dissolution of the everlasting flux."

Born in St. Louis, Mr. More was educated at Washington University and at Harvard. After teaching for two years at Bryn Mawr, he became literary editor of the *Independent* in 1901, and in 1903 joined the staff of the New York *Evening Post* and *Nation* (then edited from the same office). He retired from the editorship of the *Nation* in 1914, after adding to the luster which E. L. Godkin and W. P. Garrison had given it. Living chiefly at Princeton, he turned after 1915 more directly to philosophic and religious themes, publishing a series of volumes on Platonism, Neo-Platonism, and early Christian thought, of which *The Religion of Plato, Hellenistic Philosophies*, and *The Christ of the New Testament* may be named as especially notable.

[1] From *Shelburne Essays* (First Series). Houghton Mifflin Company. Reprinted by permission of the author and publisher.

This has been a century of strange conversions, and not least strange among these is Count Leo Tolstoi's abdication of an art in which he had won world-wide reputation for the rôle of prophet and iconoclast. "What is Art?" he has asked himself, and his published answer, the outcome of fifteen years of meditation, is a denial of all that has made art noble in the past, and a challenge to those who seek to continue that tradition in the present. Furthermore he has put his theory into practice in a long and powerful novel, *Resurrection.* Naturally such a renunciation on the part of an undisputed master in the craft caused no small commotion among poets and critics. Many of these, chiefly of the French school, shrugged their shoulders and smiled at a theory that would reject the works of Sophocles and Dante and Shakespeare as "savage and meaningless," and find in *Uncle Tom's Cabin* the acme of art toward which the ages have been tending. Others have taken the quasi-prophet more seriously, and with much ingenuity have pointed out the seeming flaws in his argument. Must I for my part confess that I have been chiefly impressed by the terrible and relentless logic of the book? It is easy to smile; it is easy to denounce the work as "literary nihilism put into practice by a converted pessimist." Pessimist and fanatic and barbarian Tolstoi may be, and to judge from his portrait alone he is all these; yet I know not how we shall escape his ruthless conclusions unless we deny resolutely his premises, and these are in part what our age holds as its dearest heritage of truth. Furthermore, his theoretic book may claim to be only the latest blow struck in a quarrel as old as human consciousness itself. Long ago Plato, himself a renegade from among the worshipers of beauty, could speak of "the ancient feud between philosophy and art," and today one of the barbarians of the North has delivered a shrewd stroke in the same unending conflict.

Least of all should we have expected to find in Greece this lurking antipathy between art and philosophy, for there, if anywhere in the world, truth and beauty seem to us to have walked hand in hand. It is curious that the school of Socrates, which did so much to introduce a formal divorce between these ideas, should have been so fond of the one word that more than any other expresses the intimate union of beauty and goodness. *Kalokagathia,* beauty-and-goodness, "that solemn word in which even the gods take delight," was ever on their lips. In the beginning, no doubt, this strangely compounded term conveyed the simple thought still dear to our own youth when a fair face seems naturally and inevitably the index of a noble soul. That indeed is the ideal which we believe the truest gentlemen of Athens actually attained; we think we see it portrayed in the statues bequeathed to us by the land; it is at least the goal toward which Greek art ever strove as the reintegration of life. But after all we must confess that this harmony of the inner and the outer vision was but an ideal in Greece, such as has now and again glanced before other eyes — only appearing not quite so fitfully there and approaching at times nearer the reality. Had it been anything more than a desire of the imagination, the history of the world would have been something quite different from the vexed pages of growth and decay which we now read. Perhaps, too, Joubert was not entirely wrong when he said that "God, being unable to bestow truth upon the Greeks, gave them poesy." Achilles, fair without and noble within, was the glory of the race; but too often the reality was like Paris, divinely beautiful and beloved of the goddess, but hollow at heart. From an early date the wise men of the land foresaw the threatened danger. Pythagoras, who described the poets tortured in Hell, was not the only prophet to denounce their travesty of the gods; nor was Solon the only sage who looked askance on the stage.

But Socrates, the first man of the Western world to attain to full self-consciousness, was the first also to ask seriously, What are truth and goodness? and What is beauty? And though in general he would deprive beauty of its peril, by reducing it to a mere matter of utility, yet at times he seems as a philosopher to have recognized its doubtful allurements. Xenophon reports an amusing conversation with his master on the nature of kissing, wherein Socrates in his usual style of badinage hints at this hidden peril. "Know you not," says he, "that this monster, whom you call beauty and youth, is more terrible than venomous spiders? These can sting only by contact, but that other monster injects his poison from a distance if a man but rest his eyes upon him." In another book we read Socrates's misgivings in regard to the current meaning of the word *Kalokagathia*. He with his contemporaries had supposed that a necessary harmony existed between virtue and a man's outer semblance, until experience brought its cruel awakening. Beauty, which as a Greek he could not omit from the composition of a full man, became thenceforth for him, as for the rest of the world, mere grace of inner character, scarcely distinguishable from goodness itself. This idea is naïvely developed in a conversation with the gentleman of the *Oeconomicus*, where Socrates asks his old friend how despite his homely exterior he has won the reputation of uniting perfect beauty and goodness.

If we are a little surprised to hear the contemporary of Phidias and Sophocles speak doubtfully of the office of beauty, what shall we think of his disciple Plato, who was himself in youth a poet, and who in manhood was master of all styles, and able to drape in the robes of fancy the barest skeleton of logic?   He, if anyone, has given us "the sweet foode of sweetly uttered knowledge," and we further may say of him, with Sir Philip Sidney, "almost hee sheweth himselfe a passionate lover, of that unspeakable and everlasting beautie to be seene by the eyes of the minde, onely cleered by fayth"; and yet Plato knew and could avow that "to prefer beauty to virtue was the real and utter dishonor of the soul."   I can imagine that to one bred on the visions of poetry and by birth a worshiper of all the fair manifestations of nature, nothing could be more disconcerting than to follow the changes of Plato's doctrine in this regard.   In the earlier dialogues physical come- liness is but a symbol of inner grace, a guide to lead us in the arduous and perilous ascent of the soul; and his theory of love was to become the teacher of idealism to a new world.   In *The Republic* the cardinal virtues are blent into one perfect harmony of character so alluring as to seem the reflection in his mind of all the visual charm he had seen in Hellas.   But even here his change of attitude is apparent; this same dialogue contains that bitter diatribe against poetry and music which would banish inexorably all the magicians of art from his ideal state, because they draw the mind from the contemplation of abstract truth to dwell upon her deceptive imitations.   The world has not forgotten and will never forget how these greatest Athenians turned away their eyes from what had given their land its splendid pre- dominance.   Socrates's question, What is beauty? was the "little rift within the lute," that was to widen until the music of Greece became hushed forever.

We may liken the texture of art to that floating garment of gauze, inwoven with a myriad forms and symbols, in which the goddess Natura was wont to appear to the visionary eyes of the schoolmen: we may liken it to the curtain that hung in the temple before the holy of holies; and the rending of the curtain from top to bottom may signify a changed aspect in the warfare of our dual nature.   A new meaning and acrimony enter into the conflict henceforth.   Christianity introduced, or at least strongly emphasized, those principles that were in the end to make such an utter revolt as Tolstoi's.   With the progress of the new era, the feud between philosophy and art will take on a thousand different disguises, appearing now as a contest between religion and the senses, and again as a schism within the bosom of the

church itself.   To the followers of Christ, the indwelling of divinity is
no longer made evident by beauty of external form, for their incarnate
deity came to them as one in whom there was "no form nor comeliness" nor any "beauty that we should desire him."   Instead of magnanimity and magnificence the world shall learn to honor humility; a
different sense shall be given to the word "equality," and the individual soul will assume importance from its heavenly destiny, and not
from its earthly force or impotence; the ambition to make life splendid
shall be sunk in humanitarian surrender to the weak; the genial command of the poet, "Doing righteousness make glad your heart," shall
be changed to the shrill cry of the monk, "But woe unto those that
know not their own misery; and woe yet greater unto those that love
this miserable and corrupted life!"   Not that the old desire of loveliness shall be utterly routed from the world; but more and more it will
be severed from the life of the spirit, and appear more and more as
the seducer, and not the spouse, of the soul. . . .

This is not the place to follow the conflict of our dual nature
through all the ramifications of history.   Those who wish to study it
in its most dramatic movement may turn to the story of England in the
seventeenth century, or read *John Inglesant*, where it developed into a
romance of curious fascination.   And to us of America at least the
struggle of that period must always possess singular interest; for out
of it grew the intellectual life of our nation, and even today the
poverty of our art and literature is partly due to the fact that our
strongest colonists brought with them only one fraction of the endless
feud.

For the feud is not settled and can never be settled while human
nature remains what it is.   Today the man who approaches the
higher intellectual life is confronted by the same question that
troubled Plato.   He who can choose without hesitation between art
and religion, or between the new antinomy of literature and science,
has climbed but a little way on the ladder of experience.   There was a
parable current among the Greeks, and still to be found in our modern
school readers, which tells how the youthful Hercules in the pathway of
life was met by two women who represented virtue and pleasure, and
who bade him choose between the careers they offered.   And it has often
seemed to me that the fable might be applied without much distortion
to many an ardent man who in his youth goes out into the solitudes to
meditate on the paths of ambition — his choice lying not between
virtue and pleasure, but between the philosophic and the imaginative
life.   As he sits musing in some such solitude of the spirit, we can

discern two feminine forms approach him, very tall and stately — one of them good to look upon and noble in stature, clad in modest raiment, and with a brooding gaze of austerity in her eyes as if troubled by no vision of turbid existence; the other more radiant in face, and richer and more alluring in form, with wide open eyes that might be mirrors for all the delightful things of nature, and dressed in a floating transparent robe wherein are woven figures of many strange flowers and birds.   She of the fluttering garment comes forward before the other, and greets the youth effusively, and bids him follow her, for she will lead him by a pleasant path where he shall suffer no diminution of the desires of his heart, neither be withheld from the fullness of earthly experience, but always he shall behold a changing vision of wonder of beauty, and in the end be received into the palace of Fame. Here the youth asks by what name she is known, and she replies: "My friends call me Fancy, and I dwell in the meadows of Art, but my enemies call me Illusion."   In the meanwhile the other woman has drawn near, and now she says to the young man: "Nay, follow me rather, and I will show you the true value of life.   I will not deceive you with cunning seductions of the eye and ear that lead only to distraction in the end.   The road in which I shall guide you lies apart from the vanities and triumphs of earthly hopes; the way of renunciation will seem hard to tread at first, but slowly a new joy of the understanding will be awakened in you, born of a contempt for the fleeting illusions of this world, and in the end you shall attain to another and higher peace that passeth understanding.   I am named Insight, and by some my home is called Philosophy and by others Religion."   I can fancy that some such parting of the ways has come to many of those who by choosing resolutely have won renown as artists or seers. I can believe that some who have elected the smoother path have even in the full triumph of success felt moments of regret for the other life of ascetic contemplation. . . .

Count Tolstoi accepts without reservation the plain precepts of the Gospel, and demands our adherence to the strict letter of the law. This may be well, although possibly it denotes something of the false logic of fanaticism to dwell so persistently on the one command, "Resist not evil."   But deeper than the commands lies the spirit of Christ; and he who follows the law of the Gospel without heeding the spirit, wherein does he differ from the Pharisees of the old dispensation whom Christ so vehemently denounced?

If you ask in what respect Tolstoi misses the heart of true religion and of Christ, I would reply in the words of a famous French woman,

"*La joie de l'esprit en marque la force*" — the joy of the spirit is the measure of its force. It may seem trifling to confront the solemn exhortation of a prophet with the words of Ninon de l'Enclos, whose chief claim on our memory is the scandalous story of her grandson, who killed himself on discovering that he had fallen in love unwittingly with his own grandmother; and yet I know not where a saner criticism could be found of the arrogant dogmatism of this Russian bigot. There is no joy in Tolstoi, and lacking joy he lacks the deepest instinct of religion. I know that here and there a sentence, or even a page, may be quoted from Tolstoi that sounds as if he had discovered joy in his new faith, and I know that he respects volubly the glad tidings that are said to have made the angels sing as they never sang before; but it needs no more than a glance at the rigid, glaring eyes of the old man to feel that the soul within him feeds on bitter and uncharitable thoughts, and it needs but a little familiarity with his later work in fiction to learn that the ground of his spirit is bitterness and denunciation and despair.

It is natural that a writer of Tolstoi's gloomy convictions should deny the validity of beauty and should call the Greeks ignorant savages because they believed in beauty. His own later work shows an utter absence of the sense of beauty and joy. The drama called *La Puissance des Ténèbres* — I do not know that it has ever been translated into English — is one of the most revolting and heart-sickening productions of the past century. The imagination of the author has apparently dwelt on unclean objects until it has become crazed with a mingled feeling toward them of attraction and repulsion.

Count Tolstoi takes his law of righteousness from the Sermon on the Mount, and that is well; but he has forgotten the song of joy that runs like a golden thread through that discourse — "Blessed are they that mourn; for they shall be comforted. . . . Rejoice, and be exceeding glad." Out of the preaching of Christ proceeds the wonderful and beautiful lesson of the fowls of the air and of the lilies of the field; out of the preaching of Tolstoi comes the loathsome *Powers of Darkness*. Or, if we look for a more modern instance, we may read the *Fioretti* of St. Francis of Assisi, than whom no one has trod nearer to the footsteps of Christ. The parables and poems of St. Francis are all aglow with passionate joy and tenderness and beauty.

I do not mean that sorrow and denunciation are banished from the teaching of Christ. But the sorrow of Christ is not the uncharitable cry alone of one whose spirit has been wounded by seeing wrong and injustice in the world. Does it need a prophet to tell us the times are

out of joint?   Nor is it the anguish of a spirit that has retreated bitterly upon itself because the world does not respond to his own personal
demands.   It is rather the brooding pity of one who sees that the
fashion of this world passeth away, and that rich and poor alike are
in the bondage of sin.   There is in him neither the rancor of class
hatred nor the wail of personal disillusion.   The world is dark to him
because it lies outside the great and wonderful radiance of the Kingdom of Heaven.   If I read aright the fragmentary record of Christ's
life it was more filled with the joy of spiritual insight than with the
bitterness of earthly despair.

And this is not the nature of Christianity alone, but of true faith
wherever found.   We hear much of the pessimism of Buddha, and
Schopenhauer is supposed to have sucked thence the poison of his
philosophy;   but in reality the doctrine of Buddha in its pure form is
one of unspeakable gladness.   He dwelt much on the transitory
nature of this world and on the misery of human life, but he dwelt
far more on the ineffable peace and joy of deliverance.   There is the
pessimism of one whose vision is wholly downward, and who sees only
the bleakness of earthly life;   there is another so-called pessimism of
one whose vision is ever upward, and to whom, therefore, the world
seems a clog on his progress toward perfect happiness, and such, if it be
pessimism at all, is the pessimism of Buddha.   Only a reader familiar
with the Buddhist books can have any notion of the overwhelming
spirit of gladness and simple charity that pervades them.   There is in
one of them the story of a prince who is converted and leaves the luxury
of a palace to join the brotherhood;   and we are told that in the night-
time the brothers heard him walking outside in the grove and crying to
himself, *Aho! Aho!* for his joy was so great that he could not sleep.

In a word, the sadness of true religion is negative, the joy positive.
Faith is the deliberate turning of the eye from darkness to light.   If
the words of the preacher close the doors in our breasts and bring
to us a contracted feeling of depression, we may know that his denunciation of the world is because the world has turned to ashes in his
mouth and not because he has attained to any true vision of the peace
of the spirit.

It is because there is no note of spiritual joy in Tolstoi when he
speaks from his own heart and lays aside the borrowed jargon of
Christianity, it is because there is in him only the bitterness of a great
and smitten soul, it is because there is in him no charity or tenderness,
but only the bleakness of disillusion, that he must be counted in the
end an enemy to faith and not an upbuilder of faith.

I have dwelt thus at length on Tolstoi's theory of the new art and on his religion of humanitarianism from which this theory springs, rather than on his practice of art as shown in the novel *Resurrection*, because his theoretic writing seemed to me more fruitful and suggestive, and because — let me confess it — the novel has awakened in my mind a repugnance strongly at variance with the eulogistic reception it has gained at large. There is undoubtedly superabundant force in the book; there is the visual power, so common in Russian novels, which compels the reader to see with his own eyes what the author describes; there is profound skill of characterization, clothing the persons of the story in flesh and blood; but with all this, what have we in the end but "the expense of spirit in a waste of shame"?

It would be an easy task to point out how perfectly the novel follows the author's theory, and how completely it presents him as a decadent with the humanitarian superimposed. There is the same utter inability to perceive beauty as connected with a healthy ideal of character, and a consequent repudiation of beauty altogether. There is the same morbid brooding on sex which lent so unsavory a reputation to the *Kreutzer Sonata*. It should seem that the author's mind had dwelt so persistently and intensely on this subject as to induce a sort of erotic mania taking the form at once of a horrid attraction and repulsion. We are sickened in the same way with endless details of loathsome description that are made only the more repellent by their vividness; nor can I see how the fascination of such scenes as the trial and the prison can be based on any worthier motive than that which collects a crowd about some hideous accident of the street. It is not science, for it is touched with morbid emotionalism. It is not true art, for it contains no element of elevation. It is not right preaching, for it degrades human nature without awakening any compensating spiritual aspiration. It is, when all has been said, the same spirit of unclean decadence as that which led Baudelaire to write his stanzas on *Une Charogne*, and it classes Tolstoi in many respects with that corrupt school which he so heartily detested. The travesty of life presented in the book may be explained — I do not know — by the barbarous state of Russian civilization. The coarseness of details, however, may well be charged to the individual mind of the man who while describing in his memoirs the burial of his own mother dilates on the odor of the body. This is not a pleasant fact to mention, but is in itself worth a volume of argument. Christianity was thrust upon the northern heathen at the point of sword and pike: it should seem as if this propagator of humanitarianism was bent on making converts by trampling under foot all the finer feelings and fairer instincts, all the decorum and suavity, of human nature.

Such, at present, is the most notable phase of the ancient feud, so far at least as it concerns literature; and from the horns of this dilemma — the mockery of art for art's sake on one side, and on the other the dubious and negative virtue of the humanitarians — I find no way of escape, unless the world discovers again some positive ideal which beauty can serve. And if you say that this conflict is only one phase of an ever changing and never solved antinomy of human nature, and that the conception of the good and beautiful was an empty word of the philosophers, certainly I shall not attempt to answer in terms of logic, for I myself have been too long haunted by a similar doubt. And yet I seem to see dimly and figuratively the shadow of a solution. Call it a dream if you will; but what else was the vision of Jacob when he lay asleep and beheld a ladder stretching from the earth to the sky? Or the journey of Dante up the Mountain of Purgatory and from planet to planet? Or Dionysius's doctrine of the hierarchy of angels and principalities and powers reaching in unbroken succession from man to the Supreme Being?

Somewhere in that same visionary land I beheld a great mountain, whose foot was in a valley of eternal shadows, and whose head was lost in the splendor of the pure empyrean. At first the eye was bewildered and could see only the strange contrast of the gloom below and the whiteness above; but as I looked longer, I discerned a path that stretched from one to the other up the whole length of the slope, uniting them by gradual changes of light and shade. On this pathway were countless human souls, some toiling upward, others lightly descending, but none pausing, for there seemed to be at work within them some principle of unrest which forever impelled them this way or that. And their journey was a strange and mystic pilgrimage, through ever-varying scenes, between the deep abyss far below, where monstrous creatures like the first uncertain births of Chaos wallowed in the slime and darkness, and high above the regions made dim with excess of light, where in the full noonday figures of transcendent glory seemed to move. And I saw that of all the pilgrims a few lifted their eyes aloft to the great white light, and were so ravished by its radiance that the objects before their feet were as if they did not exist. And of these few one here and there pressed on valiantly and in time was himself rapt from view into the upper radiance; but the others were blinded by the light, and lost their foothold, and were hurled headlong into the loathsome valley. And I saw a few others whose eyes turned by some horrid fascination to the abyss itself, and thither they rushed madly, heedless of every allurement by the way. But by far the greater number kept their regard fixed modestly on the path just above or below, according as the spirit within led them to ascend or descend. And these seemed to walk ever in a kind of earthly paradise; for the light, streaming down from the empyrean and tempered to their vision by wont, fell upon the trees by the roadside and on the flowering shrubs innumerable and on the mountain brooks, and gilded all with wonderful and inexpressible beauty. And those that gazed above were filled with such joy at the fresh world before them that they climbed ever upward and never rested, for always some scene still fairer lured them on. And as they climbed, the light grew brighter and more clear, and the path more beautiful and easier to ascend, and so without seeming toil or peril they too passed from sight. But those others who cast their eyes on the pathway below were drawn in the same way by the beauty of the scene where the golden light glanced on the trees; and with much ease and satisfaction to themselves they paced down and still downward, following the shifting vision and dallying with pleasure on the way, and never observed how the light was growing dimmer and the road more precipitous, until losing balance they were thrown headlong into the noisome valley.

So the division and conflict of human nature appeared to me in a parable; but whether the vision had any meaning or was only an idle fancy, I do not know.

"TEN O'CLOCK"[1]

J. A. McNeil Whistler

JAMES ABBOTT MCNEILL WHISTLER was not only a great artist; he was one of the leaders of a special school of thought in art — the school which, breaking sharply from Victorian tradition, preached the gospel of art for art's sake. Not being primarily a literary man, he never gave his exposition of this doctrine the currency attained by Pater, Oscar Wilde, and Arthur Symons; but in all his varied work as painter, decorator, etcher, and lithographer he held strictly to it. Historical interest, moral interest, and sentimental interest he rigidly excluded from whatever he touched. To him the didacticism of such a canvas as Millais's "Christ in the House of His Parents," the literary quality of Rossetti's "Proserpine," were repugnant; and Turner's "Fighting Teméraire" was made fine *in spite of* its historical quality by its magnificence of design, color, and handling. He believed that beauty is the end of art, and not "emotions entirely foreign to it." While he wished to divorce painting from tradition, from mediaevalism, and above all from mere storytelling and anecdote, he sought beauty in the everyday world about him; and he found it in the fogs of London streets, the smoke-dimmed sunsets of the Thames, the hues of flesh and fabrics, the blue and silver of a wave-tossed sea, the black and white of an icebound river. His portrait of a woman he would make not a study in character, as Sargent did, but a "Harmony in Gray and Green" or an "Arrangement in Pink and Purple." He believed, like Pater, in insulating art from the innumerable activities of the contemporaneous world; he did not in the least believe, with Ruskin and William Morris, that it is an integral part of life, but that it is a haven to be kept inviolate from crude reality.

Born at Lowell, Massachusetts, in 1834, and trained in Paris and London (though he owed little to any master), Whistler spent the greater part of his productive career in the latter city, where he died in 1903. He married an Englishwoman, and much of his best-known work both in etching and painting deals with English subjects. He experimented in many mediums. Some critics place his etchings above those of Rembrandt; his studies in water color were slight but always exquisite; in pastel painting he was always successful, often triumphant; his lithographs of Thames subjects and London churches are admirable. But it is his paintings that are most famous; the portrait of Carlyle, now in Glasgow, the portrait of his mother, now in the Luxembourg, "The Old Battersea Bridge," "The Cremorne Gardens," "The Music Room." His eccentric personality made a sharp impression upon his times. He was arrogant, sharp of tongue, acidulously witty, something of a poseur in manner and dress, and addicted to controversy. His libel suit against Ruskin, who had attacked one of his nocturnes as "a pot of paint flung in the face of the public," gave him a rare opportunity to defend his ideas of art. These ideas he also expounded in a number of essays, often satirical, sometimes flippant, but always witty and pointed: "Art vs. Art Critics," "Ten O'Clock," and "The Gentle Art of Making Enemies" being the best known.

[1] From "*Ten O'Clock.*" Houghton Mifflin Company (copyright, 1888, by J. A. McNeil Whistler). Reprinted by permission.

I

Art is upon the Town! — to be chucked under the chin by the passing gallant — to be enticed within the gates of the householder — to be coaxed into company, as a proof of culture and refinement.

If familiarity can breed contempt, certainly Art — or what is currently taken for it — has been brought to its lowest stage of intimacy.

The people have been harassed with Art in every guise, and vexed with many methods as to its endurance. They have been told how they shall love Art, and live with it. Their homes have been invaded, their walls covered with paper, their very dress taken to task — until, roused at last, bewildered and filled with the doubts and discomforts of senseless suggestion, they resent such intrusion, and cast forth the false prophets, who have brought the very name of the beautiful into disrepute, and derision upon themselves.

Alas! ladies and gentlemen, Art has been maligned. She has naught in common with such practices. She is a goddess of dainty thought — reticent of habit, abjuring all obtrusiveness, purposing in no way to better others.

She is, withal, selfishly occupied with her own perfection only — having no desire to teach — seeking and finding the beautiful in all conditions and at all times, as did her high priest Rembrandt, when he saw picturesque grandeur and noble dignity in the Jews' quarter of Amsterdam, and lamented not that its inhabitants were not Greeks.

As did Tintoret and Paul Veronese among the Venetians, while not halting to change the brocaded silks for the classic draperies of Athens.

As did, at the Court of Philip, Velasquez, whose Infantas, clad in inaesthetic hoops, are, as works of Art, of the same quality as the Elgin marbles.

No reformers were these great men — no improvers of the ways of others! Their productions alone were their occupation, and, filled with the poetry of their science, they required not to alter their surroundings — for, as the laws of their art were revealed to them, they saw, in the development of their work, that real beauty which, to them, was as much a matter of certainty and triumph as is to the astronomer the verification of the result, foreseen with the light given to him alone. In all this, their world was completely severed from that of their fellow creatures with whom sentiment is mistaken for poetry; and for whom there is no perfect work that shall not be explained by the benefit conferred upon themselves.

Humanity takes the place of Art, and God's creations are excused by their usefulness. Beauty is confounded with virtue, and, before a work of Art, it is asked, "What good shall it do?"

Hence it is that nobility of action, in this life, is hopelessly linked with the merit of the work that portrays it; and thus the people have acquired the habit of looking, as we should say, not *at* a picture, but *through* it, at some human fact, that shall, or shall not, from a social point of view, better their mental or moral state. So we have come to hear of the painting that elevates, and of the duty of the painter — of the picture that is full of thought, and of the panel that merely decorates.

II

A favorite faith, dear to those who teach, is that certain periods were especially artistic, and that nations, readily named, were notably lovers of Art.

So we are told that the Greeks were, as a people, worshipers of the beautiful, and that in the fifteenth century Art was engrained in the multitude.

That the great masters lived in common understanding with their patrons — that the early Italians were artists — all — and that the demand for the lovely thing produced it.

That we of today, in gross contrast with this Arcadian purity, call for the ungainly, and obtain the ugly.

That, could we but change our habits and climate — were we willing to wander in groves — could we be roasted out of broadcloth — were we to do without haste, and journey without speed, we should again *require* the spoon of Queen Anne, and pick at our peas with the fork of two prongs. And so, for the flock, little hamlets grow near Hammersmith, and the steam horse is scorned.

Listen! There never was an artistic period.

There never was an Art-loving nation.

In the beginning, man went forth each day — some to do battle, some to the chase; others, again, to dig and to delve in the field — all that they might gain and live, or lose and die. Until there was found among them one, differing from the rest, whose pursuits attracted him not, and so he stayed by the tents with the women, and traced strange devices with a burnt stick upon a gourd.

This man, who took no joy in the ways of his brethren — who cared not for conquest, and fretted in the field — this designer of quaint patterns — this deviser of the beautiful — who perceived in nature about him curious carvings, as faces are seen in the fire — this dreamer apart, was the true artist.

And when, from the field and from afar, there came back the people, they took the gourd — and drank from out of it.

And presently there came to this man another — and, in time, others — of like nature, chosen by the Gods — and so they worked together; and soon they fashioned, from the moistened earth, forms resembling the gourd. And with the power of creation, the heirloom of the artist, presently they went beyond the slovenly suggestion of Nature, and the first vase was born, in beautiful proportions.

And the toilers tilled, and were athirst; and the heroes returned from fresh victories, to rejoice and to feast; and all drank alike from the artists' goblets, fashioned cunningly, taking no note the while of the craftsman's pride, and understanding not his glory in his work; drinking from the cup, not from choice, not from a consciousness that it was beautiful, but because, forsooth, there was none other!

And time, with more state, brought more capacity for luxury, and it became well that men should dwell in large houses, and rest upon couches, and eat at tables; whereupon the artist, with his artificers, built palaces, and filled them with furniture, beautiful in proportion and lovely to look upon.

And the people lived in marvels of art — and ate and drank out of masterpieces — for there was nothing else to eat and drink out of, and no bad building to live in; no article of daily life, or luxury, or of necessity, that had not been handed down from the design of the master, and made by his workmen.

And the people questioned not, *and had nothing to say in the matter*.

So Greece was in its splendor, and Art reigned supreme — by force of fact, not of election — and there was no meddling from the outsider. The mighty warrior would no more have ventured to offer a design for the temple of Pallas Athene than would the sacred poet have proffered a plan for constructing the catapult.

And the Amateur was unknown — and the Dilettante undreamed of!

And history wrote on, and conquest accompanied civilization, and Art spread, or rather its products were carried by the victors among the vanquished from one country to another. And the customs of cultivation covered the earth, so that all peoples continued to use *what the artist alone produced*.

And centuries passed in this using, and the world was flooded with all that was beautiful, until there arose a new class, who discovered the cheap, and foresaw fortune in the facture of the sham.

Then sprang into existence the common, the tawdry, the gewgaw.

The taste of the tradesman supplanted the science of the artist, and what was born of the million went back to them, and charmed them, for it was after their own heart; and the great and the small, the statesman and the slave, took to themselves the abomination that was tendered, and preferred it — and have lived with it ever since!

And the artist's occupation was gone, and the manufacturer and the huckster took his place.

And now the heroes filled from the jugs and drank from the bowls — with understanding — noting the glare of their new bravery, and taking pride in its worth.

And the people — this time — had much to say in the matter — and all were satisfied. And Birmingham and Manchester arose in their might — and Art was relegated to the curiosity shop.

III

Nature contains the elements, in color and form, of all pictures, as the keyboard contains the notes of all music.

But the artist is born to pick, and choose, and group with science, these elements, that the result may be beautiful — as the musician gathers his notes, and forms his chords, until he brings forth from chaos glorious harmony.

To say to the painter, that Nature is to be taken as she is, is to say to the player, that he may sit on the piano.

That Nature is always right is an assertion artistically as untrue as it is one whose truth is universally taken for granted. Nature is very rarely right, to such an extent even, that it might almost be said that Nature is usually wrong: that is to say, the condition of things that shall bring about the perfection of harmony worthy a picture is rare, and not common at all.

This would seem, to even the most intelligent, a doctrine almost blasphemous. So incorporated with our education has the supposed aphorism become, that its belief is held to be part of our moral being, and the words themselves have, in our ear, the ring of religion. Still, seldom does Nature succeed in producing a picture.

The sun blares, the wind blows from the east, the sky is bereft of cloud, and without, all is of iron. The windows of the Crystal Palace are seen from all points of London. The holiday-maker rejoices in the glorious day, and the painter turns aside to shut his eyes.

How little this is understood, and how dutifully the casual in nature is accepted as sublime, may be gathered from the unlimited admiration daily produced by a very foolish sunset.

The dignity of the snow-capped mountain is lost in distinctness, but the joy of the tourist is to recognize the traveler on the top. The desire to see, for the sake of seeing, is, with the mass, alone the one to be gratified, hence the delight in detail.

And when the evening mist clothes the riverside with poetry, as with a veil, and the poor buildings lose themselves in the dim sky, and the tall chimneys become campanili, and the warehouses are palaces in the night, and the whole city hangs in the heavens, and fairyland is before us — then the wayfarer hastens home; the working man and the cultured one, the wise man and the one of pleasure, cease to understand, as they have ceased to see, and Nature, who, for once, has sung in tune, sings her exquisite song to the artist alone, her son and her master — her son in that he loves her, her master in that he knows her.

To him her secrets are unfolded, to him her lessons have become gradually clear. He looks at her flower, not with the enlarging lens, that he may gather facts for the botanist, but with the light of the one who sees, in her choice selection of brilliant tones and delicate hints, suggestions of future harmonies.

He does not confine himself to purposeless copying, without thought, each blade of grass, as commended by the inconsequent, but, in the long curve of the narrow leaf, corrected by the straight tall stem, he learns how grace is wedded to dignity, how strength enhances sweetness, that elegance shall be the result.

In the citron wing of the pale butterfly, with its dainty spots of orange, he sees before him the stately halls of fair gold, with their slender saffron pillars, and is taught how the delicate drawing high upon the walls shall be traced in slender tones of orpiment, and repeated by the base in notes of graver hue.

In all that is dainty and lovable he finds hints for his own combinations, and *thus* is Nature ever his resource and always at his service, and to him is naught refused.

Through his brain, as through the last alembic, is distilled the refined essence of that thought which began with the Gods, and which they left him to carry out.

Set apart by them to complete their works, he produces that wondrous thing called the masterpiece, which surpasses in perfection all that they have contrived in what is called Nature; and the Gods stand by and marvel, and perceive how far away more beautiful is the Venus of Melos than was their own Eve.

THE IMPRESSIONISTS[1]

Morris Davidson

At the time the illustrious Manet was shocking and defying the critics and the bourgeois with his daring pictures, Europe was thrilling to the discoveries of science. France, as the newspapers might have expressed it, was becoming "science conscious." Pasteur and his pupil, Metchnikoff, were holding the interest of the public. It was only a few years before Edison was to startle the Paris Exposition with his phonograph, and the whole world with his incandescent lamp. Literature, as we have seen, followed along, led by Zola, Flaubert, the Goncourt brothers, and others less distinguished. Music was experimenting with new combinations and harmonies, the innovations of the German, Wagner, serving to goad young composers to cold laboratory research in sounds. It remained only for painting to enlist under the banner of the scientists.

Courbet, alone among the painters of his time, had foreseen the new trend a generation earlier. Young painters now turned back to his work. There was nothing in it as dazzling as Manet's virtuosity, but its point of view was in keeping with the new objectivity. The question was: Could painters go beyond Courbet in scientific approach? Would they have to examine nature through microscopes as Zola was doing in his writings? The musicians indicated a different direction. They dealt with new combinations of notes. Why not new combinations of color? Color was the unexplored field. The Englishman Turner had left the world amazing watercolor sketches of a brilliance and light and intensity unmatched in the history of painting. Who knew what secrets color would yield if approached scientifically? Young painters began a laboratory investigation of color.

They discovered certain truths. For example, shadow or darkness was not the absence of light, outdoors, but only a different-colored light. If the sun shone on a dirt road the road appeared yellow. If a house or tree threw a shadow across the road, the shadow was not brown nor an indiscriminate dark, but was just as light as the yellow sunlight; only it was the opposite color, violet.

[1] From *Understanding Modern Art*, by Morris Davidson. Reprinted by permission of Coward-McCann, Inc.

Again they discovered that there was no such thing as color *be-longing* to an object, or *local* color. A table was not gray or brown. The light reflected on the table made it appear gray or brown. Optical science taught that the light reflects upon the retina of the eye, the human lens, and causes a particular color to appear, depending upon the number or frequency of vibrations. We see things red, green, or yellow not because there are such colors, but because the eye receives certain vibrations. These in turn depend upon the quality of the light which surfaces reflect.

If we walk up to a tree it appears green. If we stand off from the tree and half close our eyes to shut out distracting detail, we see the sunlit foliage yellow and the shadows a brilliant blue. The light reflected by the leaves gives them their color.

Constable revealed the charm and reality of atmosphere. He showed that the condition of the air and the time of day altered the color of objects. The scientific painters seized upon this theory also. So that between reflected light and atmosphere, local color was thrown over as an illusion and deception.

But these are not all of the discoveries. Outline was shown not to exist in nature. It was an artifice that indicated where two masses, each of different color, came together. If the color matched nature accurately, why have outline? And as for the masses of color they only appear red or yellow or green, because they reflect with greater or less frequency, as has been said. In reality all masses of color, except the pure or primary colors, red, yellow, and blue, are composed of all the colors in the rainbow; gray consists of spots of every color as does brown. The difference in their appearance is the result only of the proportionate number of color atoms. For example, green appears green because there are more blue and yellow spots apparent in it than any other spots. If all spots were present in an equal pro-portion we should have the white light of the prism. When we mix our pigments equally, however, we do not attain this white light be-cause the body of the pigment deadens the color, the luminosity. Instead we get brown. Any color *except* red, yellow, and blue, the Impressionists discovered, is composed of spots of red, yellow, and blue and any of their combinations.

The net result of all this scientific investigation was to make painters turn their backs on museums and art schools and devote their talents to catching upon canvas the fugitive accidents of nature. The way in which fleeting light affected the *surface* color was the object of their studies. Form was forgotten. Composition was reduced to the most simple arrangement. The scientist-painters devoted themselves entirely to watching the changes of nature.

Claude Monet was the leader of these innovators. He was an able artist besides being a hard-working one. He went out into a field and painted a haystack at nine o'clock, again at ten-thirty, and still again at twelve, in order to show how the little specks or atoms of color in the hay changed from hour to hour. It mattered little that his subject was a stack of hay. It could just as well have been a bale of spinach.

To the Salon in Paris of 1863, Monet sent a picture of a sunset. In that year the authorities were generous enough to hang in one gallery all the rejected pictures, and the sunset was one of them. The jokers and wags had a pleasurable time in this room at the expense of the unlucky artists. They stopped to examine the new color analysis in Monet's sunset and noted the title: Impression. From that time on, the name Impressionism was given to the work of the scientific colorists who painted all things in spots of pure color, or component elements of a color.

The word "Impressionist" was really a misnomer. Manet with his dashing portraits and nudes was more an impressionist than any of these colorists. The famous Sargent, who could make one stroke take the place of nine, was certainly so. Whistler's nocturnes were the very essence of impressionism. But none of these painters are today included among the Impressionists. The industrious, meticulous color-analyzers attempted to dissect nature by formula and actually permitted themselves no impressions at all. Yet a freak of fortune dubbed them all by that name.

The most astounding thing about the scientist-painters is that they attracted to their cold researches in color the most tender and poetic artists: lyricists and sentimentalists. The lacy sylvan dells of Corot were translated literally into the new color systems. Impressionism gradually swung into a dreamy pursuit of nuances, little changes in harmonies of color; this effeminacy was reflected in the poetry of the period, and even more in the music. We have only to listen to a composition of Debussy to be aware of the whole movement of the Impressionists toward odd little harmonies, exquisitely sweet, but devoid of any classical construction. . . .

The names of two other Impressionists are generally linked with Monet. Camille Pissaro, a Portuguese Jew, was the real theorist of the group. While his own pictures have not the intensity achieved by Monet, his range is wider. He was by nature the true impressionist, in the sense that Manet was. A quick dab of color suggested life

and movement to him.   By means of variegated spots he was able
to catch the illusion of moving crowds, the bustle of a Paris street.
The very lack of definition created a rapidity of movement that literal
painting could never attain.

The Englishman Sisley was the third eminent member of the group.
His work betrays his racial origin.   The lyrical attitude becomes at
times cloyingly sweet, but there is no denying the delicacy of nuance
and the fascination of his sensitive brushwork.   In his landscapes
surface prettiness is stressed out of all proportion to the art qualities.
To him can be attributed the English and American tendencies in
academic landscape painting.

Monet, Pissaro, and Sisley remain the distinguished triumvirate of
Impressionism.   In spite of the fact that the new theories and formulas tended to make painting foolproof — "any child can work it" —
these are the only names written in the history of the movement.
It is true the Impressionists counted in their number the great master
Degas, but Degas was an aloof genius whose personal power was
greater than theories. . . .

We spoke before of the widespread interest in painting brought
about by the Impressionist formula.   What was this formula?   It
consisted mainly of two precepts, or more properly, recipes.   First,
everything was to be painted in pure colors; no browns, nor blacks,
nor grays were permissible since these colors were composed of atoms
of red, yellow, blue, violet, orange, and green.   Second, whatever was
touched by sunlight was yellow, while shadow was blue or violet.
A road was yellow in sunlight and blue in shadow.   A spot of red
judiciously placed tended to relieve a picture of its monotony.   To see
the practical application of this formula we have only to visit an
artists' colony in the summer and watch the hundreds of amateurs at
work.   The scene which meets their eye is translated into the terms
of their formula.   Thus art becomes in their hands a kind of domestic
science.   An enormous amount of concoctions have been created in
the name of Monet since his acceptance by official art circles. . . .
The whole democratic movement of the last thirty years toward
colors, meaningless, inane, but *pretty*, comes from Impressionism.

We must see, however, that Impressionism aided the development
of modern painting in two ways.   First, it contributed a scientific
understanding of color; and second, it disgusted, with its inanity,
those virile artists who required a personal method of expression.
These came to be called the Post-Impressionists.   They were as
hardy a lot of painters as has been seen since the Renaissance.

THE POST-IMPRESSIONISTS[1]

Eugen Neuhaus

EUGEN NEUHAUS was born at Barmen, Germany, in 1879, and educated at the Royal School for Applied Arts in Berlin. Coming to the United States in 1904, and settling in California, he devoted himself to painting. He quickly gained a reputation as a landscape painter, and has exhibited in Chicago, Philadelphia, and other large American cities. In 1915 he was chairman of the Western Advisory Committee of the Fine Arts Department of the San Francisco Exposition. At present he is professor and head of the department of art in the University of California. He has written *The Appreciation of Art* (1924) and numerous other books and articles on art.

If we begin with the Impressionists as a starting point of our inquiries, we may speak of "modern" tendencies as Post-Impressionism, a chronological term, coined in England by Mr. Roger Fry to describe what has been generally included in the terms Cubism, Futurism, and other isms, many of them short-lived, all evidences of the revolutionary trend in art.

The main argument of defenders of present-day modernism is that a new idea in art has always been greeted with hostility; the truth of this contention is beyond dispute, and it would be a waste of ink to argue that point. The experiences of Turner, of the Barbizon men, of Whistler, and of the Impressionists are sufficient evidence of this. But in these, which for their time were radical, "new" movements, the function of academic art as that of representing recognizable forms is maintained. This function is, on the contrary, disregarded in certain modernistic art expressions. The difference amounts to a clean break, and the position of the present-day modernist, in so far as he discards the representation of recognizable forms, is not comparable to that of the Impressionist, of the Realist. Every serious student of art will admit that the function of art is not the copying of nature. It will soon be a hundred years since it was very convincingly demonstrated that the camera can do this better than the artist; and still all art, if we except music, is to a degree imitative in that by comparison it reminds us of some fact perceived by the intellect. Now some of the moderns have cast the idea of objective representation to the winds, in the belief that by expressing their inner selves

[1] From *The History and Ideals of American Art*, by Eugen Neuhaus. Reprinted by permission of the author and Stanford University Press.

through abstract forms, unhampered by recognizable figures involving obligation to the church, the state, natural facts, anecdote, decoration, or what not, they can more forcibly give us an idea of their emotional life, which they consider of paramount interest to themselves and which they would like the public also to accept as of paramount importance.[1]

Thus to ignore the requirement of representation is unfortunately the habit of zealous defenders of abstract modern art, and for them to admit this requirement would mean the placing of these works outside the realm of art, in the generally accepted sense. To look, then, for recognizable forms in such works is a waste of time, because in every instance the idea involved can be clear only to its creator.

We quote Professor Oliver S. Tonks: "Under such circumstances it is fair to ask if such painting is art? If art is concerned with the transmission of an idea, of an emotion, it is self-evident that if the idea taken is so nebulous that it can be comprehended only by the artist himself, a picture so presenting the idea falls outside the realm of art."[2] We may call it graphic psychology, but it assuredly is not art in the heretofore accepted sense. The question may well be raised, then, whether the mediums of graphic art — drawing, painting, etching — may be used to express emotional qualities in abstract terms, or whether perhaps music or some new art may not be the better means of accomplishing this end. Many of the abstractions of the modernist artists are perfectly meaningless if we ignore their titles, which suggest realities, as in the case of the much discussed "Nude Descending the Stairs" by Marcel DuChamp. Nobody would recognize any reality in such works, although no aesthetically sensitive person would deny that the form combinations in them are interesting and stimulating.

Although we cannot "understand" them, we may "see" in such works many qualities in themselves desirable. They frequently possess architectural strength, a sense of plastic organization and of rhythmic motion; above all, stimulating patterns of form and color sequences, even when there is in the work no meaning that the intellect can grasp.

In so far, therefore, as the modernist recognizes representation as a necessary function of art, we observe in his creations not only a logical evolution from the immediately preceding movement but also a restatement of principles and qualities of plastic design centuries old

[1] This is Expressionism, as opposed to Impressionism.
[2] *The Arts*, Vol. VII, No. 4, April 1925.

but lost sight of through preoccupation with other, less significant ideals. Any observing person will quickly discover the great debt of the modern to the Byzantine and the Italian Primitives, whose work is devoid of the technical sophistication against which the modern so violently reacts. This modern "reaction," in its deliberate ignoring of technical cleverness and trickiness of the academic schools, has caused many objectors to modernism to feel that in certain circles a premium is put at present on technical incompetency and carelessness.

There is hardly a question today that the work of the Frenchman, Cézanne,[1] must be regarded as the starting point for Post-Impressionism; in fact, a rapidly growing group of intelligent and sincere art workers firmly believe that Cézanne ranks with the great innovators of all ages and that his name will acquire the same significance with respect to the art of his time as those of Giotto, Michelangelo, Titian, Velasquez, El Greco, Rembrandt, Whistler, and Monet to their respective civilizations. Cézanne's name today at any rate appears firmly established as the father of an influence which has opened new avenues of approach, enabling the artist to avoid the discouragement of following outworn formulas which at best would make of him an honest but meaningless plagiarist.

Undeniably this new influence has been in some instances exploited beyond the point of a reasonable interpretation of Cézanne's original aims, and in other cases it has been mildly and innocuously incorporated in the work of the academic traditionalists in the hope of lifting their work out of the commonplace into new and significant terms. Cézanne's art is the natural evolution from Impressionism, in which technique completely destroyed form in the academic sense, giving it a special meaning adapted to the representation of light and atmosphere. In Cézanne's work, form becomes less and less imitative but more subordinated to the requirements of plastic "design," not of the Whistlerian type acquired from the study of Japanese prints but the three-dimensional, plastic quality that we may observe in Chinese paintings and the Italian Primitives. His rhythms of form expressed in terms of geometric planes as we see them in his still-lifes, landscapes, and portraits are to the person of aesthetic sensibilities a source of the greatest pleasure. Cézanne's concepts have stimulated a fresh study and reëvaluation of every artist of the past in which these important qualities may be recognized.

El Greco suddenly has thus been rediscovered as a beacon light of modernism shining brightly over a sea of thoughtless traditionalism.

[1] First introduced to an American public in New York in 1910.

He is enthroned alongside the Italian Primitives as a great modern, and the plastic quality of his form combined with his extraordinary independence and originality in the matter of color have lifted him to the very highest pinnacle of fame and have caused a Greco vogue almost equal to that of Cézanne.

It was inevitable and logical that the rendering of forms into geometric terms in Cézanne's art should lead equally to a complete abandonment of natural form in favor of geometrical plastic abstraction. Pablo Picasso, a Spaniard from Malaga, who was early transplanted in Paris, is commonly accepted as the author of this development, which became known as Cubism. In Cubism this rendering of form and color into geometric three-dimensional expression has been carried into all the plastic arts — architecture, sculpture, painting, and the moving picture. In architecture and sculpture it has achieved new and striking values, particularly in the construction of skyscrapers, where the principle can be easily and pleasantly recognized even by the most rabid reactionary. There is no doubt that Cubism in painting, within the limits of representation, has enormously stimulated an understanding and a recasting of plastic form, and its value to modern art will be acknowledged by generations to come. The fanatical exploitation of this idea of abstraction could not but lead to a complete rejection of every traditional philosophy and method, and the appearance of Futurism, while hardly an evolution from Cubism, is in no sense illogical. Promulgated by an Italian writer named Marinetti in 1910, it was as short-lived as it was radical.

Futurism quickly collapsed because it carried the slogan "Away from nature" into "Away from everything." As we have seen, everything new has come out of something of the past; the new always has built, even though lightly, upon the past. Futurism as a complete negation of every tradition had no relation to the past. As a bold attempt to start anew with a complete rejection of the heritage of the past, it represents a singular phenomenon in the history of art. We may not question the honesty of the leaders of this movement, any more than we may question the honesty of their followers, who, in many instances, had a solid academic basis upon which to build their new departures. That there are those who have seized upon these new ideas as an easy means toward cheap and sensational successes is also apparent. The precarious position of the modern thus has been made doubly difficult.

Aside from Cézanne and Picasso, Matisse appears to have affected modern art everywhere. The chief aim of Futurism to resolve forms into terms of dynamic movement, as opposed to the static mathematical formula of Cubism, appears in Matisse's work as highly simplified rhythmical exaltations of form and color. Another French modernist, Gauguin, shook the dust of civilization off his feet and invaded the tropics to escape modern life and to achieve simple combinations of form and color in highly decorative terms. The study of the exotic since his day has become the fashion in many quarters, and artists have turned to the study of exotic art forms to remote corners of the world, in the hope of discovering new formulas as well as discovering themselves. In these modern departures simplification and abstraction of design are indicated as a means toward the expression of subjective emotion, and a deliberate neglect of the realities in an objective sense is apparent.

A reaction which aims at a new objectivity combining plastic form with intense realism has already made its appearance. It is not a return to the empty mechanical surface truth of the camera reflected in generations of uninspired academicians, but is an intensely realistic and convincingly plastic expression of natural symbols in which the inner meaning of the subject is brought out in terms of strongly rhythmical forms, forms which appear as modifications of the Cubistic idea plus the feeling for dynamic force exploited by Futurism. Representation once more triumphs. The abstractionist apparently has had his day, and the age-old experience based upon the law of change is causing a revival of objective form which has a genuine quality of plastic expression. The man in the street who likes pictures is again happy to find that here are ones which both he and the sophisticated critic like, that over them they may cease making faces at each other.

THE FUTURE OF AMERICAN ART[1]

Eugen Neuhaus[2]

While it is thus quite evident that America has been very productive of art, we may ask ourselves whether she had developed an art of her own, an art characteristically American, possessed of a national flavor, like that of Italy, Spain, or some other of the older European countries. It is clear that before a country can be said to have produced an art of its own its artists must show a national strain in their work. Such a strain until very recently has been the exception rather than the rule in American art. Particularly in the past the number of foreign-born artists in America has been very large, and even in recent times many of the native-born artists have but one generation of native ancestry behind them. Moreover, we are a heterogeneous people. For these reasons the doubt of a definite national quality in our art appears well-grounded.

It is quite obvious that our art has not traditions of centuries of patient toil and struggle, traditions of its own. On the contrary, an obvious indebtedness to foreign sources and ideals in both subject matter and technical knowledge will be at once discovered by the student of history of American art. He may ask not only the question, "Is there really an American art?" but also "What of the future of art in America?"

If we bear in mind the peculiar quality of our national structure and its history, its political and social traditions, and the various racial qualities of our population, we may question whether the usual comparison with individual European countries is applicable or fair. Politically, unless we except a brief period during the Civil War, we are very different from Europe, united and unified as we are by adherence to a Constitution which has little of European ideals in it; we all feel responsive to a common cause and a common authority. In the racial characteristics of our population and the regional diversity of scenery and climate we are, on the other hand, comparable to the whole of Europe rather than to an individual national unit. Today the peculiar national flavor that once characterized the art of Raphael, of

[1] From *The History and Ideals of American Art*, by Eugen Neuhaus. Reprinted by permission of the author and Stanford University Press.

[2] For biographical note, see page 639.

Da Vinci, of Velasquez, or of Rembrandt is no longer typical, in the same sense, of the leaders of modern European art. The art of modern Europe has become modified by the modern intercommunication of ideas. Art everywhere today, not only in America, has a marked tendency toward cosmopolitanism. It is true that in a manner this has always been so; Greece in part drew its inspiration from the Orient, Italy its in turn from the Greeks. The whole of Europe acknowledges its indebtedness to Italian culture. In modern times all have followed the road that led to the fountainheads of knowledge and inspiration — to Athens, Rome, Madrid, and Paris. Art exhibitions of today, whether in Vienna, London, Rome, or Berlin, are proof that the genuineness of art is not affected by more or less arbitrary political boundaries. For many reasons, no doubt, as the world grows older this process becomes accelerated. America, a modern nation, has fortunately been able to profit more from this than any other country. Though a giant in size, yet a fledgling among older nations, it could take advantage of the accumulated achievement of older nations nurtured in art. That it has shown great adaptability and intelligence in doing so nobody will deny.

American art in its variety is a true reflection of the variety of its population and the traditions they have brought to bear upon it. Moreover, it is becoming increasingly true of those of our artists we may truly call American that they are showing a peculiar responsiveness to their own environment, whether they have been placed there by accident or by choice, and that they have the courage of their convictions in telling us about it in unadulterated terms. No more typical and lasting art has come out of tradition than has come out of the individuality of our truly American artists such as Homer, Bellows, and Kent. Every artist drifts: he wanders, he exposes himself to all that life offers, until eventually he becomes a part of that particular environment which offers the peculiar combination of form and color and ideas that best serves his vision of that world we call art.

That there have been and are today in America many who are merely satisfied to show skill or cleverness after the formulas of others is quite evident, but no matter how pleasing or pretty their works may be they are not art in the best sense. This type will always exist here, and everywhere, and we must not judge American art by it. Undoubtedly America with its highly diversified regional characteristics in natural environment and industrial activity offers the finest materials for a real American art, an art which is going to absorb the best energies and gifts of our talented men and women. In the degree in which the public will strengthen their faith in their own institutions and will believe in the beauty of their own environment we shall have a truly independent American art. An intelligent and truly patriotic public is as much a factor in the development of an American art as is the artist, whose strength must come from the encouragement given to him by his society as well as from his artistic conviction.

There are voices, and they are gaining in strength, which predict for American art a great future comparable in scope and splendor to the revival of art in Europe during the fifteenth century. Many of the basic conditions which were responsible for the Renaissance in Italy we undoubtedly possess: wealth, power, confidence, energy, enthusiasm, and native talent. We may indeed confidently look forward to America's achieving an art which will truly reflect American life and American institutions. The argument that we are too young is growing less and less valid with the progress of time. American art will develop its finest flower only if it looks forward and learns to trust, to follow, its own impulses, its own vision.

The language of its expression, the language of form and color, American art has in common with Europe and the world at large. It is a language understood anywhere; it is universal.

THE ORIGIN OF MUSIC[1]

Edward A. MacDowell

EDWARD ALEXANDER MACDOWELL was born in New York City in 1861, the son of a prosperous business man of Scottish blood and artistic tastes. Reared in an atmosphere of culture, he had a thorough musical training, first under Spanish-American teachers in New York, then in Paris (where Debussy was a fellow student), and finally in Germany, where in 1882 he called upon Franz Liszt with the manuscript of his first concerto. Liszt encouraged him with characteristic generosity, and MacDowell shortly realized that his gifts were not as a pianist — as he had theretofore supposed — but as a composer. For the next half-dozen years, until 1888, he spent most of his time in Germany, composing some of his finest works in a small cottage near Wiesbaden. On his return to America he took up residence in Boston, where he composed, taught, and gave numerous performances and recitals. By 1895 his more important compositions frequently found a place in the programs of American and European orchestras. The one important misstep of his life was his acceptance in 1896 of the professorship of music in Columbia University. Here he accomplished a great deal. He attracted large though badly prepared classes; he organized an excellent orchestra and held departmental concerts; and he even composed a half-dozen Columbia Songs in an effort to improve undergraduate music. But the university was not yet ready to regard music as a regular part of its curriculum on the terms which MacDowell desired, and gave no academic credit for music courses. Still larger plans were also defeated. "I proposed," MacDowell wrote later, "that music be taken out of the faculty of philosophy, and architecture out of the school of mines, and with belles lettres form a faculty of fine arts, to complete which painting and sculpture would be indispensable. Owing to my inability to persuade rich men of New York into endowing a chair of painting and sculpture, the scheme, though approved by the powers that be, was not realized." In 1905 he resigned. Next year his health began to break, and mental collapse was followed in 1908 by death. His fine musical gift was essentially lyrical, and though he wrote admirable songs, sonatas, and concertos he never attempted opera. His published volume of *Critical and Historical Essays* (1912), made up of lectures at Columbia, expounds his belief that art progresses best by the development of national and racial impulses.

Darwin's theory that music had its origin "in the sounds made by the half-human progenitors of man during the season of courtship" seems for many reasons to be inadequate and untenable. A much more plausible explanation, it seems to me, is to be found in the theory of Theophrastus, in which the origin of music is attributed to the whole range of human emotion.

[1] From *Critical and Historical Essays*, by Edward A. MacDowell. Reprinted by permission of Mrs. Edward A. MacDowell and Arthur P. Schmidt Company, publishers.

When an animal utters a cry of joy or pain it expresses its emotions in more or less definite tones; and at some remote period of the earth's history all primeval mankind must have expressed its emotions in much the same manner. When this inarticulate speech developed into the use of certain sounds as symbols for emotions — emotions that otherwise would have been expressed by the natural sounds occasioned by them — then we have the beginnings of speech as distinguished from music, which is still the universal language. In other words, intellectual development begins with articulate speech, leaving music for the expression of the emotions.

To symbolize the sounds used to express emotion, if I may so put it, is to weaken that expression, and it would naturally be the strongest emotion that would first feel the inadequacy of the new-found speech. Now what is mankind's strongest emotion? Even in the nineteenth century Goethe could say, "'Tis fear that constitutes the godlike in man." Certainly before the Christian era the soul of mankind had its roots in fear. In our superstition we were like children beneath a great tree of which the upper part was as a vague and fascinating mystery, but the roots holding it firmly to the gound were tangible, palpable facts. We feared — we knew not what. Love was human, all the other emotions were human; fear alone was indefinable.

The primeval savage, looking at the world subjectively, was merely part of it. He might love, hate, threaten, kill, if he willed; every other creature could do the same. But the wind was a great spirit to him; lightning and thunder threatened him as they did the rest of the world; the flood would destroy him as ruthlessly as it tore the trees asunder. The elements were animate powers that had nothing in common with him; for what the intellect cannot explain the imagination magnifies.

Fear, then, was the strongest emotion. Therefore auxiliary aids to express and cause fear were necessary when the speech symbols for fear, drifting further and further away from expressing the actual thing, became words, and words were inadequate to express and cause fear. In that vague groping for sound symbols which would cause and express fear far better than mere words, we have the beginning of what is gradually to develop into music.

We all know that savage nations accompany their dances by striking one object with another, sometimes by a clanking of stones, the pounding of wood, or perhaps the clashing of stone spearheads against wooden shields (a custom which extended until the time when shields and spears were discarded), meaning thus to express something that words cannot. This meaning changed naturally from its original one of being the simple expression of fear to that of welcoming a chieftain; and, if one wishes to push the theory to excess, we may still see a shadowy reminiscence of it in the manner in which the violinists of an orchestra applaud an honored guest — perchance some famous virtuoso — at one of our symphony concerts by striking the backs of their violins with their bows.

To go back to the savages. While this clashing of one object against another could not be called the beginning of music, and while it could not be said to originate a musical instrument, it did, nevertheless, bring into existence music's greatest prop, rhythm, an ally without which music would seem to be impossible. It is hardly necessary to go into this point in detail. Suffice it to say that the sense of rhythm is highly developed even among those savage tribes which stand the lowest in the scale of civilization today — for instance, the Andaman Islanders, of whom I shall speak later; the same may be said of the Tierra del Fuegians and the now extinct aborigines of Tasmania; it is the same with the Semangs of the Malay Peninsula, the Ajitas of the Philippines, and the savages inhabiting the interior of Borneo.

As I have said, this more or less rhythmic clanking of stones together, the striking of wooden paddles against the side of a canoe, or the clashing of stone spearheads against wooden shields, could not constitute the first musical instrument. But when some savage first struck a hollow tree and found that it gave forth a sound peculiar to itself, when he found a hollow log and filled up the open ends, first with wood, and then — possibly getting the idea from his hide-covered shield — stretched skins across the two open ends, then he had completed the first musical instrument known to man: namely, the drum. And such as it was then, so is it now, with but few modifications.

Up to this point it is reasonable to assume that primeval man looked upon the world purely subjectively. He considered himself merely a unit in the world, and felt on a plane with the other creatures inhabiting it. But from the moment he had invented the first musical instrument, the drum, he had created something outside of nature, a voice that to himself and to all other living creatures was intangible, an idol that spoke when it was touched, something that he could call into life, something that shared the supernatural in common with the elements. A God had come to live with man, and thus was unfolded the first leaf in that noble tree of life which we call religion. Man now began to feel himself something apart from the world, and to look at it objectively instead of subjectively.

To treat primitive mankind as a type, to put it under one head, to make one theorem cover all mankind, as it were, seems almost an unwarranted boldness. But I think it is warranted when we consider that, aside from language, music is the very first sign of the dawn of civilization. There is even the most convincingly direct testimony in its favor. For instance:

In the Bay of Bengal, about six hundred miles from the Hoogly mouth of the Ganges, lie the Andaman Islands. The savages inhabiting these islands have the unenviable reputation of being, in common with several other tribes, the nearest approach to primeval man in existence. These islands and their inhabitants have been known and feared since time immemorial; our old friend Sinbad the Sailor, of *Arabian Nights* fame, undoubtedly touched there on one of his voyages. These savages have no religion whatever, except the vaguest superstition — in other words, fear; and they have no musical instruments of any kind. They have reached only the rhythm stage, and accompany such dances as they have by clapping their hands or by stamping on the ground. Let us now look to Patagonia, some thousands of miles distant. The Tierra del Fuegians have precisely the same characteristics, no religion, and no musical instruments of any kind. Retracing our steps to the Antipodes we find among the Weddahs or "wild hunters" of Ceylon exactly the same state of things. The same description applies without distinction equally well to the natives in the interior of Borneo, to the Semangs of the Malay Peninsula, and to the now extinct aborigines of Tasmania. According to Virchow their dance is demon-worship of a purely anthropomorphic character; no musical instrument of any kind was known to them. Even the simple expression of emotions by the voice, which we have seen is its most primitive medium, has not been replaced to any extent among these races since their discovery of speech, for the Tierra del Fuegians, Andamans, and Weddahs have but one sound to represent emotion: namely, a cry to express joy; having no other means for the expression of sorrow, they paint themselves when mourning.

It is granted that all this, in itself, is not conclusive; but it will be found that no matter in what wilderness one may hear of a savage beating a drum, there also will be a well-defined religion.

Proofs of the theory that the drum antedates all other musical instruments are to be found on every hand. For wherever in the anthropological history of the world we hear of the trumpet, horn, flute, or other instrument of the pipe species, it will be found that the drum and its derivatives were already well known. The same may be said of the lyre species of instrument, the forerunner of our guitar (kithara), tebuni, or Egyptian harp, and generally all stringed instruments, with this difference: namely, that wherever the lyre species was known, both pipe and drum had preceded it. We never find the lyre without the drum, or the pipe without the drum; neither do we find the lyre and the drum without the pipe. On the other hand, we often find the drum alone, or the drum and pipe without the lyre. This certainly proves the antiquity of the drum and its derivatives.

I have spoken of the purely rhythmical nature of the pre-drum period, and pointed out, in contrast, the musical quality of the drum. This may seem somewhat strange, accustomed as we are to think of the drum as a purely rhythmical instrument. The sounds given out by it seem at best vague in tone and more or less uniform in quality. We forget that all instruments of percussion, as they are called, are direct descendants of the drum. The bells that hang in our church towers are but modifications of the drum; for what is a bell but a metal drum with one end left open and the drum stick hung inside?

Strange to say, as showing the marvelous potency of primeval instincts, bells placed in church towers were supposed to have much of the supernatural power that the savage in his wilderness ascribed to the drum. We all know something of the bell legends of the Middle Ages, how the tolling of a bell was supposed to clear the air of the plague, to calm the storm, and to shed a blessing on all who heard it. And this superstition was to a certain extent ratified by the religious ceremonies attending the casting of church bells and the inscriptions molded in them. For instance, the midday bell of Strasburg, taken down during the French Revolution, bore the motto:

> I am the voice of life.

Another one in Strasburg:

> I ring out the bad, ring in the good.

Others read:

> My voice on high dispels the storm.

> I am called Ave Maria
> I drive away storms.

I who call to thee am the Rose of the World and am called Ave Maria.

The Egyptian sistrum, which in Roman times played an important rôle in the worship of Isis, was shaped somewhat like a tennis racquet, with four wire strings on which rattles were strung. The sound of it must have been akin to that of our modern tambourine, and it served much the same purpose as the primitive drum: namely, to drive away Typhon or Set, the god of evil. Dead kings were called "Osiris" when placed in their tombs, and sistri put with them in order to drive away Set.

Beside bells and rattles we must include all instruments of the tambourine and gong species in the drum category. While there are many different forms of the same instrument, there are evidences of their all having at some time served the same purpose, even down to that strange instrument about which Du Chaillu tells us in his *Equatorial Africa*, a bell of leopard skin, with a clapper of fur, which was rung by the wizard doctor when entering a hut where someone was ill or dying. The leopard skin and fur clapper seem to have been devised to make no noise, so as not to anger the demon that was to be cast out. This reminds us strangely of the custom of ringing a bell as the priest goes to administer the last rites.

It is said that first impressions are the strongest and most lasting; certain it is that humanity, through all its social and racial evolutions, has retained remnants of certain primitive ideas to the present day. The army death reveille, the minute gun, the tolling of bells for the dead, the tocsin, etc., all have their roots in the attributes assigned to the primitive drum; for, as I have already pointed out, the more civilized a people becomes, the more the word-symbols degenerate. It is this continual drifting away of the word-symbols from the natural sounds which are occasioned by emotions that creates the necessity for auxiliary means of expression, and thus gives us instrumental music.

Since the advent of the drum a great stride toward civilization had been made. Mankind no longer lived in caves but built huts and even temples, and the conditions under which he lived must have been similar to those of the natives of Central Africa before travelers opened up the Dark Continent to the caravan of the European trader. If we look up the subject in the narratives of Livingstone or Stanley we find that these people lived in groups of coarsely thatched huts, the village being almost invariably surrounded by a kind of stockade. Now this manner of living is identically the same as that of all savage tribes which have not passed beyond the drum state of civilization: namely, a few huts huddled together and surrounded by a palisade of bamboo or cane. Since the pith would decompose in a short time, we should probably find that the wind, whirling across such a palisade of pipes — for that is what our bamboos would have turned to — would produce musical sounds, in fact, exactly the sounds that a large set of Pan's pipes would produce. For after all, what we call Pan's pipes are simply pieces of bamboo or cane of different lengths tied together and made to sound by blowing across the open tops.

The theory may be objected to on the ground that it scarcely proves the antiquity of the pipe to be less than that of the drum; but the objection is hardly of importance when we consider that the drum was known long before mankind had reached the "hut" stage of civilization. Under the head of pipe, the trumpet and all its derivatives must be accepted. On this point there has been much controversy. But it seems reasonable to believe that once it was found that sound could be produced by blowing across the top of a hollow pipe, the most natural thing to do would be to try the same effect on all hollow things differing in shape and material from the original bamboo. This would account for the conch shells of the Amazons which, according to travelers' tales, were used to proclaim an attack in war; in Africa the tusks of elephants were used; in North America the instrument did not rise above the whistle made from the small bones of a deer or of a turkey's leg.

That the Pan's pipes are the originals of all these species seems hardly open to doubt. Even among the Greeks and Romans we see traces of them in the double trumpet and the double pipe. These trumpets became larger and larger in form, and the force required to play them was such that the player had to adopt a kind of leather harness to strengthen his cheeks. Before this development had been reached, however, I have no doubt that all wind instruments were of the Pan's pipes variety; that is to say, the instruments consisted of a hollow tube shut at one end, the sound being produced by the breath catching on the open edge of the tube.

Direct blowing into the tube doubtless came later. In this case the tube was open at both ends, and the sound was determined by its length and by the force given to the breath in playing. There is good reason for admitting this new instrument to be a descendant of the Pan's pipes, for it was evidently played by the nose at first. This would preclude its being considered as an originally forcible instrument, such as the trumpet.

Now that we have traced the history of the pipe and considered the different types of the instrument, we can see immediately that it brought no great new truth home to man as did the drum.

The savage who first climbed secretly to the top of the stockade around his village to investigate the cause of the mysterious sounds would naturally say that the Great Spirit had revealed a mystery to him; and he would also claim to be a wonder-worker. But while his pipe would be accepted to a certain degree, it was nevertheless second in the field and could hardly replace the drum. Besides, mankind had already commenced to think on a higher plane, and the pipe was reduced to filling what gaps it could in the language of the emotions.

The second strongest emotion of the race is love. All over the world, wherever we find the pipe in its softer, earlier form, we find it connected with love songs. In time it degenerated into a synonym for something contemptibly slothful and worthless, so much so that Plato wished to banish it from his "Republic," saying that the Lydian pipe should not have a place in a decent community.

On the other hand, the trumpet branch of the family developed into something quite different. At the very beginning it was used for war, and as its object was to frighten, it became larger and larger in form, and more formidable in sound. In this respect it only kept pace with the drum, for we read of Assyrian and Thibetan trumpets two or three yards long, and of the Aztec war drum which reached the enormous height of ten feet, and could be heard for miles.

Now this, the trumpet species of pipe, we find also used as an auxiliary "spiritual" help to the drum. We are told by M. Huc, in his *Travels in Thibet*, that the llamas of Thibet have a custom of assembling on the roofs of Lhassa at a stated period and blowing enormous trumpets, making the most hideous midnight din imaginable. The reason given for this was that in former days the city was terrorized by demons who rose from a deep ravine and crept through all the houses, working evil everywhere. After the priests had exorcised them by blowing these trumpets, the town was troubled no more. In Africa the same demonstration of trumpet-blowing occurs at an eclipse of the moon; and, to draw the theory out to a thin thread, anyone who has lived in a small German Protestant town will remember the chorals which are so often played before sunrise by a band of trumpets, horns, and trombones from the belfry of some church tower. Almost up to the end of the last century trombones were intimately connected with the church service; and if we look back to Zoroaster we find the sacerdotal character of this species of instrument very plainly indicated.

Now let us turn back to the Pan's pipes and its direct descendants, the flute, the clarinet, and the oboe. We shall find that they had no connection whatever with religious observances. Even in the nineteenth century novel we are familiar with the kind of hero who played the flute — a very sentimental gentleman always in love. If he had played the clarinet he would have been very sorrowful and discouraged; and if it had been the oboe (which, to the best of my knowledge, has never been attempted in fiction) he would have needed to be a very ill man indeed.

Now we never hear of these latter kinds of pipes being considered fit for anything but the dance, love songs, or love charms. In the beginning of the seventeenth century Garcilaso de la Vega, the historian of Peru, tells of the astonishing power of a love song played on a flute. We find so-called "courting" flutes in Formosa and Peru, and Catlin tells of the Winnebago courting flute. The same instrument was known in Java, as the old Dutch settlers have told us. But we never hear of it as creating awe, or as being thought a fit instrument to use with the drum or trumpet in connection with religious rites. Leonardo da Vinci had a flute-player make music while he painted his picture of Mona Lisa, thinking that it gave her the expression he wished to catch — that strange smile reproduced in the Louvre painting. The flute member of the pipe species, therefore, was more or less an emblem of eroticism, and, as I have already said, has never been even remotely identified with religious mysticism, with perhaps the one exception of Indra's flute, which, however, never seems to have been able to retain a place among religious symbols. The trumpet, on the other hand, has retained something of a mystical character even to our day. The most powerful illustration of this known to me is in the *Requiem* by Berlioz. The effect of those tremendous trumpet calls from the four corners of the orchestra is an overwhelming one, of crushing power and majesty, much of which is due to the rhythm.

To sum up. We may regard rhythm as the intellectual side of music, melody as its sensuous side. The pipe is the one instrument that seems to affect animals — hooded cobras, lizards, fish, etc. Animals' natures are purely sensuous; therefore the pipe, or to put it more broadly, melody, affects them. To rhythm, on the other hand, they are indifferent; it appeals to the intellect, and therefore only to man.

This theory would certainly account for much of the potency of what we moderns call music. All that aims to be dramatic, tragic, supernatural in our modern music, derives its impressiveness directly from rhythm.[1] What would that shudder of horror in Weber's *Freischütz* be without that throb of the basses? Merely a diminished

[1] The strength of the "Fate" motive in Beethoven's fifth symphony undoubtedly lies in the succession of the four notes at equal intervals of time. Beethoven himself marked it *So pocht das Schicksal an die Pforte* ("Thus Fate knocks at the door").

chord of the seventh. Add the pizzicato in the basses and the chord sinks into something fearsome; one has a sudden choking sensation, as if one were listening in fear, or as if the heart had almost stopped beating. All through Wagner's music dramas this powerful effect is employed, from *The Flying Dutchman* to *Parsifal.* Every composer from Beethoven to Nicode has used the same means to express the same emotions; it is the medium that prehistoric man first knew; it produced the same sensation of fear in him that it does in us at the present day.

Rhythm denotes a thought; it is the expression of a purpose. There is will behind it; its vital part is intention, power; it is an act. Melody, on the other hand, is an almost unconscious expression of the senses; it translates feeling into sound. It is the natural outlet for sensation. In anger we raise the voice; in sadness we lower it. In talking we give expression to the emotions on sound. In a sentence in which fury alternates with sorrow, we have the limits of the melody of speech. Add to this rhythm, and the very height of expression is reached; for by it the intellect will dominate the sensuous.

SUGGESTION IN MUSIC[1]

Edward A. MacDowell[2]

In speaking of the power of suggestion in music I wish at the outset to make certain reservations. In the first place I speak for myself, and what I have to present is merely an expression of my personal opinion; if in any way these should incite to further investigation or discussion, my object will in part have been attained.

In the second place, in speaking of this art, one is seriously hampered by a certain difficulty in making oneself understood. To hear and to enjoy music seems sufficient to many persons, and an investigation as to the causes of this enjoyment seems to them superfluous. And yet, unless the public comes into closer touch with the tone poet than that objective state which accepts with the ears what is intended for the spirit, which hears the sounds and is deaf to their import, unless the public can separate the physical pleasure of music from its ideal significance, our art, in my opinion, cannot stand on a sound basis.

The first step toward an appreciation of music should be taken in our preparatory schools. Were young people taught to distinguish between tones as between colors, to recognize rhythmic values, and were they taught so to use their voices as to temper the nasal tones of speech, in after life they would be better able to appreciate and cherish an art of which mere pleasure-giving sounds are but a very small part.

Much of the lack of independence of opinion about music arises from want of familiarity with its material. Thus, after dinner, our forefathers were accustomed to sing catches which were entirely destitute of anything approaching music.

Music contains certain elements which affect the nerves of the mind and body, and thus possesses the power of direct appeal to the public — a power to a great extent denied to the other arts. This sensuous influence over the hearer is often mistaken for the aim and end of all music. With this in mind, one may forgive the rather puzzling remarks so often met with; for instance, those of a certain English bishop, that: "Music did not affect him either intellectually or emotionally, only pleasurably," adding, "Every art should keep within

[1] From *Critical and Historical Essays*, by Edward A. MacDowell. Reprinted by permission of Mrs. Edward A. MacDowell and Arthur P. Schmidt Company, publishers.

[2] For biographical note, see page 647.

its own realm; and that of music was concerned with pleasing combinations of sound." In declaring that the sensation of hearing music was pleasant to him, and that to produce that sensation was the entire mission of music, the bishop placed our art on a level with good things to eat and drink. Many colleges and universities of this land consider music as a kind of boutonnière.

This estimate of music is, I believe, unfortunately a very general one, and yet, low as it is, there is a possibility of building on such a foundation. Could such persons be made to recognize the existence of decidedly unpleasant music, it would be the first step toward a proper appreciation of the art and its various phases.

Mere beauty of sound is, in itself, purely sensuous. It is the Chinese conception of music that the texture of a sound is to be valued; the long, trembling tone-tint of a bronze gong, or the high, thin streams of sound from the pipes are enjoyed for their ear-filling qualities. In the Analects of Confucius and the writings of Mencius there is much mention of music, and "harmony of sound that shall fill the ears" is insisted upon. The Master said, "When the music maker Che first entered on his office, the finish with the Kwan Ts'eu was magnificent. How it filled the ears!" Père Amiot says, "Music must fill the ears to penetrate the soul." Referring to the playing of some pieces by Couperin on a spinet, he says that Chinese hearers thought these pieces barbarous; the movement was too rapid, and did not allow sufficient time for them to enjoy each tone by itself. Now this is color without form, or sound without music. For it to become music, it must possess some quality which will remove it from the purely sensuous. To my mind, it is in the power of suggestion that the vital spark of music lies.

Before speaking of this, however, I wish to touch upon two things: first, on what is called the science of music; and secondly, on one of the sensuous elements of music, which enters into and encroaches upon all suggestion.

If one were called upon to define what is called the intellectual side of music, he would probably speak of "form," contrapuntal design, and the like. Let us take up the matter of form. If by the word "form" our theorists meant the most poignant expression of poetic thought in music, if they meant by this word the art of arranging musical sounds into the most telling presentation of a musical idea, I should have nothing to say: for if this were admitted instead of the recognized forms of modern theorists for the proper utterance, we should possess a study of the power of musical sounds which might truly justify the title of musical intellectuality. As it is, the word "form" stands for what have been called "stoutly built periods," "subsidiary themes," and the like, a happy combination of which in certain prescribed keys was supposed to constitute good form. Such a device, originally based upon the necessities and fashions of the dance, and changing from time to time, is surely not worthy of the strange worship it has received. A form of so doubtful an identity that the first movement of a certain Beethoven sonata can be dubbed by one authority "sonata form" and by another "free fantasia," certainly cannot lay claim to serious intellectual value.

Form should be a synonym for coherence. No idea, whether great or small, can find utterance without form, but that form will be inherent to the idea, and there will be as many forms as there are adequately expressed ideas. In the musical idea, *per se*, analysis will reveal form.

The term "contrapuntal development" is to most tone poets of the present day a synonym for the device of giving expression to a musically poetic idea. *Per se*, counterpoint is a puerile juggling with themes, which may be likened to high-school mathematics. Certainly the entire web and woof of this "science," as it is called, never sprang from the necessities of poetic musical utterance. The entire pre-Palestrina literature of music is a conclusive testimony as to the non-poetic and even uneuphonious character of the invention.

In my opinion, Johann Sebastian Bach, one of the world's mightiest tone poets, accomplished his mission, not by means of the contrapuntal fashion of his age, but in spite of it. The laws of canon and fugue are based upon as prosaic a foundation as those of the rondo and sonata form; I find it impossible to imagine their ever having been a spur or an incentive to poetic musical speech. Neither pure tonal beauty, so-called "form," nor what is termed the intellectual side of music (the art of counterpoint, canon, and fugue), constitutes a really vital factor in music. This narrows our analysis down to two things: namely, the physical effect of musical sound, and suggestion.

The simplest manifestations of the purely sensuous effect of sound are to be found in the savage's delight in noise. In the more civilized state, this becomes the sensation of mere pleasure in hearing pleasing sounds. It enters into folk song in the form of the "Scotch snap," which is first cousin to the Swiss jodel, and is undoubtedly the origin of the skips of the augmented and (to a lesser degree) diminished intervals to be found in the music of many nations. It consists of the trick of alternating chest tones with falsetto. It is a kind of quirk in the voice which pleases children and primitive folk alike, a simple thing which has puzzled folklorists the world over.

The other sensuous influence of sound is one of the most powerful elements of music, and all musical utterance is involved with and inseparable from it. It consists of repetition, recurrence, periodicity.

Now this repetition may be one of rhythm, tone tint, texture, or color, a repetition of figure or of pitch. We know that savages, in their incantation ceremonies, keep up a continuous drum beating or chant, which, gradually increasing in violence, drives the hearers into such a state of frenzy that physical pain seems no longer to exist for them.

The value of the recurring rhythms and phrases of the march is well recognized in the army. A body of men will instinctively move in cadence with such music. The ever-recurring lilt of a waltz rhythm will set the feet moving unconsciously, and as the energy of the repetition increases and decreases, so will the involuntary accompanying physical sympathy increase or decrease.

Berlioz jokingly tells a story of a ballet dancer who objected to the high pitch in which the orchestra played, and insisted that the music be transposed to a lower key. Cradle songs are fashioned on the same principle.

This sensuous sympathy with recurring sounds, rhythm, and pitch has something in common with hypnotism, and leads up to what I have called suggestion in music.

This same element in a modified form is made use of in poetry, for instance, in Poe's "Raven,"

Quoth the raven, nevermore,

and the repetition of color in the same author's "Scarlet Death." It is the mainspring (I will not call it the vital spark) of many so-called popular songs, the recipe for which is exceedingly simple. A strongly marked rhythmic figure is selected, and incessantly repeated until the hearer's body beats time to it. . . .

There are two kinds of suggestion in music: one has been called tone-painting, the other almost evades analysis.

The term "tone-painting" is somewhat unsatisfactory, and reminds one of the French critic who spoke of a poem as "beautiful painted music." I believe that music can suggest forcibly certain things and ideas as well as vague emotions encased in the so-called "form" and "science" of music.

If we wish to begin with the most primitive form of suggestion in music, we shall find it in the direct imitation of sounds in nature.

We remember that Helmholtz, Hanslick, and their followers denied to music the power to suggest things in nature; but it was somewhat grudgingly admitted that music might express the emotions caused by them. In the face of this, to quote a well-known instance, we have the "Pastoral" symphony of Beethoven, with the thrush, cuckoo, and thunderstorm. The birds and the storm are very plainly indicated; but it is not possible for the music to be an expression of the emotions caused by them, for the very simple reason that no emotions are caused by the cuckoo and thrush, and those caused by thunderstorms range all the way from depression and fear to exhilaration, according to the personality of individuals.

That music may imitate any rhythmic sounds or melodic figure occurring in nature, hardly needs affirmation. Such devices may be accepted almost as quotations, and not be further considered here. The songs of birds, the sound made by galloping horses' feet, the moaning of the wind, etc., are all things which are part and parcel of the musical vocabulary, intelligible alike to people of every nationality. I need hardly say that increasing intensity of sound will suggest vehemence, approach, and its visual synonym, growth, as well as that decreasing intensity will suggest withdrawal, dwindling, and placidity.

The suggestion brought about by pattern is very familiar. It was one of the first signs of the breaking away from the conventional trammels of the contrapuntal style of the sixteenth and seventeenth centuries. The first madrigal of Thomas Weelkes (1590) begins with the words, "Sit down," and the musical pattern falls a fifth. The suggestion was crude, but it was caused by the same impulse as that which supplied the material for Wagner's *Waldweben*, Mendelssohn's *Lovely Melusina*, and a host of other works.

The fact that the pattern of a musical phrase can suggest kinds of motion may seem strange; but could we, for example, imagine a spinning song with broken arpeggios? Should we see a spear thrown or an arrow shot on the stage and hear the orchestra playing a phrase of an undulating pattern, we should at once realize the contradiction. Mendelssohn, Schumann, Wagner, Liszt, and practically everyone who has written a spinning song, have used the same pattern to suggest the turning of a wheel. That such widely different men as Wagner and Mendelssohn should both have adopted the same pattern to suggest undulating waves is not a mere chance, but clearly shows the potency of the suggestion.

The suggestion conveyed by means of pitch is one of the strongest in music. Vibrations increasing beyond two hundred and fifty

trillions a second become luminous.   It is a curious coincidence that
our highest vibrating musical sounds bring with them a well-defined
suggestion of light, and that as the pitch is lowered we get the impression of ever-increasing obscurity.   To illustrate this, I have but
to refer you to the Prelude to *Lohengrin*.   Had we no inkling as to its
meaning, we should still receive the suggestion of glittering shapes in
the blue ether.

Let us take the opening of the "Im Walde" symphony by Raff
as an example; deep shadow is unmistakably suggested.   Herbert
Spencer's theory of the influence of emotion on pitch is well known
and needs no confirmation.   This properly comes under the subject
of musical speech, a matter not to be considered here.   Suffice it to
say that the upward tendency of a musical phrase can suggest depression, the intensity of which will depend upon the intervals used.
As an instance we may quote the "Faust" overture of Wagner, in
which the pitch is used emotionally as well as descriptively.   If the
meaning I have found in this phrase seems to you far-fetched, we have
but to give a higher pitch to the motive to render the idea absolutely
impossible.

The suggestion offered by movement is very obvious, for music
admittedly may be stately, deliberate, hasty, or furious, it may march
or dance, it may be grave or flippant.

Last of all I wish to speak of the suggestion conveyed by means of
tone-tint, the blending of timbre and pitch.   It is essentially a modern
element in music, and in our delight in this marvelous and potent aid
to expression we have carried it to a point of development at which it
threatens to dethrone what has hitherto been our musical speech,
melody, in favor of what corresponds to the shadow languages of
speech: namely, gesture and facial expression.   Just as these shadow
languages of speech may distort or even absolutely reverse the meaning of the spoken word, so can tone color and harmony change the
meaning of a musical phrase.   This is at once the glory and the danger
of our modern music.   Overwhelmed by the new-found powers of
suggestion in tonal tint and the riot of hitherto undreamed of orchestral
combinations, we are forgetting that permanence in music depends
upon melodic speech.

In my opinion, it is the line, not the color, that will last.   That
harmony is a potent factor in suggestion may be seen from the fact
that Cornelius was able to write an entire song pitched upon one tone,
the accompaniment being so varied in its harmonies that the listener
is deceived into attributing to that one tone many shades of emotion.

In all modern music this element is one of the most important. If we refer again to the "Faust" overture of Wagner, we will perceive that although the melodic trend and the pitch of the phrase carry their suggestion, the roll of the drum which accompanies it throws a sinister veil over the phrase, making it impressive in the extreme.

The seed from which our modern wealth of harmony and tone color sprang was the perfect major triad. The *raison d'être* and development of this combination of tones belong to the history of music. Suffice it to say, that for some psychological reason this chord (with also its minor form) has still the same significance that it had for the monks of the Middle Ages. It is perfect. Every complete phrase must end with it. The attempts made to emancipate music from the tyranny of this combination of sounds have been in vain, showing that the suggestion of finality and repose contained in it is irrefutable.

Now if we depart from this chord a sensation of unrest is occasioned which can only subside by a progression to another triad or a return to the first. With the development of our modern system of tonality we have come to think tonally; and a chord lying outside of the key in which a musical thought is conceived will carry with it a sense of confusion or mystery that our modern art of harmony and tone color has made its own. Thus, while any simple low chords accompanying the first notes of Raff's "Im Walde" symphony, given by the horns and violins, would suggest gloom pierced by the gleams of light, the remoteness of the chords to the tonality of C major gives a suggestion of mystery; but as the harmony approaches the triad the mystery dissolves, letting in the gleam of sunlight suggested by the horn.

Goldmark's overture to *Sakuntala* owes its subtle suggestion to much the same cause. Weber made use of it in his *Freischütz*, Wagner in his *Tarnhelm* motive, Mendelssohn in his *Midsummer Night's Dream*, Tchaikovsky in the opening of one of his symphonies.

In becoming common property, so to speak, this important element of musical utterance has been dragged through the mud; and modern composers, in their efforts to raise it above the commonplace, have gone to the very edge of what is physically bearable in the use of tone color and combination. While this is but natural, owing to the appropriation of some of the most poetic and suggestive tone colors for ignoble dance tunes and doggerel, it is to my mind a pity, for it is elevating what should be a means of adding power and intensity to musical speech to the importance of musical speech itself. Possibly Strauss's *Thus Spake Zarathustra* may be considered the apotheosis of this power of suggestion in tonal color, and in it I believe we can see the tendency I allude to. This work stuns by its glorious magnificence of tonal texture; the suggestion, in the opening measures, of the rising sun is a mighty example of the overwhelming power of tone color. The upward sweep of the music to the highest regions of light has much of splendor about it; and yet I remember once hearing in London, sung in the street at night, a song that seemed to me to contain a truer germ of music.

For want of a better word I will call it ideal suggestion. It has to do with actual musical speech, and is difficult to define. The possession of it makes a man a poet. If we look for analogy, I may quote from Browning and Shakespeare.

> Dearest, three months ago
> When the mesmerizer, Snow,
> With his hand's first sweep
> Put the earth to sleep.
>
> BROWNING, "A Lover's Quarrel"

> Daffodils,
> That come before the swallow dares, and takes
> The winds of March with beauty; Violets dim,
> But sweeter than the lids of Juno's eyes.
>
> SHAKESPEARE, *Winter's Tale*

For me this defies analysis, and so it is with some things in music, the charm of which cannot be ascribed to physical or mental suggestion, and certainly not to any device of counterpoint or form, in the musical acceptance of the word.

X

AMERICA, PAST AND PRESENT

IN the course of three centuries a few thousand colonists, scattered here and there on the eastern coast of North America, have grown into a nation of one hundred and thirty millions, dominating the continent and controlling insular dependencies. They have set up the most extensive federal state and the most powerful republic in history; they have developed numerous institutions and traits peculiar to themselves. Their history has a flavor that, despite the brevity of the record, is unique. For generations they offered the world the spectacle of the freest and most individualistic, though certainly not the purest or most orderly, democracy in the world. Millions of all races and nationalities, led by "the American dream" of political liberty, social equality, and economic security, have sought their shores. What are the chief forces which have molded this nation? The answer was long given in terms of European influences; but a new response has been offered since historians have traced the effects of the frontier, of a continental domain, of great natural resources, and of racial amalgamation. Is America still the great exemplar of free institutions which John Bright pronounced it during the Civil War? Is it still the land of equal opportunity? As the youngest of nations, are its faults — the lack of intellectual distinction which Matthew Arnold once deplored, the absorption in material affairs, the love of bigness, the disorderliness and confusion — qualities which threaten its inner constitution or more superficial flaws? In what additions to the world's achievements may Americans take pride? The pages which follow are intended to answer such questions. The paper by Frederick J. Turner traces some of the deeper elements of our history; Dr. Eliot sums up our national contributions; Basil L. Gildersleeve suggests certain essential qualities of the American spirit; and Secretary Wallace tries to indicate some of the ways in which he believes America must now develop.

THE SIGNIFICANCE OF THE FRONTIER IN AMERICAN HISTORY[1]

Frederick Jackson Turner

A new outlook in American history was born when in 1893 FREDERICK JACKSON TURNER, then professor in the University of Wisconsin, read his paper on "The Significance of the Frontier" to the American Historical Association. In a statement now classic he declared that "the wilderness masters the colonist." He explained that it finds him a European in dress, manners, industries, modes of thought; that little by little, as he transforms the wilderness, it also transforms him; that the outcome is not the old Europe, but a new product that is American. Thus the advance of the frontier in every generation up to 1890 had meant the creation of a great belt of inhabitants whose ideas, desires, standards, and ways were fixed in great part by the conditions of the wilderness; their influence, reacting upon the more settled regions, had profoundly altered their culture also. "To study this advance, the men who grew up in these conditions, and the political, economic, and social results of it," said Turner, "is to study the really American part of our history." The idea of the frontier as a determinant of American civilization has proved as fruitful in this country as the idea of the geographic determination of history or the economic determination — perhaps more so. While Turner himself has written little — his chief books are *The Rise of the New West* (1906), *The Frontier in American History* (1921), and *The Significance of Sections in American History* (1932) — his essays have been full of ideas at once caught up by others; and he trained many students who as teachers and writers of American history have applied these ideas in numerous monographs and articles. His doctrine has in fact molded much American thinking ever since 1893. Its influence may be seen even in fiction; while Fenimore Cooper and Edward Eggleston deal with pioneers whose ways and ideas were already fixed when they entered the wilderness, Willa Cather in *O Pioneers* and O. E. Rölvaag in *Giants in the Earth* deal rather with pioneer individuals and communities which the frontier is transforming. The frontier may of course be made to explain too much in American history; but that it does explain a great deal, and that its passing marked the end of a distinct epoch, cannot be controverted. Along with his work on the frontier, Turner always wished to be thought of in connection with the investigation of sections as a means of understanding American life — not merely North, South, East, and West, but many interstate and intrastate sections. He believed that the national spirit, the psychology of the country, was a complex built up out of the federation of sections. And he traced manifestations of state rights primarily to sectional differences.

Turner was born in 1861 at Portage, Wisconsin, and educated at the University of Wisconsin and Johns Hopkins. After teaching at Wisconsin from 1889 to 1901, and at Harvard from 1910 to 1924, he went in 1927 to California to assume direction of the Americana section of the Huntington Library at San Gabriel. He died in 1932.

[1] From *The Frontier in American History*, by Frederick Jackson Turner. Reprinted by permission of Henry Holt and Company, publishers.

In a recent bulletin of the Superintendent of the Census for 1890 appear these significant words: "Up to and including 1880 the country had a frontier of settlement, but at present the unsettled area has been so broken into by isolated bodies of settlement that there can hardly be said to be a frontier line. In the discussion of its extent, its westward movement, etc., it cannot, therefore, any longer have a place in the census reports." This brief official statement marks the closing of a great historic movement. Up to our own day American history has been in a large degree the history of the colonization of the Great West. The existence of an area of free land, its continuous recession, and the advance of American settlement westward, explain American development.

Behind institutions, behind constitutional forms and modifications, lie the vital forces that call these organs into life and shape them to meet changing conditions. The peculiarity of American institutions is the fact that they have been compelled to adapt themselves to the changes of an expanding people — to the changes involved in crossing a continent, in winning a wilderness, and in developing at each area of this progress out of the primitive economic and political conditions of the frontier into the complexity of city life. Said Calhoun in 1817, "We are great, and rapidly — I was about to say fearfully — growing!" So saying, he touched the distinguishing feature of American life. All peoples show development; the germ theory of politics has been sufficiently emphasized. In the case of most nations, however, the development has occurred in a limited area; and if the nation has expanded, it has met other growing peoples whom it has conquered. But in the case of the United States we have a different phenomenon. Limiting our attention to the Atlantic coast, we have the familiar phenomenon of the evolution of institutions in a limited area, such as the rise of representative government; the differentiation of simple colonial governments into complex organs; the progress from primitive industrial society, without division of labor, up to manufacturing civilization. But we have in addition to this a recurrence of the process of evolution in each western area reached in the process of expansion. Thus American development has exhibited not merely advance along a single line, but a return to primitive conditions on a continually advancing frontier line, and a new development for that area. American social development has been continually beginning over again on the frontier. This perennial rebirth, this fluidity of American life, this expansion westward with its new opportunities, its continuous touch with the simplicity of primitive society, furnish the forces dominating American character. The true point of view in the history of this nation is not the Atlantic coast, it is the Great West. Even the slavery struggle, which is made so exclusive an object of attention by writers like Professor von Holst, occupies its important place in American history because of its relation to westward expansion.

In this advance, the frontier is the outer edge of the wave — the meeting point between savagery and civilization. Much has been written about the frontier from the point of view of border warfare and the chase, but as a field for the serious study of the economist and the historian it has been neglected.

The American frontier is sharply distinguished from the European frontier — a fortified boundary line running through dense populations. The most significant thing about the American frontier is that it lies at the hither edge of free land. In the census reports it is treated as the margin of that settlement which has a density of two or more to the square mile. The term is an elastic one, and for our purposes does not need sharp definition. We shall consider the whole frontier belt, including the Indian country and the outer margin of the "settled area" of the census reports. This paper will make no attempt to treat the subject exhaustively; its aim is simply to call attention to the frontier as a fertile field for investigation, and to suggest some of the problems which arise in connection with it.

In the settlement of America we have to observe how European life entered the continent, and how America modified and developed that life and reacted on Europe. Our early history is the study of European germs developing in an American environment. Too exclusive attention has been paid by institutional students to the Germanic origins, too little to the American factors. The frontier is the line of most rapid and effective Americanization. The wilderness masters the colonist. It finds him a European in dress, industries, tools, modes of travel, and thought. It takes him from the railroad car and puts him in the birch canoe. It strips off the garments of civilization and arrays him in the hunting shirt and the moccasin. It puts him in the log cabin of the Cherokee and Iroquois and runs an Indian palisade around him. Before long he has gone to planting Indian corn and plowing with a sharp stick; he shouts the war cry and takes the scalp in orthodox Indian fashion. In short, at the frontier the environment is at first too strong for the man. He must accept the conditions which it furnishes, or perish, and so he fits himself into the Indian clearings and follows the Indian trails. Little by little he transforms the wilderness, but the outcome is not the old Europe, not simply the development of Germanic germs, any more than the first phenomenon was a case of reversion to the Germanic mark. The fact is that here is a new product that is American. At first, the frontier was the Atlantic coast. It was the frontier of Europe in a very real sense. Moving westward, the frontier became more and more American. As successive terminal moraines result from successive glaciations, so each frontier leaves its traces behind it, and when it becomes a settled area the region still partakes of the frontier characteristics. Thus the advance of the frontier has meant steady movement away from the influence of Europe, a steady growth of independence on American lines. And to study this advance, the men who grew up under these conditions, and the political, economic, and social results of it, is to study the really American part of our history.

In the course of the seventeenth century the frontier was advanced up the Atlantic river courses, just beyond the "fall line," and the tidewater region became the settled area. In the first half of the eighteenth century another advance occurred. Traders followed the Delaware and Shawnee Indians to the Ohio as early as the end of the first quarter of the century. Governor Spotswood, of Virginia, made an expedition in 1714 across the Blue Ridge. The end of the first quarter of the century saw the advance of the Scotch-Irish and the Palatine Germans up the Shenandoah Valley into the western part of Virginia, and along the Piedmont region of the Carolinas. The Germans in New York pushed the frontier of settlement up the Mohawk to German Flats. In Pennsylvania the town of Bedford indicates the line of settlement. Settlements soon began on the New River, or the Great Kanawha, and on the sources of the Yadkin and French Broad. The King attempted to arrest the advance by his proclamation of 1763, forbidding settlements beyond the sources of the rivers flowing into the Atlantic; but in vain. In the period of the Revolution the frontier crossed the Alleghanies into Kentucky and Tennessee, and the upper waters of the Ohio were settled. When the first census was taken in 1790, the continuous settled area was bounded by a line which ran near the coast of Maine, and included New England except a portion of Vermont and New Hampshire, New York along the Hudson and up the Mohawk about Schenectady, eastern and southern Pennsylvania, Virginia well across the Shenandoah Valley, and the Carolinas and eastern Georgia. Beyond this region of continuous settlement were the small settled areas of Kentucky and Tennessee, and the Ohio, with the mountains intervening between them and the Atlantic area, thus giving a new and important character to the frontier. The isolation of the region increased its peculiarly American tendencies, and the need of transportation facilities to connect it with the East called out important schemes of internal improvement, which will be noted farther on. The "West," as a self-conscious section, began to evolve.

From decade to decade distinct advances of the frontier occurred. By the census of 1820 the settled area included Ohio, southern Indiana and Illinois, southeastern Missouri, and about one-half of Louisiana. This settled area had surrounded Indian areas, and the management of these tribes became an object of political concern. The frontier region of the time lay along the Great Lakes, where Astor's American Fur Company operated in the Indian trade, and beyond the Mississippi, where Indian traders extended their activity even to the Rocky Mountains; Florida also furnished frontier conditions. The Mississippi River region was the scene of typical frontier settlements.

The rising steam navigation on western waters, the opening of the Erie Canal, and the westward extension of cotton culture added five frontier states to the Union in this period. Grund, writing in 1836, declares: "It appears then that the universal disposition of Americans to emigrate to the western wilderness, in order to enlarge their dominion over inanimate nature, is the actual result of an expansive power which is inherent in them, and which by continually agitating all classes of society is constantly throwing a large portion of the whole population on the extreme confines of the State, in order to gain space for its development. Hardly is a new State or Territory formed before the same principle manifests itself again and gives rise to a further emigration; and so is it destined to go on until a physical barrier must finally obstruct its progress."

In the middle of this century the line indicated by the present eastern boundary of Indian Territory, Nebraska, and Kansas marked the frontier of the Indian country. Minnesota and Wisconsin still exhibited frontier conditions, but the distinctive frontier of the period is found in California, where the gold discoveries had sent a sudden tide of adventurous miners, and in Oregon, and the settlements in Utah. As the frontier had leaped over the Alleghanies, so now it skipped the Great Plains and the Rocky Mountains; and in the same way that the advance of the frontiersmen beyond the Alleghanies had caused the rise of important questions of transportation and internal improvement, so now the settlers beyond the Rocky Mountains needed means of communication with the East, and in the furnishing of these arose the settlement of the Great Plains and the development of still another kind of frontier life. Railroads, fostered by land grants, sent an increasing tide of immigrants into the Far West. The United States army fought a series of Indian wars in Minnesota, Dakota, and the Indian Territory.

By 1880 the settled area had been pushed into northern Michigan, Wisconsin, and Minnesota, along Dakota rivers, and in the Black Hills region, and was ascending the rivers of Kansas and Nebraska. The development of mines in Colorado had drawn isolated frontier settlements into that region, and Montana and Idaho were receiving settlers. The frontier was found in these mining camps and the ranches of the Great Plains. The Superintendent of the Census for 1890 reports, as previously stated, that the settlements of the West lie so scattered over the region that there can no longer be said to be a frontier line.

In these successive frontiers we find natural boundary lines which have served to mark and to affect the characteristics of the frontiers, namely: the fall line; the Alleghany Mountains; the Mississippi; the Missouri where its direction approximates north and south; the line of the arid lands, approximately the ninety-ninth meridian; and the Rocky Mountains. The fall line marked the frontier of the seventeenth century; the Alleghanies that of the eighteenth; the Mississippi that of the first quarter of the nineteenth; the Missouri that of the middle of this century (omitting the California movement); and the belt of the Rocky Mountains and the arid tract the present frontier. Each was won by a series of Indian wars.

At the Atlantic frontier one can study the germs of processes repeated at each successive frontier. We have the complex European life sharply precipitated by the wilderness into the simplicity of primitive conditions. The first frontier had to meet its Indian question, its question of the disposition of the public domain, of the means of intercourse with older settlements, of the extension of political organization, of religious and educational activity. And the settlement of these and similar questions for one frontier served as a guide for the next. The American student needs not to go to the "prim little townships of Sleswick" for illustrations of the law of continuity and development. For example, he may study the origin of our land policies in the colonial land policy; he may see how the system grew by adapting the statutes to the customs of the successive frontiers. He may see how the mining experience in the lead regions of Wisconsin, Illinois, and Iowa was applied to the mining laws of the

Sierras, and how our Indian policy has been a series of experimentations on successive frontiers. Each tier of new states has found in the older ones material for its constitutions. Each frontier has made similar contributions to American character, as will be discussed farther on.

Loria, the Italian economist, has urged the study of colonial life as an aid in understanding the stages of European development, affirming that colonial settlement is for economic science what the mountain is for geology, bringing to light primitive stratifications. "America," he says, "has the key to the historical enigma which Europe has sought for centuries in vain, and the land which has no history reveals luminously the course of universal history." There is much truth in this. The United States lies like a huge page in the history of society. Line by line as we read this continental page from West to East we find the record of social evolution. It begins with the Indian and the hunter; it goes on to tell of the disintegration of savagery by the entrance of the trader, the pathfinder of civilization; we read the annals of the pastoral stage in ranch life; the exploitation of the soil by the raising of unrotated crops of corn and wheat in sparsely settled farming communities; the intensive culture of the denser farm settlement; and finally the manufacturing organization with city and factory system. This page is familiar to the student of census statistics, but how little of it has been used by our historians. Particularly in eastern states this page is a palimpsest. What is now a manufacturing state was in an earlier decade an area of intensive farming. Earlier yet it had been a wheat area, and still earlier the "range" had attracted the cattle herder. Thus Wisconsin, now developing manufacture, is a state with varied agricultural interests. But earlier it was given over to almost exclusive grain-raising, like North Dakota at the present time.

The Atlantic frontier was compounded of fisherman, fur trader, miner, cattle raiser, and farmer. Excepting the fisherman, each type of industry was on the march toward the West, impelled by an irresistible attraction. Each passed in successive waves across the continent. Stand at Cumberland Gap and watch the procession of civilization, marching single file — the buffalo following the trail to the salt springs, the Indian, the fur trader and hunter, the cattle raiser, the pioneer farmer — and the frontier has passed by. Stand at South Pass in the Rockies a century later and see the same procession with wider intervals between. The unequal rate of advance compels us to distinguish the frontier into the trader's frontier, the rancher's frontier, or the miner's frontier, and the farmer's frontier. When the mines and the cowpens were still near the fall line the traders' pack trains were tinkling across the Alleghanies, and the French on the Great Lakes were fortifying their posts, alarmed by the British trader's birch canoe. When the trappers scaled the Rockies, the farmer was still near the mouth of the Missouri.

Why was it that the Indian trader passed so rapidly across the continent? What effects followed from the trader's frontier? The trade was coeval with American discovery. The Norsemen, Vespuccius, Verrazani, Hudson, John Smith, all trafficked for furs. The Plymouth pilgrims settled in Indian cornfields, and their first return cargo was of beaver and lumber. The records of the various New England colonies show how steadily exploration was carried into the wilderness by this trade. What is true for New England is, as would be expected, even plainer for the rest of the colonies. All along the coast from Maine to Georgia the Indian trade opened up the river courses. Steadily the trader passed westward, utilizing the older lines of French trade. The Ohio, the Great Lakes, the Mississippi, the Missouri, and the Platte, the lines of western advance, were ascended by traders. They found the passes in the Rocky Mountains and guided Lewis and Clark, Frémont, and Bidwell. The explanation of the rapidity of this advance is connected with the effects of the trader on the Indian. The trading post left the unarmed tribes at the mercy of those that had purchased firearms — a truth which the Iroquois Indians wrote in blood, and so the remote and unvisited tribes gave eager welcome to the trader. "The savages," wrote La Salle, "take better care of us French than of their own children; from us only can they get guns and goods." This accounts for the trader's power and the rapidity of his advance. Thus the disintegrating forces of civilization entered the wilderness. Every river valley and Indian trail became a fissure in Indian society, and so that society became honeycombed. Long before the pioneer farmer appeared on the scene, primitive Indian life had passed away. The farmers met Indians armed with guns. The trading frontier, while steadily undermining Indian power by making the tribes ultimately dependent on the whites, yet, through its sale of guns, gave to the Indian increased power of resistance to the farming frontier. French colonization was dominated by its trading frontier; English colonization by its farming frontier. There was an antagonism between the two frontiers as between the two nations. Said Duquesne to the Iroquois, "Are you ignorant of the difference between the king of England and the king of France? Go see the forts that our king has established and you will see that you can still hunt under their very walls. They have been placed for your advantage in places which you frequent. The English, on the contrary, are no sooner in possession of a place than the game is driven away. The forest falls before them as they advance, and the soil is laid bare so that you can scarce find the wherewithal to erect a shelter for the night."

And yet, in spite of this opposition of the interests of the trader and the farmer, the Indian trade pioneered the way for civilization. The buffalo train became the Indian trail, and this became the trader's "trace"; the trails widened into roads, and the roads into turnpikes, and these in turn were transformed into railroads. The same origin can be shown for the railroads of the South, the Far West, and the Dominion of Canada. The trading posts reached by these trails were on the sites of Indian villages which had been placed in positions suggested by nature; and these trading posts, situated so as to command the water systems of the country, have grown into such cities as Albany, Pittsburgh, Detroit, Chicago, St. Louis, Council Bluffs, and Kansas City. Thus civilization in America has followed the arteries made by geology, pouring an ever richer tide through them, until at last the slender paths of aboriginal intercourse have been broadened and interwoven into the complex mazes of modern commercial lines; the wilderness has been interpenetrated by lines of civilization growing ever more numerous. It is like the steady growth of a complex nervous system for the originally simple, inert continent. If one would understand why we are today one nation, rather than a collection of isolated states, he must study this economic and social consolidation of the country. In this progress from savage conditions lie topics for the evolutionist.

The effect of the Indian frontier as a consolidating agent in our history is important. From the close of the seventeenth century various intercolonial congresses have been called to treat with Indians and establish common measures of defense. Particularism was strongest in colonies with no Indian frontier. This frontier stretched along the western border like a cord of union. The Indian was a common danger, demanding united action. Most celebrated of these conferences was the Albany congress of 1754, called to treat with the Six Nations, and to consider plans of union. Even a cursory reading of the plan proposed by the congress reveals the importance of the frontier. The powers of the general council and the officers were, chiefly, the determination of peace and war with the Indians, the regulation of Indian trade, the purchase of Indian lands, and the creation and government of new settlements as a security against the Indians. It is evident that the unifying tendencies of the Revolutionary period were facilitated by the previous coöperation in the regulation of the frontier. In this connection may be mentioned the importance of the frontier, from that day to this, as a military training school, keeping alive the power of resistance to aggression, and developing the stalwart and rugged qualities of the frontiersman.

It would not be possible in the limits of this paper to trace the other frontiers across the continent. Travelers of the eighteenth century found the cowpens among the canebrakes and pea-vine pastures of the South, and the cow drivers took their droves to Charleston, Philadelphia, and New York. Travelers at the close of the War of 1812 met droves of more than a thousand cattle and swine from the interior of Ohio going to Pennsylvania to fatten for the Philadelphia market. The ranges of the Great Plains, with ranch and cowboy and nomadic life, are things of yesterday and of today. The experience of the Carolina cowpens guided the ranchers of Texas. One element favoring the rapid extension of the rancher's frontier is the fact that in a remote country lacking transportation facilities the product must be in small bulk, or must be able to transport itself, and the cattle raiser could easily drive his product to market. The effect of these great ranches on the subsequent agrarian history of the localities in which they existed should be studied.

The maps of the census reports show an uneven advance of the farmer's frontier, with tongues of settlement pushed forward and with indentations of wilderness. In part this is due to Indian resistance, in part to the location of river valleys and passes, in part to the unequal force of the centers of frontier attraction. Among the important centers of attraction may be mentioned the following: fertile and favorably situated soils, salt springs, mines, and army posts.

The frontier army post, serving to protect the settlers from the Indians, has also acted as a wedge to open the Indian country, and has been a nucleus for settlement. In this connection mention should also be made of the government military and exploring expeditions in determining the lines of settlement. But all the more important expeditions were greatly indebted to the earliest pathmakers, the Indian guides, the traders and trappers, and the French voyageurs, who were inevitable parts of governmental expeditions from the days of Lewis and Clark. Each expedition was an epitome of the previous factors in western advance.

From the time the mountains rose between the pioneer and the seaboard, a new order of Americanism arose. The West and the East began to get out of touch of each other. The settlements from the sea to the mountains kept connection with the rear and had a certain solidarity. But the over-mountain men grew more and more independent. The East took a narrow view of American advance, and nearly lost these men. Kentucky and Tennessee history bears abundant witness to the truth of this statement. The East began to try to hedge and limit westward expansion. Though Webster could declare that there were no Alleghanies in his politics, yet in politics in general they were a very solid factor.

The exploitation of the beasts took hunter and trader to the west, the exploitation of the grasses took the rancher west, and the exploitation of the virgin soil of the river valleys and prairies attracted the farmer. Good soils have been the most continuous attraction to the farmer's frontier. The land hunger of the Virginians drew them down the rivers into Carolina, in early colonial days; the search for soils took the Massachusetts men to Pennsylvania and to New York. As the eastern lands were taken up migration flowed across them to the west. Daniel Boone, the great backwoodsman, who combined the occupations of hunter, trader, cattle raiser, farmer, and surveyor, learning, probably from the traders, of the fertility of the lands of the upper Yadkin, where the traders were wont to rest as they took their way to the Indians, left his Pennsylvania home with his father, and passed down the Great Valley road to that stream. Learning from a trader of the game and rich pastures of Kentucky, he pioneered the way for the farmers to that region. Thence he passed to the frontier of Missouri, where his settlement was long a landmark on the frontier. Here again he helped to open the way for civilization, finding salt licks, and trails, and land. His son was among the earliest trappers in the passes of the Rocky Mountains, and his party are said to have been the first to camp on the present site of Denver. His grandson, Colonel A. J. Boone, of Colorado, was a power among the Indians of the Rocky Mountains, and was appointed an agent by the government. Kit Carson's mother was a Boone. Thus this family epitomizes the backwoodsman's advance across the continent.

The farmer's advance came in a distinct series of waves. In Peck's *New Guide to the West*, published in Boston in 1837, occurs this suggestive passage:

Generally, in all the western settlements, three classes, like the waves of the ocean, have rolled one after the other. First comes the pioneer, who depends for the subsistence of his family chiefly upon the natural growth of vegetation, called the "range," and the proceeds of hunting. His implements of agriculture are crude, chiefly of his own make, and his efforts directed mainly to a crop of corn and a "truck patch." The last is a rude garden for growing cabbage, beans, corn for roasting ears, cucumbers, and potatoes. A log cabin, and, occasionally, a stable and corn-crib, and a field of a dozen acres, the timber girdled or "deadened," and fenced, are enough for his occupancy. It is quite immaterial whether he ever becomes the owner of the soil. He is the occupant for the time being, pays no rent, and feels as independent as the "lord of the manor." With a horse, cow, and one or two breeders of swine, he strikes into the woods with his family, and becomes the founder of a new county, or perhaps state. He builds his cabin, gathers around him a few other families of similar tastes and habits, and occupies till the range is somewhat subdued, and hunting a little precarious, or, which is more frequently the case, till the neighbors crowd around, roads, bridges, and fields annoy him, and he lacks elbow room. The preëmption law enables him to dispose of his cabin and corn-field to the next class of emigrants; and, to employ his own figures, he "breaks for the high timber," "clears out for the New Purchase," or migrates to Arkansas or Texas, to work the same process over. . . .

Another wave rolls on. The men of capital and enterprise come. The settler is ready to sell out and take the advantage of the rise in property, push farther into the interior and become, himself, a man of capital and enterprise in turn. The small village rises to a spacious town or city; substantial edifices of brick, extensive fields, orchards, gardens, colleges, and churches are seen.

Omitting those of the pioneer farmers who move from the love of adventure, the advance of the more steady farmer is easy to understand. Obviously the immigrant was attracted by the cheap lands of the frontier, and even the native farmer felt their influence strongly. Year by year the farmers who lived on soil whose returns were diminished by unrotated crops were offered the virgin soil of the frontier at nominal prices. Their growing families demanded more lands, and these were dear. The competition of the unexhausted, cheap, and easily tilled prairie lands compelled the farmer either to go west and continue the exhaustion of the soil on a new frontier, or to adopt intensive culture. Thus the census of 1890 shows, in the Northwest, many counties in which there is an absolute or a relative decrease of population. These states have been sending farmers to advance the frontier on the plains, and have themselves begun to turn to intensive farming and to manufacture. A decade before this, Ohio had shown the same transition stage. Thus the demand for land and the love of wilderness freedom drew the frontier ever onward.

Having now roughly outlined the various kinds of frontiers, and their modes of advance, chiefly from the point of view of the frontier itself, we may next inquire what were the influences on the East and on the Old World. A rapid enumeration of some of the more noteworthy effects is all that I have time for.

First, we note that the frontier promoted the formation of a composite nationality for the American people. The coast was preponderantly English, but the later tides of continental immigration flowed across to the free lands. This was the case from the early colonial days. The Scotch-Irish and the Palatine Germans, or "Pennsylvania Dutch," furnished the dominant element in the stock of the colonial frontier. With these peoples were also the freed indented servants, or redemptioners, who at the expiration of their time of service passed to the frontier. Governor Spotswood of Virginia writes in 1717, "The inhabitants of our frontiers are composed generally of such as have been transported hither as servants, and, being out of their time, settle themselves where land is to be taken up and that will produce the necessarys of life with little labour." Very generally these redemptioners were of non-English stock. In the crucible of the frontier the immigrants were Americanized, liberated, and fused into a mixed race, English in neither nationality nor characteristics. The process has gone on from the early days to our own. Burke and other writers in the middle of the eighteenth century believed that Pennsylvania was "threatened with the danger of being wholly foreign in language, manners, and perhaps even inclinations." The German and Scotch-Irish elements in the frontier of the South were only less great. In the middle of the present century the German element in Wisconsin was already so considerable that leading publicists looked to the creation of a German state out of the commonwealth by concentrating their colonization. Such examples teach us to beware of misinterpreting the fact that there is a common English speech in America into a belief that the stock is also English.

In another way the advance of the frontier decreased our dependence on England. The coast, particularly of the South, lacked diversified industries, and was dependent on England for the bulk of its supplies. In the South there was even a dependence on the Northern colonies for articles of food. Governor Glenn, of South Carolina, writes in the middle of the eighteenth century: "Our trade with New York and Philadelphia was of this sort, draining us of all the little money and bills we could gather from other places for their bread, flour, beer, hams, bacon, and other things of their produce, all which, except beer, our new townships begin to supply us with, which are settled with very industrious and thriving Germans. This no doubt diminishes the number of shipping and the appearance of our trade, but it is far from being a detriment to us." Before long the frontier created a demand for merchants. As it retreated from the coast it became less and less possible for England to bring her supplies directly to the consumer's wharfs, and carry away staple crops, and staple crops began to give way to diversified agriculture for a time. The effect of this phase of the frontier action upon the northern section is perceived when we realize how the advance of the frontier aroused seaboard cities like Boston, New York, and Baltimore, to engage in rivalry for what Washington called "the extensive and valuable trade of a rising empire."

The legislation which most developed the powers of the national government, and played the largest part in its activity, was conditioned on the frontier. Writers have discussed the subjects of tariff, land, and internal improvement, as subsidiary to the slavery question. But when American history comes to be rightly viewed it will be seen that the slavery question is an incident. In the period from the end of the first half of the present century to the close of the Civil War slavery rose to primary, but far from exclusive, importance. But this does not justify Dr. von Holst (to take an example) in treating our constitutional history in its formative period down to 1828 in a single volume, giving six volumes chiefly to the history of slavery from 1828 to 1861, under the title *Constitutional History of the United States*. The growth of nationalism and the evolution of American political institutions were dependent on the advance of the frontier. Even so recent a writer as Rhodes, in his *History of the United States since the Compromise of 1850*, has treated the legislation called out by the western advance as incidental to the slavery struggle.

This is a wrong perspective. The pioneer needed the goods of the coast, and so the grand series of internal improvement and railroad legislation began, with potent nationalizing effects. Over internal improvements occurred great debates, in which grave constitutional questions were discussed. Sectional groupings appear in the votes, profoundly significant for the historian. Loose construction increased as the nation marched westward. But the West was not content with bringing the farm to the factory. Under the lead of Clay — "Harry of the West" — protective tariffs were passed, with the cry of bringing the factory to the farm. The disposition of the public lands was a third important subject of national legislation influenced by the frontier.

The public domain has been a force of profound importance in the nationalization and development of the government. The effects of the struggle of the landed and the landless states, and of the Ordinance of 1787, need no discussion. Administratively the frontier called out some of the highest and most vitalizing activities of the general government. The purchase of Louisiana was perhaps the constitutional turning point in the history of the Republic, inasmuch as it afforded both a new area for national legislation and the occasion of the downfall of the policy of strict construction. But the purchase of Louisiana was called out by frontier needs and demands. As frontier states accrued to the Union the national power grew. In a speech on the dedication of the Calhoun monument Mr. Lamar explained: "In 1789 the states were the creators of the federal government; in 1861 the federal government was the creator of a large majority of the states."

When we consider the public domain from the point of view of the sale and disposal of the public lands we are again brought face to face with the frontier. The policy of the United States in dealing with its lands is in sharp contrast with the European system of scientific administration. Efforts to make this domain a source of revenue, and to withhold it from emigrants in order that settlement might be compact, were in vain. The jealousy and the fears of the East were powerless in the face of the demands of the frontiersmen. John Quincy Adams was obliged to confess: "My own system of administration, which was to make the national domain the inexhaustible fund for progressive and unceasing internal improvement, has failed." The reason is obvious; a system of administration was not what the West demanded; it wanted land. Adams states the situation as follows: "The slaveholders of the South have bought the coöperation of the western country by the bribe of the western lands, abandoning to the new Western States their own proportion of the public property and aiding them in the design of grasping all the lands into their own hands. Thomas H. Benton was the author of this system, which he brought forward as a substitute for the American system of Mr. Clay, and to supplant him as the leading statesman of the West. Mr. Clay, by his tariff compromise with Mr. Calhoun, abandoned his own American system. At the same time he brought forward a plan for distributing among all the states of the Union the proceeds of the sales of the public lands. His bill for that purpose passed both Houses of

Congress, but was vetoed by President Jackson, who, in his annual message of December, 1832, formally recommended that all public lands should be gratuitously given away to individual adventurers and to the states in which the lands are situated."

"No subject," said Henry Clay, "which has presented itself to the present, or perhaps any preceding, Congress, is of greater magnitude than that of the public lands." When we consider the far-reaching effects of the government's land policy upon political, economic, and social aspects of American life, we are disposed to agree with him. But this legislation was framed under frontier influences, and under the lead of Western statesmen like Benton and Jackson. Said Senator Scott of Indiana in 1841: "I consider the preëmption law merely declaratory of the custom or common law of the settlers."

It is safe to say that the legislation with regard to land, tariff, and internal improvements — the American system of the nationalizing Whig Party — was conditioned on frontier ideas and needs. But it was not merely in legislative action that the frontier worked against sectionalism of the coast. The economic and social characteristics of the frontier worked against sectionalism. The men of the frontier had closer resemblances to the Middle region than to either of the other sections. Pennsylvania had been the seed-plot of frontier emigration, and, although she passed on her settlers along the Great Valley into the west of Virginia and Carolinas, yet the industrial society of these Southern frontiersmen was always more like that of the Middle region than like that of the tidewater portion of the South, which later came to spread its industrial type throughout the South.

The Middle region, entered by New York harbor, was an open door to all Europe. The tidewater part of the South represented typical Englishmen, modified by a warm climate and servile labor, and living in baronial fashion on great plantations; New England stood for a special English movement — Puritanism. The Middle region was less English than the other sections. It had a wide mixture of nationalities, a varied society, the mixed town and county system of local government, a varied economic life, many religious sects. In short, it was a region mediating between New England and the South, and the East and the West. It represented that composite nationality which the contemporary United States exhibits, that juxtaposition of non-English groups, occupying a valley or a little settlement, and presenting reflections of the map of Europe in their variety. It was democratic and non-sectional, if not national; "easy, tolerant, and contented"; rooted strongly in material prosperity. It was typical of the modern United States. It was least sectional, not only because it lay between North and South, but also because with no barriers to shut out its frontiers from its settled region, and with a system of connecting waterways, the Middle region mediated between East and West as well as between North and South. Thus it became the typically American region. Even the New Englander, who was shut out from the frontier by the Middle region, tarrying in New York or Pennsylvania on his westward march, lost the acuteness of his sectionalism on the way.

The spread of cotton culture into the interior of the South finally broke down the contrast between the tidewater region and the rest of the state, and based Southern interests on slavery. Before this process revealed its results the western portion of the South, which was akin to Pennsylvania in stock, society, and industry, showed tendencies to fall away from the faith of the fathers into internal improvement legislation and nationalism. In the Virginia convention of 1829–1830, called to revise the constitution, Mr. Leigh, of Chesterfield, one of the tidewater counties, declared:

> One of the main causes of discontent which led to this convention, that which had the strongest influence in overcoming our veneration for the work of our fathers, which taught us to contemn the sentiments of Henry and Mason and Pendleton, which weaned us from our reverence for the constituted authorities of the state, was an overweening passion for internal improvement. I say this with perfect knowledge, for it has been avowed to me by gentlemen from the West over and over again. And let me tell the gentleman from Albermarle (Mr. Gordon) that it has been another principal object of those who set this ball of revolution in motion, to overturn the doctrine of state rights, of which Virginia has been the very pillar, and to remove the barrier she has interposed to the interference of the federal government in that same work of internal improvement, by so reorganizing the legislature that Virginia, too, may be hitched to the federal car.

It was this nationalizing tendency of the West that transformed the democracy of Jefferson into the national republicanism of Monroe and the democracy of Andrew Jackson. The West of the War of 1812, the West of Clay, and Benton and Harrison, and Andrew Jackson, shut off by the Middle States and the mountains from the coast sections, had a solidarity of its own with national tendencies. On the tide of the Father of Waters, North and South met and mingled into a nation. Interstate migration went steadily on — a process of cross fertilization of ideas and institutions. The fierce struggle of the sections over slavery on the western frontier does not diminish the truth of this statement; it proves the truth of it. Slavery was a sectional trait that would not down, but in the West it could not remain sectional. It was the greatest of frontiersmen who declared: "I believe this government can not endure permanently half slave and half free. It will become all of one thing or all of the other." Nothing works for nationalism like intercourse within the nation. Mobility of population is death to localism, and the western frontier worked irresistibly in unsettling population. The effect reached back from the frontier and affected profoundly the Atlantic coast and even the Old World.

But the most important effect of the frontier has been in the promotion of democracy here and in Europe. As has been indicated, the frontier is productive of individualism. Complex society is precipitated by the wilderness into a kind of primitive organization based on the family. The tendency is anti-social. It produces antipathy to control, and particularly to any direct control. The tax-gatherer is viewed as a representative of oppression. Professor Osgood, in an able article, has pointed out that the frontier conditions prevalent in the colonies are important factors in the explanation of the American Revolution, where individual liberty was sometimes confused with the absence of all effective government. The same conditions aid in explaining the difficulty of instituting a strong government in the period of the confederacy. The frontier individualism has from the beginning promoted democracy.

The frontier states that came into the Union in the first quarter of a century of its existence came in with democratic suffrage provisions, and had reactive effects of the highest importance upon the older states whose peoples were being attracted there. An extension of the franchise became essential. It was *western* New York that forced an extension of suffrage in the constitutional convention of that state in 1821; and it was *western* Virginia that compelled the tidewater region to put a more liberal suffrage provision in the constitution framed in 1830, and to give to the frontier region a more nearly proportionate representation with the tidewater aristocracy. The rise of democracy as an effective force in the nation came in with western preponderance under Jackson and William Henry Harrison, and it meant the triumph of the frontier — with all of its good and with all of its evil elements. An interesting illustration of the tone of frontier democracy in 1830 comes from the same debates in the Virginia convention already referred to. A representative from western Virginia declared:

But, sir, it is not the increase of population in the West which this gentleman ought to fear. It is the energy which the mountain breeze and Western habits impart to those emigrants. They are regenerated, politically I mean, sir. They soon become *working politicians;* and the difference, sir, between a *talking* and a *working* politician is immense. The Old Dominion has long been celebrated for producing great orators; the ablest metaphysicians in policy; men that can split hairs in all abstruse questions of political economy. But at home, or when they return from Congress, they have Negroes to fan them asleep. But a Pennsylvania, a New York, an Ohio, or a western Virginia statesman, though far inferior in logic, metaphysics, and rhetoric to an old Virginia statesman, has this advantage, that when he returns home he takes off his coat and takes hold of the plow. This gives him bone and muscle, sir, and preserves his republican principles pure and uncontaminated.

So long as free land exists, the opportunity for a competency exists, and economic power secures political power. But the democracy born of free land, strong in selfishness and individualism, intolerant of administrative experience and education, and pressing individual liberty beyond its proper bounds, has its dangers as well as its benefits. Individualism in America has allowed a laxity in regard to governmental affairs which has rendered possible the spoils system and all the manifest evils that follow from the lack of a highly developed civic spirit. In this connection may be noted also the influence of frontier conditions in permitting lax business honor, inflated paper currency and wildcat banking. The colonial and Revolutionary frontier was the region whence emanated many of the worst forms of an evil currency. The West in the War of 1812 repeated the phenomenon on the frontier of that day, while the speculation and wildcat banking of the period of the crisis of 1837 occurred on the new frontier belt of the next tier of states. Thus each one of the periods of lax financial integrity coincides with periods when a new set of frontier communities had arisen, and coincides in area with these successive frontiers, for the most part. The recent Populist agitation is a case in point. Many a state that now declines any connection with the tenets of the Populists itself adhered to such ideas in an earlier stage of the development of the state. A primitive society can hardly be expected to show the intelligent appreciation of the complexity of business interests in a developed society. The continual recurrence of these areas of paper-money agitation is another evidence that the frontier can be isolated and studied as a factor in American history of the highest importance.

The East has always feared the result of an unregulated advance of the frontier, and has tried to check and guide it. The English authorities would have checked settlement at the headwaters of the Atlantic tributaries and allowed the "savages to enjoy their deserts in quiet lest the peltry trade should decrease." This called out Burke's splendid protest:

If you stopped your grants, what would be the consequence? The people would occupy without grants. They have already so occupied in many places. You cannot station garrisons in every part of these deserts. If you drive the people from one place, they will carry on their annual tillage and remove with their flocks and herds to another. Many of the people in the back settlements are already little attached to particular situations. Already they have topped the Appalachian Mountains.

But the English government was not alone in its desire to limit the advance of the frontier and guide its destinies. Tidewater Virginia and South Carolina gerrymandered those colonies to insure the dominance of the coast in their legislatures. Washington desired to settle a state at a time in the Northwest; Jefferson would reserve from settlement the territory of his Louisiana Purchase north of the thirty-second parallel, in order to offer it to the Indians in exchange for their settlements east of the Mississippi. "When we shall be full on this side," he writes, "we may lay off a range of states on the western bank from the head to the mouth, and so range after range, advancing compactly as we multiply." Madison went so far as to argue to the French minister that the United States had no interest in seeing population extend itself on the right bank of the Mississippi, but should rather fear it. When the Oregon question was under debate, in 1824, Smyth, of Virginia, would draw an unchangeable line for the limits of the United States at the outer limit of two tiers of states beyond the Mississippi, complaining that the seaboard states were being drained of the flower of their population by the bringing of too much land into market. Even Thomas Benton, the man of widest views of the destiny of the West, at this stage of his career declared that along the ridge of the Rocky Mountains "the western limits of the Republic should be drawn, and the statue of the fabled god Terminus should be raised upon its highest peak, never to be thrown down." But the attempts to limit the boundaries, to restrict land sales and settlement, and to deprive the West of its share of political power were all in vain. Steadily the frontier of settlement advanced and carried with it individualism, democracy, and nationalism, and powerfully affected the East and the Old World.

From the conditions of frontier life came intellectual traits of profound importance. The works of travelers along each frontier from colonial days onward describe certain common traits, and these traits have, while softening down, still persisted as survivals in the place of their origin, even when a higher social organization succeeded. The result is that to the frontier the American intellect owes its striking characteristics. That coarseness and strength combined with acuteness and inquisitiveness; that practical, inventive turn of mind, quick to find expedients; that masterful grasp of material things, lacking in the artistic but powerful to effect great ends; that restless, nervous energy; that dominant individualism, working for good and for evil, and withal that buoyancy and exuberance which comes with freedom — these are traits of the frontier, or traits called out elsewhere because of the existence of the frontier. Since the days when the fleet of Columbus sailed into the waters of the New World, America has been another name for opportunity, and the people of the United States have taken their tone from the incessant expansion which has not only been open but has even been forced upon them. He would be a rash prophet who should assert that the expansive character of American life has now entirely ceased. Movement has been its dominant fact, and, unless this training has no effect upon a people, the American energy will continually demand a wider field for its exercise. But never again will such gifts of free land offer themselves. For a moment, at the frontier, the bonds of custom are broken and unrestraint is triumphant. There is no *tabula rasa*. The stubborn American environment is there with its imperious summons to accept its conditions; the inherited ways of doing things are also there; and yet in spite of environment, and, in spite of custom, each frontier did indeed furnish a new field of opportunity, a gate of escape from the bondage of the past; and freshness, and confidence, and scorn of older society, impatience of its restraints and its ideas, and indifference to its lessons, have accompanied the frontier. What the Mediterranean Sea was to the Greeks, breaking the bond of custom, offering new experiences, calling out new institutions and activities, that, and more, the ever-retreating frontier has been to the United States directly, and to the nations of Europe more remotely. And now, four centuries from the discovery of America, at the end of a hundred years of life under the Constitution, the frontier has gone, and with its going has closed the first period of American history.

THE CREED OF THE OLD SOUTH[1]

Basil Gildersleeve

BASIL L. GILDERSLEEVE in his time stood for a rare combination of scholarly and literary distinction. He was the first professor appointed at Johns Hopkins when that institution in 1876 launched graduate study in America upon a new plane. Until his death he remained the foremost classical scholar in the country; as founder and editor of the *American Journal of Philology*, one of the foremost philologists. He liked to recall how, placed by President Gilman in an empty room at Johns Hopkins, he was told to "radiate!" The word precisely fitted him; he inspired a long generation of students and research workers by his human breadth, wit, appreciation of wide vistas of literature, and brilliant insight into scholarly problems. Meanwhile he gradually won a reputation also as a general essayist of mellow wisdom, gaiety, and literary sparkle. He could draw upon a rich fund of experience. Born in 1831 in Charleston, and educated in Charleston College and at the Universities of Berlin, Bonn, and Göttingen, he was professor of Greek at the University of Virginia when the Civil War broke out. For the next four years he combined service in the Confederate army with intervals of teaching, and in 1864 was lamed for life by a severe wound. He returned to the University of Virginia for the reconstruction years, and remained there until invited to Johns Hopkins. He thought his essay on Herodotus, prefixed to the translation by Henry Cary, his best bit of work. But the volume that attracted the most notice was *The Creed of the Old South, 1865–1915*, which combined with the title essay a paper on "A Southerner in the Peloponnesian War." Another interesting collection of lectures was entitled *Hellas and Hesperia* (1897). As his "choliambic limp" in walking was a constant reminder of his war experiences, so the lessons he had learned in the sectional struggle and the grim years of Southern want after it always enriched his teaching and writing. His satiric wit, passion for exactness and accuracy, and fearlessness of temper made his editorial department in the *Journal of Philology* for forty years a salutary force in raising the general level of scholarship not only in his field but in others allied with it; but above all he was notable for breadth of outlook. His death in 1924 removed one of the truly creative scholars of his generation.

A few months ago, as I was leaving Baltimore for a summer sojourn on the coast of Maine, two old soldiers of the war between the States took their seats immediately behind me in the car, and began a lively conversation about the various battles in which they had faced each other more than a quarter of a century ago, when a trip to New England would have been no holiday jaunt for one of their fellow travelers. The veterans went into the minute detail that always puts me to shame, when I think how poor an account I should give, if

[1] Reprinted by permission of the Johns Hopkins Press.

pressed to describe the military movements that I have happened to witness; and I may as well acknowledge at the outset that I have as little aptitude for the soldier's trade as I have for the romancer's. Single incidents I remember as if they were of yesterday. Single pictures have burned themselves into my brain. But I have no vocation to tell how fields were lost and won; and my experience of military life was too brief and desultory to be of any value to the historian of the war. For my own life that experience has been of the utmost significance, and despite the heavy price I have had to pay for my outings, despite the daily reminder of five long months of intense suffering, I have no regrets. An able-bodied young man, with a long vacation at his disposal, could not have done otherwise, and the right to teach Southern youth for nine months was earned by sharing the fortunes of their fathers and brothers at the front for three. Self-respect is everything; and it is something to have belonged in deed and in truth to an heroic generation, to have shared in a measure its perils and privations. But that heroic generation is apt to be a bore to a generation whose heroism is of a different type, and I doubt whether the young people in our car took much interest in the very audible conversation of the two veterans. Twenty-five years hence, when the survivors will be curiosities, as were Revolutionary pensioners in my childhood, there may be a renewal of interest. As it is, few of the present generation pore over *The Battles and Leaders of the Civil War*, and a grizzled old Confederate has been heard to declare that he intended to bequeath his copy of that valuable work to someone outside of the family, so provoked was he at the supineness of his children. And yet, for the truth's sake, all these battles must be fought over and over again, until the account is cleared, and until justice is done to the valor and skill of both sides.

The two old soldiers were talking amicably enough, as all old soldiers do, but they "yarned," as all old soldiers do, and though they talked from Baltimore to Philadelphia, and from Philadelphia to New York, their conversation was lost on me, for my thoughts went back into my own past, and two pictures came up to me from the time of the war.

In the midsummer of 1863 I was serving as a private in the First Virginia Cavalry. Gettysburg was in the past, and there was not much fighting to be done, but the cavalry was not wholly idle. Raids had to be intercepted, and the enemy was not to be allowed to vaunt himself too much; so that I gained some experience of the hardships of that arm of the service, and found out by practical participation what is meant by a cavalry charge. To a looker-on nothing can be finer. To the one who charges, or is supposed to charge — for the horse seemed to me mainly responsible — the details are somewhat cumbrous. Now in one of these charges some of us captured a number of the opposing force, among them a young lieutenant. Why this particular capture should have impressed me so I cannot tell, but memory is a tricky thing. A large red fox scared up from his lair by the fight at Castleman's Ferry stood for a moment looking at me; and I shall never forget the stare of that red fox. At one of our fights near Kernstown a spent bullet struck a horse on the side of his nose, which happened to be white, and left a perfect imprint of itself; and the jerk of the horse's head and the outline of the bullet are present to me still. The explosion of a particular caisson, the shriek of a special shell, will ring in one's ears for life. A captured lieutenant was no novelty, and yet this captured lieutenant caught my eye and held it. A handsomer young fellow, a more noble-looking, I never beheld among Federals or Confederates, as he stood there, bareheaded, among his captors, erect and silent. His eyes were full of fire, his lips showed a slight quiver of scorn, and his hair seemed to tighten its curls in defiance. Doubtless I had seen as fine specimens of young manhood before, but if so, I had seen without looking, and this man was evidently what we called a gentleman.

Southern men were proud of being gentlemen, although they have been told in every conceivable tone that it was a foolish pride — foolish in itself, foolish in that it did not have the heraldic backing that was claimed for it; the utmost concession being that a number of "deboshed" younger sons of decayed gentry had been shipped to Virginia in the early settlement of that colony. But the very pride played its part in making us what we were proud of being, and whether descendants of the aforesaid "deboshed," of simple English yeomen, of plain Scotch-Irish Presbyterians, a sturdy stock, of Huguenots of various ranks of life, we all held to the same standard, and showed, as was thought, undue exclusiveness on this subject. But this prisoner was the embodiment of the best type of Northern youth, with a spirit as high, as resolute, as could be found in the ranks of Southern gentlemen; and though in theory all enlightened Southerners recognized the high qualities of some of our opponents, this one noble figure in "flesh and blood" was better calculated to inspire respect for "those people," as we had learned to call our adversaries, than many pages of "gray theory."

A little more than a year afterward, in Early's Valley campaign — a rude school of warfare — I was serving as a volunteer aide on General Gordon's staff. The day before the disaster of Fisher's Hill I was ordered, together with another staff officer, to accompany the general on a ride to the front. The general had a well-known weakness for inspecting the outposts — a weakness that made a position in his suite somewhat precarious. The officer with whom I was riding had not been with us long, and when he joined the staff had just recovered from wounds and imprisonment. A man of winning appearance, sweet temper, and attractive manners, he soon made friends of the military family, and I never learned to love a man so much in so brief an acquaintance, though hearts knit quickly in the stress of war. He was highly educated, and foreign residence and travel had widened his vision without affecting the simple faith and thorough consecration of the Christian. Here let me say that the bearing of the Confederates is not to be understood without taking into account the deep religious feeling of the army and its great leaders. It is an historical element, like any other, and is not to be passed over in summing up the forces of the conflict. "A soldier without religion," says a Prussian officer, who knew our army as well as the German, "is an instrument without value"; and it is not unlikely that the knowledge of the part that faith played in sustaining the Southern people may have lent emphasis to the expression of his conviction.

We rode together toward the front, and as we rode our talk fell on Goethe and on Faust, and of all passages the soldiers' song came up to my lips — the song of soldiers of fortune, not the chant of men whose business it was to defend their country. Two lines, however, were significant:

Kühn ist das Mühen,
Herrlich der Lohn.[1]

We reached the front. An occasional "zip" gave warning that the sharpshooters were not asleep, and the quick eye of the general saw that our line needed rectification and how. Brief orders were given to the officer in command. My comrade was left to aid in carrying them out. The rest of us withdrew. Scarcely had we ridden a hundred yards toward camp when a shout was heard, and, turning round, we saw one of the men running after us. "The captain had been killed." The peace of Heaven was on his face, as I gazed on the noble features that afternoon. The bullet had passed through his official papers and found his heart. He had received his discharge, and the glorious reward had been won.

[1] " Fierce is the ordeal, glorious the reward."

This is the other picture that the talk of the two old soldiers called up — dead Confederate against living Federal; and these two pictures stand out before me again, as I am trying to make others understand and to understand myself what it was to be a Southern man twenty-five years ago; what it was to accept with the whole heart the creed of the Old South. The image of the living Federal bids me refrain from harsh words in the presence of those who were my captors. The dead Confederate bids me uncover the sacred memories that the dust of life's Appian Way hides from the tenderest and truest of those whose business it is to live and work. For my dead comrade of the Valley campaign is one of many; some of them my friends, some of them my pupils as well. The 18th of July, 1861, laid low one of my Princeton College roommates; on the 21st, the day of the great battle, the other fell — both bearers of historic names, both upholding the cause of their state with as unclouded a conscience as any saint in the martyrology ever wore; and from that day to the end, great battle and outpost skirmish brought me, week by week, a personal loss in men of the same type.

The surrender of the Spartans on the island of Sphacteria was a surprise to friend and foe alike; and the severe historian of the Peloponnesian War pauses to record the answer of a Spartan to the jeering question of one of the allies of the Athenians — a question which implied that the only brave Spartans were those who had been slain. The answer was tipped with Spartan wit; the only thing Spartan, as someone has said, in the whole un-Spartan affair. "The arrow," said he, "would be of great price if it distinguished the brave men from the cowards." But it did seem to us, in our passionate grief, that the remorseless bullet, the remorseless shell, had picked out the bravest and the purest. It is an old cry:

Ja, der Krieg verschlingt die Besten.[1]

Still, when Schiller says in the poem just quoted,

Ohne Wahl verteilt die Gaben,
Ohne Billigkeit das Glück,
Denn Patroklus liegt begraben
Und Thersites kommt zurück,[2]

his illustration is only half right. The Greek Thersites did not return to claim a pension.

[1] " Yes, war destroys the ablest."
[2] ' Gifts are distributed without plan, luck is bestowed without justice; for Patroclus lies in his grave, and Thersites comes through unscathed."

Of course, what was to all true Confederates beyond a question "a holy cause," "the holiest of causes," this fight in defense of "the sacred soil" of our native land, was to the other side "a wicked rebellion" and "damnable treason," and both parties to the quarrel were not sparing of epithets which, at this distance of time, may seem to our children unnecessarily undignified; and no doubt some of these *epitheta ornantia* continue to flourish in remote regions, just as pictorial representations of Yankees and rebels in all their respective fiendishness are still cherished here and there.   At the Centennial Exposition of 1876, by way of conciliating the sections, the place of honor in the "Art Annex" was given to Rothermel's painting of the battle of Gettysburg, in which the face of every dying Union soldier is lighted up with a celestial smile, while guilt and despair are stamped on the wan countenances of the moribund rebels.   At least such is my recollection of the painting; and I hope that I may be pardoned for the malicious pleasure I felt when I was informed of the high price that the state of Pennsylvania had paid for that work of art.   The dominant feeling was amusement, not indignation.   But as I looked at it I recalled another picture of a battle scene, painted by a friend of mine, a French artist, who had watched our life with an artist's eye. One of the figures in the foreground was a dead Confederate boy, lying in the angle of a worm fence.   His uniform was worn and ragged, mud-stained as well as blood-stained; the cap which had fallen from his head was a tatter, and the torn shoes were ready to drop from his stiffening feet; but in a buttonhole of his tunic was stuck the inevitable toothbrush, which continued even to the end of the war to be the distinguishing mark of gentle nurture — the souvenir that the Confederate so often received from fair sympathizers in border towns.   I am not a realist, but I would not exchange that homely toothbrush in the Confederate's buttonhole for the most angelic smile that Rothermel's brush could have conjured up.

Now I make no doubt that most of the readers of *The Atlantic* have got beyond the Rothermel stage, and yet I am not certain that all of them appreciate the entire clearness of conscience with which we of the South went into the war.   A new patriotism is one of the results of the great conflict, and the power of local patriotism is no longer felt to the same degree.   In one of his recent deliverances Mr. Carnegie, a canny Scot who has constituted himself the representative of American patriotism, says, "The citizen of the republic today is prouder of being an American than he is of being a native of any state in the country."   What it is to be a native of any state in the country,

especially an old state with an ancient and honorable history, is something that Mr. Carnegie cannot possibly understand. But the
"today" is superfluous. The Union was a word of power in 1861 as
it is in 1891. Before the secession of Virginia a Virginian Breckinridge
asked: "If exiled in a foreign land, would the heart turn back to
Virginia, or South Carolina, or New York, or to any one state as the
cherished home of its pride? No. We would remember only that we
were Americans." Surely this seems quite as patriotic as Mr.
Carnegie's utterance; and yet, to the native Virginian just quoted,
so much stronger was the state than the central government that, a
few weeks after this bold speech, he went into the war, and finally
perished in the war. "A Union man," says his biographer, "fighting
for the rights of his old mother, Virginia." And there were many men
of his mind, noted generals, valiant soldiers. The University Memorial, which records the names and lives of the alumni of the University
of Virginia who fell in the Confederate war, two hundred in number —
this volume, full "of memories and of sighs" to every Southern man of
my age, lies open before me as I write, and some of the noblest men
who figure in its pages were Union men; and the Memorial of the
Virginia Military Institute tells the same story with the same eloquence. The state was imperiled, and parties disappeared; and of
the combatants in the field, some of the bravest and the most conspicuous belonged to those whose love of the old Union was warm
and strong, to whom the severance of the tie that bound the states
together was a personal grief. But even those who prophesied the
worst, who predicted a long and bloody struggle and a doubtful result,
had no question about the duty of the citizen; shared the common
burden and submitted to the individual sacrifice as readily as the
veriest fire-eater — nay, as they claimed, more readily. The most
intimate friend I ever had, who fell after heroic services, was known
by all our circle to be utterly at variance with the prevalent Southern
view of the quarrel, and died upholding a right which was not a right
to him except so far as the mandate of his state made it a right; and
while he would have preferred to see "the old flag" floating over a
united people, he restored the new banner to its place time after time
when it had been cut down by shot and shell.

Those who were bred in the opposite political faith, who read their
right of withdrawal in the Constitution, had less heart-searching to
begin with than the Union men of the South; but when the state
called there were no parties, and the only trace of the old difference
was a certain rivalry which should do the better fighting. This ready

response to the call of the state showed very clearly that, despite varying theories of government, the people of the Southern states were practically of one mind as to the seat of the paramount obligation. Adherence to the Union was a matter of sentiment, a matter of interest. The arguments urged on the South against secession were addressed to the memories of the glorious struggle for independence, to the anticipation of the glorious future that awaited the united country, to the difficulties and the burdens of a separate life. Especial stress was laid on the last argument; and the expense of a separate government, of a standing army, was set forth in appalling figures. A Northern student of the war once said to me, "If the Southern people had been of a statistical turn, there would have been no secession, there would have been no war." But there were men enough of a statistical turn in the South to warn the people against the enormous expense of independence, just as there are men enough of a statistical turn in Italy to remind the Italians of the enormous cost of national unity. "Counting the cost" is in things temporal the only wise course, as in the building of a tower; but there are times in the life of an individual, of a people, when the things that are eternal force themselves into the calculation, and the abacus is nowhere. "Neither count I my life dear unto myself" is a sentiment that does not enter into the domain of statistics. The great Athenian statesman who saw the necessity of the Peloponnesian War was not above statistics, as he showed when he passed in review the resources of the Athenian empire, the tribute from the allies, the treasure laid up in the House of the Virgin. But when he addressed the people in justification of the war, he based his argument, not on a calculation of material resources, but on a simple principle of right. Submission to any encroachment, the least as well as the greatest, on the rights of a state means slavery. To us submission meant slavery, as it did to Pericles and the Athenians; as it did to the great historian of Greece, who had learned this lesson from the Peloponnesian War, and who took sides with the Southern states, to the great dismay of his fellow radicals, who could not see, as George Grote saw, the real point at issue in the controversy. Submission is slavery, and the bitterest taunt in the vocabulary of those who advocated secession was "submissionist." But where does submission begin? Who is to mark the point of encroachment? That is a matter which must be decided by the sovereign; and on the theory that the states are sovereign, each state must be the judge. The extreme Southern states considered their rights menaced by the issue of the presidential election. Virginia and the border states were more deliberate; and Virginia's "pausing" was the theme of much mockery in the state and out of it, from friend and from foe alike. Her love of peace, her love of the Union, were set down now to cowardice, now to cunning. The Mother of States and Queller of Tyrants was caricatured as Mrs. Facing-both-ways; and the great commonwealth that even Mr. Lodge's statistics cannot displace from her leadership in the history of the country was charged with trading on her neutrality. Her solemn protest was unheeded. The "serried phalanx of her gallant sons" that should "prevent the passage of the United States forces" was an expression that amused Northern critics of style as a bit of antiquated Southern rodomontade. But the call for troops showed that the rodomontade meant something. Virginia had made her decision; and if the United States forces did not find a serried phalanx barring their way — a serried phalanx is somewhat out of date — they found something that answered the purpose as well.

The war began, the war went on. Passion was roused to fever heat. Both sides "saw red," that physiological condition which to a Frenchman excuses everything. The proverbial good humor of the American people did not, it is true, desert the country, and the Southern men who were in the field, as they were much happier than those who stayed at home, if I may judge by my own experience, were often merry enough by the camp fire, and exchanged rough jests with the enemy's pickets. But the invaded people were very much in earnest, however lightly some of their adversaries treated the matter, and as the pressure of the war grew tighter the more somber did life become. A friend of mine, describing the crowd that besieged the Gare de Lyon in Paris, when the circle of fire was drawing round the city, and foreigners were hastening to escape, told me that the press was so great that he could touch in every direction those who had been crushed to death as they stood, and had not had room to fall. Not wholly unlike this was the pressure brought to bear on the Confederacy. It was only necessary to put out your hand and you had touched a corpse; and that not an alien corpse, but the corpse of a brother or a friend. Every Southern man becomes grave when he thinks of that terrible stretch of time, partly, it is true, because life was nobler, but chiefly because of the memories of sorrow and suffering. A professional Southern humorist once undertook to write in dialect a Comic History of the War, but his heart failed him, as his public would have failed him, and the serial lived only for a number or two.

The war began, the war went on. War is a rough game. It is an omelet that cannot be made without breaking eggs, not only eggs in *esse*, but also eggs in *posse*. So far as I have read about war, ours was no worse than some other wars. While it lasted, the conduct of the combatants on either side was represented in the blackest colors by the other. Even the ordinary and legitimate doing to death was considered criminal if the deed was done by a ruthless rebel or a ruffianly invader. Non-combatants were especially eloquent. In describing the end of a brother who had been killed while trying to get a shot at a Yankee, a Southern girl raved about the "murdered patriot" and the "dastardly wretch" who had anticipated him. But I do not criticize, for I remember an English account of the battle of New Orleans, in which General Pakenham was represented as having been picked off by a "sneaking Yankee rifle." Those who were engaged in the actual conflict took more reasonable views, and the annals of the war are full of stories of battlefield and hospital in which a common humanity asserted itself. But brotherhood there was none. No alienation could have been more complete. Into the cleft made by the disruption poured all the bad blood that had been breeding from colonial times, from Revolutionary times, from constitutional struggles, from congressional debates, from "bleeding Kansas" and the engine house at Harper's Ferry; and a great gulf was fixed, as it seemed forever, between North and South. The hostility was a very satisfactory one — for military purposes.

. . . When social relations were resumed between the North and the South — they followed slowly the resumption of business relations — what we should call the color-blindness of the other side often manifested itself in a delicate reticence on the part of our Northern friends; and as the war had by no means constituted their lives as it had constituted ours for four long years, the success in avoiding the disagreeable topic would have been considerable if it had not been for awkward allusions on the part of the Southerners, who, having been shut out for all that time from the study of literature and art and other elegant and uncompromising subjects, could hardly keep from speaking of this and that incident of the war. Whereupon a discreet, or rather an embarrassed silence, as if a pardoned convict had playfully referred to the arson or burglary, not to say worse, that had been the cause of his seclusion.

Some fifteen years ago Mr. Lowell was lecturing in Baltimore, and during the month of his stay I learned to know the charm of his manner and the delight of his conversation. If I had been even more prejudiced than I was, I could not have withstood that easy grace, that winning cordiality. Everyone knew where he had stood during the war, and how he had wielded the flail of his "lashing hail" against the South and the Southern cause and "Southern sympathizers." But that warfare was over for him, and out of kindly regard for my feelings he made no allusion to the great quarrel, with two exceptions. Once, just before he left Baltimore, he was talking as no other man could talk about the Yankee dialect, and turning to me he said with a half smile and a deep twinkle in his eye, "I should like to have you read what I have written about the Yankee dialect, but I am afraid you might not like the context." A few days afterward I received from him the well-known preface to the Second Series of *The Biglow Papers*, cut out from the volume. It was a graceful concession to Southern weakness, and after all I may have been mistaken in thinking that I could read the Second Series as literature, just as I should read the Anti-Jacobin or the Two-penny Post Bag. In fact, on looking into the Second Series again, I must confess that I cannot even now discover the same merits that I could not help acknowledging in the First Series, which I read for the first time in 1850, when I was a student in Berlin. By that time I had recovered from my boyish enthusiasm over the Mexican War, and as my party had been success-ful, I could afford to enjoy the wit and humor of the book, from the inimitable Notices of an Independent Press to the last utterance of Birdofredum Sawin; and I have always remembered enough of the contents to make a psychological study of the Second Series a matter of interest, if it were not for other things.

On the second occasion we were passing together under the shadow of the Washington Monument, and the name of Lee came by some chance into the current of talk. Here Mr. Lowell could not refrain from expressing his view of Lee's course in turning against the govern-ment to which he had sworn allegiance. Doubtless he felt it to be his duty to emphasize his conviction as to a vital clause of his creed, but it instantly became evident that this was a theme that could not be profitably pursued, and we walked in silence the rest of the way — the author of the line

Virginia gave us this imperial man,

and the follower of that other imperial man Virginia gave the world; both honest, each believing the other hopelessly wrong, but absolutely sincere.

I have tried in this paper to reproduce the past and its perspective, to show how the men of my time and of my environment looked at the problems that confronted us. It has been a painful and, I fear, a futile task. So far as I have reproduced the perspective for myself it has been a revival of sorrows such as this generation cannot understand; it has recalled the hours when it gave one a passion for death, a shame of life, to read our bulletins. And how could I hope to reproduce that perspective for others, for men who belong to another generation and another region, when so many men who lived the same life and fought on the same side have themselves lost the point of view not only of the beginning of the war, but also of the end of the war; not only of the inexpressible exaltation, but of the unutterable degradation? They have forgotten what a strange world the survivors of the conflict had to face. If the state had been ours still, the foundations of the earth would not have been out of course; but the state was a military district, and the Confederacy had ceased to exist. The generous policy which would have restored the state and made a new union possible, which would have disentwined much of the passionate clinging to the past, was crossed by the death of the only man who could have carried it through, if even he could have carried it through; and years of trouble had to pass before the current of national life ran freely through the Southern states. It was before this circuit was complete that the principal of one of the chief schools of Virginia set up a tablet to the memory of the "old boys" who had perished in the war — it was a list the length of which few Northern colleges could equal — and I was asked to furnish a motto. Those who know classic literature at all know that for patriotism and friendship mottoes are not far to seek, but during the war I felt as I had never felt before the meaning of many a classic sentence. The motto came from Ovid, whom many call a frivolous poet; but the frivolous Roman was after all a Roman, and he was young when he wrote the line — too young not to feel the generous swell of true feeling. It was written of the dead brothers of Briseis:

Qui bene pro patria cum patriaque iacent.[1]

The sentiment found an echo at the time, deserved an echo at the time. Now it is a sentiment without an echo, and last year a valued personal friend of mine, in an eloquent oration, a noble tribute to the memory of our great captain, a discourse full of the glory of the past, the wisdom of the present, the hope of the future, rebuked the sentiment as idle in its despair. As well rebuke a cry of anguish, a cry of desolation out of the past. For those whose names are recorded on that tablet the line is but too true. For those of us who survive it has

[1] "Who gloriously fell for fatherland and with fatherland."

ceased to have the import that it once had, for we have learned to work resolutely for the furtherance of all that is good in the wider life that has been opened to us by the issue of the war, without complaining, without repining. That the cause we fought for and our brothers died for was the cause of civil liberty, and not the cause of human slavery, is a thesis which we feel ourselves bound to maintain whenever our motives are challenged or misunderstood, if only for our children's sake. But even that will not long be necessary, for the vindication of our principles will be made manifest in the working out of the problems with which the republic has to grapple. If, however, the effacement of state lines and the complete centralization of the government shall prove to be the wisdom of the future, the poetry of life will still find its home in the old order, and those who loved their state best will live longest in song and legend — song yet unsung, legend not yet crystallized.

FIVE AMERICAN CONTRIBUTIONS TO CIVILIZATION[1]

Charles W. Eliot

CHARLES W. ELIOT will be remembered chiefly as the most influential educator of his time in America; the leader who, taking charge of Harvard University in 1869 and remaining president until 1909, not only recreated that institution but gave a quickening impulse to advanced education throughout the nation. But he was a man of versatile interests, and his weight of character, his learning, his public spirit, and his wisdom gave him influence in a large number of fields. He was always active as an independent in politics, taking part in the Mugwump movement, becoming a strong anti-imperialist, and later warmly supporting Woodrow Wilson's chief policies. No advocate of international peace in the United States was better known; he wrote and spoke much on the subject, and became a devoted champion of the League of Nations. He was also a religious and moral leader of much power; a Unitarian in faith, the exponent of an optimistic philosophy of life, and a constant preacher of philanthropy and of strenuous activity as leading to the "durable satisfactions" of life. A man of great physical and mental vigor, he was incessantly busy, constantly concerned with altruistic effort, and always serene of spirit. In his published writings he expounded his religious convictions as to the spiritual nature of the world, and his moral conviction that duty and service are the sole roads to happiness. Of three books in this field, *The Happy Life* (1896), *The Religion of the Future* (1909), and *The Durable Satisfactions of Life* (1910), he regarded the first as the most important. He also published a thoughtful collection of essays upon general social and political topics, *American Contributions to Civilization* (1897). Always interested in the more popular forms of education, late in life he made the assertion that a man might acquire a liberal education by reading fifteen minutes a day in a five-foot shelf of books, and then supported it by editing the *Harvard Classics*. This collection of fifty volumes showed the catholic range of his reading, his appreciation of the best in letters, and his ethical and scientific bent.

Eliot was born in 1834 of the best New England stock, his father having been mayor of Boston, and was educated at Harvard, where his chief interests — apart from English literature — were mathematics and science, and where he profited greatly from the teachings of Agassiz, Asa Gray, and Jeffries Wyman. After teaching mathematics and chemistry at Harvard, and studying for a time abroad, he was appointed professor of mathematics at the Massachusetts Institute of Technology in 1865. It was from this post that he was called to the presidency of Harvard. A considerable group of eminent university presidents became prominent in the United States in the last quarter of the nineteenth century — Andrew D. White, James McCosh, Daniel Coit Gilman, James B. Angell; but in scope of influence Eliot was easily foremost. He died in 1926.

[1] From *American Contributions to Civilization and Other Essays and Addresses*, by Charles W. Eliot. Used by permission of D. Appleton-Century Company, Inc.

Looking back over forty centuries of history, we observe that many nations have made characteristic contributions to the progress of civilization, the beneficent effects of which have been permanent, although the races that made them may have lost their national form and organization, or their relative standing among the nations of the earth. Thus, the Hebrew race, during many centuries, made supreme contributions to religious thought; and the Greek, during the brief climax of the race, to speculative philosophy, architecture, sculpture, and the drama. The Roman people developed military colonization, aqueducts, roads and bridges, and a great body of public law, large parts of which still survive; and the Italians of the Middle Ages and the Renaissance developed ecclesiastical organization and the fine arts, as tributary to the splendor of the church and to municipal luxury. England, for several centuries, has contributed to the institutional development of representative government and public justice; the Dutch, in the sixteenth century, made a superb struggle for free thought and free government; France, in the eighteenth century, taught the doctrine of individual freedom and the theory of human rights; and Germany, at two periods within the nineteenth century, fifty years apart, proved the vital force of the sentiment of nationality. I ask you to consider with me what characteristic and durable contributions the American people have been making to the progress of civilization.

The first and principal contribution to which I shall ask your attention is the advance made in the United States, not in theory only, but in practice, toward the abandonment of war as the means of settling disputes between nations, the substitution of discussion and arbitration, and the avoidance of armaments. If the intermittent Indian fighting and the brief contest with the Barbary corsairs be disregarded, the United States have had only four years and a quarter of international war in the one hundred and seven years since the adoption of the Constitution.[1] Within the same period the United States have been a party to forty-seven arbitrations — being more than half of all that have taken place in the modern world. The questions settled by these arbitrations have been just such as have commonly caused wars; namely, questions of boundary, fisheries, damage caused by war or civil disturbances, and injuries to commerce. Some of them were of great magnitude, the four made under the Treaty of Washington (May 8, 1871) being the most important

---

[1] This address was delivered in 1896.

that have ever taken place. Confident in their strength, and relying on their ability to adjust international differences, the United States have habitually maintained, by voluntary enlistment for short terms, a standing army and a fleet which, in proportion to the population, are insignificant.

The beneficent effects of this American contribution to civilization are of two sorts: in the first place, the direct evils of war and of preparations for war have been diminished; and secondly, the influence of the war spirit on the perennial conflict between the rights of the single personal unit and the powers of the multitude that constitute organized society — or, in other words, between individual freedom and collective authority — has been reduced to the lowest terms. War has been, and still is, the school of collectivism, the warrant of tyranny. Century after century, tribes, clans, and nations have sacrificed the liberty of the individual to the fundamental necessity of being strong for combined defense or attack in war. Individual freedom is crushed in war, for the nature of war is inevitably despotic. It says to the private person: "Obey without a question, even unto death; die in this ditch, without knowing why; walk into that deadly thicket; mount this embankment, behind which are men who will try to kill you, lest you should kill them; make part of an immense machine for blind destruction, cruelty, rapine, and killing." At this moment every young man in continental Europe learns the lesson of absolute military obedience, and feels himself subject to this crushing power of militant society, against which no rights of the individual to life, liberty, and the pursuit of happiness avail anything. This pernicious influence, inherent in the social organization of all continental Europe during many centuries, the American people have for generations escaped, and they show other nations how to escape it. I ask your attention to the favorable conditions under which this contribution of the United States to civilization has been made.

There has been a deal of fighting on the American continent during the past three centuries; but it has not been of the sort which most imperils liberty. The first European colonists who occupied portions of the coast of North America encountered in the Indians men of the Stone Age, who ultimately had to be resisted and quelled by force. The Indian races were at a stage of development thousands of years behind that of the Europeans. They could not be assimilated; for the most part they could not be taught or even reasoned with; with a few exceptions they had to be driven away by prolonged fighting, or subdued by force so that they would live peaceably with the whites.

This warfare, however, always had in it for the whites a large element of self-defense — the homes and families of the settlers were to be defended against a stealthy and pitiless foe. Constant exposure to the attacks of savages was only one of the formidable dangers and difficulties which for a hundred years the early settlers had to meet, and which developed in them courage, hardiness, and persistence. The French and English wars on the North American continent, always more or less mixed with Indian warfare, were characterized by race hatred and religious animosity — two of the commonest causes of war in all ages; but they did not tend to fasten upon the English colonists any objectionable public authority, or to contract the limits of individual liberty. They furnished a school of martial qualities at small cost to liberty. In the War of Independence there was a distinct hope and purpose to enlarge individual liberty. It made possible a confederation of the colonists, and, ultimately, the adoption of the Constitution of the United States. It gave to the thirteen colonies a lesson in collectivism, but it was a needed lesson on the necessity of combining their forces to resist an oppressive external authority. The War of 1812 is properly called the Second War of Independence, for it was truly a fight for liberty and for the rights of neutrals, in resistance to the impressment of seamen and other oppressions growing out of European conflicts. The Civil War of 1861–1865 was waged, on the side of the North, primarily to prevent the dismemberment of the country, and secondarily and incidentally to destroy the institution of slavery. On the Northern side it therefore called forth a generous element of popular ardor in defense of free institutions; and though it temporarily caused centralization of great powers in the government, it did as much to promote individual freedom as it did to strengthen public authority.

In all this series of fightings the main motives were self-defense, resistance to oppression, the enlargement of liberty, and the conservation of national acquisitions. The war with Mexico, it is true, was of a wholly different type. That was a war of conquest, and of conquest chiefly in the interest of African slavery. It was also an unjust attack made by a powerful people on a feeble one; but it lasted less than two years, and the number of men engaged in it was at no time large. Moreover, by the treaty which ended the war, the conquering nation agreed to pay the conquered nation eighteen million dollars in partial compensation for some of the territory wrested from it, instead of demanding a huge war indemnity, as the European way is. Its results contradicted the anticipations both of those who advocated and of those who opposed it. It was one of the wrongs which prepared the way for the great rebellion; but its direct evils were of moderate extent, and it had no effect on the perennial conflict between individual liberty and public power.

In the meantime, partly as the results of Indian fighting and the Mexican War, but chiefly through purchases and arbitrations, the American people had acquired a territory so extensive, so defended by oceans, gulfs, and great lakes, and so intersected by those great natural highways, navigable rivers, that it would obviously be impossible for any enemy to overrun or subdue it. The civilized nations of Europe, western Asia, and northern Africa have always been liable to hostile incursions from without. Over and over again barbarous hordes have overthrown established civilizations; and at this moment there is not a nation of Europe which does not feel obliged to maintain monstrous armaments for defense against its neighbors. The American people have long been exempt from such terrors, and are now absolutely free from this necessity of keeping in readiness to meet heavy assaults. The absence of a great standing army and of a large fleet has been a main characteristic of the United States, in contrast with the other civilized nations; this has been a great inducement to immigration, and a prime cause of the country's rapid increase in wealth. The United States have no formidable neighbor, except Great Britain in Canada. In April, 1817, by a convention made between Great Britain and the United States, without much public discussion or observation, these two powerful nations agreed that each should keep on the Great Lakes only a few police vessels of insignificant size and armament. This agreement was made but four years after Perry's naval victory on Lake Erie, and only three years after the burning of Washington by a British force. It was one of the first acts of Monroe's first administration, and it would be difficult to find in all history a more judicious or effectual agreement between two powerful neighbors. For eighty years this beneficent convention has helped to keep the peace. The European way would have been to build competitive fleets, dockyards, and fortresses, all of which would have helped to bring on war during the periods of mutual exasperation which have occurred since 1817. Monroe's second administration was signalized, six years later, by the declaration that the United States would consider any attempt on the part of the Holy Alliance to extend their system to any portion of this hemisphere as dangerous to the peace and safety of the United States. This announcement was designed to prevent the introduction on the American continent of the horrible European system — with its balance of power, its alliances offensive and defensive in opposing groups, and its perpetual armaments on an enormous scale. That a declaration expressly intended to promote peace and prevent armaments should now be perverted into an argument for arming and for a belligerent public policy is an extraordinary perversion of the true American doctrine.

The ordinary causes of war between nation and nation have been lacking in America for the last century and a quarter. How many wars in the world's history have been due to contending dynasties; how many of the most cruel and protracted wars have been due to religious strife; how many to race hatred! No one of these causes of war has been efficacious in America since the French were overcome in Canada by the English in 1759. Looking forward into the future, we find it impossible to imagine circumstances under which any of these common causes of war can take effect on the North American continent. Therefore, the ordinary motives for maintaining armament in time of peace, and concentrating the powers of government in such a way as to interfere with individual liberty, have not been in play in the United States as among the nations of Europe, and are not likely to be.

Such have been the favorable conditions under which America has made its best contribution to the progress of our race. . . .

The second eminent contribution which the United States have made to civilization is their thorough acceptance, in theory and practice, of the widest religious toleration. As a means of suppressing individual liberty, the collective authority of the church, when elaborately organized in a hierarchy directed by one head and absolutely devoted in every rank to its service, comes next in proved efficiency to that concentration of powers in government which enables it to carry on war effectively. The Western Christian Church, organized under the Bishop of Rome, acquired, during the Middle Ages, a centralized authority which quite overrode both the temporal ruler and the rising spirit of nationality. For a time Christian church and Christian state acted together, just as in Egypt, during many earlier centuries, the great powers of civil and religious rule had been united. The Crusades marked the climax of the power of the church. Thereafter, church and state were often in conflict; and during this prolonged conflict the seeds of liberty were planted, took root, and made some sturdy growth. We can see now, as we look back on the history of Europe, how fortunate it was that the colonization of North

America by Europeans was deferred until after the period of the Reformation, and especially until after the Elizabethan period in England, the Luther period in Germany, and the splendid struggle of the Dutch for liberty in Holland. The founders of New England and New York were men who had imbibed the principles of resistance both to arbitrary civil power and to universal ecclesiastical authority. Hence it came about that within the territory now covered by the United States no single ecclesiastical organization ever obtained a wide and oppressive control, and that in different parts of this great region churches very unlike in doctrine and organization were almost simultaneously established. It has been an inevitable consequence of this condition of things that the church, as a whole, in the United States has not been an effective opponent of any form of human rights. For generations it has been divided into numerous sects and denominations, no one of which has been able to claim more than a tenth of the population as its adherents; and the practices of these numerous denominations have been profoundly modified by political theories and practices, and by social customs natural to new communities formed under the prevailing conditions of free intercourse and rapid growth. The constitutional prohibition of religious tests as qualifications for office gave the United States the leadership among the nations in dissociating theological opinions and political rights. No one denomination or ecclesiastical organization in the United States has held great properties, or has had the means of conducting its ritual with costly pomp or its charitable works with imposing liberality. No splendid architectural exhibitions of church power have interested or overawed the population. On the contrary, there has prevailed in general a great simplicity in public worship, until very recent years. Some splendors have been lately developed by religious bodies in the great cities; but these splendors and luxuries have been almost simultaneously exhibited by religious bodies of very different, not to say opposite, kinds. Thus, in New York City, the Jews, the Greek Church, the Catholics, and the Episcopalians have all erected, or undertaken to erect, magnificent edifices. But these recent demonstrations of wealth and zeal are so distributed among differing religious organizations that they cannot be imagined to indicate a coming centralization of ecclesiastical influence adverse to individual liberty.

In the United States, the great principle of religious toleration is better understood and more firmly established than in any other nation of the earth. It is not only embodied in legislation, but also completely recognized in the habits and customs of good society. Elsewhere it may be a long road from legal to social recognition of religious liberty, as the example of England shows. This recognition alone would mean, to any competent student of history, that the United States had made an unexampled contribution to the reconciliation of just governmental power with just freedom for the individual, inasmuch as the partial establishment of religious toleration has been the main work of civilization during the past four centuries. In view of this characteristic and infinitely beneficent contribution to human happiness and progress, how pitiable seem the temporary outbursts of bigotry and fanaticism which have occasionally marred the fair record of our country in regard to religious toleration! If anyone imagines that this American contribution to civilization is no longer important — that the victory for toleration has been already won — let him recall the fact that the last years of the nineteenth century have witnessed two horrible religious persecutions: one, of the Jews by Russia, and the other, of the Armenians by Turkey.

The third characteristic contribution which the United States have made to civilization has been the safe development of a manhood suffrage nearly universal. The experience of the United States has brought out several principles with regard to the suffrage which have not been clearly apprehended by some eminent political philosophers. In the first place, American experience has demonstrated the advantages of a gradual approach to suffrage, over a sudden leap. Universal suffrage is not the first and only means of attaining democratic government; rather, it is the ultimate goal of successful democracy. It is not a specific for the cure of all political ills; on the contrary, it may itself easily be the source of great political evils. The people of the United States feel its dangers today. When constituencies are large, it aggravates the well-known difficulties of party government, so that many of the ills which threaten democratic communities at this moment, whether in Europe or America, proceed from the breakdown of party government were elaborated where suffrage was limited and constituencies were small. Manhood suffrage has not worked perfectly well in the United States, or in any other nation where it has been adopted, and it is not likely very soon to work perfectly anywhere. It is like freedom of the will for the individual — the only atmosphere in which virtue can grow, but an atmosphere in which sin can also grow. Like freedom of the will, it needs to be surrounded with checks and safeguards, particularly in the childhood of the nation; but, like freedom of the will, it is the supreme good, the goal of perfected democracy. Secondly, like freedom of the will, universal suffrage has an educational effect, which has been mentioned by many writers, but has seldom been clearly apprehended or adequately described. This educational effect is produced in two ways. In the first place, the combination of individual freedom with social mobility, which a wide suffrage tends to produce, permits the capable to rise through all grades of society, even within a single generation; and this freedom to rise is intensely stimulating to personal ambition. Thus every capable American, from youth to age, is bent on bettering himself and his condition. Nothing can be more striking than the contrast between the mental condition of an average American belonging to the laborious classes, but conscious that he can rise to the top of the social scale, and that of a European mechanic, peasant, or tradesman, who knows that he cannot rise out of his class, and is content with his hereditary classification. The state of mind of the American prompts to constant struggle for self-improvement and the acquisition of all sorts of property and power. In the second place, it is a direct effect of a broad suffrage that the voters become periodically interested in the discussion of grave public problems, which carry their minds away from the routine of their daily labor and household experience out into larger fields. The instrumentalities of this prolonged education have been multiplied and improved enormously within the last fifty years. In no field of human endeavor have the fruits of the introduction of steam and electrical power been more striking than in the methods of reaching multitudes of people with instructive narratives, expositions, and arguments. The multiplication of newspapers, magazines, and books is only one of the immense developments in the means of reaching the people. The advocates of any public cause now have it in their power to provide hundreds of newspapers with the same copy, or the same plates, for simultaneous issue. The mails provide the means of circulating millions of leaflets and pamphlets. The interest in the minds of the people which prompts to the reading of these multiplied communications comes from the frequently recurring elections. The more difficult the intellectual problem presented in any given election, the more educative the effect of the discussion. Many modern industrial and financial problems are extremely difficult, even for highly educated men. As subjects of earnest thought and discussion on the farm, and in the workshop, factory, rolling mill, and mine, they supply a mental training for millions of adults, the like of which has never before been seen in the world.

In these discussions, it is not only the receptive masses that are benefited; the classes that supply the appeals to the masses are also benefited in a high degree. There is no better mental exercise for the most highly trained man than the effort to expound a difficult subject in so clear a way that the untrained man can understand it. In a republic in which the final appeal is the manhood suffrage, the educated minority of the people is constantly stimulated to exertion, by the instinct of self-preservation as well as by love of country. They see dangers in proposals made to universal suffrage, and they must exert themselves to ward off those dangers. The position of the educated and well-to-do classes is a thoroughly wholesome one in this respect: they cannot depend for the preservation of their advantages on land-owning, hereditary privilege, or any legislation not equally applicable to the poorest and humblest citizen. They must maintain their superiority by being superior. They cannot live in a too safe corner.

I touch here on a misconception which underlies much of the criticism of universal suffrage. It is commonly said that the rule of the majority must be the rule of the most ignorant and incapable, the multitude being necessarily uninstructed as to taxation, public finance, and foreign relations, and untrained to active thought on such difficult subjects. Now, universal suffrage is merely a convention as to where the last appeal shall lie for the decision of public questions; and it is the rule of the majority only in this sense. The educated classes are undoubtedly a minority; but it is not safe to assume that they monopolize the good sense of the community. On the contrary, it is very clear that native good judgment and good feeling are not proportional to education, and that among a multitude of men who have only an elementary education, a large proportion will possess both good judgment and good feeling. Indeed, persons who can neither read nor write may possess a large share of both, as is constantly seen in regions where the opportunities for education in childhood have been scanty or inaccessible. It is not to be supposed that the cultivated classes, under a régime of universal suffrage, are not going to try to make their cultivation felt in the discussion and disposal of public questions. Any result under universal suffrage is a complex effect of the discussion of the public question in hand by the educated classes in the presence of the comparatively uneducated, when a majority of both classes taken together is ultimately to settle the question. In practice, both classes divide on almost every issue. But, in any case, if the educated classes cannot hold their own with the uneducated, by means of their superior physical, mental, and moral qualities, they are obviously unfit to lead society. With education should come better powers of argument and persuasion, a stricter sense of honor, and a greater general effectiveness. With these advantages, the educated classes must undoubtedly appeal to the less educated, and try to convert them to their way of thinking; but this is a process which is good for both sets of people. Indeed, it is the best possible process for the training of freemen, educated or uneducated, rich or poor.

It is often assumed that the educated classes become impotent in a democracy, because the representatives of those classes are not exclusively chosen to public office. This argument is a very fallacious one. It assumes that the public offices are the places of greatest influence; whereas, in the United States, at least, that is conspicuously not the case. In a democracy, it is important to discriminate influence from authority. Rulers and magistrates may or may not be persons of influence; but many persons of influence never become rulers, magistrates, or representatives in parliaments or legislatures. The complex industries of a modern state, and its innumerable corporation services, offer great fields for administrative talent which were entirely unknown to preceding generations; and these new activities attract many ambitious and capable men more strongly than the public service. These men are not on that account lost to their country or to society. The present generation has wholly escaped from the conditions of earlier centuries, when able men who were not great landowners had but three outlets for their ambition — the army, the church, or the national civil service. The national service, whether in an empire, a limited monarchy, or a republic, is now only one of many fields which offer to able and patriotic men an honorable and successful career. Indeed, legislation and public administration necessarily have a very second-hand quality; and more and more legislators and administrators become dependent on the researches of scholars, men of science, and historians, and follow in the footsteps of inventors, economists, and political philosophers. Political leaders are very seldom leaders of thought; they are generally trying to induce masses of men to act on principles thought out long before. Their skill is in the selection of practicable approximations to the ideal; their arts are arts of exposition and persuasion; their honor comes from fidelity under trying circumstances to familiar principles of public duty. The real leaders of American thought in this century have been preachers, teachers, jurists, seers, and poets. While it is of the highest importance, under any form of government, that the public servants should be men of intelligence, education, and honor, it is no objection to any given form, that under it large numbers of educated and honorable citizens have no connection with the public service. . . .

Timid or conservative people often stand aghast at the possible directions of democratic desire, or at some of the predicted results of democratic rule; but meantime the actual experience of the American democracy proves: (1) that property has never been safer under any form of government; (2) that no people have ever welcomed so ardently new machinery, and new inventions generally; (3) that religious toleration was never carried so far, and never so universally accepted; (4) that nowhere have the power and disposition to read been so general; (5) that nowhere has governmental power been more adequate, or more freely exercised, to levy and collect taxes, to raise armies and to disband them, to maintain public order, and to pay off great public debts — national, state, and town; (6) that nowhere have property and well-being been so widely diffused; and (7) that no form of government ever inspired greater affection and loyalty, or prompted to greater personal sacrifices in supreme moments. In view of these solid facts, speculations as to what universal suffrage would have done in the seventeenth and eighteenth centuries, or may do in the twentieth, seem futile indeed. The most civilized nations of the world have all either adopted this final appeal to manhood suffrage, or they are approaching that adoption by rapid stages. The United States, having no customs or traditions of an opposite sort to overcome, have led the nations in this direction, and have had the honor of devising, as a result of practical experience, the best safeguards for universal suffrage, safeguards which, in the main, are intended to prevent hasty public action, or action based on sudden discontents or temporary spasms of public feeling. These checks are intended to give time for discussion and deliberation, or, in other words, to secure the enlightenment of the voters before the vote. If, under new conditions, existing safeguards prove insufficient, the only wise course is to devise new safeguards.

The United States have made to civilization a fourth contribution of a very hopeful sort, to which public attention needs to be directed, lest temporary evils connected therewith should prevent the continuation of this beneficent action. The United States have furnished a demonstration that people belonging to a great variety of races or nations are, under favorable circumstances, fit for political freedom. It is the fashion to attribute to the enormous immigration of the last fifty years some of the failures of the American political system, and particularly the American failure in municipal government, and the introduction in a few states of the rule of the irresponsible party foremen known as "bosses." Impatient of these evils, and hastily accepting this improbable explanation of them, some people wish to depart from the American policy of welcoming immigrants. In two respects the absorption of large numbers of immigrants from many nations into the American commonwealth has been of great service to mankind. In the first place, it has demonstrated that people who at home have been subject to every sort of aristocratic or despotic or military oppression become within less than a generation serviceable citizens of a republic; and, in the second place, the United States have thus educated to freedom many millions of men. Furthermore, the comparatively high degree of happiness and prosperity enjoyed by the people of the United States has been brought home to multitudes in Europe by friends and relatives who have emigrated to this country and has commended free institutions to them in the best possible way. This is a legitimate propaganda vastly more effective than any annexation or conquest of unwilling people, or of people unprepared for liberty.

It is a great mistake to suppose that the process of assimilating foreigners began in this century. The eighteenth century provided the colonies with a great mixture of peoples, although the English race predominated then, as now. When the Revolution broke out, there were already English, Irish, Scotch, Dutch, Germans, French, Portuguese, and Swedes in the colonies. The French were, to be sure, in small proportion, and were almost exclusively Huguenot refugees, but they were a valuable element in the population. The Germans were well diffused, having established themselves in New York, Pennsylvania, Virginia, and Georgia. The Scotch were scattered through all the colonies. Pennsylvania, especially, was inhabited by an extraordinary mixture of nationalities and religions. Since steam navigation on the Atlantic and railroad transportation on the North American continent became cheap and easy, the tide of immigration has greatly increased; but it is very doubtful if the amount of assimilation going on in the nineteenth century has been any larger, in proportion to the population and wealth of the country, than it was in the eighteenth. The main difference in the assimilation going on in the two centuries is this, that in the eighteenth century the newcomers were almost all Protestants, while in the nineteenth century a considerable proportion have been Catholics. One result, however, of the importation of large numbers of Catholics into the United States has been a profound modification of the Roman Catholic Church in regard to the manners and customs of both the clergy and the laity, the scope of the authority of the priest, and the attitude of the Catholic Church toward public education. This American modification of the Roman Church has reacted strongly on the church in Europe.

Another great contribution to civilization made by the United States is the diffusion of material well-being among the population. No country in the world approaches the United States in this respect. It is seen in that diffused elementary education which implants for life a habit of reading, and in the habitual optimism which characterizes the common people. It is seen in the housing of the people and of their domestic animals, in the comparative costliness of their food, clothing, and household furniture, in their implements, vehicles, and means of transportation, and in the substitution, on a prodigious scale, of the work of machinery for the work of men's hands. This last item in American well-being is quite as striking in agriculture, mining, and fishing as it is in manufactures. The social effects of the manufacture of power, and of the discovery of means of putting that power just where it is wanted, have been more striking in the United States than anywhere else. Manufactured and distributed power needs intelligence to direct it: the bicycle is a blind horse, and must be steered at every instant; somebody must show a steam drill where to strike and how deep to go. So far as men and women can substitute for the direct expenditure of muscular strength the more intelligent effort of designing, tending, and guiding machines, they win promotion in the scale of being, and make their lives more interesting as well as more productive. It is in the invention of machinery for producing and distributing power, and at once economizing and elevating human labor, that American ingenuity has been most conspicuously manifested. The high price of labor in a sparsely settled country has had something to do with this striking result; but the genius of the people and of their government has had much more to do with it. As proof of the general proposition, it suffices merely to mention the telegraph and telephone, the sewing machine, the cotton gin, the mower, the reaper, and threshing machine, the dish-washing machine, the river steamboat, the sleeping-car, the boot and shoe machinery, and the watch machinery. The ultimate effects of these and kindred inventions are quite as much intellectual as physical, and they are developing and increasing with a portentous rapidity which sometimes suggests a doubt whether the bodily forces of men and women are adequate to resist the new mental strains brought upon them. However this may prove to be in the future, the clear result in the present is an unexampled diffusion of well-being in the United States.

These five contributions to civilization — peacekeeping, religious toleration, the development of manhood suffrage, the welcoming of newcomers, and the diffusion of well-being — I hold to have been eminently characteristic of our country, and so important that in spite of the qualifications and deductions which every candid citizen would admit with regard to every one of them, they will ever be held in the grateful remembrance of mankind. They are reasonable grounds for a steady, glowing patriotism. They have had much to do, both as causes and as effects, with the material prosperity of the United States; but they are all five essentially moral contributions, being triumphs of reason, enterprise, courage, faith, and justice, over passion, selfishness, inertness, timidity, and distrust. Beneath each one of these developments there lies a strong ethical sentiment, a strenuous moral and social purpose. It is for such work that multitudinous democracies are fit.

In regard to all five of these contributions, the characteristic policy of our country has been from time to time threatened with reversal — is even now so threatened. It is for true patriots to insist on the maintenance of these historic purposes and policies of the people of the United States. Our country's future perils, whether already visible or still unimagined, are to be met with courage and constancy founded firmly on these popular achievements in the past.

THE UNIFORMITY OF AMERICAN LIFE[1]

James Bryce[2]

To the pleasantness of American life there is one, and only one, serious drawback — its uniformity. Those who have been struck by the size of America, and by what they have heard of its restless excitement, may be surprised at the word. They would have guessed that an unquiet changefulness and turmoil were the disagreeables to be feared. But uniformity, which the European visitor begins to note when he has traveled for a month or two, is the feature of the country which Englishmen who have lived long there, and Americans who are · familiar with Europe, most frequently revert to when asked to say what is the "crook in their lot."

It is felt in many ways. I will name a few.

It is felt in the aspects of nature. All the natural features of the United States are on a larger scale than those of Europe. The four great mountain chains are each of them longer than the Alps. Of the gigantic rivers and of those inland seas we call the Great Lakes one need not speak. The center of the continent is occupied by a plain larger than the western half of Europe. In the Mississippi valley, from the Gulf of Mexico to Lake Superior, there is nothing deserving to be called a hill, though, as one moves westward from the great river, long soft undulation in the great prairie begins to appear. Through vast stretches of country one finds the same physical character maintained with little change — the same strata, the same vegetation, a generally similar climate. From the point where you leave the Alleghanies at Pittsburgh, until after crossing the Missouri, you approach the still untilled prairie of the West, a railway run of some thousand miles, there is a uniformity of landscape greater than could be found along any one hundred miles of railway run in Western Europe. Everywhere the same nearly flat country, over which you cannot see far, because you are little raised above it, the same fields and crops, the same rough wooden fences, the same thickets of the same bushes along the stream edges, with here and there a bit of old forest; the same solitary farmhouses and straggling wood-built villages. And when one has passed beyond the fields and farmhouses,

[1] From *The American Commonwealth*, by James Bryce. By permission of The Macmillan Company, publishers.

[2] For biographical note, see page 3.

there is an even more unvaried stretch of slightly rolling prairie, smooth and bare, till after five hundred miles the blue line of the Rocky Mountains rises upon the western horizon.

There are some extraordinary natural phenomena, such as Niagara, the Yellowstone geysers, and the great canyon of the Colorado River, which Europe cannot equal.   But taking the country as a whole, and remembering that it is a continent, it is not more rich in picturesque beauty than the much smaller western half of Europe.   There is a good deal of pretty scenery and a few really romantic spots in the long Alleghany range, but hardly anything so charming as the best bits of Scotland or southern Ireland, or the English lakes.   The Rocky Mountains are pierced by some splendid gorges, such as the famous canyon of the Arkansas River above South Pueblo, and some most impressive wide prospects, such as that over the Great Salt Lake from the Mormon capital.   But neither the Rocky Mountains, with their dependent ranges, nor the Sierra Nevada can be compared for variety of grandeur and beauty with the Alps; for although each chain nearly equals the Alps in height, and covers a greater area, they have little snow, no glaciers, and a singular uniformity of character.   One finds, I think, less variety in the whole chain of the Rockies than in the comparatively short Pyrenees.   There are indeed in the whole United States very few quite first-rate pieces of mountain scenery rivaling the best of the Old World.   The most impressive are, I think, two or three of the deep valleys of the Sierra Nevada (of which the Yosemite is the best known), and the superb line of extinct volcanoes, bearing snowfields and glaciers, which one sees, rising out of vast and somber forests, from the banks of the Columbia River and the shores of Puget Sound.   So the Atlantic coast, though there are pretty bits between Newport and the New Brunswick frontier, cannot vie with the coasts of Scotland, Ireland, or Norway; while southward from New York to Florida it is everywhere flat and generally dreary.   In the United States people take journeys proportionate to the size of the country. A family thinks nothing of going twelve hundred miles, from St. Louis to Cape May (near Philadelphia), for a seaside holiday.   But even journeys of twelve hundred miles do not give an American so much change of scene and variety of surroundings as a Parisian has when he goes to Nice, or a Berliner to Berchtesgaden.   The man who lives in the section of America which seems destined to contain the largest population, I mean the states on the upper Mississippi, lives in the midst of a plain wider than the plains of Russia, and must travel hundreds of miles to escape from its monotony.

When we turn from the aspects of nature to the cities of men, the uniformity is even more remarkable. With five or six exceptions to be mentioned presently, American cities differ from one another only herein: that some of them are built more with brick than with wood, and others more with wood than with brick. In all else they are alike, both great and small. In all the same wide streets, crossing at right angles, ill-paved, but planted along the sidewalks with maple trees whose autumnal scarlet surpasses the brilliance of any European foliage. In all the same shops, arranged on the same plan, the same Chinese laundries, with Li Kow visible through the window, the same ice cream stores, the same large hotels with seedy men hovering about in the dreary entrance hall, the same street cars passing to and fro with passengers clinging to the doorstep, the same locomotives ringing their great bells as they clank slowly down the middle of the street. I admit that in external aspect there is a sad monotony in the larger towns of England also. Compare English cities with Italian cities, and most of the former seem like one another, incapable of being, so to speak, individualized as you individualize a man with a definite character and aspect unlike that of other men. Take the Lancashire towns, for instance, large and prosperous places. You cannot individualize Bolton or Wigan, Oldham or Bury, except by trying to remember that Bury is slightly less rough than Oldham, and Wigan a thought more grimy than Bolton. But in Italy every city has its character, its memories, its life and achievements wrought into pillars of its churches and the towers that stand along its ramparts. Siena is not like Perugia, nor Perugia like Orvieto; Ravenna, Rimini, Pesaro, Fano, Ancona, Osimo, standing along the same coast within seventy miles of one another, have each of them a character, a sentiment, what one may call an idiosyncrasy, which comes vividly back to us at the mention of its name. Now, what English towns are to Italian, that American towns are to English. They are in some ways pleasanter; they are cleaner, there is less poverty, less squalor, less darkness. But their monotony haunts one like a nightmare. Even the irksomeness of finding the streets named by numbers becomes insufferable. It is doubtless convenient to know by the number how far up the city the particular street is. But you cannot give any sort of character to Twenty-ninth Street, for the name refuses to lend itself to any association. There is something wearisomely hard and bare in such a system.

I return joyfully to the exceptions. Boston has a character of her own, with her beautiful Common, her smooth environing waters, her

Beacon Hill crowned by the gilded dome of the State House, and Bunker's Hill, bearing the monument of the famous fight.   New York, besides a magnificent position, has in the grandeur of the buildings and the tremendous rush of men and vehicles along the streets as much the air of a great capital as London itself.   Chicago, with her enormous size and the splendid warehouses that line her endless thoroughfares, leaves a strong though not wholly agreeable impression.   Richmond has a quaint Old World look which dwells in the memory: few cities have a sea front equal in beauty to the lake front of Cleveland. Washington, with its wide and beautifully graded avenues, and the glittering white of the stately Capitol, has become within the last twenty years a singularly handsome city.   And New Orleans — or rather the Creole quarter of New Orleans, for the rest of the city is commonplace — is delicious, suggesting old France and Spain, yet a France and Spain strangely transmuted in this new clime.   I have seen nothing in America more picturesque than the Rue Royale, with its houses of all heights, often built round a courtyard, where a magnolia or an orange-tree stands in the middle, and wooden external staircases lead up to wooden galleries, the house fronts painted of all colors, and carrying double rows of balconies decorated with pretty ironwork, the whole standing languid and still in the warm soft air, and touched with the subtle fragrance of decay.   Here in New Orleans the streets and public buildings, and specially the old City Hall, with the arms of Spain still upon it, speak of history.   One feels, in stepping across Canal Street from the Creole quarter to the business parts of the town, that one steps from an old nationality to a new one, that this city must have had vicissitudes, that it represents something, and that something one of the great events of history, the surrender of the northern half of the New World by the Romano-Celtic races to the Teutonic.   Quebec, and to a less degree Montreal, fifteen hundred miles away, tell the same tale: Santa Fe in New Mexico repeats it.

It is the absence in nearly all the American cities of anything that speaks of the past that makes their external aspect so unsuggestive. In pacing their busy streets and admiring their handsome city halls and churches, one's heart sinks at the feeling that nothing historically interesting ever has happened here, perhaps ever will happen.   In many an English town, however ugly with its smoke and its new suburbs, one sees at least an ancient church, one can discover some fragments of a castle or a city wall.   Even Wigan and Northampton have ancient churches, though Northampton lately allowed the

North-Western Railway to destroy the last traces of the castle where Henry II issued his assize.   But in America hardly any public building is associated with anything more interesting than a big party convention; and nowadays even the big conventions are held in temporary structures, whose materials are sold when the politicians have dispersed.   Nowhere, perhaps, does this sense of the absolute novelty of all things strike one so strongly as in San Francisco.   Few cities in the world can vie with her either in the beauty or in the natural advantages of her situation; indeed, there are only two places in Europe — Constantinople and Gibraltar — that combine an equally perfect landscape with what may be called an equally imperial position. Before you there is the magnificent bay, with its far-stretching arms and rocky isles, and beyond it the faint line of the Sierra Nevada, cutting the clear air like mother-of-pearl; behind, there is the roll of the ocean; to the left, the majestic gateway between mountains through which ships bear in commerce from the farthest shores of the Pacific; to the right, valleys rich with corn and wine, sweeping away to the southern horizon.   The city itself is full of bold hills, rising steeply from the deep water.   The air is keen, dry, and bright, like the air of Greece, and the waters not less blue.   Perhaps it is this air and light, recalling the cities of the Mediterranean, that make one involuntarily look up to the top of these hills for the feudal castle, or the ruins of the Acropolis, which one thinks must crown them.   I found myself so looking all the time I remained in the city.   But on none of these heights is there anything more interesting, anything more vocal to the student of the past, than the sumptuous villas of the magnates of the Central Pacific Railway, who have chosen a hilltop to display their wealth to the city, but have erected houses like all other houses, only larger.   San Francisco has had a good deal of history in her forty years of life; but this history does not, like that of Greece or Italy, write itself in stone, or even in wood. . . .

Everywhere the same system of state governments, everywhere the same municipal governments, and almost uniformly bad or good in proportion to the greater or smaller population of the city; the same party machinery organized on the same methods, "run" by the same wirepullers and "workers."   In rural local government there are some diversities in the names, areas, and functions of the different bodies, yet differences slight in comparison with the points of likeness.   The schools are practically identical in organization, in the subjects taught, in the methods of teaching, though the administration of them is as completely decentralized as can be imagined, even the state commissioner having no right to do more than suggest or report. So it is with the charitable institutions, with the libraries, the lecture courses, the public amusements. All these are more abundant and better of their kind in the richer and more cultivated parts of the country, generally better in the North Atlantic than in the inland states, and in the West than in the South. But they are the same in type everywhere. It is the same with social habits and usages. There are still some differences between the South and the North; and in the Eastern cities the upper class is more Europeanized in its code of etiquette and its ways of daily life. But even these variations tend to disappear. Eastern customs begin to permeate the West, beginning with the richer families; the South is more like the North than it was before the war. Travel where you will, you feel that what you have found in one place that you will find in another. The thing which hath been, will be: you can no more escape from it than you can quit the land to live in the sea.

Last of all we come to man himself — to man and to women . . . their fundamental beliefs and their superficial tastes, their methods of thinking and their fashions of talking, are what most concern their fellow men; and if there be variety and freshness in these, the uniformity of nature and the monotony of cities signify but little. If I observe that in these respects also the similarity of type over the country is surprising, I shall be asked whether I am not making the old mistake of the man who fancied all Chinese were like one another, because, noticing the dress and the pigtail, he did not notice minor differences of feature. A scholar is apt to think that all business men write the same hand, and a business man thinks the same of all scholars. Perhaps Americans think all Englishmen alike. And I may also be asked with whom I am comparing the Americans. With Europe as a whole? If so, is it not absurd to expect that the differences between different sections in one people should be as marked as those between different peoples? The United States are larger than Europe, but Europe has many races and many languages, among whom contrasts far broader must be expected than between one people, even if it stretches over a continent.

It is most clearly not with Europe, but with each of the leading European peoples that we must compare the people of America. So comparing them with the people of Britain, France, Germany, Italy, Spain, one discovers more varieties between individuals in these European peoples than one finds in America. Scotchmen and Irishmen are more unlike Englishmen, the native of Normandy more unlike the native of Provence, the Pomeranian more unlike the Wurtemberger, the Piedmontese more unlike the Neapolitan, the Basque more unlike the Andalusian, than the American from any part of the country is to the American from any other. Differences of course there are between the human type as developed in different regions of the country — differences moral and intellectual as well as physical. You can generally tell a Southerner by his look as well as by his speech. A native of Maine will probably differ from a native of Kentucky, a Georgian from an Oregonian. But these strike even an American observer much as the difference between a Yorkshireman and a Lancastrian strikes the English, and is slighter than the contrast between a middle class southern Englishman and a middle class Scotchman, slighter than the differences between a peasant from Northumberland and a peasant from Dorsetshire. Or, to take another way of putting it: If at some great gathering of a political party from all parts of the United Kingdom you were to go round and talk to, say, one hundred, taken at random, of the persons present, you would be struck by more diversity between the notions and the tastes and mental habits of the individuals comprising that one hundred than if you tried the same experiment with a hundred Americans of the same education and position, similarly gathered in a convention from every state in the Union.

I do not in the least mean that people are more commonplace in America than in England, or that the Americans are less ideal than the English. Neither of these statements would be true. On the contrary, the average American is more alive to new ideas, more easily touched through his imagination or his emotions, than the average Englishman or Frenchman. I mean only that the native-born Americans appear to vary less, in fundamentals, from what may be called the dominant American type than Englishmen, Germans, Frenchmen, Spaniards, or Italians do from any type which could be taken as the dominant type in any of those nations. Or, to put the same thing differently, it is rather more difficult to take any assemblage of attributes in any of these European countries and call it the national type than it is to do the like in the United States.

These are not given as the impressions of a traveler. Such impressions, being necessarily hasty, and founded on a comparatively narrow observation, would deserve little confidence. They sum up the conclusions of Europeans long resident in America, and familiar with different parts of the country. They are, I think, admitted by the most acute Americans themselves. I have often heard the latter dilate on what seems to them the one crowning merit of life in Europe — the variety it affords, the opportunities it gives of easy and complete changes of scene and environment. The pleasure which an American finds in crossing the Atlantic, a pleasure more intense than any which the European enjoys, is that of passing from a land of happy monotony into regions where everything is redolent with memories of the past, and derives from the past no less than from the present a wealth and a subtle complexity of interest which no new country can possess.

Life in America is in most ways pleasanter, easier, simpler than in Europe; it floats in a sense of happiness like that of a radiant summer morning. But life in any of the great European centers is capable of an intensity, a richness blended of many elements, which has not yet been reached in America. There are more problems in Europe calling for solution; there is more passion in the struggles that rage round them; the past more frequently kindles the present with a glow of imaginative light. In whichever country of Europe one dwells, one feels that the other countries are near, that the fortunes of their peoples are bound up with the fortunes of one's own, that ideas are shooting to and fro between them. The web of history woven day by day all over Europe is vast and of many colors: it is fateful to every European. But in America it is only the philosopher who can feel that it will ultimately be fateful to Americans also; to the ordinary man the Old World seems far off, severed by a dissociating ocean, its mighty burden with little meaning for him.

Those who have observed the uniformity I have been attempting to describe have commonly set it down, as Europeans do most American phenomena, to what they call democracy. Democratic government has in reality not much to do with it, except in so far as such a government helps to induce that deference of individuals to the mass which strengthens a dominant type, whether of ideas, of institutions, or of manners. More must be ascribed to the equality of material conditions, still more general than in Europe, to the fact that nearly everyone is engaged either in agriculture, or in commerce, or in some handicraft, to the extraordinary mobility of the population, which in migrating from one part of the country to another brings the characteristics of each part into the others, to the diffusion of education, to the cheapness of literature and universal habit of reading, which enable everyone to know what everyone else is thinking, but above all to the newness of the country, and the fact that four-fifths of it has been made all at a stroke, and therefore all of a piece, as compared with the slow growth by which European countries have developed. Newness is the cause of uniformity, not merely in the external aspect of cities, villages, farmhouses, but in other things also, for the institutions and social habits which belonged a century ago to a group of small communities on the Atlantic coast, have been suddenly extended over an immense area, each band of settlers naturally seeking to retain its customs, and to plant in the new soil shoots from which trees like those of the old home might spring up. The variety of European countries is due not only to the fact that their race elements have not yet become thoroughly commingled, but also that many old institutions have survived among the new ones; as in a city that grows but slowly, old buildings are not cleared away to make room for others more suited to modern commerce, but are allowed to stand, sometimes empty and unused, sometimes half adapted to new purposes. This scarcely happens in America. Doubtless many American institutions are old, and were old before they were carried across the Atlantic. But they have generally received a new dress, which, in adapting them to the needs of today, conceals their ancient character; and the form in which they have been diffused or reproduced in the different states of the Union is in all those states practically identical.

In each of the great European countries the diversity of primeval and mediaeval times, when endless varieties of race, speech, and faith existed within the space of a few hundred miles, has been more or less preserved by segregative influences. In America a small race, of the same speech and faith, has spread itself out over an immense area, and has been strong enough to impose its own type, not only on the Dutch and other early settlers of the Middle States, but on the immigrant masses which the last forty years have brought.

May one, then, expect that when novelty has worn off, and America counts her life by centuries instead of decades, variety will develop itself, and such complexities, or diversities, or incongruities (whichever one is to call them) as European countries present, be deeper and more numerous?

As regards the outside of things this seems unlikely. Many of the small towns of today will grow into large towns, a few of the large towns into great cities, but as they grow they will not become less like one another. There will be larger theatres and hotels, more churches (in spite of secularist lecturers) and handsomer ones; but what is to make the theatres and churches of one city differ from those of another? Fashion and the immense facilities of intercourse tend to wear down even such diversities in the style of building or furnishing, or in modes of locomotion, or in amusements and forms of social intercourse, as now exist.

As regards ideas and the inner life of men, the question is a more difficult one. At present there are only two parts of the country where one looks to meet with the well-marked individualities I refer to. One of these is New England, where the spirit of Puritanism, expressed in new literary forms by Emerson and his associates, did produce a peculiar type of thinking and discoursing, which has now, however, almost died out; and where one still meets, especially among the cultivated classes, a larger number than elsewhere of persons who have thought and studied for themselves, and are unlike their fellows. The other part of the country is the Far West, where the wild life led by pioneers in exploration, or ranching, or gold-mining has produced a number of striking figures, men of extraordinary self-reliance, with a curious mixture of geniality and reckless hardihood, no less indifferent to their own lives than to the lives of others. Of preserving this latter type there is, alas, little hope; the swift march of civilization will have expunged it in thirty years more.

When one sees millions of people thinking the same thoughts and reading the same books, and perceives that as the multitude grows, its influence becomes always stronger, it is hard to imagine how new points of repulsion and contrast are to arise, new diversities of senti- ment and doctrine to be developed. Nevertheless I am inclined to believe that as the intellectual proficiency and speculative play of mind which are now confined to a comparatively small class become more generally diffused, as the pressure of effort toward material suc- cess is relaxed, as the number of men devoted to science, art, and learning increases, so will the dominance of what may be called the business mind decline, and with a richer variety of knowledge, tastes, and pursuits, there will come also a larger crop of marked individuali- ties, and of divergent intellectual types.

Time will take away some of the monotony which comes from the absence of historical associations: for even if, as is to be hoped, there comes no war to make battlefields famous like those of twenty-five years ago, yet literature and the lives of famous men cannot but attach to many spots associations to which the blue of distance will at last give a romantic interest. No people could be more ready than are the Americans to cherish such associations. Their country has a short past, but they willingly revere and preserve all the memo- ries it has bequeathed to them.

OUR CHANGING CHARACTERISTICS[1]

James Truslow Adams

JAMES TRUSLOW ADAMS, who was born in Brooklyn in 1878 and educated at Brooklyn Polytechnic Institute and Yale University, devoted his early career to business. In 1912 he gave up his seat on the New York Stock Exchange, and soon afterward settled at Bridgehampton, Long Island, to devote himself to historical work. His original interest was in Persian culture, but he was drawn into the American field by two volumes which he wrote on local annals — *Memorials of Old Bridgehampton* (1916) and *History of the Town of Southampton* (1918). It was natural for him to turn from the colonial history of these towns to colonial New England, and he first made a large reputation by his *Founding of New England* (1921), a work of distinctly iconoclastic character and fine literary quality. This was followed in due course by two other volumes, *Revolutionary New England*, and *New England in the Republic*, bringing the record of the section from 1620 down to 1850. A book of less scholarly nature, but equally fertile in ideas (for Mr. Adams is confessedly more interested in interpretation than any other facet of history), *The Epic of America*, became a best-seller in America and found many readers in foreign countries. It is particularly valuable for its breadth of outlook and its grasp of the great forces which have molded the American people. Mr. Adams has also produced a two-volume history of the United States, more factual in character, called *The March of Democracy;* a study of social life in the colonial period, *Provincial America;* and an interesting study of a great American line, *The Adams Family.* In recent years he has spent much time in England, and has written many essays upon American life which are interesting for their detachment as well as penetration.

I

There are few things more difficult to generalize about without danger of valid objections than national character. The exceptions to any generalization at once begin to appear destructively numerous. A concept of a Frenchman must include not only such diverse types as the Gascon, the Parisian, and the Breton, but also the innumerable differences between individuals of these and other types in what is a rather small country which for long has been culturally and politically unified.

When we attempt the task in America it would seem to be hopeless. Who *is* an American? Is he the descendant of a Boston Brahman, of a Georgian cotton planter, or a newly arrived Armenian, Hungarian, or Italian? Is the typical American a clerk on the fifty-fourth story of a

[1] From *The Tempo of Modern Life*, by James Truslow Adams. Reprinted by permission of Albert & Charles Boni, Inc., publishers.

Wall Street office building or a farm hand of the machine age guiding in isolation a power plow along a furrow which stretches endlessly over the horizon? Is he a scientist working for pitiful pay and the love of science in some government bureau in Washington, or a one hundred per cent go-getter in a Chamber of Commerce whose ideas of progress are limited to increase of wealth and population? Is he Hamilton or Jefferson, Lincoln or Harding, Roosevelt or Coolidge, Emerson or Barnum?

The task of defining national character in such a conflicting welter of opposites is dismaying enough, and yet a fairly clear notion is of prime importance for any number of very practical purposes. The modern business man doing business on a national scale, making mass appeal to our whole hundred and twenty millions at once; the states-man, domestic or foreign, trying to forecast the success or failure of an idea or a policy; the genuine patriot interested in the highest de-velopment of his civilization — these and others must all take account of that real if vague concept which we call the national character. It is from the third point of view that we are concerned with the topic in the present article.

There are many signs that our world is approaching a new and critical stage. Deeply embedded in the structure of the universe there is a power or force that is continually at work molding chaos into cos-mos, formlessness into forms. These forms, or patterns, belong to the spiritual as well as to the physical plane of reality. A scale of values, an ethical system, a philosophy of life appear to be as "natural" and inevitable a part of the web and woof of that strange and inexplicable phantasmagoria that we call the universe as are crystals, corals, or living embodiments of the form-producing force in the plant or animal body.

For generations now we have been witnessing the gradual break-down of old forms until we have reached the very nadir of formlessness in our whole spiritual life. But there are, as I have said, many indications that we are about to witness a new stage, the embryo stage of new forms.

For the most part this play of cosmic forces is independent of con-sciousness or will in individuals. The atoms know not and care not why or how they combine to make quartz crystals or a living cell of protoplasm. To a greater extent than we care to admit, perhaps, the higher forms — our scales of values, our philosophies — are also inde-pendent of conscious molding by ourselves. They are not wholly so, however, and if, as has recently been said, more and more of us here in America as elsewhere "are looking for a new set of controlling ideas capable of restoring value to human existence," it is evidence of the interplay between the blind form-making force of physical nature and the consciousness of man. What these ideas will be, will depend largely upon the soil in which they will be rooted, the soil of our national character.

It is also clear that the form in which life, either physical or spiritual, is embodied is of transcendent importance for the individual. If living cells are arranged in the form of a bird, both the powers and limitations of the individual are wholly different from those of the individual when they are arranged in the form of a fish. Similarly in the spiritual world, powers and limitations depend largely upon the forms within which the spirit has its being. Because they are so largely intangible, we are likely to lose sight of the fact that these forms — scales of values, systems of thought, philosophies of life — all afford the spirit peculiar powers and impose peculiar limits.

What of the new forms? Arising from and in large part molded by the national character, are they likely to afford wider scope for man's highest aspirations, to enlarge the powers of the spirit, or to place limits and bind them closer to the earth? What of the national character itself?

Let us for the present discussion avoid the more difficult problem of a complete analysis and seek to establish a trend, often a simpler task, in the spiritual as in the physical world. Are our characteristics changing, and, if so, in what direction? Can we, in the first place, establish any definite points of reference which will be tangible and certain? I think we can.

Man expresses himself in his arts, and among these none is more illuminating than the earliest and most practical, that of architecture. It is one, moreover, in which we as Americans excel.

We need not greatly concern ourselves with the inchoate beginnings of our nationality in the first few generations of early settlement in the wilderness of the Atlantic seaboard. The physical tasks were almost overwhelmingly hard and there was little opportunity for a distinctly American expression of either old or new spiritual life. By the time there was, we find that the spirit of the colonies had expressed itself in an architectural form, characteristic with minor variations throughout all of them.

When we speak of "colonial architecture," what at once comes to our mind is the home, the dwelling house of Georgian type, modeled on the English but with a delicacy and refinement surpassing most of the models overseas. From New England to the Far South these homes had outwardly a perfection of form and inwardly a proportion, a refinement of detail, a simplicity that all clearly sprang from the spirit of the time.

We may note quickly, in passing, several points in regard to them. The high point of the architecture was domestic. They were homes. They had an air of spaciousness, of dignity. They were aristocratic in the best sense. They were restrained and disciplined. Display or vulgarity were unthinkable in connection with them. They evidenced an ordered and stratified society. They held peace and rest. They were simple, unostentatious, and profoundly satisfying. They were shelters for a quiet life, alien from haste.

Let us, using the same architectural measure, pass from this first flowering of the American spirit to the very instant of today. The great contribution of twentieth century America to the art of building is the skyscraper, of which we may take the office building as both the earliest and most typical example. What are some of its usual characteristics?

The buildings are commercial, not domestic. Their very *raison d'être* is financial, the desire to get the most money possible from a given plot of ground. Their bulk is huge but they are not spacious, save perhaps for their entrance halls in some instances. They are democratic in the physical sense of herding within their walls thousands of persons of every possible sort. In their primary insistence upon mere size and height regardless of every other element, they are undisciplined and unrestrained. Peace or rest is unthinkable within their walls with the incessant movement of thousands of hurrying individuals, and elevators moving at incredible speed.

They are lavish in their ostentation of expense on the ground floor, bare and unsatisfying above. A "front" of vulgar cost is built to hide the emptiness of the countless floors beyond the reach of the first casual glance from the street. Yet every small and growing community cries for them, and we hold them to the world as our characteristic achievement in art, as our most significant contribution in that most telltale of all arts, the housing of man's chief interest.

II

Here, then, we have two points of reference tangible enough to be noted by all men, because they are physical in structure, yet full of spiritual implications for our task. When we turn to other means

of establishing our trend, such as literature, newspapers, our methods
of living, the wants we create and strive to satisfy, our social ways of
contact, our national ideals as expressed in political campaigns and
policies, and other means less obvious than the buildings in which
we live or work or express our spiritual aspirations, what do we find?
I think we find the same trends indicated above, amplified and
emphasized.

It is, if I may repeat myself to prevent misunderstanding, only with
these trends and not with the whole complex national character that
I am here concerned.   As a historian, and with no wish to make a case
but only to report what I find, certain trends in the past century
appear to me to be clearly indicated.   Let me note them just as from
time to time I have jotted them down, without at first trying either
to order or explain them.

These trends are the substitution of self-expression for self-discipline;
of the concept of prosperity for that of liberty; of restlessness for rest;
of spending for saving; of show for solidity; of desire for the new or
novel in place of affection for the old and tried; of dependence for self-
reliance; of gregariousness for solitude; of luxury for simplicity; of
ostentation for restraint; of success for integrity; of national for local;
of easy generosity for wise giving; of preferring impressions to thought,
facts to ideas; of democracy for aristocracy; of the mediocre for the
excellent.

For the most part I do not think any observer would quarrel with
the validity of most of the above list.   Discipline, self or other, has
almost completely vanished from our life.   In earlier days it was
amply provided by school, family, and social life, by ideals and
religious beliefs.   Today it is not only absent in all these quarters
but is preached against by psychologists and sociologists, decried by
the new pedagogy, and even legislated against in school and prison.

Nothing is imposed any longer, from learning one's ABC's to honor-
ing one's parents.   Everything is elective, from college courses to
marital fidelity.   The man or woman who casts all discipline to the
winds for the sake of transient gratification of selfish desires, who
denies obligations and duties, is no longer considered a libertine or a
cad but merely a modernist pursuing the legitimate end of self-
expression.

For a considerable time evidence has been accumulating that the
national rallying cry has become an economic balance sheet.   Perhaps
one of the chief values of the whole prohibition muddle has been to
serve as a mirror for the American soul.   In the arguments advanced

for and against, in the spiritual tone of the discussion, we can see all too well reflected the moving ideals of the American people, and the argument that carries most weight would clearly appear to be that of prosperity. Balanced against this, the questions of personal liberty, class legislation, or constitutional propriety are but as straw weighed against iron.

Prohibition is only one of the many mirrors that reflect the same truth. In innumerable cases of business practice and of legislation it has become evident that when personal freedom and initiative have to be balanced against the prosperity of the moment according to the business methods of the moment, prosperity wins. The one liberty that is still valued is the liberty to exploit and to acquire. That liberty will be defended to the death, but other liberties, such as freedom of thought and speech, have become pale and unreal ghosts, academic questions of no interest to the practical man.

Who cares in the slightest about the innumerable cases of encroachment on personal liberties on the part of both state and federal governments in the past ten years so long as business is good? Who cares about the methods employed by our police? Who is willing to give thought to the treatment frequently meted out to foreigners by our immigration officials — treatment that could hardly be surpassed by the old Russian régime at its worst, treatment that we could not stand a moment if accorded to *our* citizens by any foreign government? No, personal liberty as a rallying cry today receives no answer. But we will elect any man President who will promise us prosperity.

There is as little question of our growing restlessness. By rail, boat, automobile, or plane we are as restless as a swarm of gnats in a summer sunbeam. "We don't know where we're going but we're on our way" is the cry of all. Even the babies get their rest by traveling at forty miles an hour swung in cradles in Ford cars. That much of the movement is mere restlessness and does not spring from a desire to see and learn may easily be observed by watching the speed of our new tourists when they travel, and by listening to their comments when they have to stop to look at anything. As for the "nature" they claim to go to see, they are ruining our whole countryside with appalling indifference.

The home itself has yielded and has ceased to afford any sense of permanence and security. In the old days a home was expected to serve for generations. In the South, frequently property was entailed and the family was assured of a continuing center where it could cluster. A year ago, on October first, a hundred thousand families in New York City moved from one apartment to another, in many instances for no better reason than that they were bored with the one they had occupied a twelvemonth.   Our multimillionaires build palaces, and in a few years abandon them to country clubs or office buildings.

As for thrift and saving, with the entire complex of spiritual satisfactions that go with an assured future, they have not only notoriously been thrown overboard but are vigorously denounced by advertising experts like Bruce Barton and great industrial leaders like Henry Ford.   "We should use, not save," the latter teaches the American people while they mortgage their homes, if they own them, to buy his cars.   On every side we are being taught not to save but to borrow. The self-respect and satisfaction of the man of a generation ago who did not owe a penny in the world is being replaced by the social-respect and deep dissatisfaction of the man who has borrowed to the limit to live on the most expensive scale that hard cash and bank credit will allow.

With this has naturally come a preference for show to solidity.   A witty and observing foreigner has said that Americans put all their goods in the shop window.   In every vein the insidious poison is at work.   A man who toiled and saved to own his home would see to it that it was well built and substantial.   The man who expects to move every year cares for nothing more than that the roof will not fall until he gets out, provided the appearance is attractive.   In an advertisement of houses for sale in a New York suburb recently one of the great advantages pointed out was that the roofs were guaranteed for three years.

The first thing that every business firm thinks of is show.   Its office or shop must look as if there were unlimited resources behind it.   Even a savings bank, whose real solidity should be seen in its list of investments and whose object is to encourage thrift, will squander hugely on marbles and bronze in its banking room to impress the depositor.

The same motive is at work in our intellectual life.   One has only to glance at the advertisements of the classics, of language courses, of "five foot shelves" and note the motives that are appealed to for desiring culture.   Nor are our schools and colleges exempt from the same poison.   The insistence on degrees after a teacher's name, the regulating of wage scales in accordance with them, the insistence on a professor's publishing something which can be listed, are as much part of the same trend as is the clerk's wanting to be cultured so as to pass from a grilled window to an assistant-assistant executive's desk.

III

We could expand the above examples almost indefinitely and continue through the remainder of the list. But it is all obvious enough to anyone who will observe with fresh eyes, and ponder. Both for those who may agree or disagree with me, let us pass to some of the other questions that arise in connection with the trends I have noted. Do they in any way hang together? Do they make a unified whole or are they self-contradictory and hence probably mistaken? Do they derive from any conditions in our history that would make them natural and probable, or are they opposed to those conditions? If they are real, do they represent a transient phase or a permanent alteration in our character?

As we study them carefully, it seems to me that they do hang together remarkably and ominously well. A person, for example, who is restless, rather than one who cares for rest and permanence, would naturally prefer the new to the old, the novel for the tried, impressions instead of difficult and sustained thought. Both these characteristics, again, naturally cohere with the desire for show rather than solidity, and for self-expression rather than self-discipline.

With these same qualities would go the love of gregariousness rather than solitude, of luxury rather than simplicity, and, easily belonging to the same type of character, we would find the desire to spend ousting the desire to save, and the substitution of prosperity for liberty and of success for integrity. With such a succession of substitutions, that of dependence for self-reliance is not only natural but inevitable, and so with the other items in the trend. They all fit into a psychological whole. There is no self-contradiction to be found among them.

But is there any connection to be found between them and our history? Are they qualities that might be found to have developed with more or less logical and psychological necessity from the conditions of American life which have separated the period of the colonial home from that of the seventy-story office building? I think here again we find confirmation rather than contradiction.

I have no intention to rival Mr. Coolidge by writing the history of America in five hundred words. All I can do in my limited space is to point to certain facts and influences.

Until well into the eighteenth century, there had been no very great change in the character of the American to mark him off from his English cousin. The wilderness and remoteness had, indeed, had some effect, but this was small compared with the later effects of what we have come to call "the West." Leaving out a few minor strains — such as the Dutch, Swedes, and the earlier Germans — the settlers were almost wholly British, who sought, in a somewhat freer atmosphere and with somewhat wider economic opportunity, to reproduce the life they had left.

The continent open to them was of limited extent. Beyond a comparatively narrow strip lay the long barrier of the Appalachians and the claims of the French. The strip itself contained no great natural resources to arouse cupidity or feverish activity. The character of the colonists had become a little more democratic, a little more pliant, a little more rebellious and self-reliant than that of their cousins of similar social ranks at home. That was all. They might differ with the majority of both Englishmen and Parliament over questions of politics and economics, but those were differences of interest and policy, not of character.

There lay ahead, however, the operation of two factors that were to prove of enormous influence — the exploitation of the American continent, and the immigration from Europe. We cannot here trace this influence step by step chronologically, but we must summarize it. "The West" — there were successively many of them — unlike the colonial America, was of almost limitless extent and wealth. There were whole empires of farm land and forest, mines that made fortunes for the lucky almost overnight, reservoirs of gas and oil that spawned cities and millionaires.

All did not happen in a day, but it did happen within what might almost be the span of one long life. In ages past an Oriental conqueror might sack the riches of a rival's state, a king of Spain might draw gold from a Peruvian hoard, but never before had such boundless opportunities for sudden wealth been opened to the fortunate among a whole population which could join in the race unhampered.

In the rush for opportunity, old ties and loyalties were broken. A restlessness entered the American blood that has remained in it ever since. In American legend, the frontier has become the Land of Romance and we are bid to think of the pioneers as empire-builders. A very few may have dreamed of the future glory of America rather than of private gain, but it is well not to gild too much the plain truth, which is that in the vast majority of instances, the rush was for riches to be made as quickly as might be. In the killing of a million buffaloes a year, in the total destruction of forests without replanting, in the whole of the story in all its aspects there were few thoughts for a national destiny not linked with immediate personal gain at any expense to the nation. In this orgy of exploitation it is not difficult to discover the soil in which some of the elements of the changed trend in American character had its roots.

Another factor was also at work which combined with the above in its effects. The racial homogeneity of our earlier colonial days was broken by the millions of immigrants who came to us of racial stocks other than our own. Our first character had been that of seventeenth and eighteenth century Englishmen, not greatly altered until the Revolution. It was unified and stable, but the West and Europe both operated to undermine its stability.

On the one hand, the influence of the West, with the loosening of old bonds, its peculiar population, and its opportunities of limitless expansion and wealth greatly altered old ideals and standards of value. On the other, the steady infusion in large numbers of Germans, Irish, Swedes, Norwegians, Jews, Russians, Italians, Greeks, and other races also bore a conspicuous part in making the national character less uniform and stable. I am not concerned with their several contributions of value, but merely with the fact that the introduction of such foreign swarms tended to destroy a unified national character.

By the latter part of the nineteenth century, two things had thus happened. In the first place, the real America had become the West, and its traits were becoming dominant. One of these was restlessness, not only a willingness but a desire to try any new place or thing and make a complete break with the old. Moreover, although the frontier may breed some fine qualities, it is a good deal like the farm in the respect that although it may be a fine place to come from, it is a soul-killing place in which to remain. It bred emotion rather than thought, and to a considerable extent substituted new material values for the spiritual ones of the older America.

In the rush for wealth — whether won from forests or mines; farms tilled, raped, and abandoned for fresher soil; real estate values from fast-growing cities; lands fraudulently obtained from a complaisant government — restraint, self-discipline, thought for the future ceased to be virtues. With all this came a vast optimism, a belief that everything would become bigger and better, and, because the standards of success were economic, better because bigger. Wealth was the goal, and the faster things got bigger — towns, cities, the piles of slain buffaloes, the area of forests destroyed — the quicker one's personal wealth accumulated. Statistics took on a new significance and spelled the letters of one's private fate.

At the same time, by the latter half of the nineteenth century another thing had happened, as we have said. Partly from the effects of the West and partly from immigration, the old, stable American-English character had become unstable, soft, pliant, something which could be easily molded by new influences. It could readily take the impress of an emotion, a leader, a new invention. It was full of possibility, both of good and evil.

Suddenly this new, unformed, malleable national character, already warped to a large degree toward material values, was called upon to feel the full force of the influences flowing from the fruition of the industrial revolution. Invention followed invention with startling rapidity. Life itself became infinitely more mobile. Scientists, engineers, manufacturers threw at the public contrivance after contrivance of the most far-reaching influence upon man's personal and social life without a thought of what that influence might be beyond the profit of the moment to the individual manufacturer.

Choice became bewildering in its complexity. The national character had become unstable. It was in a real sense unformed and immature, far more so than it had been a century earlier. It had also lost belief in the necessity of restraint and discipline. It had accepted material standards and ideals. It was in far more danger of being overwhelmed by the ideals of a new, raw, and crude machine age than was perhaps any other nation of the civilized group.

With an ingenuity that would have been fiendish had it not been so unthinking and ignorant, the leaders of the new era used every resource of modern psychology to warp the unformed character of the people, to provide the greatest possible profit to the individuals and corporations that made and purveyed the new "goods." Our best and worst qualities, our love of wife and children, our national pride, our self-respect, our snobbery, our fear of social opinion, our neglect of the future, our lack of self-restraint and discipline, our love of mere physical comfort have all been played upon to make mush of our characters in order that big business might thrive. Even our national government, whether wittingly or not, undertook to inflame our American love of gambling and our desire to "get rich quick" regardless of effect on character.

IV

Taking all the molding influences of the past century and more into account, it is little wonder, perhaps, that our national characteristics exhibit the trend noted. The situation, serious as it is, might be less so had it occurred at a time when the spiritual forms in the world at large — its scales of values, its ethical systems, its philosophies of life — were intact. But as we have noted, they have been largely destroyed; and at the very time when new forms are in process of arising, largely to be molded by the national characters of the peoples among whom they arise, our own is in the state pictured above. The question whether our new characteristics are temporary or permanent thus becomes of acute significance.

"Race" is a word of such vague and undefined content as to be of slight help to us, but if we take the whole history of the Western nations from which we derive, I think we may say that the characteristics noted above may be classed as acquired and not inherited. Biologists consider such not to be permanent and heritable, though the analogy with biology again is so vague as to afford little comfort.

More hopeful, I think, is the fact that these new characteristics appear to have derived directly from circumstances, and that these circumstances themselves have been in large part such as have passed and will not recur again. Immigration and "the West" have ceased to be continuing factors in our development. Their effects remain and must be dealt with, but neither factor will continue to intensify them. The tides of immigration have been shut off. There is significance in the fact that "the Wests" which won under Jefferson, Jackson, and Lincoln were defeated in 1896 under Bryan.

"The West" of today is a new West in which conditions, and to a large extent ideals, are different. Yet its greatest contribution to our national life and character remains that broadening and deepening of the dream of a better and a richer life for all of every class which was the cause of its earlier victories and which goes far to redeem its less noble influences. The nation as a whole is entering upon a new era in which all the conditions will be different from any experienced heretofore. Territory, resources, opportunities are none of them any longer unexploited and boundless. What the future may hold, we cannot tell, but in fundamental influences it will be different from the past. The menacing factor that remains is that of mass production and the machine.

Also, we have spoken thus far only of the trend in characteristics, not of our character as a whole. In that there are certain noble traits which remain unaltered, or have matured and strengthened. It is possible, now the warping influences of the past century have to some extent disappeared, that the national character may develop around them as a core, that we shall forget in manhood the wild oats sown in our youth.

But age acquires no value save through thought and discipline. If we cannot reinstate those, we are in danger of hampering rather than aiding in that reconstruction of the spiritual life of man that is the inevitable and most vital task now before the nations. We must either forward or retard it. We are too great to live aloof. We could not if we would, and upon the trend of our character depends to a great extent the future of the world.

Nor let us forget that although fortune has poured her favors in our lap, there is a Nemesis that dogs the steps of all, and we cannot lightly scorn the growing enmity of half the world. Are we to treat the machine age and mass production only as a new and different "West," or are we at last, in growing up, to learn wisdom and restraint? Are we going to change the trend in our character, or is it to become fixed in its present form, a danger to ourselves and a menace to mankind?

BEYOND THE FRONTIER [1]

Henry A. Wallace

HENRY AGARD WALLACE, formerly a Republican, and the son of Henry C. Wallace, who had been Secretary of Agriculture in the Harding Cabinet, became Secretary of Agriculture under President Franklin D. Roosevelt in 1933. He played the most prominent rôle in launching and guiding the great experiment in agricultural planning and control under the A.A.A. (Agricultural Adjustment Administration). While doing this, and overseeing the routine affairs of his department, he found time to write many articles and one important book (*New Frontiers*, 1934) upon the new problems facing the nation. Born in 1888 in Adair County, Iowa, Mr. Wallace was educated at the Iowa State College, and was editor of *Wallace's Farmer* (later *Iowa Homestead and Wallace's Farmer*), one of the leading Western farm journals, from 1924 until he was made Secretary of Agriculture.

When those forty thousand undisciplined slaves, the Children of Israel, left Egypt, it was possible for them to reach their promised land within a few months. But they were not fit to march a straight course, enter and take possession. The older men and women among them thought of everything in terms of the fleshpots of Egypt. Before the promised land could be attained it was necessary for the younger generation, hardened by travels in the wilderness, to come to maturity.

We have been forced away from the fleshpots. When our stock market crashed in 1929 it was plain that we would have to abandon them. We, too, know something about a new land and how it may be reached, but we are not yet fit to go in and take possession. Too many of us would like one last round with those fleshpots and golden calves. It may be that many of our younger people have been sufficiently hardened by suffering in our economic wilderness. But all will have to come to a more effective maturity before the new land can be fully possessed. Advance guards sent out to estimate the cost of the march tell us that there are giants in the way.

I am sometimes accused of undue idealism; but I know very well that it will not do to hope too much of the generation of which I am a part. It is simply impossible for us to let go overnight of the habits and beliefs of a lifetime. Younger people, if they will, can easily accomplish changes which seem impossible to older people.

[1] From *New Frontiers*, by Henry A. Wallace. Reprinted by permission of Reynal and Hitchcock, Inc., publishers.

Unfortunately, many of the oncoming generation now in our schools, or idling in our homes, are handicapped by an inheritance of past concepts, bitterly complicated by the present stalemate. They are stirred into potentially menacing forms of protest by the fact that the present world does not seem to want their services. If misled by demagogues and half-baked educators, they may be inclined to assume more and more that the world owes them not only a living but a limousine. Their restlessness and present disillusionment can be fatal or infinitely constructive, depending upon which side they wake up on.

After all, we middle-aged, middle-course, people have some hard thinking and many hard jobs to do, before we can reasonably expect to arouse our young to hope for an enduring democracy. Talk alone will not lead them to consolidate the position we now strive to hold, and push forward to something better.

The Children of Israel's problems did not come to an end after they had crossed the borders, or even after they had taken possession of their promised land. Their real troubles as a people had then only begun. They had put behind them a vague, nomadic wandering, but they still had to adapt themselves in some measure to the commercial features of the Canaanite civilization. Their old frontier was gone. They had to work on new frontiers. These problems, in many respects strikingly modern, provoked the strife and turmoil which resulted in the tremendous literature of the prophets and the historical records contained in Chronicles and Kings. Amos, that farmer prophet of the hill country of Judah, first raised in dramatic form the problem of social justice, fair treatment of debtors, and balanced prices.

Physically, and in other ways also, the basic structure of our land of yesterday had been torn to pieces. By the raw pioneer rules of first stakes we have encamped as migrants and have taken greedily and unevenly of its wealth. A few of us, in consequence, have much more than we can comfortably or decently spend or handle; yet most of us have too little for comfort, decency, and hope of a general progress.

We face, moreover, these hard facts: First, the land frontier of the United States is gone. Depression can no longer be solved by shipping the unemployed West. We must learn to live with each other. We have no longer enormous unexploited natural resources awaiting only the touch of young and vigorous hands to be transformed into fabulous individual wealth.

Second, the wealth that may be drawn by the shrewdest of a

rapidly expanding population is now drawing to an end. In the old days, expanding population, and the million or so of people we received annually from Europe, enlarged certain of our cities so rapidly that tremendous real estate values were reared. Today, immigration is mostly shut out. Our birth rate is decreasing. It appears that by 1950 our population will probably reach its peak, around a hundred and fifty million people, and then start declining. Our rural areas, especially in the South, furnish most of the present population increase. Most of our cities are growing only in so far as they suck in the surplus population from farms and small towns; and this surplus is falling off.

Third, enormous decentralizing forces are beginning to influence the psychology and eventually the location of many of our city families. Hard roads, trucks, autos, high-line electricity, and the increasing love of city people for good air, sunshine, trees, and natural surroundings, will inevitably result in drawing millions of Americans back into the open.

As we dimly discern these forces which will be at work among us for years to come, we wonder just what, in the new combination, will give to the new life the same unity that our old life obtained, simply as a result of fears and hopes centering in the frontier.

The old frontier was real. There were Indians and fear of foreign conquest. People in the older colonies or states had to stand together against actual perils on the edge of a new civilization.

Their determination to stand together was continually renewed by romantic tales of many unknown kinds of wealth out on the frontier, of precious metals and fertile valleys, although as a matter of fact, the old frontier was all too often a place of ragged barbed-wire fences, dusty roads, unpainted shacks. Nevertheless, the hopes and fears that existed in the old frontier furnished a unity to our national life. For a hundred and fifty years we felt it was manifest destiny to push onward, until the Pacific coast was reached, until all the fertile lands between had been plowed and bound together by railroads and paved highways.

The obvious physical task to which we set ourselves has been accomplished; and in so doing, we have destroyed in large measure the thing which gave us hope and unity as a people.

We now demand a new unity, a new hope. There are many spiritual and mental frontiers yet to be conquered, but they lead in many different directions and our hearts have not yet fully warmed to any one of them. They do not point in an obvious single direction as did that downright physical challenge which, for so many generations, existed on the Western edge of our life. Now we have come to the time when we must search our souls and the relationship of our souls and bodies to those of other human beings.

Can we build up a unified, national cultural life, unique, outstanding, one that will reinforce the cultural life of the entire world? Can we leave something that contributes toward giving life meaning, joy, and beauty for generations to come?

During the sixteenth, seventeenth, eighteenth, and nineteenth centuries, ideas took possession of our fathers and grandfathers which made them resolute hard workers, men of iron, equally good as Indian fighters, pioneer farmers, and captains of industry. They suffered and forged ahead in the world, believing that there was something prophetically worthy in all they did. Progress westward, landward, and wealth-ward was their continual urge. They exploited not only natural resources but the generations which came after. We glorify these men, grabbers and exploiters that they were, and marvel at their conquests. But they did not know how to live with each other and they did not know how to teach the American nation to live with other nations.

The keynote of the new frontier is coöperation just as that of the old frontier was individualistic competition. The mechanism of progress of the new frontier is social invention, whereas that of the old frontier was mechanical invention and the competitive seizure of opportunities for wealth. Power and wealth were worshiped in the old days. Beauty and justice and joy of spirit must be worshiped in the new.

Many of the most lively, intimate expressions of spirit spring from the joyous, continuous contact of human beings with a particular locality. They feel the age-long spirit of this valley or that hill, each with its trees and rocks and special tricks of weather, as the seasons unfold in their endless charm. If life can be made secure in each community and if the rewards of the different communities are distributed justly, there will flower in every community not only those who attain joy in daily, productive work well done; but also those who paint and sing and tell stories with the flavor peculiar to their own valley, well-loved hill, or broad prairie. And so we think of co-operative communities not merely in a competent commercial sense but also from the standpoint of people who are helping unfold each other's lives in terms of the physical locality and tradition of which they are a part.

In this way, every community can become something distinctly precious in its own right. Children will not try to escape as they grow up. They will look ahead to the possibility of enriching the traditions of their ancestors. They will feel it is a privilege to learn to live with the soil and the neighbors of their fathers. Such communities will be strung like many-colored beads on the thread of the nation, and the varied strings of beads will be the glory of the world.

The pettiness of small communities will disappear as their economic disadvantages disappear. The people of small communities, rid of the pettiness which grows of economic fear, will be free to realize that community success may be truly measured only in terms of contribution to a spirit of world unity, even though political and economic ties may be very loose.

In the old days, we could not trust ourselves with joy and beauty because they ran counter to our competitive search for wealth and power. Men of the old days, whether Protestant or Catholic, accepted implicitly the discipline of the Protestant Ethic (see Weber's *The Protestant Ethic and the Spirit of Capitalism*). The men of the new day must have their social discipline comparable in its power with that of the inner drive toward the hard-working, competitive frugality of the old frontier. People may actually work harder than they did on the old frontier, but their motive will be different. They may make and use more mechanical inventions. They may do more to increase the wealth-producing power of the race.

But their efforts will, of necessity, be continually moved by the spirit of coöperative achievement. They will devise ways in which the monetary mechanism can be modified to distribute the rewards of labor more uniformly. They will work with disinterested spirit to modify the governmental and political machinery so that there is a balanced relationship between prices, an even flow of employment, and a far wider possibility of social justice and social charity.

So enlisted, men may rightfully feel that they are serving a function as high as that of any minister of the Gospel. They will not be socialists, communists, or Fascists, but plain men trying to gain by democratic methods the professed objectives of the communists, socialists, and Fascists: security, peace, and the good life for all.

In their efforts they will not allow their work to be divided or embittered by the dogma or prejudice of any narrow, superficially logical, political or religious sect.

Some will seek for the fountains of an abundant life in renewed artistic, religious, and scientific inspiration. They will not, I trust, accept the animal view of human nature, put forth by the biologists and the economists of the nineteenth century. Of necessity, they will recognize competitive individualists and competitive nations and deal with them as the anachronisms they are, treating them kindly, firmly, and carefully.

But the new frontiersman will be continually seeking for his fellows those satisfactions which are mutually enriching. The nature of these satisfactions can only be faintly shadowed now. They exist in a land as strange and far as was America in 1491. In this land of ageless desire we are all striving newcomers. It is not a mushy, sentimental frontier, but one of hard realities, requiring individual and social discipline beyond that of the old frontiers. It lies within us and all about us. A great seer of the human heart who lived nineteen hundred years ago called it the Kingdom of Heaven. He knew that the tiny spark of divine spirit found in each individual could be fanned into an all-consuming flame, an intense passion for fair play, man to man, and man to woman, in the little time that we are here. In the Sermon on the Mount, He spoke of the rules of the Kingdom of Heaven.

The land beyond the new frontier will be conquered by the continuous social inventions of men whose hearts are free from bitterness, prejudice, hatred, greed, and fear; by men whose hearts are aflame with the extraordinary beauty of the scientific, artistic, and spiritual wealth now before us, if only we reach out confidently, together.

Frontier freebooter democracy of the purely individualistic type is definitely gone unless civilization lapses back into the Dark Ages and starts over again. To maintain the good points of the old individualism and the old democracy, and yet to enable modern methods to operate over an entire continent, without injury to the rest of the world, is a challenge to our utmost sympathetic ingenuity.

At this point all of the great leaders of the past have failed. The world has never been ripe for a general success. But today our scientific understanding, our mechanical inventive power, our widespread methods of transportation and communication make possible fulfillment of the individual in the unity of the whole.

Hitherto, such talk would have been mere words and empty ideas. No one of us yet thinks clearly in this field. But millions of the unemployed, and hard-pressed farmers, as they look at the tragic waste of empty factories and idle resources, are groping in a new direction. The good things of the past, including the finer traits of rugged individualism, can make their contribution to the triumph of social, coöperative ideals, over competitive bitterness.

This means hard, definite, precise work. There may even be an Armageddon such as Theodore Roosevelt spoke of as he searched the Scripture and felt his way toward the dawn of this day.

But even though there may be grievous work, careful study, and hard fighting, the essential thing is that our spirits be continually renewed by the vision of the ageless operations that bind all humanity together. In the final analysis, our nation must serve itself by serving the world, just as you and I in serving ourselves must keep steadily in mind the needs of this nation.

These are some of the general considerations that occur as we try to peer beyond new frontiers. Because they are general in nature, they may seem to involve too exclusively a reliance upon good intentions; and to provide too little of a concrete pattern for a better order.

Good intentions are not enough — not even good intentions backed by enlightened realization of need for less selfishness and more coordination of effort. Good intentions always have characterized human kind. The fact of aspiration is the one unfailing bulwark of stubborn hope that man can learn to master the world in a way that really expresses "peace on earth, good will to men."

But there is need to express aspiration toward the ultimate in terms of today. There is need to set up such social forms as will give the human heart opportunity for translating its altruistic impulses into practical action.

Perhaps we can set up a few principles by which to judge proposals. It is essential, for example, that we come more often and more fully to coördinate the thing that is individually wise and the thing that is socially wise. We can examine each proposed new step on this basis.

From the standpoint of guiding principles for the future, there is a design drawn from the far past which seems to be appropriate, because it suggests the maximum development of individual diversity within the limitations of the whole. Mediaeval painters used to put it in one corner of their work. It is the design used by Nicholas Roerich for the Banner of Peace and incorporated in the Roerich Pact for the protection of cultural treasures. The design represents three spheres — symbolic of the Trinity — within a larger circle. The circle represents of course the idea of unity. With its universal application it is not surprising that this symbol has been used in all ages — one may find it, perhaps, upon a Christ of Memling, an Ikon of St. Sergius, or a Tibetan Banner. This design has great depths of meaning in this infinitely more complex world of today. The uniqueness of each individual and each community must be realized, but always (instinctively, by the necessity of inner compulsion) with reference to the national and world community. All individuals, classes, and nations which approach the future with beauty of spirit might well unite their economic, social, and cultural endeavors within this imagined circle of unifying freedom.

Those who struggle beyond the new frontier will be those who know how to obey economic traffic lights, and drive social machines on the right-hand side of the road. They will have a flair, an unconscious instinct akin to the good sportmanship of the British upper class, that will lead them to ask continually and intelligently in their business dealings: "Is it fair?"

At the moment perhaps, the developments of such measures in this new world — they have been imperfectly developed in the old world — doubtless seems as remote as the flying life of the butterfly seems to the leaf-eating caterpillar.

A thousand years ago, the concept of a "nation" was entirely strange to most people; yet two hundred years ago most people in Western Europe saw the idea of a nation as something real, and they had an almost religious feeling about their own particular nation. The intense national loyalties that developed during the sixteenth, seventeenth, and eighteenth centuries were decidedly useful from the standpoint of enabling the mediaeval communities to approach a larger life. National loyalties were rather simple in the days when there was little trading between the nations and when the communities within nations were largely self-sufficing.

Today we realize that greatly intensified communication, transportation, and new methods of machinery have put the simple nationalism of the eighteenth century out of date. The new nationalism will not be a simple loyalty, but a very complex one, vigorously expressed in making an individual success in a particular community, but also realizing in the end that all of us, regardless of race or color, must learn to live together peaceably on the face of this earth.

This requires a greatly increased number of people with a truly modern community feeling. I think that facts, not words, may make that feeling more general the world over.

In this country, the transition from the old to the new is bringing forth a larger number of young men who have this basic community feeling and who turn as naturally to the social opportunities opened up by the New Deal as do plants to the life-giving sun.

It is extremely heartening to see, as I do, here and there in private life and in government service, men who have definitely turned their backs on the mere accumulation of wealth for more satisfying possibilities on the new frontiers.

When this country's attention was centered upon money-making, the successful were additionally rewarded by common adulation. The younger generation quite naturally sought the same cheap reward. I am sure that, had their elders set them saner objectives in life, they would have pursued these ends with as great avidity, for youth naturally follows the guiding hands of those whom it respects. While many a youth finds himself limited at the very start by the lack of industrial, commercial, agricultural, and professional opportunities and by the competition of millions of unemployed, there is another type quick to see the large tasks of the future and to step forward with eager minds and hands.

For those who see now that the men who led us into chaos have nothing to give except another selfish fling and more chaos, new frontiers beckon with meaningful adventures. . . .

Putting our lands and factories in order is more than a day's job and holds many unforeseeable problems.

Putting our jobs in order and arranging our wages and hours of labor with the object of greater joy in work, leisure, and play will supply many a social engineer with his life's work.

Putting our houses in order in city and town and on the farm is a challenge to any architect's sense of beauty, of harmony between men, his shelter, his neighbors, and his natural environment.

Putting our democratic political and educational institutions in order, so that the new order of the land and factory and home is constantly brought to higher standards of creative living, calls for almost limitless wisdom.

In every one of these and other new directions, there are challenges and accomplishments far more real than those that rewarded the old pioneers who carried our civilization beyond the Alleghanies. The Indians, wild animals, and disease of this new world are the forces of prejudice, fear, greed, and suspicion, even now stirring and shouting.

THE TEMPO OF POLITICAL CHANGE[1]

Allan Nevins

ALLAN NEVINS was educated at the University of Illinois. After service on the editorial staffs of the *Nation, Evening Post, Herald,* and *World* in New York, and as professor of history in Cornell University, he became professor of history in Columbia University. His books include *The American States During and After the Revolution; The Evening Post: A Century of Journalism; The Emergence of Modern America; American Social History Recorded by British Travellers; Frémont; Grover Cleveland: A Study in Courage; Henry White: Thirty Years in American Diplomacy,* and *Abram S. Hewitt, With Some Account of Peter Cooper.*

For the sixteen years between 1918 and 1934 Americans have been living in a world of incessant and tremendous political changes. Yet until the last year they have taken little or no part in these changes; they have held the passive rôle of spectators. Once-great nations have crashed into fragments; once-hopeful democracies have turned to dictatorships; socialist or labor governments have taken the helm in lands where aristocracy had been all but unchallenged since the Plantagenets and Hohenstaufens. The most populous nation in the Western world has become a gigantic experiment in communism. The greatest empire the globe has seen has ceased to be an empire and become a commonwealth, a loose alliance of free nations. The ancient Orient has heaved and swayed under the impulses of revolution. "Like wrecks of a dissolving dream," old political fabrics have passed away and new structures have arisen. But amid these seething currents the United States had stood still. Its people felt that they had good reason for their immobility. Other nations had emerged from the World War trembling with exhaustion, loaded with intolerable debts, racked with social discontent. The United States had emerged richer than ever before, more powerful, more self-satisfied — and more selfishly intent upon risking none of its gains.

Not merely did America during these years stand unmoved in a changing world; it watched the swirling currents of the time sweep past in directions which left it isolated, and which implied a rejection of its example. After the war a score of nations, new and old, equipped or reëquipped themselves with governments. Not one modeled its constitution after that of the United States. Even those which

---

[1] From *The University of Buffalo Studies,* May 1934.

accepted the principles of democracy declined our presidential system and chose the parliamentary system. Moreover, not one imitated the cautious and restricted policy of the United States with respect to social and economic problems. They insisted unanimously that their new governments should exercise a vigorous and far-reaching control over social and economic affairs. They adopted these divergent policies in the face of the fact that the United States in 1918 had attained to an unapproached pinnacle of wealth, power, and prestige. Our mighty war effort had astonished the world. Our President had gone to Paris to be universally acclaimed as the greatest living leader of democracy. But when they grappled with the realities of government, and the realities of the relation between government and public welfare, these nations turned their backs upon the American system.

In this fact reflective Americans might well have seen a ground for uneasiness. There had been a time when the United States was both a symbol of wise political change and the archetype of all progressive democracies. When we set up our Constitution in 1787, with George III King of England, with Catherine the Great on the Russian throne, with Louis XVI at Versailles, our government was the hope of liberal minds the world over. When a generation later the republics of South America came into existence, they modeled their constitutions, in no small degree, upon the example we had set. When a generation later we fought our Civil War, the Old World hung upon the conflict as a supreme test of political liberalism. Henry Adams heard John Bright in 1863 tell the workingmen of London that the United States was the great exemplar of progressive democracy. European Privilege, said Bright, hated us. "It has beheld thirty millions of men happy and prosperous, without emperors, without kings, without the surroundings of a court, without nobles, except such as are made by eminence in intellect and virtue, without state bishops and state priests, without great armies and navies, without a great debt and great taxes — and Privilege has shuddered at what might happen to old Europe if that great experiment should succeed." But that was seventy years ago. What European in the last generation has pointed to the United States as a preëminent example of political progressivism, of social liberalism? What Old World radical, in the ten years after the Great War, failed to think of the United States as on the side of inertia and conservatism?

The fact is undeniable that for two long generations preceding 1933 the United States was far more conservative than progressive — that politically it was often even reactionary. The last shots of the Civil

War ushered in the corrupt and tyrannical régime in politics which one historian has called the Tragic Era, and the turbulent scramble in economic affairs which another historian has called the Great Barbecue. An era of lethargy succeeded. It was broken from time to time by spasmodic movements for reform; but after the World War we were still capable of relapsing into blind, sluggish inertia. We called for a *safe* government — and found that a decade of it left us in direr peril than ever before. We thought we could continue indefinitely to be an individualistic and provincial democracy — and sharply awoke to the fact that we are not in the eighteenth century, but well advanced in the twentieth.

There is nothing strange or deeply censurable in our long conservatism with respect to politics and politico-economic affairs. Historically, there are a dozen reasons for our sluggish temper. One great reason beyond doubt lies in our Anglo-Saxon heritage. The common political tradition of the English-speaking peoples, which we share, is a conservative tradition. Tennyson did not write merely that freedom broadens down from precedent to precedent; he wrote that it broadens *slowly down*. Violent radicalism is repugnant to the race. The French Revolution filled George Washington and Edmund Burke with the same horror. When Elihu Root defined popular government as organized self-control, he expressed a belief that may be traced back to Runnymede. A second great reason for our conservatism lies in our written Constitution. This instrument was framed under the influence of the eighteenth century idea of checks and balances. With its carefully enumerated powers, with its attempt at an exact coördination of functions, with its rigid, unyielding specifications, it has always been a restraining influence. Its authors did not regard it as a charter of democracy; they regarded it rather as a check upon democracy. Moreover, our veneration for the Constitution, criticized long ago by Jefferson, has indubitably grown to exaggerated proportions. Many people have made it a fetish; a Cabinet officer a few years ago referred proudly to the religious faith which believes in its "divine origin"! And as a third great reason for our political conservatism, we must not overlook our material wealth. With a richly-stored continent to exploit, for one hundred fifty years we have been the most prosperous people on the planet. Nothing suppresses discontent like the full dinner-pail; nothing induces caution like property.

There have been minor reasons as well. One is that the best leadership available in America has not in general gone into political affairs. It has heretofore been attracted chiefly to industry and business, with their larger constructive opportunities, their more glittering prizes of power as well as wealth. Our great magnates of transportation, banking, and manufacturing, our Morgans, Carnegies, and James J. Hills, would have looked contemptuously on the ordinary political career. The result is that while bold enterprise has been displayed in finance and industry, second-rate minds have usually ruled the political sphere. Still another reason lies in the fact that our party politics, with its incessant bustle and excitement, has offered a frequent illusion of progress where none existed. We thought our quadrennial campaigns, with their parades, rallies, speeches, and newspaper rhetoric, decided something — when they were often mere sound and fury. Despite all the pother and din, our wagon of government creaked forward at snail's pace. Again, our nation has been unified but slowly. It required steam, electricity, the internal combustion engine, the radio, to knit the country together. Decentralized government does not lend itself to swift and radical change, and in many departments of national life it is only since 1901, when Theodore Roosevelt became President, that we have moved toward a truly centralized authority.

It cannot be doubted, by anyone who gives careful study to our national past, that we have paid some severe penalties for our indolent conservatism. We too often took the easy attitude that the Fathers of the Republic, the makers of the Constitution, had done so much for us that we had little need to do anything for ourselves. While we recognized that our society had imperfections, we felt it patriotic to assume that the American stream, if but given time, would scour itself clean. We refused to face even our manifest failures. With fewer problems to meet than crowded Europe, we botched some of them lamentably. Every other nation which had slavery, including the British Empire, Brazil, and Russia, abolished it without firing a shot, but we did so only after four years of bloody war. Great Britain, dismayed by the insidious corruption of her civil service, got almost completely rid of it by the middle of the nineteenth century. We, less dismayed by our far more impudent spoils system, did not even begin our piecemeal reform till the federal law of 1883. We had no policy on immigration, but accepted every element that the Old World flung upon our shores. We had no considered policy as regarded our vast national domain; we gave it to corporations in lavish grants, and when we ceased that extravagance, let it be stolen. As late as 1900 the average American had not learned the word "conservation." While we boasted that we had no great standing army, we were the only nation in the world to let a colossal organization of veterans systematically loot its Treasury. Year by year we permitted our government to drift further into the control of plutocratic forces.

It is quite true that, late in the nineteenth century, a heterogeneous body of reformers arose. There were tariff reformers, civil service reformers, municipal reformers, believers in direct government. Their work was spasmodic in energy, and narrow in outlook, while it now seems naïve in purpose — but it was valuable for all that. It is true also that in the first fifteen years of the twentieth century two men, Theodore Roosevelt and Woodrow Wilson, caught a larger vision of change. They saw that the individualistic and provincial democracy was dead. They realized that a great new coöperative democracy, with expert and responsible leadership furnished by a centralized government, must take its place. But the American people were slow to accept their teachings. They hearkened unwillingly when Herbert Croly wrote in *The Promise of American Life* in 1912 that the time was fast coming when our nation must emancipate itself from its "traditional illusions," and understand that only under a "nationalized organization," acting to plan our whole economy, could we realize the democratic ideal.

Thus it was that, in the languor after the World War, a majority of Americans believed that we could go back of Woodrow Wilson, back of Theodore Roosevelt's New Nationalism, to the old conservatism which had so often approached stagnation. Inaction could again be veiled in consecrated phrases. We would return to normalcy. Government would stand aside and do nothing but keep the ring while rugged individualism did everything. The business of the country, remarked Mr. Coolidge, is business. As for foreign affairs, we would simply wash our hands of them. The kind of government was best which, at home and abroad, risked least.

Whatever may be said of the want of heroism and idealism in this course, we can now see that it lacked the simpler requisite of common sense. It was founded upon several glaring miscalculations. We believed, for one thing, that Europe would recover and readjust itself much more rapidly than it has done. President Wilson had thought it advisable that we lend a steadying hand to Europe; most Americans after him thought that unnecessary. The result was that Europe half rose, lurched, staggered eccentrically, and fell. We paid our full share of the penalty in impaired trade, demoralized exchanges, debt moratoria, repudiated bonds, and general fear of the future.

We miscalculated, again, in thinking that we had a stable and well-balanced economic system at home. Business indeed seemed to prosper. But agriculture, the primary foundation of our well-being, passed from debility to utter prostration. Various industries, notably textiles and coal, suffered from chronic disorganization and over-competition, their hundreds of thousands of workers stumbling in an unconquerable murk of poverty. Still other industries had what their leaders at last bitterly termed "profitless prosperity." Our whole economic mechanism was badly geared, ill-lubricated, unplanned. We miscalculated, once more, in thinking that we had a financial system adequate to any strain. We even boasted that the Federal Reserve had made another panic and depression impossible. We erred, above all, in believing that this greatest of industrial nations, with its ever-thickening population, its violently conflicting interests, its intricate problems of technology, its difficult position in a sick world, needed only a passive government. We had learned better long before the inauguration of Franklin D. Roosevelt, when business and finance turned in desperation to the new Administration with a frank confession of their incompetence, their helplessness, and their overwhelming fear.

Since March 4, 1933, we seem to have been thrust out into a swiftly moving, indeed a steadily accelerating, current of political change. Never before in time of peace has the tempo of experiment, reorganization, and reform been so rapid. Is this a temporary phenomenon, or does it open a permanent new phase of American life? Are we only in a morning-after mood, experimenting with purgatives and tonics; or are we trying to write a new chapter in our history? From any point of view we have much to do. We have to recover our prosperity; to restore a fair balance between agriculture and industry, production and consumption; to deal with our staggering debts, public and private; to meet a thousand minor emergencies. Will many of the new elements introduced into our government be sloughed away when we return to general health? We may differ greatly upon the wisdom or unwisdom of specific measures of the New Deal; and yet assuredly thoughtful people will hope that the vigor and rapidity of political change in the United States have been permanently stimulated.

Without venturing upon the uncertain ground of prophecy, we can say that the new tempo ought to be maintained, and that a new and far less conservative era ought to be opening. It should be a true dawn, not a false dawn. And for our hope that it may so prove we may assign several reasons. The decade of political stagnation in which we indulged ourselves between 1921 and 1931 must alone make it necessary to move fast and far to catch up. The mere fact that the rest of the globe has been striding feverishly along new paths, again, renders it important for us in some ways to stride with it. Some of the changes abroad have been far from meaning real progress — we have only to look at Germany to see that. And yet the general tendency everywhere is to place increased powers, economic, political, and social, in the hands of the central government. This is true in England and in Russia, in Italy and in Germany, in Spain and in Japan. Measures of state control in one nation often compel similar measures in another. When Germany regulates her commerce by quotas, France must do the same. When Great Britain controls the value of her currency through a stabilization fund, the United States has to act likewise. A world-wide movement, in short, is under way, and it will not easily be checked. But above all, in the past year we have been recognizing an unescapable change in the basic conditions of our national life. Our new measures, broadly regarded, are simply a resumption of the work which Theodore Roosevelt and Woodrow Wilson had begun nearly a generation ago.

We must shift to new paths; we must shake off the illusion that we can prosper as an individualistic and provincial democracy, and realize that our true ideal is the coöperative commonwealth, under planned governmental leadership. One great vice of Americans has always been their intellectual insincerity. We liked to think we were democratic when we were not. We liked to believe we were progressive when we were not. In time of trouble we evaded a fundamental responsibility by tackling a superficial responsibility. We met lawlessness by talking of crime waves and shaking up the police force. We dealt with lost markets by passing a tariff bill which had been condemned by the unanimous voice of our expert economists, but which James E. Watson assured us would bring back prosperity within thirty days. But this time, after our last sobering shock, we perceive that the fundamental responsibilities of 1934 are not to be met by attacks on surface abuses. Nothing less than the whole problem has to be dealt with by comprehensive national forethought. One part of our task involves the reorganization of our entire agricultural life by cutting down overproduction, lopping off marginal lands, returning to a more leisurely and more pastoral farm existence. Another part of the task involves the reorganization of our entire industrial mechanism by checking our furious excess output, stopping lawless competitive warfare, standardizing labor costs at a decent level, and introducing, under Federal oversight, that self-government of industry which has long been desired by business leaders. The experiments represented by the A.A.A., T.V.A., and the rest may fail; if so, we must try other experiments. We cannot return to 1929; we must go on to a more carefully planned, more truly balanced national life.

"The future of mankind," John Stuart Mill once told John Morley, "will be gravely imperiled if great questions are left to be fought out between ignorant change and ignorant opposition to change." That certainly can be said of the portion of mankind contained in the United States. Ignorance on both sides can be avoided only if it is realized that change — and rapid change — is inevitable, and that the questions involved must be taken up with promptness and diligence if they are to be canvassed rationally, and if the best judgment is to be brought to bear upon them. Some of the political errors of the last twelvemonth in the United States are obviously attributable to the excessive haste with which a grim emergency has finally compelled action upon problems too long postponed. The United States has always been a liberal nation. It has clung instinctively to the faith of Jefferson and Mill that all the great sources of human suffering are more or less conquerable by human effort, and that this effort is best applied by individuals working in a liberty as untrammeled as possible. But since the time of these older thinkers the basic conditions of liberalism have changed beyond recognition. What the author of the Declaration of Independence chiefly feared was the pressure of institutions upon the individual, weighing him down, binding his hands, destroying his individuality. But that principle helped to open the door to *laissez faire* in the industrial sphere, with all its abuses. It is a principle so outmoded, so paralyzed and futile, that it has tended to bring all liberalism into disrepute. We have a world far more highly industrialized than any Jefferson dreamed of, resting upon a new scientific and technological basis, with enormous possibilities of abundance, of leisure, of individual freedom; but a world at the same time so fettered by economic practice and law, by social custom, by nationalistic prejudices, that the richer possibilities of liberty mean little.

There are several possible roads. One is drift — and we have had ample experience of the result to which it leads. One is the attempt to achieve reform and a better world by violence — a course followed in other lands with little success, and repugnant to the American temper. The third is to mobilize the best social intelligence of the time, and to give it a wider application in the institutions of society and government by welcoming change, by encouraging reasonable and informed experimentation. This will require abandonment of the adult infantilism to which the nation fondly clung through most of the period from Grant to Coolidge. We cannot continue to act as if we were an isolated land, when actually a myriad of economic, social, and cultural forces bind us to the remainder of the world. We cannot continue to act as if we were still a semi-rural people, cushioned by unused lands against the shocks of panic and depression, when actually we are one of the most highly industrialized of nations. We cannot act as if our problems of class, of race, of poverty, of ignorance were so simple that the mere chanting of the word "democracy" will abolish them, when actually they are alarmingly grave and growing graver. We cannot afford to act as if governmental effort and collective intelligence were evils, as if planned social action were a peril, when actually they offer the only road under modern conditions to safety and the good life. Recognition that the republic has attained adult stature and must move with adult rapidity, decision, and energy will avert great material misfortunes. But it will do more — it will furnish spiritual rewards that lie beyond any yet attained by the American people.

This, to be sure, is a task which will require decades rather than years. We have seen only the beginning. Secretary Wallace was correct when he said that, spectacular though our new undertakings appear, they are but a foreshadowing of far vaster changes that must eventually be carried through. In this momentous labor the oncoming generation of college-trained men and women should play the principal part. One great difficulty with the limited and naïve reform movements of the past lay in the nature of their appeal. They were presented as moral challenges, when actually reform should always be an intellectual challenge. The old idea was that we needed a revivalistic awakening, a greater spiritual fervor, and all would be well. Our politics would be "purified"; our democracy, with the good men overthrowing the wicked special interests, would press on to new triumphs. But we do not need good intentions most; we need brains. We do not need moral fervor in denouncing wicked interests; we need expert skill in seeing that the economic efficiency of the special interests is all retained, and yet somehow better bent to the common good — its fruits more equitably distributed. If the new tempo in political affairs does not present an intellectual challenge, then it falls short of its proper aim. A constructive national policy is essentially a series of the most difficult problems imaginable.

A MODERN BOOKLIST

(Many older books of great value are omitted; they may easily be obtained by using older bibliographies.)

I. THE CHANGING POLITICAL WORLD

ISAIAH BOWMAN, *The New World* (rev. ed., 1930); RAYMOND L. BUELL, *Europe: A History of Ten Years* (1929); C. DELISLE BURNS, *A Short History of the World, 1918–1928* (1928); WILLIAM H. CHAMBERLIN, *Russia's Iron Age* (1934) and *The Russian Revolution 1917–1921* (2 vols., 1935); GROVER CLARK, *The Great Wall Crumbles* (1935); GEORGE D. H. COLE, *The Intelligent Man's Review of Europe Today* (1930); WILLIAM H. DAWSON, *Germany under the Treaty* (1933); FRANCIS DELAISI, *Political Myths and Economic Realities* (1925); WILHELM DIBELIUS, *England* (1930); HERBERT FEIS, *Europe the World's Banker* (1930); AGNES HEADLAM-MORLEY, *The New Democratic Constitutions of Europe* (1929); MAURICE G. HINDUS, *Humanity Uprooted* (1929) and *The Great Offensive* (1933); JAMES F. HORRABIN, *An Atlas of Current Affairs* (1934); WALTER C. LANGSAM, *The World since 1914* (rev. ed., 1935); HAROLD D. LASSWELL, *World Politics and Personal Insecurity* (1935); W. K. KOROSTEWITZ, *The Rebirth of Poland* (1928); EVERETT DEAN MARTIN, *Farewell to Revolution* (1935); ARTHUR ROSENBERG, *History of Bolshevism, from Marx to the First Five Years' Plan* (1934); BERTRAND RUSSELL, *Freedom vs. Organization, 1814–1914* (1934); OWEN RUTTER, *The New Baltic States and Their Future* (1925); JOHN STRACHEY, *The Coming Struggle for Power* (1932); NORMAN THOMAS, *The Choice before Us; Humanity at the Crossroads* (1934); LEON TROTSKY, *History of the Russian Revolution* (3 vols., 1932–1933); ACHILLE VIALLATE, *Economic Imperialism and International Relations during the Last Fifty Years* (1923); LUIGI VILLARI, *The Expansion of Italy* (1930) and *The Fascist Experiment* (1926); LEONARD S. WOOLF, *After the Deluge* (1931).

II. THE CHANGING ECONOMIC WORLD

CHARLES A. BEARD, *The Open Door at Home* (1934); ARTHUR L. BOWLEY, *Some Economic Consequences of the Great War* (1930); C. DELISLE BURNS, *Leisure in the Modern World* (1932); THOMAS N. CARVER, *The Present Economic Revolution in the United States* (1925); STUART CHASE, *A New Deal* (1932) and *The Economy of Abundance* (1934); GEORGE D. H. COLE, *A Guide through World Chaos* (1932) and *What Everyone Wants to Know about Money* (1933); LEWIS COREY, *The Decline of American Capitalism* (1934); MAURICE H. DOBB, *Russian Economic Development since the Revolution* (rev. ed., 1931); RICHARD T. ELY, *Studies in the Evolution of Industrial*

Society (1903); JOHN T. FLYNN, *Security Speculation: Its Economic Effects* (1934); ROY F. HARROD, *International Economics* (1933); LEO HAUSLEITER, *The Machine Unchained* (1933); FRED HENDERSON, *The Economic Consequences of Power Production* (1931); FRANCIS W. HIRST, *Wall Street and Lombard Street* (1931); HENRY V. HODSON, *Economics of a Changing World* (1933); CALVIN B. HOOVER, *The Economic Life of Soviet Russia* (1931); JOHN M. KEYNES, *Laissez Faire and Communism* (1926); HARRY W. LAIDLER, *Concentration of Control in American Industry* (1931); LEAGUE OF NATIONS, *The Course and Phases of the World Economic Depression* (rev. ed., 1932), *World Economic Survey* (1932), and *The Agricultural Crisis* (2 vols., 1931–1932); ALEXANDER LOVEDAY, *Britain and World Trade* (1931); WESLEY C. MITCHELL and OTHERS, *Recent Economic Changes in the United States* (2 vols., 1929); SIR CHARLES MORGAN-WEBB, *The Money Revolution* (1935); HAROLD S. MOULTON and ASSOCIATES, *America's Capacity to Consume* (1934); RAMSAY MUIR, *The Interdependent World and Its Problems* (1933); LEWIS MUMFORD, *Technics and Civilization* (1934); EDWIN G. NOURSE and ASSOCIATES, *America's Capacity to Produce* (1934); JOHN H. RICHARDSON, *Economic Disarmament* (1931); ISAAC M. RUBINOW, *The Quest for Security* (1934); SIR ARTHUR SALTER, *Recovery* (1932); SIR ARTHUR SALTER and OTHERS, *The World Economic Crisis* (1932); THORSTEIN VEBLEN, *The Engineers and the Price System* (1921); JOHN W. WHEELER-BENNETT, *The Wreck of Reparations* (1933).

III.   THE CHANGING SOCIAL WORLD

JANE ADDAMS, *Twenty Years at Hull House* (1912); CAROLINE BAUER, *Modern Housing* (1934); PAUL BLANSHARD, *Outline of the British Labor Movement* (1923); HENRY N. BRAILSFORD, *Property or Peace* (1934); KENNETH BURKE, *Permanence and Change* (1935); C. DELISLE BURNS, *Short History of International Intercourse* (1924); MARJORIE R. CLARK, *History of the French Labor Movement* (1930); GEORGE D. H. COLE, *Guild Socialism and Social Theory* (1921); JOHN R. COMMONS and JOHN B. ANDREWS, *The Principles of Labor Legislation* (1927); WILLIAM CUNNINGHAM, *Christianity and Social Questions* (1910); MAURICE R. DAVIE, *Social Aspects of Mental Hygiene* (1925); STANLEY P. DAVIES, *Social Control of the Mentally Deficient* (1930); ROBERT C. DEXTER, *Social Adjustment* (1927); ABRAHAM EPSTEIN, *Insecurity: A Challenge to America* (1933); CHARLES R. FAY, *Coöperation at Home and Abroad* (1925); JULIAN HUXLEY, *Science and Social Needs* (1935); ROBERT W. KELSO, *Poverty* (1929); HARRY LAIDLER, *Socializing Our Democracy* (1935); LEWIS L. LORWIN and JEAN A. FLEXNER, *The American Federation of Labor* (1933); ROBERT S. and HELEN LYND, *Middletown* (1929); FRANCIS S. MARVIN, *The Unity of Western Civilization* (3rd ed., 1930); GEORGIANA P. MCENTEE, *The Social Catholic Movement in Great Britain* (1921); REINHOLD NIEBUHR, *Reflections on the End of an Era* (1934); WILLIAM F. OGBURN and OTHERS, *Social Change and the New*

Deal (1934); JOSÉ ORTEGA Y GASSET, *The Revolt of the Masses* (1932); PRESIDENT'S RESEARCH COMMITTEE, *Recent Social Trends in the United States* (2 vols., 1933); JOHN H. RANDALL, *A World Community* (1930); LOUIS N. ROBINSON, *Penology in the United States* (1921); JOHN H. RYAN, *A Better Economic Order* (1935); RICHARD H. TAWNEY, *The British Labor Movement* (1925); NORMAN THOMAS, *Human Exploitation* (1934); EDITH E. WOOD, *The Housing of the Unskilled Wage-Earner* (1919).

IV. WAR AND WORLD ORDER

DEVERE ALLEN, *The Fight for Peace* (1930); NORMAN ANGELL, *The Great Illusion* (1914), *Peace and the Plain Man* (1935), and *The Unseen Assassins* (1932); STANLEY H. BAILEY, *The Framework of International Society* (1932); ARTHUR C. F. BEALES, *History of Peace* (1931); LÉON BLUM, *Peace and Disarmament* (1932); FLORENCE B. BOECKEL, *Between War and Peace* (1928); HENRY N. BRAILSFORD, *If We Want Peace* (1932); KARL A. BRATT, *That Next War?* (1931); RUSSELL M. COOPER, *American Consultation in World Affairs for the Preservation of Peace* (1934); HELEN M. CORY, *The Compulsory Arbitration of International Disputes* (1932); MERLE E. CURTI, *The American Peace Crusade, 1835-1860* (1929); G. LOWES DICKINSON, *War, Its Nature, Cause and Cure* (1923); HELMUTH C. ENGELBRECHT and FRANK C. HANIGHEN, *Merchants of Death* (1934); GUGLIELMO FERRERO, *Militarism* (1903); INTER-PARLIAMENTARY UNION, *What Would Be the Character of the Next War?* (1932) and *What Would Be the Character of a New War?* (1933); INTERNATIONAL LABOR ORGANIZATION, *The International Labor Office, The First Decade* (1931); DAVID STARR JORDAN, *The Human Harvest* (1907); PRINCE KROPOTKIN, *Mutual Aid* (Section on War) (1917); JOHN H. LATANÉ, *From Isolation to Leadership* (1925); LEAGUE OF NATIONS, *Ten Years of World Coöperation* (1931); SALVADOR DE MADRI-ARAGA, *Disarmament* (1929); THEODORE MARBURG, *The Development of the League of Nations Idea* (1932); LAURA W. MCMULLEN, *Building the World Society* (1931); LUCIA T. A. MEAD, *Law or War?* (1928); FELIX MORLEY, *The Society of Nations* (1932); RAMSAY MUIR, *Nationalism and Internationalism* (1917); DENYS P. MYERS, *World Disarmament* (1932); GEORGE H. PERRIS, *A Short History of War and Peace* (1911); ARTHUR PORRITT, *The Causes of War* (1932); PITMAN B. POTTER, *Introduction to the Study of International Organization* (3rd ed., 1928); K. B. SCHMIDT and ADOLF GRABOWSKY, *The Problem of Disarmament* (1933); GEORGE SELDES, *Iron, Blood and Profits* (1934); JAMES T. SHOTWELL, *War as an Instrument of National Policy and Its Renunciation* (1929); LAURENCE STALLINGS, *The First World War: A Photographic History* (1933); FLORENCE G. TUTTLE, *Alternatives to War* (1931); THORSTEIN VEBLEN, *An Inquiry into the Nature of Peace, and the Terms of Its Perpetuation* (1917); HAROLD M. VINACKE, *International Organization* (1934); GRAHAM WALLAS, *The Great Society* (1914); H. G. WELLS, *The Work, Wealth, and Happiness of Man-*

kind (1932) and *The Shape of Things to Come* (1933); JOHN W. WHEELER-BENNETT, *The Disarmament Deadlock* (1935); BENJAMIN H. WILLIAMS, *The United States and Disarmament* (1931).

V. SCIENCE AND THE MODERN WORLD

ROBERT H. BAKER, *The Universe Unfolding* (1932); BERNHARD BAVINK, *The Natural Sciences, An Introduction to the Scientific Philosophy of Today* (1932); EDWIN G. BORING, *History of Experimental Psychology* (1929); FLORIAN CAJORI, *History of Mathematics* (1919); BEVERLEY L. CLARKE, *The Marvels of Modern Chemistry* (1932); EDWIN G. CONKLIN, "Science and the Faith of the Modern" (*Scribner's*, Nov., 1925); RICHARD T. COX, *Time, Space, and Atoms* (1933); SIR WILLIAM C. D. DAMPIER-WHETHAM, *History of Science* (1932); CHARLES DARWIN, *Origin of Species* (1887) and *Voyage of the Beagle* (1909); DAVID DIETZ, *The Story of Science* (1934); HERBERT DINGLE, *Modern Astrophysics* (1924) and *Science and Human Experience* (1932); SIR ARTHUR S. EDDINGTON, *The Nature of the Physical World* (1929); HAIG G. GARBEDIAN, *The Major Mysteries of Science* (1933); BENJAMIN GINZBURG, *The Adventure of Science* (1930); JOHN B. S. HALDANE, *The Philosophical Basis of Biology* (1931); WILLIAM O. HOTCHKISS, *The Story of a Billion Years* (1933); THOMAS HUXLEY, *Collected Essays* (1894); SIR JAMES H. JEANS, *The Universe around Us* (1933), *The Mysterious Universe* (1932), and *Through Time and Space* (1934); EDWIN A. KIRKPATRICK, *The Sciences of Man in the Making* (1932); JOHN LANGDON-DAVIES, *Man and His Universe* (1930); HYMAN LEVY, *The Universe of Science* (1933); RICHARD S. LULL, *The Ways of Life* (1925); HIRAM P. MAXIM, *Life's Place in the Cosmos* (1933); JOSEPH MCCABE, *The Riddle of the Universe Today* (1934); ROBERT A. MILLIKAN, *Electrons* (+ and −) *Protons, Photons, Neutrons and Cosmic Rays* (1935), *Elements of Electricity* (1920), and *Evolution in Science and Religion* (1927); CONWY L. MORGAN, *Emergent Evolution* (1923) and *The Scientific Basis of Evolution* (1932); MAX K. E. L. PLANCK, *The Universe in the Light of Modern Physics* (1931); PAUL RADIN, *The Racial Myth* (1934); LAWRENCE V. REDMAN and AUSTIN V. H. MORY, *Romance of Research* (1933); BERTRAND RUSSELL, *The Scientific Outlook* (1931) and *Selected Papers* (1927); VERA SANFORD, *Short History of Mathematics* (1930); WILLIAM T. SEDGWICK and HARRY W. TYLER, *Short History of Science* (1917); HARLOW SHAPLEY, *Flights from Chaos* (1930); ROBERT SHAFER, *Progress and Science* (1922); MAYNARD SHIPLEY, *The War on Modern Science* (1927); EDWIN E. SLOSSON, *Chats on Science* (1924) and *Creative Chemistry* (1930); HERBERT SPENCER, *The Classification of the Sciences* (1870), *Essays* (1885), and *Autobiography* (1904); SIR J. ARTHUR THOMSON, *Modern Science* (1929) and *The Outlines of Science* (1922); ROBERT S. WOODWORTH, *Contemporary Schools of Psychology* (1931).

VI. RELIGION AND MORALS

GEORGE P. ADAMS, *Idealism and the Modern Age* (1919); SAMUEL ALEXANDER, *Moral Order and Progress* (1906) and *Space, Time, and Deity* (1920); BERNARD BOSANQUET, *Essays and Addresses* (1899) and *Value and Destiny of the Individual* (1913); JOHN BURROUGHS, *Accepting the Universe* (1920); MARY W. CALKINS, *The Persistent Problems of Philosophy* (1912); JOHN DEWEY, *Creative Intelligence* (1917) and *Human Nature and Conduct* (1927); DURANT DRAKE, *Problems of Conduct* (1914); IRWIN EDMAN, *Human Traits and Their Social Significance* (1920); WALTER G. EVERETT, *Moral Values* (1918); JOHN FISKE, *Through Nature to God* (1899); HARRY E. FOSDICK, *As I See Religion* (1932); JUNE P. GUILD, *Living with the Law* (1928); VISCOUNT HALDANE, *The Philosophy of Humanism* (1922) and *Autobiography* (1929); LEONARD T. HOBHOUSE, *Morals in Evolution* (1906) and *The Rational Good* (1921); WILLIAM E. HOCKING, *The Meaning of God in Human Experience* (1912); DEAN WILLIAM R. INGE, *Outspoken Essays* (two series, 1919); LAWRENCE P. JACKS, *Religious Perplexities* (1922); JOSEPH A. LEIGHTON, *Man and the Cosmos* (1922); WALTER LIPPMANN, *A Preface to Morals* (1929); JACQUES LOEB, *The Mechanistic Conception of Life* (1912); ARTHUR C. McGIFFERT, *The Rise of Modern Religious Ideas* (1915); JOHN M. E. McTAGGART, *Human Immortality and Pre-Existence* (1915); H. L. MENCKEN, *Treatise on Right and Wrong* (1934); PAUL ELMER MORE, *The Sceptical Approach to Religion* (1934); CARDINAL JOHN H. NEWMAN, *Apologia Pro Vita Sua* (1858); REINHOLD NIEBUHR, *Moral Man and Immoral Society* (1932); GEORGE H. PALMER, *The Problem of Freedom* (1911) and *Altruism, Its Nature and Varieties* (1919); HOWARD M. PARSHLEY, *Science and Good Behavior* (1928); GEORGE T. W. PATRICK, *The World and Its Meaning* (1925); JAMES B. PRATT, *The Psychology of Religious Belief* (1907); RALPH B. PERRY, *The Present Conflict of Ideals* (1918); BENJAMIN RAND, *The Classical Moralists* (1909); JOSIAH ROYCE, *The Problem of Christianity* (1913) and *The Spirit of Modern Philosophy* (1892); BERTRAND RUSSELL, *The Analysis of Mind* (1922); ARTHUR L. SWIFT, ed., *Religion Today* (1933); ALFRED N. WHITEHEAD, *Adventures in Ideas* (1933).

VII. EDUCATION IN ITS MODERN ASPECTS

ROBERT C. ANGELL, *The Campus* (1928); WILLIAM C. BAGLEY, *Education, Crime and Social Progress* (1931); RALPH A. BEALS, *Aspects of Post-Collegiate Education* (1935); WALTON S. BITTNER and HERVEY F. MALLORY, *University Teaching by Mail* (1933); ABERDEEN O. BOWDEN and IDA C. CLARKE, *Tomorrow's Americans* (1930); WILLIAM BOYD, *The History of Western Education* (1921); WERRETT W. CHARTERS, *The Teaching of Ideals* (1927); SHEPARD B. CLOUGH, *Making Fascists* (1929); GEORGE A. COE, *Educating for Citizenship* (1932); JOHN J. COSS, ed., *Five College Plans* (1931); GEORGE S. COUNTS, *The Social Foundations of Education* (1934) and *The American Road to Culture* (1930); ELLWOOD P. CUBBERLEY, *Public Education in the United States* (1919); MERLE E. CURTI, *Social Ideas of American Educators* (1935); JOHN DEWEY, *School and Society* (1899) and *Democracy and Education* (1916); JOHN and EVELYN DEWEY, *Schools of Tomorrow* (1915); JOHN P. GAVIT, *College* (1925); FRANK P. GRAVES, *A Student's History of Education* (1915); A. L. HALLQUEST, *The University Afield* (1926); MARIUS HANSOME, *World Workers' Educational Movements* (1931); JOSEPH K. HART, *Education for an Age of Power* (1935); HAMILTON HOLT, *The Rollins College Adventure in Education* (1928); HENRY JOHNSON, *Introduction to the History of the Social Sciences in Schools* (1932); CHARLES H. JUDD, *Education and Social Progress* (1934); FRITZ KELLERMAN, *The Effect of the World War on European Education* (1928); WILLIAM H. KIL-PATRICK, *Education for a Changing Civilization* (1927); CLARENCE C. LITTLE, *The Awakening College* (1930); EVERETT DEAN MARTIN, *The Meaning of a Liberal Education* (1933); ALEXANDER MEIKLEJOHN, *The Experimental College* (1932); CHARLES E. MERRIAM, *Civic Education in the United States* (1934); J. P. MONROE, *New Demands in Education* (1912); ARTHUR E. MORGAN, *What Is College For?* (1930); NATHANIEL PEFFER, *Educational Experiments in Industry* (1932) and *New Schools for Older Students* (1926); FREDERICK W. ROMAN, *The New Education in Europe* (1930); BERTRAND RUSSELL, *Education and The Modern World* (1932); WILLIAM S. and LENA SADLER, *Piloting Modern Youth* (1931); HOWARD J. SAVAGE and OTHERS, *American College Athletics* (1929); DAVID SNEDDEN, *Toward Better Educations* (1931); HERBERT SPENCER, *Education, Intellectual, Moral, Physical* (1861); MARION TALBOT, *The Education of Women* (1910); CHARLES F. THWING, *The American and the German University* (1928); REXFORD G. TUGWELL and LEON H. KEYSERLING, *Redirecting Education* (2 vols., 1934–1935); THORSTEIN VEBLEN, *The Higher Learning in America* (1918).

VIII. LITERATURE AND THE MODERN SCENE

LASCELLES ABERCROMBIE, *The Theory of Poetry* (1924); RICHARD ALDINGTON, "The Poet and His Age" in *Literary Studies and Reviews* (1924); WILLIAM ARCHER, *The Old Drama and the New* (1923); MATTHEW ARNOLD, *Essays in Criticism* (1865–1888); IRVING BABBITT, *The New Laokoön* (1910), *Literature and the American College* (1908), and *On Being Creative* (1932); GAMALIEL BRADFORD, *Biography and the Human Heart* (1932); BENJAMIN G. BRAWLEY, *New Survey of English Literature* (1925); DOROTHY BREWSTER and JOHN A. BURRELL, *Modern Fiction* (1934 ; WILLIAM C. BROWNELL, *Standards* (1917), *French Traits* (1896), and *The Genius of Style* (1924); VICTOR F. CALVERTON, *The Liberation of American Literature* (1932); HENRY S. CANBY, *The Age of Confidence* (1934); SAMUEL M. CROTHERS, *The Modern Essay* (1926); JOHN W. CUNLIFFE, *English Literature in the Last Half-Century* (1923); G. LOWES DICKINSON, *The Greek View of Life* (1932); MAX EASTMAN, *Enjoying Poetry* (1925); ARTHUR ELOESSER,

Modern German Literature (1933); NORMAN FOERSTER, *American Criticism* (1928) and *Humanism and America* (1930); EDWARD M. FORSTER, *Aspects of the Novel* (1927); RICHARD GARNETT, *History of Italian Literature* (1900); ISAAC GOLDBERG, *Studies in Spanish American Literature* (1920); GRANVILLE HICKS, *The Great Tradition* (1933); RENÉ LALOU, *Contemporary French Literature* (1924); ÉMILE H. LEGOUIS and LOUIS F. CAZAMIAN, *History of English Literature* (1926–1927); LUDWIG LEWISOHN, *Expression in America* (1932); AMY LOWELL, *Tendencies in Modern American Poetry* (1921); JAMES RUSSELL LOWELL, *Among My Books* (1870–1876) and *My Study Windows* (1871); JOHN L. LOWES, *Convention and Revolt in Poetry* (1926); PERCY LUBBOCK, *The Craft of Fiction* (1921); PRINCE MIRSKY, *Contemporary Russian Literature* (1926); CHARLES E. MONTAGUE, *Dramatic Values* (1925); PAUL ELMER MORE, *The Shelburne Essays* (11 vols., 1904–1921) and *The Demon of the Absolute* (1928); EDWIN MUIR, *Transition: Essays on Contemporary Literature* (1926); HAROLD G. NICOLSON, *The Development of English Biography* (1928); VERNON L. PARRINGTON, *Main Currents in American Thought* (3 vols., 1927–1930); LEWIS RUCKOW, *Contemporary Political Thought in England* (1925); GEORGE SANTAYANA, *The Sense of Beauty* (1905), *Little Essays Drawn from the Writings of George Santayana* (1920), *Winds of Doctrine* (1926), and *Soliloquies in England and Later Soliloquies* (1924); GEORGE BERNARD SHAW, *Dramatic Opinions and Essays* (1907); STUART P. SHERMAN, *Americans* (1922), *The Genius of America* (1923), and *On Contemporary Literature* (1917); ALEXANDER SMITH, "The Art of the Essay," in *Dreamthorp* (1914); WILLIAM R. THAYER, *The Art of Biography* (1920); LESLIE A. WARREN, *Modern Spanish Literature* (2 vols., 1929); EDITH WHARTON, *The Writing of Fiction* (1927); GEORGE E. WOODBERRY, *The Torch* (1920).

IX. ART AND THE MODERN MIND

MARION BAUER, *Twentieth Century Music; How It Developed and How to Listen to It* (1933); ADOLPHE BAULER, *La Sculpture Moderne* (1924); CLIVE BELL, *Since Cézanne* (1922), *An Account of French Painting* (1932), *Art* (1924), *Civilization* (1928), *Enjoying Pictures* (1934), *Landmarks in Nineteenth Century Painting* (1927), *On British Freedom* (1923), *Peace At Once* (1915), *Potboilers* (1918), and *Proust* (1929); C. H. CAFFIN, *History of American Painting* (1907); SIDNEY CASSON, *Some Modern Sculptors* (1929); THOMAS CRAVEN, *Modern Art* (1934) and *Men of Art* (1931); SHELDON W. CHENEY, *Expressionism in Art* (1934); ROBERT L. DUFFUS, *The American Renaissance* (1928); GEORGE DYSON, *The New Music* (1926); ARTHUR J. EDDY, *Cubists and Post-Impressionism* (rev. ed., 1919); DAVID EWEN, *Composers of Today* (1934); ELIE FAURE, *Modern Art* (1924); HAROLD N. FOWLER, *A History of Sculpture* (1916); EGON FRIEDELL, *Cultural History of the Modern Age* (3 vols., 1928); HELEN GARDNER, *Art through the Ages* (1926); TALBOT F. HAMLIN, *The American Spirit in*

Architecture (1926); W. J. HENDERSON, *How Music Developed* (1898); JOHN T. HOWARD, *Our American Music* (1931); RUPERT HUGHES, *Contemporary American Composers* (1900); JAMES HUNEKER, *Ivory Apes and Peacocks* (1914) and *Unicorns* (1917); E. RILLA JACKSON, *American Art* (1928); HENRY E. KREHBIEL, *Music and Manners in the Classical Period* (1898), *How to Listen to Music* (1929), and *Studies in the Wagnerian Drama* (1891); JOHN LA FARGE, *Considerations on Painting* (1895); HENRY C. LAHEE, *Annals of Music in America* (1922); CHARLES MARRIOTT, *Modern Movements in Painting* (1920); FRANK JEWETT MATHER, *The American Spirit in Art* (1927), *The Collectors* (1912), *Concerning Beauty* (1935), *The Additional Sentence in Anglo-Saxon* (1893), *Do the Arts Make for Peace?* (1912), *Estimates in Art* (1931), *A History of Italian Painting* (1932), *Homer Martin, Beauty in Landscape* (1912), *Isaac Master, A Reconstruction of the Work of Gaddo Gaddi* (1932); *Modern Painting, A Study of Tendencies* (1927), *The Portraits of Dante Compared with the Measurements of His Skull and Reclassified* (1921) and *Ulysses in Ithaca* (1926); JULIUS A. MEIER-GRAEFE, *Modern Art* (1908); EDWIN A. PARK, *New Backgrounds for a New Age* (1927); SIR CHARLES H. H. PARRY, *The Evolution of the Art of Music* (1897); CHANDLER R. POST, *A History of European and American Sculpture from the Early Christian Period to the Present Day* (1921); MAURICE RAYNAL, *Modern French Painting* (1928); PAUL ROSENFELD, *An Hour with American Music* (1929); OSCAR G. T. SONNECK, *Suum Cuique: Essays in Music* (1916); LORADO TAFT, *American Sculpture* (1924); THOMAS E. TALLMADGE, *The Story of Architecture in America* (new ed., 1927); JAMES McNEILL WHISTLER, *Eden versus Whistler* (1899), *The Gentle Art of Making Enemies* (1909), and *Ten O'Clock* (1904); REGINALD H. WILENSKI, *Modern Movement in Art* (1927).

X. AMERICA, PAST AND PRESENT

JAMES T. ADAMS, *Provincial Society, 1690–1763* (1927) and *The Epic of America* (1931); JANE ADDAMS, *Twenty Years at Hull House* (1910) and *The Second Twenty Years* (1930); CHARLES A. BEARD, *Economic Interpretation of the Constitution* (1913); CHARLES and MARY BEARD, *Rise of American Civilization* (2 vols., 1932); MARY R. BEARD, *Short History of the Labor Movement* (1925); CARL BECKER, *Declaration of Independence* (1922); STEPHEN VINCENT BENÉT, *John Brown's Body* (1928); ALBERT J. BEVERIDGE, *Life of John Marshall* (4 vols., 1916–1919); CLAUDE G. BOWERS, *Jefferson and Hamilton* (1925); LORD CHARNWOOD, *Lincoln* (1929); HIRAM M. CHITTENDEN, *The American Fur Trade of the Far West* (1935); JOHN R. COMMONS, *Races and Immigrants in America* (1920); EDWARD S. CORWIN, *John Marshall and the Constitution* (1919); WILLIAM E. DODD, *Statesmen of the Old South* (1911); RALPH WALDO EMERSON'S *Journals* (10 vols., 1909–1914); HENRY P. FAIRCHILD, *Immigration* (1913); ALBERT B. FAUST, *German Element in the United States* (1927); CARL R. FISH, *The Rise of the*

Common Man (1927); WALTER L. FLEMING, *The Sequel of Appomattox* (1919); PAUL L. FORD, *The True George Washington* (1903); EDWIN L. GODKIN, *Problems of Modern Democracy* (1897); BURTON HENDRICK, *The Age of Big Business* (1921); FRANCIS W. HIRST, *Life and Letters of Thomas Jefferson* (1926); MILDRED HOWELLS, *Life in Letters of William Dean Howells* (2 vols., 1928); JOHN F. JAMESON, *The American Revolution Considered as a Social Movement* (1926); JOHN ALLEN KROUT, *Annals of American Sport* (1929); ROBERT LA FOLLETTE, *Autobiography* (1913); JESSE MACY, *The Anti-Slavery Crusade* (1921); L. K. MATHEWS, *The Expansion of New England* (1909); JAMES F. MUIRHEAD, *The Land of Contrasts* (1900); ALLAN NEVINS, *American Social History by British Travellers* (1923); and *The Emergence of Modern America* (1927); JOHN G. NICOLAY and JOHN HAY, *Abraham Lincoln* (10 vols., 1917); SAMUEL P. ORTH, *The Boss and the Machine* (1921); ERNEST S. OSGOOD, *The Day of the Cattleman* (1929); THOMAS NELSON PAGE, *Social Life in Old Virginia before the War* (1898); ALBERT B. PAINE, *Life of Mark Twain* (1929); FRANCIS PARKMAN, *The Oregon Trail* (1919); JAMES PARTON, *Life of Jackson* (1883); JACOB RIIS, *How the Other Half Lives* (1890) and *The Making of an American* (1924); PHILIP A. ROLLINS, *The Cowboy* (1922); THEODORE ROOSEVELT, *Chapters of a Possible Autobiography* (1913); ALBERT H. SANFORD, *The Story of Agriculture in the United States* (1916); CARL SCHURZ, *Reminiscences* (3 vols., 1907–1908); JOHN R. SPEARS, *American Merchant Marine* (1910); NATHANIEL W. STEPHENSON, *Lincoln* (1921); WILLIAM G. SUMNER, *Hamilton* (1904); HOLLAND THOMPSON, *The Age of Invention* (1921); ALEXIS DE TOCQUEVILLE, *Democracy in America* (1835); FREDERICK J. TURNER, *Rise of the New West* (1906); BOOKER T. WASHINGTON, *Up from Slavery* (1909); ANDREW D. WHITE, *Autobiography* (1905); WILLIAM A. WHITE, *Masks in a Pageant* (1928); BRAND WHITLOCK, *Forty Years of It* (1925); JUSTIN WINSOR, *The Westward Movement* (1897); JOHN S. WISE, *The End of an Era* (1902); JAMES BRYCE, *The American Commonwealth* (2 vols., 1888).